The Tenochca Empire of Ancient Mexico

The Tenochca Empire of Ancient Mexico

The Triple Alliance of Tenochtitlan, Tetzcoco, and Tlacopan

By Pedro Carrasco

UNIVERSITY OF OKLAHOMA PRESS : NORMAN

Library of Congress Cataloging-in-Publication Data

Carrasco Pizana, Pedro, 1921–
    The Tenochca Empire of ancient Mexico : the triple alliance of Tenochtitlan, Tetzcoco,
and Tlacopan / by Pedro Carrasco.
        p.   cm. — (The civilization of the American Indian series : v. 234)
    Includes bibliographical references.
    ISBN 0–8061–3144–6 (cl. : alk. paper)
    1. Aztecs—Politics and government.   2. Tezcucan Indians—Politics and government.
3. Tepanecas—Politics and government.   I. Title.   II. Series.
F1219.76.P75C36   1999
972'.018—dc21   99–26789
                                                                                                              CIP

The Tenochca Empire of Ancient Mexico: The Triple Alliance of Tenochtitlan, Tetzcoco, and Tlacopan is
Volume 234 in The Civilization of the American Indian Series.

The paper in this book meets the guidelines for permanence and durability of the Committee
on Production Guidelines for Book Longevity of the Council on Library Resources, Inc.

Text design by Gail Carter.

1   2   3   4   5   6   7   8   9   10

Contents

Sources

Terminology

Identification of Towns

On the Spelling of Nahuatl

Plan of the Book

PART ONE

The Tripartite Structure and the Political-Territorial Categories

The Dependent Kingdoms of Each of the Three Capitals

The Tripartite Division in the Subject Areas of the Empire

The Intermingling of Territories

Motolinía's "Memorial tetzcocano" and the "Memorial
de los pueblos de Tlacopan"

The Memorial of Don Hernando Pimentel of Tetzcoco

The Tlacopanec Memorial in the Codex Osuna

The Codex Mendoza and Related Tenochca Documents

The Calpixques of Tenochtitlan in Sahagún's *Historia*

PART TWO

The Three Kingdoms of the Alliance

Tenochtitlan, Capital of the Colhua-Mexicas

The Tributaries of Tlacopan within Its Own Domain
and the Domains of the Other Two Capitals

> Estancias in the Tenochca Domain and in Chalco
>
> Estancias in Tlalhuic
>
> Tributary Towns in Matlatzinco
>
> Tributary Towns in the Northern Basin

PART THREE
The Distant Regions Subject to the Empire

Native Kingdoms, Tributary Provinces, and Military Colonies

The Establishment of Tributary Units

The Governance of the Tributary Provinces

The Distribution of Tribute

The Three Sectors of the Empire

The Tepanec Kingdoms and the Establishment of Tenochca
Predominance in the West

The Provinces in the Valley of Toluca and the Southern Part
of the Cuauhtlalpan in the Codex Mendoza

> Tolocan
>
> Ocuillan
>
> Malinalco
>
> Xocotitlan

The Frontier with Michoacan

The Provinces in the Balsas Basin and the Costa Grande in
the Codex Mendoza

> Tlachco
>
> Tepecuacuilco
>
> Cihuatlan
>
> Tlappan
>
> Tlalcozauhtitlan
>
> Quiauhteopan
>
> Yohualtepec

PART FOUR

The Territorial Entities within the Organization of the Empire

Maps

Tables

Preface to the English Edition

This edition is a close translation of the Spanish original, *Estructura político-territorial del Imperio tenochca: La Triple Alianza de Tenochtitlan, Tetzcoco y Tlacopan*, albeit with some changes. The division into chapters has been reorganized to reduce the number of chapters from thirty-three to thirteen. I have also made some additions, usually brief but in some instances longer, as in chapter 8 (originally chapters XXI to XXIII), which I have expanded.

I have also made some deletions and revisions. I have omitted the section on the "Pintura de México" (chapter III.2 in the original), but I have incorporated my conclusions about this document into the discussion of the works of Itlilxochitl in the section on sources in chapter 1. I have also relocated the passages in Durán and Tezozomoc on the extent of the Empire (chapter IV.2) to chapter 1. I have shortened some notes, and in these cases the reader is referred to the Spanish edition.

Quotations from sources written in Spanish have been for the most part shortened or paraphrased. Although some sources have been translated and published in English, in this book the translations have been made directly from the Spanish. In quotations from sources published in Spanish I have at times made slight changes in the division into paragraphs.

Errors, errata, and omissions in the Spanish edition have called for a few minor changes. When new information has been added, the text has been revised. For example, changes in the identification of Acazacatla and other towns required a change in the discussion of the Empire's frontier north of Tlaxcallan. I have also made a few references to publications that appeared after the Spanish edition.

The maps have been redrawn, some with only minor changes or additions. Others have been divided into two parts to provide more space for including additional names of towns mentioned in the text.

The translation from the Spanish has been made by H. B. Genereux, with some revisions and additions by the author, who has also prepared the translations from the Nahuatl.

Preface to the First Spanish Edition

This book began in 1979 as an article titled "Political Geography of the Aztec Empire," my contribution to a volume in honor of Donald Brand, a book that was never published. Later, in 1986, the Instituto Nacional de Antropología e Historia (INAH), then under the direction of Enrique Florescano, invited me to organize a research project at the Departamento de Etnohistoria together with its director, Jesús Monjarás-Ruiz. We took as a theme the organization of the Triple Alliance and after several meetings of the members of the project decided on a collective work that would cover the principal aspects of that theme. The participants were not only personnel of the Departamento de Etnohistoria but also several scholars from the Centro de Investigaciones y Estudios Superiores en Antropología Social (CIESAS). However, we soon realized that there would not be enough contributions to produce a book in which all the topics would conform to a single plan and be discussed with the same criteria; some topics had to be omitted. Therefore I decided to divide the results of this project into two parts. One has resulted in this book, devoted to the territorial structure; the other is to be a collection of essays on the Triple Alliance, written by members of the project, that we hope to publish in the near future. It will include my first contributions to the project on aspects of the economic and political organization not included in this volume, together with articles, by other participants in the project, for the most part concerning the frontiers of the Empire. Another result of our meetings was the decision to publish some of the source material, including documents concerning the lands of Doña Isabel de Montezuma that Emma Pérez Rocha and I had studied in the Archivo de Indias, which will be edited for publication by Pérez Rocha. Rafael Tena has worked on editing and translating several documents on the indigenous nobility that will be part of a volume to be prepared by other members of the Departamento de Etnohistoria.

During the writing of this book I also gave lectures on its basic theme at the Escuela Nacional de Antropología de México and at Brandeis University, the State University of New York at Albany, the Graduate Center of the City University of New York, the International Congress of Americanists at Amsterdam, and the Sociedad de Geografía e Historia de Guatemala. A summary of this book is part of my contribution on the political organization and territorial structure of the Triple Alliance for a volume on Mesoamerica at the beginning of the sixteenth century prepared by the Consejo Nacional para la Cultura y las Artes (*Temas mesoamericanas,* edited by S. Lombardo and E. Nalda [Mexico: INAH and CNCA, 1996]). A somewhat expanded version of the initial article offered to Professor Brand was published with the title "The Territorial Structure of the Aztec Empire," in *Land and Politics in the Valley of Mexico,* edited by Herbert R. Harvey (Albuquerque: University of New Mexico Press, 1991).

I decided to prepare this book on the territorial structure when I joined the Centro de Estudios Históricos of the Colegio de México in 1990. Most of the work was done under the auspices of that institution, to which I express my gratitude for the support given to me. To Alicia Hernández, director of the Centro de Estudios Históricos, I owe the invitation to publish it in the series of the Fideicomiso Historia de las Américas. The exchange of ideas with the participants in the project supported by the INAH was a constant stimulus to complete this book. I am especially obliged to Jesús Monjarás-Ruiz, who never doubted that I would finish this lengthy task.

The archival material used for this book was obtained years before it was begun. In Mexico I worked in the Archivo General de la Nación in 1960 and 1961, with assistance from the Unión Panamericana, and in the Archivo de Indias in Seville in 1963–64, with a subsidy from the American Council of Learned Societies. During the final stage of preparing the book I worked in the Library of Brandeis University; the assistance of the library staff in obtaining interlibrary loans was essential, and I wish to express my thanks to them.

The Tenochca Empire of Ancient Mexico

Chapter 1

INTRODUCTION

The most important political entity in pre-Spanish Mesoamerica was the Tenochca Empire, founded in 1428 when the rulers of the three kingdoms of Tenochtitlan, Tetzcoco, and Tlacopan formed an alliance that eventually controlled not only the Basin of Mexico but also a large area extending from the Gulf coast to the Pacific; from the frontiers with Metztitlan, the Chichimecs, and the Tarascan kingdom of Michoacan, in the north and northwest, to the Isthmus of Tecuantepec and Xoconochco in the southeast.

The words that have been used to designate this political entity have sometimes been questioned. Terms such as *kingdom* and *empire* were criticized by Morgan and his followers, who saw the society of ancient Mexico as simply a variant of that of the Iroquois or the Pueblos of New Mexico; it is now universally acknowledged that a complex civilization developed in central Mexico, as in the entire Mesoamerican cultural area.[1] The word *empire* itself implies a large-scale state organization in which one people dominates others and, similarly, one king is supreme over other subordinate rulers; the concept of emperor as king of kings expresses this concisely. Both ideas can be applied to the Mesoamerican political units of greatest complexity.

There has also been a lack of agreement about the name of the people who were the dominant group of this political entity. Early colonial writers called them Mexicanos, in contrast with other groups such as Tepanecs or Tlaxcaltecs. The adjective *mexicano* was also applied to the political unit ruled by Moteuczoma, but this usage became awkward after Mexico became an independent nation. A term such as *Mexican Empire* is hardly suitable, evoking as it does the empires of Iturbide or Maximilian. The phrase "ancient Mexicans" or similar expressions solve the problem, but the name *Aztec* came into frequent use in order to have a term that would avoid such inconveniences. Some scholars still use Aztec to refer to the Mexicas,[2] but recently others have applied the name to all the people of the Basin of Mexico, extending the name to people such as the Tepanecs, Acolhuas, or Chalcas, and in spite of the fact that a large number of people in the Basin spoke Otomi. Archaeologists have also applied the name *Aztec* to types of ceramics and chronological periods.

But who were the Aztecs? Suffice it to say that in the sixteenth century no ethnic group called themselves Aztec. In some historical traditions the name was used for people originally from the legendary city called Aztlan who migrated towards the south and entered the Basin of Mexico. Following the instructions of Huitzilopochtli, their patron god, they changed their name to Mexitin and eventually settled on an island in the central lake, where they founded the city of Mexico, hence the gentile name *Mexica*.

In the late 1940s Barlow criticized the use of the word *Aztec*, and his arguments are still valid.[3] Since Barlow's article and the publications of the Seminario de Cultura Náhuatl, the use of Nahua (and/or Nahuatl) and Mexica predominates in Mexico among anthropologists and historians, although to a certain extent the use of Mexicanos for the pre-Spanish people and for the Nahuatl language continues. This usage is also followed by ethnohistorians in the United States.

I have avoided the term *Aztec* in this book. It is of no use for understanding the ethnic complexity of ancient Mexico and for identifying the dominant element in the political entity we are studying. I will use Nahuatl for the language and speakers of the language and appropriate gentile names for individual migratory groups and the peoples of regional polities and towns. Thus, the Mexicas are the people who took this name when so instructed by their god and founded the city of Mexico with its twin settlements of Tenochtitlan and Tlatelolco. As a label for the empire, *Mexica* might do except for the very uneven position of the Tlatelolca within the Empire. If we wish to choose an ethnic qualifier that will define the ethnic group, city, and dynasty that were dominant in the Empire, and given that Tenochtitlan was the principal capital city and its king the most powerful ruler, the word that best serves this purpose is *Tenochca*.

The phrase "Triple Alliance" is useful because it emphasizes the tripartite nature of the governing center of the Empire, making clear that from its inception segmentation was an essential characteristic of the political structure. In this book, therefore, "the Empire" means the Tenochca Empire, formed by the alliance of Tenochtitlan, Tetzcoco, and Tlacopan.

From the beginning of the Triple Alliance Tenochtitlan and its ruling dynasty dominated the others. The king of Tenochtitlan was the supreme commander of the alliance's armies and had the deciding voice in the establishment of garrisons and military colonists in strategic locations. The tribute from conquered areas was taken first to Tenochtitlan and was there distributed among the three powers. The higher status of the Tenochca kings is also evident in the marriage alliances and succession practices among the rulers of the core area.

Each of the three great kings was the sovereign in his city and its domain, which included a number of lesser kingdoms whose rulers were subordinate to the higher-ranking king of the capital city and were members of the same dynasty and/or related to it by marriage. These three domains formed the core area of the Empire, encompassing the Basin of Mexico and some adjacent areas. A geographical division was established in which each capital city was predominant in a certain part of the Basin, Tenochtitlan in the south, Tetzcoco in the northeast, and Tlacopan in the west.

The intermingling of territories was also essential to the imperial structure. In addition to its own territory in the surrounding rural area, each capital city held land within the domains of the other capitals and in the adjacent conquered areas of Chalco, Tlalhuic (present-day Morelos), and Tolocan.

As the Empire expanded, this three-part division was replicated in the distant areas. Most of the conquered towns became tributaries of the three capital cities, but each of the three capitals was predominant in the area adjoining that capital's domain in the core area. The degree of control exercised by the Empire varied greatly in the distant regions; the situation of some is not well known, and probably they paid tribute only occasionally.

Outside the Empire there were still some independent polities. These were, in the east, the three Nahuatl-speaking kingdoms in the region that the peoples of the Basin called *tlatepotzca* (tramontane): Cholollan, Tlaxcallan, and Huexotzinco. Surrounded by subjects and allies of the Empire, they were its most powerful enemies and the ones of greatest cultural prestige; their rulers were invited to the great celebrations that took place in Tenochtitlan, and they fought against the cities of the Empire in ritual or "flower" wars (*xochiyaoyotl*). Others were, towards the north, Metztitlan, on the frontier with the Chichimecs; in the west, the Tarascan kingdom of Michoacan; and to the south, on the coast of Guerrero, Yopitzinco, the land of the Yopis. All of these were also at times invited to Tenochtitlan.

Other independent peoples, east of Metztitlan, were the Otomis of Tototepec and Hueyacocotlan.[4] Farther north were several Huaxtec chiefdoms. North of the Empire, from the Tarascan frontier to the Huaxteca, were Chichimec groups who had a lesser degree of political complexity and territorial integration. Very little is known about their relations with the Empire. In the southern part of Oaxaca the Mixtec kingdom of Tototepec controlled a large part of the coast. In the isthmus, the Empire's neighbors were the Nahua realm of Coatzacualco, the kingdom of Chiappan (Chiapa de Corzo, Chiapas), and the Mayance-speaking peoples of Tabasco, Chiapas, and Guatemala.

The nature of the frontiers is not discussed in detail, but we can easily detect different situations. In some areas the Empire was in immediate confrontation with other strong polities, and both had tribute-paying dependencies and military strongholds. This was the situation on the borders with Michoacan, the tramontane polities, and Metztitlan. Yet even here, variations in the nature of the frontier can be identified. In the western and southern boundaries with the tramontane kingdoms the Empire exercised strong control. Up to the boundary line there were kingdoms of the core area or well-controlled polities such as those in the Tepeyacac province. On the other hand, north of Tlaxcallan were small states, such as Tetellan, Zacatlan, and Iztaquimaxtitlan, that can be defined as military allies on whom no strong tributary demands were imposed.

In other areas the Empire had expanded sporadically without succeeding in imposing lasting tribute obligations or establishing fortresses. Such was probably the situation in the areas facing the Mixtec kingdom of Tototepec as well as the Huaxtec area in the northeast, with its many independent chiefdoms. In eastern Oaxaca were independent or almost independent small polities surrounded by areas where the Empire maintained more steady control or had local allies. There the approximate extent of the Chinantec kingdom of Coatlicamac is ascertainable, but probably there were other independent units of a similar nature in the mountainous Tzapotec, Mixe, and Chontal areas. In the isthmus the garrison of Atzaccan and the tributary or allied polities such as Cuauhcuetzpaltepec, Malinaltepec, Xaltepec, and Tecuantepec marked the frontier area where the Empire faced Coatzacualco and Chiappan, but much of the boundary is not well known. The maps in this book indicate the ill-defined external boundaries with broken lines, but no attempt is made to identify the boundaries of independent or rebellious polities within the confines of the Empire in areas such as eastern Oaxaca.

For the most part, in studying the Empire scholars have been primarily concerned with two questions: the process of its expansion and its territorial extent at the arrival of the Spanish.

The traditional histories of Tenochtitlan, best known from the works of Durán and Tezozomoc, narrate the reign of each sovereign, giving special attention to his wars and conquests. Other sources, such as the first part of the Codex Mendoza, list the cities defeated or conquered by each Tenochca king. The *Matrícula de tributos* and the second part of the Codex Mendoza present in pictorial form the distant tributary regions, indicating the towns that comprise each one and the tribute they pay. Following these sources, Aragón, in the first modern study on this topic, examined the extent of the Empire using the data on conquests rather than analyzing the documents on tribute.[5]

Scholars have relied on Barlow's monograph on the extent of the Empire for locating the different tributary units of the Empire. Although he also studied the conquests of the Tenochca kings, Barlow based his work almost exclusively on the

Tenochca sources on tribute, that is, the *Matrícula de tributos* and the Codex Mendoza.[6] However, he did not discuss the administrative nature of these units nor their role within the imperial organization. He used the term *province* for a group of towns listed on the same page of the *Matrícula* and added to each province neighboring places mentioned as tributaries in other sources, primarily the *Relaciones geográficas*, so his work amounts to a compilation and identification of those places that paid tribute.[7] Gibson used a greater number of sources, advanced considerably the identification of the places enumerated in the Tetzcoco and Tlacopan sources, and in addition gave a better general picture of the territorial organization of the Empire.[8] Others have researched the organization of the kingdoms of Tetzcoco and Tlacopan, but without integrating all this material with that on Tenochtitlan to elucidate the structure of the Empire as a whole.[9]

In addition to his monograph on the extent of the Empire, Barlow investigated the sequence and location of its conquests, but he was not able to complete his work; some of his material has only recently been published.[10] Kelly and Palerm cataloged the conquests of the Tenochca kings in a study that is still the most useful modern compilation of data on the conquests of each king, with their geographical locations and maps.[11] These authors did not investigate the role of conquered places within the organization of the Empire, but they did note the importance of the problem and pointed out how the defeat of a given place could have variable consequences, from the taking of booty to the permanent collection of tribute by stewards of the Empire, the settlement of Mexica colonists, and the establishment of fortresses in strategic places.[12] Later, Tschohl went more thoroughly into the question of conquests, especially those of Ahuitzotl and the second Moteuczoma.[13] It would be useful to determine the consequences of each conquest in regard to the political and tributary organization of the Empire; unfortunately, that is not always possible.

The aim of this book is to go beyond the mere cataloging and locating of conquests and tributary towns. It will take in the total structure of the Empire, including the three parts of the alliance; define the different types of territorial entities that comprised the Empire; and determine how they came to be organized under different conditions of economic and political domination and performed different functions within the imperial organization.

The analysis presented here relies to a large extent on the information in Tetzcoca and Tlacopan sources for defining the tripartite structure of the Empire and also for interpreting certain data from the Tenochca sources on the internal organization of the Tenochca part of the Empire. It puts forth the structure of the Empire from its ruling center, with its tripartite structure, both in the core area ruled directly by the three great kingdoms of the alliance and in the distant conquered areas. An explanation of all the variations in the territorial structure of the individual kingdoms that made up each of the three parts of the alliance and of each of the conquered regions is beyond the scope of this book. It is certainly a topic that deserves further research and an analysis based on regional studies.[14]

In the modern state, people and territory are closely related. Borders are well marked and delineate a contiguous area. The state exercises exclusive sovereignty within its territory and has jurisdiction over all its inhabitants. This western model of nation-state is not the most suitable for studying ancient Mexico, where there were no clearly defined borders and where different political entities could share, in differing degrees of domination, people and territory in the same region. It would be more useful to compare Mesoamerica with other precapitalist complex societies. One must also identify the indigenous political categories, but without abandoning the aim of defining the questions of political and economic organization that arise in the comparative study of imperial structures at the worldwide level, and choose the criteria suitable for such a study.

In this work I emphasize a fundamental aspect of the study of Mesoamerica and other complex societies: social segmentation and its connection with territoriality.[15] Segments are to be understood as the subdivisions of a political entity that generally comprise both territory and a population of distinctive cultural characteristics, each subdivision with collective responsibility for the performance of specialized functions within the total organization. This leads us to the question of who exercises jurisdiction over a particular people and territory. Jurisdiction and rights to goods and services of different kinds may be combined (that is, the ruler or official receives his income from the same social segment that he governs), or they can be separate (that is, the source of his income is not the same place and people that he governs). The tasks of government may be the responsibility of one person or else divided among various officials, each with authority over a different governmental function, such as the administration of justice, the collection of tribute, or military service. On the other hand, the territory of each social segment may be either contiguous or scattered over various regions and intermingled with those of other segments. Clearly, the latter is a structure that gives to all the segments of a political entity access to the resources of all the territories it controls. All this is of capital importance for maintaining social solidarity and an efficient economic organization. In ancient Mexico segmentation and territoriality were also connected with land tenure and the nature of the *calpolli* (ward, barrio), questions that will come up again in the course of this work.

The constituent kingdoms of the Empire that formed the highest level of segmentation were, in turn, divided into segments or subdivisions, frequently called *parcialidades*. Thus, Mexico comprised two cities, Tenochtitlan and Tlatelolco; Tetzcoco had six ethnic subdivisions; in Azcapotzalco and Tlacopan there were separate ethnic subdivisions of Tepanec and Mexica. Xochimilco was divided into three parts and Cuitlahuac into four; the different realms of Chalco and their subdivisions are well documented. Outside of the Basin, Matlatzinco, Tlaxcallan, Cholollan, and Huexotzinco also had such subdivisions.

Segmentation was the basis of the frequent factionalism that was characteristic of the internal organization of pre-Spanish political entities. It was an important factor in the conflicts that broke out at the highest levels of political organization, such as the Triple Alliance and the Tepanec empire that preceded it. In the conflicts between major polities, the different parts of a given kingdom would take sides with one or the other of the contending powers, as can be seen in the wars that led to the formation of the Triple Alliance under Tenochca predominance. The historical traditions describe the largest political entities as groups of allied cities, alliances whose disintegration was linked to factional conflicts among their principal components. This is how the fall of Tollan and Colhuacan came about, and the well-known case of the league of Mayapan in Yucatan indicates that this process was not limited to the central highlands.[16]

However, although segmentation and territorial intermingling contributed to the factionalism that could bring about the disintegration of political entities, they also served as an integrating mechanism both for the governing class and for the political-territorial units. The ruling estate of the Empire was made up of the rulers of the various political-territorial segments, or kingdoms, that comprised it; they were, in Zorita's classic formulation, "los señores supremos," or *tlatoque*. These were the kings who governed the Empire—thirty according to some sources—who were not isolated rulers of independent states but rather constituted an entire social and politically integrated level. Lords and nobles (*teteuctin* and *pipiltin*), who functioned as government officials, made up a lower rank of the nobility. Some were relatives of the kings; others, persons of plebeian origin promoted for their merit. Kings and officials formed a privileged estate that can be defined as the ruling class; they held public power and enjoyed the economic privileges that went with their positions.[17]

Sources

Sources of many different kinds have been used for this book. Some will be analyzed in detail (see chapter 4), and the materials they contain on certain topics are discussed in the relevant chapters. Sources of an ethnographic kind that describe the political organization contain in general few data, although what they do have is important. The principal sources of this sort are the Codex Mendoza; Motolinía; Sahagún,[18] especially book 8 of his *Historia General de las Cosas de Nueva España*, which treats of kings and government; and Zorita.[19] But on the whole the best information is found in documents, or parts of them, that can be classified in three principal categories: historical chronicles, lists of conquests, and lists of the territorial components of the Empire.

Some historical chronicles are written in a narrative style, sometimes without chronological precision; others are strictly organized in the form of annals. Within the narrative type, Durán and Tezozomoc are the most important for Tenochca history and Ixtlilxochitl for Tetzcoco. Torquemada treats of both kingdoms; there are no chronicles of Tlacopan.

The two principal sources on Tenochca history, Durán and Tezozomoc,[20] are probably versions derived from a hypothetical prototype that Barlow called "Crónica X."[21] In some respects the two histories differ considerably. Tezozomoc uses Nahuatl terminology much more frequently so that his version seems closer to the supposed prototype, and he gives more information on cultural traits.[22] His text is often obscure and contains many errors made in copying. Durán's text is more polished and reflects a more European mind set. In addition, both develop certain points in their particular ways, sometimes using sources other than the prototypical "Crónica X."

Both writers organize their histories according to the reigns of the Tenochca sovereigns and give detailed accounts of those kings' wars, although with very little specific information on the chronology of each campaign. They also provide some data concerning the political organization of each conquered region before and after incorporation into the Empire. In addition, they contain detailed accounts of certain other important events, such as the funerals and installations of the Tenochca kings, public works, and the great religious celebrations. Thus, in contrast to the generalizations found in many other sources, they provide a collection of concrete cases that document the role of the different components of the Empire in the total organization. These descriptions also make it possible to discern the territorial categories defined in the Tetzcoca and Tlacopan sources. Both chronicles emphasize the predominance of Tenochtitlan but also make clear the important, although subordinate, role of the other two capitals. However, they have little information on the initial composition of the alliance or the rights held by Tetzcoco and Tlacopan in the distant tributary provinces. These chronicles also make clear the contrast between the core area and the distant subjugated regions and emphasize the importance of the kingdoms of the southern basin, as dependencies of Tenochtitlan, in all the activities of the Empire.

These chronicles will be used, in the chapters that treat the different conquered regions, for the information they provide on the political situation before those areas were conquered and on the changes imposed by the imperial power. Chapter 13 will discuss the different ways the territorial entities participated in the military organization, in public works, and in the great religious and political ceremonies held in Tenochtitlan.

The Tetzcoca sources provide the best information on the initial constitution of the Triple Alliance. Ixtlilxochitl is the most thorough in his historical account, but Motolinía and Torquemada, who also used Tetzcoca materials, provide key data about the tripartite structure of the Empire.

Ixtlilxochitl is also the principal source on the kingdom of Tetzcoco.[23] Some of the documents he used are known in pictorial form—for example, the Codex Xolotl and Mapa Quinatzin—but to interpret them the Spanish text of the chronicler is absolutely necessary. Ixtlilxochitl must also have used the documents that are the basis of Motolinía's "Memorial tetzcocano," which is included in his *Memoriales*, and parts of the *Anales de Cuauhtitlan*, which will be discussed later. As a member of the Teotihuacan ruling family, related to the Tetzcoca dynasty, Ixtlilxochitl was acquainted with the documentation on this important Acolhua kingdom. As in all the available historical chronicles, he emphasizes the importance of his own people, especially in the period before the Triple Alliance. More than other writers he uses Spanish terminology in describing political institutions and omits almost entirely their religious aspects. Nevertheless, Ixtlilxochitl gives a convincing vision of pre-Spanish society that essentially confirms other sources. He also gives important data about the tripartite structure and the components of the Empire similar to those of other sources that are basically catalogs of territorial units.

One might expect that Ixtlilxochitl would give greater importance to the Acolhuas and their king, Nezahualcoyotl, than might be justified. Yet Ixtlilxochitl's account is especially valuable in this respect. The predominant role of Tenochtitlan can be detected even in his account of the war against Azcapotzalco, in spite of his emphasis on Nezahualcoyotl in the restoration of the Chichimec empire. Ixtlilxochitl also describes quite clearly the predominance of the Tenochca, not only in military matters but also in their control of the tribute for the three capitals that was brought together in Tenochtitlan and in the decisions of Moteuczoma Xocoyotzin that diminished the importance of Tetzcoco.

Ixtlilxochitl's most polished work is the *Historia Chichimeca*, which also has the most material about the formation of the Triple Alliance and its later history. His other works are drafts, summaries, and notes that often have additional information, especially on the earlier periods. The most important are known under the names of *Sumaria relación*, *Relación sucinta*, and *Compendio histórico*. These works are all published in his *Obras históricas*. The document called "Pintura de México" is a simple catalog of place names without any explanation about its origin or its meaning.[24] Barlow thought it was a basic source or "primitive catalog" from which Ixtlilxochitl quoted "long fragments."[25] A comparison with other sources, including the writings of Ixtlilxochitl, shows that the "Pintura de México" is simply a list of the towns that formed part of the Acolhua kingdom and of towns conquered by the Triple Alliance. It might have been part of a longer document similar to that of the memorials of Tetzcoco and Tlacopan discussed below, but most probably it is an inventory of place names extracted from Ixtlilxochitl's own writings rather than a separate and original source. It adds practically nothing to what is better described in his other works and will be used as a source only when it provides some data not found elsewhere in the chronicler's writings.[26]

Torquemada was able to use the same sources on Tetzcoco as Ixtlilxochitl. In addition he knew Motolinía's work and also the Tenochca tradition, as put forth in Durán and Tezozomoc. Torquemada's work is largely a reelaboration of known documents, but he also used other sources of information and offers some data of great value, even though their provenance is not always known.[27]

The histories organized in the form of annals provide a better chronology of events, but their accounts tend to be very brief and at times give only the sequence of conquests. Some, such as the Codices Telleriano-Remensis and Vaticano-Ríos, are pictorial documents, several with brief legends added. Other sources, such as the *Anales de Cuauhtitlan*, the *Anales de Tlatelolco*, and the narratives of Chimalpahin, must have been based at least in part on pictorial documents but have come down to us only in the Nahuatl text or in Spanish, as, for example, the "Historia de los Mexicanos por sus Pinturas." Some of these sources are compilations of the annals of several cities.

What has come to be known as the *Anales de Cuauhtitlan* is a collection of different documents included in the manuscript called the Codex Chimalpopoca.[28] They are largely annals of various cities, with very brief reports on the events of each year, but some accounts are longer and contain digressions that go beyond the limits of the year in which they are included. Of special importance for our topic are three of the documents included at the end, after the historical annals: (1) another version of Motolinía's "Memorial tetzcocano," described below; (2) a list of the kings who were ruling when the Spanish arrived in 1519; and (3) one of the versions of a possible primordial document that we might entitle "List of Conquests of the Tenochca Kings."[29]

There are several versions of this hypothetical "List of Conquests," each of which is part of a more extensive source. They identify each king, give the duration of his reign, and enumerate his conquests; basically they contain little more than lists of toponyms without any dates. Although the sequence of the toponyms varies from one version to another, the similarities concerning the total number of places and their names suggest that these lists come from a common source.[30] Two of them—the lists included in the Codex Mendoza and the *Leyenda de los Soles*—are almost identical except in the order of enumeration.[31] In two other documents, the *Anales de Cuauhtitlan* and a letter from Pablo Nazareo to the king of Spain, the lists are almost the same; the toponyms are in the same order and there are very few variants. The lists in the *Anales de Tlatelolco* are similar but follow a different order and have more variants in the toponyms.[32] The Codex Mendoza list is especially useful, for it gives the glyphs and written forms for all the towns listed and is therefore essential when there are problems in the interpretation of toponyms. Barlow gave preference to the *Anales de Cuauhtitlan* because he believed that the conquest lists in that document were in chronological order, an arrangement that the artist of the Codex Mendoza had undone.

The conquests of the first kings of Tenochtitlan, from Itzcoatl to Tizoc, as enumerated in these lists are in accord with the narrations of the chronicles; the few toponyms they add are all identifiable. But the lists of the last two kings, Ahuitzotl and Moteuczoma Xocoyotzin, include several conquests that do not appear in other sources. Torquemada includes some of them in his historical and chronological account, but he does not always indicate where they are. Some have unidentifiable names that are not in the historical chronicles, in reports such as the *Relaciones geográficas*, or in modern toponymy; others are toponyms that occur frequently, but the lists do not say which one is indicated.

All these lists differ in the order in which names appear, and we do not know how the ordering of each source can be explained. At times a series of toponyms can be located in the same area, but one cannot be certain that they were conquered in a single campaign. The list may follow a geographical order even when places in a particular area were conquered at different times. There are also places that are close together geographically but are far apart in the list. Thus, in determining the geographical location of certain place names, one cannot depend on their position in the lists.

Occasionally the sources give different toponyms for the same position in the lists. In some of these cases the names, although different, can be understood as alternative readings of the same glyph; in others they can be considered as equivalent because they are places with two names or else towns that were part of the same political unit. Interpretations of this type are risky in locating a place, however, unless they are supported by other facts. In any case, these lists never provide information on the motive for a particular war, the local political organization, or the imposition of tribute. For this reason I do not cite them systematically.[33] They are valuable for our topic principally because they demonstrate that during the reigns of the last two kings there were conquests, in Oaxaca and the Pacific coast, that are not listed in the tributary provinces; one must conclude, therefore, that the tribute registers do not give a complete picture of the extent of the Empire. Shorter lists in Sahagún of the conquests of each Tenochca king do not seem to be based on the same sources as those discussed above.[34]

In addition to the material provided in historical chronicles and lists of conquests, other documents catalog the components of the Empire and therefore are basic for this study. Of primary importance are the registers of tribute paid to

Tenochtitlan. Two pictorial versions exist: the *Matrícula de tributos*, with legends in Nahuatl or Spanish, and the second part of the Codex Mendoza, with legends and extensive commentary in Spanish. Another such record, in Spanish, is included in the *Información de 1554*, written in response to an inquest by the Crown concerning tribute. It is based on the interpretation given by various indigenous witnesses of a painting that must have been almost identical to the two already mentioned. These three related documents are those that have been commonly used to determine the total extent of the Empire and to identify its dominions. The pictorial data provide little more than the names of the provinces and their component towns, together with the amounts of tribute in kind. Only the Codex Mendoza has commentaries on the administrative organization, but these are not entirely dependable, since they apply the same formula to all the provinces and we know from other sources that there were important regional differences. In any case, it presents a Tenochca point of view in which the other two parts of the Empire—Tetzcoco and Tlacopan—do not appear at all.

From Tetzcoco and Tlacopan come other documents of great importance having to do with petitions to the Spanish Crown by the governors of those cities, descendants of the native rulers. To provide a basis for the privileges solicited, they describe the extent of these two kingdoms and define distinct groups of components of the Empire, with different economic and political functions, in a form better organized than that of the Codex Mendoza. From Tetzcoco we have Motolinía's "Memorial tetzcocano" and another related version of this same material included in the *Anales de Cuauhtitlan*; both must have been based on the same pictorial document. Another source of the same type but shorter is the Memorial de Don Hernando Pimentel, and there is also the Mapa Quinatzin, which depicts the dependent kingdoms and towns of Tetzcoco. The chronicles of Ixtlilxochitl and Torquemada contain material related to all these Tetzcoca sources. From the Tepanec capital we have only one source, the "Memorial de los pueblos de Tlacopan."

All these documents from Tetzcoco and Tlacopan are essential for defining the internal composition of those two parts of the Triple Alliance, since they distinguish between the center of the Empire, with its component kingdoms, and the distant conquered regions that paid tribute to the three allied capitals, and also because within that central zone they distinguish between cities ruled by their own kings and towns of tenant farmers (*renteros*), whereas other writers give all these places as a series of toponyms with no explanation of their political and economic characteristics. These sources therefore require extensive commentary; they are discussed in chapter 4, which sets forth the political-territorial categories of the Empire.[35]

Other documents of great value are the *Relaciones geográficas*, prepared from 1579 to 1585. All answer the same questionnaire and therefore lend themselves to systematic comparisons. They present some difficulties of interpretation in material referring to pre-Spanish political institutions owing to the brevity with which most of them treat this matter, to their having been written sixty years after the Spanish Conquest, and to the fact that some of the persons responsible did not take their commission seriously and failed to search for competent informants. But in spite of their deficiencies, for many places these reports are the only sources of information available, and some are of extraordinary value, as, for example, Pomar's report on Tetzcoco and Muñoz Camargo's on Tlaxcallan.[36] All of them are indispensable for defining the jurisdictions of the indigenous communities in the first half-century of the colony. On this same topic, the reports on the bishoprics of Mexico, Puebla, and Oaxaca, and colonial rosters of tributary towns such as the *Suma de visitas* and the *Libro de las tasaciones*, are also essential. To understand the tripartite structure of the Empire and the circumstances prevailing at its beginning, we must give more importance to the Tetzcoco and Tlacopan sources than they have usually received. They contain basic information that the Tenochca sources do not record, but they also present divergences and contradictions. To formulate the history of the expansion and the territorial organization of the Empire, we must always keep in mind the different origins of the limited data available. Often the information on a certain topic comes from only one of these sources and there is no way to verify it. At other times the sources contradict each other and it is not always possible to reconcile them. Each fact must be presented together with its source; the regional or dynastic identification of the source will alert the reader to the possibility of a partisan bias.

Terminology

Sources written in Nahuatl and in Spanish present some problems in the concepts and words used to describe territorial and political entities. In general, Nahuatl terminology is not well defined in either dictionaries or other sources; at times one has to infer the meaning from the context, and the documentation is not always sufficient to solve these problems. Those who wrote in Spanish used the terminology of European society of that time; this has raised some doubts about its applicability to the society of ancient Mexico. But modern historians and anthropologists have sometimes forced the data in the sources into categories of contemporary history or theories favored in their time and thus have frequently distorted indigenous institutions as much as or more than the Spanish friars and officials did. In any case, the choice of words, such as tribe, state, kingdom, and others, for a discussion of pre-Spanish society implies from the start a certain interpretation that is not always justified.

The meaning of the Nahuatl terms that denote territorial and political entities must be made clear, but for analyzing the data one has to use English words that are also the terminology of the social sciences and lend themselves to a comparative study of different societies. The application of such terms to the indigenous society will be explained along with the expressions used in Nahuatl. Nahuatl terms reveal concepts peculiar to the society that used them, but they also combine meanings that must be distinguished, and the texts may be too ambiguous to express distinctions necessary for a historical and sociological analysis. In this book I will not extend the use of Nahuatl terms beyond the cases in which their meaning and applicability are well documented in the sources.

The basic political-territorial entity is the *altepetl,* literally "water-hill," usually translated into Spanish as "pueblo," a term that is discussed below.[37] To indicate this concept on a larger scale it is preceded by *huey* (large, big), as in *huey altepetl,* which is here translated as "city." One also finds *tlatocaaltepetl,* meaning "a town that governs, a town with a king, a city"; this may be a colonial expression.

Molina's dictionary translates altepetl as "pueblo, o rey," but the meaning of *rey,* "king," is not well attested, although some passages in the ceremonial speech addressed to the people of the city in the presence of the king can be interpreted this way.[38]

The altepetl includes both the urban or civic center and all the territory pertaining to the city, including its rural zone. It is clear in other entries in Molina that this distinction can be defined through phrases or compound words that modify the basic idea of altepetl.[39] The following are the principal entries in his dictionary:

Altepenayotl. principal ciudad, que es cabeça de reyno [principal city, which is the head of a kingdom]. . . .

Totecuacan. cibdad matriz o metropolitana [mother city or metropolis; literally, the Nahuatl means "place of our lords"]. . . .

Matriz de las cibdades. *altepenanyotl. totecuacan.*[40]. .

Altepeyolloco. el riñon o medio de la ciudad [the kidney or middle of the city; literally, the Nahuatl means "heart of the city"]. . . .

Altepetlianca. subjecto o comarca de ciudad o pueblo, o aldea de ciudad [subject settlement, or region of a city or town, or village of a city. Simeón, in his *Diccionario,* follows Olmos in defining *anca,* used with the possessive *I-,* as "*yanca,* su igual o lo que está unido a otra cosa" (its equal or that which is united to something else)]. . . .

Altepemaitl. aldea, o aldeano [village, or villager; literally, "hand (or arm) of the city"]. . . .

Altepemame. aldeas o aldeanos. . . .

Ima ycxi yn altepetl. aldea de la ciudad o barrio [literally, "its hand, its foot of the city"].

The use of "hands and feet" as a metaphor for the villages pertaining to a city, or for the villagers, is well attested.[41] It is a construction similar to that of *atlapalli cuitlapilli* (wings and tail) for the common people. The *Historia tolteca-chichimeca* uses the expression *yn ima yn icxi* (their hands and feet) for the twenty towns of the great city of Tollan, which—after the fall of the city—left the area and dispersed, each group to earn its own town (*quitlatlamaceuito yn imaltepeuh*).[42] The same source refers to Cholollan as *ytzontecon yn toltecayotl* (head of the Toltecadom), while the people of the barrios (*calpoleque*) were *yn yma yn ihicxi in tolteca* (the hands and feet of the Tolteca).[43]

The terminology in Molina and in the *Historia tolteca-chichimeca* appears to be adequate for the analysis presented here, since each capital of the Triple Alliance was the head of a group of dependent cities; the capitals could then be the heads, and the dependent cities, their hands and feet. However, in the available Nahuatl texts one finds only *tlatocaaltepetl* (governing city) or *tzontecomatl* (head). Given the scarcity of Nahuatl texts that treat of these topics, nothing can be taken as certain.

In the Spanish-Nahuatl part of his *Dictionary* Molina gives some of these expressions to translate the Spanish *provincia* or *comarca* (region):

> comarca de pueblo [*sic*]. *altepenauac. altepetlianca. altepemaitl.* . . .
> provincia. *vey altepetl.*

In Spanish, *pueblo* is generally used to translate altepetl. In the sources written in Spanish, pueblo expresses the whole gamut of the usual meanings of this word: any type of settlement or inhabited place; an ethnic group or "nation"; a rural place inhabited by peasants, in contrast to the city; the masses in contrast to the rulers and the nobility. In this study, *city* will be used to designate a large settlement, or altepetl, governed by a king of importance in the total political organization; it was the seat of the government and the governing class and had the greatest concentration of artisans and merchants, who provisioned the government and the rest of the inhabitants. This use of city is justified, therefore, in the sociological sense, as the center of a population internally differentiated in the division of labor and by social stratification. Whenever necessary to make distinctions, city will be used to emphasize the fact that we are speaking of the capital of a kingdom, the seat of the government, and the economic and ceremonial center. *Village* will be used for a settlement of peasants and tenant farmers to call attention to this difference. Quite often not enough information is available to describe each settlement on those terms; I will use *town* as the equivalent of the Spanish pueblo.

A more problematical Nahuatl term that designates a territorial entity is *calpolli*, or *calpulli*. In Spanish this is usually translated as "barrio," but at times a Nahuatlism, *calpul* (pl. *calpules*) is used. In the scholarly literature since the late nineteenth century it has been taken to mean a peasant community, a kin group, or both. Actually, this word has many meanings and cannot be equated with a technical term from the social sciences. In general it can be said that it applies to the segments in which a social group is divided at different levels of segmentation; that it can have various economic, political, and ceremonial functions; and that its members (or some of them) hold to the notion of a common origin. At the highest level of social segmentation one finds calpolli used in some of the historical traditions as they enumerate the different groups that began their migration towards the south from a place of common origin; in other sources the same groups are called altepetl. In their place of origin they were part of the same political-territorial entity; at the end of their migration they founded separate towns. On the other hand, within a given town we find denoted as calpolli social segments that are in turn subdivided into units also called calpolli; in that sense the usual Spanish equivalent is barrio. Another term associated with calpolli is *tlaxilacalli*, which at times is used practically as a synonym but seems to refer principally to the territorial extent of the group, while calpolli refers to the political, administrative, and ceremonial aspects. A related word, *calpolco*, is used for the room or house where certain political or ceremonial activities of the people of the calpolli are carried on. As Vetancurt says, frequency in the use of these words varied over time; in the colonial era what was formerly called calpolli was called tlaxilacalli. We cannot here go into all the problems related to the social units called calpolli, nor is it necessary, since we are concerned primarily with the higher level of social segmentation in the three capital cities of the Triple Alliance and some of their dependent cities.[44]

Nahuatl terminology does not provide an unequivocal word to designate the imperial structure; words that express the concept of ruling have a wide range of meanings. The verb *tlatoa* means "to speak, to order, to govern, to reign." In Molina, *tlatoani* is translated as "hablador o gran señor" (speaker or great lord), the verb *tlatocati* as "ser señor o príncipe" (to be a lord or prince), and *tlatocayotl* as "señorío, reyno, corona real, o patrimonio" (lordship, kingdom, royal crown, or patrimony), that is, the rank and dominion of a tlatoani; it could be used for empire and for the modern concept of the state. In the Spanish-Nahuatl section Molina does not translate *emperador* but uses the same Spanish word, and for *Ymperio* he gives "Emperador ytlatocayo." Chimalpahin translates empire and emperor as "huey tlahtocayotl" and "huey tlahtohuani."[45]

There were different degrees of power among the kings, but they are not well noted in Nahuatl terminology; only the context can indicate this. The king of greatest importance is *huey tlatoani*, "great king." In this study I will use *king* as equivalent to tlatoani. The plural of tlatoani is *tlatoanime* or *tlatoque*; the latter form is also used in a wider sense to mean "lords."[46]

Another Nahuatl term for a person of high status is *teuctli* (pl. *teteuctin*); the office or rank of a person with this title is *teucyotl*. Teuctli is applied to persons in authority at various levels of the social and political hierarchy. It is part of a title of the three kings of the alliance;[47] of the heads of noble houses;[48] of various officials, for example, judges;[49] and of tribute collectors or local chiefs.[50] Teuctli is, in addition, part of the name of several gods, which is never the case with tlatoani.[51] Molina also gives teuctli to mean the master of servants or slaves.[52] Documents about this title and the *teccalli*, or noble houses, are most abundant in the tramontane region, both in the independent realms and in the Tepeyacac region conquered by the Empire. However, since this terminology has to do primarily with the internal structure of each one of the component kingdoms of the Empire, they will not be dealt with here.[53]

The terms *señor* and *señorío* are very common in the Spanish sources; here I will translate señor as "ruler" or "king" and occasionally as "lord." Señorío will be "kingdom" or "realm." In works written in the first century of the colonial period, the word *imperio* (empire) is relatively infrequent compared to *reino* (kingdom) or señorío, and emperador is rarely used, but these terms are found in López de Gómara, Tezozomoc, and, above all, Ixtlilxochitl and Torquemada. Durán states that the king of Mexico was almost equivalent to an emperor or monarch.[54]

"Triple Alliance" is basically a modern expression, although it was used by the eighteenth-century writer Clavijero.[55] A similar phrase used by Ixtlilxochitl—"imperio de las tres cabezas" (empire with three heads)—combines the two concepts of a large political entity and of segmentation in three parts, thus supporting the use of "Triple Alliance."[56]

The Nahuatl expression closest to "Triple Alliance" is *excan tlahtolloyan* or *excan tlahtolloc*, which Chimalpahin employs in his account of the foundation of Colhuacan, a city that governed together with two others, first with Tollan and Otompan and later with Coatlichan and Azcapotzalco.[57] Literally these phrases mean "the place of government in three parts," or "there is government in three parts," from the verb *tlatoloa*, which Molina translates as "tratarse de algún negocio y entender en el remedio dél" (to deal with some affair and be engaged in the remedy for it). In referring to the alliance of Tenochtitlan, Tetzcoco, and Tlacopan, the *Anales de Cuauhtitlan* say they were *tlatoloyan catca* (places of government).[58] In the Codex Osuna the phrase *yn etetl tzontecomatl* (the three heads) designates the three capitals of the Empire.[59] As we have seen, there is an indigenous basis for using the names of parts of the body for the divisions of a social entity (head in contrast with hands and feet), but tzontecomatl (Sp. *cabeza*, "head") corresponds also to the Spanish term *cabecera* (head town), which must have reinforced this usage in colonial documentation.

Certain Spanish words, such as *provincia*, *sujeto*, *estancia*, and *parcialidad*, were used in colonial Mexico with particular meanings, which should be examined. The word *provincia* is used in the sources to designate a region. The name of a province is usually related to a town or its people or to a region that has a distinctive Nahuatl name. There are many examples, such as Acolhuacan, Cohuixco, Cuauhtlalpan, Cuauhtenco, Coatlalpan, Teotlalpan, and so on, that will be mentioned many times in what follows. Sometimes, but not always, such a region is a political entity. Durán writes of the province of Tetzcoco or of Tlacopan when referring to the territory controlled by those cities. In some cases the reference is to a conquered entity that pays tribute; for example, Durán writes of the province of Cuetlaxtlan when narrating its conquest and the imposition of tribute.[60] A tributary entity, as such, would be in Nahuatl *calpixcayotl* (steward), as in the pertinent article in Molina, although the term refers to the office instead of the territory. It is significant that Molina translates provincia as "vey altepetl" but does not use provincia to translate altepetl, even though one of his equivalents for *altepeianca* is "comarca de ciudad" (the city's territory).[61]

Province in the sense of a territorial unit governed by the Empire to which it pays tribute is a usage of modern writers. Here it will be used for discussing the territorial entities of the Codex Mendoza, as a term sanctioned by usage. I will avoid it in other instances when speaking of tributaries of the component kingdoms of the Empire or of documents—such as the *Memorial de Tlacopan*—that in some instances differ notably from the Codex Mendoza without giving precise information on the nature of the entities described. I will also use province in its primary meaning of a region with common geographical, ethnic, or political features, following the usage of the sources that are cited. In some cases I will add quotation marks or will use the term *region* when it is necessary to avoid confusion with the tributary provinces of the Codex Mendoza.

Parcialidad is used frequently in the sources to designate the principal divisions of a political entity or a city, with emphasis on territorial and political aspects, each as a unit with its own ruler; at times its members (or their rulers) share a particular ethnic affiliation. The Nahuatl name may be either calpolli or *tlayacatl*.[62] I will use the Spanish word when the Nahuatl terms are not given in the sources.

Sujeto (subject) is a term used with several meanings in the sixteenth century to denote the different ways in which a town was subject to another;[63] often this results in ambiguity because the nature of the subordination is not sufficiently explained. In general, I will use sujeto, following the sources, simply to identify the political subordination of a given place. As for the characteristics of the place thus identified, it could be a kingdom or town subject to another, but for the most part it is a rural dependency of a town or city and would thus be equivalent to what other texts call barrio or estancia.

An estancia is usually a rural unit, agricultural or—in the colonial era—a cattle ranch, but it can also mean an inhabited place that is a dependent of another place and therefore is the same as barrio.

Barrio is equivalent to calpolli but can also designate an inhabited place out-side the urban center of the political-territorial unit to which it pertains. In this sense it may coincide with estancia.

Identification of Towns

Different kinds of sources are needed to identify all the places that comprise each of the territorial entities of the Empire. I have used both colonial sources and mod-ern maps and censuses. Because of resettlements enforced during the colonial pe-riod, such as the *congregaciones* of many towns, the locations given for a number of places are only approximate, but I believe they are sufficient for our purpose. In certain regions such as the Gulf coast, some populations were moved to places at a considerable distance; probably more detailed regional studies will show that the pre-Spanish settlement was far from the location here suggested. Intensive use of archaeological material would of course be very helpful for problems of location, and there is a great need for studies that would combine the use of published sources with archival research and archaeological explorations.

From the first century of colonial rule there are well-known documents that help to identify pre-Spanish settlements, above all the *Suma de visitas* and the *Rela-ciones geográficas*. When necessary they will be supplemented with similar reports on the various bishoprics and with tribute documents such as the *Libro de las tasaciones*. The indexes of documents in the Archivo General de la Nación have been very useful, especially those published by Mario Colín on the state of Mexico, for find-ing places whose identity is doubtful. At times they only define the boundaries of a certain place or state that was a sujeto of a certain cabecera; in other cases they tell of a congregación or a population transfer that at least helps in identifying the region in which a certain place was found. Gerhard's work is especially useful for documenting the vicissitudes of many towns and changes made to their names during the colonial period.

A great number of pre-Spanish communities have survived to the present day with only minor changes in their geographical location; in such cases the ancient places can be identified with their present-day successors. To identify modern towns I have used the volumes of *Integración territorial* from the 1980 census for the states of Morelos, Hidalgo, Mexico, Guerrero, and Puebla. The volumes for other states were not yet published when I was preparing this study; censuses from other years were used instead, especially the volume of *Integración territorial* from the census of 1950, which covers the whole country. When a pre-Spanish town is identified with a modern community that is not itself a municipal cabecera, the *municipio* in which it is found is also given. In a great many cases I have not considered it necessary to give additional information.

In this book the towns that constituted a given territorial unit are given in listings within the text or in tables. When the information about the towns comes from only one source, or there are very few differences among the sources, the list is presented in two columns; the first lists the toponyms and the second gives the identification with bibliographical references in parentheses. When there is more than one source with important differences, the data are arranged in a table with a separate column for each source, to make comparisons easier. If the identification information cannot fit within the table, it will be put in the text that follows or in a two-column list. More detailed information about the identification and other characteristics of each place is given in the text that follows the tables or lists, with bibliographical references in footnotes. As a rule, to make an identification I cite the oldest and most systematic colonial source, followed by the modern toponym according to the official name in the census. In the most complicated cases—as a matter of course when a town no longer exists—I make use of the pertinent colonial sources.

The tables and lists for each territorial entity are accompanied by maps; in some cases several entities are included in one map. The location of the toponyms in these maps corresponds to that of the modern towns, which do not always coincide exactly with the old ones. When there are doubts, I put a question mark before the location proposed in the tables or the symbol that marks the place in the map. Problems of location are explained in the table or in the text that accompanies it. At times the toponym in question is found in several regions, and it is impossible to be sure that the one shown on the map is correct; in other cases we know that the pre-Spanish town was moved to another site far from the old one, and there is no dependable information about where it was originally.

The maps I have used are those of the Comisión Geográfica Exploradora from the end of the nineteenth century; they register some places that do not appear in more recent maps. Several pages of the *Carta de la República Mexicana* a la 100 000ª, prepared by the Secretaría de Estado del Departamento de Fomento, cover the Basin of Mexico. The page numbers are 19-I(H) (first edition 1888, published in 1896); 19-I(M) (first edition 1909, published in 1909); 19-I(N) (first edition 1888, published in 1891), and 19-I(I) (first edition 1888, published in 1894). The same commission prepared the maps for the states of Morelos (1:100,000 in 1910) and Puebla (1:250,000 in 1908). I have also made use of the maps published about 1930 by the Secretaría de Agricultura, among them that of the state of Hidalgo (1:200,000), and, from the map of the republic (1:500,000), the sheets for San Luis Potosí, Tampico, Guanajuato, Pachuca, Mexico, Puebla, Coatzacoalcos, Chilpancingo, Oaxaca, Tuxtla Gutiérrez, and Pochutla.

On the Spelling of Nahuatl

When quoting sources written in Nahuatl, I keep to the orthography of the manuscript or of the edition used, although at times I change the division of words, the punctuation, and the use of capital letters. In the lists of towns in tributary provinces, the components of political units, and the conquests of the different kings, I spell the toponyms as in the sources used.

Otherwise I follow, with some modifications, the traditional spelling that has been most frequently used in colonial documents since the seventeenth century and by modern scholars. For the labialized velar stop I use *cu-* before a vowel and *-uc* after a vowel; I write *u* followed by a vowel as *hu*; instead of *ç*, I always use *z* before *a* and *o*, and the back vowel is always *o*. Thus I write Moteuczoma and Cuauhnahuac and not Motecuhçuma or Quauhnauac. Since glottal stops are only occasionally marked in the documents and vowel length is shown in a very few special texts, I do not indicate either.

Names of pre-Spanish places are generally given in the classical form. Some writers have suggested alternate etymologies and therefore spellings for a few of these; I have chosen the spelling that is closest to the modern forms. Thus I write Coyoacan and Tolocan, even though Coyohuacan and Tollocan are probably correct. Proper nouns often appear in very corrupt forms, written by scribes who obviously did not know Nahuatl. I occasionally add in brackets *sic* or *sic pro* and the probably correct form. Personal or place names that appear very seldom and in a corrupt form I spell as in the source.

For present-day communities I use the official names as spelled in the censuses. Thus, Huaxyacac refers to the pre-Spanish settlement, and Oaxaca is always the name of the modern state or its capital. The index of place names at the end of this book clarifies the equivalences between the classical and modern forms as well as the variants, at times chaotic, used in the sources quoted.

When adapting to English Nahuatl gentile and occupational names, I omit the final *-atl* of nouns ending in *-ecatl* but only the final *-tl* when *-catl* follows a consonant or a vowel other than *e*; in many of these nouns an awkward consonant cluster would result from deleting the ending. Therefore the people of Tollan are Toltec; Mexica and Chalca designate the people of Mexico and Chalco. To form the plural of anglicized Nahuatl nouns I simply add a final *-s*.

My translations from Nahuatl do not always follow exactly those already published, although I have considered them. If I differ substantially from the translation of the edition used, I have indicated this in a note. In some cases I present the Nahuatl text and its translation in two columns to make clear how the two correspond; at other times the Nahuatl text is given in the notes.

Plan of the Book

From the creation of the Triple Alliance, about 1428, until the Spanish Conquest, initiated in 1521, the political entity we are studying lasted almost a century. Within this time, the period about which the problems set forth here can be discussed is limited by the nature of the sources available. The Tenochca documents on tributary provinces refer to the time of Moteuczoma Xocoyotzin. Sources on the extent of the imperial domains coming from Tetzcoco and Tlacopan also present the situation that prevailed at the arrival of the Spanish, although for certain aspects of the organization Tetzcoca sources emphasize the early period of the Empire, when this city was strongest. We do not have comparable data about the different historical periods. Data on the political organization of the Empire, including the territorial structure, are scarce, disconnected, frequently confusing, and at times contradictory. It is difficult, therefore, to present the information on hand as a series of well-documented facts that conform to a plan determined by the connections among different aspects of the structure we are examining. Consequently this study follows a thematic ordering of the territorial structure of the Empire during the whole century of its existence without dividing it into periods but indicating when possible when the events related took place. To a great extent the discussion of the different topics must start with the evaluation of the sources, pointing out the limitations and complications that affect their interpretation.

This book is divided into four parts. Part one—chapters 2, 3, and 4—presents the basic characteristics of the imperial structure. Chapter 2 outlines the main features of the Empire's segmentary structure, specifically the tripartite organization that is the basis for the organization of this book. From the moment of its founding each of the three allied cities had a separate domain consisting of a group of kingdoms directly related to their capital by political, dynastic, and ethnic affiliation, and a clear distinction was made between this core area and the regions conquered by the alliance as a unit. Furthermore, the tripartite organization of the core area was extended to the conquered regions, and each of the three allied capitals became predominant in a sector of the expanding Empire. A further basic feature was the intermingling of territories, each of the three parties sharing in land distributions and in tribute from the domains of all three and from the distant areas conquered by the three allies together. Chapter 3 sketches the development of the Empire's structure throughout its history, starting with the political conditions at the moment of its establishment. It relates the conquests of each Tenochca king and the manner in which they modified the territorial structure of the alliance and the balance of power among its three parts. Chapter 4 is a detailed analysis of the different types of territorial categories, discussing individually the principal sources in order to demonstrate that these categories—defined better in the sources from Tetzcoco and Tlacopan—are also applicable to the Tenochca domain.

The domains of the three great kingdoms of the Triple Alliance are treated in part two (chapters 5 to 7), each separately, with its capital, dependent kingdoms, and towns of peasant tributaries, the latter situated primarily in the capital's own domain but also in those of the other two capitals.

Part three (chapters 8 to 12) covers the distant regions subject to the Empire. First, chapter 8 presents their organization based on the continuation of the conquered local kingdoms under different degrees of control and the tributary provinces established for collecting tribute. The procedures for dividing the tribute among the three capitals of the alliance are also discussed. This chapter further examines the division of the whole area subject to the Empire into three sectors, each corresponding to one of the kingdoms of the alliance and related to one of the directions of the universe. From this point of view, a comparison is made of the Codex Mendoza and the "Memorial de los pueblos de Tlacopan." The next chapters of this part (9, 10, and 11) review all the areas subject to the Triple Alliance, ordering them according to this tripartite division, always combining and comparing the Tenochca sources with those from Tetzcoco and Tlacopan. Chapter 12 is concerned with the military garrisons, settled in conquered regions with colonists from the basin, that were coordinated with the services of the local kingdoms for military activities.

The final part (chapter 13) sets forth the role played by the different territorial entities of the Empire. The core area supplied the personnel for military campaigns, raw materials and workers for public works, and settlers for the conquered areas. The elite of the ruling cities played the leading roles in the great political and religious ceremonies.

In conclusion, following the last chapter is a general summary of the topics investigated in this study.

PART ONE

The Tripartite Structure and the Political-Territorial Categories

Chapter 2

THE TRIPARTITE STRUCTURE

After Tenochtitlan and Tetzcoco defeated the Tepanecs, their rulers Itzcoatl and Nezahualcoyotl decided to include Totoquihuatzin of Tlacopan as the third member of the alliance and thus established a new political order in the Basin. From the moment the Triple Alliance was founded, the decisions made by the victors illustrate the organizational features basic to the territorial structure of the new regime. Three of those features were aspects of the segmentary structure on which the Empire was based.

In each of the three capital cities the king would govern his own domain directly and without interference, continuing an already existing political and dynastic organization. Each of the three great kings kept under his rule a group of kingdoms, each with its own dynasty and ethnic tradition. The king of Tenochtitlan ruled the Colhua-Mexica kingdoms, the king of Tetzcoco the Acolhua-Chichimec kingdoms, and the king of Tlacopan the Tepanec kingdoms. In this way, each of the three parts of the alliance included a capital city with its great king and the lesser kingdoms with their dependent kings. A tripartite organization was thus established by the founding kings. The entire region that comprised the alliance was divided into three parts, each defined geographically as the domain of one of the three capitals.

Next this tripartite division was extended beyond the core area of the Basin. The three great kings decided that in all future conquests one of the three would be preeminent in one of three sectors of the Empire. Beyond the Basin the area of each sector was adjacent to the domain of one of the ruling capital cities within the core area, with Tenochtitlan predominant in the south, Tetzcoco in the northeast, and Tlacopan in the northwest. Finally, in some of the areas first conquered by the Empire each capital took possession of separate towns, but as a rule the distant conquered regions paid tribute to the Empire as a unit, and their tribute was then shared by the three capitals. From the beginning there was, therefore, a series of distributions of conquered towns, of exchange of rights to the land, and of participation in tribute income that resulted in the scattering and consequently the intermingling of the territorial possessions of the three capitals, and of their rights to tribute, throughout the entire Empire. This intermingling constituted a third basic feature of the imperial structure. To a certain extent the three allied kingdoms were equivalent parts of the imperial structure, but a functional differentiation among them was established that gave predominance to the Tenochca king as director of the imperial armies. The proportion in which conquered lands and tribute were divided also favored Tenochtitlan, as did the practice of taking the tribute from conquered areas to Tenochtitlan before distributing it among the three kingdoms.

The tripartite structure and the predominance of Tenochtitlan are the reasons for the double title of this book.[1] The basic features of the territorial structure of the Empire continued throughout the century of its existence, but the constant process of expansion was accompanied by changes in the organization that increased the Tenochca predominance. These basic features are discussed in more detail in the rest of this chapter; the historical development of the imperial structure is outlined in chapter 3.

The Dependent Kingdoms of Each of the Three Capitals

The distinction between the dependent kingdoms that formed the domains of the three great kingdoms in the core area of the Empire and the distant conquered areas that paid tribute to all three is clear in a letter from Motolinía, who states that Tetzcoco, Tlacopan, and Mexico were each a kingdom with ten provinces and many subject towns. In addition, they divided among themselves the tribute from 160 provinces and towns.[2] The same author, in his *Memoriales*, when speaking of the installation ceremonies of the kings, states again that the sovereign of each of the three allied capitals had a group of kings directly subject to him. Those directly subject to Mexico went there to be confirmed as kings after first being elected by the principals of their provinces. Similarly, the towns and provinces directly subject to Tetzcoco and Tlacopan went to their sovereigns to be confirmed as kings, because "in this and other matters these two sovereigns recognized no superior."[3]

Motolinía is an early source worthy of belief, but the statement that there were ten kingdoms subject to each of the three capitals seems to be no more than the application of a formula—one which is not confirmed in the sources that provide the names of the cities subject to each capital. In another passage Motolinía himself refers to Tetzcoco's fifteen "provinces," which must be the dependent kingdoms of the great king of the Acolhua, and to ten provinces of Tlacopan, but he does not say how many provinces pertained to Tenochtitlan.[4] If the total number of kings was thirty, the number of Tenochtitlan's dependencies would have been five.

López de Gómara also reports that there were thirty kings in the Empire, each with a hundred thousand vassals, and three thousand lords of towns, also with many vassals. The thirty kings resided in Tenochtitlan a certain part of the year, and when they returned to their lands and kingdoms, they were obliged to leave a son or brother as security so that they would not rise in rebellion.[5] Gómara does not distinguish among the three allied capitals, nor does he name any of the subject kingdoms, but fortunately there are other sources that make it possible to identify the kingdoms that made up each of the three parts of the alliance.

Ixtlilxochitl relates that when the Triple Alliance was formed, each of the kings of the three allied cities had under his direct rule a certain number of kings of related dynastic affiliation: fourteen kings under the king of Tetzcoco, nine under the king of Tenochtitlan, and seven under the king of Tlacopan. He presents this organization as the result of the policy successfully advocated by Nezahualcoyotl in spite of the fact that Itzcoatl was reluctant to include Tlacopan as a third part of the Empire. The allied kings then decided to restore the subordinate kings of the Basin to their kingdoms, Itzcoatl restoring the nine kingdoms pertaining to the royal house of Mexico and Totoquihuatzin the seven that had pertained to Azcapotzalco. One more was added to the thirteen of the royal house of Tetzcoco, so altogether thirty kings were the grandees of the whole Empire. They were present in person at the courts of the three great kings, or else their sons were there; the acknowledgment they owed was only their homage and presence and to report in time of war with their vassals to serve their great king, without any other tribute or duty.[6]

The kingdoms whose rulers were restored by the three allied kings, or at least some of them, had sided with the Tepanecs and had to be overcome by force.[7] The internal factionalism of political entities is of great importance in the history of ancient Mexico and is closely related to the territorial structure. Nezahualcoyotl was opposed by the kings of Acolman and Coatlichan,[8] and cities of the Colhua domain such as Xochimilco and Cuitlahuac, stubborn holdouts during the war against the Tepanecs, were conquered later by Itzcoatl.[9] On the other hand, the lord of Tlacopan was said to have secretly favored Mexico and Tetzcoco.[10] These conflicts will not be analyzed here; let it be taken as proved that each of the three parts of the alliance consisted of a number of cities under the great king of the capital.

Ixtlilxochitl enumerates the Acolhua cities whose kings Nezahualcoyotl restored under the sovereignty of Tetzcoco. These were initially Huexotla, Coatlichan, Chimalhuacan, Tepetlaoztoc, Acolman, Tepechpan, Tezoyocan, Chiucnauhtlan, Teotihuacan, and Otompan. Later he confirmed the kings of Tollantzinco, Cuauhchinanco, and Xicotepec, and installed one of his sons in the new kingdom of Chiauhtlan, thus making a total of fourteen kings.[11]

Ixtlilxochitl does not name the nine cities within the Tenochca domain nor the seven that pertained to Tlacopan. The Tlacopan sources define the kingdoms of the Tepanec domain; the principal ones were Coyoacan, Cuauhtitlan, Apazco, Tollan, and Xilotepec.[12] But no source provides a specific list of the kingdoms of the Tenochca domain, a lack that explains why it has not been well defined, or even recognized, by various writers. Barlow, who makes his own subdivision of the territories of the Empire, speaks of the "old Tepanec domain" and the "old Acolhua domain," but he does not take into account the existence of a Tenochca domain, which had taken over the old Colhua polity of the southern Basin of Mexico. Actually, Barlow's "heart of the Empire" (Citlaltepec, Tlatelolco, and Petlacalco) corresponds to such a Tenochca domain, but he does not discuss the political category of the towns in this area. He defines the old Tepanec domain as the region subject to the Tepanecs before the formation of the Empire; his old Acolhua domain includes the first conquests of Nezahualcoyotl after the defeat of Azcapotzalco, and he adds other towns without sufficient reason to do so, as he himself admits.[13]

Nevertheless, when recounting the war against Azcapotzalco, Ixtlilxochitl names the cities of the Tepanec empire that were subjugated and incorporated into the Empire, the Tepanec cities into the domain of Tlacopan and the Colhua and the Chinampanec cities into that of Tenochtitlan. Likewise, he gives the list of various places, "cities, towns, and villages that are on the lake and around it belonging to the two kingdoms of Mexico and Tlacopan," where Nezahualcoyotl secured the right to receive the tribute called *chinampaneca tlacalaquilli*, that is, the tribute of the Chinampan region. This makes it possible to delineate the region dominated by those two capitals and identify approximately the cities with kings that, on the formation of the Triple Alliance, were direct dependents of Tenochtitlan or Tlacopan. The nine kingdoms of Tenochtitlan included the four kingdoms of Colhuacan, Itztapalapan, Mexicatzinco, and Huitzilopochco—referred to in the sources as *nauhteuctin*, literally "the Four Lords"—in the vicinity of Huixachtecatl (Cerro de la Estrella), and further south, Xochimilco, Cuitlahuac, and Mizquic in the Chinampan area. Two other cities are included: Tenayocan, northwest of Tenochtitlan, and Ecatepec, where the northern lakes drained into Lake Tetzcoco.[14]

Thus, the three allied capitals with their dependent kingdoms formed the core area of the Empire. Basically it occupied the Basin of Mexico, with the exception of Chalco, but it also extended beyond the Basin's eastern rim to include Tollantzinco and the higher slopes towards the Gulf coast, and in the northwest the Otomi areas north of the Basin and the mountains between the Basin and the Valley of Toluca. In the major cities of this core area resided the governing elite and skilled craftsmen, while in the rural areas the peasant population was organized into tributary units, *calpixcazgos*, supplying the cities. Some adjoining areas—Chalco, Tlalhuic, and Tolocan—were governed by kings of a lesser category, but they will be considered here as part of the core area. These lesser kingdoms gave the same services in war and construction that were typical of the allied cities.

They were also areas in which each of the three capitals had its own calpixcazgos in contrast with the distant conquered areas, where joint control prevailed. Their situation was intermediate between the cities of the alliance and the distant subjects of the Empire. Some changes in their status took place during the growth of the Empire that—although not always well documented—demonstrate an increased integration into the core area.

The Tripartite Division in the Subject Areas of the Empire

A second fundamental policy agreed upon by the rulers of the three constituent kingdoms of the Triple Alliance was that the initial territory of the Empire, formed by the domains of the three allied cities, would be expanded by dividing the lands obtained by future conquests into three parts or sectors. The best accounts of this are those of Ixtlilxochitl and Torquemada, based on Tetzcoca sources used by both authors. Ixtlilxochitl gives this agreement as the decision of Nezahualcoyotl, who after the triumph over the Tepanecs "divided all the land, already won or to be won, into five parts; [of] four [parts] he took half for himself, and the other half for his uncle the king of Mexico equaling himself to him in authority, and the fifth part to the king of Tlacopan."[15]

Torquemada describes the tripartite division of the Empire's territory in terms of the cardinal points. To Tenochtitlan would go the part that extends from the city to the east and thence towards the south until almost reaching the west; to Tlacopan the part that goes from the west until almost at the north; and to Tetzcoco the area from before the north to the east, where it shared the boundary with Tenochtitlan. Although all three kings might go to war in a given military campaign, the one who would be called the lord of the conquered region would be "that one whose lot had been to receive that part." If one king went alone to war, he would take all the tribute; if all three participated, they shared it.[16] Other sources confirm this division into three sectors, although there are some problems in applying the formula to the concrete data on the different conquests.[17]

Within these subjugated areas survived the underlying political organization, which was basically that established before the imperial conquest. Native rulers were kept in charge of internal affairs under different degrees of domination, but always as part of a system of indirect rule. Over them the Empire established an additional structure of tributary provinces for the collection of tribute and of military colonies and garrisons for control and expansion. The tribute collectors and the military commanders also intervened in the local political organizations, and high officials from the three capitals were occasionally sent to subject areas for particular matters.

The groups of cities governed by their own kings, each subject to one of the three capitals, and the distribution of all the conquered areas according to a tripartite division of the world are the key features in the political and territorial structure of the Empire. On this basis Map 2-1 presents a schematic picture of the different components of the Empire.

The Intermingling of Territories

From the beginning the intermingling of territories was an essential part of the policy of the three allied kings. Land was to be distributed in the kingdoms that became part of their own domains in the core area. The three allies would also share the tribute from all future conquests. Within each sector, in the core and beyond, each capital received rights to land and tribute in such a manner that the possessions of no one of the three were exclusively within its own geographic sector; each also had possessions in the sectors of the other two parties.

In the Tenochca histories that relate the defeat of Azcapotzalco, Coyoacan, and Xochimilco, lands in these cities were given to the lords, warriors, temples, and barrios of Tenochtitlan.[18] Similarly, in the Tetzcoca accounts of the reorganization made by Nezahualcoyotl in his own Acolhua domain, land was distributed among all the sociopolitical entities of his kingdom.[19]

The Tenochca and Tetzcoca histories present two different versions, apparently contradictory, of events in the early years of the Triple Alliance that are discussed further in the next chapter, on the history of the Empire. Following the Tetzcoca tradition, Ixtlilxochitl describes in detail a campaign by Nezahualcoyotl against Itzcoatl, as a consequence of which tribute from the Chinampan region of Tenochtitlan and Tlacopan was given to Tetzcoco.[20] The Tenochca tradition tells instead of a feigned war in which Nezahualcoyotl let himself be vanquished by Moteuczoma Ilhuicamina, with the result that Tenochtitlan acquired lands in Acolhuacan.[21] It is possible to accept a good deal of both traditions, since the predominance of Tetzcoco is placed in the days of Itzcoatl, and Moteuczoma's victory came later; thus, they might reflect a change in the balance of power between the two founding cities of the Empire. Nevertheless, these stories express the partisan point of view of each city, and the historicity of these traditions deserves further discussion.[22] What is of interest for this analysis is the fact that, from the beginning, each of the two founding cities of the Empire obtained possessions in the domain of the other.

A brief report in the Tratado de Teotihuacan is a help in understanding this situation. It states that when Nezahualcoyotl apportioned lands, he gave some "here" (which appears to mean the Acolhuacan) to various Acolhua and Mexica kings, and in the same way, these kings gave lands to the kings of "here." The cities that participated in this exchange were Tetzcoco, Huexotla, Coatlichan, Tepetla-

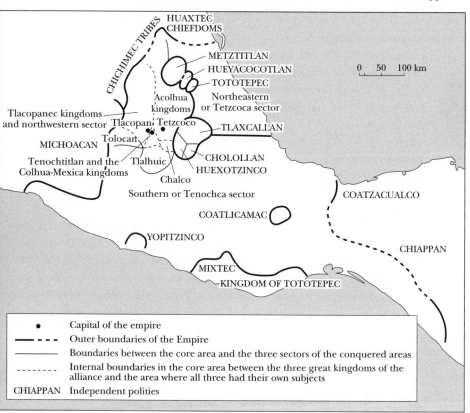

MAP 2-1. The Empire of the Triple Alliance

oztoc, Tezoyocan, Acolman, Chiucnauhtlan, Tenochtitlan, Tlatelolco, and Ecate-pec.[23] This concise statement illustrates the organizational practice that we are concerned with—that is, the exchange of rights to land, comparable to a trading contract or an exchange of gifts between allied rulers. In accordance with this principle, Tetzcoco had possessions in the Tenochca and Tlacopaneca domains, already mentioned in reference to the so-called Chinampan tribute; Tenochtitlan received tribute from towns in the Tetzcoca and Tlacopaneca domains; and, al-though to a lesser extent, Tlacopan had possessions in the domains of Tenochtitlan and Tetzcoco.[24]

On the other hand, there were regions conquered by the Triple Alliance, es-pecially Tlalhuic (Morelos), Chalco, and later Matlatzinco, where, as the new ter-ritory was divided, each capital obtained its own separate possessions.[25]

If in some towns, especially in the core area, each of the three capitals had its own lands, in areas conquered by the Triple Alliance the tribute that the subject towns paid was usually divided in stipulated proportions; the formula most often cited gave two-fifths to Tenochtitlan, two-fifths to Tetzcoco, and one-fifth to Tlacopan. Thus, the three allied kingdoms shared the resources of the Empire in different ways. At first glance there seem to have been two main procedures that were very different. There was distribution of lands when in a certain region each kingdom was given its lands separately, but there was a sharing of tribute when each received part of what was collected in common. Sometimes one or both of these procedures can be discerned, but other reports are contradictory. In regard to the tributary provinces that paid tribute to the three capitals, some sources suggest that in a given province there were stewards, or tribute collectors, from each of the three capitals, although they do not specify whether each one collected the tribute of certain towns or whether the tribute of the whole province was brought to one town to be divided later among the three stewards.[26] Ixtlilxochitl states that in some provinces Nezahualcoyotl put in place his own stewards to collect the tribute, of which the other two received no share, while in other provinces the three kings shared the tribute that was taken to Tenochtitlan, where it was apportioned to the stewards of each king.[27] Given that the tribute goods were concentrated in Tenochtitlan, the Tenochca king was in an advantageous position for influencing their distribution, as happened in the case of the Chinampan tribute when Moteuczoma Xocoyotzin ordered that it should no longer be paid to king Nezahualpilli of Tetzcoco.[28]

The nature of the territorial entities was closely related to land tenure. The towns and villages that were the source of tribute in goods and services for the members of the ruling estate are described as their possessions, thus raising the question of the relation between rights to the land and the participation of its owners in the political system. In this essay it will not be possible to discuss in detail all the many aspects of land tenure, but it is necessary to deal with certain problems that have to do with the definition of territorial entities.[29] Specifically we have to ask whether these were personal properties and the right to the income obtained from them was independent of giving services to the sovereign, or whether they were office lands that served as a kind of remuneration for services rendered. We also have to know, in each case, whether the land in question includes the inhabitants, who enjoy certain rights to these same lands. If the right of the nobles was that of receiving goods and labor from the peasants, one would have to know who assessed the property and collected the tribute. Moreover, the question of whether the noble owners exercised jurisdiction over the inhabitants of their lands is also of fundamental importance.

In a document that describes the preparation of the Codex Mendoza it is said that this codex depicts the distribution of towns by Moteuczoma to "the principal lords [señores principales] of this city of Mexico and the fee [*feudo*] given to him by those entrusted [*encomendatarios*] with the tribute from his towns." This is given as an antecedent of the distribution that Cortés made to Spaniards.[30] It is not entirely clear who were these "encomendatarios," nor what rights to the land they might have acquired. The text cited makes them similar to encomenderos, but the most probable answer is that they were those whom the commentator of the Codex Mendoza calls "gobernadores" or "calpixques," that is, governors or tribute collectors, officials of the Empire.

The chronicles of Durán and Tezozomoc describe the apportionment of lands to the kings and nobles of Tenochtitlan in the cities in the south of the Basin, and other documents give an inventory of the lands of Ahuitzotl and Moteuczoma, all of them located in the core area of the Empire.[31] When Axayacatl distributed lands in Tolocan, he not only gave lands to the kings of cities in the Basin but also kept some for himself or for his brother Ahuitzotl.[32] The Memorial of Don Hernando Pimentel lists towns where the kings of Tetzcoco had certain lands won as individuals (*caballerías ganadas por sus personas*) and other towns where they had tenants and lands that had been won in war (*ganaron por guerra donde tenían renteros y tierras*). These may well have been two distinct categories of tenure, but the explanation is insufficient.[33] The king of Tlacopan also had lands of his own,[34] and the king of Teotihuacan, in the Acolhuacan, had "war lands" in different towns, probably all in Chalco, that had been given to him by Nezahualcoyotl.[35] Documentation from the early years of the colony prove the existence of lands held by the subordinate kings and the nobles, sometimes called patrimonial lands as distinct from lands that went with the office held; nevertheless, the difference between these two types of lands is never well explained.

Concrete examples of patrimonial or personal lands, registered in other documents, suggest that donations of land and tribute would be made to relatives of the kings who held positions in the government or to warriors who would be given lands for their achievements; their heirs would be required to give military service. As in the case of Ahuitzotl and Moteuczoma, all these examples are from the core area. The lands were in the same regions as the tribute payers who provisioned the capitals, and the beneficiaries also received payments in kind.[36] This raises the question whether the tribute from these lands was included in the tribute collected by the royal stewards. Ixtlilxochitl makes the distinction in a concrete example: When Nezahualpilli recompensed his brother Axoquentzin for his victory over Chalco, "he designated certain places to be his, and a certain amount of the tribute that was collected from Chalco."[37]

However, there is seldom sufficient data to make a clear distinction between these two procedures. This is true not only because of the incompleteness and frequent ambiguity of the sources, but also because there was an institutional order that combined both procedures. What is described as donations of land may actually be concessions of tribute. There is a case from Cuauhtitlan that exemplifies this situation: In the year 3 Tecpatl, 1508, land in Tehuiloyocan was given (*motlalmacaque*) to the nobles of Tenochtitlan and Tlatelolco. In the presence of king Moteuczoma of Tenochtitlan and king Aztatzontzin of Cuauhtitlan the land was divided and put in the hands of the steward (*calpixqui*) of Acxotlan; the nobles were not in charge. That is, although the fields that are to produce tribute for each noble are defined, it is the steward who is put in charge of the lands and has the authority to administer them.[38]

Thus, when the Tratado de Teotihuacan and other sources speak of the donation of lands, we must ask ourselves whether this might not be the same situation as in Cuauhtitlan, where grants of land are said to be given to the nobles but, according to the additional information supplied, there has really been only a concession of tribute.

The reverse is also found. When the concession of tribute is described, it is usually identified according to the place or fields from which the tribute comes, but without defining the authority over the land the person given the lands might have acquired. This makes it difficult to determine to what extent it is a question of rights to tribute or ownership of the land—or, in other words, if the right to the income from a certain place is based on ownership of the land and includes the right to organize production and require payments in kind or labor from its occupants, or if it is simply the right to the tribute, or part of it, as a consequence of a concession from the lord of the land, whose stewards collect it for the individual to whom it has been granted.[39] This gives prominence to the fact, already noted, that the kings ordered the payment of part of the tribute as gifts to their relatives, officials, and individuals to be rewarded for merit. The giving of lands or of tribute were forms of payment that probably were combined in procedures not sufficiently explained in the sources.

As a result of the policy of distributing lands (or rights to tribute) in the same town among the different components of a social entity, almost all of them had lands in the same areas, and the inhabitants of one town made payments to various lords.[40] These phenomena are closely related and result in the intermingling of rights to the lands and tribute that are found at all levels of the social structure. Tenochtitlan, Tetzcoco, and Tlacopan each had holdings in the territories of the other two, and in addition, the three capitals had separate possessions in various tributary regions such as Tlalhuic, Chalco, and Tolocan. In other words, in each region there were possessions of the three capitals. In a similar fashion, Tenochtitlan and the cities of the Four Lords had lands in the region of Itztapalapan; an old map shows the intermingling of strips of land that go from the top of the hills to the lake shore and belonged to Tenochtitlan, Iztacalco, Colhuacan, Itztapalapan, and Mexicatzinco. Likewise, the kings of other Tenochca, Acolhua, and Tepanec cities had possessions not only in their own domains but also in those of their neighbors and even in the other two parts of the Empire. The individual properties of each ruler and nobleman were distributed in different areas,[41] and the residents of the different barrios of a cabecera had lands in the dependent villages.[42] The exchanges of lands, or tribute from them, among allied rulers permit one to say, as Gibson pointed out, that Mexico and Tetzcoco paid tribute to each other.[43]

Intermingling also results from the policy of taking in immigrants, as did the kings of Tetzcoco, who settled various groups of Toltec culture in all the cities of the kingdom. It is also a consequence of the practice of founding colonies with settlers from the various segments of a complex political entity, as was done by Tetzcoco in Calpullalpan and by the three cities of the Triple Alliance in the colonies of Oztoman and Huaxyacac.

The intermingling of lands and political units also touches on the question of boundaries and frontiers. It was a general practice in Mesoamerica for various towns or groups of towns to occupy a certain territory within which their dependent settlements were intermingled. It is said of several polities that the different head towns did not have well-marked boundary lines because their subject towns or villages were intermingled.[44]

This intermingling of lands and ethnic settlements is the accumulated effect of the distribution of lands and the migrations of peoples that took place at different times, but it also seems to have been a conscious policy as a way of forging alliances and establishing predominance in a region. This occurred not only in the Triple Alliance but also in earlier times and political units and perhaps in all of Mesoamerica.

Torquemada defines this practice as part of the policy of king Techotlalatzin of Tetzcoco, who, before the Tepanec empire was constituted, established twenty-six "cabezas" (head towns) of kingdoms and "provinces," appointing their kings or confirming those who were already in place. Later he established another thirty-nine "provinces" in which he named the rulers, making a total of sixty-five, and distributed all the land according to ethnic segments so that in each town he distributed people according to their numbers. If a Tepanec town had six thousand residents, he took two thousand from that town and sent them to another Metzotec or Chichimec town, from which he took two thousand and sent them to the Tepanec town from which he had transferred the first two thousand. Torquemada continues with more details about this procedure and also identifies the Colhuas, Chichimecs, and Acolhuas as those who were transferred.[45]

There is no description of such a systematic policy in the Triple Alliance, but some examples of colonization—as in Huaxyacac, Oztoman, and Cuextlaxtan—exemplify a procedure that, applied frequently, would have an effect similar to that of the policy of Techotlalatzin.

In conclusion, the procedures for sharing resources that have been identified (distribution and sharing) are found at various levels of the social structure: among the three allied capitals, among the dependent kingdoms of each capital, among the nobles of the city when conquered lands were distributed, and among the subdivisions of a town that shared the lands of the community. As a consequence, the settlements of the different kinds of people who comprised a political entity, and their rights to the land or to goods and services from the inhabitants of the land, were scattered and intermingled throughout that entity's territory.

The intermingling of social units was part of the segmentation of the political entities into cabeceras, parcialidades, or barrios—with different cultural traditions and specializations in the social division of labor—that were the basis for the factionalism of political life but also acted as a mechanism of integration by keeping them together and interdependent within a common structure.[46]

These principles are manifest in different ways in the territorial entities of the Triple Alliance. Before discussing these forms of political-territorial organization in detail in each of the three kingdoms of the Triple Alliance, we will first analyze the manner in which the different territorial categories are described in the sources that provide information on the extent and organization of the Empire.

Chapter 3

HISTORICAL DEVELOPMENT OF THE IMPERIAL STRUCTURE

The Tenochca Empire represents the culmination of a period of growing political integration following the collapse of an older political system in which the dominant power had been the city of Tollan.[1] Its structure, however, was built upon principles that had been part of the Mesoamerican tradition for a long period of time.

The decline and abandonment of Tollan led to an extensive migration of peoples who had been part of the Toltec political system and had settled in the Basin and neighboring areas, where they established their own separate political units and eventually developed larger political structures on the Toltec model. Other groups from the areas bordering on the Mesoamerican frontier also moved south and entered the Basin, but with a simpler level of cultural complexity. According to their traditions they were hunters when they arrived and without the temples and images typical of the Mesoamerican religion. All these peoples arriving from the north were called Chichimecs, a term that could refer more specifically to the hunter-gatherers but was applied to all those groups, even those of Toltec ancestry, who came from the north. A period of cultural and political recovery took place during which the interaction between these two types of peoples led to the acculturation of the Chichimecs to a typical Mesoamerican, specifically Toltec, culture and to the development of wider political units.

The leading polities in the Basin were Colhuacan, whose people were of the most direct Toltec ancestry and ruled the southern Basin; Azcapotzalco, capital of the Tepanecs, also of Toltec culture but with Chichimec influences; and Tetzcoco, where a dynasty ruled that prided itself on its Chichimec ancestry. But these Chichimecs had long since become acculturated and had incorporated various groups of Toltec ancestry, first the Acolhuas, who gave their name to the region Acolhuacan, and later other groups, among them Colhuas and Mexicas. The Mexicas were late immigrants who from the beginning had a Mesoamerican culture, engaged in cultivation, and built shrines during their migration, although they also had Chichimec influences. They established a kingdom in Chapoltepec but were defeated by the older powers of the area and fell into the orbit of the Colhuas and the Tepanecs. Eventually they settled in Mexico, where they established two cities: Tenochtitlan, which took a king of Colhua ancestry, and Tlatelolco, whose king stemmed from the Tepanec dynasty of Azcapotzalco.

The Tepanecs became the dominant power of the entire Basin during the reign of Tezozomoc of Azcapotzalco. He established his sons and his daughters' husbands as local rulers in various towns of the Basin and in the southern tramontane area. Very closely associated with his rule were the two Mexica cities, Tlatelolco and Tenochtitlan. Both had military functions in the organization of the Tepanec empire and received part of the tribute obtained by Tezozomoc from the subjugated towns.[2] Shortly after the beginning of the Tepanec empire, Tenochtitlan conquered the kingdoms of Colhuacan and Tenayocan, and its first king, Acamapichtli, won the Chinampan cities (Xochimilco, Cuitlahuac, and Mizquic) and Cuauhnahuac, thus establishing the basis for Tenochtitlan's predominance in the southern part of the Basin with which it would enter into the Triple Alliance.[3] The second Tenochca king, Huitzilihuitl, participated in various military campaigns carried out by the Tepanec empire and also gave a daughter in marriage to King Ixtlilxochitl of Tetzcoco. After the Acolhuacan had been completely subjugated by the Tepanecs, Tezozomoc named two of his sons as kings of Acolman and Coatlichan and gave dominion over Tetzcoco to the king of Tenochtitlan and over Huexotla to the king of Tlatelolco. All these kings shared in the tribute of the Acolhuacan.[4]

After the death of Tezozomoc, his heir was overthrown by Maxtla, king of Coyoacan, who installed himself in Azcapotzalco as the new Tepanec sovereign. The king of Tenochtitlan, Chimalpopoca, grandson of Tezozomoc, was no longer in favor with the new regime and was killed by the Tepanecs. The Mexicas then made Itzcoatl king and allied themselves against the Tepanecs with Nezahualcoyotl of Tetzcoco, whose father, Ixtlilxochitl, had perished in the struggle against Tezozomoc.

The war against the Tepanecs was led by Tenochtitlan and Tetzcoco. When their forces had defeated Azcapotzalco and other cities of its empire, Tenochtitlan and Tetzcoco formed the Triple Alliance together with Tlacopan, formerly a lesser Tepanec city. The historical traditions of the two major cities differ about the relative power of their sovereigns. According to the Tetzcoca writer Ixtlilxochitl, Nezahualcoyotl proposed accepting Tlacopan as the new capital of the Tepanecs and the third city of the alliance. Itzcoatl, although reluctant, agreed, and it was decided that in the future conquered areas would fall into three sectors, each under one of the kings of the alliance.[5] According to this same tradition, Nezahualcoyotl was the victor in an early contest with Tenochtitlan in which he won the so-called Chinampan tribute, given by the towns in the southern part of the Basin that was the center of the Tenochca and Tlacopanec domains.[6]

What is most probable is that Tetzcoco and especially Tlacopan had been from the beginning more subject to Tenochtitlan than would be expected from the formula of a tripartite alliance that Ixtlilxochitl presents. At the end of the war against the Tepanecs, Tenochtitlan still maintained the superiority over Tetzcoco that it had acquired in the time of Tezozomoc of Azcapotzalco. Torquemada states very clearly that the Acolhuacan belonged to Itzcoatl, since Tezozomoc had given him part of that kingdom and Itzcoatl had won the other part by defeating Maxtla. However, it was Iztcoatl's wish that Nezahualcoyotl should be restored to sovereignty over his kingdom, and the two together conquered the rebel kings of the Acolhuacan. When the defeated kings begged Itzcoatl to give them back to Nezahualcoyotl, whom they wished to obey as their sovereign, Itzcoatl graciously agreed.[7]

According to the Mexica chronicles, the supremacy of the Tenochca sovereign was present from the beginning of the alliance. At the time of the war against the Tepanecs, Nezahualcoyotl was the nephew of Itzcoatl, since his father, King Ixtlilxochitl of Tetzcoco, had married a daughter of the Tenochca king Huitzilihuitl— the type of matrimonial alliance in which the superior king gives a daughter to a subordinate king. This kind of alliance was continued, and the kings who succeeded Nezahualcoyotl were sons of Mexica princesses. At the end of his reign Itzcoatl, as he was dying, ordered that the king of Tetzcoco should be the second king of the land and the king of Tlacopan the third. According to another tradition, Itzcoatl reduced all the conquered kingdoms to only three—Mexico, Tetzcoco, and Tlacopan.[8]

Tetzcoco's subordinate status is made clear in other sources. The *Anales de Cuauhtitlan* record that on 4 Acatl 1431, Nezahualcoyotl was installed as king by Itzcoatl in Tenochtitlan, and only later in 1433 established himself in Tetzcoco.[9] Chimalpahin also makes clear the subordination of Tetzcoco in his account of the submission, or "entrance" (*hualcalacque*), of the Tetzcocas to Tenochtitlan in 1427.[10] Later, in 4 Acatl 1431, Nezahualcoyotl was installed as king when Itzcoatl had already been reigning for five years in Tenochtitlan and a year after Tlacopan had submitted to Tenochtitlan. And he adds: "Then were also defeated the Acolhua Tetzcocas. And although the Acolhuas were defeated, the war lasted only half a day and was over by dinner time. The Tetzcocas capitulated; Nezahualcoyotl had arranged it; and when they were defeated, the victors were the Tenochca Mexicas."[11]

The relación geográfica of Cempohuallan reports that during the reign of Itzcoatl there was a transfer of villages in the northern part of the Acolhuacan to Tenochtitlan, which is further evidence of Tenochtitlan's superiority.[12] However, in Durán's account it was Itzcoatl's successor, Moteuczoma Ilhuicamina, who conquered Tetzcoco in a feigned war arranged ahead of time with Nezahualcoyotl and acquired lands for the Mexicas in the Acolhuacan.[13] Perhaps there was some confusion about chronology in this chronicle as a result of the fact that Ilhuicamina was *tlacatecatl* under Itzcoatl and played an active role in the war against the Tepanecs.[14]

All the sources agree that Tlacopan was the least important of the three allied cities. As one source has it, when Maxtla of Coyoacan enthroned himself in Azcapotzalco, the legitimate ruler, son of the previous king, saw fit to leave the city and went to Tlacopan.[15] According to Ixtlilxochitl, Totoquihuatzin of Tlacopan "was secretly on the side of Nezahualcoyotzin and the Mexica lords, who were his close relatives."[16] Chimalpahin reports that Tlacopan surrendered to Tenochtitlan during Itzcoatl's reign at the same time as Azcapotzalco, Coyoacan, and the Chinampanec cities.[17] He further states that in 1428 the people of Tlacopan "gave themselves into the hands of the Mexicas, when they surrendered, and the Colhuas also submitted to Mexico,"[18] and in 3 Tochtli 1430 a Tlacopanec leader named Tlacacuitlahua and the king of Tlacopan, Acolnahuacatl Tzacualcatl, surrendered to Tenochtitlan.[19] Tlacopan's position as subordinate to Tenochtitlan is evident in that since Itzcoatl's reign the kings of several cities of the Tepanec group were of the Tenochca dynasty, and also in that Tlacopan received a smaller portion of tribute than the other two capitals of the Empire.

In the war against Azcapotzalco both Tenochtitlan and Tetzcoco had to defeat the cities of their own domains that had gone over to the Tepanecs. Acolman and Coatlichan, for many years components of the Acolhua-Chichimec kingdom, were governed by kings imposed on them by Tezozomoc of Azcapotzalco, and they fought on the side of the Tepanecs. After the defeat, their kings were restored and they became dependencies of Tetzcoco.[20]

The Tenochca sources recognize the privileged position of Tetzcoco and Tlacopan, although at times they present the creation of the Empire as a series of conquests starting with the defeat of Coyoacan and Azcapotzalco. But the victories recorded in the lists of conquests and the Tenochca chronicles should be understood as different types of military events, similar to those described for the Acolhuacan in the Tetzcoco sources. Thus, the lists of Itzcoatl's conquests include towns in the core area that became part of the Triple Alliance in its beginning— that is, instead of conquests they were towns in the Tepanec, Colhua, and Acolhua regions in which there had been military action during the war against Maxtla of Azcapotzalco. These "conquests" of Itzcoatl were Azcapotzalco, Coyoacan, Teocalhueyacan, Cuahuacan, Tlacopan, Atlacuihuayan, Mixcoac, Cuauhximalpan, Cuauhtitlan, Tecpan, and Huitzitzilpan, all of them Tepanec towns. But Acolhuacan-Tetzcoco is also in the list. That is, the other two parts that formed the Triple Alliance are given as "conquered." In addition, Tlatelolco and the cities in the southern part of the Basin—Mizquic, Cuitlahuac, and Xochimilco—also appear as conquests.[21] These cities comprised the old Colhua kingdom, over which Tenochtitlan already claimed sovereignty during the period of Tepanec predominance, even though Xochimilco's king had been put in place by Tezozomoc of Azcapotzalco.[22] The situation of these cities is comparable to that of the Acolhua cities, such as Coatlichan, that had been defeated by Nezahualcoyotl. The kings of Tenochtitlan and Tetzcoco had to reassert their power in their own traditional domains. All this is in effect a record of the formation of the core area of the Triple Alliance, as Ixtlilxochitl and Torquemada describe it.[23]

Once the Triple Alliance had been established, each of the three capitals was free to undertake its own conquests, but most conquests were carried out with the collaboration of the three kings. Nevertheless, all the conquered areas were associated more closely with one or another of the three ruling kingdoms.

Each of these capitals was ruled by its own dynasty, thus continuing those that had ruled, each in its own domain, before the Triple Alliance was formed. The dynasty of Colhua antecedents founded by Acamapichtli ruled in Tenochtitlan; in Tetzcoco the royal lineage begun by their leader, Xolotl, continued; and in Tlacopan a member of the Tepanec dynasty governed. In the Tenochca kingdom, once the alliance was established, succession was to a collateral relative, that is, a brother or nephew of the previous ruler, and the kings that followed were the sons of mothers belonging to the same lineage. In Tetzcoco and Tlacopan succession was lineal, from father to son. The kings of Tetzcoco were the sons of Tenochca mothers; the maternal line of the kings of Tlacopan is not well known.[24]

Itzcoatl and Nezahualcoyotl carried their military campaigns beyond the core area formed by the three allied kingdoms. The expansion of the Empire followed the routes laid down previously by Tezozomoc of Azcapotzalco towards the lowlands of present-day Morelos. Under Itzcoatl the Triple Alliance conquered Cuauhnahuac and inflicted a first defeat on Chalco, where lands were divided among the capitals of the Empire. Farther south, the chronicles place within Itzcoatl's time the conquest of several towns in the present-day state of Guerrero, where the expansion continued under his successors.[25] Itzcoatl sent several of his sons to be the rulers of cities that define the Tenochca sphere of influence in this initial period: Ecatepec and Itztapalapan, which were part of the Tenochca domain, as well as Xilotepec, Apan, and Atotonilco in the Tlacopan domain.[26]

At his death, Itzcoatl was succeeded in 1440 by a son of Huitzilihuitl, Moteuczoma Ilhuicamina; during the latter's reign Nezahualcoyotl continued to rule in Tetzcoco. The conquest lists of this period still include towns that were part of the three great kingdoms of the alliance; thus, it seems that the tripartite structure of the Empire was still taking shape. Numerous conquests by Ilhuicamina are recorded in the northwestern, or Tepanec, domain within the core area. The most important were Hueypochtlan, Atotonilco de Tula, Axocopan, Tollan, Xilotepec, and, more towards the east, Atotonilco el Grande. Although they include the Tepanec kingdoms of Tollan and Xilotepec, these places coincide almost completely with the cabeceras of the tributary provinces that the Codex Mendoza gives for that region; it seems reasonable to conclude that this indicates the establishment of those provinces.[27] All this signals the first increase of Tenochca power in territories that may have come into the Triple Alliance as the dominion of Tlacopan. There is a parallel here with the acquisition by Itzcoatl (or Moteuczoma), in the prearranged war with Tetzcoco, of the cities in the northern part of the Acolhua kingdom, which became the tributary province of Acolman.

Other towns in the conquest lists of Ilhuicamina show the continued expansion of the recently established Empire, with the participation of the three kings and the creation of tributary provinces that made payments to the three capitals. Thus, they gained more towns south of the Basin, in Tlalhuic and Cohuixco, where Itzcoatl had already made conquests. These also came to be under Tenochca predominance, although Tetzcoco established a calpixcazgo in Tlalcozauhtitlan.[28] The conquests toward the Huaxteca were probably the work of Nezahualcoyotl and signify the Acolhua predominance in the northeastern sector of the Empire, with Tochpan and Tziuhcoac as the principal provinces.[29]

The expansion that began with the conquest of Tepeyacac reached Coaixtlahuacan and continued in two directions, toward the Gulf coast and towards the Valley of Oaxaca. The conquest of Huaxyacac resulted in the establishment of the colony of that name that from then on was the center of imperial domination in the region. The expansion towards the coast reached Cuetlaxtlan and Cuauhtochco. It also incorporated Tochtepec, more often cited in the Tetzcoca tradition than in the Tenochca; probably Tetzcoco played a dominant role in the conquest of Tochtepec, since it established its own calpixcazgo.[30]

Moteuczoma was succeeded in 1469 by Axayacatl, offspring of a son of Itzcoatl and a daughter of Moteuczoma. At almost the same time, the king of Tlacopan died and was succeeded by his son Chimalpopoca; shortly thereafter Nezahualcoyotl died and was succeeded by his son Nezahualpilli. The two new kings ruled throughout the reign of Axayacatl. Following the death of Nezahualcoyotl, the chronicles, including the Tetzcoca sources, attribute a less important role to Tetzcoco. Nezahualpilli participated in the wars of the Empire, but he did not play a role comparable to that attributed to Nezahualcoyotl in the first conquests of the Empire.

During the reign of Axayacatl, Tlatelolco was defeated when its king, Moquihuix, rebelled against Tenochtitlan and tried in vain to obtain the support of cities that had been part of the Tepanec empire of Azcapotzalco. From then on Tlatelolco was no longer ruled by its own king but was under the command of military governors. The fall of Tlatelolco, whose role under the Tepanecs had been as important as that of Tenochtitlan, if not more so, coincided with the Tenochca expansion in the western sector. Axayacatl—with the participation of Nezahualpilli—carried out campaigns in the Tolocan region, where he established the tributary province headed by the city of that name, and the conquest of Xiquipilco, Tenantzinco, Xocotitlan, and Ocuillan is also recorded. Part of this region probably came into the Empire under Tlacopan as part of.the old empire of Azcapotzalco, but under Axayacatl it was reorganized and enlarged, coming under Tenochca predominance, although Tlacopan and, to a lesser extent, Tetzcoco also had separate possessions there. Perhaps these western towns had not entered completely into the imperial organization as part of the domain of Tlacopan, or they rebelled during the Tlatelolco war. The threat posed by the Tarascan kingdom also impelled Axayacatl's activity in this region. It all led as a consequence to the reorganization of the domain with which Tlacopan entered the alliance and reinforced the influence of Tenochtitlan in the west, especially with the departure of some of the Matlatzincas to Michoacan and the division of lands in Tolocan. Although Tlacopan and Tetzcoco were also allotted lands, the Tenochca predominance is unquestionable. Axayacatl also made conquests in the Huaxteca and consolidated control over Tepeyacac and Cuetlaxtlan.[31]

The reign of Axayacatl's successor, his brother Tizoc, began in 1481; during Tizoc's rule there were no changes in the kings of Tetzcoco and Tlacopan. Tizoc is credited with very little in new acquisitions for the Empire. He carried on the war in the west but failed in his attempt to conquer Metztitlan.[32]

Ahuitzotl succeeded his brother Tizoc in 1486. During Ahuitzotl's entire reign Nezahualpilli continued to rule in Tetzcoco; in Tlacopan, Chimalpopoca died in 1489 and was succeeded by his son, the second Totoquihuatzin.

In his first campaign, Ahuitzotl waged war in the west against Chiappan, Xiquipilco, Cuahuacan, Cillan, Mazahuacan, Xocotitlan, and Xilotepec.[33] With the exception of Chiappan, these places are mentioned among the conquests of previous kings; it is noteworthy that Cuahuacan appears again after a first conquest by Itzcoatl. It was the head town of the Tenochca tributary province situated within the domain of Tlacopan. One sees here the final consolidation of the Tenochca expansion in the west, begun under Axayacatl, that strengthened the Tenochca predominance over the Tlacopanec kingdoms in that region. There are no reports of such an effective penetration by Tenochtitlan in the Tetzcoca domain in the Acolhuacan nor in the neighboring regions in the northeast sector.

Ahuitzotl, like Ilhuicamina, was a great conqueror who extended the Empire's boundaries considerably. He directed new campaigns on the Tarascan frontier, where he established military colonies in the Oztoman region, won the tributary province of Cihuatlan on the Costa Grande, and conquered other towns along the coast in Acapolco and the Costa Chica. He also undertook more wars in the Huaxteca and in Oaxaca, whence he began the military and commercial expansion to Tehuantepec and Xoconochco. In addition, commercial expeditions to Xicallanco were started during his reign.[34]

Ahuitzotl was succeeded in 1502 by his nephew, a son of Axayacatl, Moteuczoma Xocoyotzin, who was killed in 1520 when the Spanish occupied Tenochtitlan. In Tetzcoco, Nezahualpilli died in 1515 and was succeeded by his son Cacama, who, like Totoquihuatzin of Tlacopan, died during the war of the Spanish Conquest, which put an end to the Empire.

Moteuczoma Xocoyotzin waged war in several regions but was most active in Oaxaca, where he fought again against local kingdoms that had not been thoroughly subjugated previously. He made new conquests, among which Tlachquiauhco was outstanding, but he did not succeed in dominating the entire region. The Mixtec kingdom of Tototepec, on the coast, maintained its independence, and, according to some reports, the cities of the Mixteca were rebelling when the Spanish arrived. Moteuczoma also won new territories in the center of Veracruz, although they are not recorded as tributaries in the Codex Mendoza or in the "Memorial de los pueblos de Tlacopan."[35]

Surrounded by the Empire, Tlaxcallan and Chololan maintained their independence, although it is said of the latter that three of its subdivisions sided with Tlaxcallan and the other three favored Moteuczoma. Huexotzinco was defeated by the Empire shortly before the arrival of Cortés.

The balance among the three kingdoms of the alliance changed during its history with the growth of the power of Tenochtitlan, whose king directed the military activities of the Empire. The expansion under the last two kings, Ahuitzotl and Moteuczoma, took place principally in the southern sector of the Empire associated with Tenochtitlan, thus increasing the income from tribute sent to Tenochtitlan and administered from there. The supremacy of the Tenochca sovereign also increased during this period of territorial expansion. Seeing Tetzcoco as a rival for power within the alliance, Moteuczoma plotted an ambush of Nezahualpilli's army in a war with Tlaxcallan and used the Tetzcoca king's defeat to justify the revocation of the Chinampan tribute that Tetzcoco had been receiving since the days of Nezahualcoyotl. When Nezahualpilli sent his ambassadors to complain, Moteuczoma replied that the Empire was now to be governed by only one of the three kings and that he was the supreme ruler.[36] It is possible that in other regions Moteuczoma also took possession of provinces that might have belonged to Tetzcoco, such as Tochtepec and Tlalcozauhtitlan. Soon after this, at

Nezahualpilli's death, his son Cacama, born of a Tenochca mother, ascended the throne of Tetzcoco with Moteuczoma's support. But another son, Ixtlilxochitl, disputed the succession, and the great Acolhua kingdom was divided between the two brothers.[37] All this augmented the Tenochca influence in the Acolhua zone and is also evidence of the erosion of the tripartite structure.

The political-territorial structure presented here—the contrast between the core area and the conquered regions and the extension of the tripartite organization to the conquered areas—is in accord with the formula decided upon at the beginning of the alliance, according to the Tetzcoca sources. An examination of the concrete data on the expansion of the Empire shows that such a formula is useful for understanding the information available, although it must be modified on various points. The growth of the domain of Tenochtitlan in the northwest sector shows that the dependent kingdoms of Tlacopan outside the Basin were limited to Teotlalpan and Xilotepec. Farther west, in the Valley of Toluca, although Tlacopan had its own towns and villages there, the power of Tenochtitlan predominated. The "Memorial de Tlacopan" does not count that region among those that paid tribute to the three capitals. In the northeast sector associated with Tetzcoco, the conquests of the Empire reinforced the dominion of Tenochtitlan in regions such as Atlan and parts of the coast, which are never recorded as belonging to the provinces of the Tetzcoca sector. And as we have seen, Nezahualpilli lost his rights to the tribute of Chinampan.

The organization of the Empire as an alliance of three kingdoms, each with its own domain that included several dependent kingdoms, and the distinction between the core area formed by these three parts and the distant regions subjugated by the Empire were kept throughout all its history. As the Empire developed, certain changes modified the structure in ways that increased in successive steps the supremacy of Tenochtitlan.

Chapter 4

THE POLITICAL-TERRITORIAL CATEGORIES IN THE SOURCES

The various territorial units that made up the Empire performed different functions within its organization, and these functions are related to the occupations and social levels of their members. In order to determine the basic categories within the political-territorial structure of the Empire, the Tenochca documents—the *Matrícula de tributos* and the Codex Mendoza—are not the best place to start. Although these sources are the most complete as to lists of tributary towns and the nature and quantity of the tribute paid, they contain very little information on the social and political characteristics of each province, usually presenting all of the provinces as entities of the same kind. It is better to start with the documentation from Tetzcoco and Tlacopan, which, although less detailed about tribute, makes it possible to identify the different categories of territorial units on the basis of their economic obligations, their political status within the Empire, and the social level of their inhabitants.

Motolinía's "Memorial tetzcocano" and the "Memorial de los pueblos de Tlacopan"

The key documents are the "Memorial de los pueblos de Tlacopan,"[1] which originated in that city, and, for Tetzcoco, one of the inserts in Motolinía's work that I will label Motolinía's "Memorial tetzcocano."[2] The importance of these documents, both written in Spanish, lies in the lists they provide of the towns pertaining to each of these two kingdoms arranged in categories that make clear their political and economic characteristics—information that is basic to the interpretation presented in this book.

At the end of the *Anales de Cuauhtitlan* is a document in Nahuatl that complements Motolinía's "Memorial tetzcocano" in several respects.[3] Both these texts can be considered as different versions of material originating from a common corpus of pictorial documents. The lists of towns pertaining to Tetzcoco in the *Anales de Cuauhtitlan* are practically the same as those given by Motolinía, but they do not include the description of the towns' sociopolitical characteristics given by the Franciscan. On the other hand, the *Anales de Cuauhtitlan* provides essential information on the nature and quantity of tribute paid by the provinces of the Empire that is lacking in Motolinía; this will be discussed here only tangentially, since it is peripheral to the main concerns of this study. The Tlacopan and Tetzcoco memorials consist only of text, but there are allusions to pictures that must have been similar to those of the *Matrícula de tributos*, and the version in the *Anales de Cuauhtitlan* contains a few glyphs in the last line of the text.[4] For both Tlacopan and Tetzcoco there are chronicles and documents that add important data on the topic of interest here.

It is clear that the two documents written in Spanish—the "Memorial de los Pueblos de Tlacopan" and Motolinía's "Memorial tetzcocano"—are closely related. Both are organized in the same way, and some passages in them, as will be seen, are almost identical. The resemblance no doubt results from their both having been prepared to be sent together with petitions directed to the Spanish Crown by the caciques of the two cities.

In a letter written in 1552, Don Antonio Cortés of Tlacopan states that in addition to its many tributary towns, the kingdom of Tlacopan shared with Mexico and Tetzcoco part of the tribute from 123 provinces and towns, "as will be seen in a list that accompanies this [letter]." This list could have been the "Memorial de Tlacopan," although the figure of 123 towns spoken of in the letter is not in accord with the numerous toponyms of the "Memorial," which add up to 347 towns paying tribute to the three capitals.[5] When Don Antonio's letter speaks of 123 provinces and towns whose tribute Tlacopan shared with Mexico and Tetzcoco, he must be referring to something different from the arrangement of the "Memorial." Perhaps this list of 123 towns was a slightly different version mentioned in another letter from Don Antonio Cortés, in 1561, in which with words identical to those of the earlier letter he alludes to a list (memoria) sent with his letter without saying how many towns it contained.[6] In any case it is clear that on more than one occasion lists of the towns subject to Tlacopan were prepared to be sent to Spain, and the letters quoted here explain the origin of the "Memorial de Tlacopan."[7] A pictorial document (1565) inserted into the Codex Osuna is yet another list of subject towns prepared in Tlacopan that coincides closely with part of the "Memorial de Tlacopan," as will be seen below.

No letter has survived from the cacique of Tetzcoco that refers specifically to a list of the towns pertaining to Tetzcoco, but there is a *real cédula*, addressed to the Audiencia in 1557, that refers to such a letter. According to this document, Don

Hernando Pimentel, cacique of Tetzcoco, together with other noblemen, had stated that in past times the government had three heads, Mexico, Tetzcoco, and Tlacopan, and that Tetzcoco used to have many subject towns and had shared with Mexico and Tlacopan the tribute from 123 provinces and towns contained in a memorial that they presented to the Council of the Indies.[8] Although the date when this memorial was sent is not given, the statement about 123 towns suggests that it was a document prepared at the same time as the one sent by Don Antonio Cortés, according to his letter dated 1552. In addition, Don Hernando Pimentel, writing to the king in 1554 for permission to go to Spain, claimed the city of Tetzcoco and its sujetos as his own, "as cacique and legitimate heir."[9] Probably he wished to continue the matter that he had raised two years earlier, as had Don Antonio Cortés of Tlacopan.

Later, in 1558, another royal cédula refers to a communication from Don Hernando Pimentel in which he states— without any mention of Tlacopan—that the former kings of Tetzcoco and Mexico had their own provinces and lands and divided among themselves the tribute from many other provinces. The Audiencia was ordered to make a report with the testimony of witnesses that Don Hernando would provide and to send it to the Council of the Indies.[10]

It is obvious that Motolinía's "Memorial tetzcocano" must have been written in connection with the "Memorial de Tlacopan," since they share a similar organization and coincide literally in some phrases. The allusion to 123 towns in documents from both Tetzcoco and Tlacopan also suggests that the two capitals collaborated in preparing the memorials sent to Spain.[11] However, another memorial by Don Hernando Pimentel has survived in which he lists the possessions of the kings of Tetzcoco in pre-Spanish times. In several respects it is organized differently from Motolinía's "Memorial tetzcocano" and gives greater importance to the personal rights of the kings; it shows no resemblance to the documents of Tlacopan. Therefore, it must have been prepared independently, perhaps in connection with the petition referred to in the royal cédula of 1558 or the report that the cédula ordered to be made. This document, which I call the Memorial of Don Hernando Pimentel, is discussed in the next section of this chapter. Some of the sources used by Ixtlilxochitl must have been related in some way to all these memorials, especially the documents Ixtlilxochitl calls royal registers (*padrones reales*) of Tetzcoco.[12]

There is no evidence that a descendent of the Tenochca rulers participated in these particular petitions made by the caciques of Tetzcoco and Tlacopan. A few years later (1562) the three Indian governors of the old imperial capitals wrote a letter in which they requested restitution for their old possessions, but nothing is said about a list of towns formerly under the rule of their cities.[13]

In order to define the different categories that comprised each of the three parts of the Triple Alliance, the memorials of Tetzcoco and Tlacopan are the most explicit on several points of primary importance and will be the starting point of this analysis. Since the Tetzcoca sources are the most informative, they will be considered first.

Motolinía's "Memorial tetzcocano" alludes to the pictorial document from which his data were taken and gives the best explanations of the nature of the different groups of towns. His source depicted groups of toponymical glyphs, each with additional drawings showing the peasants in the towns, the kings who governed the cities, and the stewards who collected the tribute. The tribute itself is not given in Motolinía's memorial, but it is in the related version in the *Anales de Cuauhtitlan*. Together they provide information on six kinds of towns that will be examined in detail in the course of this book. The six categories are described in the text in the following order:[14]

1. Towns subject to Tetzcoco, with their own kings who were married to daughters of Nezahualcoyotl, "who along with his daughters gave to their husbands the rulership [señorío]." These towns served only in construction and in supplying firewood for half a year. All these towns are in the Acolhuacan.[15]

2. Towns made up of peasants, in which "there were no kings but stewards [mayores y principales] who governed them. They were all as tenants [renteros] of the king of Tetzcoco. In addition to their tribute the king of Tetzcoco had in all these towns many plots of land that the people cultivated for him." The peasants also contributed firewood for half a year. All these towns are also in the Acolhuacan.[16]

3. Towns that paid tribute to the three capitals of the Empire and that correspond to the tributary province of Tochpan in the Codex Mendoza.

4. Towns that paid tribute to the three capitals of the Empire and that correspond to the tributary provinces of Tlatlauhquitepec, Tlapacoyan, and Tziuhcoac in the Codex Mendoza.[17]

5. Other towns that paid tribute to the three capitals and that correspond to the province of Tochtepec in the Codex Mendoza.

6. Cuauhnahuac, together with other towns, whose tribute all went to Tetzcoco.[18]

The towns in groups 1, 2, and 6 comprise the Acolhua kingdom of Tetzcoco; they are discussed below in chapter 6. Groups 3, 4, and 5, towns that paid tribute to the three capitals, according to other sources are only part of the many conquered regions that paid tribute to the Empire. They correspond approximately to the Tetzcoca sector as defined by Torquemada; they are discussed in chapter 11. As to the government of these towns, the memorial says only that the stewards of each of the three kings of the alliance collected the tribute.

The material from Tlacopan is very similar to that of Tetzcoco. The "Memorial de Tlacopan" is organized in the same way as Motolinía's "Memorial tetzcocano." The description of the towns of tenants is almost identical in both documents, and the enumeration of the obligations of the cities, whose kings, as we will see, were subject to Tlacopan, also contains sentences that are very similar.

The manuscript is divided into eight main sections, with headings that define the nature of the towns in each list. These sections, except for the first three and the last, are in turn subdivided into paragraphs.[19]

The first three sections, which have no corresponding category in Motolinía's "Memorial tetzcocano," are described as follows:

1. The first towns listed were "subject to the cabecera of Tlacopan."

2. A second group of towns had been distributed to Spaniards residing in Tlacopan.

3. The next five towns pertained to Juan Cano and did not acknowledge the rule by Tlacopan.

In terms of pre-Spanish territorial categories, the distinctions among these three categories are irrelevant, since they relate to Spanish administrative decisions. Other sources show that the first two formed the rural district of Tlacopan and the towns in the third were also sujetos of Tlacopan.

4. The fourth section lists subjects to Tlacopan whose people "gathered here to go to war, and their tribute obligations were given here"; they also brought to the city construction material and craft products. This section is subdivided into five paragraphs. As will be seen when discussing the kingdom of Tlacopan, each paragraph enumerates one of the cities that were direct dependencies of Tlacopan together with its subject towns.[20] This section corresponds to the first category in Motolinía's "Memorial tetzcocano," which in a more detailed definition explains that they were ruled by their own kings.

5. The fifth section is defined with almost the same words as Motolinía's second category. The lists of settlements are grouped into paragraphs described as either towns or hamlets where the tenants of the king of Tlacopan lived.[21]

These five sections delineate the kingdoms and the tributary towns of the Tepanec capital; all this is discussed in chapter 7. They include all the regions that formed part of the Empire in the northwest sector and pertained to Tlacopan, according to Torquemada, but one does not find in that area any of the towns that, according to other sections of the "Memorial de Tlacopan," paid tribute to the three capitals of the alliance. All other towns in this area are those listed in section 4 as part of the kingdoms that constituted the Tepanec kingdom of Tlacopan. However, as will be seen, in this northwestern sector there were also towns that paid tribute to Tenochtitlan or to Tetzcoco. Obviously, in this area as in Tlalhuic the three capitals had separate holdings, but the "Memorial de Tlacopan" lists only those of the Tepanec capital.

The last three sections comprise the towns that paid tribute to the Empire as a unit; they include the northeastern and southern regions that, according to Torquemada, pertained to Tetzcoco and Tenochtitlan, respectively.

6. The sixth section begins with a heading that states: "These towns and provinces that follow paid tribute to Mexico, Tezcuco, and Tlacupan; their tribute was distributed by these three kings of Mexico, Tezcuco, and Tlacupan." It includes regions also mentioned in the Tetzcoca documents: six groups of towns headed by Tochpan, Tziuhcoac, Tochtepec, Tlapacoyan, Tlatlauhquitepec, and Chinantlan. The towns in Tochpan and Tziuhcoac are almost the same ones as those in the Tetzcoca documentation, which includes Tlapacoyan and Tlatlauhquitepec together with Tziuhcoac, but without listing the towns that were their dependents. Chinantlan is missing in Motolinía's "Memorial tetzcocano." This section is discussed in chapter 11, which is devoted to the provinces of the Empire in the northeastern sector, except for Tochtepec, which is discussed as part of the southern sector in chapter 10.

7. The seventh section has this heading: "Also, these other towns and provinces, whose tribute was [in] three [parts], distributed by these three kings of Mexico, Tetzcoco, and Tlacopan, are the following." This section contains four paragraphs, each headed by towns that are not cabeceras of tributary provinces in other sources: Cempohuallan includes towns on the Gulf Coast; Cozcatlan, towns in the Mixteca Alta and Baja; Tlachmalacac, towns in interior Guerrero; and the paragraph headed by Oztoman lists towns from the coast of Guerrero and the central valleys of Oaxaca.

8. The heading of the eighth section is the same: "And also these other towns and provinces whose tribute was [in] three [parts] distributed by the three kings of Mexico, Tetzcoco, and Tlacopan, are the following." The entire region of the isthmus, from Tototepec to Tehuantepec and Xoconochco, is included in one paragraph.

The "Memorial de Tlacopan" lists the entire extent of the Empire, making it possible to see the sequence in which the whole area is ordered. In contrast with Codex Mendoza, which follows a counterclockwise direction, the "Memorial de Tlacopan" proceeds clockwise. Beginning in the northwest, the region associated with Tlacopan (sections 1 to 5), it continues with the towns that paid tribute to the three capitals. Here, it presents first those in the Tetzcoca sector in the northeast (section 6) and then those in the Tenochca or southern sector (sections 7 and 8). In the southern sector the paragraphs go from east to west: Cempohuallan (7.1), Cozcatlan (7.2), Tlachmalacac 7.3), and Oztoman (7.4). But the sequence turns back towards the east within this last paragraph, going along the coast and into Oaxaca, and ends in paragraph 8, which contains Tecuantepec and Xoconochco.

Table 4-1 presents a comparison of the memorials of Tetzcoco and Tlacopan. These two sources agree on the principal characteristics of the Empire's territo-

TABLE 4-1.
Territorial Categories in the Memorials of Tetzcoco and Tlacopan

"Memorial de los pueblos de Tlacopan"*	Motolinía's "Memorial tetzcocano"†
The cabecera: 1. Sujetos of Tlacopan 2. Towns granted to Spaniards 3. Towns granted to Juan Cano	
4. Cities with kings subordinate to Tlacopan	1. Cities with kings subordinate to Tetzcoco
5. Towns and estancias of tenants in the Basin, Tlalhuic, and Valley of Toluca	2. Towns of tenants in the Basin 6. Sujetos in Cuauhnahuac
6. Six areas in the northeast and east paying tribute to the three capitals:	Three areas paying tribute to the three capitals:
1. Tochpan 2. Tziuhcoac 3. Tochtepec 4. Tlapacoyan 5. Tlatlauhquitepec 6. Chinantlan	3. Tochpan 4. Tlatlauhquitepec, Tlapacoyan, and Tziuhcoac 5. Tochtepec
7. Areas in the south paying tribute to the three capitals:	
1. Cempohuallan (Gulf Coast) 2. Cozcatlan (Mixteca) 3. Tlachmalacac (Guerrero) 4. Oztoman (coast of Guerrero and Valley of Oaxaca)	
8. Areas in the southeast paying tribute to the three capitals:	
Isthmus and Xoconochco	

* Numbers refer to section and paragraph (Zimmermann 1970:5–8).
† Numbers refer to paragraphs in the sequence in which they appear in the document (Motolinía 1971:394–96).

rial structure. Both make the same distinction between the kingdoms that were dependencies of one or another of the allied capitals and the areas conquered jointly by the three allied kings, which were tributaries of all three imperial capitals as a unit. However, they differ in that the Tetzcoco document covers only the imperial provinces of its own sector, while the Tlacopan document lists all the tributary provinces, including those of the Tenochca and Tetzcoca sectors.

The concrete data from these sources make clear that each of the constituent parts of the core area was made up of (1) the capital and its district, (2) a group of cities with their own kings subject to the great king of the capital, and (3) towns inhabited by peasants, as tenants, and administered by stewards. In these settlements there were royal lands, but it is not clearly explained whether they were cultivated by tributary peasants or by a different category of tenants.

Several sources attest to the existence of two different types of peasants in ancient Central Mexico. Some held lots, for which they paid tribute, from the land of their towns and barrios. Others were settled in the office lands and patrimonial lands of kings and noblemen; these were what the two memorials call tenants (renteros). Other sources also use *terrazgueros* in Spanish or the Nahuatl *mayeque* or *tlalmaitl*. I will refer to them as tenants. While both memorials use the same terminology, there is a noteworthy difference in the way they apply the category of towns of tenants to the specific towns they list. Motolinía uses the term to define the status of the inhabitants of the sixteen calpixcazgos in the great kingdom of Tetzcoco, but he does not include those situated in the capital itself (the calpixcazgos of Tetzcoco and Atenco), which do not appear anywhere in this document, although Ixtlilxochitl describes them together with the others. Nor does Motolinía use this definition for the possessions of Tetzcoco in Cuauhnahuac, which are listed in another paragraph without any description at all. In contrast, the Tlacopan memorial applies the definition of tenants to the most distant possessions of Tlacopan— in the Basin, in Tlalhuic, and in Matlatzinco—while those situated in the capital's rural zone and its immediate vicinity are classified only in terms of whether, during the colonial period, they were under the rule of Tlacopan or had been granted to Juan Cano and other Spaniards. Nothing is said about stewards or the goods or services that they gave.

This raises the problem of whether all the towns that the two documents place under the same definition of tenants correspond to a single category or whether each of the two capitals used different criteria in applying the term *tenants* to the lists of towns prepared separately in each city. These tenants probably lived in towns that were different in their political status and their location with respect to the capital of the kingdom. Specifically, they could be towns within the rural district of the capital, towns outside the capital but inside the kingdom's own domain, possessions of the capital in more distant areas within the domain of another kingdom, or, finally, areas subject to the alliance where each of the three kingdoms had its own possessions. In this way, although the almost identical descriptions of category 2 in Motolinía's "Memorial tetzcocano" and category 5 in the "Memorial de Tlacopan" could be applied to various groups of subject towns, neither of the memorials applies that description to all of them but only to some; in putting together groups of towns, each document combines various sociopolitical and geographical criteria without indicating systematically which are being used. This might explain why Ixtlilxochitl describes as provinces under stewards all these different categories of towns, making a distinction only in their geographical location.[22]

Before moving on to the Tenochca sources, I will discuss other documents from Tetzcoco and Tlacopan that amplify the reports on those two kingdoms and are basically in agreement with the categories defined in the memorials reviewed above. The already mentioned Memorial of Don Hernando Pimentel from Tetzcoco is discussed below. The chronicles of Ixtlilxochitl and Torquemada were probably based on documents related to Motolinía's "Memorial tetzcocano," but there is no need to discuss them here in their entirety. The relevant data will be discussed in the appropriate chapters in this book. The Mapa Quinatzin treats only the towns in Motolinía's groups 1 and 2 and is discussed in chapter 6. As for sources on Tlacopan, the Codex Osuna includes a document that depicts the dependencies of Tlacopan and its dependent kingdoms together with their subject towns; that is, it presents groups 1 to 5 of the "Memorial de Tlacopan" and is also discussed below, in this chapter.

The Memorial of Don Hernando Pimentel of Tetzcoco

The Memorial of Don Hernando Pimentel was first published, in part, by Orozco y Berra. He includes a note by Ramírez, from whom he had obtained the manuscript, explaining that it was taken from a memorial addressed to the king by Don Hernando Pimentel Nezahualcoyotl, cacique and governor of the province of Tetzcoco, son of Coanacochtzin and grandson of Nezahualpilli, former rulers of Tetzcoco.[23]

Don Hernando was governor of Tetzcoco from 1545 to 1564. He must have prepared his memorial at about that time from materials similar to those used for Motolinía's "Memorial tetzcocano" and the related document in the *Anales de Cuauhtitlan*. However, it differs in certain ways from Motolinía and should be examined as an independent document. The beginning of the published text explains that the intention of the memorial was to let the king of Spain know the extent of the province of Tetzcoco at the time Cortés arrived by listing the "towns and provinces" that were "under dominion and rule of the said uncle of mine [Cacamatzin] and of the city of Tetzcoco."

Don Hernando arranges the possessions of Tetzcoco in a different order from that of Motolinía's *Memorial,* grouping them in five categories. The definitions he gives of each of these categories are not as clear as the distinction that Motolinía makes between cities governed by kings and towns of tenant farmers, but they do show that these groups differed in political status and tributary obligations. This memorial also lacks detailed lists of tribute and services such as those in the *Anales de Cuauhtitlan* and the *Historia chichimeca* of Ixtlilxochitl.

In the following lists Don Hernando's five categories are numbered with Roman numerals, and the towns within each one are listed with Arabic numbers.

I. The first category begins with a list of nine towns, following which it is stated that "all the above towns were designated and assigned to service in the household of the said lord." The towns are the following: 1. Otompan with its sujeto; 2. Tepeapulco with its sujeto; 3. Ahuatepec; 4. Cuauhtlantzinco; 5. Tzinquilucan; 6. Tepetlaoztoc; 7. Azapuchco; 8. Coatepec; 9. Iztapaluca.

In comparing this with Motolinía's "Memorial tetzcocano" and other sources, one sees that Otompan was the only one of these towns ruled by a king; all the others were towns of tenants.

II. The second category is that of "the towns that my ancestors gained in war, in which they had tenants and land." These are: 1. Tulancingo; 2. part of Chalco; 3. Acoac (*sic pro* Tziuhcoac); 4. Tuchpa; 5. part of Cuauhnahuac; 6. Tlatlauhtepec (Tlatlauhquitepec); 7. Tuchtepec; 8. part of Toluca; 9. Tlalcotzauhtitlan.

The towns in this list are also found in Motolinía's "Memorial tetzcocano" and the *Anales de Cuauhtitlan*, although in different categories (see Table 4-2). They coincide with the towns that according to Ixtlilxochitl were conquered by Nezahualcoyotl together with the other two allied kings and in which he placed his own stewards.[24] Don Hernando's statement that the ruler of Tetzcoco held part of Chalco, of Cuauhnahuac, and of Toluca indicates that he was not entitled to all the tribute from those areas, thus distinguishing his possessions from those of Tenochtitlan and Tlacopan in the same three areas.

III. The third category has no equivalent in Motolinía or the *Anales de Cuauhtitlan*. It is defined as "towns where [the ancestors of Don Hernando] had fields gained personally." One might think that the reference is to lands acquired as personal belongings, perhaps merited by performance in battle, but the difference between this and the preceding category is not adequately explained. What is most likely is that these were what other sources call patrimonial lands in contrast to royal or office lands (tierras de señorío). The list is as follows: 1. Azcaputzalco; 2. Suchimilco; 3. Cuauhtlapa; 4. Huacalco; 5. Cuauhtitlan; 6. Tacuba (Tlacopan); 7. Aticpac; 8. Cuyuacan; 9. Tepozotlan; 10. Ecatepec; 11. Tultitlan; 12. Chicoloapa.

Almost all these towns can be easily located in the southern and western part of the Basin. Half are kingdoms of the Tepanec domain: Tlacopan, Azcapotzalco, Tepotzotlan, Cuauhtitlan, Toltitlan, Coyoacan. Two others are in the Tenochca domain: Xochimilco and Ecatepec. The rest are smaller and less important. Chicualoapan was in the southern part of the Acolhuacan near Coatepec and Chimalhuacan; the identity of the rest is less certain. The area occupied by these towns is similar to that of the Chinampan towns in the Tenochca and Tepanec domains, which paid tribute to Nezahualcoyotl according to Ixtlilxochitl, although the toponyms only partly coincide.[25] The inclusion of Chicualoapan suggests that it is not simply a matter of the Chinampan tribute obtained from Tenochtitlan, since that town had long been part of the Acolhua domain.[26]

IV. The fourth category is that of "towns that divided their tribute among Mexico, Tetzcuco, and Tacuba." There were five:1. Coayxtlavuacan; 2. Avlizapan (*sic*); 3. Cuauhtuchco; 4. Tepeaca; 5. Cuetlachtlan.

None of these are included in Motolinía's "Memorial." They correspond to the cabeceras of tributary provinces in the Codex Mendoza, except for Ahuilizapan, which in that codex is part of the province of Cuauhtochco. According to Ixtlilxochitl, they were towns conquered by Nezahualcoyotl and his allies, but he does not say that Nezahualcoyotl put his own stewards there.[27]

V. The fifth category is defined as "towns adjacent to the city of Tetzcoco [that were] sujetos paying tribute to the said city" and were the following: 1. Huexotla; 2. Coatlichan; 3. Chimalhuacan; 4. Aculma; 5. Tepechpa; 6. Chiuconauhtla; 7. Tezayuca; 8. Tlalanapan; 9. Papalotlan; 10. Cempoallan; 11. Oztoticpac; 12. Teutivuacan; 13. Xicotepec; 14. Pahuatlan; 15. Tlaculultepec; 16. Papaloticpac.

Following this list Don Hernando states that "all the said towns given above used to be sujetos of this said city of Tetzcoco and they had in it their houses and paid tribute and obeyed the lord of Tetzcoco and not any other." He adds that Cortés took away all those towns, leaving under Tetzcoco only four sujetos, namely Huexotla, Coatlichan, Chiauhtla, and Tezayuca (*sic*).

Most probably this statement refers to the towns in this fifth category, although since it comes at the end of the document it could refer to all the towns listed in Don Hernando's memorial. According to the description in Motolinía's "Memorial tetzcocano," most of the towns in category V are cities ruled by kings, but there are several towns of tenants. Thus, Don Hernando's categories I and V together correspond to the first two categories of Motolinía's "Memorial" (cities with kings and towns of tenants), but the towns are combined in a different way: each group includes one or more cities as well as towns of tenants. These two categories bring to mind, therefore, the two halves of the Acolhuacan that according to Ixtlilxochitl and Torquemada alternated in provisioning the palace and included, each one, both cities and towns of tenants (see p. 154–60). However, Don Hernando's category I has only one city, Otompan, and all the other cities are in category V; the distribution of the towns of tenants also differs from that of Ixtlilxochitl and Torquemada. As for tribute, group I, headed by Otompan, gave service in the household of the ruler of Tetzcoco, and group V, headed by Huexotla, paid tribute to the city of Tetzcoco, but the nature of their tribute and services is not explained.

Don Hernando's personal interest as a descendant of the kings of Tetzcoco is evident, since he emphasizes that (1) the towns in category I were intended for service to the lord of Tetzcoco; (2) those of group II had been won by his ancestors, who had been given tenant farmers and lands; and (3) the property in category III they had won by merit. He puts in the last place (V) the towns that paid tribute to the city of Tetzcoco. Don Hernando seems to distinguish between the royal office lands and the personal or patrimonial lands of the kings. He differs also from Motolinía in that he puts together in category II the towns in the Tetzcoca sector of the Empire (Tziuhcoac, Tochpan, Tlatlauhquitepec, Tochtepec) that according to Motolinía paid tribute to the three capitals; towns that were divided among the three allied cities (part of Chalco, part of Cuauhnahuac, and part of Toluca); an Acolhua kingdom (Tollantzinco); and a tributary province in the southern sector of the Empire (Tlalcozauhtitlan).

Table 4-2 compares the data from the Memorial of Don Hernando Pimentel with other sources. The order in which the document lists the categories has been changed in the table in order to facilitate a comparison with the information from other Tetzcoca sources.

The Tlacopanec Memorial of the Codex Osuna

The Codex Osuna contains several pictorial documents, prepared in the year 1565 with legends in Nahuatl and Spanish, that provide information on public works in the city of Mexico and the payments given to Spanish officials. It consists of thirty-nine folios. On the first, unnumbered, are the words, "Painting of the governor, judges, and councilmen of Mexico." The rest bear two sets of numbers, from 2 to 39 and from 464 to 501, indicating that these thirty-nine pages had been incorporated into a much larger collection of documents in which their place is indicated by the second foliation.[28] There are references (482r, 492r, 500r) to the visita of Licenciado Valderrama and to Don Esteban de Guzmán, governor of Xochimilco, who was the *juez de residencia* in Mexico from 1552 to 1557. Chávez Orozco, in his 1947 edition of this codex, included a transcription of related documents from the Archivo General de la Nación, from 1557 to 1567, which deal with the activities of Don Esteban de Guzmán and the same subjects as the pictorial documents that comprise the Codex Osuna.

One document, made up of three folios (496r–498v), is very different from the rest of the codex. It is not concerned with public works or the goods and services provided to Spaniards, but simply depicts the towns that belonged to Tlacopan. The pictures are accompanied by legends, and there is an explanatory paragraph at the end; all the texts are in Nahuatl except for a few words on the title page and the final paragraph.[29] I will call this document the Tlacopanec Memorial of the Codex Osuna, a title drawn from the text in the document itself (496r, 498v).

This memorial is in three parts. The first page (496r) serves as a title page; the glyphs of the three capitals of the Triple Alliance are painted, with four lines of text

TABLE 4-2.

The Territorial Categories in the Memorial of Don Hernando Pimentel

Memorial of Don Hernando Pimentel	Data from Other Tetzcocan Sources
V. Towns adjacent to Tetzcoco, paying tribute to the city [Includes the Acolhua cities and some of the towns of tenants]	These two categories cut across the two parts of Torquemada and Ixtlilxochitl and across Motolinía's dichotomy of cities with kings and towns of tenants.
1. Towns assigned to the service of Tetzcoco's palace [Includes Otompan and towns of tenants]	
III. Towns where Pimentel's ancestors had lands gained personally [In the southern part of the Basin]	These are in part the same towns that paid the Chinampan tribute to Tetzcoco, but under a different type of tenure.
II. Towns that Pimentel's ancestors gained in war in which they had lands and tenants	
1. Tollantzinco	Kingdom and calpixcazgo of Tetzcoco
2. Towns in Chalco	Tetzcoco's holdings in Chalco
8. Towns in Tolocan	Tetzcoco's holdings in Tolocan
5. Towns in Cuauhnahuac	Tetzcoco's holdings in Tlalhuic
3. Tziuhcoac	Imperial tributary provinces in the Tetzcocan sector included in Motolinía
4. Tochpan	
6. Tlatlauhquitepec	
7. Tochtepec	
9. Tlalcozauhtitlan	Not in Motolinía and *Anales de Cuauhtitlan*, but mentioned in Ixtlilxochitl
IV. Towns whose tribute was divided by Tenochtitlan, Tetzcoco, and Tlacopan	Imperial tributary provinces (Codex Mendoza) outside the Tetzcocan sector, not included in Motolinía
1. Coaixtlahuacan	
2. Ahuilizapan	
3. Cuauhtochco	
4. Tepeyacac	
5. Cuetlaxtlan	

beneath them. The second part (496v–498r) depicts all the towns that belonged to Tlacopan together with their governors, and a brief legend under each one gives its name. The last page (498v) has only a text. This last page and the text on the first page describe the purpose of the document and help in understanding the list of towns. The text that appears on the first page (496r) beneath the glyphs of the three capitals states briefly the nature of the content:

Yzca inilnamicoco yn etetl	This is the memory of the three
tzontecomatl yn altepetl	capital cities
yn nican Nueva España	here in New Spain,
Mexico, Tetzcuco, Tlacuban.	Mexico, Tetzcoco, Tlacopan.
Yn Mexico yehuatl quitl[30]	To Mexico, the tribute
in isquich ytech pohui altepetl	all belongs to the city,
yhuan yn Tetzcuco.	and to Tetzcoco.
Auh yn Tlacuba ca ye nican	And [as to] Tlacopan, here
ycuiliuhtoc tlapalacuilolpan	is written in the painting
in isquich ytech pohui.	all that belongs to it.

The text on the final page (498v) comments on the content of the document and gives the place and date of its composition:

Ynin altepetl inisquich omoteneuh	All these towns named,
inizqui governadores	all the governors
yn tlatoque catca.	were kings.
Auh yn tepaneca	And the Tepanec
yn tlatlacateuctin catca.	were kings.
Inisquich ytech pohui Mexico	All belongs to Mexico
yhuan yn Tetzcuco.	and Tetzcoco.
Auh yn Tlacuban ytech pohui	And what belongs to Tlacopan
ynin yehuantini omoteneuhque.	[are] those named here.
Çan icentequiuh catca	Its entire contribution was
yaoquizque tepehuanime	to be warriors, conquerers
No yuhqui Mexico,	Thus [it was] in Mexico,
no yuhqui Tetzcuco.	also thus in Tetzcoco.
Auh atle Justicia ompa	And no justice was there
quichihuaya	administered [in the towns]
ynisquich yntech popohuia	it all belonged to
yn etetl tzontecomatl.	the three capitals.
Çan yeppa oncan mochihuaya	Only in three places was
Justicia	justice made

yn Mexico, yn Tetzcuco,	Mexico, Tetzcuco,
yn Tlacuban.	Tlacopan.
Yn aço miquiztli	If it was a [case of] death
	[that is, capital punishment]
mochi oncan motzontequia	they all judged there,
imeistin mononotzaya.	the three conferred.
Omochiuh memorial Tlacuban	This memorial was made in Tlacopan,
a viij dias	on the eighth day
del mes de henero de 1565 años.	of the month of January 1565.

This document is clearly similar to the "Memorial de Tlacopan." It calls to mind the two letters from Don Antonio Cortés (1552 and 1561) that spoke of sending a memorial relating how Tlacopan, in addition to having many sujetos of its own, shared the tribute of other towns with Mexico and Tetzcoco. Undoubtedly, more than once during those years Don Antonio Cortés and the governing body of Tlacopan prepared memorials concerning their possessions as part of the Triple Alliance, and on those memorials they based their petitions to the Crown asking for certain privileges. The "Memorial de Tlacopan" is one version of the memorial alluded to in the letters quoted above. This document from the Codex Osuna includes part of the same documentation, but it cannot be the memorial spoken of in the 1561 letter of Don Antonio Cortés, for it was not written until 1565 and it does not include the material concerning the imperial tributary provinces that Tlacopan shared with the other two capitals. It might have been a partial copy of a pictorial document like the one that was the basis of the "Memorial de Tlacopan" but included only what was relevant to the investigation with which the Codex Osuna is concerned.

This list from the Codex Osuna does not include the direct dependencies of Tlacopan that make up the first section of the "Memorial de Tlacopan"; they must have been considered a constituent part of the capital. Perhaps the legend that accompanies the glyph for Tlacopan (496v) refers to these dependencies in saying "Tacuban ysquichi ytech pohui" (all this belongs to Tlacopan), although it is also possible that this legend refers to all the towns depicted in the codex. Some of these correspond to the dependencies of Tlacopan that, according to sections 2 and 3 of the "Memorial de Tlacopan," were possessions of Juan Cano or other Spaniards. The rest of the towns depicted coincide with those described in section 4 of this memorial as towns subject to Tlacopan that gathered there in time of war and to be told their tribute obligations; they also brought to the city building material and craft products. The explanation on the last page of this document in the Codex Osuna also agrees with that in the "Memorial de Tlacopan", in which military service is indicated as the principal obligation of those towns. In other words, both documents describe the same group of towns with the same military obligation to the Tepanec capital.

The obligation to provide labor and material, as Gibson has shown, continued under the colonial regime for the public works directed from Mexico City. Although this particular document does not mention tribute in goods or labor, all the other documents in the Codex Osuna are about that subject, and a clear definition of the old jurisdiction of the kingdom of Tlacopan would have been relevant to these matters. That part of the codex (492r–495v) which precedes the document discussed here is a pictorial account of "the food given to doctor Puga in Tula and Tetepango and what they were paid for it." Other documents mention the lime brought by Tzompanco and Citlaltepec for repairs on the royal house and for works in Chapultepec (463v–464r). In documents from the Archivo General de la Nación there are also orders from Viceroy Velasco that Tlacopan, Coyoacan, and Cuauhximalpan contribute lime for work to be done on the tecpan (palace) in Mexico.[31] All these towns were dependencies of Tlacopan. It may be that others also took part in the activities under investigation, because the foliation of the Codex Osuna shows that a great deal of the original documentation has been lost, and the publication of material from the Archivo General de la Nación does not entirely complete it.

The fact that this document is presented in connection with litigation concerning public works in Mexico may be the reason why Xilotepec is not included, since it was no doubt too distant to give such services. Nor does Xilotepec appear in the colonial summonses that Gibson studies.[32] This also explains why the document does not include the towns, listed in the "Memorial de Tlacopan," that paid tribute to the three capitals, since they were under no obligation to take part in the colonial public works that the Codex Osuna documents.

A comparison of the explanatory text of this document from the Codex Osuna with section 4 of the "Memorial de Tlacopan" and with the related text in Motolinía's "Memorial tetzcocano" demonstrates that the towns listed were the cities (with their subject towns) governed by kings who were directly subject to Tlacopan. The only important difference between the list of the "Memorial de Tlacopan" and that of the Codex Osuna is that the latter does not include Xilotepec and its sujetos. The Tlacopanec Memorial of the Codex Osuna is especially valuable in that it shows in pictorial form the category of the governors of each town in such a way that, case by case, distinguishes between the cabeceras with their kings and the towns subject to them, a distinction that in the "Memorial de Tlacopan" one can only infer from the grouping and order of the toponyms listed.

In pages 496v to 498r of this document each town is represented by a glyph with its name written in the legend. The encomendero is represented by the head and shoulders of a bearded Spaniard with a hat, connected by a line to the town of his *encomienda*. A crown indicates that the city paid tribute to the Crown. Some towns have no indication of an encomendero. One is Tlacopan; the others must have been sujetos of Tlacopan or of a town paying tribute to an encomendero or to the Crown. The category of the indigenous ruler or official of a town is shown in three ways: (1) by a *xihuitzolli* (a crown or headband) and speech scrolls, (2) by a xihuitzolli and the head of a beardless man wearing a hat, or (3) by the head alone, usually linked to the glyph of the city by a line. Evidently three categories of indigenous rulers are depicted. The first two were tlatoani and teuctli, in accordance with the glyphs; the text on folio 498v uses the titles of tlatoque and tlacateteuctin. Those depicted by a head only can be considered as lords of a lower category or as officials. Some towns are depicted with no local ruler indicated; they must have been under stewards or other lesser officials. Each city with a tlatoani is preceded by a rhombus that separates the groups of cities subject to each kingdom. Azcapotzalco has two lords, one with a stone as a glyph, indicating that he was the lord of the Tepanec parcialidad.

Table 4-3 is a schematic representation of the content of these folios, with annotations on the data that interest us here. A number has been added to each toponym to indicate the order in which the painting should be read.[33]

The Codex Mendoza and the Related Tenochca Documents

Three related documents, the *Matrícula de tributos,* the Codex Mendoza, and the *Información . . . de 1554,* take in the whole Empire and provide the most complete catalog of tributary towns and cities. These are the sources that require a most detailed analysis. Although they do not distinguish among the different kinds of dependencies, as do the memorials from Tetzcoco and Tlacopan, a comparison with these sources, using also scattered data from other Tenochca materials, will show that the political categories outlined above are valid for understanding how the Tenochca sources deal with the domains of the three capitals and with the imperial structure as a whole. The Tenochca chronicles and ethnographic sources do not list systematically all the tributary provinces of the Empire; information must be sought among the data provided on other topics. Among the sources with ethnographic material, Sahagún provides a useful list of the twenty calpixques in charge of the insignia worn by warriors on military campaigns. The final section of this chapter is devoted to that list. The narrative chronicles of Durán and Tezozomoc, although they provide the best accounts of various conquests and other activities of the Empire, never give an explicit categorization of the territorial entities.[34] They provide extensive listings of the components of the Empire as they describe their participation in military campaigns and in political and ceremonial events; the significance of this material in supporting the categorization of political and

TABLE 4-3.
The Tepanec Rulers in Codex Osuna*

fol. 496v — fol. 497

1. Tlacuba tlatoani	2. Azcapotzalco two lords	3. Tzaucyocan lord	4. Quahuacan lord	5. Huitzitzilapan lord	6. Ocelotepec lord	7. Tlalachco lord	8. Chichicquauhtla lord
9. Tepehuexoyocan	10. Ocoyacac	◆ 11. Coyohuacan tlatoani	12. Atlacuihuayan lord	13. Atlauhpolco lord	14. Xalatlauhco lord	15. Capolloac lord	16. Cohuatepec lord
17. [◆ Cuauhtli]tlan tlatoani	18. Toltitlan teuctli	19. Tepotzotlan teuctli	20. Huehuetocan lord	21. Otlazpan lord	22. Tepesic teuctli	23. Tzompanco lord	24. Citlaltepec (torn edge)

fol. 497v — fol. 498r

◆ 25. Tullan tlatoani	26. Xiuhpacoyan lord	27. Atlitlalacyan lord	28. Michmaloyan lord	29. Nestlalpan lord	30. Teçontepec lord	31. Tlemaco lord	32. Mizquiyahualla lord
33. Thaahuililpan lord	34. Chilquauhtla lord	35. Yzmiquilpan lord	◆ 36. Apazco tlatoani	37. Atotoniltonco lord	38. Axocopan lord	39. Tecpatepec lord	40. Ytzcuincuitlapil[co] tlatoani
41. . . . tepanco lord	42. Tezcatepec lord	43. Hueypochtlan lord	44. Tequisquiac lord	45. Xilotzinco lord			

NOTE: The numbering of towns has been added to show the sequence in which the glyphs should be read. The rhombus is drawn as in the document; its meaning is not explained in the MS, but it precedes the glyphs of towns ruled by a tlatoani. The material in brackets reconstructs the parts of the legends missing at the torn edges of the document.

territorial units derived from the analysis of the sources of the catalog type is discussed in chapter 13.

The *Matrícula de tributos* and the second part of the Codex Mendoza are pictorial documents that depict a number of what have come to be called tributary provinces, each page containing a column of glyphs that represent the names of the towns in each province, along with pictures of the tribute they paid.[35] The *Matrícula* has no explanatory material except the legends alongside the glyphs and pictures that represent place names and the kind and quantity of each product paid as tribute. The Codex Mendoza has similar legends and also explanations of the contents of each page, written separately on pages without pictures. The third source related to these two, the *Información de 1554*, was written in answer to the same questionnaire from the Crown that was the basis of Zorita's well-known work. It contains the statements by several witnesses that explain a document that must have been similar to the *Matrícula de tributos*.[36]

Nothing is known about the origin of the *Matrícula de tributos;* the Codex Mendoza was prepared for the Viceroy Mendoza. A report by the encomendero Gerónimo López concerning the distribution of encomiendas to Spaniards includes information on the preparation of a document that appears to be the Codex Mendoza. If so, it is the earliest information we have about this particular source. López relates that in the house of a master painter, one Francisco Gualpuyogualcal, he saw a book with parchment covers and asked what it was. The painter showed it to him, "in secret," and said the viceroy had ordered him to make a book

> in which he was to put all the land from the founding of this city of Mexico and the lords who had governed it and ruled until the coming of the Spaniards and the battles and encounters they had and the taking of this great city and all the provinces that it ruled and [all the areas] subject to it and the distribution that Motezuma [*sic*] made of these towns and provinces to the principal lords of this city and the fee (*feudo*) given to him by each one of the grantees (encomendatarios) from the tribute of the towns that he held and the plan that he [Moteuczoma] had in the said distribution and how he drew up the towns and provinces for that [purpose]. This was the origin of these personal and domestic services and it was not something that the Spanish installed as something new and following this the distribution of the said towns and provinces [was] made by the Marqués del Valle and others who [later] governed.[37]

This report identifies the artist, but we do not know who wrote the many comments in this codex. Gerónimo López also provides information on the nature of the tributary units that is unrelated to the legends and explanations in the Codex

Mendoza. At first glance the language of his report suggests that some towns or provinces were distributed to the principal lords of Tenochtitlan in a form similar to the encomiendas of the Spanish. However, the most probable meaning of the text is that the "encomendatarios" were the individuals who in the Codex Mendoza and the *Matrícula* are called governors or stewards.

Scholars who have studied and edited these two pictorial documents have concentrated on describing them and on making a correct reading of the annotatins and glyphs, primarily in order to identify the towns and the nature and quantity of the tribute depicted.[38] There are still problems to be solved about these topics, especially in regard to quantities and payment periods. There are also problems as to whether these documents present an assessment of the tribute required or are registers of tribute actually received, and in any case, to what year or years the report refers. These problems are not discussed here, because our primary concern is the territorial structure of the Empire.[39] What is more relevant to our subject is the question of whether all the tribute went to the Triple Alliance as a unit or only to Tenochtitlan. It seems more probable that all the tribute was sent to Tenochtitlan; the tribute from the Tenochca provinces would have been for the exclusive use of that kingdom, but a share of the tribute from the imperial provinces would have been distributed to Tetzcoco and Tlacopan.

These sources provide information on the tributary provinces of the Empire and their tribute payments in a more detailed and systematic manner than do the Tetzcoco and Tlacopan memorials, but they present the data without explaining the nature of each "province" in terms of the economic and political categories so clearly described in the documents from the other two capitals. They make no distinction between the towns paying tribute to Tenochtitlan and those paying tribute to the three capitals of the Empire. Therefore, the content of these Tenochca documents must be analyzed and compared with the data from other sources in light of the territorial structure described in the sources from the other two capitals of the Empire, as explained above. The basis of the discussion will be the Codex Mendoza, because it is the most complete—several pages are missing in the *Matrícula*—and because it is the only document that provides information on the administrative organization.[40] The *Matrícula* has no annotations on this matter. The *Información de 1554* is too brief; it does not usually give a list of all the towns in each province, and as to the organization for collecting tribute, it says only that it was collected by persons chosen by Moteuczoma and the local rulers for this purpose. These persons, called in their language *tequitlato,* took the tribute to their rulers and gave an account of it.[41]

The three parts of the Codex Mendoza differ in contents. The first gives the history of Tenochtitlan in the form of annals from the beginning of its existence and depicts the Tenochca kings from Acamapichtli to Moteuczoma Xocoyotzin, each with a list of the towns he conquered. There is a painting of the city of Ten-ochtitlan on the first page; it may simply represent the foundation of the city as the beginning of its history, or it may also be intended to represent the center of the territorial structure given in the second part. In any case, it does not include information on the rural villages within the city's territory that could be compared with the data in the "Memorial de los Pueblos de Tlacopan" on the Tepanec capital.

The material in the second part is almost identical with that of the *Matrícula de tributos*. It consists of a series of pages, each depicting a group of towns and the tribute they paid. This is the part that has always been used to determine the extent of the Empire and must be examined carefully in order to discuss the political-territorial categories of the Empire. The third part is essentially ethnographic, with depictions of family life and the political organization.

These three basic documents—the Codex Mendoza, the *Matrícula*, and the *Información de 1554*—present the series of tributary provinces in the same order. In his 1949 essay based on the two pictorial documents, Barlow regroups the provinces according to ideas that are foreign to the codices and arranges the provinces in sections titled "The Tarascan Frontier," "The Old Tepanec Domain," "The Old Acolhua Domain (North, Southwest, and Southeast)," "The Mixtec-Tzapotec Zone," and "The Heart of the Empire." It is much more likely that the order followed in the documents reflects the organization of the Empire, and this should be taken into account for any analysis.[42]

Table 4-4 lists the component entities of the Empire in the order in which the three documents present them; see also Map 4-1. The sequence in which the different provinces are arranged in the pictorial codices calls for a discussion of the order of the folios as well as the disposition of the pictures and the commentary on each one.

The *Matrícula* as it is today is bound in the form of a book. Boturini had described it in his catalog as "A register [matrícula] of tributes. . . . It is sixteen leaves of Indian paper, although something is missing at the beginning and the end."[43] But he does not say whether they were loose pages or if they had already been bound. In its present state the pages, made of *amate* (bark cloth), are pasted together verso against verso so that the pages of the book have pictures on each side. In the fragmentary sheets (the first, second, third, and fourth) or those with pieces torn off the edges, the amate is pasted on pieces of paper of a size to complete the page, as can be noticed even in the facsimile editions. If one examines the codex there is no doubt that this is so, but none of those who have studied the *Matrícula* have called attention to this fact.[44] In its original form the codex could have been either a series of separate leaves or a screenfold that had been cut into pieces in order to paste one against the other to form leaves with pictures on both sides.

The order in which the tributary provinces are described in the *Información de 1554* is the same as that of the *Matrícula* and the Codex Mendoza except for the province of Apan, as is indicated in Table 4-4. Three of the witnesses described the verso before the recto of the sheet that in the *Matrícula* is now folio 8. If the document presented to the witnesses consisted of separate sheets, this variation from the sequence could be more easily understood than if it had been in the form of a screenfold or a book.

The three parts of the Codex Mendoza are indicated by inscriptions that mark the beginning and end of each part, except for the beginning of the first part and the end of the third. They are written in italic script, different from the Spanish legal script (*letra procesal*) of the rest of the document. The contents of the codex, both the paintings with legends and the explanations for each page, suggest that the inscriptions that indicate the end of the first part and the beginning of the second have been misplaced. The list of cities conquered by Moteuczoma Xocoyotzin ends on folio 16v; 17r is blank. The following folio (17v) is in a style completely different from that of the first part and more like that of the second. In the left-hand margin and across the bottom of the page is a series of toponymical glyphs corresponding to towns in the Basin of Mexico; in the center of the page, instead of pictures of tribute goods as in the second part, there are glyphs of towns located in distant parts of the Empire. Some are accompanied by glyphs of governors with military ranks, indicating that these are the imperial garrisons. Folio 18r has more of these glyphs for distant towns and their governors together with an explanatory text; it ends with the inscription "fin de la partida primera de esta ystoria" (end of the first part of this history). Folio 18v (numbered 19 in the manuscript) begins with the heading "La segunda parte de la historia" (the second part of the history), and below this there is an explanation of the content of the following folio (19r), which depicts the tribute and services owed by Tlatelolco. The codex continues with all the tributary provinces depicted in the style typical of the second part. The annotation "fin de la parte segunda" is written at the end of the text on Oxitipan but before the picture of this province. The heading "La partida tercera de esta historia" (the third part of this history) precedes the Spanish text of the ethnographic part of the codex (56v, numbered 57).[45]

According to the placement of the inscriptions that indicate the beginning and end of the three parts, folios 17v and 18r would be part of the lists of kings and their conquests, but that idea cannot be supported by data from any other source.[46] Probably these inscriptions in italic script, different from the script used by the commentator, were added by someone who did not understand the contents of the document. It is obvious that those pages do not pertain to the section on conquests but to that on the imperial provinces. The text of the commentary on 18r, quoted below, supports this interpretation, and furthermore, the contents of those two folios correspond to the first two folios of the *Matrícula*, a document that does not contain a section on conquests. Unfortunately the first folio of the *Matrícula* is only

TABLE 4-4.
The Imperial Tributary Provinces According to the Tenochca Sources

Codex Mendoza*	Matrícula de tributos†	Información . . . de 1554‡
The military district in the basin:		
Citlaltepec, 17v	—	—
Distant military districts:§		
Quecholtetenanco, 17v	—	—
Cuauhtochco, 17v	—	—
Izteyocan, 17v	—	—
Huaxyacac, 17v	1—1r	—
Çoçolan, 17v	1—1r	—
Poctepec, 17v	1—1r	—
Oztoman, 18r	1—1r	—
Atlan, 18r	2—1v	—
Teçapotitlan, 18r	2—1v	—
Atzacan, 18r	2—1v	—
Xoconochco, 18r	2—1v	—
Provinces paying tribute in kind:		
1. Tlatilulco, 19r	3—2r	—
2. Petlacalcatl, 20r—v	4—2v	1. Petlacalcalco
3. Acolhuacan (Acolmecatl), 21v—22r	5—3r	2. Aculma
4. Quauhnahuac, 23r—v	6—3v	3. Cuernavaca
5. Huaxtepec, 24v—25r	7—4r	4. Guastepeque
6. Quauhtitlan, 26r	8—4v	5. Cuautitlan
7. Axocopan, 27r	—	6. Axacuba
8. Atotonilco [de Tula], 30r	—	7. Atotonilco
9. Hueypuchtlan, 29r	9—5r	8. Teopochitlan
10. Atotonilco [el Grande], 30r	10—5v	9. Atotonilco
11. Xilotepec, 31r	11—6r	10. Xilotepeque
12. Quahuacan, 32r	12—6v	11. Quahuacan
13. Tuluca, 33r	13—7r	12. Toluca
14. Ocuilan, 34r	14—7v	13. Ocuila
15. Malinalco, 35r top	15 left—8r	—
16. Xocotitlan, 35r bottom	15 right—8r	—
—	—	14 (15). Apan
17. Tlachco, 36r	16—8v	15 (14). Tlachco
18. Tepequacuilco, 37r	17—9r	16. Tepequaquilco
19. Cihuatlan, 38r	18—9v	17. Çiguatlan
20. Tlapan, 39r	19—10r	18. Tlapa
21. Tlalcoçauhtitlan, 40r top	20 left—10v	19. Çacatlan‖

Table 4-4 continued

Codex Mendoza*	Matrícula de tributos†	Información . . . de 1554‡
22. Quiauhteopan, 40r center	20 center—10v	20. Tequisquitlan‖
23. Yoaltepec, 40r bottom	20 right—10v	21. Ichcaatoyaque‖
24. Chalco, 41r	21—11r	22. Chalco
25. Tepeacac, 42r	22—11v	23. Tepeaca
26. Coayxtlahuacan, 43r	23—12r	24. Cuestlavaca
27. Coyolapan, 44r	24—12v	25. Cuilapan
28. Tlachquiauco, 45r	—	26. Tlaxiaco
29. Tochtepec, 46r	—	27. Tochitepeque
30. Xoconochco, 47r	25—13r	28. Soconusco
31. Quauhtochco, 48r	26—13v	29. Quautuchco
32. Cuetlaxtlan, 49r	27—14r	30. Cotlastla
33. Tlapacoyan, 50r	28—14v	31. Tlapacoya
34. Tlatlauhquitepec, 51r	29—15r	32. Tlatlauquitepeque
35. Tuchpa, 52r	30—15v	33. Tochpan
36. Atlan, 53r	31—16r	34. Atlan
37. Çtzicoac, 54r	32—16v	35. Çicoaque
38. Oxitipan, 55r	—	36. Oxitipan

*Provinces paying tribute in kind are numbered according to their position in the manuscript; the military districts are not numbered.
†The first number given is that of the plate as in the edition by Castillo Farreras (1974); the second is that of the foliation of the codex in its present state. The numbers of the provinces are not given in this column.
‡Scholes and Adams 1957. All the witnesses give the provinces in the same order except that the first, third, and fifth put Tlachco before Apan and the second, fourth, and sixth do the opposite. Apan is the equivalent of Malinalco and Xocotitlan in the pictorial sources.
§Alongside seven towns are pictures of their governors; these would be the cabeceras. The other towns would be subject to one or another of the cabeceras. See chapter 12.
‖In these cases the *Información* names the town of the province that is last in the list of the Codex Mendoza. Tequisquitlan is the same as Xala in the Codex Mendoza; the same glyph has been read in two different ways. See the discussion of these provinces in chapter 10.

partly preserved; the half that is missing probably contained the glyphs for Quecholtetenanco, Cuauhtochco, and Itzteyocan. Also missing are all the towns in the Basin that may possibly have been on another sheet, which has been lost.

The nature of the groups of towns depicted in the second part is set forth in the commentary on the reign of Moteuczoma in the first part, where it is said that the forty-four towns that he conquered paid a great deal of tribute, as can be seen in the figures and their explanations (14v). It then adds that Moteuczoma took extreme care to see that the tribute was paid according to how he had assessed it, "and for this [purpose] he had his calpixques and agents installed in all the towns of his vassals, as governors who ruled them, gave orders, and governed, and as he

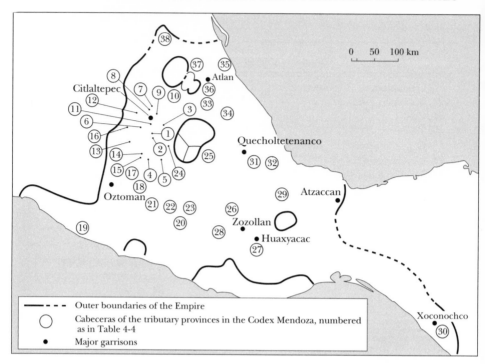

MAP 4–1. Tributary provinces and military garrisons according to the Codex Mendoza

was so feared no one dared to countermand an order or go beyond his wish and command, but were careful to carry out [his will], because he was unyielding in the execution and punishment of rebels."[47]

According to the annotation on folio 18r, the second of the two pages on which the distant garrisons of the Empire are depicted, "The towns contained and figured and named in this page and the previous page were governed by the caciques and principals of Mexico installed by the lords of Mexico for the protection and good government of the natives and so that they would have complete charge of collecting and ordering to be collected the rents and tributes that they were obliged to give and pay to the kingdom of Mexico and for the security of the towns so that they would not rebel."

A comparison of this commentary with those of the following pages shows that they express many of the same ideas, but the comment just quoted does not adhere strictly to the glyphs that it accompanies, since they do not represent the tribute that those towns had to pay. These pictures represent the garrisons established in various parts of the Empire, together with certain towns in the Basin under the direct control of Tenochtitlan.

All the following pages depict towns that paid tribute in kind. Folio 19r, which depicts Tlatelolco, is the first to include pictures of the goods given as tribute, but the explanatory text on folio 18v (numbered 19) says nothing about the administrative organization.

Folio 19v (numbered 20) contains a commentary on how the province of the *petlacalcatl* depicted on 20r and 20v was governed: "The lords of Mexico had placed a governor called petlacalcatl although in each town they had put a calpixque that is like a steward who is in charge of having the rent and tribute collected that the said towns paid to the kingdom of Mexico and all the said stewards reported to the said petlacalcatl as their governor."

The commentary on the province of Acolhuacan (21r) states there were "twenty-six towns in which the lords of Mexico since they were conquered by them had put calpixques in each one of them and in the most principal [one] a governor ruled over all of them so that he would keep them in peace and justice and make them pay their tribute and so that they would not rebel."

The annotation on Cuauhnahuac (22v) says: "So that the towns [would be] well administered and governed the lords of Mexico had put in each one of them calpixques and over all the calpixque[s] a governor, [a] principal person from Mexico and likewise the calpixques were Mexicas, which was done and provided by the said lords for the security of the land so that they would not rebel."

A shorter statement is made about the Huaxtepec towns (24r): "As in the above a Mexica governor and calpixques resided in them put there by the hand of the lords of Mexico."

Regarding Cuauhtitlan (25v) it is said that they paid tribute "as has been mentioned in the preceding sections," and almost the same is said about Axocopan (26v) and Atotonilco [de Tula] (27v). There is no further commentary on the governing of the provinces until the province of Tepeyacac (41v), where "in each town there were Mexica calpixques and the same order and administration and government as in the other towns and provinces described above, and thus in the rest to be brief, the towns and the tribute they gave will only be numbered; in what concerns the government of these towns by their calpixques it will be understood in what follows that they had the same order and government."

It is clear that for this commentator the same procedure was followed in all the tributary provinces: Each town has a Mexica calpixque and over the calpixques there was a governor (in one case also called calpixque) to collect the tribute and watch over the security of the province. This is, then, a formula that the commentator used as the norm to be applied to all the provinces, although he is not specific on all points in every case. Data from other sources, as we shall see, show that the situation was more complex.[48]

Economically and politically the towns painted in the two codices are of different kinds, from cities with their own kings to rural villages described in the memorials of Tetzcoco and Tlacopan as inhabited by tenants. Not all the cities with kings subject to Tenochtitlan are represented; only Huitzilopochco, Olac Xochimilco, Cuitlahuac, and Mizquic, in the province of Petlacalco, are shown, and Ecatepec in the province of Acolhuacan. Not shown are Colhuacan, Mexicatzinco, Itztapalapan, and Tenayocan. Of the cities with Tepanec kings, we find Cuauhtitlan and Xilotepec, the cabeceras of their respective provinces. Of the cities with kings subject to Tetzcoco, Acolman is the cabecera of the province of Acolhuacan, which includes Tezoyocan and Tepechpan. Tollantzinco is listed in the province of Atotonilco el Grande.

Thus it is obvious that the criterion used in the Codex Mendoza and the *Matrícula* is very different from that found in the memorials of Tetzcoco and Tlacopan. The fact that there are glyphs for cities such as Cuitlahuac, Cuauhtitlan, or Tollantzinco does not mean that their entire tribute went to Tenochtitlan and that the cities not represented did not pay anything. The cities painted in these codices must be those in which there were Tenochca possessions and stewards to collect the tribute for Tenochtitlan. The cities not represented were not points for collection; perhaps they paid tribute and labor to their own kings and to the king of the capital city to which they were subject, but they did not pay tribute to Tenochtitlan, or rather, they did not pay tribute in the products shown in these codices. This explains why the same town may appear on different pages—as a tributary town and as a garrison—or be spoken of in other sources as having different obligations. This is not a matter of contradiction but results from the multiple obligations that a city might have and the various types of landholders and tenant farmers that there might be within the territory of a city.

On the other hand, the Codex Mendoza and the *Matrícula* do not include many towns that, according to other sources, were conquered or at least obliged to pay tribute. Towns of little importance that were omitted were probably towns or villages administered by the calpixques of the towns depicted in these codices. But there must be another explanation in the case of important towns, such as many towns in the Balsas Basin, along the coasts, and on the Isthmus of Tecuantepec, that are not included in the Codex Mendoza but were part of the imperial system. We will, therefore, review all the pages of these two codices to see if different categories of tributary towns can be identified according to what we have seen in the documents from the other two capitals of the Empire, and later we will compare them with other sources, such as the *Relaciones geográficas* and the various lists of conquests.

From the Tetzcoco and Tlacopan material we know there was an extensive rural area with villages that provisioned the capitals; in this area there were also lands of nobles and commoners rewarded for merit. The question then arises, are there similar data in the Tenochca material?

In regard to Tenochtitlan, the area of the city proper has been ably identified by Caso, and we also know that the city had dependencies nearby on the chinampa islets and on the mainland. Gibson has compiled the data on the villages pertaining to the City of Mexico, both of Tenochtitlan and of Tlatelolco.[49] These were located to the south and north of the city, principally in the same areas of the Basin that appear on folio 17v and in the province of Petlacalco. Tezozomoc names the parcels of land distributed to the magnates of the city and to the gods of the barrios in Azcapotzalco, Coyoacan, Xochimilco, and Chalco.[50] Some of these towns appear also in the *Matrícula* and the Codex Mendoza: Popotla, won from Azcapotzalco, appears on folio 17v of the Codex Mendoza, as does Chalco Atenco, and in the province of Petlacalco (20r) are listed Olac Xochimilco, Tepepulan (in Chalco), and (A)toyac (in Coyoacan).

What is most intriguing about folios 17v–18r of the Codex Mendoza is that they include towns both in the Basin and in the distant conquered regions. Along the left-hand and bottom margins of folio 17v there is a series of place name glyphs painted in the same style and position as the glyphs of tributary towns in the rest of the codex. They are Citlaltepec, Tzompanco, Xaltocan, Acalhuacan, Coatitlan, Huixachtitlan, Coatlayauhcan, Acolnahuac, Puputlan, Iztacalco, and Chalco Atenco, all of which are located in the Basin. In the space in which tribute is painted on all the other pages are larger glyphs for several other towns, all of them outside the Basin, some with the glyphs of their governors: Quauhtochco, Quecholtetenanco (glyph without a legend), Huaxac (*sic pro* Huaxyacac), Izteyocan, Çoçolan, and Poctepec. Folio 18r has only glyphs of distant towns and their governors: Oztoma, Atzacan, Atlan, Xoconochco, and Teçapotitlan.

At first the combination on one page of towns in the Basin and distant towns whose governors are depicted seems enigmatic.[51] R. van Zantwijk found a key to the interpretation of these pages in Tezozomoc's account of how, in order to repopulate Oztoman and Alahuiztlan, the order was given to transfer settlers from the three powers of the Empire; to govern them, twenty married principales would be sent from Iztacalco, Popotlan, Coatlayauhcan, and Acolnahuac. Van Zantwijk concludes that the towns whose glyphs are painted in the margin were obliged, instead of paying tribute in kind, to provide settlers for the imperial garrisons in the conquered provinces, which are painted on that part of the page where tribute is usually depicted.[52] The military role of the towns headed by Citlaltepec is clear, but local sources show that this area also contained towns paying tribute to Tetzcoco and Tlacopan; more data are needed in order to clarify the obligations of these towns.

Within the territorial structure of the Empire, all the towns on folios 17v and

18r in the Codex Mendoza were basically military colonies, that is, settlements that instead of paying tribute in kind gave military service and functioned as garrisons. Since the eleven towns in the Basin were ancient settlements, they would serve, according to Tezozomoc's description, as a source of settlers and officials for the distant garrisons established in conquered regions. Both the eleven towns in the Basin and the distant garrisons were military posts governed directly from Tenochtitlan. The separation in both these documents of the military garrisons and the tributary towns makes clear that the organization of the military districts was different from that of the tributary provinces. This is of primary importance for comparing these documents with the "Memorial de los Pueblos de Tlacopan," which makes no such distinction.

Folio 19r of the Codex Mendoza (plate 3, torn, in the *Matrícula*) depicts Tlatelolco, whose status was somewhat special. In the early days of the Empire Tlatelolco had its own king, but after the war with Tenochtitlan, Tlatelolco was ruled by military governors (*cuauhtlatoque*) appointed by the Tenochcas. The Codex Mendoza indicates certain specialized forms of tribute to be given by Tlatelolco, such as repairing the temple of Huitznahuac and giving ground cacao and pinole as provisions for war, along with cloaks and warriors' garments. Tlatelolco's situation resembles that of the cities with kings, under Tetzcoco and Tlacopan, whose obligations were principally public works and military assistance, but it also resembles the garrisons on 17v and 18r, also under the rule of military governors. It is also possible that Tlatelolco, with its military governors, could have been the cabecera of the eleven towns represented in the margin of 17v, some of which were subject to Tlatelolco during colonial times.[53]

The province on folios 20r–20v of the Codex Mendoza is headed by the glyph for Petlacalco; above it is written "governador petlacalcatl." The abbreviation pu° (pueblo) that came next has been crossed out. Only a fragment remains of the corresponding plate of the *Matrícula*, and the glyph for the cabecera is missing, but the legend says, "All this was the tribute [or task] of the petlacalcatl" (ynin mochi ytequiuh catca yn petlacalcatl). Petlacalco means "storehouse" or "treasury," and nothing indicates that it was the name of a town; petlacalcatl was the chief steward.[54] The towns in this province were in the region ruled directly by Tenochtitlan, where there were several cities governed by kings of the Tenochca dynasty. Of the towns listed, four had kings: Huitzilopochco, Olac Xochimilco, Cuitlahuac, and Mizquic. There is no need to think that these kingdoms brought all their tribute and services to the Petlacalco. There were stewards in those kingdoms to administer the local Tenochca possessions, and the sites listed in this province were, at least in part, the lands that Tenochtitlan took for itself following the defeat of Coyoacan, Xochimilco, and Chalco.[55] Part of this province corresponds also to the region where Nezahualcoyotl established his Chinampan tribute district; the difference is that the Codex Mendoza lists the holdings of Tenochtitlan, while Ixtlilxochitl enumerates those of Tetzcoco. Therefore Citlaltepec, Tlatelolco, and the province of Petlacalco were the direct dependencies of Tenochtitlan in its own domain within the Basin.

Following Petlacalco is the province that comprises the Acolhuacan, or kingdom of Tetzcoco, in the eastern part of the Basin; its cabecera was probably Acolman. Only two of the kingdoms of Tetzcoco appear: Tepechpan and Tezoyocan. Some of the other towns are also listed in the Acolhua sources as inhabited by tenants of the king of Tetzcoco, but a good many in the region of Temazcalapan, as is known from other sources, paid tribute to Tenochtitlan.[56] This province represents, therefore, the Tenochca organization for collecting the tribute due to Tenochtitlan within the domain of Tetzcoco.

Two provinces comprise the region called Tlalhuic: Cuauhnahuac (23r–v) and Huaxtepec (24v–25r). Tetzcoco and Tlacopan also had possessions there. The "Memorial de Tlacopan" gives a list of Tlacopan's villages of tenants in this region and also includes Cuauhnahuac and Huaxtepec among the towns paying tribute to the three capitals. There were local kings—who are not mentioned as directly subject to any of the three capitals of the alliance—in Cuauhnahuac, Tepoztlan, Yauhtepec, Huaxtepec, and Yacapichtla; all these towns appear in the Codex Mendoza, and Tenochtitlan had many more sujetos there than did the other capitals. These two provinces comprise, therefore, the towns in that region pertaining to Tenochtitlan.

The provinces that follow are in the area where the dependent kingdoms of Tlacopan are found: Cuauhtitlan (26r); Axocopan (27r), lacking in the *Matrícula*; Atotonilco [de Tula] (28r), lacking in the *Matrícula*; Hueypochtlan (29r); Xilotepec (31r); and Cuahuacan (32r). The towns depicted on these pages must be those that pertain to Tenochtitlan. The cities with Tepanec kings represented in these provinces are only two: Cuauhtitlan and Xilotepec. The province of Cuahuacan coincides fairly well with the region that, according to the "Memorial de Tlacopan," consisted of the direct dependencies of that city. All these provinces will be considered as the possessions of Tenochtitlan within the Tlacopan domain.

In the sequence of provinces described thus far, Atotonilco [el Grande] (30r) is also listed. This province includes Tollantzinco, governed by a king subject to Tetzcoco, and Tzihuinquilocan, a settlement established by Nezahualcoyotl, but it is not certain that all the other towns were within the Tetzcoca domain. Probably there was some overlapping of jurisdictions.

The province of Tolocan is depicted next (33r). As in Cuauhnahuac and Huaxtepec, Tetzcoco and Tlacopan also had possessions in Tolocan.

The provinces of Ocuillan (34r), Malinalco (35r), and Xocotitlan (35r) appear only in the Tenochca sources. Malinalco may well have been an exclusive tributary of Tenochtitlan. The Malinalcas were of the same origin as the Mexicas and were closely allied with them during the migration to the Basin. Xocotitlan, the principal Mazahua town, is near Ixtlahuacan, one of the towns of tenant farmers subject to Tlacopan in the same section of the "Memorial de Tlacopan" in which Tolocan also is found. It should also be remembered that Mazahuacan was given to Tlacopan when the Triple Alliance was established. The *Información de 1554* does not include the provinces of Malinalco and Xocotitlan, but instead adds a province, Apan, that is lacking in the Codex Mendoza. One group of witnesses described it between the provinces of Ocuillan and Tlachco; another group put it between Tlachco and Tepecuacuilco. As will be shown in chapter 5, it should be considered equivalent to Malinalco and Xocotitlan, which share a common page in the pictorial sources.

Starting with Tlachco, the remaining provinces of the Codex Mendoza are described in the other available sources as tributaries of the three capitals of the Empire, without any clear information whether each capital had its own separate holdings except in the case of Chalco (41r). But although Chalco is located in the Basin, the Codex Mendoza and related sources, which follow a political-geographical order, do not include it until much later, after the provinces in the present-day state of Guerrero and before Tepeyacac. This suggests that it was considered to be one of the kingdoms conquered by the Empire as a unit. Yet some of the towns in Chalco pertaining to Tenochtitlan are included in the province of Petlacalco, Tlapechuacan is included in one of the tribute districts of Tetzcoco, and the possessions of Tlacopan in Chalco are included in a group of tributaries in the southern part of the Basin. The political situation of Chalco varied in the course of the history of the Empire. One might conclude that parts of this province were incorporated separately into the domains of each one of the three capitals and that the province in the Codex Mendoza registers other tribute demands on Chalco to be divided among the three capitals.[57]

Taking all this into account, we can arrange the possessions of the Tenochca kingdom in categories similar to those of the other two kingdoms of the alliance as described in the memorials of Tetzcoco and Tlacopan.

1. The capital, which included the island with its civic-religious center, is not mentioned in the Tenochca sources as a tributary unit. Some rural dependencies on the islets in the vicinity, and also various towns that in colonial times were villages of Tenochtitlan and Tlatelolco, are listed in the provinces of Citlaltepec and Petlacalco, located in the territory of Tenochtitlan and of the kingdoms that were its dependencies.

2. The cities with kings subject to Tenochtitlan, which have been identified in the historical sources, are not found in the *Matrícula* or in the Codex Mendoza as a separate category. This contrasts with the memorials of Tetzcoco and

Tlacopan, which give lists of cities with kings that were dependencies of those capitals. The kingdoms of the Tenochca domain appear in the Codex Mendoza only when they are the seat of stewards who would have in their charge the holdings within these kingdoms that belonged to Tenochtitlan.

3. The groups of tributary towns (or calpixcazgos) corresponding to what the memorials of Tetzcoco and Tlacopan describe as towns of tenants are all in territory pertaining to one or another of the three parts of the alliance. However, these Tenochca tribute registers, unlike the memorials from Tetzcoco and Tlacopan, do not make any statements about land tenure among peasants in tributary settlements. What is clear from the comparison of all sources is that each of the three capitals had tributary towns both in its own domain and in the domains of the other two. The provinces organized for the collection of the tribute sent to Tenochtitlan, listed in the Codex Mendoza and related sources, can be classified in the following manner:

a. Provinces of towns paying tribute to Tenochtitlan in the area containing the cities whose kings were direct subordinates of Tenochtitlan: the military district of the Basin headed by Citlaltepec, Tlatelolco, and Petlacalco. The kings of Tetzcoco and Tlacopan also had possessions in these regions, as Tenochtitlan held lands in their domains, which are the next categories, *b* and *c*.

b. Provinces of towns paying tribute to Tenochtitlan in the dependent kingdoms of Tetzcoco: Acolman and part of Atotonilco el Grande.

c. Provinces of towns paying tribute to Tenochtitlan in the dependent kingdoms of Tlacopan: Cuauhtitlan, Axocopan, Atotonilco de Tula, Hueypochtlan, Xilotepec, and Cuahuacan.

4. Three areas in the center of the Empire that were not governed by kings directly subject to one or another of the three capitals. It seems that they were subject to the Empire as a whole, although they were under Tenochca predominance, but nevertheless each of the three capitals had separate possessions in these areas. The Codex Mendoza lists possessions of Tenochtitlan in Tlalhuic (Cuauhnahuac and Huaxtepec), Chalco, and Tolocan.[58]

The tributary provinces in these four categories were the Tenochca part of the core area of the Empire, which is described in chapter 5. They paid tribute to Tenochtitlan, while other towns in those same regions paid tribute to Tetzcoco and Tlacopan and are identified in the sources from those two capitals. The rest of the tributary provinces painted in the *Matrícula* and the Codex Mendoza correspond to the regions that the memorials of Tetzcoco and Tlacopan describe as tributaries of the Empire as a whole, whose tribute was divided among the three capitals. This tribute was taken to Tenochtitlan, but—according to the general procedure described by Ixtlilxochitl—part of it was then distributed to the two other capitals (see chapter 8). The Codex Mendoza, like the "Memorial de Tlaco-

TABLE 4-5.

The Tributary Provinces of the Codex Mendoza Compared with the
Territorial Categories of the Memorials of Tetzcoco and Tlacopan.

Codex Mendoza	"Memorial de Tlacopan"*	Tetzcocan Sources†
The Core Area		
	Tlacopan and its sujetos (secs. 1, 2, and 3)	Tetzcoco "with its barrios and hamlets" (Ixtlilxochitl)
[Military district of the Basin] Citlaltepec (fol. 17v)		
[Distant military districts] Oztoman, etc. (fols. 17v–18r)		
	Cities with kings subject to Tlacopan (sec. 4)	Cities with kings subject to Tetzcoco (Motolinía)
[Tributaries of Tenochtitlan in its own domain]	Tributaries of Tlacopan in its own domain (sec. 5)	Tributaries of Tetzcoco in its own domain (Motolinía; Ixtlilxochitl)
1. Tlatelolco 2. Petlacalcatl		
[Tributaries of Tenochtitlan in the domain of Tetzcoco]	Tributaries of Tlacopan in the domains of Tenochtitlan and Tetzcoco (sec. 5)	Tributaries of Tetzcoco in the domains of Tlacopan and Tenochtitlan
3. Acolhuacan 10. Atotonilco [el Grande]		Tribute of the Chinampan (Ixtlilxochitl)
[Tributaries of Tenochtitlan in the domain of Tlacopan]		
6. Cuauhtitlan, 7. Axocopan 8. Atotonilco [de Tula] 9. Hueypochtlan 11. Xilotepec 12. Cuahuacan		
[Tributaries of Tenochtitlan in Tlalhuic]	Tributaries of Tlacopan in Tlalhuic (sec. 5)	Tributaries of Tetzcoco in Tlalhuic
4. Cuauhnahuac 5. Huaxtepec		Cuauhnahuac (Motolinía)

Table 4-5 continued

Codex Mendoza	"Memorial de Tlacopan"*	Tetzcocan Sources[†]
[Tenochtitlan Tributaries in the Valley of Toluca]	Tlacopan Tributaries in the Valley of Toluca (sec. 5)	Tetzcoco Tributaries in the Valley of Toluca (Pimentel)
13. Tolocan		
14. Ocuillan		
15. Malinalco		
16. Xocotitlan		

The Subjugated Regions

17. Tlachco	Tlachmalacac (sec. 7.3)	
18. Tepecuacuilco		
19. Cihuatlan		
20. Tlappan		
21. Tlalcozauhtitlan		Tlalcozauhtitlan (Ixtlilxochitl)
22. Quiauhteopan		
23. Yohualtepec		
24. Chalco		
25. Tepeyacac		Tepeyacac (Pimentel)
26. Coaixtlahuacan	Cozcatlan (sec. 7.2)	Coaixtlahuacan (Pimentel)
27. Coyolapan	Oztoman (sec. 7.4)	
28. Tlachquiauhco		
29. Tochtepec	Tochtepec (sec. 6.3) Chinantlan, etc. (sec. 6.6)	Tochtepec (Motolinía)
30. Xoconochco	Tototepec (sec. 8)	
31. Cuauhtochco	Cempohuallan (sec 7.1)	Cuauhtochco (Pimentel)
32. Cuetlaxtlan		Cuetlaxtlan (Pimentel) Ahuilizapan (Pimentel)
33. Tlapacoyan	Tlapacoyan (sec. 6.4)	Tlapacoyan (Motolinía)
34. Tlatlauhquitepec	Tlatlauhquitepec (sec. 6.5)	Tlatlauhquitepec (Motolinía)
35. Tochpan	Tochpan (sec. 6.1)	Tochpan (Motolinía)
36. Atlan	Cempohuallan (sec. 7.1)	
37. Tziuhcoac	Tziuhcoac (sec. 6.2)	Tziuhcoac (Motolinía)
38. Oxitipan		

NOTE: The characterization of the politico-territorial categories follows the Tlacopan and Tetzcocan sources. In the case of Tenochtitlan they are defined within square brackets in accordance with the interpretation given in this chapter.

*The sections and paragraphs are numbered as in Table 4-1. The towns in sections 7 and 8 are very different from the provinces in the Codex Mendoza. Here, only the town that heads each paragraph is indicated. A more detailed comparison is given in Table 8-1.

[†]Memorial of Motolinía in Motolinía 1971:394–96. From Ixtlilxochitl (1975–77, 2:89–97, 106–108) are included only the provinces where Nezahualcoyotl named stewards.

TABLE 4-6.

The Twenty Calpixques in Sahagún's *Historia*

Calpixques in Sahagún*	Provinces in the Codex Mendoza
1. petlacalcatl	2. Petlacalco
2. aztacalcatl	—
3. quauhnaoac calpixquj	4. Cuauhnahuac
4. oaxtepec calpixquj	5. Huaxtepec
5. cuetlaxtecatl	32. Cuetlaxlan
6. tochpanecatl	35. Tochpan
7. tziuhcoacatl	37. Tziuhcoac
8. tepequacujlcatl	18. Tepecuacuilco
9. hoappanecatl	Ohuapan, included in 18. Tepecuacuilco
10. coaixtlaoacatl	26. Coaixtlahuacan
11. tlappanecatl	20. Tlappan
12. tlachcotecatl	17. Tlachco
13. matlatzincatl	13. Tolocan
14. ocujltecatl	14. Ocuillan
15. xilotepecatl	11. Xilotepec
16. atotonjlcatl	8. Atotonilco [de Tula]
17. axocopanecatl	7. Axocopan
18. itzcujncujtlapilcatl	—
19. atocpanecatl	Atocpan, included in 9. Hueypochtlan
20. ayotzintepecatl	Ayotzintepec, included in 29. Tochtepec

*Sahagún 1954:51, 52 (book 8, chap. 17).

pan," takes in the whole Empire, although the two documents differ on the composition of the provinces. In contrast, the Tetzcoca sources are concentrated on the northeastern or Tetzcoca sector and give little information on the sectors of Tlacopan and Tenochtitlan. All these tributary provinces in the conquered regions that paid tribute to the three capitals have not been enumerated in the preceding discussion of the Codex Mendoza; they are treated in chapters 9, 10, and 11. Another very different category is that of the military districts, which did not pay tribute in kind. The military district in the Basin is discussed in chapter 5, and the distant garrisons in chapter 12.

Table 4-4 has listed the territorial categories according to the Tenochca sources; Table 4-5 compares them with the memorials of Tetzcoco and Tlacopan, analyzed above. The pages, or provinces, are given in the same order as in the Codex Mendoza. Part one of Table 4-5 includes the military districts—of the Basin and the distant regions—which appear only in the Tenochca sources, as well as the territorial entities that constitute the three great kingdoms of the core area. Part two of Table 4-5 comprises the provinces that paid tribute to the three kingdoms.

The Tetzcoca sources name primarily the provinces in the Tetzcoca sector. In the Codex Mendoza and the "Memorial de Tlacopan" the enumeration is more complete, but the territorial organization is different, especially in the southern or Tenochca sector of the Empire. Later chapters will compare in detail the organization presented in the different sources for each region.

The Calpixques of Tenochtitlan in Sahagún's Historia

Sahagún's *Historia general*, in describing the preparations that took place in Tenochtitlan for a military campaign, gives a list of twenty calpixques who were in charge of the military insignia. Their names refer to the areas that contributed these goods and thus provide a picture of the extent of the Empire. The king (tlatoani) summoned the generals (*tlacochcalcatl* and tlacatecatl) to plan the campaign and ordered the warriors (*quauhtlocelotl*) to be ready. He summoned the calpixques and ordered them to bring all the valuable insignia and cloaks to be distributed to the nobles and warriors. Finally, the king called on the kings of Tetzcoco, Tlacopan, and the Chinampan and ordered the commoners to go forth to war.[59]

This passage in Sahagún provides the most extensive list of calpixques that exists in the Tenochca sources, aside from the Codex Mendoza and related documents. Table 4-6 gives the list of calpixques, in the order in which Sahagún's text gives them, and compares their names with the provinces of the Codex Mendoza, starting with Tlatelolco. The correspondence is evident, but for some towns additional commentary is necessary.

Only two towns in Sahagún's list are missing in the Codex Mendoza. Itzcuincuitlapilco (18), today in the municipio of San Agustín Tlaxiaca, Hidalgo, is a well-known town that the "Memorial de Tlacopan" identifies as one of the sujetos of the kingdom of Apazco, among which are also Axocopan and Hueypochtlan, cabeceras of provinces in the Codex Mendoza. The other is Aztacalco (2), for which there are two possible locations in the Basin, one a barrio of Tenochtitlan in the parcialidad of Moyotla,[60] and the other a town, Santa María Aztacalco (or Astacalco), to the east or northeast of Lake Xaltocan.[61] Matlatzincatl (13) is equivalent to Tolocan.

If we take this list of twenty calpixques as equivalent to a list of the tributary provinces of the Empire, we have a picture somewhat different from that presented in the Codex Mendoza. Reyes has analyzed the order in which the provinces appear in this list from the point of view of cosmological principles and finds that it can be subdivided into five groups, each with four calpixques, that correspond to the center of the earth and the four cardinal directions.[62] The first four calpixcazgos form the center, and the four groups of four that follow correspond to the east, south, west, and north. But there are two towns that do not fit into this scheme:

TABLE 4-7.
Sahagún's Twenty Calpixques and the World Directions

Direction	Calpixques in Sahagún*	Provinces in the Codex Mendoza
Center	1. petlacalcatl	2. Petlacalco
	2. aztacalcatl	—
	3. quauhnaoac calpixquj	4. Cuauhnahuac
	4. oaxtepec calpixquj	5. Huaxtepec
East	20. ayotzintepecatl	Ayotzintepec in 29. Tochtepec
	5. cuetlaxtecatl	32. Cuetlaxtlan
	6. tochpanecatl	35. Tochpan
	7. tziuhcoacatl	37. Tziuhcoac
South	8. tepequacujlcatl	18. Tepecuacuilco
	9. hoappanecatl	Ohuapan in 18. Tepecuacuilco
	10. coaixtlaoacatl	26. Coaixtlahuacan
	11. tlappanecatl	20. Tlappan
West	12. tlachcotecatl	17. Tlachco
	13. matlatzincatl	13. Tolocan
	14. ocujltecatl	14. Ocuillan
	15. xilotepecatl	11. Xilotepec
North	16. atotonjlcatl	8. Atotonilco [de Tula]
	17. axocopanecatl	7. Axocopan
	18. itzcujncujtlapilcatl	—
	19. atocpanecatl	Atocpan in 9. Hueypochtlan

*Sahagún 1954:51, 52 (Bk. 8, chap. 17).

Tepecuacuilco (in present-day Guerrero) cannot be part of the group of the east, and Ayotzintepec, in the Chinantec region of Oaxaca, cannot be associated with the north. Reyes then suggests that Tepecuacuilco would be in the Sierra de Puebla, corresponding to Tlatlauhquitepec in the Codex Mendoza, and Ayotzintepec would be a present-day place called Estación Tortugas, to the north of Tollantzinco, which would be in the province of Atotonilco el Grande.[63] It is preferable to think that Ayotzintepec, the last town on the list, was the first of those located away from the center and through an error was put at the end. This is understandable if the list was copied from a painting or map that depicted all those towns around the center. If this explanation is accepted, the ordering of the towns in five groups of four, as Reyes suggests, would be as shown in Table 4-7, and there is no need to change the location of well-known toponyms represented in the Codex Mendoza.

Sahagún's text lists only twenty calpixques, a number considerably less than

TABLE 4-8.
Sahagún's Twenty Calpixques Compared with the Provinces in the Codex Mendoza

Sahagún*	Codex Mendoza Equivalent in Sahagún	Not in Sahagún
1. petlacalcatl	2. Petlacalco	
2. aztacalcatl	[3. Acolhuacan]	
3. quauhnaoac calpixquj	4. Cuauhnahuac	
4. oaxtepec calpixquj	5. Huaxtepec	
		38. Oxitipan
7. tziuhcoacatl	37. Tziuhcoac	
		36. Atlan
6. tochpanecatl	35. Tochpan	
		34. Tlatlauhquitepec
		33. Tlapacoyan
5. cuetlaxtecatl	32. Cuetlaxtlan	
		31. Cuauhtochco
		30. Xoconochco
20. ayotzintepecatl	29. Tochtepec	
		28. Tlachquiauhco
		27. Coyolapan
10. coaixtlaoacatl	26. Coaixtlahuacan	
		25. Tepeyacac
		24. Chalco
		23. Yohualtepec
		22. Quiauhteopan
		21. Tlalcozauhtitlan
11. tlappanecatl	20. Tlappan	
		19. Cihuatlan
9. hoappanecatl	in 18. Tepecuacuilco	
8. tepequacujlcatl	18. Tepecuacuilco	
12. tlachcotecatl	17. Tlachco	
		16. Xocotitlan
		15. Malinalco
14. ocujltecatl	14. Ocuillan	
13. matlatzincatl	13. Tolocan	
		12. Cuahuacan
15. xilotepecatl	11. Xilotepec	
		10. Atotonilco [el Grande]
18. itzcujncujtlapilcatl	—	
19. atocpanecatl	9. Hueypochtlan	
16. atotonjlcatl	8. Atotonilco [de Tula]	
17. axocopanecatl	7. Axocopan	
		6. Cuauhtitlan

*Sahagún 1954:51, 52 (book 8, chap. 17).

the thirty-eight provinces in the Codex Mendoza. One might think that the latter, as Reyes proposes, were also organized in five divisions conforming to the directions of the universe. Table 4-8 compares Sahagún's list with all the provinces of the Codex Mendoza. The column on the left gives Sahagún's list, with the order of the names of the calpixques slightly changed, within each group of four, to align them with the provinces of the Codex Mendoza. These are put into two columns; the first comprises those that are equivalent to the calpixques in Sahagún, and those not in Sahagún's list are in the second column.

In Sahagún's list, the sequence of names begins in the center and continues clockwise, starting in the east and then proceeding south, west, and north; within each group the towns do not follow a systematic order. This clockwise arrangement is contrary to that of the Codex Mendoza, in which the provinces are arranged, after the central group, counterclockwise, beginning with the north and then moving to the west, south, and east. Therefore in Table 4-8, after the center (numbers 1–4), Sahagún's list reads from top to bottom, while that of the Codex Mendoza reads from bottom to top. As we saw, the "Memorial de Tlacopan," like Sahagún's text, also presents the sections in a clockwise arrangement, but it begins with Tlacopan and the Tepanec kingdoms in the northwest, continuing with the imperial provinces of the northeast and ending with those in the south.

The groups in Sahagún's list correspond to the cardinal points. This is different from Torquemada's scheme, in which it is the lines of demarcation among the three parts of the Empire that are oriented to the cardinal points. Therefore, it is not possible to interpret this list according to Torquemada's tripartite division, used in this study as the basis for presenting the provinces. But the ordering of the material according to the directions of the universe and the different ways of numbering the sequence, clockwise or counterclockwise, are questions that need not be discussed here. Our principal interest is to see how this list is related to the obligations of the calpixques within the territorial and economic organization of the Empire.

Some calpixques in Sahagún's list administered towns that are not in the Codex Mendoza and others that are included, but not as cabeceras of provinces. Aztacalco was probably located as given above in the region east of Xaltocan. It was close to towns such as Ecatepec, Tizayocan, and Temazcalapan that were in the province of Acolman (Acolhuacan) and may denote this province in Sahagún's list.[64] However, it is near Xaltocan, in the military district of Citlaltepec, and furthermore, Tlatelolco had sujetos in this same area; it is also possible that Aztacalco also represents that region and includes the province of Cuauhtitlan. Itzcuincuitlapilco was in the kingdom of Apazco. Its geographical location suggests that it was part of the province of Axocopan or of Hueypochtlan, but it is also possible that in Sahagún's list it occupies the place of Atotonilco (el Grande). In the Codex

Mendoza the province of Tepecuacuilco is represented by both Tepecuacuilco and Ohuapan. From other sources we know that Ohuapan was one of the principal collection centers in this province (see p. 273). Ayotzintepec was not a cabecera of a province in the Codex Mendoza; it was one of the towns in the province of Tochtepec, but its calpixque together with the calpixque of Chinantlan are given special mention as suppliers of rabbit fur to Moteuczoma Xocoyotzin (see p. 340).

These twenty calpixques could be those of higher rank within the total organization, but—given the context in which Sahagún's *Historia* presents the list—it seems more likely that they were simply the calpixques charged with providing the insignia stored at Tenochtitlan, and also that these calpixques were not those who went to the provinces as tribute collectors but were stationed in Tenochtitlan in charge of the storehouses. In any case, it is not said that they administered all the tribute that came to Tenochtitlan, but that they were the ones who cared for the highly valued insignia. Sahagún's text alludes to provisions for war, and the Spanish version speaks several times of goods other than the insignia, but in the Nahuatl text it is clear that the list of calpixques is related to their providing insignia and richly decorated cloaks.

A comparison of the provinces represented in this list of twenty calpixques with the provinces that gave insignia as tribute shows that there is not a strict correlation between them. Most of the insignia came from the provinces in the north and west. The provinces in the east and south gave few insignia as tribute, and yet they are represented in the list by the same number of calpixques. There seems to have been an intent to give equal representation to the five directions of the Empire, but it is striking that among the provinces of the Codex Mendoza that are not on the list of twenty calpixques, we find precisely those that did not contribute military insignia, and that the only province in the south that gave an important quantity of insignia is represented by two calpixques, those of Tepecuacuilco and Ohuapan.[65] Therefore, this list in Sahagún cannot be considered a picture of the total organization of the imperial tributary provinces but only of the organization for providing military insignia. If we had lists of the stewards in charge of costumes for religious ceremonies, of food, or of other goods, perhaps we would find that the composition of these groups of stewards would be different. If so, this idea could also explain some of the differences between the Codex Mendoza and the "Memorial de los Pueblos de Tlacopan." The regional groupings of the Empire's subject towns that sent representatives to Tenochtitlan on certain occasions—as described by Durán and Tezozomoc—also differ in significant ways from the provinces of the Codex Mendoza, the "Memorial de los Pueblos de Tlacopan," and this text of Sahagún's.

This chapter has dealt with the principal sources of information on the three kingdoms of the Triple Alliance—Tenochtitlan, Tetzcoco, and Tlacopan. The next three chapters present the organization of each of these three kingdoms within the core area. The material on each kingdom is arranged in the same way, according to the relevant political-territorial categories. Later chapters will discuss the regions that, being subject to the Empire as a unit, paid tribute to the three capitals and, finally, the organization of military colonies and garrisons.

PART TWO

The Three Kingdoms of the Alliance

Chapter 5

THE COLHUA-MEXICA KINGDOM OF TENOCHTITLAN

Tenochtitlan, Capital of the Colhua-Mexicas

Tenochtitlan, as one of the two cities situated on an island in the lake, shared with Tlatelolco the name Mexico. Its dominant position within the Empire implied the greatest concentration of the characteristics typical of an urban center. It was the seat of the governing class, who were not required to pay tribute and served in administrative, military, and religious positions. The city included a great number of public buildings related to these activities: palaces, storerooms, temples, and the residences of priests. From the members of the governing class officials were recruited to serve in the subjugated areas as governors and tribute collectors.

The rulers of the dependent kingdoms went to the capital for their installation ceremonies and maintained residences there for their visits to the capital. The kings of Tetzcoco and Tlacopan also had residences in the city, and there were houses to provide lodging for the rulers of independent kingdoms when they were invited to Tenochtitlan for the great civic and religious ceremonies.[1] The tributary towns of the Empire had houses in Tenochtitlan for the use of the stewards and the remittance of tribute,[2] and there were temples to house the gods of the subjugated areas.[3] As the dominant city of the alliance, Tenochtitlan exercised a certain preponderance over the other two capitals, which for the religious celebrations and military campaigns provided assistance to Tenochtitlan in a manner similar to that required of the kingdoms that were direct dependencies of the city.

Before the Spanish Conquest, Tenochtitlan was divided into four parcialidades, or principal barrios, and this division continued throughout the colonial period. The boundaries between these parcialidades ran from north to south and from east to west so that each one occupied a quarter of the city, Atzacualco (San Sebastián) in the northeast, Cuepopan (Santa María) in the northwest, Moyotla

(San Juan) in the southwest, and Teopan (San Pablo) in the southeast.[4] The histories of the Mexica migration usually give the names of seven original calpolli: Tlacatecpan, Tlacochcalco, Cihuatecpan, Chalman, Huitznahuac, Yopico, and Izquitlan. Four of these can be identified with the four parcialidades: Tlacatecpan with Atzacualco, Tlacochcalco with Cuepopan, Cihuatecpan with Moyotla, and Chalman with Teopan.[5] Huitznahuac was also in Teopan and Yopico in Moyotla;[6] the location of Izquitlan is not certain. The Nahuatl name for these parcialidades is either calpolli, the same term applied to the migration groups, or tlayacatl.[7] Sources giving the later history of the city name various other calpolli or temples whose connection with the four or seven original calpolli is not clear. The social function of the parcialidades and calpolli is obviously related to the ceremonial organization, since their names refer directly to temples, patron gods, and residences of the priests (calmecac),[8] but their location and their relation to governmental or military activities are more difficult to establish.[9]

In regard to the economy, there were in addition to the governing element a great many craftspeople and merchants in both Tenochtitlan and Tlatelolco, and in both cities there were marketplaces where a great variety of goods circulated, attended by large numbers of buyers and sellers.

The city's needs were supplied through this market system and also by the tribute from the royal or state lands and the tributary provinces, as well as from the lands assigned to institutions and to individual members of the governing class. The Tenochca kings and other members of the nobility held patrimonial lands, and land was also assigned to the temples and the young men's houses (telpochcalli). In the rural domain of the capital were fields for the use of the barrios of the city and their members.[10]

Tenochtitlan's position on an island has led to the assumption that the capital as a social unit coincided with the island and its urban population. But it is very clear in the sources that there were also dependencies of the city on various islets and on the mainland that constituted a rural extension of the capital similar to that which is better documented for Tetzcoco and Tlacopan. The principal sources about the rural extension of Tenochtitlan in pre-Spanish times are the pages of the Codex Mendoza and the Matrícula de tributos depicting Citlaltepec, Tlatelolco, and Petlacalco, even though these documents do not make clear which of these places are rural villages pertaining to the city and which are more distant dependencies located in other kingdoms. These tributary provinces will be discussed below, but it will be useful to examine first other sources, including colonial data, about the estancias pertaining to Tenochtitlan and Tlatelolco not located on the island.

A report by Zorita in 1562 on the tribute due to Tenochtitlan and Tlatelolco describes the urban nature of these two cities. The residents were warriors and members of the upper class who paid no tribute except for certain minor, and voluntary, services, and there was no need for cultivated land since "the other towns in the region paid tribute to this [city]." Zorita adds that what little land there was had been taken over by the Spaniards for various purposes, and since most of the Indians in the city were craftsmen, they went to the marketplace to buy food brought in from outside the city. He also comments on the difficult situation of Indians in the subject towns, since the Spaniards had taken most of their land and left them barely enough for their own needs. Part of the city's needs would have been provided for by these towns.[11]

A somewhat later document, a memorial written by the indigenous residents of the city of Mexico after the reforms of Valderrama, addresses the same problems. It emphasizes the importance in pre-Spanish times of the tribute that was brought into the city as well as the status of the Indians who as rulers were exempt from tribute and service. All residents, "lords and commoners," were supplied with food from the tribute that came from the subject provinces. In addition, the nobility had further income from their extensive patrimonial lands within the city and in the surrounding region. Since the coming of the Spanish, the Mexicas, who had formerly "served only to be rulers" of this country, had been left with neither lands nor vassals to supply them with the necessaries of life.[12]

Gibson has put together material on several estancias of Tenochtitlan and Tlatelolco in colonial times that were located in well-defined areas of the Basin. North of Lakes Tzompanco and Xaltocan were Santa Ana Zacatlan, San Bartolo Cuauhtlalpan, and San Lucas Xoloc, estancias of Tlatelolco. On the eastern side of Lake Xaltocan, San Francisco Cuauquiquitla (or Cuauhtlihizca), San Pablo Tecalco, and San Pedro Ozumba (Ozumbilla) pertained to Tenochtitlan, and to Tlatelolco, San Andrés Tecalco, Santa María Ozumbilla, and—more to the west—San Pablo de las Salinas. On the western shore of Lake Tetzcoco, Tolpetlac, Xaloztoc, and others were also estancias of Tlatelolco. In the southern part of the Basin, on the lake shore between Itztapalapan and Tlapitzahuayan, were several estancias of Tenochtitlan (Los Reyes, Santa Marta, and Aztahuacan) and in Chalco of both Tenochtitlan (Reyes Acatlixcoatlan, San Juan Coxtocan, Santiago Tepepollan) and Tlatelolco (part of Santiago Tepepollan and Tepoztlan).[13]

Thus, it is quite clear that the city of Mexico had held important possessions in various areas of the Basin. Zorita's data include little information about the extent of these lands because by that time the Spanish had taken possession of them, but the description in the memorial referred to above and the data collected by Gibson show that even during the Colonial period both Tenochtitlan and Tlatelolco had significant rural holdings in the Basin.

Although the existence of rural villages of tenant farmers is well documented, it is difficult to establish a distinction, as is made in the "Memorial de Tlacopan," between what could have been the capital district and rural settlements within the dependent kingdoms. And there is the related problem of the difficulty, in some cases, of determining whether they are barrios and lands of the city and its barrios or individual possessions of the nobles of the city. On the one hand, the historical traditions describe settlements in various places that later are said to be rural dependencies of the capital: Iztacalco, Mixiuhcan, and so on. On the other hand, traditions concerning the establishment of Tenochca control over neighboring towns tell of the appropriation of lands, principally in areas pertaining to Azcapotzalco, Coyoacan, Xochimilco, and Chalco, some of which appear later as estancias of Tenochtitlan. These lands were given to the tlatoani, to the cihuacoatl and other nobles of the city, and also to distinguished warriors and to the calpolli (or their gods). In other words, these "estancias" included lands held under different forms of tenure, and the nobles and institutions of the capital would have had possessions scattered among all the different dependencies.[14] This material will be considered below, together with the tributary towns of Tenochtitlan within its own domain that are listed in two of the provinces of the Codex Mendoza.

The Dependent Kingdoms of Tenochtitlan

There is no source that gives a list of the kingdoms directly subject to Tenochtitlan such as those describing the kingdoms subject to Tetzcoco and Tlacopan. Nevertheless, the information available is sufficient to state that the situation in the Tenochca domain was similar to that of the other two kingdoms of the alliance.

When Ixtlilxochitl, in his account of the beginning of the Triple Alliance, tells of the installation of fourteen kings under the sovereignty of Tetzcoco, nine under that of Tenochtitlan, and seven under Tlacopan, he names the kings and their realms subject to Nezahualcoyotl but does not identify the nine kingdoms subject to Tenochtitlan or those of Tlacopan. However, he provides indirectly the necessary information when he refers to the towns defeated during the Tepanec war that became part of the domains of Tenochtitlan and of Tlacopan and when he enumerates the towns in those two domains that paid to Tetzcoco the so-called tribute of the Chinampan area. The kingdoms in those domains are obviously those subordinate to either Tenochtitlan or Tlacopan. Ixtlilxochitl further alludes to the subordinate kingdoms of the Tenochca domain in his account of Tlatelolco's war against Axayacatl (see below).

Table 5-1 compares three enumerations, from different works by Ixtlilxochitl, of the towns subdued during the war against Azcapotzalco,[15] together with the list of places paying the Chinampan tribute to Tetzcoco.[16]

Six of these towns were Tepanec: Azcapotzalco, Coyoacan, Tlacopan, Toltitlan, Tepotzotlan, and Cuauhtitlan. The identity of Tepanoayan is not clear in the sources, but it is a toponym associated with the Tepanecs. In these lists it could refer to the Tlalnepantla region, between Tenayocan and Toltitlan.

TABLE 5-1.

Extent of the Tenochca and Tlacopan Domains at the Formation of the Alliance

Towns Defeated during the Tepanec War			Later Tributaries of Tetzcoco in
"Compendio histórico"*	"Sumaria relación"†	"Historia chichimeca"‡	the Chinampan§
			1. Barrio of Xoloco in Tenochtitlan
1. Azcapotzalco	1. Azcapotzalco	1. Azcapotzalco	3. Azcapotzalco
2. Tenayuca	2. Tenayuca	4. Tenayocan	4. Tenayocan
	3. Tepanohuayan	5. Tepanoaya	
	4. Tultitlan	6. Toltitlan	7. Toltitlan
3. Cuauhtitlan	5. Cuauhtitlan	7. Quauhtitlan	6. Cuauhtitlan
			5. Tepotzotlan
4. Xaltocan	6. Xaltocan	8. Xaltocan	
			8. Ecatepec
5. Tlacopan	7. Tacuba	3. Tlacopan	2. Tlacopan
6. Coyohuacan	8. Coyohuacan	2. Coyohuacan	10. Coyohuacan
		9. Huitzilopochco	
7. Culhuacan	9. Culhuacan	10. Colhuacan	
			9. Huixachtitlan
8. Xochimilco	10. Xochimilco	11. Xochimilco	11. Xochimilco
9. Quitlahuac		12. Cuitlahuac	
10. Mizquic			
			12. Cuexomatitlan

*Ixtlilxochitl 1975–77, 1:444.
†Ibid., 376–77.
‡Ibid., 2:80.
§Ibid., 1:446; 2:87–88.

The nine towns that were dependencies of Tenochtitlan in the zone defined by Ixtlilxochitl would be the four kingdoms of Colhuacan, Itztapalapan, Mexicatzinco, and Huitzilopochco, south of the city, usually considered as a unit, although only Colhuacan is listed; Xochimilco, Cuitlahuac, and Mizquic in the area of the southern lakes; Tenayocan on the mainland, bordering the Tepanec region; and Ecatepec, to the west of the drainage of the northern lakes towards Lake Tetzcoco. Among the towns in the Chinampan that paid tribute to Tetzcoco, Huixachtitlan takes the place of Colhuacan and Huitzilopochco, and Cuexomatitlan, of Cuitlahuac and Mizquic. Map 5-1 depicts the dependent kingdoms of Tenochtitlan.

Various sources contain information on the kingdoms of the Tenochca domain in later periods. Ixtlilxochitl in his version of the revolt headed by Moquihuix against Axayacatl, identifies the kings who were in league with Moquihuix. Although Ixtlilxochitl is not specific about what role they may have played in the battle with Axayacatl, their status as subjects of Tenochtitlan is made clear. They owed neither tribute nor vassalage to Axayacatl, but were "subjects [of Tenochtitlan] and of the Mexica party" (eran sujetos y del bando del nombre mexicano),

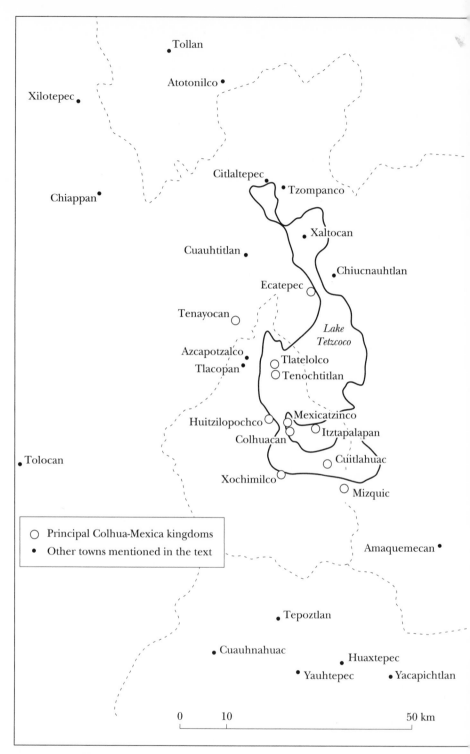

MAP 5–1. The dependent kingdoms of Tenochtitlan

that is to say, their kingdoms were within the Tenochca sector of the Triple Alliance.[17] The kings named were Xilomantzin of Colhuacan, Zoanenemitl and Tlatolatl of Cuitlahuac, and Quauhyacatl of Huitzilopochco.

As recorded in the Florentine Codex, when the Spaniards came to the Basin, on leaving Chalco—that is, on entering the territory directly under the rule of Tenochtitlan—they went first to Cuitlahuac, where the kings who ruled the Chinampanec kingdoms of Xochimilco, Cuitlahuac, and Mizquic gathered. They then went on to Itztapalapan, where they convened "the kings called the Four Lords" (in tlatoque nauhtecutli mitoa) of Itztapalapan, Mexicatzinco, Colhuacan, and Huitzilopochco.[18] Here we have again the seven kings from the southern part of the Basin. In earlier times these towns had constituted part of a political entity led by Colhuacan, founded when the various groups migrating from Tollan had settled there.[19] Dominion over these towns later passed to Tenochtitlan when Acamapichtli overcame Colhuacan. Together with Tenayocan and Ecatepec they add up to nine, the number of kingdoms subject to Tenochtitlan, according to Ixtlilxochitl.

In Table 5-1, Xaltocan is listed among the conquered towns, but it is not included in the list of towns from which Tetzcoco received the Chinampan tribute. Xaltocan had been conquered in the final years of Tezozomoc of Azcapotzalco; its king fled to Metztitlan, and the town of Xaltocan was abandoned. No new settlers moved in there for the next few years.[20] Probably Ecatepec was then the principal Tenochca town in that area; its last king, of the Tenochca dynasty, became governor of Tenochtitlan during the colonial period and was the father of the chronicler Hernando Alvarado Tezozomoc.[21] Although Xaltocan was of secondary importance during the Triple Alliance, the genealogy of its rulers is known; they married Tenochca women, but only the last king had a wife of royal rank, a daughter of Axayacatl.[22] This alone marks Xaltocan as a sujeto of Tenochtitlan; in addition, it appears on the page of the Codex Mendoza that depicts towns with military obligations. However, Tetzcoco also had the right to receive tribute from Xaltocan.[23]

In the third section of the Codex Mendoza is a painting of Moteuczoma's palace as a building on two levels (fol. 69r). On the higher level there are three rooms or "houses" (casas); in the highest one, in the center, Moteuczoma is depicted; the legend above it says, "Moteuczoma's throne room where he held court and passed judgment." On his left, another house is labeled as the lodging of the rulers of Tetzcoco and Tlacopan, "who were Moteuczoma's friends." On his right was the lodging of the lords of Tenayocan, Chiucnauhtlan, and Colhuacan, "who were Moteuczoma's friends and confederates." [24] Nothing is said about the political functions of these three kings in comparison with others. Geographically, Colhuacan, in the southern part of the Basin, represents the principal nucleus of the Tenochca domain, while Tenayocan is a bridgehead in the Tepanec territory and Chiucnauhtlan another in the Acolhuacan.

Tenayocan, within the Tepanec region, is depicted in the Codex Mendoza at the beginning of the first section (2r) together with Colhuacan as the first conquests by the Mexicas, before the reign of Acamapichtli. It may have been a conquest achieved while in the service of the Tepanecs, although Tenayocan is mentioned once as one of the Tepanec towns when the Tepanecs were defeated in 1430.[25] Later, it is not counted among the towns that were dependencies of Tlacopan. Tenayocan is lacking in the "Memorial de los pueblos de Tlacopan" and the Codex Osuna, and furthermore, several Tenochca princes were sent there as rulers.[26]

The description of the king of Chiucnauhtlan as "friend and confederate" of Moteuczoma does not agree with other sources, according to which this town had been part of the Acolhua political system since before the Empire was formed, and it appears in all the lists of the kingdoms of Tetzcoco. It would make more sense to find Ecatepec instead of Chiucnauhtlan in this passage of the Codex Mendoza. Perhaps Chiucnauhtlan had obligations to both Tetzcoco and Tenochtitlan, or it changed later on from the Tetzcoca domain to the Tenochca. It is also possible that there were two kings in Chiucnauhtlan, one subject to Tetzcoco and the other to Tenochtitlan.[27]

The painting of Moteuczoma's palace in the Codex Mendoza could be an abbreviated representation of a council of the kings of the Tenochca domain that would correspond to the group of kings of the Acolhua domain depicted in the Mapa Quinatzin, and the rulers of the three kingdoms named in the Codex Mendoza could be the heads of different sectors of the kingdom. The room with the three "confederates" of Moteuczoma would also correspond to the council Sahagún called *tlacxitlan*, in the chapter in which he describes Moteuczoma's palace. The council members, not enumerated, were "tlatoque tlazopipilti tecutlatoque," that is, kings, princes, and judges.[28] It is possible that the area dominated by Tenochtitlan was greater than the group of nine of which Ixtlilxochitl speaks. At any rate, whatever its extent at the beginning of the alliance, in later years the number of towns with kings that were dependencies of Tenochtitlan increased.

The dynastic affiliation of local kings can give us important clues about whether they were subject to the Tenochca sovereign. The kings of Tetzcoco gave their daughters as wives to local subordinate kings. In Tenochtitlan, although there were also cases of this procedure, the predominant custom was to establish as local kings the sons of a Tenochca king; some were born of mothers who were princesses of the kingdom where they were to be installed, and others married a princess of the local dynasty when they were sent to the town they were to rule.[29] Unfortunately, the information available is not as complete as one might wish. Some of these princes were established as kings during the reign of Moteuczoma Xocoyotzin, and it is difficult to know whether they founded a new kingdom or if a royal Tenochca prince was appointed to a rulership already controlled by the Tenochca dynasty. We do know that Tenochca princes ruled in Itztapalapan, Huitzilopochco, Olac Xochimilco, Azcapotzalco Mexicapan, Tenayocan, Ecatepec, Tollan, Tecuanipan Huitzoco in Amaquemecan, Xilotepec, and Apan.[30]

Three of the Chinampanec towns—Xochimilco, Cuitlahuac, and Mizquic— had been founded by the Xochimilcas.[31] Xochimilco had to be overcome by force during the Tepanec war, but nevertheless Itzcoatl ordered that the king of Xochimilco was to be made one of his close associates, who would be allowed to stand and eat in his presence and give an opinion on all that had to be done. This was a highly esteemed honor and a great favor not previously bestowed on any lord.[32] Ixtlilxochitl also gives a list of the lords of Xochimilco, who seem to be related to the two principal parcialidades of that town, Tepetenchi and Tecpan. In the third parcialidad, called Olac, a nephew of Moteuczoma Xocoyotzin was the ruler.[33]

Cuitlahuac was divided into four parts and was governed by a dynasty of rulers, described as *nahualteuctin* (magician lords), descended from Mixcoatl.[34] The kings of Mizquic were of Toltec stock; their god was Quetzalcoatl.[35] Several towns in the northern part of Tlalhuic and southern Chalco were also considered to be of Xochimilca origin, and at least some of them, such as Tetellan, Hueyapan, and Nepopoalco, gave tribute and military service to Xochimilco.[36]

The region of Tlalhuic was incorporated into the Empire from its beginning, and each of the three capitals of the Empire administered its own holdings in this area. There is not enough information to know whether the kings of Tlalhuic were among those directly subject to the Mexica capital. These kingdoms had long had close relations with Tenochtitlan. Moteuczoma Ilhuicamina was the son of Huitzilihuitl and a princess of Cuauhnahuac; according to one report Huitzilihuitl married the heiress of the kingdom of Cuauhnahuac, which the two then ruled together.[37] In the year 8 Acatl 1487 new kings were installed in Cuauhnahuac, Tepoztlan, Huaxtepec, and Xiloxochitepec (or Yauhtepec); probably this marks the beginning of rulers with closer ties to the Empire than those of their predecessors.[38] The *Relaciones geográficas* describe the government by local rulers in Tepoztlan, Huaxtepec, and Yacapichtlan. Those of Huaxtepec recognized the authority of Moteuczoma Ilhuicamina, and their calpixque was from Mexico. They were governed by their "natural lord," with two judges to dispense justice and, in the religious organization, two principal priests, one from Xochimilco and the other from Tenochtitlan. According to the *Relación geográfica* of Yacapichtlan, this town was governed by its own lords as "absolute rulers," and the Mexica could not conquer them. Still, it is said that when they waged war with Huexotzinco they sent captives to Moteuczoma.[39]

In Chalco the kings installed after being conquered by the Empire were established by the Tenochca sovereigns, married Tenochca princesses, and went to Tenochtitlan for the required fasting before their installation ceremony, all of which makes clear that they were directly subordinate to Tenochtitlan (see p. 286).

Tlatelolco, at the beginning of the Triple Alliance, had its own dynasty of

Tepanec origin. It seems to have been one of the kingdoms subject to Tenochtitlan, even though their kings were of Tepanec descent. Their situation must have been conflictive; the Codex Mendoza records not only its conquest by Itzcoatl but also the death of King Cuauhtlatoa.[40] Years later, after King Moquihuix was defeated by Axayacatl, there were no more kings in Tlatelolco until Cuauhtemoc, who was the son of Ahuitzotl and one of Moquihuix's daughters.[41]

Several towns of the Tlacopan domain had kings from the Tenochca dynasty. Some of these towns had two or more lords with the title of king, and this must be kept in mind in some cases for which there are no clear data about the political dependence of a city. For example, Azcapotzalco had two parcialidades, Azcapotzalco Tepanecapan and Azcapotzalco Mexicapan, each with a king. In Tlacopan, the parcialidad that later took the advocation of All Saints (Sanctorum) was called Tiliuhcan Tlacopan and had its own king of Tenochca stock.[42] In the case of Tollan it is noteworthy that its kings had long been of the Tenochca dynasty, and yet Tollan appears in the lists of dependencies of Tlacopan. It may be relevant that there were two towns named Tollan: Tollan Xicocotitlan and Tollan Xippacoyan. It is not clear whether there were two distinct dynastic lines.

Two of Itzcoatl's sons were sent as rulers to towns in this Tlacopanec region, which suggests that those towns were incorporated into the initial political system of the alliance in its earliest days. Iztacmixcoatzin went as king to Xilotepec and Chalchiuhtlatonac was established in Apan. On the other hand, a daughter (whose name is not given) married a commoner from Atotonilco, who was made king because of his wife's rank, and their son became the next king, called Itzcoatl after his grandfather.[43] Itzcoatl the senior gave another daughter to the first Chichimec settler in Tolnacochtla, who went there from Azcapotzalco and later submitted to the king of Tenochtitlan.[44]

When writing about Ahuitzotl, Torquemada names Cuitlahuac as king of Itztapalapan, Tezozomoctli as governor of Azcapotzalco ("no longer with the title of king but of governor"), and Ixtlilcuechahuacatzin as king of Tollan, stating that "all these were named by the Mexican kings as those who acknowledged vassalage."[45] In regard to the kings of the Acolhuan region, in the Codex Mendoza the king of Chiucnauhtlan is given as an ally of Moteuczoma even though all the other data include this town among the dependencies of Tetzcoco.

Some of the towns that can be considered in the category of kingdoms associated with Tenochtitlan do not appear in the Codex Mendoza or related sources that give the lists of tributary provinces, a clear indication that these documents—differing in this from the Tetzcocan and Tlacopan memorials—were not intended to give a list of towns with kings that were dependencies of Tenochtitlan. Among those that are missing are Colhuacan, Itztapalapan, Mexicatzinco, Tollan, Azcapotzalco Mexicapan, Tiliuhcan Tlacopan, and Tenayocan. Other kingdoms in the Tenochca domain do appear in the Codex Mendoza, but not in such a way as to invalidate what has been said, since it does not imply the inclusion of the entire town but only the obligation of certain towns in the kingdom to give tribute or services. The page that shows the Petlacalco, the storehouse of Tenochtitlan, includes Huitzilopochco, Olac Xochimilco, Cuitlahuac, and Mizquic. Moteuczoma had installed a Tenochca king in Olac, the least important of the three cabeceras of Xochimilco, a fact that suggests that the other cabeceras, Tecpan and Tepetenchi, were not included. If all the four cabeceras that comprised Cuitlahuac had been included, Cuitlahuac would have been a town of disproportionate importance in relation to all the others on that page.[46] What we have here is simply a list of collection centers (*calpixcan*) where there were stewards and probably lands attached to the calpixcan. Thus, when the name of an important town is given, this does not mean that the whole town would be a tributary entity but simply that it was where the calpixcan was located.

The obligations of these kings and their towns to Tenochtitlan are not defined in a concise formula as are their equivalents in the kingdoms of Tetzcoco and Tlacopan, but the information in several sources on the subject kingdoms of Tenochtitlan indicates the same situation as in the other two parts of the Empire. It has already been pointed out that the dependent kings of Tenochtitlan participated in the council called tlacxitlan. As to the services provided by these towns, according to the chronicles of the Tenochca kings, the towns of the Four Lords and of the Chinampan area are usually listed as preeminent among those convened for war or public works. Their obligations are thus similar to those of the dependent kingdoms of Tlacopan and Tetzcoco.[47] The reports in the *Relaciones geográficas* of three of the kingdoms of the Four Lords agree with this; all three declared themselves subjects of Moteuczoma. The people of Itztapalapan were praised as valiant and industrious, and for this reason the king chose many of their men to be captains in his armies, especially because they were trustworthy; they were exempt from tribute.[48] Similarly, the people of Mexicatzinco were warriors who did nothing other than military service and were therefore exempt from tribute,[49] and those of Colhuacan gave personal services and soldiers in time of war.[50] Chalco and the towns of the "serranía" or Cuauhtlalpan (Forest Land)[51] participated in military campaigns and public works just as did Xochimilco, the Chinampanecs, and the Four Lords, suggesting again that their rulers were directly subordinate to Tenochtitlan.

The Tributaries of Tenochtitlan within Its Own Domain

Three of the provinces in the Codex Mendoza should be considered as direct dependencies of the Tenochca capital in its own domain. One comprises the eleven towns in the Basin headed by Citlaltepec (17v), which is missing in the *Matrícula* and had military obligations; another is Tlatelolco; and the third, Petlacalco, which was the responsibility of the chief steward (petlacalcatl) of Tenochtitlan. Map 5-2 represents these three provinces; the lists that follow enumerate their component towns. Within the area occupied by these provinces, the towns pertaining to Tetzcoco or Tlacopan were minimal in comparison with those that Tenochtitlan held within the domains of those two capitals.

CITLALTEPEC (CODEX MENDOZA, 17v)

1.	Citlaltepec	Citlaltepec (RG 7:196–97). San Juan Zitlaltepec in Zumpango, Mexico.
2.	Tzonpanco	Zumpango (RG 7:197, 205). Zumpango de Ocampo, Mexico.
3.	Xaltocan	Saltoca (SV, par. 502; RG 6:230–31). San Miguel Jaltocan in Nextlalpan, Mexico.
4.	Acalhuacan	Acalvacan, estancia of Tlatelolco (AGI, Justicia, no. 5; Montoto 1927–32, 1:83). Located to the north of Ecatepec (Palerm 1973:209).[52]
5.	Coatitlan	Coatitlan (Vetancurt 1961, 3:201). Santa Clara Coatitla in Ecatepec, Mexico.
6.	Huixachtitlan	On the Mexica migration route, located between Coatitlan and the mountain called Chiquihuite (Tezozomoc 1975:283). It was perhaps the barrio of Ecatepec that is written Guyjahtiquipal (Huixachticpac?) in the relación of Chiconauhtlan (RG 6:232 and n. 26; cf. Barlow 1949b: 129–30).
7.	Coatlayauhcan	Magdalena de las Salinas. (González Aparicio 1973: map, square f-IX).[53]
8.	Acolnahuac	San Bernabé Aculnahuac, estancia of Tlatelolco bordering on Azcapotzalco (Barlow 1949b: 129–30).
9.	Puputlan	San Esteban Popotla, one of the towns where the Mexicas acquired land after the defeat of Azcapotzalco (Tezozomoc 1975:253). Don Antonio Cortés of Tlacopan claimed this as his property in 1561 (see p. 179).
10.	Iztacalco	Ixtacalco in the Federal District.
11.	Chalco atenco	Chalcoatengo (SV, par. 242). Chalco de Díaz Covarrubias, Mexico.[54]

Citlaltepec (1) and Tzompanco (2) were part of the kingdom of Cuauhtitlan, a kingdom of the Tlacopan group. Xaltocan (3) is listed in Motolinía's "Memorial

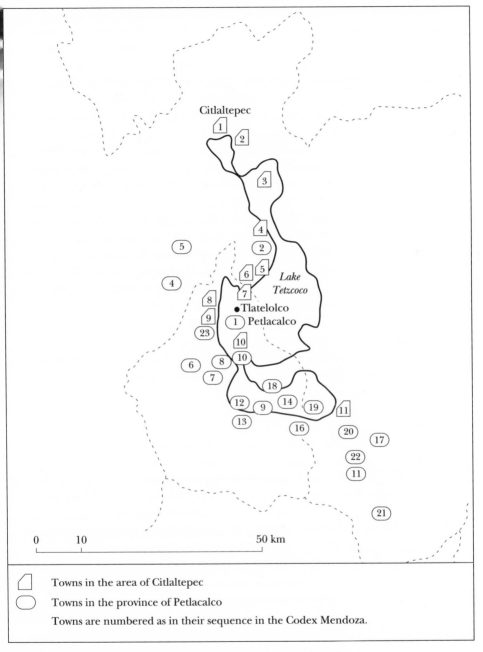

Citlaltepec

Lake
Tetzcoco

●Tlatelolco

Petlacalco

0   10   50 km

Towns in the area of Citlaltepec

Towns in the province of Petlacalco

Towns are numbered as in their sequence in the Codex Mendoza.

MAP 5–2. The tributaries of Tenochtitlan within its own domain

tetzcocano" among the towns of tenant farmers of the Acolhua kingdom, but Xaltocan was governed by a local dynasty that probably was a dependency of Tenochtitlan.

The old Otomi kingdom of Xaltocan had been defeated by Tezozomoc of Azcapotzalco shortly before the formation of the Triple Alliance, and its inhabitants had scattered. The king went to Metztitlan, which was part of his domain, and the rural Otomi population was taken in by Techotlalatzin of Tetzcoco; other Otomis went to Tlaxcallan. Xaltocan was resettled in 8 Acatl 1435 by Acolmantlacas, Colhuas, Tenochcas, and Otomis. The first ruler of Xaltocan under the Empire was a descendant of the old kings of Xaltocan, but he married a daughter of Itzcoatl, and his successors also wed noble Mexica women.[55] Also in 1435 the Tenochcas and Tlatelolcas designated land as Mexica (*mexicatlalli*) in Toltepec and Tepeyacac, and water rights for Tlatelolco (*tlatilolcaatl*) in Cuachilco.[56] All this indicates Mexica dominion in this region. Citlaltepec, Tzompanco, and Xaltocan are the towns of greatest political importance in this list, although their presence on this folio may simply indicate that within them there were lands or subject towns of Tenochtitlan. All the other places are of less importance; some of them appear in colonial documentation as estancias of Tenochtitlan or of Tlatelolco.[57]

The eleven towns in the Basin and the distant garrisons depicted together in the Codex Mendoza (17v–18r) were probably on separate pages in the *Matrícula de tributos,* and therefore the distinction between these two groups of settlements was indicated more clearly than in the Codex Mendoza.[58] The fact that during the colonial period many of these places were still estancias of the city of Mexico suggests that this list of eleven towns, like the province of Petlacalco, could be equivalent to the rural district of the capital as described for Tlacopan and Tetzcoco, that is, towns outside the urban nucleus but administered as part of the city.

To understand the political situation of these eleven towns it is important to note that the majority were steps along the Mexica migration route from Tollan to Chapoltepec. According to the *Crónica Mexicayotl* the route was as follows (towns in this province of Citlaltepec are in italics): Tollan, Atlitlallacyan, Tequixquiac, Atenco, *Tzompanco,* Cuachilco, *Xaltocan,* Epcoac, Ecatepec, *Acalhuacan,* Tolpetlac, *Huixachtitlan,* Tecpayocan, Atepetlac, *Coatlyayauhcan,* Tepepanco, *Acolnahuac,* Techcatitlan, Chapoltepec.[59] It seems that during their migration the Mexica left, in the towns where they stopped along the way, small nuclei of population which were later integrated into the Mexica domain.[60] This does not invalidate the idea that they had military obligations, which is consistent with the dominant rank of the population of Tenochtitlan and with the strategic position of these towns; all are where the Tenochca domain borders on those of Tepanecs and Acolhuas, and the last town was in Chalco on the lake shore.

These eleven towns are found only in the Codex Mendoza. There is no equivalent page in the *Matrícula*. They may have been depicted on a page that has disappeared; there would not have been sufficient space for them on the fragments that have been lost from the incomplete pages that remain. Given that some of them were estancias of Tlatelolco in colonial times, it is possible that they were formerly its sujetos. Barlow thought that they might have paid some of the tribute given by Tlatelolco according to the following page (19r) in the Codex Mendoza.[61] Another interpretation, first proposed by van Zantwijk, is that the obligations of all these towns were military.[62]

According to the relación geográfica of Citlaltepec, the king of Mexico distributed the towns among the Chichimec lords who came from Colhuacan (two hundred leagues from this area), and Citlaltepec was given to a certain Ecatotzin, who lived until after the arrival of the Spaniards. Citlaltepec paid tribute in kind: decorated cotton cloths, birds, feathers, *chalchihuites*, fish, mats, other small items, and slaves captured in war.[63] The military function of this town is emphasized in the description of their system of government. The ruler, who was elected for his courage and strength, had many captains distributed in a number of places, all with many soldiers under their command as garrisons ready for whatever might happen. The town and its domain carried on wars with Tlaxcallan, Chiappan, Metztitlan, and other very large towns.[64]

It should be noted that these eleven towns did not occupy a compact region but are placed along a strategic line on the borders of Tenochtitlan with Tlacopan and Tetzcoco.[65] Tenochtitlan shared some towns, such as Xaltocan or Popotlan, with Tetzcoco or Tlacopan, which also had possessions in this region (see p. 144).

Documentation for the towns of San Juan Ixhuatepec and Santa Isabel Tollan in the vicinity of Huixachtitlan (6) tells of the donation of land, made by Itzcoatl after the war with Azcapotzalco, to people of the four barrios of Tenochtitlan; the names of the grantees seem to be titles or gentile names derived from the names of temples or barrios. These were probably settlements of nobles or commoners rewarded for military achievements.[66] The Codex Cozcatzin contains similar data about settlements located between Iztacalco (10) and Chalco Atenco (11).[67] All these documents deserve further study. I suggest provisionally that these lands were granted by Itzcoatl to noble or meritorious warriors and their descendents under some type of military tenure; that is, the possessors had the obligation of giving military service in time of war. These towns would comprise part of the settlements in the province headed by Citlaltepec in the Codex Mendoza. However, not all the inhabitants of that region would have only military obligations. The data from Xaltocan and other towns, which will be discussed below, show that there were also peasants obliged to pay tribute in kind.

Farther north in Acolhua territory, according to the *Anales de Cuauhtitlan*, an area of war land (*cuauhtlalpan*, literally "eagle land") was established in Tizayocan, near Xaltocan, with the participation of Citlaltepec and Tzompanco, the towns in first and second place on the list of this series of towns.[68] This is further evidence that this was a military district and that Tenochtitlan and Tetzcoco shared control over a good part of the region.

TLATELOLCO (CODEX MENDOZA, 19R)

This province comprises only the town of that name. Two kings of Tlatelolco are depicted—Cuauhtlatoa and Moquihuix—who were defeated by Itzcoatl and Axayacatl of Tenochtitlan; therefore, the codex must refer to the period in which Tlatelolco no longer had a king of its own and was under the command of military governors.

According to Chimalpahin, Cuauhtlatoa was defeated during the reign of Itzcoatl. The vanquished king went to Tenochtitlan, where he died during the reign of Moteuczoma Ilhuicamina. Nothing is said about the circumstances of his stay in Tenochtitlan.[69] Torquemada relates that Cuauhtlatoa became Itzcoatl's enemy for having sought help from neighboring kings to destroy the Tenochcas, but the conflict did not break out until the reign of Ilhuicamina, who fought the Tlatelolcas and killed their king.[70] Nevertheless, other sources ascribe a long reign to Cuauhtlatoa, contemporaneous with the reigns of Itzcoatl and Ilhuicamina, and make him a participant in the conquests of these two Tenochca kings.[71]

A second defeat of the Tlatelolcas took place when the new king, Moquihuix, tried to usurp the power of Axayacatl but failed in his attempt to obtain the support of other kings in the Basin. After the victory, the Tenochcas divided up the lands that Tlatelolco held in "Chiquiuhtepec, Cuauhtepec, and, within the area of Azcaputzalco, Chilocan, Tempatlacalcan, and many other towns."[72] These towns are located north of Azcapotzalco. Tempatlacalcan must be Tepetlacalco, one of the towns in the province of Petlacalco. Chilocan is present-day Chiluca in Atizapán de Zaragoza, Mexico; Cuauhtepec is Santa María Cuauhtepec in the extreme north of the Federal District; and Chiquiuhtepec is the Cerro del Chiquihuite, north of La Villa, between Ticomán and Cuauhtepec.[73] They are thus in the region of the military district of Citlaltepec, near Huixachtitlan and also Ixhuatepec and Tollan (Santa Isabel Tula), which have been discussed above together with the province of Citlaltepec.

The Tenochcas also shared the income from the Tlatelolco marketplace. Durán says that this was because the Tlatelolcas did not have any more land.[74] It is difficult to reconcile a total takeover of land with the data discussed above on the estancias of Tlatelolco, which still existed in colonial times. Perhaps that statement referred only to royal lands, or it may be that land was restored or acquired when Tlatelolco's political position improved during the reign of Moteuczoma Xocoyotzin and the town again had its own king. In the Codex Mendoza the tribute paid by Tlatelolco consisted of *cacahuapinolli* (ground cacao) and *chianpinolli* (ground chía), blankets, and warrior costumes. Durán and Tezozomoc explain that the pinolli was for the provisions needed for going to war; they also mention biscuits, or *tlaxcaltotopochtli*—that is, toasted tortillas. Other obligations were to carry equipment and provisions for military campaigns and to repair the temple of Huitznahuac.[75] Barlow suggests that the eleven towns in the Citlaltepec group could have contributed to the tribute payments painted on the Tlatelolco page.[76] It is also possible that Tlatelolco kept possession of its numerous estancias in the Basin all through its history and that they produced part of the raw material for preparing the provisions they were required to give. Another part, such as cacao, would have been either obtained in the marketplace, or, if it was tribute from other provinces, furnished to the cooks of Tlatelolco by the calpixques.

The military governors appointed by the Tenochca king after the death of Moquihuix were given the titles of tlacatecatl and tlacochcalcatl. These were the same titles as those of the governors of several of the distant garrisons depicted in the Codex Mendoza, which suggests a similar political situation. Not until four years before the Spanish Conquest was the monarchy restored under Cuauhtemoc.[77] The tribute Tlatelolco paid in kind was, as has been pointed out, of a military kind: warrior emblems, provisions and transportation in time of war.

PETLACALCO (CODEX MENDOZA, 20R)

1. Petlacalcatl	This is the name given in the legend, but the glyph can be read as the toponym Petlacalco, the name given in the *Información de 1554*. In the *Matrícula* the glyph of the cabecera is on the damaged part of the page, but the legend says that the tribute went to the petlacalcatl (Barlow 1949b: 132; Scholes and Adams 1957:29, 67).
2. Xaxalpan	San José Jajalpa, barrio of Ecatepec, Mexico.
3. Yopico	Probably the barrio of this name in Chiucnauhtlan, which places it near the previous town (*Proceso inquisitorial* 1910:5),[78] but Yopico was also a barrio in the parcialidad of San Juan Moyotla in Tenochtitlan (Caso 1956:13).
4. Tepetlacalco	San Jerónimo or San Lucas Tepetlacalco in Tlalnepantla, Mexico.
5. Tecoloapan	San Mateo Tecoloapan in Atizapan de Zaragoza, Mexico.
6. Tepechpan	This is the same name as that of the Acolhua town to the north of Tetzcoco, but the glyph (a house over a

stone and a mat) is not the same.[79] This town in Petlacalco could be the Tepechpan (or Tepezpan in the
Spanish text) that was one of the places where the
cacique of Coyoacan had servants (ytech poui
tepantlaca; Carrasco y Monjarás-Ruiz 1978:184).
The *Información de 1554* gives Texopetlaque, which
agrees with the Nahuatl word for foundation, *xopetlatl*
or *xopechtli*. Because the glyph can be read in several
ways, it could also identify the town we are concerned
with as Texopeco, bordering on Cuitlahuac
(AC, 63, sec. 218).

7. Tequemecan   San Sebastián Tequemecan, barrio of Coyoacan
(Carrasco y Monjarás-Ruiz 1976:78, 145; 1978:169,
189).

8. Huicilopuchco   Ochilobusco (SV, sec. 444). Huitzilopochco, present-
day Churubusco in the Federal District.

9. Colhuacinco   Asunción Colhuacacingo, barrio of Xochimilco
(Vetancurt 1961, 3:155; Torquemada 1975–83, 7:552);
or San Cristóbal Colhuacatzinco, estancia of Temazcalapan, sujeto of Tepechpan (RG 7:222, 246).

10. Coçotlan   San Pedro Cotzotlan, barrio of Huitzilopochco
(Navarro de Vargas 1909:583).

11. Tepepulan   San Mateo or Santiago Tepopula in Tenango
del Aire, Mexico. It was acquired by the Mexicas
during Ilhuicamina's war against Chalco
(Tezozomoc 1975:305).

12. Olac   The glyph indicates that it was in Xochimilco. Olac
Xochimilco was one of the three cabeceras of that
town (Vetancurt 1961, 3:153).

13. Acapan   Barrio of Xochimilco (Zavala y Castelo 1:84; Belén
Acampa in Vetancurt 1961, 3:155);
or San Miguel Acapan in Tenanco, Chalco (AGI,
Mexico 665, 2d book).

14. Cuitlahuac   Present-day Tlahuac in the Federal District.

15. Tezcacoac   This is a barrio name in several towns—Ecatepec
(Vetancurt 1961, 3:200), Itztapalapan (parish records
of Itztapalapan, notes provided by Eduardo Corona),
Colhuacan (S. Cline 1986:54, 145), and Tenanco in
Chalco (AGN, Tierras 2914, exp. 2, fol. 157v).

16. Mizquic   Present-day Mixquic in the Federal District.

17. Aochpanco   This must be the tract of land called Auxpango in
                       Tlalmanalco (Colín 1966: par. 2984).[80]
18. Tzapotitlan   Former subject of Cuitlahuac (AH-INAH, Anales
                       Antiguos de México y sus Contornos, no. 25).
                       Present-day Santiago Zapotitlan to the north of
                       Tlahuac in the Federal District.
19. Xico   The former islet in Lake Chalco.
20. Toyac   This could be Atoyac, a frequent toponym, perhaps
                       Santa María Atoyac, estancia of Tlalmanalco be-
                       tween Tlalmanalco and Chalco Atenco (AGI, Mexico
                       210, no. 33). Today Atoyac is a rancho in Chalco,
                       Mexico.
                       There was also Santa Cruz Atoyac, a barrio of
                       Coyoacan (Carrasco and Monjarás-Ruiz 1976:78, 81,
                       170, 187).
21. Tecalco   Tecalco (SV, par. 515).
                       San Mateo Tecalco in Ozumba, Mexico.
22. Tlaçoxiuhco   Tlazoxiuco was a barrio of Tenanco in Chalco (AGN,
                       Tierras 2914, exp. 2, fol. 157v).[81]
23. Nextitlan   Today this is the name of a street and a development
                       east of Popotlan (González Aparicio 1973: map).

We have seen that Petlacalco was the palace storehouse in Tenochtitlan and petlacalcatl the principal steward. The commentary in Codex Mendoza states that there were eighteen towns, although twenty-three glyphs are depicted. Apparently the glyph for Petlacalco was not counted as a town, since the legend reads it as the title petlacalcatl and the word pueblo (town) has been crossed out. The commentator must also have neglected to count the four towns (10 to 13) across the bottom of folio 20r on a horizontal line, like the pictures of tribute items, and not in the vertical line on the left of folios 20r–v, like all the other towns. Most towns on this list were in the Chinampanec region, where Itzcoatl took possession of lands in Coyoacan, Xochimilco, and Chalco.[82]

According to the *Información de 1554* this province had forty-three towns, but only seventeen are named, all of them in the Codex Mendoza except Chimalpan, which can be either San Lorenzo Chimalpa in Chalco, Mexico, or San Sebastián Chimalpa in Los Reyes (La Paz), Mexico.[83] Perhaps these forty-three towns included the eleven towns headed by Citlaltepec that are missing in the first fragmentary sheets of the *Matrícula*.

Durán refers to this province when enumerating the stewards who brought goods for the inauguration of the great temple in the reign of Ahuitzotl. First in line were the stewards of the city of Mexico, who brought tribute of great value, followed by the Xochimilcas and Chinampanecs.[84] The corresponding text in Tezozomoc names in first place the petlacalcatl and then the steward of Chinantlan.[85] Like Citlaltepec, this province is comparable to the calpixcazgo of "Tetzcoco con sus barrios y aldeas" pertaining to the Acolhua king (see p. 148).

Other Dependencies of Tenochtitlan in the Basin

There are various local documents with information on other possessions of Tenochtitlan. Some, located in the southern part of the Basin, could have been part of the province of Petlacalco, which would be consistent with the statement in the *Información de 1554* that this province included more towns than those shown in the Codex Mendoza. Other towns in the northern Basin may have been part of the Citlaltepec district.

A map of the area of Itztapalapan was presented by this town in order to object to a grant of land requested by a Spaniard. It shows the terrain that goes from the mountains called Tlatoca, Mazatepetl, Teyo, Tetlaman, and Cuexomatl to the shore of Lake Tetzcoco. The land in question was the region of Santa María Aztahuacan, Santa Marta, Santiago Cahualtepec, and Reyes Acaquilpan. The map shows the whole area divided by lines into twenty-seven strips, each extending from the top of the mountain range down to the shore, and a town's name is written on each strip. The names—Mexicatzinco, Tenochtitlan, Iztacalco, Itztapalapan, and Colhuacan—are repeated several times, always in the same order from west to east. These towns are three of the kingdoms of the Four Lords, located on the eastern side of the strait connecting Lakes Xochimilco and Mexico, plus Tenochtitlan and Iztacalco.[86] Similar material is found in the Codex Cozcatzin, although not in the form of a map but only a simple drawing of strips of land labeled as belonging to Mexicatzinco, Tenochtitlan, Iztacalco, Itztapalapan, and Colhuacan, the same towns in the same order as on the map from the Archivo General de la Nación. Legends along the edge or within one of the strips identify their location in Reyes Acaquilpan or Santa Marta Aztahuacan.[87] These two places were barrios of Iztacalco, which was part of the province of Citlaltepec; it is therefore probable that these barrios were also in that same province.[88] The Mexicas took possession of Acaquilpan and Aztahuacan during Ilhuicamina's war against Chalco.[89]

Although the documents do not give details about the tenure of these lands, it is clear that they must have been distributed to those kingdoms in the Tenochca domain when the Mexicas took possession of them. This is one more example of the way in which the possessions of several towns were intermingled in a rural zone. Since all the dividing lines go from the top of the mountain range to the lake shore, each section would include land in the different environments of this area.

Another place shared by Tenochtitlan and Tlatelolco was Ximilpan, in the area of Tlacopan. The Oidor Tejada, who had an interest in obtaining land there, arranged an exchange with the Indian landowners, to whom he gave other lands that he had been granted in the Chalco region. As a result, a register of the Indians of Ximilpan who were given lands in Chalco has survived; all of them are identified as residents of certain barrios of Tenochtitlan or Tlatelolco.[90] That is, Ximilpan was a rural area whose land was divided among people from various barrios of Mexico. The toponym Ximilpan is relatively frequent.[91] The place in question was probably south of Tlacopan, where a street with that name still exists. It is also possible that it is the same Ximilpan gained by Itzcoatl when he defeated the Tepanecs.[92]

Other dependencies of Tenochtitlan are referred to in a letter written in 1532 by several Indian nobles of the city. In addition to reclaiming their individual possessions, they describe the tribute sources of the city. Four towns, which had been settled by Mexicas but were now destroyed, paid tribute that maintained the entire populace: Xoconochco, Metuxco, Xaltocan, and Acaccan. The city also had held lands, which it no longer possessed, in Chalco, Tlacopan, Coatepec, Matlatzinco, Coyoacan, and many other areas.[93]

Xaltocan is without doubt the same town that is listed in the province of Citlaltepec. It had important connections with Tenochtitlan, as this and other documents demonstrate, but it is also given as subject to Tetzcoco (see p. 144). Xoconochco may be a town of the same name in Metepec, Mexico, a town that was part of the tributary province of Tolocan,[94] or perhaps the site called Xoconochnopaltitlan, Xoconochpalyacac, or Xoconochyacac in the area between Tenochtitlan and Azcapotzalco.[95] Metuxco could be the present-day San Antonio Ometusco in Axapusco, Mexico, near Otompan, a region where there were tributaries of Tenochtitlan,[96] but there were also places with this name in Chalco and Tepotzotlan.[97] Acaccan (Atzaccan?) has not been identified. The tributaries in other provinces, alluded to in this letter, will be discussed in the relevant chapters of this book.

The Codex Mendoza illustrates an important difference between the two provinces that occupy the southern and northern parts of the Basin. The cabeceras of the Colhua and Chinampanec kingdoms were in Petlacalco, in the south. In regard to tribute, the provisions contributed by this region were equal to those of Chalco, which defines it as a region of primary importance for the supplying of Tenochtitlan. In the north, the obligations of the towns headed by Citlaltepec were principally military, although local reports show that there were there also estancias of Mexico and its rulers. This distinction between north and south in the Tenochca domain in the Basin suggests a comparison with the two parts of the Acolhuacan.[98] There is no explicit definition of this duality, such as that given for the Acolhua domain in several Tetzcoca sources; it may have been connected with the old division between the two Mexica cities of Tenochtitlan and Tlatelolco.

The Tributaries of Tenochtitlan within the Domain of Tetzcoco

Tenochtitlan had important possessions in the Tetzcoca domain that are listed in two provinces of the Codex Mendoza, Acolhuacan (Acolman in the *Matrícula*) and part of Atotonilco el Grande. Both are shown in Map 5-3.

Acolhuacan [Acolman] (Codex Mendoza, 21–22r)

1.	Acolhuacan [Acolman]	Acolman (SV, par. 19).
		Acolman de Nezahualcoyotl, Mexico.
		[Acolhua kingdom, Table 6-1, no. 7.]
2.	Huicilan	Estancia of Tizayocan (DA, 54).
		Huitzila in Tizayuca, Hidalgo.
3.	Totolcinco	Former sujeto of Tecciztlan (RG 7:240–41).
		Totolcingo in Acolman, Mexico.
4.	Tlachyahualco	Santa Ana Tlachyahualco, sujeto of Tepechpan (RG 7:221, 246).
5.	Tepechpa	Tepechpa (SV, par. 512).
		Tepexpan in Acolman, Mexico.
		[Acolhua kingdom, Table 6-1, no. 8.]
6.	Aztaquemeca	Santo Domingo Aztacameca in Axapusco, Mexico.
		[Tenants of Tetzcoco, Table 6-4, no. 9.]
7.	Teacalco	San Juan Teyacalco, sujeto of Temazcalapan (DA, 57).
		San Juan Teacalco, like Temazcalapan a sujeto of Tepechpan (RG 7:222, 246–47).
		Teacalco in Temazcalapa, Mexico.
8.	Tonanytla	Santa María Tonanitla in Jaltenco, Mexico.
9.	Cempoalan	Cempoala (RG 6:73ff.).
		Zempoala, Hidalgo.
		[Tenants of Tetzcoco, Table 6-4, no. 13.]
10.	Tepetlaoztoc	Tepetlaoztoc (RG 8:48, 50).
		Tepetlaoxtoc, Mexico.
		[Acolhua kingdom, Table 6-1, no. 6.]
11.	Ahuatepec	Aguatepec in Otumba, Mexico.
		[Tenants of Tetzcoco, Table 6-4, no. 5.]
12.	Tiçatepec	Location unknown.

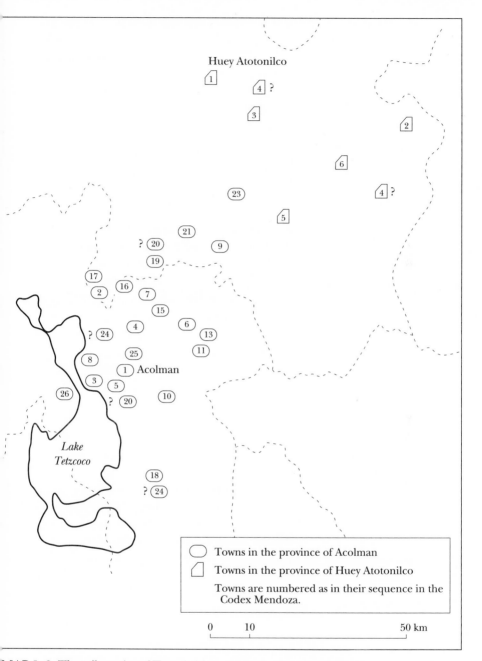

Huey Atotonilco

Lake
Tetzcoco

Acolman

	Towns in the province of Acolman
	Towns in the province of Huey Atotonilco
	Towns are numbered as in their sequence in the Codex Mendoza.

0   10   50 km

MAP 5–3. The tributaries of Tenochtitlan within the domain of Tetzcoco

13.	Contlan	Contla, rancho in Otompan (Colín 1966: par. 1727). A map in AGN (Tierras 1719, exp. 2) places it next to Xaltepec (Jaltepec in Axapusco, Mexico).
14.	Yxquemecan	Location unknown.
15.	Matixco	Santa María Maquixco, sujeto of Tepechpan (RG 7:222, 246, 250). Santa María Maquixco in Temazcalapa, Mexico, or Maquixco, barrio of Teotihuacan, Mexico.
16.	Temazcalapan	Sujeto of Tepechpan (RG 7:221–22, 246). Temascalapa, Mexico.
17.	Tiçayucan	Teçayuca (SV, par. 524). Tizayuca, Hidalgo. [Tenants of Tetzcoco, Table 6-4, no. 10.]
18.	Tepetlapan	Tepetlapa, one of the cabeceras of Coatepec (RG 6:130).
19.	Calyahualco	Estancia of Tezontepec (SV, par. 523).
20.	Teçoyucan	Tetzoyucan (RG 8:47, 48, 50). Tezoyuca, Mexico. [Acolhua kingdom, Table 6-1, no. 9.] However, the glyph (not clear in the *Matrícula*) can also be read as Tezontepec (Teçuntepeque in SV, par. 523). Villa de Tezontepec, Hidalgo.
21.	Tlaquilpan	Tlaquilpan (RG 6:74–85). San Pedro Tlaquilpan in Zempoala, Hidalgo.
22.	Quauhquemecan	Location unknown.
23.	Epaçuyucan	Epazoyuca (RG 6:83). Epazoyucan, Hidalgo.
24.	Ameyalco	Santa María Ameyalco, sujeto of Coatepec (RG 6:130), or rancho in Tecamac, Mexico (Colín 1966:406).
25.	Quauhyocan	San Marcos Quauhyoca, sujeto of Tecciztlan (RG 7:225).
26.	Ecatepec	Ecatepeque (RG 6:232). Ecatepec de Morelos, Mexico.

In both the *Matrícula* (1) and the Codex Mendoza (21v) the glyph for the cabecera of this province is the same: an arm with water flowing from the shoulder. In the codex the legend is "acolhuacan puº acolmecatl calpixqui" (the town of Acolhuacan; the Acolman tribute collector). In the *Matrícula* the legend next to the glyph says, "la insignia de Acolman acolmecatl" (the insignia of Acolman, the man of Acolman); in two other legends referring to tribute, the name of the tribute collector, which was first written *tetzcocatl*, has been corrected to *acolmecatl*. The *Información de 1554* also gives Acolman as the cabecera.[99]

Some of the places in this province are known to have been Acolhua kingdoms or towns of Tetzcoco tenants. They are indicated in the list with references in brackets to the tables in the chapter on the kingdom of Tetzcoco, in which the data on these two types of settlements have been compiled.[100] The kingdoms are Acolman (1), Tepechpan (5), Tepetlaoztoc (10), and possibly Tezoyocan (20), unless this has been written by mistake instead of Tezontepec. The towns of tenants are Aztaquemecan (6); Cempohuallan (9); Ahuatepec (11), which was the cabecera of a Tetzcoca calpixcazgo; and Tizayocan (17). In these towns the lands and sujetos of Tetzcoco coexisted with those of Tenochtitlan.

Some towns in this province of Acolman do not appear in any other sources that list the tributaries of Tetzcoco: Tlachyahualco (4), Teacalco (7), Tonanitlan (8), Tizatepec (12), Contlan (13), Ixquemecan (14), Matixco (15), Temazcalapan (16), Tepetlapan (18), Calyahualco (19), Ameyalco (24), and Cuauhyocan (25). Others appear as pertaining to Tetzcoco only in the list that Durán gives of the towns subject to Tetzcoco represented at the dedication of the temple of Tenochtitlan during the reign of Ahuitzotl: Huitzilan (2), Totoltzinco (3), Tlaquilpan (21), and Epazoyocan (23).[101] Probably this list of Durán mixes towns belonging to Tetzcoco with those that, within the Acolhua kingdom, paid tribute to Tenochtitlan, since he states that Mexica people were settled on Tetzcoca lands, which they cultivated, and some of them were tenants (*terrazgueros*) of the kings of Mexico.[102]

Durán's list includes eight other towns that are not in this province in the Codex Mendoza, nor do they appear as tributaries of Tetzcoco in any other source. They are the following:

Tecciztlan was where Tenochtitlan put its boundary markers during Ilhuicamina's war against Nezahualcoyotl.[103] During the colonial period it was the cabecera of the *corregimiento* that included Acolman, Tepechpan, and Teotihuacan.[104] In the Codex Mendoza the province of Acolman included Totoltzinco (3), which was a sujeto of Tecciztlan. The others are Zacatzontitlan, which was near Calpullalpan;[105] Oztoyocan, an estancia of Epazoyocan (23);[106] Tecoac, today a rancho in Texcoco, Mexico; Tlatzcayocan, which has not been identified;[107] Apan, near Tepepolco;[108] Tzacuallan, like Tlaquilpan (21) in 1580 a cabecera resettled together with Cempohuallan;[109] and Tezontepec, present-day Villa de Tezontepec, Hidalgo, which perhaps corresponds to Teçoyucan (20) in this list in the codex. The *Información de 1554* states that the province of Acolman had thirty-five towns, nine more than in the Codex Mendoza; some were perhaps those named by Durán.[110]

It seems, therefore, that many towns in this province did not pay tribute to

Tetzcoco but only to Tenochtitlan. These possessions of Tenochtitlan in Tetzcoca territory must have been those acquired at the beginning of the alliance, during Moteuczoma Ilhuicamina's war against Tetzcoco.[111] The relación geográfica of Cempohuallan related that Cempohuallan, Tlaquilpa, and Tecpilpan all passed from Nezahualcoyotl to the kingdom of Tenochtitlan in the reign of Itzcoatl. However, Tecpilpan is not listed in the Codex Mendoza. In the same relación it is said that this region began to pay tribute to Tenochtitlan during the reign of Itzcoatl, but at first only obsidian knives and a canoe each year. Ahuitzotl, for the inauguration of the temple, demanded tribute in cloaks, maize, and birds, and this continued through the reign of Moteuczoma Xocoyotzin.[112]

During Ilhuicamina's campaign against Tetzcoco, the Mexicas got as far as Totoltzinco and Tecciztlan, where they marked the boundary with the Acolhuas. When this campaign ended, lands in Tezontepec, Tuchatlauhtli, Temazcalapan, and Atzompan were distributed to Moteuczoma, the *cihuacoatl*, and the principals and valiant warriors, with stewards assigned from Coyoacan and Xochimilco.[113] Two of these towns are in the province of Acolman: Totoltzinco (3) and Temazcalapan (16). Tezontepec, as we have seen, could be the town that the Codex Mendoza legend calls Tezoyuca (20). In Atzompan, present-day Ozumbilla, there were springs of fresh water along the shore of lake Xaltocan. Tuchatlauhtli, or Tochatlauhco, was a sujeto of Acolman.[114] In Tochatlauhtli the Acolhuas were defeated in the war against the Cuextecas and Totonacas, who had gone to Tzompanco to do battle, with the result that a war land was established in Tizayocan, number (17) in the Acolman list.[115] There was then a division of lands recorded as follows:

Ye yquac ynyn moman quauhtlalli	Then the eagle land was established
yn ompa Tiçayocan	in Tizayocan
moxoxotlac yn tlalli	the boundaries were drawn.
ca yn oncan Tiçayocan	Indeed in Tizayocan
quauhtlalpan	was the eagle land.
axcan Acolhuacan tlalli	Now it is land of Acolhuacan
ypan yaotlalpan catca	where the battleground was;
ca axcan ompa mani xoxotitimani	now it is covered with vegetation.
Quauhtitlan, Toltitlan,	Cuauhtitlan, Toltitlan,
Cuitlachtepec	Cuitlachtepec,
yn quauhtlalli quicuique.	took the eagle land.[116]

In other words, there was a war land in Tezayocan, which was in the Acolhuacan, but lands in this town were given to the three towns just named that were part of the Tlacopan kingdom.

There is more information on the Tizayocan region that also records the estancias of the three capitals of the alliance in that area. According to the Acolhua sources, Tizayocan was one of Tetzcoco's towns of tenant farmers, but it is not stated which Tetzcoca calpixcazgo it was in. This is similar to the case of Xaltocan, which was also among the sujetos of Tetzcoco, although it is not named among the calpixcazgos of that capital and is in the military district of Citlaltepec.[117] In spite of the distance, Tizayocan was in the province of Otompan in 1534. In 1573 it was one of the sujetos of Otompan that, along with Cuauhtlatzinco and Ahuatepec, tried to separate themselves from their cabecera.[118] It seems that both Tizayocan and Xaltocan were part of the war land, described in the *Anales de Cuauhtitlan*, that was shared with Tenochtitlan and, to a lesser extent, with Tlacopan.[119]

In this same area were several towns called Tecalco. The present-day San Pablo Tecalco, in the municipio of Tecamac, Mexico, was probably the Tecalco of the *Suma de visitas*, between Chiucnauhtlan and Acolman, that comprised two estancias (Tecalco and Atengo) of the caciques of Mexico and two others (Calco and Viznauatengo) of the caciques of Tlatelolco.[120] In this same sector there was Santiago Tecalco and San Andrés Tecalco, a sujeto of Tlatelolco.[121] There was also a Tecalco among the towns of tenant farmers of Tlacopan (see p. 204). In addition, among the lands of Doña Isabel de Montezuma there was a Tecalco in Ecatepec and another in Acolman.[122] Thus, various estancias named Tecalco pertained to different lords or towns and survived into colonial times with the same indigenous name, but they were distinguished by the names of different patron saints.

Ecatepec, the last town listed in the Tenochca province of Acolhuacan, is always defined in the sources as belonging to Tenochtitlan and never in Tetzcoca territory. However, Tizayocan (17), which is listed in this province, used to be a sujeto of Ecatepec.[123] In the description of the campaign against Tetzcoco mentioned above, the war is said to have begun on the western shore of the lake in Chiquiuhtepec and Toltepec.[124] Ecatepec would be the point where the Tenochca domain proper connected with this Tenochca tributary province in Tetzcoca territory.

Most of the towns in this province are in the northern part of the Acolhuacan. This accords with the fact that the kingdoms of Acolman and Tepechpan, included in this province, are precisely those that, although situated in the center of the Acolhuacan, had estancias north of the Cerro Gordo.[125]

Only two towns were located in Coatepec, in the southern Acolhuacan: Tepetlapan (18) and Ameyalco (24). Contla (13) could be the town of this name in Chalco and would be the southernmost town in the province, but if so, it would be far from all the other towns in the list; it is most likely the town of the same name near Otompan.[126] The location of Tizatepec is not known. The Teotenancas migrated to a town by this name, near Tolyahualco in Xochimilco,[127] but it is too far away to be the one in this province.

Most of the region under the acolmecatl calpixqui coincides with the calpixcazgo of Tecpilpan, one of the eight tribute collection districts in the Tetzcoca organization that Ixtlilxochitl describes (see p. 153). At the time when the *Relaciones geográficas* were being compiled, Tecpilpa was one of the four cabeceras resettled in Cempohuallan; the other three were Tzacuallan, Tlaquilpan, and Cempohuallan itself.[128] These relaciones tend to emphasize the connection with Tenochtitlan, and therefore one can assume that the data on the government of these towns refer to the dependencies of the Mexica capital. The Cempohuallan relación states that the four towns it comprised and their sujetos were governed by leaders they called *tlacatecuhtles* (*sic pro tlacateuctli*); the relación includes a map in which several of these personages are painted with a headband and seated on the *icpalli* (reed seat).[129]

Atotonilco [el Grande] (Codex Mendoza, 30r)

1.	Atotonilco	Atotonilco (SV, par. 21).
		Atotonilco el Grande, Hidalgo.
2.	Acaxochitla	Acaxochitlan, Hidalgo.
3.	Quachqueçaloyan	Coauqueçaloya (SV, par. 133; Gerhard 1986:346).
		Huasca de Ocampo, Hidalgo.
4.	Hueyapan	Ranchería in Huasca de Ocampo, Hidalgo, or *ejido* (collective farm) in Cuautepec, Hidalgo.
5.	Çtzihuinquilocan	Singuilucan, Hidalgo.
6.	Tulancingo	Tulancingo, adjacent to Acatlan (SV, par. 22).
		Tulancingo, Hidalgo.

In the Codex Mendoza the toponym Atotonilco is used for the cabeceras of two tributary provinces. On their respective pages the glyphs are the same and cannot be distinguished, but the other towns listed in each province make it possible to identify the cabeceras; one is the present-day Atotonilco de Tula (28r) and the other, Atotonilco el Grande. Both Atotonilcos appear on the page where the conquests of Moteuczoma Ilhuicamina are illustrated (8r), but their glyphs differ in size; obviously the larger one indicates Atotonilco el Grande and the smaller one, the other. Because the towns on this page are arranged in a geographical sequence, those depicted on either side of the two Atotonilcos also aid in identifying them. Atotonilco de Tula, with the smaller glyph, is between Hueypochtla and Axocopan; Atotonilco el Grande, with the larger glyph, is before Tlapacoyan. The Nahuatl names would therefore be Atotoniltonco and Huey Atotonilco. Some other sources also use Atotoniltonco for Atotonilco de Tula.[130]

The first four towns in this province are not found in the lists of Tetzcoco's possessions. Tollantzinco or Tulancingo (6) was one of the dependent kingdoms of Tetzcoco and cabecera of a Tetzcoca calpixcazgo. The town of Tzihuinquillocan

(5) was founded by Nezahualcoyotl when he conquered Tollantzinco, which had rebelled shortly after the establishment of the Triple Alliance. The rebels "burned down the forts where the king kept his garrisons (located in three towns: Macanacazco, Tlayacac, and Chiquiuhtepec), killing all the soldiers that Nezahualcoyotl had in the garrisons." After the victory, Nezahualcoyotl founded a town there with settlers from Tetzcoco and named it Tzihuinquilocan, and it became part of his patrimony.[131] If later it was a garrison of the Empire, this would reenforce the possibility that this province of Atotonilco el Grande had been connected with the region of Tizayocan and with Xaltocan (in the military zone of Citlaltepec) as the military base in the northern part of the Basin from which expeditions would leave for Metztitlan and the Huaxteca (Oxitipan).

The province of Atotonilco el Grande has a certain frontierlike character in terms of both the old Tetzcoca kingdom and the Triple Alliance. When Xolotl took possession of the land, its boundaries included Metztitlan, Cuachquezaloyan (3), Atotonilco, and Cuahuacan.[132] This Atotonilco could be Atotonilco de Tula, but more probably it is Atotonilco el Grande, which is mentioned with the Metzcas and Tepehuas after Quinatzin's war against those towns.[133] In Tizoc's campaign against Metztitlan the Tenochca forces went from Tezontepec to Atotonilco el Grande, where the Tetzcoca king awaited him, with his people.[134] It is clear that the position of this town was of strategic importance against the Metztitlan frontier.

The Tributaries of Tenochtitlan within the Domain of Tlacopan

Several provinces in the Codex Mendoza—Cuauhtitlan, Axocopan, Atotonilco de Tula, Hueypochtlan, Xilotepec, and Cuahuacan—correspond to the area of the Tlacopan domain. The province of Cuahuacan coincides approximately with the district of Tlacopan; the others are in kingdoms that were direct dependencies of the Tepanec capital. All are shown on Map 5-4.

The province of Cuahuacan includes towns also listed in the first three sections of the "Memorial de Tlacopan," which enumerate the direct dependencies of the Tepanec capital. These are identified in the following list by a note, between square brackets, giving, first, the number of the section in the "Memorial de Tlacopan" (as [MTl]) and, second, the order in which each occurs on that section. The towns in this province of the Codex Mendoza that do not appear in the "Memorial de Tlacopan" are also in the same region.

CUAHUACAN (CODEX MENDOZA, 32R)

1. Quahuacan   Cahuacán in Nicolás Romero, Mexico.
                             [MTl 2-10]

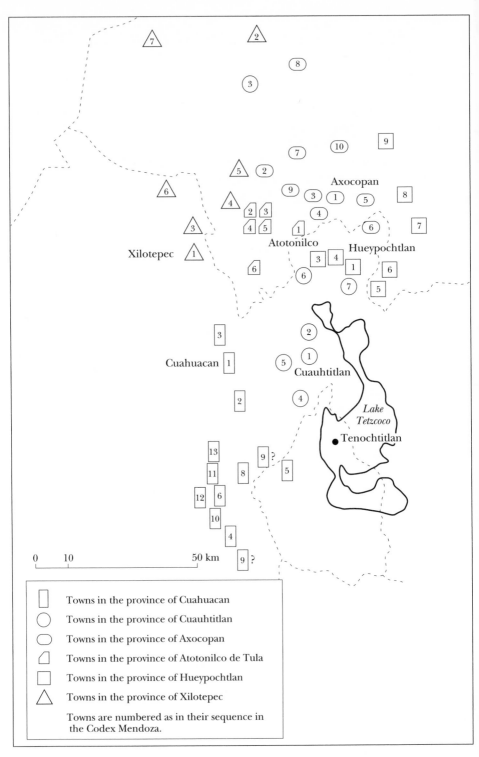

MAP 5–4. The tributaries of Tenochtitlan within the domain of Tlacopan

2. Tecpa Tequepa, bordering on Ocelotepec (SV, par. 418).
San Miguel Tecpan in Jilotzingo, Mexico.
[MTl 2-9]

3. Chapolmoloyan Chapolmalloyan, bordering on Cuauhtitlan
(AC, 21). Town adjacent to Chiappan
(Colín 1967: pars. 488, 2099).
[MTl 1-10]

4. Tlalatlauco Xalatlaco (DA, 112–13).
Jalatlaco, Mexico.

5. Acaxochic Santa Fe, D.F. (Tezozomoc 1975: 530).

6. Ameyalco San Miguel Ameyalco in Lerma, Mexico.

7. Ocotepec Location unknown.

8. Huizquilocan Huixquilucan de Degollado, Mexico.
[MTl 1-7]

9. Coatepec Quatepec, estancia of Xalatlauhco (DA, 114).
San Bartolo Coatepec in Huixquilucan, Mexico.
There is also San Nicolás Coatepec de las Bateas
in Tianguistenco, Mexico.
[MTl 3-5]

10. Quauhpanoayan Quapanoaya (DA, 232).
San Juan Coapanoaya in Ocoyoacac, Mexico.
[MTl 3-3]

11. Tlallachco Talasco, adjacent to Huitzitzilapan (SV, par. 782).
Santa María Atarasquillo in Lerma, Mexico;
or San Sebastián Tlallachco, north of Tequixquiac
(DA, 66–7).
[MTl 2-1]

12. Chichiquauhtla Chichiguautla (SV, par. 113).
Concepción or San Francisco Xochicuautla in
Lerma, Mexico.
[MTl 2-2]

13. Huitzicilapa Vçiçilapa (SV, par. 782).
San Agustín or San Lorenzo Huitzitzilapan in
Lerma, Mexico.
[MTl 2-3]

Before the Triple Alliance was constituted, Cuahuacan had been an important kingdom since the Chichimecs settled there. It was still important during the empire of Tezozomoc of Azcapotzalco, and perhaps that is why the cabecera of this Tenochca province was established there. There is no information about whether

Cuahuacan had its own king as one of the group of dependent kingdoms of Tla-copan, although it is cited as one of the seven powerful towns that joined Chiap-pan in rebelling against Ahuitzotl.[135]

The provinces described in the following sections were tributaries of Tenoch-titlan within the area occupied by the dependent kingdoms of Tlacopan.

CUAUHTITLAN (CODEX MENDOZA, 26R)

1. Quauhtitlan   Quautitlan (SV, par. 487).
Cuauhtitlan, Mexico.
2. Tehuiloyocan   Tehuiloyocan (DA, 263).
Teoloyucan, Mexico.
3. Alhuexoyocan   Albaxuyuca, adjacent to Chilguautla
(SV, par. 112). Alfajayucan, Hidalgo.
4. Xalapan   San Pablo Xalapa in Tlalnepantla, Mexico.
5. Tepoxaco   Tepujaco in Tepotzotlan, Mexico;
or Tepojaco in Tizayuca, Hidalgo.
6. Cuezcomahuacan   Barrio of Tequixquiac (DA, 67).
Bordering on Cuauhtitlan (AC, 21).
7. Xilocinco   Xilocingo (SV, par. 795).
Jilotzingo in Hueypoxtla, Mexico.

According to the *Información de 1554,* this province included Cuauhtitlan to-gether with fourteen towns whose names are not given.[136]

Tenochtitlan was not the only kingdom that had possessions in Cuauhtitlan. The lands of Atlixelhuian were distributed to Tlacopan, Azcapotzalco, Tlatelolco, Colhuacan, Itztapalapan, and Mexicatzinco, that is, to the Tepanec capital and to towns within the Tenochca sector, while the ruler of Cuauhtitlan had land in Chalco and Matlatzinco.[137]

AXOCOPAN (CODEX MENDOZA, 27R)

1. Axocopan   Axacuba (SV, par. 8).
Ajacuba, Hidalgo.
2. Atenco   Atengo (SV, par. 548).
Atengo in Tezontepec de Aldama, Hidalgo.
3. Tetepanco   Tetepango, Hidalgo.
4. Xochichiuca   Xuchichiuhca, sujeto of Axocopan (RG 8:132).
5. Temohuayan   Temoayan (PNE 5:68).
Temoaya, east of Axocopan (RG 8:128, 134).
Present-day Benito Juárez in San Agustín Tlaxiaca,

		Hidalgo. It appears as Temoaya in the Mapa del Estado de Hidalgo, Secretaría de Agricultura y Fomento 1926.
6.	Tezcatepec	Located between Hueypochtlan and Axocopan, one-quarter league from Tozantlalpan, present-day Tezontlalpan de Zapata in Hueypoxtla, Mexico. (SV, par. 217; RG 8:147; DA, 188).
7.	Mizquiyahuala	Mizquiaguala (SV, par. 347). Mixquiahuala, Hidalgo.
8.	Yzmiquilpan	Yzmiquilpa (SV, par. 293). Ixmiquilpan, Hidalgo.
9.	Tlaahuililpan	Tlaualilpa (SV, par. 555). Tlahuelilpan, Hidalgo.
10.	Tecpatepec	Tecpatepec, adjacent to Axocopan (SV, par. 8). Tepatepec in Francisco I. Madero, Hidalgo.

ATOTONILCO [DE TULA] (CODEX MENDOZA, 28R)

1.	Atotonilco	Atotonilco (SV, par. 1). To distinguish it from Huey Atotonilco, this town is sometimes called Atotoniltonco (see above under the province of Atotonilco el Grande). Atotonilco de Tula, Hidalgo.
2.	Guapalcalco	Huapalcalco in Tollan (AGN, Vínculos 256:15r, 52r, 63r; Rosas Herrera 1946:157).
3.	Queçalmacan	The glyph can also be read as Quetzalhuacan.[138] Quetzalhuacan in Tollan (AGN, Vínculos 256:63r).
4.	Acocolco	Acocolco in Tollan (Rosas Herrera 1946:156). Acoculco in Tula de Allende, Hidalgo.
5.	Tehuehuec	A site where Moteuczoma had lands in the area of Tollan (AGI, Patronato 245-R.3, 9r).
6.	Otlazpan	Vllaspa (*sic*; SV, par. 781). A town later resettled with Tepexic.
7.	Xalac	Location unknown.

HUEYPOCHTLAN (CODEX MENDOZA, 29R)

1.	Hueypuchtla	Gueypustla (SV, par. 258). Hueypoxtla, Mexico.
2.	Xalac	Location unknown.

3. Tequixquiac   Tequisquiaque (SV, par. 533).
                  Tequixquiac, Mexico.
4. Tetlapanaloyan   Tlapanaloya (SV, par. 534).
                     Tlapanaloya in Tequixquiac, Mexico.
5. Xicalhuacan   Estancia of Tizayuca (DA, 54).
6. Xomeyocan   Jomeyuca, estancia of Tolguayuca (SV, par. 524);
                or Xomeyucan, estancia of Tlapanaloya
                (SV, par. 534).
7. Acayocan   Acayuca in Zapotlan de Juárez, Hidalgo.
8. Tezcatepetonco   Perhaps Tezcatepec (SV, par. 546; RG 8:146).
                     Tepetongo in San Agustín Tlaxiaca, Hidalgo.
9. Atocpan   Atocpa (PNE 5:66).
              Actopan, Hidalgo, or San Bartolo Actopan in
              Temazcalapa, Mexico.

XILOTEPEC (CODEX MENDOZA, 31R)

1. Xilotepec   Xilotepec (RG 9:216ff.).
                Jilotepec de Abasolo, Mexico.
2. Tlachco   Tasquillo, Hidalgo, or Tlaxcoapan, Hidalgo.
3. Tzayanalquilpa   Çayanaquilpa (SV, par. 106).
                     Soyaniquilpan, Mexico.
4. Michmaloyan   Michimaloya (SV, par. 397).
                  Michimaloya in Tula, Hidalgo.
5. Tepetitlan   Tepetitlan (SV, par. 560).
                 Tepetitlán, Hidalgo.
6. Acaxochitla   Acazuchitlán in Jilotepec, Mexico.
7. Tecoçauhtlan   Tecuzautla in Xilotepec (RG 9:217).
                   Tecozautla, Hidalgo.

Table 5-2 shows the relationship between the kingdoms of the Tlacopan domain and the provinces paying tribute to Tenochtitlan that were located within that domain.[139] These provinces do not coincide with the Tlacopanec kingdoms in the same area; instead, they cut across each other.[140] The table compares the towns in these provinces of the Codex Mendoza with the dependent kingdoms of Tlacopan. Three of the Tenochca cabeceras (Axocopan, Atotonilco de Tula, and Hueypochtlan) are in the kingdom of Apazco. Atotonilco de Tula included a town in Cuauhtitlan and four others in the immediate neighborhood of Tollan itself, as can be seen in the list given above of towns in that province. Hueypochtlan included the southern and eastern parts of the kingdom of Apazco, and Axocopan took in the northern part of that kingdom as well as towns in the northern and southern areas of the kingdom of Tollan. The province of Cuauhtitlan included a town in the kingdom of Apazco, and Xilotepec province had a town in the kingdom of Tollan.

According to Torquemada's definition, the northwestern, or Tlacopan, sector of the Empire would include the Lerma Valley and the region of Toluca and its environs. But in this area, according to the "Memorial de Tlacopan," there were no dependent kingdoms pertaining to Tlacopan. Instead, Tolocan and other nearby towns, Ixtlahuacan, and Ahuazhuatepec (cabecera of Xiquipilco), were among the towns and estancias of tenants belonging to Tlacopan, forming a region that coincides approximately with the provinces of Tolocan and Xocotitlan in the Codex Mendoza. Thus, it seems that Tlacopan and Tenochtitlan had separate posses-

TABLE 5-2.

Tributary Provinces of Tenochtitlan in the Tlacopan Domain
Compared with the Dependent Kingdoms of Tlacopan

Tributaries (Codex Mendoza)	Kingdoms in Which They Were Located*
1. Quauhtitla	Cuauhtitlan 1 (1)
2. Tehuiloyocan	
3. Alhuexoyocan	
4. Xalapan	
5. Tepoxaco	
6. Cuezcomahuacan	
7. Xilocinco	Apazco 11 (45)
1. Axocopan	Apazco 3 (38)
2. Atenco	
3. Tetepanco	Apazco (42)
4. Xochichiucan	
5. Temohuayan	
6. Tezcatepec	Apazco 7 (43)
7. Myzquiyahuala	Tollan 5 (32)
8. Yzmiquilpan	Tollan 7 (35)
9. Tlaahuililpan	Tollan 8 (33)
10. Tecpatepec	Apazco 4 (39)
1. Atotonilco [de Tula]	Apazco 2 (37)
2. Guapalcalco	
3. Queçalmacan	
4. Acocolco	
5. Tehuehuec	
6. Otlazpan	Cuauhtitlan (21)
7. Xalac	

Table 5-2 continued

Tributaries (Codex Mendoza)	Kingdoms in Which They Were Located*
1. Hueypochtlan	Apazco 9 (43)
2. Xalac	
3. Tequixquiac	Apazco 10 (44)
4. Tetlapanaloyan	Apazco 8
5. Xicalhuacan	
6. Xomeyocan	
7. Acayocan	
8. Tezcatepetonco	
9. Atocpan	Apazco 5
1. Xillotepec	Xilotepec 1
2. Tlachco	
3. Tzayanalquilpa	
4. Michmaloyan	Tollan 2 (28)
5. Tepetitlan	
6. Acaxochitla	
7. Tecoçauhtla	Xilotepec 3

*The second column indicates the kingdom in which each town was located, followed by the number that shows its place within the list of subjects in each kingdom, according to the "Memorial de Tlacopan" and, in parentheses, according to the Codex Osuna. See chapter 4.

sions in this area, and the provinces of Xocotitlan and Tolocan in the Codex Mendoza were not among those that paid tribute to the three capitals of the Empire but represent only the part that paid to Tenochtitlan. Similarly, the provinces of Ocuillan and Malinalco in the Codex Mendoza are not in the "Memorial de Tlacopan," either among the kingdoms or the towns and estancias of tenant farmers pertaining to Tlacopan or among those that paid tribute to the three capitals. It is most probable that they paid tribute exclusively to Tenochtitlan (see chapter 9).

The Tributaries of Tenochtitlan in Tlalhuic

A comparison of the sources that list the tributaries of the three capitals of the alliance shows that in some regions each one of the three had separate possessions of its own. The cases that are well documented are those of Tlalhuic, Tolocan, and Chalco. Two of the tributary provinces of Tenochtitlan in the Codex Mendoza are in Tlalhuic—Cuauhnahuac and Huaxtepec—and list the tributaries of Tenochtitlan. Both provinces are shown on Map 5-5.[141]

MAP 5–5. The tributaries of Tenochtitlan in Tlalhuic

Cuauhnahuac (Codex Mendoza, 23r–v)

1. Quauhnahuac   Cuernavaca, Morelos.
2. Teocalcinco   San Juan Teocalcingo (AGN-HJ 290, fol. 1707v), six leagues from Cuernavaca (AGI, Patronato 16, no. 2, R. 32). It has been identified as Teocalcingo in Atenango del Río, Guerrero, which is much farther away (Barlow 1949b: 75; Gerhard 1986:99, 116). Another possibility is Teocalcingo, former estancia of Ocuillan (SV, par. 419), present-day Lomas de Teocalcingo, ranchería of Ocuila, Mexico. There is another Teocalcingo, also very distant, in Zacualpa, Mexico.
3. Chimalco   Panchimalco in Jojutla, Morelos. [Panchimalco]
4. Huicilapan   Huitzillac, Morelos. [Huitzillan]
5. Acatl ycpac   Acatlipa in Temixco, Morelos.
6. Xochitepec   Xochitepec, Morelos.
7. Miacatla   Miacatlán, Morelos.
8. Molotla   Location unknown.[142]
9. Coatlan   Coatlán del Río, Morelos.
10. Xiuhtepec   Jiutepec, Morelos.
11. Xoxoutla   Jojutla de Juárez, Morelos.
12. Amacoztitla   Amacuzac, Morelos [number 13 in the *Matrícula*].
13. Yztla   Puente de Ixtla, Morelos [number 12 in the *Matrícula*].
14. Ocpayucan   Ocopayuca, subject of Cuauhnahuac (CDI 12:560). Bordered on Acamistlauaca, near Tasco (SV, par. 37).
15. Iztepec   (?) Gerhard (1970a: 34) identifies it as the former Iztayuca (or Izteocan) northwest of Cuauhnahuac.[143]
16. Atl icholoayan   Atlacholoaya in Xochitepec, Morelos.

According to the *Información de 1554*, twenty-four towns paid tribute together with Cuauhnahuac; their names are not given.[144] Those listed in the Codex Mendoza and the *Matrícula* are essentially the same; in the above list, variants in the *Matrícula* are indicated between brackets. Cuauhnahuac (1) and Miacatlan (7) are also among the possessions of Tetzcoco; Xoxouhtla (11), Amacoztitlan (12), and perhaps Molotla (9) and Iztepec (15) are among those of Tlacopan (see pp. 173 and 201). This province coincided with the kingdom of Cuauhnahuac, whose sovereign, related to the Tenochca dynasty, was probably directly subject to Tenochtitlan.

Huaxtepec (Codex Mendoza, 24v–25r)

1. Huaxtepec   Oaxtepec in Yautepec, Morelos.
2. Xochimilcacinco   In Las Amilpas (RG 6, 200; Barlow 1949b: 79).
3. Quauhtlan   Cuautla, Morelos.
4. Ahuehuepan   In Las Amilpas (RG 6:200; Barlow 1949b: 79).
                     Perhaps San Juan Ahuehueyo in Ayala, Morelos.
5. Anenecuilco   Anenecuilco de los Mata in Ayala, Morelos.
6. Olintepec   Olintepec in Ayala, Morelos.
7. Quahuitlyxco   Cuautlixco in Cuautla, Morelos.
8. Çompanco   Estancia of Xochimilcatzinco in Las Amilpas
                     (RG 6:200).
9. Huicilan   Huitzililla in Ayala, Morelos.
10. Tlaltiçapan   Tlaltizapán, Morelos.
11. Coacalco   Oacalco in Yautepec, Morelos.
12. Yzamatitlan   Itzamatitlan in Yautepec, Morelos.
13. Tepoztlan   Tepoztlan, Morelos.
14. Yauhtepec   Yautepec, Morelos.
15. Yacapichtla   Yecapixtla, Morelos.
16. Tlayacapan   Tlayacapan, Morelos.
17. Xaloztoc   Jaloxtoc in Ayala, Morelos.
18. Tecpacinco   Tepalcingo, Morelos.
19. Ayoxochapan   Axochiapan, Morelos.
20. Tlayacac   Tlayecac in Ayala, Morelos.
21. Tehuizco   Teuhizco (*sic*), sujeto of Totolapan (PNE 6:7; Teuixco
                     in RG 8:159).
22. Nepopoalco   Nepopualco in Totolapan, Morelos (Maldonado
                     1990:104), or Nepopoalco, next to Hueyapan
                     (SV, par. 505; RG 7:265).
23. Atlatlauca   Atlatlahucan, Morelos.
24. Totolapan   Totolapan, Morelos.
25. Amilcingo   Estancia of Cuautla in Las Amilpas (RG 6:200).
                     East of Cuautla in the Mapa de Morelos de la
                     Comisión Geográfica Exploradora 1910.
                     There is another Amilcingo in Temoac, Morelos.
26. Atlhuelic   Alveleca, sujeto of Yautepec (CDI 12:560). Alhuelica,
                     in Yautepec (AGN-HJ 289, exp. 100 passim).
                     Atlihueyan in Yautepec, Morelos.

The possessions of Tetzcoco in this region included Olintepec (6) and Yautepec (14); Anenecuilco (5) also pertained to Tlacopan (see pp. 173 and 201).

The province of Huaxtepec included several kingdoms of Xochimilca affiliation: Tepoztlan (13) and those of the region called Cuauhtenco, which included
Tlayacapan (16), Atlatlauhcan (23), and Totolapan (24).[145] Other kingdoms were
Tlalhuica: Huaxtepec (1), Yauhtepec (14), and Yacapichtla (15). The towns numbered 9, 10, and 26 were sujetos of Yautepec.

The dependencies of Huaxtepec made up the region called Amilpan (Las
Amilpas, "irrigated fields"); the towns in the above list from 2 to 8 and also 25 were
in this area. The sujetos of Yacapichtla (15) comprised the area called Tlalnahuac
and included the towns numbered 17 to 20. During the colonial period there were
lawsuits about whether Las Amilpas and the Tlalnahuac area had pertained to
their colonial cabeceras in the pre-Spanish era or had been separate entities.[146] At
least in part they must have been settled by colonists from other towns. Moteuczoma Ilhuicamina had pleasure gardens created in Huaxtepec and brought workers there from Cuetlaxtlan.[147] It was also said that Huaxtepec itself was Moteuczoma's garden and by his order was looked after by certain Indian calpixques
from Totomihuacan and Cozcatlan.[148] Ayahualco, in Las Amilpas, was settled by
newcomers from Chalco, Mexico, Xochimilco, and other towns.[149] The people of
Yacapichtla were Tlalhuicas, while those in the Tlalnahuac area were Mexicas.[150]
The situation of the kings in this region in relation to the Triple Alliance is not entirely clear. Probably they were direct dependents of Tenochtitlan.[151]

Tribute from the towns in Las Amilpas went to Mexico, Xochimilco, Tetzcoco, Ecatepec, and Itztapalapan[152]—that is, to two of the capital cities, Tenochtitlan and Tetzcoco, and also to certain kingdoms in the Tenochca group. In regard
to the Xochimilca towns in the region of Cuauhtenco, the *Relaciones geográficas* state
that the people of Totolapan, Tlayacapan, and Atlatlauhcan did not pay tribute to
Moteuczoma because they served him only in his wars against Chalco, Huexotzinco, Tlaxcallan, and Cholollan, and Moteuczoma provided them with the necessary weapons.[153]

Some towns farther east—Tetellan, Hueyapan, and the Nepopoalco adjoining Hueyapan—paid tribute to Tenochtitlan; they were also dependencies of Xochimilco, to which they gave tribute in goods and labor for public works and men
for war parties.[154] Neighboring Ocuituco sent flowers to Moteuczoma.[155] However, Tetellan and Hueyapan are mentioned as sujetos of Cuauhquechollan, one
of the towns in the tributary province of Tepeyacac (see p. 291).

Chapter 6

THE ACOLHUA-CHICHIMEC KINGDOM OF TETZCOCO

Tetzcoco, Capital of the Acolhua-Chichimecs

Of the three capitals of the Triple Alliance, Tetzcoco is the one for which we have the best documentation of its political situation as the head of a group of kingdoms—the Acolhua cities—whose rulers were direct dependents of the Chichimecateuctli of Tetzcoco.[1] The urban character of Tetzcoco, its division into barrios, and the existence of an extensive rural area are also well documented. As the political and religious center of the kingdom, the city housed a large proportion of the ruling estate. Within its territory were the residences and pleasure gardens of the kings and the nobility, administrative buildings such as palaces and storehouses, and houses maintained there by the tributary districts.[2] There were also a great ceremonial center and other structures for religious observances and a large marketplace; the population also included many artisans. As Hicks has pointed out, the highest concentration of these urban elements was in the central area, although the settlement pattern as a whole was rather dispersed, and some institutions, such as the palace of Tetzcotzinco, were at a distance from the center.[3]

Ixtlilxochitl's description of the city of Tetzcoco "with its barrios and hamlets" makes clear the existence of a rural zone that was an essential part of the city. A steward was put in charge of collecting all the revenue due to the city and was also responsible for the maintenance of the king's household and court for seventy days, with specific amounts of the foodstuffs stipulated for each day.[4] Ixtlilxochitl does not give a list of the rural settlements nor describe their geographical extent, and Motolinía's "Memorial tetzcocano" does not give a list of towns in the township of Tetzcoco comparable to the list in the "Memorial de los pueblos de Tlacopan" for the Tepanec capital. Nevertheless, other sources make up for this lack; Hicks has compiled abundant material on the city of Tetzcoco and its territory that illustrates the importance of both an urban center and an extensive rural zone. Calpollalpan and certain towns north of Atenco were also part of its territory.

Tetzcoco was divided into six parcialidades inhabited by groups of immigrants who had settled in Tetzcoco at different moments of its history. In Quinatzin's time the Tlailotlaques and Chimalpanecs came to Tetzcoco from the Chalco area. The Tlailotlaques, who worshiped Tezcatlipoca, came from "beyond the Mixteca" and are described as learned men and expert artisans, especially noted for their skill in painting the pictorial documents that recorded the historical traditions; the Chimalpanecs descended from the Chichimecs who had established themselves in the Chalco region. Techotlalatzin, successor to Quinatzin, took in four Toltec "nations" from Colhuacan—Mexitin, Colhuas, Tepanecs, and Huitznahuas—giving them barrios to settle in. Later, Nezahualcoyotl made a very orderly arrangement in the city, dividing it into six barrios: Mexicapan, Colhuacan, Tepanecapan, Huitznahuac, Chimalpan, and Tlailotlacan.[5]

The sources written in Spanish call these subdivisions parcialidades or barrios; the Nahuatl name must have been calpolli, since neighboring Calpollalpan (land of calpolli) was thus named because it was settled by people from the same six barrios of Tetzcoco.[6] This organization of the city was comparable to that of the calpolli of the Mexica migration and their establishment in barrios of Tenochtitlan.

Aside from the traditions about the establishment of the six parcialidades in Tetzcoco there are no early sources that list all the sections of the city and its rural settlements. The area covered by Tetzcoco and its villages is well described in Vetancurt, but this is a late report from the end of the seventeenth century that reflects changes introduced during the colonial epoch. Moreover, it refers principally to the ecclesiastical organization, with twenty-four chapels, nineteen of which were in the city, and twenty-nine villages (pueblos de visita), attended by the city's priest, divided among five parcialidades.[7] Still it is useful as a reference point for this discussion.

Vetancurt first lists the chapels in the city: the Hospital del Santo Sepulcro named Hueicalco, San Pedro Colhuacan, San Pablo Huitznahuac, Concepción de Quauhxincan, San Lorenzo Tecpan, San Juan Mexicapa, San Sebastián Chimalpan, Trinidad Tlalnepantla, Santa María Tlayotlacan (*sic pro* Tlailotlacan), San Mateo Tlatelco, Santa Ana Teocaltitlan, Santo Tomás Tetzotzonca, Santa Ursula Tepozhuacan, Santa Catalina Tepozhuacan, San Gregorio Amanalco, Santa Inés Ahuehuetitlan, Santa Cruz Tecpan, and Phelipe (*sic*), San José Atlihuetzian. At the end of the list are the names of two churches near the city: Santo Tomás, in a rancho, and San Simón Cihuatecpan, which was considered part of the cabecera.

Next he enumerates twenty-nine villages in the five parcialidades, with three nearby chapels. The first parcialidad, called "del Monte," comprises Santa María Tetzcotzinco, Purificación de Tenochco, San Joaquín Quauhiacac, San Juan Tetzontla, Santa María Tecoanolco, Santa Catalina Ayauhcalco, San Miguel Tecuilan (*sic pro* Tlaixpan),[8] San Nicolás Tlaminca, and San Gerónimo Zoquiyapan, with two chapels: Santa Inés Tepantla and San Bartolomé Quauhiacac.

In the second parcialidad are located San Buenaventura Tezoyocan, Resurrección Tepetlynahuac, San Mateo Istlahuacan, Santiago Mexicapan, Assumpción de Quanala, San Lucas Huitzilhuacan, and Reyes de Totitlan.

The third parcialidad includes San Salvador Atenco, San Miguel Chiconcohuac, Santa María Magdalena Panohuayan, San Francisco Acuzcomac (*sic pro* Acuezcomac), San Pedro Calmimilolco, San Andrés Tlilapan, and San Miguel Tlaixpan (*sic pro* Tocuillan).

The fourth contains Santo Toribio Papalotlan, Corpus Cristi Xoxocotla, Espiritu Santo Tlateyocan, Circuncisión Texopan, and the chapel of Santos Reyes.

In the fifth parcialidad are San Cristóbal Nexquipayac and Santa María Iztapa.

Upon finishing this enumeration Vetancurt notes that to the north of the city there was the church and village of Nuestra Señora de la Purificación de Tulantonco.

The pre-Spanish extent of Tetzcoco and its villages was not exactly the same as in this list of Vetancurt's. He includes, in the second parcialidad, the town of Tezoyocan, which appears in older sources as separate from Tetzcoco with its own king.[9] Also, the inclusion of Papalotlan in the district of Tetzcoco is not well documented in other sources. According to Ixtlilxochitl, Nezahualcoyotl appropriated it for the royal chamber; perhaps it was made part of the capital (see p. 145).

Nevertheless, Vetancurt's report comes close to what must have been the rural district proper to which Ixtlilxochitl refers. It was a very broad area, including land from the shores of the lake to the top of the mountains.[10] Some estancias of Tetzcoco that were beyond the neighboring kingdom of Chiauhtlan should be added to Vetancurt's list.[11] Also it is probable that the Calpollalpan region towards the east was part of the capital district. This area is never spoken of as a city with its own king but as a dependency of Tetzcoco. It might have been included in one of the calpixcazgos such as that of Tetzcoco itself, or that of Tepepolco, or it might well have had a special status as a frontier zone.

Some of the barrios in this list reflect the names of the immigrant groups of the historical traditions, but there are many others, including some in the center of the city. Torquemada explains that the parcialidades in which the towns of the Acolhuacan had been divided since the time of Techotlalatzin "were divided into calpules [calpolli] which are barrios," and one parcialidad might have three, four, and more calpolli, according to the number of the inhabitants.[12] The areas settled by the original groups, as in the traditions, should be seen as what Torquemada calls parcialidades, each one of which could include several calpolli. In Vetancurt's list the names of the six parcialidades are found in the center of the city, and Hicks has related them to archaeological remains.[13] In addition, each of the parcialidades would have several barrios, some of which extended into the rural area.

This rural area must have contained a goodly number of country people who lived in the calpixcazgo designated as "Tetzcoco with its barrios and hamlets" and also in that of Atenco, which the sixteenth-century documents consider barrios or estancias of the city. The calpixcazgo of Atenco comprised the third of Vetancurt's parcialidades and part of the fifth. It occupied the lake shore west of the city, while that of Tetzcoco took in the area to the east; these two calpixcazgos are discussed below.

The Dependent Kingdoms of Tetzcoco

The Tetzcoca sources explain the position within the kingdom of the cities governed by kings who were dependents of the great king of the Acolhuacan. Ixtlilxochitl relates that, when the Triple Alliance was founded, each of the three parts comprised a certain number of cities with their own kings: fourteen under Tetzcoco, nine under Tenochtitlan, and seven under Tlacopan. But it is Motolinía's "Memorial tetzcocano" that gives the best short description of the cities subordinate to the great king of Tetzcoco, as follows:

> Of these towns named and painted here the head and principal rulership is Tetzcoco, and the others have their names [indicated]: they were all subject to the king (señor) of Tetzcoco, and each town had a king after he married a daughter of the king of Tetzcoco, and that is why these women are painted here: all were daughters of a great king of Tetzcoco, called Nezahualcoyotzin, who, together with his daughters, gave the rulership to their husbands.
>
> The figures and names of the towns they ruled are written above their heads. That sign and picture at the back of their heads is the name of each one by which their proper name was known and painted as is declared for two or three [of them].
>
> These that are here within this house are father and son, two very great kings that reigned here for eighty-six years: the father was called Nezahualcoyotzin, and the son Nezahualpilli.
>
> Vehxutla [Huexotla]; Couatlichan [Coatlichan]; Chimalhuacan; Otompan; Teotihuacan; Acolma; Tepechpan; Teconyucan [Tezoyocan]; Chiyaputla [Chiauhtlan]; Chihuinahutla [Chiucnauhtlan]; Tollancinco; Quauhchinanco; Xicotepec; Pauatla.
>
> These towns depicted here gave no tribute other than labor to build and repair the houses and works of the king and the temples, and for those they looked for and brought lime, stone, wood, and all the materials [necessary], and they also provided firewood for half a year, and the palace alone used in one day a pile [of wood] as tall as a man and ten brazas wide, that held more than 400 Indian loads.[14]

These fourteen cities governed by kings are almost the same that Ixtlilxochitl names in the "Historia chichimeca" on enumerating the kingdoms that Nezahual-coyotl restored after the defeat of the Tepanecs.[15] The only difference is that this author includes Tepetlaoztoc but not Pahuatlan, and in this he agrees with the se-ries of kings depicted in the interior of the palace of Tetzcoco in the Mapa Quin-atzin.[16] In his "Compendio Histórico," Ixtlilxochitl also includes Pahuatlan among the towns conquered along with Tollantzinco, but without saying whether it had its own king; in another passage, in the "Historia chichimeca," he gives Totona-pan instead of Pahuatlan.[17] The corresponding text in the *Anales de Cuauhtitlan*—after the phrase "Tetzcoco mochi yn tlatocayotl Nezahualcoyotzin Nezahualpiltz-intli" (Tetzcoco, the whole kingdom, Nezahualcoyotzin, Nezahualpiltzintli)—enumerates fifteen cities and includes both Tepetlaoztoc and Pantlan (*sic pro* Pahu-atlan?) together with the thirteen cities in common with the other sources cited above.[18] There are thus a total of fifteen cities governed by kings.

In his *Memoriales*, Motolinía states that "the city of Tetzcoco was the second in importance in the country, and similarly its king was the second king of the coun-try. He ruled over fifteen provinces as far as the province of Tozapan, which is on the coast of the Northern Sea."[19] According to Torquemada, the kings of Ten-ochtitlan and Tetzcoco were equals, and as proof he states that when, after the de-feat of the Tepanecs, Itzcoatl claimed the position of supreme ruler, Nezahu-alcoyotl sent an army to Tenochtitlan to maintain his own position.[20] He then adds to his information, referring to Motolinía:

> This equality of [both] kings is avowed by Fray Toribio Motolinía with these words: The kingdom of Tetzcoco was equal to that of Mexico and reached to the Northern Sea, where he had many towns and provinces that paid him tribute and were subject to Tetzcoco when the Spaniards came to this land; and it is so, that I have in my possession ancient paintings of that kingdom in which fifteen large provinces are depicted, each of which is a very extensive kingdom and each of these provinces has many cities, towns, and villages; and if when the Spaniards entered the country, they found that Mo-teuczoma was [the] great king, not however that he was [king] of all of New Spain, but that since they entered lands conquered by Moteuczoma, and they [the people] did not acknowledge any other lord, they said that all were his vassals; the truth being that Tetzcoco had its own kingship like that of Mex-ico and there was no inequality between them; I say this so that it will not sound wrong when something about this is heard.[21]

In another passage Motolinía states that "there were, then, subject to Tezcoco many provinces and towns, as I intend to show here painted and all were reduced to six cabeceras, and there they gave obedience and had recourse, and there the tribute was collected, and they also went there for litigation although instead of the judges [en lugar de los jueces (*sic*)] all were present in the palace."[22]

In describing the government of Tetzcoco, Torquemada returns to Motolinía and relates the fifteen "provinces" to the six cabeceras. He says that the king of Tetzcoco had judges as advisers and adds: "This kingdom had fifteen subject provinces, but not all of them had these high judges immediate [to the king]; therefore one of these most prudent kings ordered that there should be six courts, like chanceries, in six particular towns, to which all the said provinces were reduced, and to which people came from the whole kingdom to take care of their affairs according to how jurisdiction was distributed or according to what place was more convenient because of proximity."[23]

The reference to paintings suggests that he alludes to the source of Motolinía's "Memorial tetzcocano," but neither of these two writers names the "provinces" and audiencias. Probably in both documents the kingdom of Tetzcoco includes the capital city and fifteen dependent kingdoms, and the six audiencias were perhaps in the six kingdoms that Ixtlilxochitl describes as the most important.[24]

Table 6-1 gives the complete list of the kingdoms that were dependencies of Tetzcoco in the order in which they appear in the *Anales de Cuauhtitlan*; the sequence of toponyms in the other two sources is also indicated, and the names of the kings have been added. Map 6-1 represents all these kingdoms. The Mapa Quinatzin coincides completely with Ixtlilxochitl as to the names of the kings of fourteen cities. The disposition of the glyphs of cities and kings in the Mapa Quinatzin is discussed below.

The different order in which the cities are listed in Ixtlilxochitl and the other two sources suggests regional groupings as indicated on the table. Most of the cities are in the eastern part of the Basin; of these, the three cities south of Tetzcoco—Huexotla, Coatlichan, and Chimalhuacan—make up one group; north of Tetzcoco, Teotihuacan and Otompan are another. The other cities in the Basin are located along the lake shore from the vicinity of Tetzcoco towards the north. A separate group is formed by the more distant cities in the Valley of Tollantzinco and the eastern slopes of the highlands, an area referred to in Ixtlilxochitl and Torquemada as La Sierra: Tollantzinco, Cuauhchinanco, Xicotepec, and Pahuatlan.

Durán's list of towns subject to Tetzcoco does not indicate which ones were kingdoms, but he names all those located in the Basin, and listed in Table 6-1, except Chiauhtlan; of those in La Sierra he names only Tollantzinco.[25]

The kings of these cities participated in the highest councils of government in the kingdom of Tetzcoco. The kings of Teotihuacan and Otompan had the rank of "captain," and each was in charge of a tribunal. The king of Teotihuacan heard

TABLE 6-1.

The Cities with Kings That Were Dependents of Tetzcoco

Anales de Cuauhtitlan*	Motolinía[†]	Ixtilxochitl[‡]	Names of Kings According to the Mapa Quinatzin and Ixtlilxochitl
1. Huexotla	1	1	Tlazolyaotzin
2. Coatlichan	2	2	Motoliniatzin
3. Chimalhuacan	3	3	Tezcapoctzin
4. Otompan	4	11	Quecholtecpantzin
5. Teotihuacan	5	10	Quetzalmamalitzin
6. Tepetlaoztoc	—	4	Cocopintzin
7. Acolman	6	5	Motlatocazomatzin
8. Tepechpan	7	6	Tencoyotzin
9. Tezoyocan	8	7	Techotlalatzin
10. Chiauhtlan	9	9	Cuauhtlatzacuilotzin
11. Chiucnauhtlan	10	8	Tezozomoctzin
12. Tollantzinco	11	12	Tlalolinztin
13. Cuauhchinanco	12	13	Nauhecatzin
14. Xicotepec	13	14	Quetzalpaintzin
15. Pantlan	14. Pahuatlan	—	

*AC, 64.
[†]Motolinía 1971:394.
[‡]Ixtlilxochitl 1975–77, 2:89.

the cases of nobles from the "province" called La Campiña (the countryside); the king of Otompan took care of the affairs of commoners from the same region.[26]

Some of these cities (Tepechpan, Tepetlaoztoc, and Tezoyocan) are also listed in the tributary province in the Codex Mendoza (21v–22r) that includes cities of the Acolhuacan. In other words, they would give part of their tributary obligations to Tenochtitlan; within their territory there would be towns pertaining to the Tenochca king and officials to collect his tribute. Acolman was probably the seat of the Tenochca tribute collector for this province, since he is referred to as acolmecatl calpixqui (see p. 116).

Chiucnauhtlan is a special case. As in the Tetzcoca sources, Durán also locates it in the "province" of Tetzcoco.[27] Nevertheless its ruler appears in the Codex Mendoza (69r), with those of Tenayocan and Colhuacan, as one of three who were the "friends and confederates of Moteuczoma" (sus amigos y confederados de Moteuczuma). It is possible that there were two towns named Chiucnauhtlan (see p. 100).

Probably there were other cities that also had rulers with the title of tlatoani,

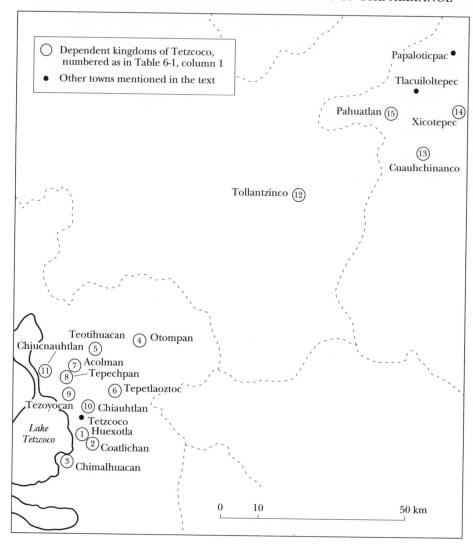

MAP 6–1. The dependent kingdoms of Tetzcoco

but they would have been of a lower rank and without the political role in the government of the Acolhua kingdom of the cities listed above.

The dynasties that reigned in the dependent cities of Tetzcoco were descended either from the Chichimec chiefs who migrated to the Acolhuacan at the same time as the Chichimecs of Xolotl or from the Acolhua rulers established by Xolotl in Huexotla and Coatlichan.[28] In contrast, the dynasty of Chimalhuacan was connected to the Tolteca-Colhuas.[29] Motolinía's "Memorial tetzcocano," quoted above, states that the kings of these cities married daughters of the king of Tetzcoco, specifically, the daughters of Nezahualcoyotl, who gave each of the kings a kingdom along with a daughter. The only dynasty fully documented is that of Teotihuacan.[30] The matrimonial alliances of the other kingdoms are less well known, but there are several cases that support Motolinía's generalization. A different situation is found in Chiauhtlan. Here, when the Empire was founded, Nezahualcoyotl established his son Cuauhtlatzacualotzin, and later Nezahualpilli installed a younger son of Nezahualcoyotl's, born to one of his concubines.[31] This is similar to the Tenochca custom of establishing sons of the ruler of the capital as kings of dependent cities. In Xicotepec the king restituted by Nezahualcoyotl was Quetzalpaintzin. The recently published Codex de Xicotepec does not mention him but does record later rulers, whose rules of succession and kinship with the kings of Tetzcoco are not fully ascertainable. It is possible that Cipactli, first mentioned in 1440, was a son of Nezahualcoyotl, while Coatl, the last ruler, might have married a daughter of Moteuczoma Xocoyotzin.[32]

In the text quoted above from Motolinía's "Memorial tetzcocano" he points out that the cities governed by kings subject to Tetzcoco were obliged to provide materials and labor for construction and to supply firewood. According to Ixtlilxochitl, the recognition that these kings gave "was only homage and attendance [at court], and in time of war to report with their vassals to serve their kings, without any other tribute and acknowledgment [of authority]."[33] According to the relación geográfica of Acolman, this town recognized the ruler of Tetzcoco only by providing men in time of war; tribute in kind went to the ruler of Acolman.[34] Except for the tribute of firewood, these obligations are obviously related to the social and political level of the urban population, which included the personnel of government and highly skilled artisans.

Most of the Acolhua kingdoms were in the Basin. The situation of the kingdoms in La Sierra was somewhat different. Ixtlilxochitl, on giving the list of kings restored to their kingdoms, speaks first of those in the Basin and adds that "in the course of time" Nezahualcoyotl restored the kings of Tollantzinco, Cuauhchinanco, and Xicotepec. Farther on he states that this happened after having confirmed his friendship with the Tlaxcaltecs and determined the boundaries with them. Nezahualcoyotl then went to war with Tollantzinco, where he restored Tlalolintzin as king. Cuauhchinanco surrendered peacefully. Nezahualcoyotl confirmed its king as ruler, and also the king of Xicotepec, and proceeded to win the whole area of Totonapan.[35] Then Nezahualcoyotl and the kings of Tenochtitlan and Tlacopan went on to conquer Cuauhnahuac and several other towns, after which he had to defeat again the people of Tollantzinco, who had destroyed his garrisons. In spite

TABLE 6-2.
The Domain of Tetzcoco in the Sierra

Torquemada*	Ixtilxochitl[†]	H. Pimentel[‡]	Motolinía[§]
1. Tollantzinco	Tollantzinco	Tollantzinco	Tollantzinco
2. Xicotepec	Xicotepec	Xicotepec	Xicotepec
3. Cuauhchinanco	Cuauhchinanco		Cuauhchinanco
4. Pahuatlan	Pahuatlan	Pahuatlan	Pahuatlan
5. Tlacuiloltepec		Tlacuiloltepec	
6. Papaloticpac		Papaloticpac	

*Torquemada 1975–83, 1:232.

[†]Ixtlilxochitl 1975–77, 1:382, 446; 2:114.

[‡]Tollantzinco is counted among the towns won by war, where the kings of Tetzcoco had lands and tenants. The rest are the last ones on the list of tributary towns in the environs of Tetzcoco. See p. 59–60.

[§]Cities in the Sierra with kings subject to Tetzcoco (Motolinía 1971:394). The list in AC (64, sec. 225) has Pantlan in place of Pahuatlan.

of this rebellion, Nezahualcoyotl kept the king of Tollantzinco as one of the fourteen grandees of the kingdom, but obliged him to pay tribute in clothing and beans and provide labor for the royal gardens. He installed a steward in Tollantzinco to see to this, and also founded a town called Tzihuinquillocan with people from Tetzcoco.[36]

Table 6-2 brings together the data on cities in La Sierra that pertained to Tetzcoco. Only Ixtlilxochitl and Motolinía state specifically that the cities they enumerate were ruled by kings. There is no information about who governed Tlacuiloltepec and Papaloticpac.

In addition to the data he provides on labor and tribute in goods, Torquemada explains the administrative service given by the rulers of La Sierra: "From all the provinces of La Sierra (Tulantzinco, Xicotepec, Quauhchinanco, Pahuatlan, Tlacuiloltepec, Papaloticpac, and other very large and populous towns) there were many lords and captains who were present at his court [of Nezahualcoyotl] and had their particular halls in the palace, where they were daily attending to all matters that came up, concerning war or the good government of their republics."[37]

Ixtlilxochitl states that the king was responsible for the tribute that Nezahualcoyotl imposed on Tollantzinco, but the organization for the production of tribute in clothing and beans that the peasants of the region would give must have been different from that of the governmental services that Torquemada cites.[38] As we have seen, the distinction between the two types of obligations, one imposed on the cities and the other on the villages of tenants, is well defined in Motolinía's "Memorial tetzcocano."

Cuauhchinanco, situated towards the eastern end of the Tetzcoca domain, served as the point of departure for the campaigns in the Huaxteca.[39] Together with other officials from the three capitals of the Empire, a principal of Cuauhchinanco took part in resolving a dispute over lands between Chillan and Mecatlan in La Sierra de Puebla.[40]

The Tetzcoca sources that enumerate the towns subject to the capital and describe their obligations follow one of two different procedures. Some reports make a distinction between cities governed by their own kings and villages of peasants administered by stewards. Others define two extensive geographical units in the Basin that include both cities and peasant villages, each of which provides tribute and services for half the year. We will look first at the sources that describe the obligations of groups of peasant villages and then the reports that describe two tributary halves. The Mapa Quinatzin resolves the apparent contradictions between the different forms of organization.

The Tributaries of Tetzcoco within Its Own Domain

The Tetzcoca sources present more detailed information on the tributaries pertaining to the Acolhua capital than the Tenochca sources give about theirs. In addition to the key data in Motolinía's "Memorial tetzcocano," which coincides with the "Memorial de los pueblos de Tlacopan," there are several other sources that describe different ways of organizing the tributaries according to the nature of the tribute and services given, such as providing firewood or caring for the king's gardens.

Motolinía's "Memorial tetzcocano" and the "Memorial de los pueblos de Tlacopan" describe with almost identical words groups of towns that did not have kings of their own but were governed by "mayores y principales." Motolinía states:

> These sixteen towns that are pictured here were subject to Tetzcoco, and there was no king in them but elders and principals who ruled them. They were all as tenant farmers of the ruler of Tetzcoco, and in addition to their tribute the ruler of Tetzcoco had in these towns many fields that they cultivated for him, and [that is why] those Indians are [pictured] here with their *huictles* [*sic pro huictli*, "spades"] in their hands, . . . with which they cultivate the land in this New Spain. They also provided firewood for the king's household for half the year.
>
> There were others who provided firewood to the temples of the devil: they used much more than in the palace; almost all the firewood was oak: the two together used both day and night more than a thousand loads of wood, without [counting] the loads of pitch-wood they used for lighting. They also brought many loads of dried bark that gave good light and extremely good coals.

Couatepec; Yeztapacoca [Itztapallocan]; Papalotla; Xaltoca; Auatepec; Oztoticpac; Couatlacinco [Cuauhtlatzinco]; Axapuchco; Azcaymeca [Aztaque-mecan]; Tizayuca; Tlauanapa [Tlallanapan]; Tepepulco; Cempuallan; Coyoc; Oztotltlatlahucan; Achichitlacohyocan [Achichilacachocan].[41]

The corresponding list in the *Anales de Cuauhtitlan* is almost the same as that in Motolinía; it does not include Cuauhtlatzinco or Cempohuallan, but adds Tetliz-taca.[42]

The economic contribution, as it is described, was basically agricultural prod-ucts and the labor necessary for cultivation. As we have seen in discussing the cities governed by kings, firewood for the palace was the obligation of these cities dur-ing half the year. This source now adds that the subject towns gave firewood the other half of the year, and also that firewood for the temples was the obligation of "others," who are not named. According to a passage in Torquemada, they would probably be the young priests of the temples, while the firewood for the palace would be contributed by the young men of the telpochcalli (youths' house).[43]

Together with Motolinía's "Memorial," Ixtlilxochitl is the source that gives the most information on the organization of the peasant towns and the tribute they paid. His most useful report, in the "Historia chichimeca," is an account of the reor-ganization of the Acolhuacan by Nezahualcoyotl after his victory over the Tepanecs.

First Nezahualcoyotl restored a number of kings to their positions of author-ity. Along with the names of the kings and their cities, Ixtlilxochitl adds that Neza-hualcoyotl appropriated certain towns for himself: "Coatepec, Itztapalocan and others located in that area," and also "Xaltocan, Papalotlan and others." Later he explains that all the rest of the land was divided into eight tribute districts (calpix-cazgos). For each one of these Ixtlilxochitl gives the name of the calpixque, his place of residence, and the number of towns and villages he was in charge of, al-though without giving their names. Six of these calpixcazgos supplied the palace with food during a certain number of days. After listing the calpixques, Ixtlilxo-chitl adds: "This was what belonged to Nezahualcoyotl, which was the royal pat-rimony (*realengo*), without counting more than 160 villages and hamlets that he dis-tributed to his sons, relatives, and meritorious persons."[44]

But it is not clear whether "this" refers only to the towns that Nezahualcoyotl put under stewards or to these towns together with those that he appropriated. Two of the latter (Coatepec and Itztapallocan) were in one of the calpixcazgos (Tetitlan), but others (Xaltocan and Papalotlan) are not mentioned. It is possible that they were included in other calpixcazgos, since Ixtlilxochitl does not list all the towns included in each one. In the more concise account of this same topic in his *Sumaria relación*, Ixtlilxochitl states that Nezahualcoyotl, after restoring the kings, kept for his chamber (*recámara*) the towns of Cohuatepec, Iztapalocan, Xaltocan,

Tepepolco, Cempohuallan, Aztaquemecan, Ahuatepec, Axapochco, Oztoticpac, Tizayocan and many other towns that he founded. In each one of them he put a calpixque to be in charge of collecting the tribute.[45]

Thus this account of Nezahualcoyotl's organization of his realm combines into one category, that of his chamber, all those towns that were direct dependencies of the king of Tetzcoco (and not of the kings subordinate to Tetzcoco). This includes the towns that, according to the "Historia chichimeca," the king had appropriated for himself (*adjudicó para sí*) as well as the calpixcazgos of the royal patrimony (de realengo).[46] However, in other passages the expression "towns of the chamber" implies a closer relationship with the monarch. Thus, in his discussion of the system of land tenure, Ixtlilxochitl defines the palace lands (*tecpantlalli*) as "lands belonging to the palaces and chamber of the kings or lords, and the natives settled on them were called tecpanpouhque, which means people belonging to the chamber and palace of those kings and lords."[47]

Probably he uses recámara with this meaning of tecpantlalli when he states that the towns of Calpollalpan, Mazaapan, Yahualiuhcan, Atenco, and Tzihuinquilocan would pertain to the king's chamber, after having said that Nezahualcoyotl "had assigned five lots of land, the most fertile of those near the city, where for his pleasure and entertainment people work his fields, and he personally was present for their improvement, as was the case in Atenco, near the lake, and in the towns of Papalotlan, Calpolalpan, Mazaapan, and Yahualiuhcan."[48]

As we have seen, according to Motolinía, in the towns of tenant farmers the king not only received tribute but also owned many parcels of land that the people cultivated for him. It seems that when this distinction is made, "realengo" refers to the royal lands (*tlatocatlalli* or *tlatocamilli*), and lands of the chamber ("recámara") are those of the palace (tecpantlalli).[49]

The towns that Nezahualcoyotl took for himself when he reorganized his kingdom present a situation halfway between the cities ruled by their own kings and the calpixcazgos of peasants. Coatepec, Itztapallocan, Xaltocan, and Papalotlan are mentioned in the "Historia chichimeca" together with the cities whose kings were restored, because formerly they had been ruled by their own kings or had been subject to other kings, not to the king of Tetzcoco. To say that Nezahualcoyotl took them for himself or kept them for his recámara indicates that he removed their former rulers and made the towns part of the domain of Tetzcoco, in the same sense in which he uses the phrase "de realengo." Veytia, in speaking of these cities, says that they had been made crown property.[50] Nezahualcoyotl's action in regard to these cities is understandable, for the kings he deposed had sided with the Tepanecs.[51]

As told in the relación geográfica of Coatepec, during the reigns of Moteuczoma and Nezahualcoyotl, because the successor to the rulership of Coatepec was very young, the two kings designated two captains, natives of the city, "one a noble and the other of middle rank," who governed for twenty-two years. When the young man came of age, since he was not considered capable of governing, the same two kings chose a relative of the young king, "a very valiant captain," to govern with him.[52] Thus, although the local dynasty was not banished, the ruler was put in a subordinate position, with captains named by two kings of the Empire who in effect governed the town.

In Xaltocan the local dynasty of the old Otomi kingdom survived with local rulers whose marriages to Tenochca princesses suggest that they were subordinate to Tenochtitlan.[53] In addition, Xaltocan is one of the towns depicted on the same page as Citlaltepec (17v) in the Codex Mendoza. However, according to the Tetzcoca sources, Tetzcoco also had tributaries there. Other areas in the vicinity of Xaltocan were also shared by the three capitals of the Empire.[54]

There is information on only one king of Papalotlan, who ruled at the time of Techotlalatzin, Nezahualcoyotl's grandfather.[55] Nothing is said about its rulers under the Empire. This is not unusual, since Nezahualcoyotl had appropriated the town for himself. The local ruler was probably either removed or put in a subordinate position, as was the case in Coatepec.

The Calpixcazgos in the Basin

Table 6-3 presents the eight calpixcazgos organized by Nezahualcoyotl. The data in the second column are literal quotations from Ixtlilxochitl's text. The language is somewhat ambiguous in some instances (numbers 2 and 3); the number of towns in each calpixcazgo could be understood to mean all the settlements in the district or only those in addition to the steward's place of residence.

The stewards were in charge of collecting tribute and provisioning the palace. Ixtlilxochitl lists the amounts of foodstuffs needed for seventy days, provided by the steward of the first calpixcazgo, Tetzcoco; we can assume that the other calpixcazgos paid similar goods. The total number of days covered by the six calpixcazgos that supplied the palace comes to 365 days, but it is not clear how they could have been divided into two equal halves as other sources state.[56] The last two calpixcazgos did not provide food. Perhaps they supplied goods of some other kind, such as cloth and other craft products, or domestic service, or they may have paid tribute to other institutions and not to the palace. The six calpixcazgos that supplied the palace were in the central zone of the Acolhuacan, near Tetzcoco, or in the vicinity of Otompan. Of the other two, Tetitlan was in the southern end of the realm and Tecpilpan in the extreme north. Both were near the frontiers with Tlaxcallan or Metztitlan; they might have provided men and supplies for the frontier garrisons.

TABLE 6-3.

Tribute Districts (Calpixcazgos) Established by Nezahualcoyotl

Residence of the steward	Dependencies	Name of steward	Number of days to provision the palace
1. Tetzcoco	with its barrios and villages	Matlalaca	70
2. Atenco	which was the part of the city near the lake with all its towns and villages that were altogether eleven	Tochtli	70
3. Tepepolco	with all its towns and hamlets subject to it, that were altogether thirteen	Coxcoch	70
4. Axapochco	with all its hamlets and villages, that were another thirteen	Tlemati	45
5. Cuauhtlatzinco	that had twenty-seven villages and hamlets	Ixotl	65
6. Ahuatepec	with eight other villages and hamlets that were were subject to it	Cuauhtecolotl	45
7. Tetitlan	in which are the towns of Coatepec, Itztapallocan, Tlapechhuacan and their villages	Papalotl	—
8. Tecpilpan	with eight other villages and hamlets that were united with it	Cuateconhua	—

SOURCE: Ixtlilxochitl 1975–77, 2:89–90.

It is not clear how Ixtlilxochitl's eight calpixcazgos relate to his list of "towns of the king's chamber" or to Motolinía's list of towns of tenants. There is a great coincidence of place names, but the description of the calpixcazgos gives only the names of the residences of the stewards, and it is not certain whether they would include the towns in Motolinía's list that are missing in the description of the calpix-cazgos. Table 6-4 compares the lists in Motolinía's "Memorial tetzcocano" and the *Anales de Cuauhtitlan*, which contain the most toponyms, with the data Ixtlilxochitl gives on the calpixcazgos, the towns adjudicated to the king, and the towns of the king's chamber. Map 6-2 shows all the towns in the table.[57] In the following discussion the eight calpixcazgos are numbered in the sequence of Ixtlilxochitl's list as in Tables 6-3 and 6-4.

TABLE 6-4.
Towns of Tenants and Calpixcazgos as in Motolinía and Ixtlilxochitl

Towns of tenants*	Calpixcazgos†	Towns taken by the king‡	Towns of the recámara§	Fields of the king§
	1. Tetzcoco			
	2. Atenco		4. Atenco	1. Atenco
1. Coatepec 1	7. Tetitlan	1. Coatepec		
2. Itztapallocan 2	(with Coatepec,	2. Itztapalloca		
	Itztapallocan,	and others		
	Tlapechuacan)			
3. Papalotlan 3		4. Papalotlan		2. Papalotlan
4. Xaltocan 4		3. Xaltocan		
5. Ahuatepec 5	6. Ahuatepec			
6. Oztoticpan 6				
7. Cuauhtlantzinco 0	5. Cuauhtlatzinco			
8. Axapochco 7	4. Axapochco			
9. Aztaquemecan 8				
10. Tizayocan 9				
11. Tlallanapan 10				
12. Tepepolco 11	3. Tepepolco			
	8. Tecpilpan			
13. Cempohuallan 0				
14. Coyoac 12				
15. Oztotlatlauhcan 13				
16. Achichilacachocan 14				
0. Tetliztaca 15				
			1. Calpullalpan	3. Calpullalpan
			2. Mazaapan	4. Mazaapan
			3. Yahualiuhcan	5. Yahualiuhcan
			5. Tzihuinquillocan	

NOTE: Each toponym is numbered according to the order in which it appears in the source indicated. Other lists of sujetos of Tetzcoco (Torquemada 1975–83, 1:232; Ixtlilxochitl 1975–77, 2:114) do not distinguish between cities with kings and towns of tenants or calpixcazgos; see below about the two parts of the Acolhuacan, Tables 6-5 and 6-6.
*Motolinía 1971:394–95; AC, 64. The number that precedes a toponym gives the order in Motolinía; the number following the toponym gives the order in the AC. A zero indicates that the source does not mention that town.
†Ixtlilxochitl 1975–77, 2:89–90.
‡Ixtlilxochitl 1975–77, 2:89.
§Ixtlilxochitl 1975–77, 2:114.

　　1. Tetzcoco "with its barrios and hamlets" is how Ixtlilxochitl defines the first calpixcazgo. Since Atenco occupied the lake shore near the city, the calpixcazgo of Tetzcoco must have been located in the foothills and in the mountains, in two of the parcialidades described by Vetancurt.[58] The first, which includes Tetzcotzinco, he labels as "del Monte"; the other, fourth in his list, is in the area of Papalotlan. Towards the north Tetzcoco bordered on Acolman and Teotihuacan, but it is not clear whether the estancias of that area pertained to the calpixcazgo of Tetzcoco or that of Atenco.

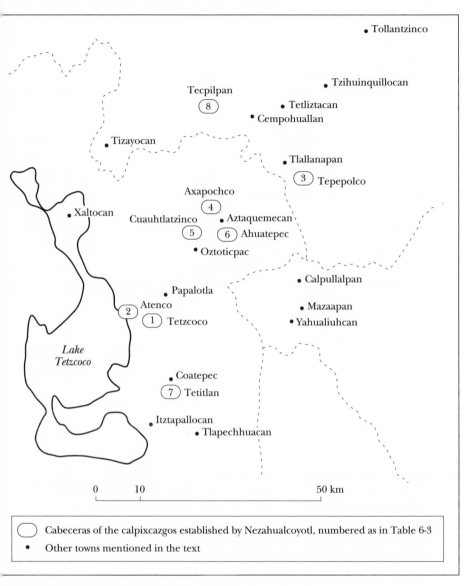

MAP 6–2. The tributaries of Tetzcoco within its own domain

According to Pomar's relación, Tetzcoco's territory extended from the lake to more than ten leagues into the mountains; its boundaries would therefore be beyond Calpollalpan on the Tlaxcallan frontier.[59] Many sources describe Calpollalpan as pertaining to Tetzcoco, and none say that it had a king of its own.[60] As we have seen, Ixtlilxochitl speaks of Calpollalpan as a town in the royal chamber of Nezahualcoyotl in which that ruler owned cultivated fields.[61] Pomar states that Nezahualcoyotl divided the land among people from all six barrios of Tetzcoco, who were sent to settle on these lands.[62] In 1545, Don Antonio Pimentel declared in his will that in his lifetime an arrangement was made as to the amount of land in Calpollalpan that was to be given to the ruler, but the people of the six parcialidades had not given over the lands according to the agreement.[63] Thus, it seems that although Nezahualcoyotl gave the lands in Calpollalpan to settlers from six parcialidades of Tetzcoco, some of them would be royal lands. After the Spanish Conquest there was a dispute about this land that resulted in the agreement Don Antonio refers to, which had not been carried out.

Don Martín, a nephew of the king of Tetzcoco, Don Pedro de Alvarado Coanacochtzin, declares in a letter that Cortés had given to Coanacochtzin lands on the border of Hueyotlipan, Tliliuhquitepec, and Calpollalpan which are "wastelands where they fought and which belonged to no one but were unoccupied." According to other data, the battlegrounds for the so-called flower wars were between Cuauhtepec and Ocelotepec, beyond Calpollalpan in the vicinity of Hueyotlipan, which pertained to Tlaxcallan.[64]

Two other towns near Calpollalpan are mentioned as containing royal lands and fields: Yahualiuhcan and Mazapan.[65] In both towns Techotlalatzin settled Otomis from the Tepanec kingdom and the "province" of Cuahuacan who had fled during the reign of Tezozomoc.[66] Probably Zoltepec (present-day San Felipe Zultepec, Tlaxcala) was in this calpixcazgo. The "Pintura de México" lists it next to Calpollalpan, and other references in Ixtlilxochitl and Muñoz Camargo locate it in the same area.[67]

2. Atenco was the second calpixcazgo in the area of Tetzcoco. It included eleven towns and villages in "the part of the city towards the lake," but Ixtlilxochitl gives only the name of Atenco, which would be the cabecera, or residence of the steward.[68] A lawsuit from 1573 between the commoners of Atenco and the principals of Tetzcoco provides valuable information on the organization of this calpixcazgo.[69] The litigation concerned lands in the area of present-day San Salvador Atenco, but the statements presented name many other places, making it possible to delineate the extent of the calpixcazgo. The name of Atenco is used with two meanings: one is the total calpixcazgo, and the other, its cabecera. The latter, in turn, comprised several places where the disputed lands were located, near the former pleasure park of the kings of Tetzcoco, in Acatetelco.[70]

The principals maintained that Nezahualpilli owned all the land in the district (*pago*) of Atenco, which was approximately two leagues long and three-quarters of a league wide. As Hicks has pointed out, this is a very large area, much greater than the lands in litigation.[71] Probably the dimensions given were not those of the district of Atenco but of the whole calpixcazgo. This idea is supported by the fact that the principals of Tetzcoco brought forth as witnesses individuals from ten barrios, who declared that they had been tenants (terrazgueros) and had paid rent for their land.[72] The towns that comprised the calpixcazgo can thus be identified. Six of the ten barrios of tenant farmers mentioned in the lawsuit are in the third of Vetancurt's parcialidades, of which San Salvador Atenco was the cabecera: Santa María Atenco, San Francisco Acuezcomac Atenco, Santa María Magdalena Panohuayan, San Miguel Tocuillan,[73] San Pablo Calmimilolco, and San Miguel Chiconcohuac. Three others are in the second parcialidad, headed by Tezoyocan: San Lucas Huitzilhuacan, Santa María Cuanallan, and Reyes Tetitlan.[74] The tenth, San Cristóbal Nexquipayac, is in the fifth parcialidad.[75]

Most of the towns of tenant farmers that figure in this lawsuit are along the shore, thus agreeing with Ixtlilxochitl's statement that the calpixcazgo of Atenco was near the lake. They occupy all of this area from Tocuillan, near the border with Huexotla, to Atenco and beyond as far as Nexquipayac, on the boundaries with Tecciztlan and Tepechpan. Vetancurt also includes in his fifth parcialidad Santa María Iztapa, which is not mentioned in the lawsuit. Cuauhtla and Huitzilhuacan are farther inland, to the north of Chiauhtlan and Tezoyocan, cities ruled by their own kings that remained surrounded by the territory of Tetzcoco. Therefore this calpixcazgo of Tetzcoco bordered upon Tepechpan and Acolman, as the relación geográfica of these towns affirms.[76]

This interpretation agrees with the extent of the calpixcazgo given above. The distance from the southernmost town, Tocuillan, to the most northern is actually about two leagues. The width of three-quarters of a league must refer to the east-west extension of the coastal strip. Only Cuanallan and Huitzilhuacan, in the interior, do not fit this description well. The territory of the Atenco calpixcazgo included several towns, and it is not easy to distinguish in the lawsuit when the statements refer to the land or the calpixcazgo as a whole and when to the cabecera, also called Atenco. It is possible that, since the calpixcazgo of Atenco is said to have occupied the lake shore, only the barrios from Nexquipayac to Tocuillan would be part of it, while Cuanallan and Huitzilhuacan, in the interior, would be part of the calpixcazgo of "Tezcoco with its barrios and villages."

Several of the witnesses for the principals of Tetzcoco said they had been in the service of previous rulers or governors of Tetzcoco as calpixques (stewards), or as a *mandón* (barrio official) or *alguacil* (constable) who went to Atenco to collect the tribute. They were from the barrios of San Juan Mexicapan, San Pablo Huitznahuac, San Pedro Colhuacan, Mazatlan, and Oztoticpac and therefore not from Atenco but from the barrios in the center of Tetzcoco.[77]

3. Tepepolco may have included Tlallanapan, frequently written Tlan-alapan,[78] one of the towns of tenant farmers that Motolinía writes about. Apan was probably the unnamed sujeto of Tepepolco that Don Hernando Pimentel refers to in his memorial.[79] Although the calpixcazgo of Tepepolco contributed to the provisioning of the palace, its position close to the frontier with Tlaxcallan suggests that its inhabitants also gave military service.[80]

4. Axapochco, 5. Cuauhtlatzinco, and 6. Ahuatepec were the three calpixcazgos located in the Valley of Otompan, the region that Ixtlilxochitl calls La Campiña. Several towns subject to Tetzcoco were in one or another of these calpixcazgos: Oztoticpac must be the town that Ixtlilxochitl describes as a sujeto of Otompan,[81] as was Aztaquemecan, near Axapochco.[82] Nopaltepec, listed in the "Pintura de México," was a sujeto of Acolman, although it was located north of Otompan.[83] The location of Coyoac is difficult to determine; it may have been the San Juan Cuyoa that was subject to Tepechpan.[84] Quatlaeca and Quauhtlat-lauhca, which Ixtlilxochitl names among the towns of La Campiña, have not been identified.[85] In the area of these three calpixcazgos there were also several towns that paid tribute to Tenochtitlan; some paid tribute to both capitals (see p. 117).

7. Tetitlan was one of the cabeceras of Coatepec, according to the relación geográfica of this town.[86] The territory under its steward included Coatepec, Itztapallocan, Tlapechhuacan,[87] and other towns whose names are not given.

Coatepec and other towns in the Tetitlan calpixcazgo were probably taken from Chalco by conquest.[88] According to Tezozomoc, Tlapechhuacan was one of the towns where Moteuczoma Ilhuicamina and other Mexica nobles were given lands after the war with Chalco.[89] The kings of Teotihuacan and Tepetlaoztoc also had lands there.[90] It seems that the towns in Chalco that paid tribute to Tetzcoco were part of the calpixcazgo of Tetitlan.

In contrast with what he says about Cuauhnahuac, Ixtlilxochitl says nothing about the naming of a steward in charge of Tetzcoco's holdings in the Chalco region; however, he includes Chalco among the towns that paid tribute to Tetzcoco, and the description of the palace in Tetzcoco mentions rooms for storing the tribute from Chalco.[91] Several lords of the Acolhuacan had possessions in Chalco. The king of Teotihuacan, Quetzalmamalitzin, received from Nezahualcoyotl "war lands" (*yaotlalpan, tepehuallalpan*), most of which were in Chalco: Mazahuacan, Calte-coyan, Ecatzinco, Tlapechhuacan, Ayahualolco, and Chalco quauhtlalpan.[92] The king of Tepetlaoztoc also had lands in Tlapechhuacan, Ecatzinco, and Caltecoyan,[93] and Axoquentzin, a prince of Tetzcoco, was given lands in the Chalco region that he had helped to conquer.[94] In his memorial, Don Hernando Pimentel lists "part of Chalco" among the areas that his ancestors won through warfare, in which they had land and tenants. Chicualoapan is included in another group of towns where "they held tracts of land won by personal merit."[95] As in the case of Tlapechhuacan, all these towns could have been part of the Tetitlan calpixcazgo.

8. Tecpilpan, at the time that its relación geográfica was written, was one of the four cabeceras congregated in Cempohuallan; the other three were Tzacuallan, Tlaquilpan, and Cempohuallan itself.[96] The name Tecpilpan does not appear in other lists of the towns of tenant farmers, but it is found in the "Pintura de México" in a group of towns that corresponds to the list of calpixcazgos given by Ixtlilxochitl in his "Historia chichimeca."[97]

The calpixcazgo of Tecpilpa must have included the nearby towns that, according to other sources, paid tribute to Tetzcoco. Tetliztaca, near Cempohuallan, because they were poor people, gave cloaks made of henequen as tribute; "the king of Tetzcoco used them only for service within his house."[98] Oztotlatlauhca, mentioned by Motolinía, was an estancia of Epazoyocan, today a well-known town of the same name in the state of Hidalgo.[99] Tezontepec, listed in the "Pintura de México,"[100] is today La Villa de Tezontepec, Hidalgo. Achichilacachocan is difficult to locate precisely.[101]

In this region there were also several towns that paid tribute to Tenochtitlan and formed the tributary province headed by the acolmecatl calpixqui. Some were also in the lists of tributaries of Tetzcoco: Ahuatepec, Aztaquemecan, Tizayocan, and Cempohuallan. Others appear only in Durán. Tecpilpan itself is counted among the towns that became part of the domain of Tenochtitlan;[102] perhaps this explains why it is not included more often among the towns subject to Tetzcoco. Probably all these towns paid tribute to both capitals.[103]

The Calpixcazgo of Tollantzinco in La Sierra

The great Acolhua kingdom of Tetzcoco, that is, the region in which the local kings were directly subordinate to the great king of Tetzcoco, included the Valley of Tollantzinco and the eastern slopes of the Central Plateau, in the area called La Sierra. In this region there are none of the so-called towns of tenants, all of which are in the eight calpixcazgos in the Basin established when Nezahualcoyotl reorganized his kingdom. Another calpixcazgo was founded later in Tollantzinco. After the war against the Tepanecs, Nezahualcoyotl had restored to his position the king of Tollantzinco, but the latter rebelled again and burned down the forts where Nezahualcoyotl had stationed garrisons (in Maçanacazco, Tlayacac, and Chiquiuhtepec), killing all the soldiers in the presidios. Thus provoked, Nezahualcoyotl raised a large army and reconquered the area. As before, the king was allowed to continue as ruler and as one of the fourteen grandees of the realm, but tribute in goods and services was imposed and a steward installed to see that the people complied with their obligations, "so that from then on they were subjugated and oppressed," as Ixtlilxochitl tells the story. Nezahualcoyotl took further action in that area, establishing a town (called Tzihuinquilocan) where the presidios had been, sending people from the city of Tetzcoco to settle there.[104]

It is not known which towns within Tollantzinco had to produce this tribute and services. Ixtlilxochitl and Torquemada, in their accounts of the calpixcazgo of Tollantzinco, treat this region as a tributary unit of the same kind as the two halves of the Acolhuacan—that is, as an area that includes both cities and peasant towns. While Ixtlilxochitl specifies tribute in clothing and beans plus labor in the forests and gardens, Torquemada—in addition to payments (*rentas*) that he does not specify— states that Tollantzinco's obligation was to give military service and also to serve in the government in Tetzcoco,[105] which was the usual obligation for cities governed by their own kings. The administrative service given in Tetzcoco would of course fall to the nobility of Tollantzinco, while the tribute in clothing, beans, and labor as gardeners would be the duty of the peasants. When Ixtlilxochitl relates the founding of Tzihuinquillocan, where the presidios had been, he notes that it was part of Nezahualcoyotl's patrimonial lands.[106] In addition, Don Hernando Pimentel includes Tollantzinco among the towns gained in war by his ancestors, "where they had tenants and lands" (see p. 59). Therefore, the social composition of La Sierra was similar to that of the Acolhuacan and included cities, towns of peasant tributaries, and royal lands.

However, the position of Tzihuinquillocan within the calpixcazgos of the Acolhuacan raises doubts; as we have seen, those of Tepepolco and Tecpilpan, in the Basin, extended as far as the vicinity of Tzihuinquillocan. In the description of the two halves of the Acolhuacan, Tzihuinquillocan is listed in the northern half before the names of towns in La Sierra begin, which seems to indicate that it was part of the calpixcazgos of the Basin. Nevertheless, the quotation from Ixtlilxochitl favors the assumption that it was included in the calpixcazgo of Tollantzinco. Macanacazco (Maçanacazco), Tlayacac, and Chiquiuhtepec have not been identified, and there is no information on their status after the calpixcazgo of Tollantzinco was established. In the Codex Mendoza the province of Atotonilco el Grande, which included Tollantzinco and Tzihuinquillocan, coincided only in part with the calpixcazgo that Nezahualcoyotl established in Tollantzinco (see p. 120).

The Two Parts of the Acolhuacan

In the material provided thus far, the payment of tribute and services given is presented in terms of two kinds of territorial entities: the cities ruled by their own kings and the peasant towns under the stewardship of a calpixque. But other reports describe an organization based on two groups of settlements, both including cities and peasant towns, that functioned as teams that alternated in providing tribute and service. The best information on this is in Torquemada and Ixtlilxochitl.

Torquemada reports the expenses of Nezahualcoyotl's palace on the basis of this king's account books ("los libros de su gasto"), authenticated by his grandson, Don Antonio Pimentel. After giving the income of the palace, Torquemada lists twenty-nine towns that provisioned the palace. They include what other sources define as either cities with kings or as villages of tenants, and they were divided into two groups. Fourteen towns served half a year: Tetzcoco, Huexotla, Coatlichan, Chiauhtlan, Tezoyocan, Papalotlan, Tepetlaoztoc, Acolman, Tepechpan, Chiauhtlan (*sic pro* Chiucnauhtlan), Xaltocan, Chimalhuacan, Itztapallocan, and Coatepec; and fifteen served the other half a year: Otompan, Teotihuacan, Aztaquemecan, Cempohuallan, Axapochco, Tlallanapan, Tepepolco, Tizayocan, Ahuatepec, Oztoticpac, Quauhtlatzinco, Coyoac, Oztotlatlauhcan, Achichilacachocan, and Tetliztacan. People from these towns brought firewood, charcoal, mats, and other things for the royal household and also did the sweeping, carried water, and performed other services. They also cultivated fields and supplied maize, although all the other provinces subject to Tetzcoco also gave a large part of the maize consumed.[107]

In the "Historia chichimeca" Ixtlilxochitl also gives a division into two groups or teams, which include both cities and peasant villages, almost identical to that of Torquemada, but the economic function he attributes to them is different. Ixtlilxochitl had similar documentation at his disposal, since he says he had used the writings of Nezahualpilli's sons.[108] His data are included in a description of Nezahualcoyotl's palaces that names the various buildings, pleasure gardens, forests, and cultivated fields. The king designated for himself five tracts of fertile land in Atenco, Papalotlan, Calpollalpan, Mazaapan, and Yahualiuhcan. For the service, adornment, and cleaning of the king's palaces were assigned Huexotla, Coatlichan, Coatepec, Chimalhuacan, Itztapallocan, Tepetlaoztoc, Acolman, Tepechpan, Chiucnauhtlan, Tezoyocan, Chiauhtlan, Papalotla, Xaltocan, and Chalco, which served half the year; the other half-year was the responsibility of the towns of La Campiña—Otompan, Teotihuacan, Tepepolco, Cempoalan, Aztaquemecan, Ahuatepec, Axapochco, Oztotipac, Tizayocan, Tlallanapan, Coyoac, Cuatlatlauhcan, Quatlaeca (*sic*), and Cuauhtlatzinco. The towns assigned to the king's chamber were Calpollalpan, Mazaapan, Yahualiuhcan, Atenco, and Tzihuinquilocan. For labor in the woods and gardens, Tollantzinco, Quauhchinanco, Xicotepec, Pahuatlan, Yauhtepec, Tepechco, Ahuacayocan, and Quauhnahuac, with their sujetos, took turns sending workers, each town taking care of a particular garden, forest, or cultivated field.[109]

Table 6-5 compares the composition of the two tributary halves according to Torquemada and Ixtlilxochitl. Evidently the two writers are describing almost ex-

TABLE 6-5.

The Two Tributary Parts of the Acolhuacan
According to Torquemada and Ixtlilxochitl

| First half | | Second half (La Campiña) | |
Torquemada*	Ixtlilxochitl†	Torquemada*	Ixtlilxochitl†
1. Tetzcoco‡		1. Otompan‡	1
2. Huexotla‡	1	2. Teotihuacan‡	2
3. Coatlichan‡	2	3. Aztaquemecan	5
4. Chiauhtlan‡	11	4. Cempohuallan	4
5. Tezoyocan‡	10	5. Axapochco	7
6. Papalotlan	12	6. Tlallanapan	10
7. Tepetlaoztoc‡	6	7. Tepepolco	3
8. Acolman‡	7	8. Tizayocan	9
9. Tepechpan‡	8	9. Ahuatepec	6
10. Chiucnauhtlan‡	9	10. Oztoticpac	8
11. Xaltocan	13	11. Cuauhtlatzinco	14
12. Chimalhuacan‡	4	12. Coyoac	11
13. Itztapallocan	5	13. Oztotlatlauhca	12. Cuauhtlatlauhcan
14. Coatepec	3	14. Achichilacachocan	
	14. Chalco	15. Tetliztaca	
			13. Cuatlaeca

*Torquemada 1975–83, 1:232. Torquemada has Chiauhtlan in both fourth and tenth place in the list; I have corrected this by putting Chiucnauhtlan in tenth place.
†Ixtlilxochitl 1975–77, 2:114. With the exception of the toponyms included in the table, those that Ixtlilxochitl gives are the same as those of Torquemada and are indicated only by the numbers of their places in the list.
‡Places identified as cities with kings. (See Table 6-1).

actly the same groups of towns, but the functions assigned to the groups in the two writers' descriptions of the contributions made are very different. Torquemada says nothing about the obligations of the cities ruled by kings that Motolinía mentions—that is, military service and labor for public works. Instead, it appears that the services that Torquemada notes were part of the obligations of the peasant towns according to Motolinía and also Ixtlilxochitl in his description of the calpixcazgos. The text from Ixtlilxochitl just quoted, on the other hand, credits the two teams only with the adornment of and service in the palaces and gardens. One might think that this organization into teams would be the basic structure for the accounts of both Torquemada and Ixtlilxochitl, but there would have been a somewhat different organization for each kind of contribution, perhaps with different groups of tributaries and stewards. This would explain the divergence between the information incorporated into the works of these two chroniclers.

Although it is not possible to identify completely this description of the two halves for provisioning the palace with what Ixtlilxochitl says about the towns of the royal chamber and the eight calpixcazgos, there are some well-defined similarities.

The first half comprises the cities with kings (except Otompan and Teotihuacan) together with those which Nezahualcoyotl appropriated for himself without restoring their kings. The second half is composed of all the peasant towns plus the two cities, Otompan and Teotihuacan, that administered them and were situated in the same area. But if this division into two halves served for organizing the supplying of provisions in two halves of the year, the data do not agree with what Ixtlilxochitl says about the calpixcazgos that provisioned the palace. Table 6-3 gives the number of days assigned to each calpixcazgo; the periods of each one—three of 70, one of 65, and two of 45 days—add up to a year. One would expect them to be grouped into two halves of the year, one half assigned to three calpixcazgos that would contribute 70, 70, and 45 days, and the other half to the three remaining calpixcazgos, which would be responsible for 70, 65, and 45 days. This would produce two half-years, one of 185 days and the other of 180 days. However it is not like that. In their ordering of the calpixcazgos, both Torquemada and Ixtlilxochitl put Tepepolco, Axapochco, Cuauhtlatzinco, and Ahuatepec in the same half, headed by Otompan; the days that they provisioned the palace according to Ixtlilxochitl add up to 225 days. In the other half there remain only Tetzcoco and Atenco, which supplied it for 140 days.

These two parts were geographical entities as well as social and economic ones. The first, with Tetzcoco as cabecera, included all of the southern section of the Acolhuacan in which are found Tetzcoco and the principal Acolhua cities—Coatlichan and Huexotla—and extended from the lake to the frontier with Huexotzinco and Tlaxcallan. It also comprised all the other cities situated farther north near the shore—that is, Tepechpan, Acolman, and Chiucnauhtlan. Therefore, it included almost all the cities in the kingdom, with a population that was predominantly Nahuatl-speaking. Only in reference to Yahualiuhcan and Mazaapan, in the mountains east of Tetzcoco, and in the estancias of Tetitlan, near Coatepec, is there any mention of Otomi-speaking people.

The second part took in the Valley of Otompan and the area north of the Cerro Gordo to the border of the kingdom of Tollantzinco. The only cities ruled by their own kings were Otompan and Teotihuacan, or, according to Don Hernando Pimentel, only Otompan, whose king governed the peasant inhabitants. From the social point of view, therefore, it was a region of peasants, most of whom were Otomi-speaking, together with a few small groups who spoke a Chichimec language.

In describing this division of the Acolhua kingdom into two parts, Ixtlilxochitl uses the expression La Campiña in referring to the second group of towns that provided service in the royal palaces. While the towns near the court served during half a year, the other half-year was the responsibility of the towns of La Campiña, named above. On another occasion he uses the same term, La Campiña, when speaking of its two cities in his account of the reorganization of the kingdom brought about by Nezahualcoyotl. He gave to Quetzalmamalitzin, king of Teotihuacan, the title of captain-general of the kingdom of the distinguished people (gente ilustre) and ordered that all litigation concerning the nobility (caballeros y gente noble) of the towns of La Campiña would be decided in Teotihuacan. In Otompan he made Quecholtecpantzin the ruler, giving him the same title, but of the commoners, and he was to settle the affairs of the common people of La Campiña.[110] Thus, rather than make a territorial division between Teotihuacan and Otompan, Nezahualcoyotl divided authority over the whole area between the two kings. Both governed in the same region, one with jurisdiction over the nobility and the other over the commoners, at least insofar as the administration of justice was concerned.

In another account of Nezahualcoyotl's reorganization of his kingdom he refers to the same area of Teotihuacan and Otompan as "all that part, that was of peasants, and different from the manners and clothing of Tetzcoco."[111] This characterization of La Campiña refers to the reign of Techotlalatzin, who—after Xaltocan was defeated by the Tepanecs—took the lands bordering Tetzcoco and ordered the Otomis from then on not to live within the cities and towns, but in villages in the mountains. He gave them Otompan for a cabecera, and as ruler a nobleman (*caballero*) called Cuauhquezaltzin. "This was how the Otomis ended, for Techotlalatzin could not accept that this nation, nor any of their descendents, should live within the republics, because these people were low and miserable."[112]

The Nahuatl terms that probably correspond to La Campiña are found in the Tratado de Teotihuacan. The region under the king of Otompan is called in Spanish "los pueblos llamados de la milpa" (the towns called of the maize field); the Nahuatl says *altepetl momillacaitoa*, literally "the towns called of farm workers."[113] The Tratado also uses the expression *mayecapan*, "place of farm hands," which also occurs in the Mapa Quinatzin.[114] Both expressions agree with Ixtlilxochitl's definition of its inhabitants as Otomi peasants. The noun *milla* also calls to mind the name La Milpa, applied to the rural area of Xochimilco.

Gibson has pointed out how the dependencies of Teotihuacan, Acolman, and Tepechpan were intermingled in the rural area north of the Cerro Gordo.[115] Ixtlilxochitl, in his account of how Tezozomoc of Azcapotzalco organized the administration of his conquests in the Tetzcoca kingdom, notes that the cities in the southern part of the Acolhuacan held many rural settlements in La Campiña. Tezozomoc took for himself Coatlichan, with all that pertained to it, and divided the rest between Tlacateotzin, lord of Tlatelolco, who was given Huexotla, and Chimalpopoca, king of Mexico, who was given the city of Tetzcoco. Ixtlilxochitl emphasizes the many towns and villages in the area and notes the intermingling of the possessions of some of the major towns. Coatlichan, which Tezozomoc claimed, at that time contained many towns of the Acolhuas, extending from the boundaries of Chalco to those of Tollantzinco, among which were Otompan, Tepepolco, and Cempohuallan. Huexotla, the other cabecera, "likewise had many towns intermingled with those of the city of Tetzcoco and of Coatlichan." The territory of the city of Tetzcoco that was given to Chimalpopoca is described simply as the rest of the towns within the area subject to its labor draft (*llamamiento*).[116] This region of La Campiña also included towns assigned to Tetzcoca nobles, and several towns in the same area paid tribute to Tenochtitlan.[117]

After the death of Nezahualpilli the conflict for the succession between Ixtlilxochitl and Cacama led to the division of the kingdom. Cacama took the south, with Tetzcoco as his capital, and Ixtlilxochitl the north, with its cabecera in Otompan.[118] In later times, after the arrival of the Spaniards, Coanacoch, who succeded Cacama, and Ixtlilxochitl confirmed the division of the kingdom. Ixtlilxochitl kept the northern half, setting the boundaries along Tepetlaoztoc, Papaluca (Papalotlan), Tenayucan (Tezayocan), Chimanauhtla (Chiucnauhtlan), and Xaltocan, and made Otompan and Teotihuacan the cabeceras of that region.[119]

The division of the Acolhuacan into two halves merits comparison with the political-territorial categories in the Memorial of Don Hernando Pimentel, as in Table 6-6. Two of its categories, the first, of towns under Otompan, and the fifth, of towns under Tetzcoco, together comprise the first two categories of Motolinía's "Memorial tetzcocano": (1) cities ruled by their own kings, and (2) the towns of tenant farmers. However, the towns are combined in a different way; each group includes both cities and towns. Don Hernando's first category puts the city of Otompan together with several of the peasant towns, defined as towns dedicated to the service of the king of Tetzcoco. The fifth he describes as subject towns in the district of Tetzcoco that paid tribute to the city, but he does not specify the tribute; this category also includes both cities and peasant towns. The first six are cities, then follow five towns, and the last is another city. Thus, this is similar to the two halves that, according to Ixtlilxochitl and Torquemada, alternated in provisioning the palace and that included, each one, both cities and peasant towns.

Nevertheless, the distribution of cities and towns between the two halves according to Don Hernando Pimentel does not coincide with that of the other two writers, as shown in Table 6-6. His first half (or first category) contains only one city, Otompan; the other half (his fifth category) includes all the other cities. The distribution of peasant towns also differs from that of Ixtlilxochitl and Torquemada. The half headed by Otompan includes the four calpixcazgos that according to Ixtlilxochitl would have provisioned the palace during 225 days. The other half, headed by Tetzcoco, according to Don Hernando, does not include any of the

TABLE 6-6.

The Two Tributary Parts of the Acolhuacan
According to Torquemada and Pimentel

Torquemada*	Pimentel	
	Under Otompan (I)	Under Tetzcoco (V)†
1. Tetzcoco		
2. Huexotla		1. Huexotla
3. Coatlichan		2. Coatlichan
4. Chiauhtla		
5. Tezoyocan		
6. Papalotlan		9. Papalotlan
7. Tepetlaoztoc	6. Tepetlaoztoc	
8. Acolman		4. Acolman
9. Tepechpan		5. Tepechpan
10. Chiucnauhtlan		6. Chiucnauhtlan
11. Xaltocan		
12. Chimalhuacan		3. Chimalhuacan
13. Itztapallocan	9. Itztapallocan	
14. Coatepec	8. Coatepec	
1. Otompan	1. Otompan and its sujeto	
2. Teotihuacan		12. Teotihuacan
3. Aztaquemecan		
4. Cempohuallan		10. Cempohuallan
5. Axapochco	7. Axapochco	
6. Tlallanapan		8. Tlallanapan
7. Tepepolco	2. Tepepolco and its sujeto‡	
8. Tizayocan		7. Tezayuca (*sic*)§
9. Ahuatepec	3. Ahuatepec	
10. Oztoticpac		11. Oztotipac
11. Cuauhtlatzinco	4. Cuauhtlatzinco	
	5. Tzinquilucan [sic]	
12. Coyoac		
13. Oztotlatlauhca		
14. Achichilacachocan		
15. Tetliztaca		

*The parts that Ixtlilxochitl gives are almost the same. He adds Chalco in the first half, and in the second lists Cuauhtlatlauhcan instead of Oztotlatlauhca; also Achichilacachocan and Tetliztaca are missing, but Cuatlaeca is added (see Table 6-5).

†Although Pimentel defines them as neighbors of Tetzcoco, his text contains several towns in the Sierra not included in this table: Xicotepec, Pahuatlan, Tlacuiloltepec, and Papaloticpac.

‡Probably Apan (RG 7:173).

§It could also be identified as the city of Tezoyocan.

calpixcazgos, but must have contained those of Tetzcoco and Atenco. On the other hand, he includes Cempohuallan, Tlallanapan, and Oztoticpac, which are peasant towns in the Otompan half in the other sources. The Otompan half can be said to comprise only peasant towns together with the city that administered them, since—in contrast to Torquemada and Ixtlilxochitl—Don Hernando does not include Teotihuacan. Therefore, it is very similar to the category of peasant towns in Motolinía's "Memorial tetzcocano." But not all the peasant towns are included; some are in the half in which the cities predominate. In this respect Don Hernando differs from Motolinía more than Torquemada and Ixtlilxochitl. The division into two halves, as it is given in all the sources, always presents the problem of not agreeing with the teams of provisioners that Ixtlilxochitl gives in his list of calpixcazgos.[120]

Two important aspects of this situation could be the basis for the disagreements among the different sources. On the one hand, the frequent intermingling of territorial entities may have modified the division into two halves that geographically could be roughly defined as north and south. Coatlichan had some sujetos in the northern region, where Otompan, Tepepolco, and Cempohuallan are located, while Huexotla at one time had also received tribute from Otompan and its sujetos. It is then possible that some towns situated geographically in the region of Otompan might have been included in the teams supplying the palace as part of the southern half.

On the other hand, although all the sources describe a system for provisioning the palace that supposes the centralized organization of the Acolhua kingdom of Tetzcoco, the division of the kingdom between Ixtlilxochitl and Cacama must have affected the organization that concerns us. It is quite possible that changes were made in the allotment of certain peasant towns to the cities.

Kingdoms, Tributary Towns, and the Two Parts of the Acolhuacan in the Mapa Quinatzin

Motolinía's "Memorial tetzcocano" and the data in Ixtlilxochitl that agree with it are centered on the distinction between cities ruled by kings and peasant towns and the consequences of that distinction concerning kinds of tribute and services that they contributed. However, the data presented above—from Torquemada, Ixtlilxochitl, and Hernando Pimentel—show that the Acolhuacan was organized into two parts, or halves, each containing both cities and peasant towns. The Mapa Quinatzin presents in pictorial form all these data on the kings of the Acolhuacan, the category of settlements (with or without kings), and the presence of those whom Motolinía calls tenants (renteros).[121] This is done in such a way that it provides the key to understanding how the different lists of tributaries could have been prepared in the written sources that have been cited. Plate 2 of this pictorial document is a plan of the royal palace in Tetzcoco. The subordinate kings, each with his name's glyph, are represented in the patio. Outside of this patio, two series of towns are depicted, one on each side of the palace. The toponyms of the cities governed by kings are indicated by both a glyph and a legend; one glyph that is only half legible (that of Papalotlan) seems to be in the same style even though it did not have a king. The peasant towns are represented, as Motolinía describes them, by a mountain with a spade and have no toponymic glyph but only a legend that gives the name of the town. In one case there is no legend; in another it is illegible. The bottom edge of the page is torn so that it lacks what must have been the continuation of the two lines of toponyms as far as the palace entrance. Table 6-7 gives a schematic diagram of the palace as depicted on Plate 2 in the Mapa Quinatzin.

In order to describe how the kings and towns are positioned in this plan of the palace, we shall assume that the east is at the top of the page, as was usually the case in indigenous and Spanish maps of the sixteenth century. Therefore, we will speak of right or left as seen from the royal room (where Nezahualcoyotl and Nezahualpilli are depicted) looking towards the entrance that opens to the west. In this way right is north and left is south, as is said in Nahuatl. On the north, or right-hand side of the patio, are the kings of Otompan, Teotihuacan, Acolman, Tepechpan, Chiucnauhtlan, Tollantzinco, and Cuauhchinanco. On the south, or left, are the kings of Huexotla, Coatlichan, Chimalhuacan, Tepetlaoztoc, Chiauhtlan, Tezoyocan, and Xicotepec. Those depicted to the right of the sovereigns ruled in the cities of the northern part of the Acolhuacan; those on the left governed the southern part and the immediate vicinity of Tetzcoco. In the west, next to the entrance, are the kings of La Sierra: the king of Cuauhchinanco, the last on the northern side, and the king of Xicotepec, the last on the southern side.

These fourteen kings are the same ones cited in the reports of Motolinía and Ixtlilxochitl. In his description of the palace of Tetzcoco, Ixtlilxochitl enumerates the kings who attended the royal council and explains how they were seated in the council room according to their rank and seniority. The room was divided into three areas, with the king in the first one. In the second, six of the kings were seated: on the right-hand side, first, the king of Teotihuacan, next, the king of Acolman, and the third, the king of Tepetlaoztoc; on the left-hand side, first, the king of Huexotla, followed by the kings of Coatlichan and Chimalhuacan. In the third part ("which was the most exterior") were the other eight kings, also arranged according to their rank and seniority: on the right-hand side, first, the king of Otompan, then the kings of Tollantzinco, Cuauhchinanco, and Xicotepec; on the left-hand side, first, the king of Tepechpan, then the kings of Tezoyocan, Chiucnauhtlan, and Chiauhtlan.[122] Table 6-8 gives the spatial distribution of these kings as described by Ixtlilxochitl.

TABLE 6-7.
Kings, Cities, and Towns of Tenants in the Mapa Quinatzin

	Teotihuacan	Otompan	Huexotla	Coatlichan	Chimalhuacan
		Nezahualcoyotl and Nezahualpilli, Kings of Tetzcoco			
no legend*					
Cuauhtlatzinco*					Tepetlaoztoc
Ahuatepec*					Chiauhtlan
Axapochco*	King of Teotihuacan	King of Otompan	King of Huexotla	King of Coatlichan	Tezoyocan
Tepepolco*	King of Acolman			King of Chimalhuacan	Acolman
Coyoac*	King of Tepechpan			King of Tepetlaoztoc	Tepechpan
Aztaquemecan*	King of Chiucnauhtlan			King of Chiauhtlan	Chiucnauhtlan
illegible*	King of Tollantzinco	King of Cuauhchinanco	King of Xicotepec	King of Tezoyocan	Papalotlan
torn	torn	torn	torn	torn	torn

*The town glyph has a spade (*huictli*).

TABLE 6-8.

Placement of the Acolhua Kings in the Palace According to Ixtlilxochitl

The Great King	
Six of the Kings	
Teotihuacan	Huexotla
Acolman	Coatlichan
Tepetlaoztoc	Chimalhuacan
The Other Eight Kings	
Otompan	Tepechpan
Tollantzinco	Tezoyocan
Cuauhchinanco	Chiucnauhtlan
Xicotepec	Chiauhtlan

This disposition of the kings according to where they sat in the council room does not coincide exactly with that of the Mapa Quinatzin, and this is not the only divergence between the Mapa Quinatzin and Ixtlilxochitl's description of the palace. Ixtlilxochitl's arrangement makes sense in terms of geography as well as rank. The six kings of highest rank are divided into two groups of three: on the right, or north, the kings of Teotihuacan, Acolman and Tepetlaoztoc; on the left, or south, the kings of Huexotla, Coatlichan and Chimalhuacan. The remaining eight, of lower rank, are also grouped geographically: on the right, the kings of La Campiña (Otompan) and of La Sierra; on the left, those who ruled in the immediate vicinity of Tetzcoco and on the lake shore. In the Mapa Quinatzin the rulers of highest rank are also placed near the king of Tetzcoco, but the king of Otompan is included with them instead of the king of Tepetlaoztoc.

In the Mapa Quinatzin the place name glyphs painted outside the palace are also arranged in two series, north and south. Those on the south side include Huexotla, Coatlichan, Chimalhuacan, Tepetlaoztoc, Chiauhtlan, Tezoyocan, Acolman, Tepechpan, Chiucnauhtlan, and, at the end, a town whose glyph is half obliterated but seems to be Papalotlan. A line of red dots connects all these glyphs but does not go as far as that of Papalotlan. All these places are cities governed by the kings depicted in the patio, again excepting Papalotlan, which did not have a king. The glyphs of other cities that had kings—Otompan and Teotihuacan—are on the north side; there are no glyphs for the cities of Tollantzinco, Cuauhchinanco, and Xicotepec, which might have been painted where the bottom edge of the page had been torn off.

The series on the north side begins in the northeast corner with the glyphs of Otompan and Teotihuacan. The legends, of which the first is half erased, say "[Otom]pan tlahtoloyan" (Audiencia of Otompan) and "Teotihuacan tlahtoloyan"

(Audiencia of Teotihuacan).[123] A line of red dots goes from these two cities to a room in which there are two lords with a legend half erased but sufficiently legible to inform the reader that this represents the council that met every eighty days in which the king of Tetzcoco, together with two appellate judges, decided cases.[124] The red line ends just above the wall that separates this room from a larger room in the center, within which Nezahualcoyotl and Nezahualpilli are painted.

Between the glyphs for Teotihuacan and the first two towns in the series that occupy all the north side there is another smudged legend that can be read as "In matlactepec once . . . tlahtoloyan . . . in onoc temayecan" (the eleven towns . . . Audiencia . . . they are where the farmhands).[125] Then follows the series of glyphs each consisting of a mountain with a spade on top of it and the toponym written in Nahuatl. On the first there seems to have been a glyph painted on the mountain, but it is very smudged and cannot be identified; either there was no legend or it had been erased. Then follow Cuauhtlatzinco, Ahuatepec, Axopochco, Tepepolco, Coyoac, Aztaquemecan, and another with a legend that is illegible. Of all these towns, Otompan and Teotihuacan are the cities ruled by kings that are included in the northern half, in the organization described above by Torquemada and Ixtlilxochitl. The rest of the towns marked with a spade are all peasant settlements, also situated in that half. Nezahualcoyotl's name glyph is painted between Ahuatepec and Axapochco; between the latter and Tepepolco is that of Nezahualpilli, indicating that the towns on that side were patrimonial (de realengo), according to Ixtlilxochitl, or, as Motolinía puts it, "tenant farmers of the king of Tetzcoco." Their status is shown by the spades painted on the glyphs. In contrast, the towns on the other side that have their own kings are depicted in a different way, each with its own and well-drawn glyphs.

How many glyphs might there have been on the torn edge of the document? In the center of the patio two braziers are painted, each with a legend saying, "matlatepetl omey oncan tlahuia in cenxihuitl" (thirteen towns make fire all year).[126] This would seem to indicate that a total of thirteen places were painted on each side of the palace. If so, then six are missing, three on each side. This supposition is confirmed by the legend, cited above, in the northeast corner of the page which refers to eleven towns that follow Otompan and Teotihuacan. But only eight are depicted; three others that would complete the thirteen for that side are missing. Given that the written sources do not agree about the number and the names of the towns in each half, it is difficult to reconstruct the names of the towns that are missing.[127]

A comparison of the towns mentioned in the different sources shows that the arrangement of the glyphs in the Mapa Quinatzin is similar to that in the reports that give an organization in two parts, each one including both cities and peasant towns.[128] On the northern side of the palace Otompan and Teotihuacan are pictured together with the peasant towns, while on the southern side, together with the cities, is Papalotlan, all of this the same as in Ixtlilxochitl's and Torquemada's first half. Don Hernando Pimentel's memorial also gives two lists that combine cities and towns, but in contrast to the Mapa Quinatzin he puts Tepetlaoztoc with Otumba and Teotihuacan with Tetzcoco. All the peasant towns in the Mapa Quinatzin appear in the lists of Ixtlilxochitl and Torquemada and in Motolinía's "Memorial tetzcocano." However, Cuauhtlatzinco is missing in the *Anales de Cuauhtitlan*, while Aztaquemecan and Coyoac do not appear in the Memorial of Don Hernando Pimentel.

Therefore, what the Mapa Quinatzin most resembles is the division into two halves of Ixtlilxochitl and Torquemada, and these two writers can give us the best idea as to which are the towns that are missing from the torn edge of the document. On the southern side of the palace, going from Papalotlan toward the west, Coatepec, Itztapallocan, and Xaltocan could have been depicted. Thus, the series would coincide with Ixtlilxochitl's enumeration, in which he combines the towns where Nezahualcoyotl restored their kings with the towns where he did not do so, instead adjudicating them to himself.[129] Reconstructed in this way, the list would also coincide with the half headed by Tetzcoco that Ixtlilxochitl and Torquemada give (without including Tetzcoco itself or Chalco, which is also on the list of Ixtlilxochitl). The series on the north side would continue with towns that other sources describe as peasant towns in the northern part of the Acolhuacan, governed by Otompan and Teotihuacan. There is not sufficient space, however, for all the additional names that Torquemada and Ixtlilxochitl provide. In the Mapa Quinatzin there is one peasant town without a name and another with an illegible legend; there must have been three glyphs more to complete the thirteen. This gives a total of five place names that are missing; the lists of Ixtlilxochitl and Torquemada offer more than five candidates.[130]

Although some problems still remain as to details, this page of the Mapa Quinatzin is of fundamental importance, because in one picture it combines the data that we have seen before described separately in the written sources. On the one hand it makes the distinction between cities with kings and peasant towns; on the other, it presents the division of the kingdom into two halves, each including both cities with kings and peasant towns, or towns of the recámara. Therefore, from a painting such as this one, a writer could take the place names to make two lists, one of the northern half and another of the south, without distinguishing between cities and towns, as is the case in Torquemada (referring to Antonio Pimentel), Ixtlilxochitl, and Hernando Pimentel. In other sources, such as Motolinía's "Memorial tetzcocano" and the *Anales de Cuauhtitlan*, the authors would have taken the information about cities with their own kings for one list, and about peasant towns for another, but without distinguishing the two halves or teams, both of which included cities and towns.

The Tributaries of Tetzcoco
within the Domains of Tenochtitlan and Tlacopan

The great king of Tetzcoco and the kings of the other Acolhua cities had possessions not only in their own cities but also in those of their neighbors in the Acolhuacan and within the other two parts of the alliance. The importance of this factor in the territorial integration of the Empire has been put forth in the Introduction. The best information available is found in the histories of Ixtlilxochitl on what he calls the tribute of the Chinampan. Don Hernando Pimentel also reports on the lands held by the kings of Tetzcoco that they had won personally, primarily within the domains of Tenochtitlan and Tlacopan. According to a shorter report in the Tratado de Teotihuacan, land was distributed among a number of Acolhua and Tenochca kingdoms in such a way that they all held lands in the territory of the others. We will begin with the more detailed information provided by Ixtlilxochitl and Hernando Pimentel.

In two different accounts of all this, Ixtlilxochitl relates that, after the defeat of the Tepanecs, a disagreement between Itzcoatl and Nezahualcoyotl resulted in the latter's going to war with Tenochtitlan and thereby winning the right to tribute from several towns within the Tenochca and Tepanec zones. This was what, in the royal registers of Tetzcoco, was called *chinampaneca tlacalaquilli* (tribute of the people of Chinampan).[131] Ixtlilxochitl's narrative is the counterpart of the very different one from the Tenochca tradition, according to which Tenochtitlan led a campaign against Tetzcoco, previously agreed to by Nezahualcoyotl, in order to justify the establishment of Tenochca possessions within the Acolhua domain. In these two passages Ixtlilxochitl lists the towns of the Chinampan in a somewhat different way. Table 6-9 brings together the toponyms cited in the two versions; they are shown in Map 6-3.

Most of these names are familiar, and there is no doubt about the identity of these cities: Tenochtitlan, Tenayocan, Ecatepec, and Xochimilco were cities in the Tenochca domain; Tlacopan, Azcapotzalco, Tepotzotlan, Cuauhtitlan, Toltitlan, and Coyoacan, in the Tepanec domain. The rest of the toponyms in this table require a more detailed discussion.

Xoloco (or Xolteco) was a barrio of Tenochtitlan in the parcialidad of Moyotla.[132] Huexachtitlan and Axoctitlan could be corrected to Huixachtitlan, a place north of Mount Tepeyac, which in several sources appears as a stopping place on the Mexica migration route and is included in the province of Citlaltepec in Codex Mendoza.[133] However, as Ixtlilxochitl uses the name, it is probably related to Mount Huixachtecatl (present-day Cerro de la Estrella), where the ceremony of the New Fire was celebrated. On the slopes of the mountain there were in pre-Spanish times four barrios of Toltec peoples (Mexica, Colhua, Huitznahua, and Tepanec)

TABLE 6-9.

Tetzcoco's Tribute Payers from the Chinampan Area

"Historia chichimeca"*	"Compendio histórico"†	Identification
1. Tenochtitlan	1. Tenochtitlan, Mexico	1. Barrio Xoloco
the barrio of Xoloco	Xolteco *(sic)*	in Tenochtitlan
2. Tlacopan	2. Tlacopan	2. Tlacopan
3. Azcaputzalco	3. Azaputzalco *(sic)*	3. Azcapotzalco
4. Tenayocan	4. Tenayocan	4. Tenayocan
5. Tepotzotlan	5. Tepotzotan *(sic)*	5. Tepotzotlan
6. Quauhtitlan	6. Quauhtitlan	6. Cuauhtitlan
7. Toltitlan	7. Toltitlan	7. Toltitlan
8. Tlecatepec *(sic pro* Hecatepec)	8. Ecatepec	8. Ecatepec
9. Huexachtitlan *(sic)*	9. Axoctitlan *(sic)*	9. Huixachtitlan
10. Coyohuacan	10. Coyohuacan	10. Coyoacan
11. Xochimilco	11. Xochimilco	11. Xochimilco
12. Cuexomatitlan	12. Iquexomatitlan *(sic)*	12. Cuexomatitlan

*Ixtlilxochitl 1975–77, 2:80.
†Ixtlilxochitl 1975–77, 1:444.

who settled in Tetzcoco and other towns after they had been expelled, in 4 Calli 1301, by King Coxcox of Colhuacan.[134] Huixachtitlan could be the name of a town near the mountain, or it might take in all the area nearby, which included the kingdoms of the Four Lords (Colhuacan, Itztapalapan, Mexicatzinco, and Huitzilopochco), which had very close ties to Tenochtitlan and were frequently cited in Tenochca history.

Cuexomatitlan was between Tlapitzahuayan and the Cerro de la Estrella, a place through which the Mexica passed in the year 1 Calli 1285 after their defeat in Chapoltepec.[135] It is also cited as between Aztahuacan and Tlapitzahuayan in Moteuczoma Ilhuicamina's campaign against Chalco.[136] The name is connected with Mount Cuexomatl, present-day Cerro de la Caldera,[137] the starting point from which, after crossing the lake toward the north, boundary markers were placed to delineate the Tenochca and Acolhua kingdoms.[138] It seems to have been in the territory of Cuitlahuac,[139] and therefore the Cuexomatitlan that paid tribute to Nezahualcoyotl would be in that kingdom.

The towns that paid the tribute of the Chinampan should be compared also with Don Hernando Pimentel's third category, which included towns where his ancestors held lands and tenants they had won personally (see p. 59). Some had long been part of the Acolhuacan, but the rest coincide basically with the towns of the Chinampan, according to Ixtlilxochitl. Table 6-10 presents the two lists; Map 6-3 represents the towns identified.

Of the towns that are found only in the Memorial of Don Hernando Pimentel,

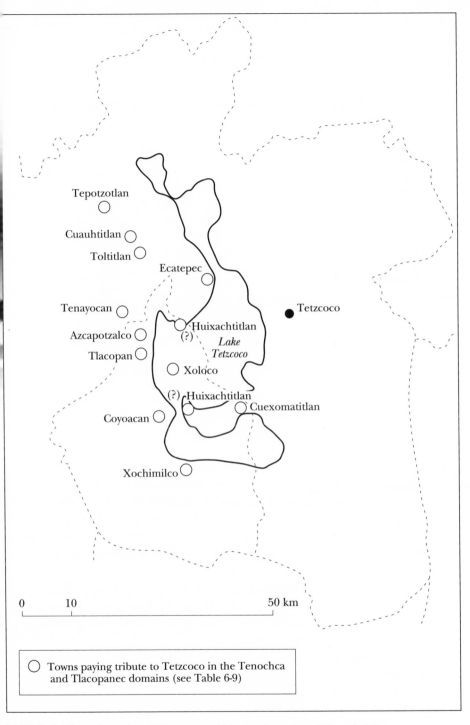

Tepotzotlan

Cuauhtitlan

Toltitlan

Ecatepec

Tenayocan

Azcapotzalco

Tlacopan

Xoloco

Coyoacan

Xochimilco

Tetzcoco

Huixachtitlan
(?)

Lake Tetzcoco

(?) Huixachtitlan

Cuexomatitlan

0   10   50 km

○ Towns paying tribute to Tetzcoco in the Tenochca
   and Tlacopanec domains (see Table 6-9)

MAP 6–3. The tributaries of Tetzcoco within the domains of Tenochtitlan
and Tlacopan

TABLE 6-10.
The Chinampan Towns Compared with the
Memorial of Don Hernando Pimentel

The Chinampan*	Pimentel[†]
1. Barrio of Xoloco in Tenochtitlan	
2. Tlacopan	6. Tacuba
3. Azcapotzalco	1. Azcaputzalco
4. Tenayocan	
5. Tepotzotlan	9. Tepozotlan
6. Cuauhtitlan	5. Cuauhtitlan
7. Toltitlan	11. Tultitlan
8. Ecatepec	10. Ecatepec
9. Huixachtitlan	
10. Coyoacan	8. Cuyuacan
11. Xochimilco	2. Suchimilco
12. Cuexomatitlan	
	3. Cuauhtlapa
	4. Huacalco
	7. Aticpac
	12. Chicoloapan

*Ixtlilxochitl 1975–77, 1:444; 2:80.
†Orozco y Berra 1960, 2:172–73.

Chicoloapan (Chicualoapan) is the present-day Chicoloapan de Juárez, Mexico. It is difficult to identify the other towns because these are frequent toponyms that are found in several areas.

Cuauhtlapa could be the present-day Santiago Cuautlalpan in the municipio of Texcoco;[140] another possibility could be Cuauhtlaapan, west of Tepotzotlan, which was a "town of tenants" of Tlacopan (see p. 203).

Huacalco can be identified with San Juan Huacalco, a town in the *delegación* of Azcapotzalco in the Federal District.[141] Another possibility is Coacalco de Berriozábal, Mexico; in colonial documents this name is sometimes written as Huacalco.[142]

Aticpac is a frequent toponym. It was the name of a temple and perhaps of a barrio in Tenochtitlan.[143] There were also barrios with this name in Coyoacan[144] and in Colhuacan.[145] It might also be La Magdalena Atlicpac in La Paz, Mexico, also called Aticpac in colonial documents.[146]

Two of these three towns, then, can be located in the vicinity of Chicualoapan or together with other towns already identified in this group of towns. Chicualoapan with its nearby villages had long been part of the Acolhuacan; it must have been part of the Tetzcoca calpixcazgo of Tetitlan and not necessarily a town won during the Tepanec war.

Most of the toponyms of the Chinampan and of Pimentel's third group are important kingdoms, but some are towns of a lesser political category. In Tenochtitlan one place is named that was only a barrio; we can assume that in a similar manner Huixachtitlan would be a place of a lower category in the region of the Four Lords, and Cuexomatitlan the same in the region of Cuitlahuac and Mizquic, where the calpixcazgos of Tetzcoco in those two kingdoms would be located. In the same manner these lists of tributary towns agree very well with those of the cities of the Tenochca domain in which they were situated (see Table 5-1).

The tribute that these towns of the Chinampan paid to Tetzcoco consisted of luxury objects. The version in the "Historia chichimeca" lists what was due from each city and town every year: large quantities of elegant cloaks trimmed with rabbit fur, special cloaks for the kings to wear at public ceremonies and festivals, and various other royal accoutrements. A steward was chosen to be in charge of collecting this tribute.[147] A shorter version in the "Compendio histórico" includes, in addition to the royal apparel, feathers, jewelry and objects made of gold, and "all the vegetables, flowers, fish, and birds that they have there."[148]

The quality of this tribute contrasts with what the same region—the province of Petlacalco in the Codex Mendoza—paid to Tenochtitlan: maize, beans, chía, and huauhtli. The province of Acolman (or Acolhuacan)—that is, the tributaries of Tenochtitlan in the kingdoms of Tetzcoco, the counterpart of these Tetzcoca possessions in the Chinampan—also paid tribute in foodstuffs. The nature of the tribute that the towns in the Chinampan paid to Tetzcoco agrees with the political category of the places that paid it; they were the principal cities of the Tenochca and Tlacopanec domains. In contrast the majority of the tributaries of Tenochtitlan in the province of Acolman were peasant towns, and there is also a reference to tenant farmers of the lords of Mexico who had settled in Tetzcoca lands.[149]

In the brief data of the Tratado de Teotihuacan, not only Tetzcoco acquired rights in the Tenochca domain. Several other Acolhua cities—Huexotla, Coatlichan, Tepetlaoztoc, Tezoyocan, Acolman, Chiucnauhtlan, and Teotihuacan—acquired lands in Tenochtitlan, Tlatelolco, and Ecatepec, all in the Tenochca domain.[150] Noblemen of Tepechpan held land in Toltitlan, Azcapotzalco, and Xochimilco.[151] The Acolhua cities that benefited from this were only half of the cities whose kings were dependents of Tetzcoco, but the group includes the most important cities in the Acolhua center—Huexotla and Coatlichan—as well as those in the northern area that were closer to the Tenochca domain—Teotihuacan, Acolman, and Chiucnauhtlan. In the area north of the Basin, where both capitals shared many pos-

sessions, Chiucnauhtlan was the principal Acolhua city and Ecatepec the principal Tenochca one.[152]

The rights that Tetzcoco had in the Chinampan did not last until the end of
the Empire. Moteuczoma Xocoyotzin revoked these rights when the Tetzcoca army
was defeated in battle by Tlaxcallan.[153]

The towns that Don Hernando Pimentel described as belonging to his ancestors are also found within the Tenochca and Tlacopan domains. However, these
lands were probably held under a different kind of tenure—that is, as the patrimonial lands of the kings, different from the royal lands. They can be compared
with the lands of the Tenochca kings that were all in the core area of the Empire,
not only in the Tenochca domain but also in those of Tetzcoco and Tlacopan.[154]
Perhaps the towns listed by Pimentel that are not in Ixtlilxochitl—Chicualoapan
and its neighbors—were not really part of the Chinampan obtained from Itzcoatl
but towns won previously in the wars with Chalco; the category of towns in Pimentel does not entirely match the description of the Chinampan as Ixtlilxochitl
gives it.

The list of Chinampan towns that paid tribute to Tetzcoco includes most of
the cities that were defeated by Tenochtitlan and Tetzcoco during the Tepanec
war and became part of the Tenochca and Tlacopan domains. There is no need to
accept literally what Ixtlilxochitl relates about a defeat inflicted on Tenochtitlan
by Nezahualcoyotl that led to the creation of the Tetzcoca calpixcazgo in the Chinampan. It is more likely that Tetzcoco acquired those towns in an exchange of
lands or rights to tribute among the capitals of the alliance, as is described briefly
in the Tratado de Teotihuacan. Each version reflects the way in which its propo-
nents upheld their claims. In any case the fact remains that each of the three capitals had possessions in the domains of the others and the towns examined in this
chapter were those that, in the domains of Tenochtitlan and Tlacopan, paid tribute to Tetzcoco.

The Tributaries of Tetzcoco in Tlalhuic

In Tlalhuic each of the three capitals, Tenochtitlan, Tetzcoco, and Tlacopan, acquired separate possessions. This is clearly explained in the "Historia chichimeca"
as Ixtlilxochitl relates the conquest of this region after Nezahualcoyotl had established the boundaries with Tlaxcallan and reestablished his control in Tollantzinco
and La Sierra, which he considered part of his own patrimony. He then joined
forces with his uncle, Itzcoatl, and Totoquihuatzin, king of Tlacopan, and the three
kings with their armies set out for "the land of the Tlalhuicas," conquered them,
and divided the lands among themselves. Nezahualcoyotl's share comprised Cuauhnahuac, the cabecera, together with nine towns. He appointed a steward to collect

their tribute, which consisted of large amounts of clothing and "a certain quantity of valuable objects of gold, precious stones, and feathers every year, the servants necessary for the royal household, and the flowers that were regularly used in the palace." The king of Mexico acquired Tepoztlan, Huaxtepec, and other towns, with the same quantity of tribute; the king of Tlacopan also received his share, described only as "the part that belonged to him."[155]

The nine towns of this Tetzcoca calpixcazgo of Cuauhnahuac are found in both Motolinía's "Memorial tetzcocano" and in the corresponding text of the *Anales de Cuauhtitlan*.[156] They are listed here, using the spelling of the *Anales de Cuauhtitlan*, together with the identification of each town.

1.	Cuauhnahuac	Cuernavaca, Morelos
2.	Atlpoyecan	Alpuyeca in Xochitepec, Morelos
3.	Miyacatla	Miacatlan, Morelos
4.	Maçatepec	Mazatepec, Morelos
5.	Tlaquiltenanco	Tlaquiltenango, Morelos
6.	Çacatepec	Zacatepec, Morelos
7.	Ollintepec	Olintepec in Ayala, Morelos
8.	Ocopetlatlan	Sujeto of Yautepec (AGN-HJ 289, exp. 100, passim), or sujeto of Huaxtepec (AGI, México, 68, Libro de cartas [book of letters], 210r).
9.	Huehuetlytzallan	Not identified.

In describing the royal palace of Tetzcoco, Ixtlilxochitl notes that there were rooms for storing the tribute from Cuauhnahuac, but he does not name the nine towns that comprised Tetzcoco's possessions in that area.[157] Only in his description of the towns that contributed labor in the royal gardens does he name, together with the towns of La Sierra, some of the towns in Tlalhuic: Yauhtepec, Tepechco, Ahuacayocan, and Cuauhnahuac.[158] The list of Nezahualcoyotl's conquests in the "Compendio Histórico" includes Quauhnahuac, Tlalhuic, Yauhtepec, Tepexco, and Abacayocan (*sic*).[159] Tepexco can be identified as the present-day town of the same name in Puebla;[160] Ahuacayocan was an estancia of Teotlalco (present-day Teotlalco, Puebla).[161] Both towns border on Morelos. The Memorial of Don Hernando Pimentel lists "a certain part of Cuauhnahuac" among the towns won by his ancestors.[162] The holdings of Tetzcoco in Tlahuic are shown in Map 6-4.

The *Anales de Cuauhtitlan* enumerate the tribute payments by this Tetzcoca calpixcazgo of Cuauhnahuac at six twenty-day periods of the year; the quantities of clothing coincide almost exactly with the data in Ixtlilxochitl.[163]

Four of Tetzcoco's towns in Tlalhuic are also listed among the tributaries of Tenochtitlan in the Codex Mendoza: Cuauhnahuac and Miacatlan in the prov-

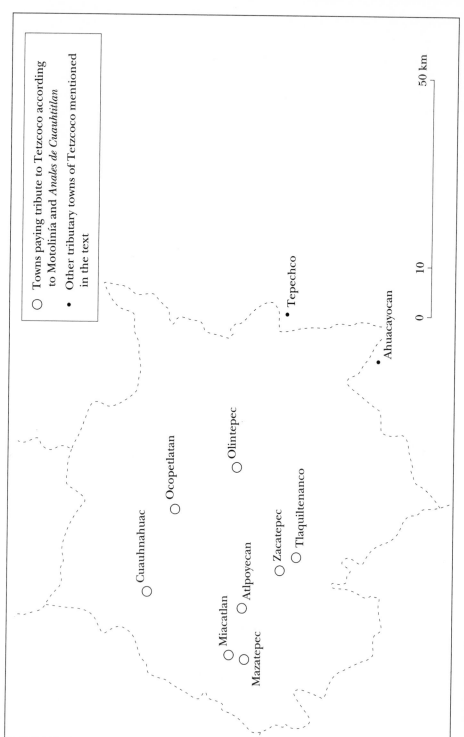

MAP 6-4. The tributaries of Tetzcoco in Tlalhuic

ince of Cuauhnahuac; Olintepec and Yauhtepec in the province of Huaxtepec. None of these towns is mentioned among the tributaries of Tlacopan. The other towns that have been located are in those same regions. According to the colonial documentation on the towns of the Marquesado, the cabecera of Tetzcoco in Las Amilpas was Olintepec, which included four towns—Chinameca, Zacapolco, Tecihuac, and Ichcatepec—distributed by Nezahualpilli among his relations.[164]

Chapter 7

THE TEPANEC KINGDOM OF TLACOPAN

Tlacopan, Capital of the Tepanecs

There are sources for the Tepanec kingdom of Tlacopan that give a thorough description of the territorial divisions of this third section of the Empire. These documents—the "Memorial de los pueblos de Tlacopan" and the Codex Osuna—have been discussed when treating the question of the political and territorial categories in the sources from Tlacopan. They demonstrate that there was an extensive rural area pertaining to the capital, but they say nothing about the social and political institutions of the capital, and there are no independent sources on these topics.[1]

The information we have on the barrios of Tlacopan is inadequate. Pérez Rocha has put together the available data,[2] but they are not sufficient to relate the barrios with different groups of settlers or with temples and patron gods, as in Tenochtitlan and Tetzcoco. Perhaps there were two parcialidades in Tlacopan, one of Mexicas and the other of Tepanecs, each with its own government, as was the case in Azcapotzalco. The kings of Tiliuhcan Tlacopan were closely connected with the Tenochca dynasty in such a way that one can assume this was a Mexica parcialidad, while Tlacopan would be Tepanec.[3]

The ethnic complexity of the area of Tlacopan is apparent in the many languages that were spoken there: Nahuatl, Otomí, Matlatzinca, Mazahua, Chocho, and Chichimec.[4] This linguistic diversity did not exist only in the urban nucleus of Tlacopan but also in the whole extent of the Tepanec domain, which included speakers of all these languages except for the unidentified Chocho. It is also possible that all these ethnic groups had representatives in the Tepanec capital, as is said to be the case of the sujetos of Tenochtitlan and Tetzcoco.

The urban institutions of Tlacopan are unknown. There was still a concentration of merchants and artisans in neighboring Azcapotzalco during the Empire; they probably had stayed there after Tlacopan became the capital of the Tepanecs.[5]

Tlacopan's position within the Triple Alliance was of lesser importance than that of the other two capitals. It received a smaller portion of the tribute from the conquered towns and probably was subordinate to Tenochtitlan from the very beginning of the Empire. In the demarcation of the area conquered by Nezahualcoyotl and Itzcoatl, the territory of Tlacopan was included in that of Tenochtitlan,[6] perhaps not only for geographical reasons but also because of its lesser importance in relation to Tenochtitlan. Ixtlilxochitl relates that Nezahualcoyotl insisted on including Tlacopan in the alliance, although Itzcoatl was not in favor of this at first.[7] It is also noteworthy that the kings of some of the kingdoms in the Tlacopanec group were of Mexica affiliation, and the towns in those kingdoms paying tribute to Tenochtitlan were very numerous.

The data from all the sources about the district of Tlacopan have been combined in Table 7-1, arranged according to the most complete report, the "Memorial de los pueblos de Tlacopan." All these rural sujetos of the Tepanec capital are shown in Map 7-1.

The towns in the first three lists in the "Memorial de Tlacopan" comprise the capital district proper. The first is defined as "the towns subject to this cabecera of Tlacupan." They occupy an extensive area—from the lake shores to the mountain range that separates the Basin from the Valley of Toluca—that includes Cepayauhtlan and Tziuhtepec near Teotenanco (present-day Tenango del Valle).

In the second list are eleven towns under a heading that states: "These towns named above still belong in the cabecera; the towns distributed to Spaniards of the said cabecera are the following." The heading of the third list says: "These five towns that follow were obtained by Juan Cano, and they serve him and do not acknowledge any rule of Tlacupan over them and their names are . . ."; the list of five towns follows. The second and third sections are both based on changes made by the colonial government. The pre-Spanish situation is not clear; there is an implication that the towns given to Spaniards had been part of Tlacopan. The towns of Juan Cano, or some of them, might have been separate.

The list in the Codex Osuna of towns subject to Tlacopan does not include any that are in the first section of the "Memorial de Tlacopan," but it does include some from the second. Of those in the third section, there are four in the Codex Osuna, two that come after Tlacopan and two others that follow Coyoacan. Other documents supply complementary data. The dowry that Cortés gave to Doña Isabel de Montezuma in 1527 included some towns in Tlacopan. Several old copies of this document have survived, and it has been published several times, but the spelling of some toponyms is doubtful.[8]

TABLE 7-1.
Settlements in the Tlacopan District

"Memorial de Tlacopan"*	Codex Osuna†	Dowry of Isabel de Montezuma‡	Letters of Antonio Cortés§	Report of 1566‖
1. Towns belonging to the cabecera				
1. Tlacupan	1. Tlacuban	1. Tacuba		
				1. Quautlalpan
2. Metztitlan				9. Meztitlan
3. Tetlolincan				11. Tetalinga
4. Tecamachalco				3. Tecamachalco
5. Cuauhximalpan				
6. Iyetepec		2. Yetebeque		4. Yetepeque
7. Vitzquillocan		3. Yzquiluca		2. Huizquilucan
8. Ayotochco		11. Goatuzco *(sic)*		10. Yaotochco
9. Chimalpan		4. Chimalpan		12. Chimalpan
10. Chapulmaloyan		5. Chapulmaloyan		8. Chapolmaloyan
11. Xilotzinco		7. Xilocingo		7. Xilozingo
12. Azcaputzal[ton]co		6. Escapuçaltongo		5. Azcapuzaltongo
13. Tziuhtepec				
14. Cepayauhtlan				
		13. Tacala *(sic)*		6. Tlacalan *(sic)*
2. Towns distributed to Spaniards				
1. Tlallachco	7. Tlalachco	10. Talauco	3. Tlallachco,e	
2. Chichicquauhtla	8. Chichicquauhtla			
3. Vitzitzilapan	5. Huitzitzilapan		6. Vitzitzilatan,e	
4. Ocelotepec	6. Ocelotepec		12. Ocelotepec,e	
5. Xilotzinco			11. Xilotzinco,e	
6. Mimiyauaapan				
7. Tzaucyocan	3. Tzaucyocan		7. Tzauciocan,e	
8. Maçatlan				
9. Tecpan				
10. Quauhuacan	4. Quahuacan		8. Quauhuacan,e	
11. Teocalveyacan			4. Teocalhueyacan,e	
3. Towns of Juan Cano				
1. Ocoyacac	10. Ocoyacac	8. Ocoyacaque	[Ocoyacac]	16. Ocuyacac
2. Tepehuexoyocan	9. Tepehuexoyocan		[Tepeuexoyocan]	14. Tesoyocan
3. Quappanouayan				15. Quapanoayan
4. Capolloac	15. Capolloac		[Capoloac]	13. Capoluac
5. Couatepec	16. Cohuatepec			

Table 7-1 continued

"Memorial de Tlacopan"*	Codex Osuna†	Dowry of Isabel de Montezuma‡	Letters of Antonio Cortés§	Report of 1566‖
	2. Azcapotzalco		10. Azcapotzalco, p	
			2. Tenanyocan, p	
			1. Ixtlahuacan, p	
			9. Popotla, e	
			5. Caltecoyan, e	
		9. Caltepeque		
		12. Tepeque		

NOTE: The towns under the dashed line are outside the region covered by the first three categories of the "Memorial de Tlacopan" or have not been identified. See the discussion in the text that follows the table.

*The categories 1, 2 and 3 in the "Memorial de Tlacopan" are defined in the text.

†Numbered as in Table 4-3. Between 10, Ocoyacac, and 15, Capolloac, the Codex Osuna lists 11, Coyoacan; 12. Atlacuihuayan; 13, Atlauhpolco; and 14, Xalatlauhco. Table 7-2 notes the rank of the local rulers.

‡AGI, Patronato 245, R9. The reading of 11, Goatuzco, is not certain.

§The towns are numbered according to the order in which they are mentioned in the 1561 letter. Estancias are marked with *e* and pueblos with *p*. The towns in brackets are from the 1552 letter.

‖AGI Justicia 1029, n°. 10.

Several petitions to the Crown from the cacique Don Antonio Cortés and other principals also mention the former dependencies of Tlacopan. A letter dated 1552 states that Capolhuac, Ocoyacac, and Tepehuexoxoyocan, given to Juan Cano, were estancias that had formerly belonged to them.[9] Another letter dated 1561 adds almost all the towns in the second section of the "Memorial de Tlacopan."[10] There is also a report from 1566 on the belongings of Tlacopan that mentions almost all the towns in the first and third sections of the memorial, all of which responded to the labor drafts (*llamamientos*) "with other natives of many other towns whose borders go as far as the province of Michoacán."[11] Many towns listed in sections 1 and 2 of the "Memorial de Tlacopan" are also found among those included in the colonial labor drafts for public works that Gibson studied.[12]

Thus, it is obvious that the towns listed in the first three sections of the "Memorial de Tlacopan" comprise the district that was a direct dependency of Tlacopan, in contrast with the other kingdoms in the Tepanec domains, listed in section 4 of the same document. Nevertheless, as in the other Tepanec kingdoms, there were also tributary towns of Tenochtitlan within the territory of Tlacopan that are listed in the Codex Mendoza in the province of Cuahuacan.

The dependencies of Tlacopan with their identification are listed below in the same order as in Table 7-1. The towns that are also in the Codex Mendoza, in the province of Cuahuacan, are identified in square brackets with the name of this province and a number indicating its place on the list.

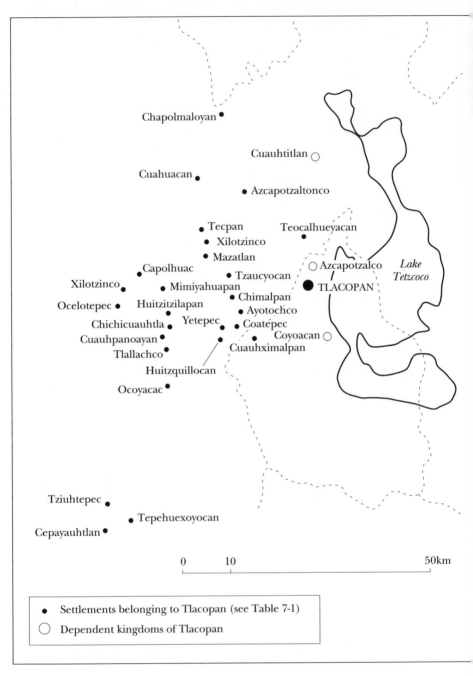

Chapolmaloyan •

Cuauhtitlan ○

Cuahuacan •

• Azcapotzaltonco

• Tecpan   Teocalhueyacan
   • Xilotzinco   •
   • Mazatlan

• Capolhuac   ○ Azcapotzalco   *Lake*
Xilotzinco •   • Tzaucyocan   *Tetzcoco*
   • • Mimiyahuapan   ● TLACOPAN
Ocelotepec •   Huitzitzilapan   • Chimalpan
              • Ayotochco
Chichicuauhtla • • Yetepec • Coatépec
Cuauhpanoayan •   •   • Coyoacan ○
   Tlallachco •   Cuauhximalpan

      Huitzquillocan

Ocoyacac •

Tziuhtepec •
     • Tepehuexoyocan
Cepayauhtlan •

0   10   50km

● Settlements belonging to Tlacopan (see Table 7-1)
○ Dependent kingdoms of Tlacopan

MAP 7–1. The district of Tlacopan

The following towns were still sujetos of the cabecera of Tlacopan and make up the longest list:

1. Tlacupan	Tacuba, Federal District.
2. Metztitlan	San Mateo Mextitlan, Naucalpan, Mexico.
3. Tetlolincan	San Lorenzo Totolinga, Naucalpan, Mexico.
4. Tecamachalco	Visita of Tlacopan (Vetancurt 1961, 3:189). San Miguel Tecamachalco in Naucalpan, Mexico.
5. Cuauhximalpan	Cuajimalpa, Federal District.
6. Iyetepec	San Juan Yetepec of the jurisdiction of Huizquilucan, near San Bartolomé Coatepec (Pérez Rocha 1982:16–18). San Juan Yautepec, Huixquilucan, Mexico.
7. Vitzquillocan	Huixquilucan de Degollado, Mexico. [Cuahuacan, 8]
8. Ayotochco	Nacaz Ayotochco, visita of Tlalnepantla (Vetancurt 1961, 3:194); or Ayutusco, estancia, sujeto of Zacualpan (DA, 134; SV, par. 109). Ayotusco (Santa Cruz or San Francisco) in Huixquilucan, Mexico. ˙
9. Chimalpan	San Francisco Chimalpan in Naucalpan, Mexico.
10. Chapulmaloyan	Town contiguous with Chiappan (Colín 1967: pars. 488, 2099). Former boundary of Cuauhtitlan (AC, 21, par. 112). [Cuahuacan, 3]
11. Xilotzinco	Jilotzingo, Mexico.
12. Azcaputzal[ton]co	In the document it is written Azcaputzalco. This must be an error for Azcapotzaltonco (Zimmermann 1970:5). San Pedro Azcapotzal- tongo in Nicolás Romero, Mexico.
13. Tziuhtepec	Ciuhtepec, sujeto of Tacuba (DA, 163). North of Tenancingo (SV, par. 531). San Pedro Zictepec in Tenango del Valle, Mexico.
14. Cepayauhtlan	Cepayauhtla, sujeto of Tacuba (DA, 164). North of Tenancingo (SV, par. 531). Zepayautla in Tenancingo, Mexico.

Cuauhximalpan (5) is also mentioned as an estancia of Coyoacan.[13] It may be that Tlacopan and Coyoacan each owned part of this town. The documentation on Coyoacan alludes to lawsuits between Tlacopan and Coyoacan over certain Indians of Cuauhximalpan,[14] and Moteuczoma also had land there.[15] This is probably one of many rural areas where several cities possessed land.

In the same area as the preceding towns there were others listed in the report of 1566. Cuauhtlalpan was probably the name of the region, not of a particular town. Tlacalan, or Tacala, can be understood—if we add the cedilla—as Tlatzallan. A town of this name, together with Xilotzinco, was the object of a dispute between Tlacopan and Teocalhueyacan.[16] Today there is Santiago Tlazala de Fabela in Isidro Fabela, Mexico, and San Nicolás Tlazala in Capulhuac, Mexico.

The following list contains the towns of Tlacopan that had been given to Spaniards as encomiendas:

1. Tlallachco   Santa María or San Mateo Atarasquillo in
                     Lerma, Mexico. (San Sebastián Tlallachco
                     north of Tequixquiac [DA, 66–67] is far from
                     the other pueblos in the list.)
                     [Cuahuacan, 11]

2. Chichicquauhtla   Chichiguautla (SV, par. 113).
                     Concepción or San Francisco Xochicuautla in
                     Lerma, Mexico.
                     [Cuahuacan, 12]

3. Vitzitzilapan   Vçiçilapa (SV, par. 782).
                     San Agustín or San Lorenzo Huitzitzilapan in
                     Lerma, Mexico.
                     [Cuahuacan, 13]

4. Ocelotepec   One of the three cabeceras of Ocelotepeque
                     (SV, par. 418).
                     Otzolotepec (Villa Cuauhtemoc), Mexico.

5. Xilotzinco   Xilocingo, one of the three cabeceras of
                     Ocelotepeque (SV, par. 418).
                     Santa Ana Jilotzingo in Otzolotepec, Mexico.

6. Mimiyauaapan   Mimiapan, one of the three cabeceras of
                     Ocelotepeque (SV, par. 418).
                     San Miguel Mimiapan in Xonacatlan, Mexico.

7. Tzaucyocan   Durán (2:274) alludes to the "mountains of
                     Tzaueyucan [*sic*], Huitzitzilpan and
                     Chichicuauhtla."
                     Çacoyuca (*sic*) bordered on Huitzitzilapan
                     (SV, par. 782).

8. Maçatlan	Santa María Mazatla in Jilotzingo, Mexico.
9. Tecpan	Tequepa (SV, par. 418).
	San Miguel Tecpan in Jilotzinco, Mexico.
	[Cuahuacan, 2]
10. Quauhuacan	Santa María Magdalena Cahuacán in Nicolás Romero, Mexico.
	[Cuahuacan, 1]
11. Teocalveyacan	An Otomí town congregated with Tenayuca in Tlalnepantla (Vetancurt 1961, 3:194.
	Cf. Sahagún 1975:75 [book 12, chap. 26]).

Then follows the list of the towns of Tlacopan that had been given to Juan Cano.

1. Ocoyacac	Ocuyaque (SV, par. 445).
	Ocoyoacac, Mexico.
2. Tepehuexoyocan	Tepexuxuca (SV, 445).
	La Asunción Tepezoyuca in Ocoyoacac, Mexico.
3. Quappanouayan	Quapanoaya (DA, 232).
	San Juan Coapanoaya in Ocoyoacac, Mexico.
	[Cuahuacan, 10]
4. Capolloac	Capuluaque (SV, par. 445).
	Capulhuac de Mirafuentes, Mexico;
	or San Mateo Capulhuac in Otzolotepec, Mexico.
5. Couatepec	Guatepeque (SV, par. 256).
	San Nicolás Coatepec de las Bateas in Tianguistenco, Mexico, or San Bartolomé Coatepec, Huixquilucan, Mexico.
	[Cuahuacan, 9]

Capulhuac and Coatepec are names that are repeatedly found in the region of Toluca. They also appear in the Codex Osuna in the group headed by Coyoacan, and this city was contiguous with Ocuila;[17] in this case they must be the present-day San Nicolás Coatepec de las Bateas and Capulhuac de Mirafuentes.

Of the towns in the table not included in the first three sections of the "Memorial de Tlacopan," Caltepeque and Tepeque have not been identified. Caltecoyan could be the town of that name in Chalco.[18] Popotla is the present-day San Esteban Popotla, in the environs of Tlacopan, also mentioned as an estancia of Tenochtitlan. In the Codex Mendoza it is listed in the military district of the Basin headed by Citlaltepec. Probably it was a sujeto of both capitals, a situation that

would have led to Vetancurt's statement that Tlacopan had a barrio of San Esteban Popotla whose inhabitants paid tribute to the governor of Mexico, although
Tlacopan administered it.[19]

Don Antonio Cortés, in his letter of 1561, labels as "estancias" the places situated in the district of Tlacopan (sections 1, 2, and 3 of the "Memorial"), but, with
the exception of Caltecoyan, he calls those outside the district "pueblos," that is,
Tenayocan, Ixtlahuacan, and Azcapotzalco. The "Memorial de Tlacopan" does
not distinguish between estancias and pueblos except in section 5. Ixtlahuacan is
a toponym frequently encountered; it is difficult to decide which is the one on this
list. Probably it is Ixtlahuaca de Rayón, Mexico; although it is far from the other
towns in the table, it is given in the "Memorial de Tlacopan" (section 5) as belonging to the Tepanec capital (see Table 7-3). Tenayocan, present-day San Bartolo Tenayuca in Tlalnepantla, Mexico, had its own king, who was a dependent of
Tenochtitlan (see p. 100); it is not cited as a Tlacopanec kingdom in either the
"Memorial de Tlacopan" or the Codex Osuna. Azcapotzalco, although its category had diminished when the Triple Alliance was formed, still had two rulers; this
situation is discussed below in the section dealing with the dependent kingdoms of
Tlacopan.

The detailed information given in the "Memorial de los pueblos de Tlacopan" on the sujetos of the cabecera contrasts with Motolinía's "Memorial tetzcocano," which has nothing comparable. This probably is a result of the fact that
Tetzcoco was under the Crown and had no Spanish encomiendas in its district.
The three lists of the "Memorial de Tlacopan" must have been made in order to
distinguish the towns that Tlacopan kept from those given to Juan Cano and other
Spaniards. It is also noteworthy that section 4, of tenant farmers, includes towns
that for the most part are outside the Tepanec boundaries, in Chalco, Tlalhuic,
and Tolocan. This differs from Motolinía's "Memorial tetzcocano," in which the
towns of tenant farmers are in the territory of the Acolhua kingdoms. Probably the
description of the towns of tenants in both memoriales could also be applied to
the towns in sections 1, 2, and 3.

There are no reports on the tribute or services provided by those towns that
comprised the rural district of the capital. They are included in the lists of towns
that responded to the labor drafts in the mid-sixteenth century,[20] but there are no
data for distinguishing among different types of settlements with inhabitants of
different social ranks and with corresponding tribute obligations, as can be per-
ceived in the case of Tetzcoco, but it is reasonable to think that there had been
something similar. The towns in the rural zone of Tlacopan must have constituted
tributary units comparable to that which Ixtlilxochitl described for the Acolhua
capital as the calpixcazgo of "Tetzcoco with its barrios and hamlets."

The Dependent Kingdoms of Tlacopan

According to Ixtlilxochitl, when the Triple Alliance was founded, Tlacopan remained at the head of seven Tepanec kingdoms. He does not identify these seven kingdoms, but in describing the region where Nezahualcoyotl obtained tributaries within the domains of Tenochtitlan and Tlacopan, he names several towns that were obviously Tepanec: Azcapotzalco, Tepotzotlan, Cuauhtitlan, Toltitlan, and Coyoacan.[21]

Torquemada also provides information on the part of the subjugated territory that Itzcoatl and Nezahualcoyotl gave to Tlacopan following the defeat of the Tepanec empire as they were constituting the alliance. Tlacopan received "a fifth of the whole," with the "province" of Mazahuacan and the mountainous area occupied by Chichimecs, "now called Otomis." Torquemada then points out that Tlacopan still governed this area; when there were labor drafts for important public works, all the towns on the western side of the mountains were included as part of Tlacopan.[22] He does not speak of seven kingdoms but of the geographical extension of the area given to Tlacopan. Considering the size of the district of Tlacopan as defined at the beginning of the "Memorial de los pueblos de Tlacopan," it might seem that Torquemada was referring to that district. But the inclusion of Mazahuacan, and the fact that the towns given to Tlacopan still responded to the labor drafts for public works during the colonial period,[23] prove that it encompassed the entire great kingdom of Tlacopan, not only the district of the capital. This would reflect the initial situation of the kingdoms with their sujetos as given in category 4 of the "Memorial de Tlacopan."

According to Motolinía, there were ten dependent kingdoms under Tlacopan, but he does not name them.[24] The account of Ixtlilxochitl is more in agreement with the concrete evidence of the Tlacopan sources. The "Memorial de los pueblos de Tlacopan" and the Tlacopanec memorial of the Codex Osuna give the best information as to which cities were governed by kings subject to Tlacopan in the sixteenth century.[25] However, it is possible that there was some difference between the cities that entered the Triple Alliance from its beginning as part of the Tlacopan kingdom and those that belonged to it when the Spanish arrived. Axayacatl's war against Matlatzinco changed considerably the situation in that region.

The "Memorial de Tlacopan" in section 4 lists the cities that gave obedience to Tlacopan, that is, the dependent kingdoms of Tlacopan together with their own sujetos. This category is defined as "the towns that gave obedience to Tlacopan and gathered here for the wars, and their tribute was assigned here, and they obtained and brought here lime, stone, wood, mats, bowls, dishes. They are the following together with their sujetos."[26] The list that follows this statement is divided into five paragraphs and contains the two different political categories to which the quotation refers. The toponyms at the head of each paragraph are those of "the towns giving obedience to Tlacopan"; the places listed under each of these are "the towns subject to them." It is possible that the cabeceras of the five groups were governed by kings, but not their sujetos. However, among them there are some that have their own kings, while others were of a lower category. Other sources, especially the Tlacopanec memorial of the Codex Osuna, indicate different categories of local governments.[27] Table 7-2 combines the data from these three sources and from the lists of towns that during the colonial era assembled for public works when summoned by Tlacopan.

As a basis for the organization of the data, the lists from the Codex Osuna have been placed in the first column of the table. Three categories of indigenous rulers are indicated in the Codex Osuna by glyphs (see Table 4-3). In Table 7-2 the different ranks are indicated by letters. There are four tlatoani (Tl) whose rank in the codex is signified by a diadem (*xiuhitzolli*) and a scroll; these are the rulers of Coyoacan, Cuauhtitlan, Tollan, and Apazco. Three teuctli (t), depicted with a xiuhitzolli and a head, are the rulers of Toltitlan, Tepotzotlan, and Tepexic. Thus, there were seven rulers of high rank, calling to mind the seven Tepanec kings under Tlacopan when the Triple Alliance was formed. The greater importance of the four cities marked with a scroll as well as a diadem is indicated in the codex by a rhombus preceding the glyph. Other towns had local rulers or officials of a lower rank who are indicated with only a head; these are marked in the table with an *s*. Although the glyphs used in the Codex Osuna indicate three categories of rulers, there is no need to think that each of them was designated with a distinctive title. According to other sources, some of those marked with an *s* also had the title of tlatoani, as, for example, Azcapotzalco. The data from the *Anales de Cuauhtitlan*, in the third column, are from the list of kings (tlatoani) ruling in the center of Mexico in 1519.[28]

The table also includes all the towns that comprised the labor draft of Tlacopan during colonial times.[29] To make a comparison with the complete lists of the labor drafts, the table also includes data from the "Memorial de Tlacopan" and from the Codex Osuna, referring to the kingdom of Tlacopan proper, which have been discussed above. These lists of the labor drafts confirm the extent of the total aggregate of dependent kingdoms of Tlacopan; they agree with the statement of Torquemada and with the fact that the towns of the Tlacopan labor draft bordered on Michoacán.[30] The documents do not specify to which of the kingdoms the towns listed belonged, but the order of enumeration in the 1563 labor draft is different from previous ones. A comparison of the sequences shows that the towns are always grouped conforming to the composition of the kingdoms in the "Memorial de Tlacopan" and the Codex Osuna.[31] This indicates that the recruiting of workers for public works was done according to the organization into kingdoms, which is different from the organization into tributary provinces for the collection of tribute in kind destined for Tenochtitlan that the Codex Mendoza presents.

Map 7-2 represents Tlacopan with the dependent Tepanec kingdoms and their sujetos. All are in the western part of the Basin and in the region immediately to the north as far as Xilotepec. Thus, the Tlacopan sector of the core area extends well beyond the Basin, as is also the case with the tributary districts discussed below. These kingdoms coincide with the nucleus of what had been the empire of Azcapotzalco under Tezozomoc.[32] The principal kings are those of Coyoacan, Cuauhtitlan, Tollan, Apazco, and Xilotepec, but a comparison of the lists raises some problems. Other sources also mention kings of several more towns, which will be discussed below.[33] The most important are Azcapotzalco, Atlacuihuayan, Toltitlan, and the dependent realms of Cuauhtitlan.

Azcapotzalco is presented in different ways in the sources used for the table. In the Codex Osuna it appears beside Tlacopan and has two lords of lower rank. One of them, with a glyph in the form of a stone, must be the ruler of Azcapotzalco Tepanecapan, while the other, without an explanatory glyph, would be the ruler of Mexicapan;[34] after Azcapotzalco the sujetos of Tlacopan are depicted. The "Memorial de Tlacopan" puts Azcapotzalco before Coyoacan in the group that seems to be the first of the dependent kingdoms of Tlacopan; other towns in this group are neighbors of Coyoacan, with which they are listed in the Codex Osuna. The labor drafts also list Azcapotzalco in a variable position. Although Azcapotzalco's importance diminished when the Triple Alliance was formed, it may have maintained a close connection with its neighbor Tlacopan as with Coyoacan; the two principal sources favor one or the other of these connections. The people of Azcapotzalco maintained that Tlacopan had usurped their territory;[35] perhaps the city itself became a dependency of Tlacopan. On the other hand, Maxtla, the last king of Azcapotzalco, had previously reigned in Coyoacan, and that connection could have continued.

Coyoacan is the first Tepanec kingdom represented with its sujetos in the Codex Osuna after the capital of Tlacopan. The towns that are together with Coyoacan are Atlacuihuayan (present-day Tacubaya in the Federal District), Tepanoayan, Atlappolco (San Pedro Atlapulco in Ocoyoacac, Mexico), Xalatlauhco (Jalatlaco, Mexico), Capolhuac (Capulhuac, Mexico), and Coatepec (San Nicolás Coatepec de las Bateas in Tianguistenco, Mexico). Of these towns, Tepanoayan is difficult to locate. As will be shown below, the historical chronicles seem to use this name for the Tepanec region, at times combined with either Azcapotzalco or Tlacopan as a second name.[36] Xalatlauhco was settled by Matlatzinca captives after Axayacatl's campaign and was given its own king,[37] but it was an older town and its name appears in the account of the Tepanec war.[38] Capolhuac and Coatepec are

TABLE 7-2. The Tepanec Kingdoms and Their Subject Towns

Codex Osuna*	"Memorial de Tlacopan"	AC	1555 Draft†	1556 Draft†	1563 Draft†
1. Tlacuban, Tl	1-1 Tlacupan	Tl	1	1	20
2. Azcaputzalco, 2s	4.1-1 Azcaputzalco	Tl	14	6	1
3. Tzaucyocan, s	2-7 Tzaucyocan		3	2	21
4. Quahuacan, s	2-10 Quauhuacan		4	3	22
5. Huitzitzilapan, s	2-3 Vitzitzilapan		8	4	31
6. Ocelotepec	2-4 Ocelotepec		7		30
7. Tlalachco, s	2-1 Tlallachco		10	5	33
8. Chichicquauhtla, s	2-2 Chichicquauhtla		9		32
	2-5 Xilotzinco		5		24
	2-6 Mimiyauaapan		6		29
	2-8 Maçatlan				
	2-9 Tecpan				
	2-11 Teocalveyacan				
9. Tepehuexoyocan	3-2 Tepehuexoyocan		11		34
10. Ocoyacac	3-1 Ocoyacac		13		25
	3-3 Quappanouayan		12		35
◆1. Coyohuacan, Tl	4.1-2 Coyouacan	Tl	2	7	
12. Atlacuihuayan, s	4.1-3 Atlacuivayan			8	
	4.1-4 Tepanouayan				
13. Atlauhpolco, s	4.1-5 Atlappolco			9	28
14. Xalatlauhco, s	4.1-6 Xalatlauhco			10	23
15. Capolloac	3-4 Capolloac			11	26
16. Cohuatepec, s	3-5 Couatepec			12	27
[◆17. Quauhtiltlan, Tl	4.2-1 Quauhtitlan	Tl	15	13	2
18. Toltitlan, t	4.2-2 Toltitlan	Tl	16	17	3
19. Tepotzotlan, t	4.2-3 Tepotzotlan	Tl	17	16	4
20. Huehuetocan, s			18		5
21. Otlazpan, s			19	18	6
22. Tepesic, t	4.2-4 Tepexic	Tl	20		7
23. Tzompanco, s	4.2-5 Tzompanco			15	8. Nextlalpan
24. Citlaltepec‡	4.2-6 Citlaltepec			14	

No. & Town	col. 1	col. 2	col. 3
◆25. Tullan, T1	19	21	36
26. Xippacoyan, s	20	22	37
27. Atlitalacyan, s	21	23	38. Tlaquepa
28. Michmaloyan, s	22	26	39
29. Nestlalpan, s	23	29	43
30. Teçontepec, s	24	28	44
31. Tlemaco, s	26	30	41
32. Mizquiyahualla, s	25	27	42. Tlacotepec
33. Tlaahuililpan, s		24	40
34. Chilquauhtla, s		25	9
35. Ytzmiquilpan, s			10
◆36. Apazco, T1		31	13
37. Atotoniltonco, s		37	11
38. Axocopan, s		32	12
39. Tecpatepec, s		38	19
40. Ytzcuincuitlapil[co], s		36	16
41. [Te] tepanco, s		35	17. Yetecomac
42. Tezcatepec, s		34	15
43. Hueypochtlan, s		33	14
44. Tequizquiac, s		39	18
45. Xilotzinco, s		40. Tolnacochtla	

Draft list:

4.3-1 Tollan — T1§
4.3-9 Atl ytlalacyan
4.3-2 Michmaloyan
4.3-3 Nextlalpan
4.3-4 Teçontepec
4.3-5 Mizquiyaualla
4.3-8 Tlaavililpan
4.3-6 Chilquauhtla
4.3-7 Itzmiquilpan
4.4-1 Hapazco — T1
4.4-2 Atotonilco
4.4-3 Axocopan
4.4-4 Tecpatepec
4.4-5 Atocpan
4.4-6 Itzcuincuitlapilco
4.4-7 Tezcatepec
4.4-8 Tetlapanaloyan
4.4-9 Veipuchtlan
4.4-10 Tequixquiac
4.4-11 Xilotzinco
4.5-1 Xilotepec — T1
4.5-2 Cacalotl ynequetzayan
4.5-3 Tecoçauhtlan
4.5-4 Acaualtzinco
4.5-5 Tlauhtla

*T1,tlatoani; t,teuctli; s,lord. See Table 4-3. Azcapotzalco has two lords.

†The numbers denote the place that a town occupies in the draft lists. The town's name is written only when it does not appear in the other Columns.

‡The edge of the document is torn; it is not possible to know whether a lord was depicted.

§This source names a king of Xippacoyan Tollan.

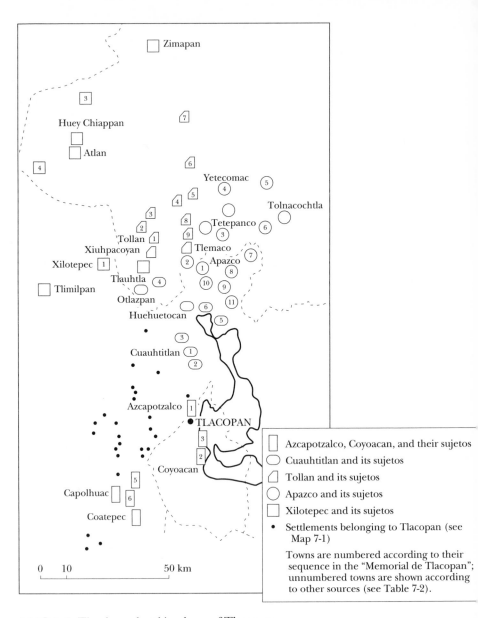

MAP 7–2. The dependent kingdoms of Tlacopan

The following labels appear within the map:

Zimapan

3

Huey Chiappan

7

Atlan

4

6

Yetecomac
4
5

5

Tolnacochtla

4 5

3
2
Tollan 1

8
9

Tetepanco
3

6

Xiuhpacoyan

Xilotepec 1

Tlemaco
2
1

Apazco
7
8

Tlauhtla 4

10 9

Tlimilpan

Otlazpan

11

Huehuetocan
6
5

3

Cuauhtitlan 1
2

Azcapotzalco 1

● TLACOPAN

3
2

Coyoacan

5

Capolhuac
6

Coatepec

Legend:

☐ Azcapotzalco, Coyoacan, and their sujetos

◯ Cuauhtitlan and its sujetos

◖ Tollan and its sujetos

◯ Apazco and its sujetos

☐ Xilotepec and its sujetos

● Settlements belonging to Tlacopan (see Map 7-1)

Towns are numbered according to their sequence in the "Memorial de Tlacopan"; unnumbered towns are shown according to other sources (see Table 7-2).

0   10   50 km

in category three of the "Memorial de Tlacopan," which includes the towns of Juan Cano, some of which belonged to Tlacopan. One can assume that this categorization did not take the indigenous jurisdiction into account and that, as in the Codex Osuna, those two towns were dependencies of Coyoacan.

The kingdom of Cuauhtitlan, according to the sources used for this table, had the following sujetos: Toltitlan (Tultitlan, Mexico); Tepotzotlan (Tepotzotlan, Mexico); Huehuetocan (Huehuetoca, Mexico); Otlazpan, which was congregated with Tepexic in the sixteenth century;[39] Tepexic (Tepeji de Ocampo, Hidalgo); Tzompanco (Zumpango, Mexico); and Citlaltepec (San Juan Citlaltepec in Zumpango, Mexico).

Other data from the *Anales de Cuauhtitlan*, not included in Table 7-2, tell us that the city was divided into four parts, and each one had two associated rulers. The most important of these—Tzompanco, Citlaltepec, Huehuetocan, and Otlazpan—were given the name of nauhteuctin, the "Four Lords."[40] Toltitlan, Tepexic, and Tepotzotlan were also within the dependency (*tlahuilanalpan*) of Cuauhtitlan. All these realms had their own rulers with the title of king (tlatoani).[41] Citlaltepec and Tzompanco were also part of the military district of the Basin registered in the Codex Mendoza.

The list of the labor draft of 1563 names a Nextlalpan that could be the old barrio of Xaltocan,[42] the present-day Santa Ana Nextlalpan, Mexico, but it also could be the Nextlalpan subject to Tollan listed below.

In the kingdom of Tollan there were twenty subject towns;[43] the sources used for Table 7-2 identify some of them. Xippacoyan, also mentioned in the traditions about Quetzalcoatl of Tollan, seems to be the present-day San Marcos in Tula de Allende, Hidalgo.[44] The others have kept their names, with slight changes, to the present day; all are in the state of Hidalgo: Atlitlalacyan (Atitalaquia), Michmaloyan (Michimaloya in Tula de Allende), Nextlalpan (Nextlalpa in Tepetitlan), Tezontepec (Tezontepec de Aldama), Tlemaco (Tlamaco in Atitalaquia), Mizquiyahuallan (Mixquiahuala), Tlaahuililpan (Tlahuelilpan), Chilcuauhtla (Chilcuauhtla), and Itzmiquilpan (Ixmiquilpan). All these towns had rulers of their own, of a lower category. According to the relación geográfica covering Atenco, Mizquiyahuallan, and Tezontepec, each of these towns had its own ruler, and they were sujetos of Tollan and of Moteuczoma, to whom they paid tribute.[45] According to the sequence of place names in the lists of the labor drafts, Tlacotepec and Tlaquepa appear to be in the kingdom of Tollan, but they have not been located.[46]

Apazco (present-day Apaxco de Ocampo, Mexico) was the cabecera of twenty towns; its first king was a certain Atlapopoca.[47] The sources of Table 7-2 identify several sujetos of Apazco, almost all of which still exist: Atotonilco (Atotoniltonco in the Codex Osuna; present-day Atotonilco de Tula, Hidalgo), Axocopan (Ajacuba, Hidalgo), Tecpatepec (Tepatepec in Francisco I. Madero, Hidalgo), Atocpan

(Actopan, Hidalgo), Itzcuincuitlapilco (Itzcuinquitlapilco in San Agustín Tlaxiaca, Hidalgo), Tetepanco (Tetepango, Hidalgo), Tezcatepec (near Tezontlalpan de Zapata in Hueypoxtla, Mexico), Tetlepanaloyan (Tlapanaloya in Tequixquiac, Mexico), Hueipochtlan (Hueypoxtla, Mexico), Tequixquiac (Tequixquiac, Mexico), and Xilotzinco (Jilotzingo in Hueypoxtla, Mexico). According to the lists of the labor drafts, the kingdom of Apazco also included Yetecomac, perhaps the present-day Tecomatlan in Ajacuba, Hidalgo,[48] and Tolnacochtla (Tornacuxtla in San Agustín Tlaxiaca, Hidalgo).

Almost all the towns depicted in the Codex Osuna had their own local rulers. The *Relaciones geográficas* add some information on several of these towns and their lords. Tecpatepec "was one of the ten towns governed by Atlapopoca, who resided in the province of Apazco"; his people came to settle there from Azcapotzalco and submitted themselves to the king of Tlatelolco, Cuacuauhpitzahuac.[49] Yetecomac was settled by people from Chiappan and was also governed by Atlapopoca of Apazco, although it recognized and paid tribute to Itzcoatzin of Tenochtitlan.[50] In this same area Tolnacochtla also submitted itself to Itzcoatl.[51] Hueypochtlan was settled first by a chief from Chiappan and later by other newcomers; it recognized and paid tribute to Moteuczoma just as did Tezontepec.[52] Axocopan was also founded by people from Chiappan, and they acknowledged the higher authority of Chimalpopoca of Tenochtitlan.[53]

According to the relación geográfica of Atlitlalacyan, which also includes Tlemaco, Atotonilco de Tula, Apazco, and Tetlapanaloyan, after the Mexica conquest the towns had Mexica tribute collectors and no natural lords, but this statement cannot be accepted as describing the government of the entire region, since other sources tell of the existence of local rulers in the kingdom of Apazco.[54]

Xilotepec (present-day Jilotepec, Mexico), the northernmost kingdom of the Tlacopanec group, bordered on the Chichimec territory beyond the Mesoamerican frontier. It is noteworthy that Xilotepec does not appear in the Codex Osuna as belonging to Tlacopan or in the lists of the labor drafts. Given that these sources are concerned with the recruitment of workers for public works in the Basin, it is to be expected that Xilotepec would not provide those services, simply because it was farther away from Tlacopan.

The "Memorial de Tlacopan" lists four subjects of Xilotepec. Cacalotl ynequetzayan has not been identified. Tlauhtla is Santiago Tlautla in the municipio of Tepeji de Ocampo, Hidalgo.[55] Tecozauhtlan (Tecozautla, Hidalgo) was one of several towns in this kingdom that contained a garrison against the Chichimecs. Another was Acahualtzinco, whose approximate location can be determined, since the relación of Querétaro lists the garrison towns against the Chichimecs, apparently in geographical order from north to south. They were Santiago Tecuzautla, San Mateo Gueychiapa (Huichapan, Hidalgo), San Josepe Atlan (San José Atlan in Huichapan, Hidalgo), Santa María Tleculutlicatzia, San Jerónimo Acagulcingo (*sic*), San Lorenzo Tlechatitla, and San Andrés Tiltmiepa (*sic*; San Andrés Timilpan, Mexico).[56] In 1601 Acahualtzinco was congregated in San José Atlan.[57] Towards the north, the kingdom of Xilotepec reached as far as Cimapan.[58]

Another toponym that must be taken into account is Mazahuacan. We have seen that, according to Torquemada, the "province" of Mazahuacan came into the Triple Alliance as a dependency of Tlacopan, but it does not appear among the Tlacopanec kingdoms in either the "Memorial de Tlacopan" or the Codex Osuna. Accounts of Ahuitzotl's war against Chiappan name Mazahuacan as one of the seven towns that were destroyed,[59] but reports on Axayacatl's war identify Mazahuacan with Xiquipilco,[60] and, on the other hand, Sahagún says the Mazahuas lived in Xocotitlan at the base of Mount Xocotepetl.[61] As in the case of Acolhuacan, Mazahuacan appears to be the name of a region that can be used as a synonym or second name of known towns such as Xiquipilco or Xocotitlan. Given its presence in the list of seven towns conquered by Ahuitzotl, it is also possible that it may be the second name of some other town as well, or an independent town that it is not possible to identify.

Later there were towns of tenants of Tlacopan in the Mazahua region. Perhaps, following Axayacatl's campaign, it was principally a dependency of Tenochtitlan, as was Tolocan. Xocotitlan had its own king in 1519 and was one of the tributary provinces of Tenochtitlan in the Codex Mendoza.[62]

There are some regional names that designate the territory of the Tepanec kingdoms, or part of them: Tlalhuacpan, Tepanoayan, and Teotlalpan. According to Durán, the king of Tlacopan was king of Tlalhuacpan, which means "the dry land."[63] Durán also uses Tlalhuacpan in referrence to Azcapotzalco and its domain during the reign of Tezozomoc.[64]

It is difficult to define Tepanoayan precisely. *Panoayan* means "crossing," or "ford," and Tepanoayan, Stone Ford; this name is also found in the Acolhuacan.[65] A place with that name in the western part of the Basin is located by Sahagún when describing the route followed by Quetzalcoatl after he left Tollan.[66] He passed through Cuauhtitlan and went on to Temacpalco (Stone Palm), identified in other sources as a mountain next to Tlalnepantla where Quetzalcoatl left his handprints.[67] He then crossed a river by placing stones in the riverbed, which explains the name Tepanoayan. Later he went to Cozcapan, a spring later named Coaapan, which can be located between Coyoacan and Xochimilco,[68] continued on to Cochtocan in Chalco,[69] and crossed the mountain pass between the volcanoes on the way to Cholollan. This tradition, therefore, locates Tepanoayan between Tlalnepantla and Coyoacan, although the exact spot is not given.

Some texts refer to Tepanoayan as a separate town, different from all the other known towns in that region. In the "Memorial de Tlacopan" it is one of the towns in the dependent kingdoms of Tlacopan, listed in the same paragraph as Azcapotzalco, Coyoacan, Atlacuihuayan, Atlappolco, and Xalatlauhco. However, Ixtlilxochitl describes the defeat of Azcapotzalco and Tlacopan by Nezahualcoyotl and Itzcoatl and then names the other conquered cities, beginning with Tepanoayan and Tenayocan. In this account Tepanoayan appears to be a separate town, unless it is an additional name of Tenayocan.[70] But Tepanoayan is also used as the name of the Tepanec region, comparable to Acolhuacan for the eastern region. In this way, the *Anales de Cuauhtitlan* refer to the capitals of the Empire as Tenochtitlan Mexico, Tetzcoco Acolhuacan, and Tlacopan Tepanoayan,[71] and Hernan Cortés, speaking of areas where the Tenochcas had gained control, includes this name with others that refer to regions: Tepanoayan, Acolhuacan, Xochimilco, and Chalco.[72] In some instances Tepanoayan is used in an ambiguous way.[73]

One can conclude that Tepanoayan was in some instances one of the Tepanec kingdoms in the region of Tlacopan, Azcapotzalco, and Tenayocan. Perhaps it was one of the ethnic parcialidades in some town with such parcialidades, as in Azcapotzalco, where there were two, Mexicapan and Tepanecapan. But Tepanoayan can also denote the Tepanec region; it is used as part of the name of Azcapotzalco and of Tlacopan and—as was Tepanecapan—is used to name the whole region dominated by them. This case is similar to those of Matlatzinco, Mazahuacan, Acolhuacan, or Chalco as well as Mexico, with its two cities of Tenochtitlan and Tlatelolco.

Another regional term is Teotlalpan, or Hueytlalpan. It means in general the north, similar to Mictlan, and can be understood as the land of the dead or of the ancestors. But it is also a well-defined area that includes the northern part of the Basin and the region of the kingdoms of Tollan and Apazco. The *Relaciones geográficas* describe several towns that were said to be in the Teotlalpan. The relación of Tequixquiac describes Tequixquiac, Citlaltepec, and Xilotzinco. Those of Atenco, Atlitlalaquia, and Tolnacochtla describe several more towns in the region of Tollan and Apazco, among them Hueypochtlan and Axocopan.[74]

The *Anales de Cuauhtitlan* contain a list of towns ruled by kings in 1519, with Cuauhtitlan the last one listed. The subdivisions of Cuauhtitlan are described as "the Four Lords: Tzompanco, Citlaltepec, Huehuetocan, Otlazpan; its dependency: Toltitlan, Tepexic, Tepotzotlan; its Great Land [*yhueytlal*], its dependency, its possession. Apazco leads 20 towns. Tollan leads 20 towns."[75] Hueytlalli, in this case, must refer to the Hueytlalpan or Teotlalpan, which also includes the two cities of Apazco and Tollan.[76]

In a list of the provinces in the archbishopric of Mexico, the province of Teotlalpan comprises the entire region north of the city of Mexico and of Acolman. In the Basin it includes Ecatepec, Cuauhtitlan, and Otompan, and towards the east, Tepepolco, Cempohuallan, Tollantzinco, Epazoyocan, Acatlan, and Cuauhchinanco.

In the northwest it was adjacent to Xilotepec and in the northeast to Metztitlan. It may be that in this source the great extent of Teotlalpan reflects colonial usage.[77]

Although the "Memorial de Tlacopan" and the Codex Osuna confirm Ixtlilxochitl's formula that there were kings subordinate to Tlacopan, there is no doubt that in several of the cities within the area of Tlacopan the kings were of the Tenochca dynasty, thus presenting a clear contrast with the situation in the Acolhuacan, where this relationship is not found. It should also be noted that in these kingdoms there is little evidence of direct lineal succession, and the imposition of Tenochca rulers was part of that irregular succession. Azcapotzalco, Atlacuihuayan, and Toltitlan are the only towns within the Tepanec realm in which there was an uninterrupted patrilineal line of local kings. The kings of Tlacopan, Atlacuihuayan, and one of the parcialidades of Azcapotzalco descended from Tezozomoc of Azcapotzalco. There is no clear evidence that the Tepanec dynasty continued in Coyoacan, and Cuauhtitlan appears to have kept its own Chichimec dynasty. What one finds instead is the presence of kings of the Tenochca dynasty in Azcapotzalco Mexicapan, Tiliuhcan Tlacopan, Toltitlan, Tollan, and Xilotepec. In Tollan the enthronement of sons of the Tenochca king is repeated in successive generations; in other towns the data are not complete enough to know whether they were individual cases or the beginning of a new line of Tenochca rulers. The marriages with Tenochca princesses in Cuauhtitlan, Coyoacan, and Xilotepec also suggest direct influence from Tenochtitlan.

The functions of these cities of the Tepanec kingdom of Tlacopan and their obligations towards the capital consisted, according to the "Memorial de Tlacopan," of military service and providing lime, stone, wood, and craft products.[78] The obligation of these towns is very similar to what is said about the corresponding category in the "Memorial tetzcocano." The Tlacopanec memorial of the Codex Osuna agrees in regard to military service, and although nothing is said about tribute in building materials, it is significant that the document was prepared specifically in regard to such demand from the Tlacopanec towns.

Van Zantwijk distinguished three types of territorial units: the kingdoms, defined in accord with the Codex Osuna; the military districts according to section 4 of the "Memorial de Tlacopan"; and the imperial tribute districts, as in the Codex Mendoza, to which he adds a few other towns.[79] Even though there are some differences between the "Memorial de Tlacopan" and the Codex Osuna concerning the towns listed, the distinction between kingdoms and military districts does not seem justifiable, since it is the kingdoms that provided both military service and personnel for public works. As to the tributary organization, the provinces in the Codex Mendoza sent their tribute to Tenochtitlan; the tributaries of Tlacopan were the towns and estancias in section 5 of the "Memorial de Tlacopan" that are discussed below.

The Tributaries of Tlacopan within Its Own Domain and the Domains of the Other Two Capitals

Tlacopan—like Tenochtitlan and Tetzcoco—had tributaries within its own domain and the domains of the other two capitals and in Tlalhuic as well as in Chalco. All these possessions are listed together in the fifth section of the "Memorial de los pueblos de Tlacopan," where they are arranged in two paragraphs of towns and two of estancias. Analysis of the list will show that in effect more important than the distinction between towns and estancias was their different geographical location, which distinguished between the towns located in the Tlacopan domain and the estancias located in other parts of the core area.

The descriptive heading of section 5 in the "Memorial de Tlacopan" reads as follows:

> These towns and estancias were subject to Tlacopan, and in them there was no lord but stewards and principals who governed them. They all were as tenants [renteros] of the lord of Tlacopan. In addition to [receiving] their tribute, the lord of Tlacopan had in these towns many fields that people cultivated for him. Because of that the Indians are here with victles [*sic*] in their hands, that are the spades used in New Spain to till the land. They also served their lxxx days each year [providing] firewood for the lord's household.[80]

This text is almost identical to the corresponding passage in Motolinía's "Memorial tetzcocano" and therefore is the best evidence that the two documents were prepared together. But there is an interesting difference between them. The "Memorial tetzcocano" says that the tenants gave firewood to the capital for half a year, and during the other half it was provided by the cities ruled by kings. In regard to firewood, where the "Memorial de Tlacopan" states that they provided firewood 80 (lxxx) days every year, Zimmermann suggests that it should be read as 180 days, which would agree with the almost identical text in the "Memorial tetzcocano." It is possible that there was an error by the scribe in writing "su lxxx" instead of "clxxx." However, a period of 80 days makes sense if we relate it to the division of this group of towns into four parts, as is seen in the list. To each part would correspond a specified period in accordance with the Nahuatl expression *nappohualtica* (literally, every 80 days), which is used for events that take place four times a year, separated by two intervals of 80 days and two others of a hundred.

The towns listed in this fifth section are divided into two basic categories, indicated by the subheadings simply as estancias or pueblos. The distinction between the two types of settlements is also found in the letter of Don Antonio Cortés of Tlacopan referred to above (see p. 184 and Table 7-1). Usually the estancias were more or less isolated settlements, with fields and peasants who cultivated them, part of a larger township; that is probably the meaning in this document. In contrast, a pueblo, or town, would be a settlement of a higher political category, probably the seat of a local ruler. In this case it is worth noting that the places called pueblos were within Tlacopan's domain.

The heading of section 5 quoted above gives a definition of the socioeconomic characteristics of these settlements that is equivalent to that in the section of Motolinía's "Memorial tetzcocano" describing the towns of tenants. Nevertheless, as has been pointed out, it appears that the two memorials used somewhat different criteria when applying this definition to their respective lists of towns. In Motolinía's memorial the towns of tenants are all in the Acolhuacan and on the frontier with Chalco, and the towns in Cuauhnahuac (Tlalhuic) are on another list without a descriptive heading. On the other hand, the "Memorial de Tlacopan" puts in its first three sections the towns of the capital's district, and in section 5 the lists of settlements of tenants of Tlacopan in the Tepanec region follow the lists of those situated in the domain of Tenochtitlan, in Chalco, and in Tlalhuic. Thus, the descriptions of both memorials define a social category of tenant farmers present in regions that differed in their political status.

Table 7-3 lists all the towns and identifies the region where they were located; they are represented in Map 7-3. As to their location, some of these towns and estancias can be readily identified, but other place names are more difficult to find.[81] When there are alternatives I have favored the identifications that show geographical consistency within each paragraph, but other possible locations are given that would scatter the settlements in each paragraph throughout a wider area.

Each of the four groups has a certain geographical unity. The first group of estancias is in the Chinampanec and Chalca regions of the southern part of the Basin, and the second, in Tlalhuic. The first group of towns is for the most part in Matlatzinco, that is, the western part of the present-day state of Mexico, from Ixtlahuacan to Tolocan and Zoquitzinco; the second, in the northern part of the Basin, is from the region of Chiappan to the region of Tizayocan. It is not clear whether the first name on each list was that of the cabecera. They are barrios or estancias of important cities (Azcapotzalco or Coyoacan, Cuauhnahuac, Cuauhtitlan, and Chiappan) but of lesser importance, as is to be expected, since they are settlements of tenants.

The territorial distribution is also significant in terms of political categories. The estancias are found outside the Tepanec domain; some were in the Chinampanec region in the southern part of the Basin that formed the Tenochca domain but where Tetzcoco had possessions—and, as can be seen in this list, where Tlacopan did also. Other estancias were in the area of Chalco and in Tlalhuic, where

TABLE 7-3.

Estancias and Towns of Tenants Subject to Tlacopan

Estancias:

A)

1. Tetzcolco	In Azcapotzalco or Coyoacan
2. Mizquic	In the Chinampanec region
3. Yaotzinco	Ayotzinco
4. Quauhatitlan	In Chalco
5. Amoloncan	In Chalco
6. Xocoyoltepec	In Chalco
7. Itztlacoçauhcan	In Chalco

B)

1. Ytzteyocan	In Tlalhuic
2. Couintepec	In Tlalhuic
3. Xoxouhtlan	In Tlalhuic
4. Xoxocotla	In Tlalhuic
5. Miyauatlan	In Tlalhuic
6. Calpilco	In Tlalhuic
7. Tecpançolco	In Tlalhuic
8. Amacoztitlan	In Tlalhuic
9. Molotlan	In Tlalhuic
10. Anenecuilco	In Tlalhuic

Towns:

A)

1. Tepeyacac	In the northern part of the Basin (Cuauhtitlan)
2. Auazuatepec	Xiquipilco
3. Xolotepec	In the northern part of the Basin (or Xocotepec, the mountain of Xocotitlan)
4. Xochiyocan	South of Teotenanco
5. Çoquitzinco	South of Teotenanco
6. Maxtlecan	South of Teotenanco
7. Tolocan	Tolocan
8. Toxinco	In Ixtlahuacan
9. Tochcalco	In Ixtlahuacan
10. Ixtlauacan	In Ixtlahuacan

B)

1. Çacapechco	In Chiappan
2. Quauhtlaapan	In the northern part of the Basin (Tepotzotlan)
3. Tequixquiyacac	Tequixquiyac
4. Nopallan	In Hueypochtlan
5. Tecalco	San Pablo Tecalco, in the northern part of the Basin

SOURCE: Zimmermann 1970:6.

MAP 7–3. The tributaries of Tlacopan within its own domain and in the domain of Tenochtitlan

some towns had their own kings and the three capitals of the alliance each had separate possessions.

The lists given below follow the arrangement of the "Memorial de Tlacopan" — that is, the regions in other parts of the core area are listed before those within Tlacopan's domain. The reason for this might be that the settlements that are listed first were the closest to the Tepanec cities and might have been among their major suppliers of agricultural goods.

Tlacopan was not the only kingdom of the Tepanec group that had possessions in regions of the core area outside its own domain. Cuauhtitlan also held lands in Chalco and in Matlatzinco;[82] the latter would have been acquired when land was distributed after Axayacatl's campaign. The *Anales de Cuauhtitlan* report that the boundary marks of the "eagle land" (cuauhtlalli) in Matlatzinco were put in place with the participation of the four parts of Cuauhtitlan.[83]

Estancias in the Tenochca Domain and in Chalco

1. Tetzcolco	Santa Apolonia Tetzcolco, barrio of Azcapotzalco (Pérez Rocha 1982:69), or Santiago Tetzcolco, barrio of Coyoacan (Carrasco and Monjarás-Ruiz 1976:78; 1978:68, 161).	
2. Mizquic	Mixquic in the Federal District.	
3. Yaotzinco	Santa Catarina Ayotzingo in Chalco, Mexico.	
4. Quauhatitlan	(?) San Martín Quauhcaltitlan in the vicinity of Atlauhtla in Chalco (García Mora 1981: fig. 17).	
5. Amoloncan	Amolo is a mountain north of Juchitepec in Chalco (García Mora 1981: fig. 1); Amolocan would be the town next to it.	
6. Xocoyoltepec	Also a holding of Tenochtitlan in Chalco (Chimalpahin 1889:144). Rancho Xocoyotepec between Pahuacan and Zoyatzinco in Chalco (García Mora 1981: fig. 1).	
7. Itztlacoçauhcan	Parcialidad of Amaquemecan in Chalco (Chimalpahin 1889:237).	

Yaotzinco (3) can be interpreted as Ayotzinco because the usual glyph for tortoise (*ayotl*) can also be read *yaotl*.[84] In Ayotzinco there seem to have been settlers from different cities in the Basin. In 1571 it was divided into four barrios: Tenochtitlan, Tlatelolco, Xochimilco, and Coyoacan.[85] This last one could have been the Tepanec dependency.

Quauhatitlan (4) may be a faulty spelling, since in the manuscript the letter *a* seems to be written over the letter *c*. There is also a Quauhacaltitlan in Atzacualpan, north of Cuauhtitlan, where lands were distributed during the reign of Moteuczoma Xocoyotzin.[86]

Amoloncan (5) is a common name. There is also San Bernabé Amolonco, which was a barrio of Azcapotzalco.[87] Almolonga and Almoloyan may be names equivalent to Amolonca and are very frequent. There was an Almolonga, an estancia of Xocotitlan;[88] another was a land site in Chiappan.[89] Almoloyan is the name of various towns in the state of Mexico.

With the exception of the first town, which might have been the cabecera, all these towns are in the Chinampan area of the Tenochca domain and in Chalco, an area in which the three capitals had separate holdings and which was primarily under Tenochca control. Two towns in this list are also recorded in the Codex Mendoza: Mizquic in the province of Petlacalco and Xocoyoltepec in that of Chalco.

Estancias in Tlalhuic

1.	Ytzteyocan	Sujeto of Cuauhnahuac (AGI, Justicia 146). Near Tetela del Monte, northwest of Cuernavaca.
2.	Couintepec	Coquentepec, in the parcialidad of San Pedro Tecpan in Cuauhnahuac (AGN-HJ, 290:1707v). San Sebastián Cuentepec in Temixco, Morelos.
3.	Xoxouhtlan	Sujeto of Cuauhnahuac (AGN-HJ, 289, exp. 102:498r; CDI, 12:560). Jojutla, Morelos.
4.	Xoxocotla	San Felipe Xoxocotla, barrio of Cuauhnahuac (AGN-HJ, 290:1708r; CDI, 12:560). Xoxocotla in Puente de Ixtla, Morelos.
5.	Miyauatlan	Miahuatlan in Amacuzac, Morelos.
6.	Calpilco	In Yauhtepec (AGN-HJ, 289, exp. 100).
7.	Tecpançolco	Not identified. The name also appears in the painting of the lands of Don Antonio Cortés Totoquihuatzin (Zimmermann 1970:13 and table 35).
8.	Amacoztitlan	Amacuzac, Morelos.
9.	Molotlan	Town in San Pedro Tecpan of Cuauhnahuac; or barrio of Yauhtepec (see note 142, chapter 5).
10.	Anenecuilco	Sujeto of Huaxtepec in Las Amilpas (CDI, 12:561; RG, 6:200). Anenecuilco de los Mata in Ayala, Morelos.

Itzteyocan is well documented in early colonial documents. In 1529, Yzteyuca and Tetela (Tetellan) were estancias within the boundaries of Cuauhnahuac, and in 1568, Tecpan Ytzteyucan was the main barrio of the seventeen in the towns of

Yzteyucan and Tetela.[90] Izteocan is listed in the parcialidad of San Juan Panchi-malco in Cuauhnahuac.[91] Tetellan, with which Itzteyocan is always associated, is the present-day Tetela del Monte northwest of Cuernavaca.

Tlalhuic was a major area in which all three capitals had their separate hold-ings. Some of the towns in this list also appear in the Codex Mendoza: Xoxocotla (4), Amacoztitlan (8), and Molotlan (9) in the province of Cuauhnahuac, and Anen-ecuilco (10) in the province of Huaxtepec. Tlacopan's share is attested not only in this Tepanec source but also in Ixtlilxochitl and in the local documentation from Tlalhuic, which also report the political authority of Tlacopan over towns in this area.[92]

Tributary Towns in Matlatzinco

1.	Tepeyacac	San Francisco Tepeyacat (*sic*), a visita of Cuauhtitlan (Vetancurt 1961, 3:166).
		San Francisco Tenopalco in Melchor Ocampo, Mexico.
2.	Auazuatepec	Ahuazhuatepeque, cabecera of Xiquipilco (SV, par. 801).
3.	Xolotepec	San Lucas Xoloc in Tecamac, Mexico, or San Mateo Xoloc in Tepotzotlan, Mexico.
4.	Xochiyocan	Santa Ana Xochuca in Ixtapan de la Sal, Mexico.
5.	Çoquitzinco	Joquicingo, Mexico.
6.	Maxtlecan	Maxtleca de Galeana in Joquicingo, Mexico.
7.	Tolocan	Toluca, Mexico.
8.	Toxinco	San Lorenzo Toxico (Colín 1968: pars. 1442, 1445, 1452, 3775).
		San Lorenzo Toxico in Ixtlahuaca, Mexico.
9.	Tochcalco	An estancia of Ixtlahuacan (SV, par. 296).
10.	Ixtlauacan	Ystlahuaca (SV, par. 296).
		Ixtlahuaca de Rayón, Mexico.

Tepeyacac (1) in other documents is spelled Tepeyac, Tepeaquilla, and Tepe-yacac. It is the same name as that of the sanctuary of Our Lady of Guadalupe, but in another location. This Tepeyacac is also mentioned in the *Anales de Cuauhtitlan* and can be identified with San Francisco Tenopalco.[93] Only this town and Xolote-pec (3) seem to be in the Basin. This would mean that the cabecera of this region was a town within the kingdom of Cuauhtitlan, one of those in the Tlacopan group.

Ahuazhuatepec (2) is a toponym found in other areas.[94] The identification here advanced is strengthened by the fact that, in a letter of 1552, Don Antonio Cortés Totoquihuatzin asked that the town of Xiquipilco be granted to him.[95]

Xolotepec (3) has several possible locations. There was a place with this name in Tlalmanalco,[96] but it is better to identify it with Mount Xoloc, near San Lucas Xoloc, a town in the municipio of Tecamac and a colonial appurtenance of Tlatelolco.[97] It had been the ancient dwelling place of the leader called Xolotl[98] and later was on the boundary between the domains of Tenochtitlan and Tetzcoco.[99] In this region of the Basin there were several estancias of Tlatelolco and Tenochtitlan; it is possible that Tlacopan also had some there.[100] There is also a San Mateo Xoloc, a town of Tepotzotlan, near Cuauhtlaapan.[101] Given that most of the towns in this group are in the region of Toluca, one can also think that Xolotepec was a scribe's error in the manuscript of the memorial, and the town is really Xocotepec, the mountain near Xocotitlan.

In Tolocan (7), after the distribution of land made by Axayacatl, Tlacopan held lands that later became the barrios of Santa María Magdalena, San Lorenzo Tlacalpa, and San Pedro Tototepec; Azcapotzalco also received several towns.[102]

The toponym Ixtlahuacan (10) is found in many areas. In this case it must be the well-known town north of Toluca, since the two previous towns on this list were in its jurisdiction. To the west, Ixtlahuacan was contiguous with Taximaroa and Maravatío;[103] that is, these possessions of Tlacopan faced the kingdom of Michoacan.

Some of these towns are also present in Codex Mendoza. In the province of Tolocan are Tolocan (7) itself and Zoquitzinco (5). Both of these and also Maxtlecan (6) were also among the possessions of Tetzcoco.[104]

Most of these towns are in the area covered by the province of Tolocan in the Codex Mendoza and in areas farther north. Tlacopan shared in the distribution of land after Axayacatl's conquests but probably had older claims to this area, since from the very beginning Mazahuacan is described as forming part of Tlacopan's domain. The more northern towns in the region of Ixtlahuaca seem to have been exclusively under Tlacopan.

Tributary Towns in the Northern Basin

1. Çacapechco   San Jerónimo Zacapechco, sujeto of Chiappan
                    (SV, par. 111; DA, 140; Colín 1966: pars. 619, 3415).
2. Quauhtlaapan   Cuauhtlaapan (AC, 8, 18, 29, 30, 46).
                    Santiago Cuauhtlalpa in Mexico.
3. Tequixquiyacac   Tequixquiac, Mexico.

| 4. Nopallan | San Ignacio Nopala in Tepeji de Ocampo, Hidalgo. |
| 5. Tecalco | One of the several towns of this name in the area of Tizayocan (see below). |

Cuauhtlaapan (2) appears in the *Anales de Cuauhtitlan*. It must be the present-day Santiago Cuauhtlalpa west of Tepotzotlan, which in certain documents is called Santiago Cuauhtlaapan.[105] An important document from Cuauhtitlan states that Tlacopan owned lands in that kingdom.[106]

The name Tequixquiyacac (3) is very similar to Tequixquiac, Mexico, a town in the northern part of the Basin listed in the "Memorial de los pueblos de Tlacopan" as a sujeto of Apazco, but there is not enough information to prove that it was the same place.

Nopallan (4) is a very frequent toponym. The location given above is the one closest to the other places on this list. Others are Nopala in Hueypoxtla, Mexico; San Mateo Nopala, formerly a town in the visita of Naucalpan;[107] and the Nopala that was in the tributary province of Xilotepec, probably the present-day Nopala de Villagrán, Hidalgo.[108]

Tecalco (5) is the name of several towns in the northern Basin. Some have been mentioned when discussing the Tenochca holdings in that area. In the sixteenth century in the region of Tizayocan there were estancias of Acolhua towns such as Tepechpan and Tecamac as well as of Tenochtitlan, Tlatelolco, and Toltitlan, a Tepanec city.[109] The *Anales de Cuauhtitlan* describe a distribution of lands in Tizayocan in which Cuauhtitlan, Toltitlan, and Cuitlachtepec, towns of the Tepanec sector, were given land.[110] It could well be that Tlacopan also had possessions there that would include this Tecalco and the Xolotepec of the preceding list.

The towns of this group are within Tlacopan's domain in the Basin but extending farther north towards the Teotlalpan and Xilotepec. Tecalco is intermingled with the holdings of Tenochtitlan and Tetzcoco.[111]

PART THREE

The Distant Regions Subject to the Empire

Chapter 8

TYPES OF TERRITORIAL UNITS

Native Kingdoms, Tributary Provinces, and Military Colonies

A detailed account of the internal organization of the conquered regions is beyond the scope of this study, but we should consider several general questions, for they bear directly on the imperial territorial organization. The basic issue concerning the political structure of the Triple Alliance, as is the case for any empire, is the manner in which the central authority is imposed and maintained in the outlying regions. In the core area there is a clear contrast between the political organization of the kingdoms that comprised the alliance and that of the tributary units, or calpixcazgos. The overlapping and intermingling of the territories of the three kingdoms are also quite clear. Something similar occurs in the conquered regions, in which the Empire kept the existing political organization but, in order to collect tribute, superimposed a system of tributary units. How the three capitals shared the resources of the conquered regions is a complex problem. One must determine whether there was a division of territory such that each one would extract its tribute separately or a division of the tribute extracted through the joint administration of the conquered areas. The data available are not entirely sufficient, but some information can be found in the historical sources, since in narrating the wars of conquest they frequently speak of the establishment of tributary units and the kind of administration imposed on them.

Zorita gives a general description of the treatment of conquered towns that is worth quoting in its entirety:

> The kings of Mexico and their allies the kings of Tetzcoco and of Tlaco-pan, in all the provinces that they conquered and regained left their natural lords (señores naturales) in their rulerships, both the highest and the inferior

ones, and they left all the commoners in possession of their lands and property and with their own customs and way of government. And [the conquerors] assigned to themselves some lands, according to what they had won, in which the commoners tilled fields for them, according to what grew in each area, and that was what they had to give them as tribute and as acknowledgment of vassalage, and the subjects went with that [tribute] to the stewards and persons that the king had established to collect it, and they took it to the persons to whom the kings of Mexico, Tetzcoco or Tlacopan had ordered them to go, each one to the king to whom he had become subject with the obligation to obey and to serve in the wars. And this was general in all the provinces they had subjugated, and they [the conquered rulers] remained as rulers as much as before, with all their realm and the governing of it, and with civil and criminal jurisdiction.[1]

Zorita notes that certain lands could be allotted to one or another of the three capitals, but for the rest he describes a general system of government based on keeping the local rulers in place and sending imperial tribute collectors. The section of Zorita's work that contains this information is based on the material provided by Francisco de las Navas, and therefore one might conclude that he is describing primarily that part of the tramontane region that had been subjugated by the Empire—that is, the tributary province of Tepeyacac.[2] Data from other sources on this region demonstrate the importance of the local rulers under the regime of the Triple Alliance and the payment of tribute in maize, two important facts in Zorita's description.

In several documents Bishop Ramírez de Fuenleal, president of the Audiencia, describes different types of sujetos in terms of their political and tributary situation. Some of these documents are related only to the colonial situation, but others describe conditions during the time of Moteuczoma Xocoyotzin. In a letter to the king of Spain in 1532, Fuenleal states that "there is another kind of sujeto, called calpixcazgo in Moteuczoma's time, and . . . in a given province he established a calpixque, what we call a steward, to receive all the tribute. And he resided in the most important town and the other towns brought there their tribute. These are not sujetos except in this respect, otherwise they were cabeceras on their own and had their own rulers."[3] In another letter that same year he makes a shorter statement to the same effect: "There are other towns they call sujetos because Moteuczoma established a calpixque or steward in a province, and many cabeceras and towns, that were independent, paid their tribute where the calpixque resided. These should not be considered sujetos."[4]

It is clear that the dominance described in these cases was exercised only in regard to tribute and did not imply political subordination to the provincial cabeceras. These statements have to be considered for the interpretation of the Codex Mendoza and related sources.

Zorita explains that when the people of a town realized that they did not have the resources to oppose the Empire's attack, they went to greet the imperial army with presents of great value and agreed to accept the Empire's god. The towns that submitted in this way without a battle "gave tribute not as vassals but as friends" who demonstrated their loyalty by bringing gifts and remaining obedient. The towns that had to be conquered by war had to pay larger tribute.[5]

A somewhat fuller account by Andrés de Tapia defines two degrees of incorporation into the Empire. In the towns that gave themselves up without fighting, the local rulers remained as such and sent tribute and "*parias*" several times a year at their own discretion; Tenochtitlan did not send stewards or collectors to these towns. The situation was very different in the towns that were conquered. The Tenochca king considered everything their people had as his own and used them as if they were slaves. The native rulers governed their people, but under the control of the stewards and collectors installed by the Mexicas. They directed the cultivation of grains, trees, and cotton, and they had large houses to which women from every town and barrio came to spin and weave. Some of the tribute was sent to other kingdoms near Mexico because they had sent men to the war of conquest.[6] Obviously these were the other kingdoms of the alliance.

Thus, Tapia gives two extremes of the degree of submission to the Empire. A more detailed description allowing for subtler variations is provided by Ixtlilxochitl. He tells of the continuance in office of local rulers and explains how they kept a certain amount of power according to the manner in which they responded to the Empire's demands. Four different degrees of submission are thus identified.

1. When the Empire decided to take action against a certain kingdom, it first sent Tenochca envoys to address the people and especially the elders of the town. The ruler "was pardoned and accepted as a friend of the Empire" if the dominion of the Triple Alliance was accepted and the ruler committed himself to "never act against the Empire," to allow freedom of trade to the Empire's merchants and freedom of movement to its people, and to send presents of "gold, precious stones, feathers and cloaks." Although it is not specified, freedom of movement must have included unobstructed passage of the imperial armies. These obligations were increased when the demands for submission had to be repeated, but obviously fidelity to the Empire, freedom of trade and movement, and the sending of valuable presents were a basic part of all requests for submission.

2. When the initial request was not accepted, a second embassy, from Tetzcoco, threatened the local ruler and noblemen with death and other punishments. If the town submitted, the people were then obliged to send tribute every year to the three kings of the Empire, but only a moderate amount, and the ruler

was pardoned together with all his noblemen and admitted "to the grace and friendship" of the three kings.

3. If the response was again negative, ambassadors sent from Tlacopan threatened to raze the town, make slaves of their prisoners, and turn the entire population into tribute payers. If the town surrendered, only the ruler was punished, and the people became subject to increased tribute demands that were to be paid from the income pertaining to the ruler. Ixtlilxochitl does not explain in what way the ruler was punished.

4. When the Empire's request was rejected for a third time, the armies of the three capitals went forth to battle. After the conquest the kingdom's lands and tribute were divided among the three kings of the alliance in the proportion of two-fifths each for Tenochtitlan and Tetzcoco, and one-fifth for Tlacopan. The defeated ruler was punished, but his heirs kept "lands and vassals appropriate to persons of their quality," and the legitimate heir succeeded to the rulership with all the obligations imposed. The conquerors left a garrison of men from the armies of the three capitals to secure the conquered area, and the rest of the army departed.[7]

In contrast with the towns that had submitted peacefully, those conquered by force had to accept the presence of representatives of the imperial powers, who established military garrisons and intervened directly in the local system of production, as implied in the redistribution of land. Ixtlilxochitl's description does not provide information on the appointment of officials; he writes of calpixques in his accounts of the conquests of Nezahualcoyotl and of the three kings of the alliance. Following the first three manners of submission, perhaps no permanent officials were appointed and the calpixques came only occasionally to collect the tribute. In the towns vanquished in battle there must have been gradations in the duties of the calpixques, some of whom were simply tribute collectors, but others had political functions. In any case, the local rulers were kept in place, but with certain limits on their authority.

It is not possible to classify all polities known to be subject to the Empire in terms of the categories defined by the authors just cited. All subject polities sent goods to Tenochtitlan whether in the form of presents or of tribute. Since the systematic records of towns subject to the Empire are registers of tribute, it is essential to know exactly what the pictorial tribute registers really represent.

The data from the Codex Mendoza, with the commentaries describing the presence of collectors or governors, suggest that the provinces recorded were those that had refused to surrender until they were conquered by the imperial armies; these were the most strictly controlled, as Ixtlilxochitl and Tapia tell us. The accounts of the chronicles that describe the imposition of tribute and the appointment of calpixques after a conquest apply concretely to many of the provinces registered in the Mendocino codex. One might assume then that towns that had submitted without a battle and only sent presents were not recorded in the Codex Mendoza, and the data from some of the *Relaciones geográficas* would support this. It could also be assumed that towns that did not pay tribute in kind but in services or in goods to be used locally, such as provisions for passing imperial armies, were not recorded. All this would also explain why many towns listed in the "Memorial de Tlacopan" as tributaries, without defining the nature of the tribute, are not depicted in the Codex Mendoza.

But as has been pointed out, the general descriptions in the commentaries of the Codex Mendoza leave room for doubt whether all the provinces recorded there were of the same type. Some provinces are within the core area; others—such as Oxitipan and Cihuatlan—are in remote areas where imperial control is not well documented. Furthermore, there is a great variation in the amount of tribute paid, and we know from other sources that there were also important differences in the power held by the rulers of the towns depicted. The general statements about the political functions of the calpixques might not be applicable to all areas. The provinces were probably under different types of submission and even within the provinces encompassing a number of polities, not all of these were necessarily subject under the same conditions.

Consequently, we should also consider the possibility that the Codex Mendoza (or even more, the original pictorial) could have been not a register of goods demanded (as were the tribute assessments in colonial times) but a record of goods received and kept under the care of the stewards in Tenochtitlan. In such a case the Codex Mendoza could include not only tribute, but also goods received as presents and even goods obtained by trade by the king's merchants in provinces such as Tochtepec and Xoconochco.

The subject polities, their native rulers, their tribute obligations, and the role of the imperial officials cannot be assumed to have constituted a uniform system applicable to all provinces depicted in the pictorial tribute registers. This is a question that has to be discussed as far as possible on the basis of specific data about each individual polity.

In the quotation given above, Zorita uses the term *señor natural* (natural lord) for the native local rulers in areas subjugated by the Empire; a number of other sources use the same term. It is an old Spanish concept that can be defined as a permanent, hereditary relationship between ruler and subjects considered to be of a familial or domestic nature, which created reciprocal legal rights and obligations as well as customary relations of fidelity and support.[8] The Spanish saw in the native polities a relationship similar to that of their own background and used the phrase "señor natural" to define the contrast with officials appointed by the imperial rulers.

The general descriptions of Ramírez de Fuenleal, Zorita, and Ixtlilxochitl

make quite clear the coexistence of local rulers and imperial calpixques who collected the tribute. A careful reading of the Codex Mendoza confirms this, since it
is known from other sources that the tributary provinces it defines rarely coincided
with local political divisions, and the towns listed as comprising the said provinces
were not separate political entities but points for the collection of tribute. If any of
these tributary provinces were political entities, they were so only to the extent
that the calpixques or other imperial envoys had assumed certain governmental
functions over the underlying political entities preserved by the Empire, not because they coincided with them.

We have seen that within the core area the Tenochca provinces depicted in
the Codex Mendoza cannot be read as representing the political organization of
that area. In the Acolhuacan the provinces of Acolman and Atotonilco el Grande
do not coincide with the political organization of the Acolhua kingdoms that were
dependencies of Tetzcoco, and the dependent Tepanec kingdoms of Tlacopan had
a territorial organization different from that of the tributary provinces in the
Codex Mendoza in the same region. A similar situation prevailed in the subjugated
regions that paid tribute to the three capitals.

In some cases the tributary provinces coincided roughly with an indigenous
political entity, but usually they contained towns from different kingdoms. The
towns listed within a province differ considerably in terms of size and political category. Some are important cabeceras with native kings who also ruled over neighboring settlements; others were smaller towns, with rulers of lesser importance,
and were part of wider native political units. Other settlements were rural dependencies of the native polities in which calpixques and tequitlatos were the local
authorities. In many cases not enough is known to ascertain the political nature of
the communities listed.

The cabeceras of a tributary province were usually established in the capitals
of native kingdoms. Tepeyacac, the most important imperial base in the tramontane area, was one of the principal Chichimec polities of the area, all of which were
also included in the province together with the Coatlalpanec towns and the Popoloca kingdom of Tepexic. Coaixtlahuacan, a Popoloca city and capital of a great
kingdom, became the cabecera of a tributary province, which also contained several Mixtec kingdoms. Tlachquiauhco was another important Mixtec kingdom;
the imperial tributary province centered there also included the kingdom of Achiotlan and a dependency of Malinaltepec. Tlappan was an extensive native polity
turned into a tributary province, although not all of its areas are represented in the
list of tributary towns. Probably a single native political unit was the basis for the
provinces of Tlachco and Tlacozauhtitlan. Quiyauhteopan coincided roughly with
the native state of Olinallan. On the Gulf coast the province of Tochpan may have
been a single native polity with two major cabeceras, in Tochpan and Papantlan.

But there is also the case of Coyolapan, where the cabecera was of secondary importance in the underlying native political organization. Coyolapan is considered to have been a late Mixtec intrusion into the valley, in which the Empire established the cabecera of the tributary province. The capital of the most important Tzapotec realm, Teotzapotlan, is not included in the province and is never mentioned as a tributary town, although it is said to have been conquered and some of its dependent kingdoms paid tribute to the Empire.

Other provinces encompassed several native polities and had perhaps formed loose confederations; the data are not sufficient. This was probably the case in Tepecuacuilco, where nothing suggests that the cabecera was more important than other towns in the same province. Similar situations existed in Yohualtepec, Xoconochco, Cihuatlan, Cuetlaxtlan, Cuauhtochco, and Tziuhcoac.

Practically all tributary provinces also included settlements of lesser importance, and this is where the identification of towns can be most difficult. The minor settlements were probably included as seats of second-level calpixques because they were centers of particular local produce, crafts, or special resources restricted to certain areas. For example, since the province of Coyolapan gave gold as tribute, one can speculate that the town in this province called Teocuitlatlan or Teocuitlapacoyan (Gold Washing) was the site of gold placers. Probably salt also came from some specific communities, but the production of most tribute items was possible in many areas within a province and cannot be connected with individual towns in the lists. Other lesser towns in the provinces might have been centers for communication and transportation.

Sometimes a small town is close to its political center, which is also listed, but others are located in areas where the native cabeceras are not included, and this may be significant for the analysis of the political control of the whole area. In the province of Tepeyacac, for example, Chiltecpintlan, Oztotlapechco, and Atezcahuacan were the old boundaries of the Chichimec polity of Totomihuacan before Tepeyacac became the center of the imperial tributary province. They were in the most distant part of the province to the south and southeast beyond towns such as Ahuatlan and Acatlan, which are not listed in the province but, according to other sources, were part of the imperial system with important military roles. A somewhat different situation is that of the province of Tlapacoyan, in which minor settlements within Tzauctlan and Iztaquimaxtitlan are included, but not the cabeceras of Tzauctlan, Tetellan, Zacatlan, and Iztaquimaxtitlan, all of them of military significance. Along similar lines, the province of Coyolapan includes at least one minor settlement in the isthmus (Tepecuatzontlan or Cuatzontepec) but not the major center, Tecuantepec. In all these cases the principal native centers probably had only military responsibilities as allies of the Empire, and some of them (such as Teotitlan and Tecuantepec) are reported as tributaries in the "Memorial de los pueblos de Tlacopan." The small communities listed in the Codex Mendoza must have given the Empire some tribute goods or perhaps some other kind of service, such as transportation.

The provinces of the Codex Mendoza sometimes cut across native jurisdictions. Thus, Tlalcozauhtitlan has among its towns a sujeto of Olinallan, the major polity in the province of Quiauhteopan. In a similar way Ocuillan has within its province an estancia of Tzompahuacan, while the town itself is listed in the province of Malinalco. This situation has parallels in the intermingling and overlapping described in the core area. If we knew more about the local political organizations, no doubt more such cases could be identified.

Therefore, the regional organization shown in the Codex Mendoza is clearly not the same as the local political organization presented in other sources. It must be accepted that what is depicted in the Codex Mendoza is only the organization superimposed on a series of indigenous political-territorial entities for the collection of tribute. Thus, the list of kings who ruled in the highland area of central Mexico in 1519, according to a document inserted in the *Anales de Cuauhtitlan*, presents a different picture from that of the Codex Mendoza and does not even distinguish between the kingdoms within the Empire and those outside.[9] Furthermore, the Tenochca histories, in describing the participation of the regional components of the Empire in the great public functions in Tenochtitlan, mix regional, ethnic, and political units with the tributary provinces in a manner very different from the definition of the provinces in the Codex Mendoza (see chapter 13).

As a rule the policy of keeping the local rulers and naming calpixques as tribute collectors was applied throughout the Empire, but the study of concrete examples in various regions shows differences in the relation between the power conserved by the local rulers and the imperial authority exercised by the calpixques or other imperial officials. The situation varies from an alliance with the Empire, as in Teotitlan (del Camino), to the expulsion of the local population and its replacement with new settlers from the Basin, as in Tzinacantepec and other places in the Valley of Toluca. In most areas the situation is not well known, but a few examples will show the nature of the regional variations.

The relación geográfica of Atlitlalacyan, referring to the cities of the Teotlalpan area, states that after the Mexica conquest the towns of that region "had no natural lord, because it was the custom of the conqueror to kill and demean the lords of the vanquished people in order better to secure it. And then they established a Mexica collector in charge of receiving the tribute from the people and of taking it to the lords of Mexico." Yet the same document qualifies the statement, saying that "this should not be understood to apply generally to all towns, because in some of them there were natural lords, although few in number, who allied themselves with the lords of Mexico and by acknowledging their sovereignty, kept their own."[10]

Atlitlalacyan is, within the core area, in the region of the Tlacopan kingdoms, near the areas of Tolocan and Chiappan, where Axayacatl and Ahuitzotl reinforced Tenochca control. This account makes the same contrast in the treatment of conquered local rulers that other sources give. However, reports of a general policy of total suppression of local rulers seem exaggerated. There are cases of the ritual sacrifice of defeated rulers,[11] but they were not all eliminated, and the treatment of subjugated local kings shows a great diversity. Although some perished as a consequence of conquest, they were replaced by individuals, usually members of the local dynasty, more willing to accept the imperial authority.

In tributary provinces such as Tlachco, or Cuetlaxtlan after its final conquest, local sources say nothing about indigenous rulers and describe as the only authority that of the imperial calpixques; this agrees with the formulaic description given in the commentaries of the Codex Mendoza on the obligations of local governors. According to the relación geográfica of Tlachco, the king of Mexico "established a governor who ruled over them and was present constantly among them, at whose death the king of Mexico appointed another one . . . , and he did not govern the entire province but only a head town with its estancias." In addition to collecting the tribute, this governor "maintained justice in their way, undoing the wrongs that they did to each other." Nevertheless, other documents show that there were local rulers in this region.[12]

According to the relación geográfica of Cuetlaxtlan, this town was governed by the Mexica calpixque installed there by Moteuczoma to collect and deliver the tribute. The Tenochca chronicles relate that after the vanquished kings were executed for having fought against the armies of the alliance, the commoners elected new lords, but at the same time, a Mexica governor was installed who was a close relative of Moteuczoma Ilhuicamina. He was not only in charge of the tribute collection and delivery, but was there also to protect the people and maintain justice. Thus, these sources indicate the continuity of local lords by saying that the people of the town elected those who were to take the place of the executed rulers, but it is also clear that the officials sent from the center had considerable authority.[13]

In certain other towns the local rulers, in administering justice, were advised by Mexica officials connected with the neighboring garrisons. Thus, it is stated in the relación of Chinantlan that, although there was a local ruler, justice was the responsibility of two men who visited the area "as judges" (como alcaldes), and that in matters concerning a principal or the imposition of the death penalty, they consulted with the Mexicas who resided in the Tochtepec garrison, seat of an audiencia from which judges were sent to the towns of the region.[14] Similarly, in Ayoxochiquillatzallan the ruler took the advice of the Mexicas in the town's garrison and in nearby Xicayan Moteuczoma had installed four Mexica principals, whose opinion was followed by the local ruler in punishing crimes.[15]

Some kingdoms entered into the imperial system as military allies. According to the relaciones of Zacatlan and Tetellan, north of Tlaxcallan, their people did not pay tribute to anybody. Those of Zacatlan sent presents to Moteuczoma; both cities received assistance from Mexico to defend themselves against the Tlaxcaltecs.[16] Other kingdoms, in the Balsas Basin on the way to Oaxaca, were subject to the Empire and gave provisions and assistance to its armies passing through to new conquests. Their relaciones deny the payment of tribute but state that they sent gifts to Mexico that were reciprocated by the Tenochca king.[17] One of these kingdoms, Acatlan in the Mixteca Baja, acknowledged Moteuczoma as the supreme ruler. There was a special storehouse to provide weapons and provisions to his armies passing through the town, and from time to time the rulers of Acatlan sent a present of cloaks and animal skins to the rulers of Mexico, who in return sent them "cloaks and other things that are made in Mexico."[18] In many cases the contributions of local rulers may have taken this form of gift exchange, although the balance of the exchange might well have favored the Empire.

The people of Acatlan claimed that they did not pay tribute because they descended from the rulers of Mexico. According to their tradition, a son of the ruler of Mexico named Mixtecatl came to dominate the whole region from Acatlan to the Mixtec kingdom of Tototepec.[19] However there are no good accounts about new Tenochca kingdoms in the subjugated regions. The naming of a new ruler of high rank coming from Mexico is attested in the case of Huaxyacac, but this was a new entity of settlers from the Basin, in which, according to the Codex Mendoza, there were military governors, and there are no data to indicate that a new local dynastic line of Tenochca origin was established.[20] In some cases matrimonial alliances, of the type practiced among the kings of the three capitals and their subordinates, were brought about. For example, daughters of Tenochca kings became the wives of the kings of Tecuantepec,[21] Tecamachalco,[22] and Tepexic.[23]

The contributions of several kingdoms to the Empire were limited to luxury objects, while payments in staples were given to the local ruler; nothing is said about imperial intervention in the local government. Probably Torquemada is referring to kingdoms such as these when he states that the kings of the three capitals of the Empire had "some provinces that gave certain goods as parias, as a gift by which they acknowledged them as lords, but this has more honor than profit."[24] The term *parias* denotes a special type of tribute from one ruler to another, in objects of high value without the direct intervention of the overlord in the production of the goods.[25] In Oaxaca important Mixtec and Tzapotec kingdoms remained, with limited intervention by the Empire. One of the most important polities of the area was the Tzapotec kingdom of Teotzapotlan (present-day Zaachila). Its king fled to Tecuantepec when the Mexicas entered the area, but the old kingdom remained under the Empire as a major underlying political unit. Teotzapotlan itself, according to its relación geográfica, paid no tribute except as a sign of friendship. Several towns still acknowledged their subordination to Teotzapotlan, although they also sent their tribute to Tenochtitlan; others denied any obligation towards the Empire.

In addition to the local rulers and the imperial tribute collectors, the picture of the organization and government of the conquered regions is completed by the garrisons and military colonies that formed territorial entities distinct from the tributary provinces. At times they intervened in the government of the kingdoms of the region, as in the examples cited above of Tochtepec and Ayoxochiquillatzallan.

It was common practice at all levels of the administration to send officials out from the capital; Ramírez de Fuenleal describes this in an opinion for the Crown on the colonial system of government. He recommended that the indigenous rulers should be detained until the tribute was paid and that constables should be sent to the towns and oblige them to pay. He gave the pre-Spanish procedure as a model, stating that "this was done by Moteuczoma, for when he sent an Indian from Mexico he was feared and was given whatever he asked for, and he arrested whomever he [Moteuczoma] ordered. All over this New Spain an Indian from Mexico was greatly feared."[26] Later, in another passage, he explains the old system further, saying that Moteuczoma ruled from Tenochtitlan by sending the persons that he thought necessary when it was suitable, and at other times he gave his orders to the persons who resided in his city representing the subject cabeceras or provinces.[27]

As will be shown, this procedure was used in the tributary organization of the conquered regions for which there were calpixques both in the provinces and in Tenochtitlan, from whence they were sent to collect the tribute. In the judicial system, the *achcacauhtin* (executors) were also sent from the capital to carry out sentences.

The practice of sending judges from the three capital cities is well described for the possessions that each held separately in Tlalhuic, where justice also pertained exclusively to the three sovereigns, each of whom sent judges to the towns of his jurisdiction.[28] Several other cases recorded in sources of various kinds demonstrate that the Tenochca king sent officials from the capital to establish new norms of government in the conquered regions or to settle disputes among the towns of the region. The following are the most important examples.

Four envoys were sent from Mexico to Tepeyacac to determine the boundaries between the principal kingdoms of the region.[29] In Cuetlaxtlan, after it had been conquered, Moteuczoma Ilhuicamina sent two officials, whose titles were *cuauhnochtli* and *tlillancalqui,* to communicate the sentence of the defeated kings, execute them, and install a Tenochca calpixque.[30] In Chalco, Ilhuicamina sent four ambassadors (*ititlahuan*) to expropriate lands in Tlalmanalco, where in addition the ruler, entitled *teohuateuctli,* was given a daughter of Moteuczoma to be his wife.[31]

The title of these envoys was *titlantli*, as in this case, or *teuctitlantli*, "envoy of the ruler," used in other texts for ambassadors or messengers with executive functions.[32]

In some colonial lawsuits between neighboring towns, explanations of the antecedents of the litigation state that formerly the rulers of Mexico had sent principals to resolve disputes over land. Two cases are from the Tlachco region, which was a tributary province.[33] Two others are from towns not listed in the provinces of the Codex Mendoza. One, from the southern Matlatzinca area, gives the antecedents of a conflict over springs of saline water between Amatepec and Texopilco; to settle this argument, Ahuitzotl sent his son Atlixcatl, who determined the boundary line between the two towns.[34] The other case occurred in the Sierra de Puebla, where Mecatlan and Coahuitlan had a dispute with Chillan about the possession of Xopala. Officials from the three capitals of the Empire and from nearby Cuauhchinanco were sent to decide this conflict.[35]

In this last case, an official from the Acolhua kingdom of Cuauhchinanco, which bordered upon Chillan, was sent as one of the imperial judges. This and the report cited above that the Tochtepec garrison sent judges to the towns of its region, suggest that the tripartite organization of the Empire and the military garrisons were the political and territorial bases for sending these envoys or visiting judges to the subject areas.

The relation between local rulers, calpixques, military governors, and special envoys is a problem that requires further study. Regional variations must have been considerable, and the frequent rebellions indicate that the organization imposed as a result of a first conquest could have changed substantially later on.[36] The following chapters (9 to 11) on the various tributary provinces of the Empire review the most important information available on the government of the political entities that these provinces encompassed. It will not be possible here to discuss systematically the native political units over which the imperial tributary organization was established, nor will it be represented in the maps. The military districts will be discussed separately in chapter 12.

The Establishment of Tributary Units

The manner in which a tributary unit or calpixcazgo was established and how it functioned is given little attention in the sources, which never contain good general descriptions of this subject. The Codex Mendoza ascribes functions in the collection of tribute and in the government to those labeled "gobernadores" of the provinces it describes, and for the most part studies of the Codex Mendoza and the *Matrícula de tributos* have concentrated on the nature and quantity of the tribute.[37] The historical chronicles of the wars undertaken by the kings of Tenochtitlan and Tetzcoco give some information on the establishment of calpixcazgos following the imperial conquests and on changes in the political organizations of the subject areas.[38]

The accounts of the different military campaigns vary considerably. Some are no more than lists of conquered towns, with no political or economic content, and it is clear that the different towns exemplify very diverse situations.[39] The list of Itzcoatl's conquests in the first part of the Codex Mendoza, for example, includes Azcapotzalco and Coyoacan (along with other Tepanec cities), which were the capitals of the political system that preceded the Triple Alliance. Others were cities in the Chinampanec area that had sided with the Tepanecs and where Tenochtitlan took control as the successor of Colhuacan; the list even includes Acolhuacan (Tetzcoco) and Tlacopan, the cities that together with Tenochtitlan established the new regime. All these cities became part of the core area of the alliance. The list also includes several other towns, such as those in the Cohuixca region, that were conquered soon after the Empire was established.[40] The lists of conquests by later kings contain towns where there was fighting but which were perhaps never incorporated into the Empire. Obviously the towns in these lists were the sites of military actions of very different kinds and with very diverse consequences for the political organization and the tribute system.

The Tenochca tradition, in Durán and Tezozomoc, tells of the establishment of calpixcazgos in the areas conquered by Moteuczoma Ilhuicamina and Ahuitzotl, recounting the cases of Tepeyacac, Cuauhtochco (together with Cuetlaxtlan), Coaixtlahuacan, Huaxyacac, and Oztoman; in all of these there are allusions to local rulers, to the naming of Mexica calpixques, and in some cases the sending of new settlers. Little of importance is said on these topics in relation to the conquests of later kings. In chapters 9 to 11, which treat the provinces paying tribute to the Empire, material will be presented about the administrative system imposed by the Empire in each region according to these and other sources.

As for the Tetzcoca tradition, Ixtlilxochitl, in the "Historia chichimeca," first describes the establishment of the eight calpixcazgos in the Basin as part of Nezahualcoyotl's reorganization of the patrimonial lands of his domain after he had regained his kingdom and defeated the Tepanecs, giving the name of each calpixque and the tribute he collected. Later, in relating the conquests of new territories by Nezahualcoyotl together with Itzcoatl of Tenochtitlan and Totoquihuatzin of Tlacopan, Ixtlilxochitl combines the enumeration of the conquests with the establishment of calpixcazgos and usually follows the same style used in his description of the calpixcazgos of the Basin, giving the name of each calpixque and the quantity of tribute. In this way he narrates the founding of the calpixcazgo of Cuauhnahuac, although in this case without giving the name of the calpixque. Ixtlilxochitl also describes the restitution of the ruler of Tollantzinco, although a calpixque was not named until later, after Nezahualcoyotl had returned to Tollantzinco to subdue the ruler once again and then named a calpixque to collect the tribute. These are possessions within the core area of the Empire that have already been discussed. The other provinces conquered by Nezahualcoyotl at that time—Tochpan, Tziuhcoac, and Tlalcozauhtitlan—are described in the other Tetzcoca sources as tributaries of the three capitals.

Of great importance for our topic is Ixtlilxochitl's account of Nezahualcoyotl's system of naming a steward for each province pertaining to Tetzcoco, while those provinces that paid tribute to the three capitals sent their tribute to Mexico to be apportioned there to the stewards of the three kings. Following his report on the province of Tlalcozauhtitlan Ixtlilxochitl states:

> This province and the others in which [Nezahualcoyotl] placed his stewards and collectors were those assigned to the kingdom of Tetzcoco without the other two kings entering into the partition. The provinces in which he did not place his stewards were those in which the revenue was divided among the three heads of this New Spain in the way described above. These tributes were taken all together to the city of Mexico and the division and distribution was made there. The stewards and agents of the three kings, received each what belonged to his lord, and the tributes that were the share of Nezahualcoyotl were kept in the city of Mexico in his old palaces. With them he rewarded all the lords of his kingdom, his sons, relatives and other meritorious persons, through the hands of the Mexica lords, so that each of them was given what he deserved for his virtue. This was the main reason why his share of the revenue that he had from the partition with the other two kings was kept in the city of Mexico.[41]

Although Ixtlilxochitl makes it quite clear that the tribute of the provinces conquered by the Empire was taken to Tenochtitlan, he does not resolve the question of whether the quantities of tribute registered in the Codex Mendoza and related sources represent the total tribute or only the portion due to Tenochtitlan. In another chapter, in describing Nezahualpilli's palace, Ixtlilxochitl states that the expenses of the palace were met by the king's income from "the provinces of his patrimony, because the tribute from the conquered provinces was kept in the storehouses that he had in Tetzcoco and in Mexico, where the distribution described above was made, so that the king could reward his sons, relatives and other lords and captains, meritorious both in war and in other occupations in which they had shown their valor and virtue."[42]

The conquered provinces for which he does not mention the naming of calpixques are Chalco (which immediately rebelled), Itzocan, Tepeyacac, Tecalco, Teohuacan, Coaixtlahuacan, Cuetlaxtlan, Hualtepec (*sic*), Cuauhtochco, Mazahuacan, and Tlapacoyan.[43] In the Codex Mendoza, Itzocan, Tepeyacac, and Tecalco are listed in the province of Tepeyacac; Hualtepec must be Yehualtepec, near Tepeyacac, and it would be in the same province.[44] The towns of Cuetlaxtlan, Cuauhtochco, and Tlapacoyan are cabeceras of provinces; Mazahuacan is the region where Xocotitlan is located. Later, Ixtlilxochitl devotes a whole chapter to the conquest of Chalco but says nothing about naming calpixques or the quantity of tribute, although he does name a storehouse where the tribute from Chalco was kept in the palace of Tetzcoco.[45]

As for the later conquests of the Triple Alliance, Ixtlilxochitl does not describe the installation of new Tetzcoca calpixques nor the division of tribute among the three capitals except in the case of the Tolocan region during the reign of Axayacatl and Nezahualpilli. The share of the king of Tetzcoco was Maxtlacan, Zoquitzinco, and other towns in which certain tribute was assigned to him, which is listed, and the cultivation of a maize field in each town. For all this he installed a calpixque. An equal amount was given to the king of Tenochtitlan, and the king of Tlacopan received "a certain part" that amounted to a fifth of the total. This conquest of Tolocan created a situation similar to that described for Cuauhnahuac at the beginning of the Empire.[46] According to Torquemada's division of the Empire into three sectors, Tochpan and Tziuhcoac would be in the Tetzcoca sector, but not Tochtepec, Cuauhnahuac, Tlalcozauhtitlan, or Tolocan.

The distinction that Ixtlilxochitl makes between the provinces where Nezahualcoyotl installed his calpixques and those that were administered by Tenochtitlan is confirmed to a certain extent in the Tenochca sources, which omit the conquest of the provinces in the Tetzcoca sector but dwell at length on Tepeyacac and Cuetlaxtlan.

In his descriptions of these two forms of organization, Ixtlilxochitl combined in the first the situation of Cuauhnahuac, where each capital held its own estancias separately, with that of the provinces in the Tetzcoca sector from which Nezahualcoyotl received all the tribute "without dividing it with the other two kings." The second form of organization would be that of the Tenochca sector, in which all the tribute was sent to Tenochtitlan, where shares were given to Tetzcoco and Tlacopan. However, according to Motolinía's "Memorial tetzcocano" and the *Anales de Cuauhtitlan*, which are cited below, as well as the "Memorial de Tlacopan," the two provinces in the Tetzcoca sector mentioned above—Tochpan and Tziuhcoac— paid tribute to the three capitals. It is possible that the procedure Ixtlilxochitl describes concerning the tribute sent to Tenochtitlan was also used to distribute the tribute that was brought to Tetzcoco—that is, shares of this tribute would be given to the calpixques of Tenochtitlan. Another possibility is that, as in Cuauhnahuac, each capital was given separate possessions. However, Ixtlilxochitl's texts do not really favor any of these interpretations. Finally, it is also possible that there were more regional differences and changes in the course of time than the sources document. Perhaps in the quotation given above Ixtlilxochitl is describing the procedure followed in the first years of the Empire; later, the preeminence of Tetzcoco and Tlacopan may have been diminished or eliminated.

The two traditions—of Tenochtitlan and of Tetzcoco—agree in that they relate the establishment of calpixcazgos as a consequence of conquests made during the first period of the Empire, under Moteuczoma Ilhuicamina and Nezahualcoyotl. The content of the chronicles changes when covering the following reigns and does not include information on the naming of calpixques, even though some accounts of their conquests coincide with what must have been the new provinces that are depicted in the Codex Mendoza, for example, Tlachquiauhco and Xoconochco. This difference in content may reflect the fact that new provinces of real importance were no longer being established. Some later military campaigns were based on the territorial structure already in existence, to punish rebellions or add new towns to existing provinces; others could have been for pillage or were failed attempts at conquest.

The Governance of the Tributary Provinces

None of our sources give a detailed account of the hierarchy of calpixques and their relations with local rulers and with other officials sent out by the Empire. The reports available are of limited scope. Some describe the officials at the royal palace, others are brief accounts of conquests that mention the appointment of calpixques, and still others describe the system for collecting revenue. The connections among all these different aspects of the system are not always easy to ascertain, nor is there a clear distinction made between kingdoms in the core area and the regions subject to the Empire.

Local sources, such as the *Relaciones geográficas*, contain invaluable information, but their reports are usually meager. While they often speak of the payment of tribute to Tenochtitlan, some refer only to the local rulers, saying nothing about imperial calpixques; others, on the contrary, mention the calpixques but not the local rulers. It is often impossible to decide whether we are dealing with different types of organizations or with differences among the sources that result from the paucity of information they provide. Torquemada gives a general picture of the Empire's revenue system that includes descriptions of officials at the court, of land tenure, and of tribute collection. His material comes from various sources, and it is not entirely clear how it should fit together, but still it can serve as a guide to coordinate scattered data from other reports.[47]

The information available makes clear that there was a large number of calpixques present at the royal court and that officials of high rank were in charge of revenue. According to Sahagún, the building called petlacalco was the store-house for all the tribute in foodstuffs, kept there in wooden bins (*cuauhcuezcomatl*). A separate building, called *calpixcacalli* or *texancalli*, was the house of the calpixques, or stewards. The term *calpixque* was also applied to the officials who in other build-ings were in charge of captives, birds, and wild animals.[48] It is not clear in Sahagún's work whether petlacalcatl and calpixqui refer to different offices; he uses the title *petlacalcatl* for one in his list of twenty calpixques (see p. 109). The Codex Mendoza, in the commentary on the province of the petlacalcatl, explains that he was the governor and each of the towns in the province had calpixques who reported to him. The Codex Mendoza also depicts the petlacalcatl in the texancalco, or "house where they gathered for public works."[49] Durán defines the petlacalcatl as the head steward in charge of the royal supplies and treasurer in charge of the royal property; he had authority over the lesser stewards in the towns and provinces.[50]

Most sources use calpixqui (or calpixque in Spanish sources) as the title of the stewards, and according to Torquemada, the king's head steward was called *huey-calpixqui* (great steward) to distinguish him from those of minor rank, of which there were many.[51] These stewards collected the tribute, took it to the hueycalpix-qui, and gave a complete and exact accounting, since "he who overstepped or did something wrong was punished by death."[52] Although the usual term for these local stewards is *calpixqui*, Torquemada calls them *tecuhtli* (teuctli) and explains that there was one in each barrio or parcialidad. The term *teuctli* has a broad meaning (lord or chief), and it is doubtful that it was a specific term for these officials.[53] They were present at the palace every day to receive orders from the hueycalpix-qui, and every year they held an election, choosing from among themselves two who were to serve that year as heads.[54]

The teuctli chose the lower officials, called *tlayacanqui* and *tequitlato*, whose duty it was to see that the people complied with the teuctli's orders.[55] The term *tequitlato* (labor chief) usually denotes the official in charge of providing laborers for public works; *tlayacanqui* (leader) is a more general term. These petty officials dealt di-rectly with the tribute payers; there were regional variations in their names, and they could also be called *tepixque* (keepers of people), or *calpuleque* (barrio chiefs).[56]

When describing how the royal revenue was collected for the kingdoms of Tenochtitlan, Tetzcoco, and Tlacopan, Torquemada presents a system similar to that which he had already described in terms of "barrios and parcialidades," now applied to the towns or provinces subject to one or another of the three kingdoms. Each kingdom had granaries and storehouses for the tribute brought in to the city "and a head steward (as we have said) with other lesser ones." A steward, or teuctli, was present in each town for the collection of tribute, holding a staff in his left hand and a fan in his right hand as a sign that he was a royal official. The staff and fan were insignia of the royal envoys, not only of the calpixques.[57] These tribute collectors reported to the accountants and stewards of the king on what they had collected and the people they had registered in the towns under their care. If they gave an inexact or falsified account, they suffered the death penalty, and even the people of their lineage were punished as relatives of traitors. Because of this, the tribute collectors were so extremely diligent that they arrested delinquent tribute payers until they paid; if the payers were poor or sick, the collectors waited until they recovered and were able to earn the tribute they owed and paid it. Finally, the collectors could take as slaves those that did not pay within a certain term and have them sold to pay the debt or to be sacrificed. These officials were very much hated by the tribute payers because they not only were insolent but also mistreated the tribute payers by words and sometimes by deeds, taking revenge on those they hated with the pretext of collecting the revenue.[58]

Local sources indicate the existence of a hierarchy of tribute collectors in the tributary provinces. In Cuetlaxtlan, for example, when the Spanish arrived they were greeted by the hueycalpixqui of that city with two other calpixques from Mictlancuauhtlan and Teociyocan and two lesser officials (tlayacanque).[59] In the provinces of Tochpan and Tziuhcoac, each of the towns depicted in the Codex Mendoza was in fact the cabecera of a group of towns, each of which probably had its minor calpixques or town officials.[60] According to Tezozomoc, in his account of the conquest of Tepeyacac and of Cuetlaxtlan, there were stewards in charge of each province both in the province itself and in Tenochtitlan.[61] General descriptions do not make this distinction, but it can be taken as the norm.

The sources do not make clear to what extent if any the imperial officials were in charge of organizing the production of goods sent as tribute. Various relaciones from Oaxaca distinguish between the payment of luxury goods to Moteuczoma and the cultivation of fields for the local ruler. It is most probable that the Empire did not intervene directly in the production of goods; although the demand for tribute would stimulate production of the goods required, local officials would be responsible for their production. This coincides with Ixtlilxochitl's statement that the tribute came from the local king's revenue.[62] But when there was a distribution of lands to the conquerors of a given town or kingdom, one can assume that the local calpixques who were responsible to the Empire would be in charge of recruiting the workers and organizing production. One example is that of Ichcatlan, in the Mixteca, where Moteuczoma deposed the local ruler, named a governor, and ordered that the former ruler should be supplied with the necessaries of life "from half the tribute." The implication is clear that the Mexicas administered all the tribute and allowed half to be assigned to the local ruler.[63] This is a topic that merits a more thorough study.

Reports about the assessment and collection of tribute are few and show different procedures connected with the types of peasant tenure. Tribute was given in kind and in labor. When a farmer held his land from his town and calpolli, he paid about a third of his crop, but labor services might also be used in the cultivation of public lands. Tenants received plots for their subsistence and also cultivated the land of their master. The best reports available refer to the core area. There must have been variations in the tributary provinces, about which very little is known.[64]

Many towns near the capital cities did not pay tribute in kind, since their contribution was to build, repair, and keep in good condition the royal palaces, providing both labor and materials. In addition, these towns supplied all the firewood that was needed for the kitchens and halls of the palace.[65] Other sources also report that the laborers and materials for construction in the imperial capitals were sent from the kingdoms of the core area.[66]

The provincial stewards who resided in Tenochtitlan looked after the goods that came in as tribute. In relating the preparations for Tizoc's coronation, Durán lists the many officials who reported to the petlacalcatl, who in turn presented them to the king. Stewards were also in charge of distributing goods from the various storehouses as ordered by the king. Sahagún refers to this procedure when he lists the stewards who brought the warriors' insignia as they were preparing for a military campaign. In another concrete example, Tezozomoc reports that when Moteuczoma ordered an effigy of himself to be made in Chapoltepec, he called the petlacalcatl and ordered him to give the sculptors the tribute that had arrived from Cuetlaxtlan. When they finished their work he ordered the petlacalcatl to pay them with cloaks and cacao out of the tribute from the Huaxteca and to summon the stewards of Tochpan and Tziuhcoac to give them more cloaks, cacao, and other foodstuffs as well as two slaves from among the captives they had in their charge so that "they could bring firewood and maize from the fields (*camellones*) they tilled."[67]

In the storehouses of Tenochtitlan there were stewards in charge of the goods needed for ceremonial activities. For example, the steward of Cuetlaxtlan guarded certain objects used by the men fasting for Huitzilopochtli.[68] In the core area the care of particular temples could also be the special responsibility of a town or province; thus, part of Tlatelolco's tribute obligation was to repair the temple of Huitznahuac.[69] The Huexotzincas were assigned to care for the Coatlan temple built under Axayacatl,[70] but there are no other examples of this sort of service demanded from the conquered areas. The stewards of certain provinces were charged also with lodging the foreign lords who came to Tenochtitlan. The steward of Cuetlaxtlan provided lodging and everything necessary for the lords of Quiahuiztlan and Cempohuallan, who were invited to Tenochtitlan by Axayacatl for the celebration of the feast of Tlacaxipehualiztli that followed the campaign against Matlatzinco.[71] The ambassadors of Yopitzinco who came to the coronation of Ahuitzotl were lodged in the houses of the stewards of Cuauhnahuac and Huaxtepec, and the Cihuacoatl ordered the "petlacalcatl, high steward of the kingdom, to take special account and care of the foreigners of Yopitzinco."[72] It is significant that the stewards were in charge of areas close to the visitors they housed while in Tenochtitlan.

Several sources refer to the royal treasury and storehouses but do not provide detailed descriptions. There is almost no information about regional and local storehouses; only for the Cuauhtochco area is there a reference to imperial storehouses, in Cuezcomatepec.[73]

Zorita reports that in each "province" there was a steward sent by the king to whom it pertained; the conquered peoples brought the tribute to the stewards, and "they took it to the persons that the kings of Mexico or Tetzcoco or Tlacopan ordered them to, each one to the king to whom the town had become subject, with the obligation to obey and to serve him in time of war."[74] It is not known for certain which were the provinces conquered individually by each of the three kings or what changes later took place. For example, Ixtlilxochitl describes Tochpan and Tziuhcoac among those conquered by Nezahualcoyotl, who appointed the stewards.[75] But according to Motolinía's "Memorial tetzcocano," the tribute from the sixty-eight towns in Tochpan was collected in certain towns where there were stewards from Tenochtitlan, Tetzcoco, and Tlacopan, who divided the tribute into three parts, each one taking the portion due to his ruler.[76]

After a conquest the victors decided upon an annual payment of tribute "of what grew or was made in that province, and then they elected governors and officials [calpixques] to preside over that province, not from among the natives of the province but from among those who had conquered them."[77] As to the social origin of the stewards, Zorita lists among the tasks of the nobles (*pilli*) that of taking the commoners to labor in the fields and other public works. He also states that the king appointed the stewards from among the nobles, but in the subject towns when there were lords of a lower rank, stewards were not needed "because the lords did what the stewards had to do."[78] Reports from Tenochtitlan also suggest that calpixques were named from among nobles of royal ancestry, but probably the reference is to the stewards of the highest ranks.[79] After the conquest of Coaixtlahuacan the widow of its king, Atonal, was sent back to Coaixtlahuacan to be the steward of the tribute goods (*cihuacalpixqui*). This is an unusual report that might indicate a possible role for women in the collection and care of tribute.[80] In general it seems that officials in the lower ranks of tequitlato and tlayacanqui were commoners, but in the higher ranks of the hierarchy they were nobles.[81]

As already pointed out, the imperial officials advised the local ruler or intervened in other ways in government. The limited information available is not sufficient to say whether this was the general rule as said in the Codex Mendoza or whether there was intervention only in certain cases. Neither is it clear whether these officials were calpixques or had titles of higher rank, such as those of the governors of the military districts.

The Distribution of Tribute

Although within the core area each capital had its own tributaries, in the distant areas conquered by the Empire there were different ways of distributing the tribute. Several sources give formulas for the share of tribute that fell to each of the three capitals, but they give little specific information about where the tribute was produced or who administered production and distribution. It should be kept in mind that those formulas for division and distribution can be applied as well to territory as to tribute, as Ixtlilxochitl does in describing the distribution of lands and tribute of the Empire in general and in the specific cases of Cuauhnahuac and Tolocan.

Zorita states that the conquered towns paid their tribute to the capital whose subjects they had become, but he also reports that the three kings held some towns in common and "divided the tribute among themselves, that from some towns in equal parts, and that from others was divided in five parts, of which the kings of Tenochtitlan and Tetzcoco each took two and the king of Tlacopan one part."[82]

According to Torquemada, at the time of the coronation of Itzcoatl the three kings agreed that a fifth should be given to the king of Tlacopan, a third of what remained to the king of Tetzcoco, and the rest to the king of Tenochtitlan as the highest authority.[83] This division gives Tenochtitlan 8/15, a little more than half of the tribute, 4/15 to Tetzcoco, and 3/15 to Tlacopan. The proportion is similar to that of the three sectors into which the whole territory of the Empire was divided according to the same writer: of the total area Tenochtitlan received the south with a little less than half; Tlacopan, in the northwest, a fourth; and Tetzcoco, in the northeast, a little more than a fourth.[84]

The memorials of Tetzcoco contain the best concrete examples available. Motolinía's "Memorial tetzcocano" gives, as does Zorita, two distinct forms of distributing the tribute among the three capitals in the provinces that it describes, and the related document in the *Anales de Cuauhtitlan* enumerates this tribute.[85] In Motolinía the tribute from the sixty-eight cities of the province of Tochpan was divided "en tres tercios" (in three thirds).[86] This expression is normally understood, when speaking of quantities, to mean three equal parts; therefore, it might seem that we have an example of the division into equal parts that Zorita notes. The Nahuatl text of the *Anales de Cuauhtitlan* says *excan* (in three parts),[87] which does not always imply equality.[88] This source enumerates the tribute paid by the province but does not specify what was paid to each of the allied capitals. It is possible that the three "tercios" were three equal parts, but the information is not precise on this point.

Motolinía himself says that the tribute of the thirty-three towns in the provinces of Tziuhcoac, Tlatlauhquitepec, and Tlapacoyan was collected by the stewards of the three principal kings and then divided into five parts, of which Tenochtitlan and Tetzcoco each took two parts and the king of Tlacopan one.[89] The corresponding data in the *Anales de Cuauhtitlan* specify the tribute that each of the three capitals received, approximately in accord with this formula.[90] Also according to Motolinía's "Memorial tetzcocano," the tribute of the province of Tochtepec was distributed among the three kings as was that of Tochpan—that is, in three tercios.[91]

In regard to the provinces in the Tetzcoca sector, Ixtlilxochitl does not agree with Motolinía. He says that the provinces where Nezahualcoyotl named calpixques were those that were part of the kingdom of Tetzcoco, and the other two kings did not share in their tribute. The provinces conquered by the Empire as a unit sent their tribute to Tenochtitlan, where two-fifths were given to Tenochtitlan, the same to Tetzcoco, and one-fifth to Tlacopan. In Cuauhnahuac there was a clear division of territory among the three capitals of the Empire; when Ixtlilxochitl states that all the tribute from Cuauhnahuac was for Tetzcoco, it should be understood that this refers only to the territory taken by the Acolhua king, since he himself also says that Nezahualcoyotl was given Cuauhnahuac together with nine towns, while to Tenochtitlan went Tepoztlan, Huaxtepec, and other towns and to Tlacopan others that he does not identify.[92]

The "Memorial de los pueblos de Tlacopan" does not specify how the three capitals shared the tribute, but in a post-Conquest inquiry made in that city, a witness declared that in the towns that the three cabeceras had conquered, they had installed their calpixques, "each one for his third part of the town."[93]

Clearly there were different ways of distributing the lands and tribute of the conquered regions. Some conquests were carried out by only one of the three kings, who then received all the tribute. At other times all three participated in the conquest and each kingdom took separately certain towns, from which it collected all the tribute. In other cases the totality of the tribute was taken to Tenochtitlan and there divided among the three capitals, but the proportions of the division were not the same in all the provinces, and we do not know if the tribute given to Tetzcoco and Tlacopan came from certain towns designated especially for them. There is not sufficient concrete data for us to know the procedure followed in each province throughout the history of the Empire. It is possible that Torquemada's formula that gives slightly more than half the tribute to Tenochtitlan refers to the provinces of the Tenochca sector, while the formula designating two-fifths for both Tenochtitlan and Tetzcoco refers to the provinces of the Tetzcoca sector.

Another question to be considered is whether in the conquered provinces there was also a distinction made between the royal lands and the patrimonial lands of kings and nobles; that is, did the tribute paid by each province also include contributions from the patrimonial lands of kings and nobles?[94] The data on the more distant conquered regions that paid tribute to the three kings of the alliance suggest that there were no patrimonial lands there of these three kings, although some of the local kings did have such possessions.

It is doubtful that one could apply to the distant provinces the statement made by Gerónimo López that the Codex Mendoza records the distribution of towns made by Moteuczoma "to the principal lords" of Tenochtitlan as "encomendatarios."[95] Probably those encomendatarios were individuals whom other sources call calpixques and provincial governors, as in the case of a certain tlacateuctli, whom the Spanish named Tapia, who held Oztoman and Alahuiztlan.[96] However, we can accept the statement that the imperial calpixques used tribute to recompense the king's relatives and officials; in other words, these payments in kind were equivalent to salaries and grants.[97]

In regard to the quality and nature of the tribute payments and their place of origin, what is most evident is the fact that the Codex Mendoza registers only tribute in kind, never in services, except in the case of Tlatelolco, which was required to repair the temple of Huitznahuac. The tribute was always in durable goods, not perishable foodstuffs such as vegetables, fruit, meat, fish, or eggs, which are cited as tribute in other sources.[98] Pottery is also lacking. There must have been other sources for such provisions, as, for example, the patrimonial lands of kings, nobles, and officials, whose inhabitants gave domestic service, firewood, and perishable food.

The accounts of the wars of conquest, with the promises of those who were defeated to pay tribute, suggest at times the payment of goods already accumulated for the local kings, as if it were a matter of ransom.[99] But Zorita says that in all the conquered provinces, as part of a permanent tributary system, there were lands set aside to produce the tribute paid to the Empire. The three kings left in place the local rulers and chose some land for themselves that the commoners cultivated, "and that was what they had to give as tribute and in recognition of vassalage."[100] In this statement there is no distinction made between the core area and the more distant regions subjugated by the Empire. The cultivation of fields implies tribute in agricultural products, which was typical of the calpixcazgos within the territories of the component kingdoms of the alliance, as well as in Chalco and the provinces of Tolocan, Ocuilan, Malinalco, and Xocotitlan, for which there is not adequate information on the condition of the local rulers.[101] Only a few of the provinces subject to the Empire outside the core area gave tribute in agricultural products, namely Tlachco, Tepecuacuilco, Tepeyacac, and Huaxyacac. All of these regions had important military obligations, and therefore such tribute was probably intended for the garrisons and the armies passing by.

However, there are reports about cultivated fields or tribute in maize for the Empire in some distant regions. Pomar says that each town on the Pacific coast cultivated a maize field, but the harvest was kept in the towns for the usual expenditures of the calpixques stationed there in the service of the king of Tetzcoco. These calpixques administered all the tribute, distributing some to those who merited it and taking the most valuable goods to the king.[102] Although Pomar is writing about Tetzcoco, he is probably describing the general practice in the distant areas, not just Tetzcoco or the Pacific coast.

Local sources confirm this practice of cultivating fields to pay part of the imperial tribute in Tlachco[103] and also in Teotzacualco, in the Mixteca (not registered in the Codex Mendoza), where fields were cultivated for the soldiers that Moteuczoma had there as a garrison.[104] Huitzillan, in the Chinantec region, is another example. The tribute paid there was for the maintenance of the governor assigned by Moteuczoma to Tochtepec, quite apart from the gifts of jewels sent to Moteuczoma.[105] In Tochtepec itself a plantation of cacao was cultivated to pay tribute to Tetzcoco.[106] Probably the tribute in maize was for the use of the local administration of the Empire and the military garrisons. When the Codex Mendoza does not record tribute in maize and other foodstuffs, it is because it was intended for local use and not to be sent to Tenochtitlan.

The cultivation of public lands and perhaps large-scale production of textiles lend themselves to intervention by the imperial calpixques, although the recruitment of workers must have been the responsibility of local officials. In the production of goods made by skilled craftsmen it is probable that the responsibility fell on local rulers, and the imperial calpixques acted simply as collectors.

Whether the Mexica calpixques administered the lands that produced the tribute would be determined by the conditions under which a kingdom became incorporated into the Empire. When Ixtlilxochitl states that the cities surrendering after the third request by the ambassadors paid tribute "out of the income pertaining to that lord," the implication is that there was no distribution of lands as was customary after a military conquest.[107] As frequently happens, the concrete cases are not sufficient to evaluate the generalizations in the sources. The report cited above on Ichcatlan in Oaxaca implies that the calpixques of Tenochtitlan controlled the tribute in foodstuffs, since it states that Moteuczoma used half the tribute to supply the local ruler with food.[108]

The goods to pay tribute in kind were as a rule local products.[109] Basic foodstuffs for the cities in the Basin came mainly from the core area; the tribute from the more distant provinces consisted of luxury goods, as is to be expected given the high cost of transportation. Almost all the distant provinces also gave warriors' suits, insignia, and shields as well as clothing of distinctive types. The place of origin of each kind of tribute confirms the rule that it was paid in local products, and it is noteworthy that each kind came from a restricted number of provinces. For example, cotton came from Cihuatlan, Cuauhtochco, Atlan, and Tziuhcoac; cochineal from Coaixtlahuacan, Coyolapan, and Tlachquiauhco; boards, beams, and firewood from Cuahuacan; canes from Tepeyacac; lime from Atotonilco de Tula and from Tepeyacac; gourds from Cuauhnahuac, Huaxtepec, Tlappan, and Xoconochco; paper from Cuauhnahuac and Huaxtepec; and copper axes from Tepecuacuilco and Quiauhteopan.[110]

There are some instances in which, of two neighboring regions, one gave raw material and the other manufactured luxury products. Thus, in the Gulf coast Tochpan's tribute was fine clothing and other luxury products, while Atlan and Tziuhcoac gave important quantities of cotton as well as clothing.[111] Similarly, Tochtepec gave fine clothing and many other luxury goods, while Cuauhtochco gave ordinary cloaks and a considerable quantity of cotton.

Some provinces paid tribute in goods that they had to acquire outside their own territory. Pomar relates how the people on the southern Pacific coast acquired some of their tribute, saying that they gave "gold dust and bricks, little bars, lip plugs and ear plugs also of gold, and slaves and precious blue feathers highly esteemed among these people, that were brought by way of trade from the provinces of Guatemala." Probably only the feathers came from Guatemala. Pomar also states that the calpixques, using some of the revenue they collected, searched for and purchased precious stones such as chalchihuites and turquoise.[112]

Several of the *Relaciones geográficas* provide more examples of tribute goods acquired through trade. The people of Tepehuitzillan (present-day Tepeucila) gave as tribute to Moteuczoma "cloaks and tiger skins that they bought from neighboring towns, and some feathers."[113] Atlatlauhcan gave cochineal, cotton cloaks, green feathers, and chalchihuites that they went to other towns to find, and these things "were traded by exchange for little cloaks of cotton, the size of a sheet of paper, that circulated among them as money."[114] Tecuicuilco paid tribute in green feathers and green stones acquired in the same way.[115]

Quiotepec gave as tribute these little cloaks used as money, described as "tapatíos, which were pillows [*cabezalejos*] of cotton, a handspan square, each of which was worth fifty cacao beans."[116] Molina defines *tlapatiotl* as the "price of that which is bought, or what is given for that which is bought." They must be the small cloaks used as money that Motolinía calls *patolcuachtli.*[117]

To understand the payment of tribute in goods obtained through exchange, we must consider the entire relationship between trade and tribute. Submission to the Empire always included freedom of trade.[118] Merchants as a rule paid tribute in the goods they traded. There were also merchants in the service of the sovereign who carried his goods to be sold and could effect the exchanges of gifts between the rulers of different kingdoms, such as those between Tenochtitlan and Xicallanco.[119] The interconnection of commercial exchange with the tribute system explains why, following the conquest of Tepeyacac, the Mexicas ordered a great market to be established, to which all the merchants of the land would come and where rich clothing, jewels, feathers, and animal skins would be sold.[120]

The people of Itztepexic declared in their relación geográfica that to find the feathers and gold that they paid as tribute they went to Tecuantepec, Xoconochco and Guatemala, hiring themselves out to carry the merchandise of traders and to cultivate lands in those areas, where they remained six or seven months or a year, while others worked at whatever the rulers of Itztepexic ordered. They were paid in gold and green feathers, which they brought back to pay their tribute.[121] This trade must have been arranged by the rulers of the participating towns, since it is doubtful that porters and farm hands, hiring themselves out, could have earned enough gold and feathers to pay the required tribute.

Given the specialization of many provinces in providing certain goods, the calpixques in Tenochtitlan who were responsible for particular kinds of goods were also responsible for different provinces. This is evident in the case of the calpixques who provided the warriors' insignia and of those who brought prisoners to be sacrificed, but it must have been so on other occasions. The same thing happens with the demand for stone, wood, lime, and sand for public works that was directed to certain towns, although in such cases supplies came largely from the core area and not from the distant provinces.

Some towns sent tribute to more than one place. In Cuauhxilotitlan there were three calpixques to collect the tribute—one in the town, another in Coaixtlahuacan, and a third in Huaxyacac.[122] Probably this is related to the fact that in the Codex Mendoza, Cuauhxilotitlan is listed in the province of Coyolapan—which included Huaxyacac—while in the "Memorial de Tlacopan" it is in paragraph 7.2, in which Coaixtlahuacan is listed. Other overlappings between the provinces of the Codex Mendoza and the sections of the "Memorial de Tlacopan" might be explained in this way. That tribute was paid both to Tenochtitlan and to other enemy kingdoms is documented in the case of Itztepexic, whose people sent tribute to Tenochtitlan and went to Huaxyacac to provide personal services, but also paid tribute to the Mixteca of Tototepec, Achiotlan, and Tlachquiauhco.[123]

The Three Sectors of the Empire

Although as a rule the distant conquered regions kept their own political organization and their own traditional rulers, the imperial organization of territorial entities superimposed on these areas for the collection of tribute also led to intervention in the local government. Variations in the degree of control and demands for tribute have been described above. In the following chapters these tributary provinces will be discussed, but first we will examine in more detail the division of the subjugated regions into three sectors corresponding to the division of the core area among the three capitals of the Empire. For this purpose it is necessary to analyze first the sources for each of the three capitals that touch on this topic, especially the "Memorial de los pueblos de Tlacopan."

As has been pointed out, some conquered towns were acquired by one of the three allied kings, while others were conquered by the Empire as a whole and paid tribute to all three capitals. However, these conquered areas were considered to be within the sphere or sector of one of the three capitals according to their geographical location in terms of the cardinal directions. Torquemada gives the most detailed information in speaking of the beginning of the alliance:

> Once the Mexicas and Tetzcocas defeated Maxtla . . . they divided the country among themselves and agreed that in the battles in which all three kings took part, they would split the tribute with which [the defeated] showed themselves to be vassals, but that in the battles that each king fought by himself the conquered peoples pertained to that king alone . . . , and when the three kings divided the country and its conquest, to the king of Mexico fell the part that looks from his city to the east and turning to the south until almost the west. And to the king of Tlacopan the area from the west till almost the north. And to the king of Tetzcoco from a little before an even line to the north to the east where the sun rises, and it shared the boundary with the Mexica king. And because of this if all three kings went to one of these areas, even if all three conquered and vanquished, not all three called themselves lords and kings of that conquest, but only he whose lot had been that part where the conquest was made. They shared these tributes but not those that they had won each one alone, because these they considered their own and not subject to partition.[124]

Geographically, these three sectors are an extension of the same division that had been made in the core area defining the domains of the three capitals of the alliance. Torquemada does not explain the exact nature of the preeminence of each capital in the provinces of its sector. It may have been a matter of the collection of tribute, the proportions in which it was divided, the rank of the stewards that each capital had in those provinces, jurisdiction over the people, or their participation in ceremonies. The specific data available on certain provinces suggest some explanations, although they cannot solve all these questions.

The sources from each of the three imperial capitals listing the subject areas reflect the tripartite organization of the Empire in different ways. The sources on Tenochtitlan do not arrange the provinces in groups, nor do they say anything explicitly that would indicate the existence of the three sectors that Torquemada describes. To Tenochtitlan was brought the tribute that was to be distributed there to the three capitals; it is natural then that the Codex Mendoza includes all the tributary provinces in the entire Empire. Furthermore, the Tenochca king was the supreme commander in their many wars, and the Codex Mendoza devotes a special section to the military colonies. Hints of a Tetzcoca sector are present only in the chronicles of Durán and Tezozomoc, which pay very little attention to the conquests and the naming of calpixques in the northeastern sector.

The Tetzcoca and Tlacopanec sources to a large extent conform to the tripartite division, but the differences among the sources of the three capitals are not only the result of the ways in which they are in accord or not with Torquemada's tripartite formula. There seem to have been differences of another sort that make necessary a careful comparison of the sources in order to consider additional explanations. Unfortunately the "Memorial de Tlacopan" does not give any information on the nature of the tribute paid; we can only examine the ways in which this source arranges the regions subject to the Empire.

The Tetzcoca sources make clear that there were areas tied to Tetzcoco that coincided with Torquemada's northeastern, or Tetzcoca sector. According to both Motolinía and Torquemada, the kingdom of Tetzcoco extended to the Gulf of Mexico and comprised fifteen "provinces." Torquemada states that he had in his possession an old pictorial document that indicated these provinces. Neither of these writers lists the provinces by name, and the number fifteen does not agree with the available data on the number of imperial tributary provinces in the Tetzcoca sector; it is most likely that they were the fourteen or fifteen kingdoms that were direct dependencies of the Acolhua king.[125] Consequently, this figure should not be taken to refer to the imperial tributary provinces in the Tetzcoca sector, even though a pictorial document such as the one alluded to by Torquemada could have been the source of Motolinía's "Memorial tetzcocano." This latter document, as has been pointed out, arranges the towns that paid tribute to the three capitals into three sections: the first corresponds to the province of Tochpan in the *Matrícula de tributos*; the second to those of Tziuhcoac, Tlapacoyan, and Tlatlauhquitepec; and the third to that of Tochtepec. The first two comprise precisely those provinces that fall within the northeast quarter of the Empire, Torquemada's Tetzcoca sector. But the third, Tochtepec, lies south of his dividing line within what would be the Tenochca sector. Oxitipan and Atlan, which, according to their geographic location would be in the Tetzcoca sector, are not included among Ixtlilxochitl's Tetzcoca provinces. These were late conquests by the Empire, accomplished under the dominion of Tenochtitlan. Atlan would also pertain to Tenochtitlan as a military garrison. The situation of Oxitipan, so distant from the other tributary provinces and hardly mentioned among the conquests, was probably exceptional.

The information in Pomar's "Relación de la ciudad y provincia de Tezcoco" confirms the statement that the Acolhua domain reached the Gulf coast and seems to refer to the Tetzcoca sector of the Empire in noting that the jurisdiction of Tetzcoco extended from the Gulf of Mexico to the Pacific, including, on the eastern side, everything except Tlaxcala and Huexotzinco.[126]

When King Ixtlilxochitl, together with Cortés, reviewed his forces, in addition to the peoples of the Acolhuacan there were fifty thousand men from Chalco, Itzocan, Cuauhnahuac, Tepeyacac, and "other parts subject to the kingdom of Tetzcoco located in the south," along with equal numbers of men from Tziuhcoac, Tlatlauhquitepec, and other provinces "located to the north and subject to Tetzcoco."[127]

Ixtlilxochitl and Coanacoch agreed in 1523 to divide the kingdom of Tetzcoco. Coanacoch, since he was the king, would stay in Tetzcoco and take for himself all the provinces that fell towards the south, namely Chalco, Cuauhnahuac, Itzocan, Tlalhuic, and the rest towards the Pacific Ocean. Ixtlilxochitl would take the other half that fell towards the north, laying his boundaries through Tepetlaoztoc, Papalotla, Tenayocan (*sic pro* Tezoyocan or Tizayocan), Chiucnauhtlan, and Xaltocan. He made Otompan and Teotihuacan the cabeceras where he built his palaces and took for himself Tollantzinco, Tziuhcoac, Tlatlauhquitepec, Pahuatlan, and all the rest as far as the North Sea and Pánuco.[128] As in other sources, Tziuhcoac and Tlatlauhquitepec are included in this account with Tetzcoco's subjects in the north, as is Pahuatlan, which some sources mention as one of the dependent kingdoms of Tetzcoco. In the south, Chalco and Cuauhnahuac (or Tlalhuic) are regions where the three capitals of the alliance each had separate possessions. Itzocan and Tepeyacac are never recorded as belonging to Tetzcoco.

In the basic Tepanec source, the "Memorial de los pueblos de Tlacopan," the three sectors of the Empire are evident but not exactly as in Torquemada's formula. This memorial arranges, in the last three sections (6, 7, and 8), the towns that paid tribute to the three kingdoms of the Empire, but it is not possible to relate each one of these sections to one of the kingdoms. Section 6 corresponds to the Tetzcoca sector as it is defined in the Tetzcoca sources; section 7 takes in the southern half, or Tenochca sector, of the Empire, plus the central and northern Gulf coast. Section 8, which includes the isthmus and Xoconochco, cannot be identified with the Tlacopan sector, but geographically it would be part of the Tenochca sector. It follows, then, that in these sections of the "Memorial de Tlacopan" there are no lists of towns that paid tribute to the three capitals in the region that, according to Torquemada, formed the northwestern or Tepanec sector. This whole region is included in the dependencies of Tlacopan or of its kingdoms (in sections 4 and 5). Some towns, such as Ocuillan and Malinalco, are not found in any of the sections of the "Memorial de Tlacopan," neither among Tlacopan's dependencies nor among those that paid tribute to the three capitals. They may have been considered part of the possessions of Tenochtitlan in the core area that are not listed in that source.

Table 8-1 and Map 8-1 compare the material in the "Memorial de Tlacopan" and the Codex Mendoza on the southern and northeastern sectors of the Empire.

Section 6 of the "Memorial de Tlacopan" is very similar to the Tetzcoca sources, although not entirely the same in all the details. This section comprises six paragraphs. Five correspond to the provinces of Tochpan, Tziuhcoac, Tochtepec, Tlapacoyan, and Tlatlauhquitepec in the Codex Mendoza; the last, Chinantlan, was probably an extension of the province of Tochtepec, since this town is included in the province of Tochtepec in the Codex Mendoza. Therefore, this section coincides with the Tetzcoca sector as defined in the Acolhua sources, which also include Tochtepec among the Tetzcoca provinces. The Tetzcoca and Tlacopan sources on Tziuhcoac and Tochpan include many more names than are in the corresponding lists in the Tenochca sources because they include towns that were under the authority of each of the stewards whose seats are named in the Codex Mendoza.

Section 7 has four large paragraphs. The first, headed by Cempohuallan (a town that is not in the Codex Mendoza), includes Atlan (a province in the Mendoza) and two towns in the province of Cuetlaxtlan as well as many other towns, most of which can be located in the central region of Veracruz, that are not in the Codex Mendoza. The second paragraph begins with Cozcatlan (not in the Codex Mendoza) and includes towns that in the Codex Mendoza are in the provinces of Tepeyacac, Coaixtlahuacan, Coyolapan, Tochtepec, Cuauhtochco, and Cuetlaxtlan, along with many other towns in the same area. The third paragraph, which begins with Tlachmalacac, includes towns that in the Codex Mendoza are listed in the provinces of Tlachco, Tepecuacuilco, Tlappan, Yohualtepec, and Tepeyacac, together with several more from the same regions, as well as Cuauhnahuac and Huaxtepec. In the fourth paragraph the best known towns are in the province of Coyolapan in the Codex Mendoza or can be located in the same region; however, the list begins with Oztoman, the fortress facing the Tarascan frontier, and extends to various towns on the Pacific coast. Section 8, with only one paragraph, corresponds to the province of Xoconochco in the Codex Mendoza, although it also includes Tecuantepec, Xochtlan, Xaltepec, and Tototepec, which heads the list. That is, it adds towns that are not in the Codex Mendoza but were conquered by the Empire and connected the Empire's possessions in Oaxaca with Xoconochco. Therefore sections 7 and 8 of the "Memorial de Tlacopan" coincide with a large part of the southern, or Tenochca sector of the Empire, although Tochtepec

TABLE 8-1.

Regions That Paid Tribute to the Three Parts of the Empire According to the "Memorial de Tlacopan" Compared with the Provinces of the Codex Mendoza

"Memorial de Tlacopan"*	Codex Mendoza†
6.1 Tochpan	35. Tochpan
6.2 Tziuhcoac	37. Tziuhcoac
6.3 Tochtepec	(29. Tochtepec)
6.4 Tlapacoyan	33. Tlapacoyan
6.5 Tlatlauhquitepec	34. Tlatlauhquitepec
6.6 Chinantlan	(29. Tochtepec)
—	38. Oxitipan
7.1 Cempohuallan	—
towns on the Gulf coast	(32. Cuetlaxtlan)
and the Sierra de Puebla	36. Atlan
7.2 Cozcatlan	26. Coaixtlahuacan
	31. Cuauhtochco
	(32. Cuetlaxtlan)
	(27. Coyolapan)
	(29. Tochtepec)
including Teotitlan del Camino	—
and the Mixteca Baja	
—	28. Tlachquiauhco
7.3 Tlachmalacac	(18. Tepecuacuilco)
	17. Tlachco
	25. Tepeyacac
	23. Yohualtepec
	20. Tlappan
	5. Huaxtepec
	4. Cuauhnahuac
—	24. Chalco
—	22. Quiauhteopan
—	21. Tlalcozauhtitlan
—	19. Cihuatlan
7.4 Oztoman,	(18. Tepecuacuilco)
with the valleys of Oaxaca	(27. Coyolapan)
and the Costa Chica	—
8. Tototepec, with Tecuantepec	—
and Xoconochco	30. Xoconochco

NOTE: A dash denotes the absence of the town or region listed in the opposite column.
*The paragraphs are numbered as in Zimmermann 1970:6–8, and the toponym is the first town listed in the paragraph.
†When towns of a province in the Codex Mendoza appear in several paragraphs of the "Memorial," the name of the province is written in parentheses opposite the paragraphs where they appear.

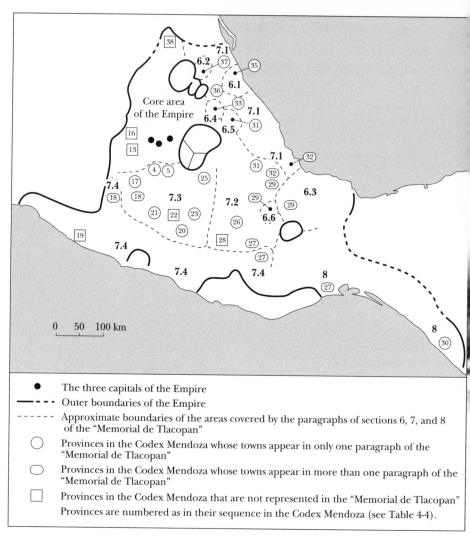

MAP 8–1. The regions paying tribute to the three capitals of the Empire, according to the "Memorial de Tlacopan," compared with the tributary provinces in the Codex Mendoza

and Chinantlan are not included here but in the Tetzcoca sector, while paragraph 7.1, headed by Cempohuallan, includes towns in Cuetlaxtlan but extends north along the coast to Tamiahua, thus embracing part of the northeastern area.

The five paragraphs of the "Memorial de Tlacopan" covering the southern sector are very different from the provinces in the Codex Mendoza. The number of paragraphs is much smaller than the number of provinces in the Codex Mendoza. Sometimes a single paragraph of the memorial (especially 7.2, and 7.3) includes several provinces of the Codex Mendoza, but there are also numerous overlappings. These will be noted in Tables 10-1, 10-2, 10-3, and 11-5 in the following chapters, which present each paragraph of the memorial and compare it with the Codex Mendoza. None of the towns heading each list are provincial cabeceras in the Codex Mendoza. Three of them (Cempohuallan, Cozcatlan, and probably Tototepec) are not even listed in the Codex Mendoza, and there is not sufficient evidence to be certain that they were the administrative cabeceras of the towns in each paragraph.

At times the "Memorial de Tlacopan" registers only one town for what in the Codex Mendoza is a whole province, such as Cuauhnahuac, Huaxtepec, Tlappan, and Yohualtepec in paragraph 7.3. At other times, on the contrary, for one town in the Codex Mendoza there is a whole group of towns in the "Memorial de Tlacopan," as can be seen in Tochpan (6.1), Tziuhcoac (6.2), and Chinantlan (6.6) in the Tetzcoca sector. Similarly, in the southern sector, paragraph 7.2 (Cozcatlan) contains several towns in the Valley of Teohuacan and La Cañada of Cuicatlan, while the Codex Mendoza registers only Cuicatlan in the province of Coaixtlahuacan.

Many important towns that are in the "Memorial de Tlacopan" are not in the Codex Mendoza, and some in the Codex Mendoza are not in the memorial. In the Mixteca Baja, the "Memorial de Tlacopan" includes towns that are entirely lacking in the Tenochca sources, but it does not include the provinces of Tlalcozauhtitlan, Quiauhteopan, or Tlachquiauhco and lists very few towns in the province of Tepeyacac. It also includes the Isthmus of Tehuantepec and many towns on the coast of Veracruz, from Cempohuallan to Tamiahua. Furthermore, the "Memorial de Tlacopan" does not include the Costa Grande (Cihuatlan province in the Codex Mendoza), but it does include the Costa Chica (7.4); in the Huaxteca it extends farther north than the province of Tziuhcoac in the Codex Mendoza but does not reach Oxitipan.

It is not easy to give a single explanation applicable to all the differences between the "Memorial de Tlacopan" and the Tenochca sources. According to the heading of the "Memorial de Tlacopan," the towns listed in sections 6, 7, and 8 paid tribute to the three capitals. If these lists included all the towns that paid tribute to one or another of the three capitals, we would find in them all the towns in the Codex Mendoza, which is not the case. Hypothetically it could be assumed that each one of the three capitals would have possessions in the subject areas, principally in its own sector, and the sources of each capital would register the towns from which they obtained their tribute. The majority would pay to the three capitals, but others to only one of them. The "Memorial de Tlacopan," then, would represent Tlacopan's organization for collecting its share of the tribute, even if, according to other sources, it was delivered in Tenochtitlan. The towns listed in these three sections of the "Memorial de Tlacopan" but not in the Codex Mendoza would be dependencies exclusively of Tlacopan, or, at least, the towns from which came the tribute that was due to Tlacopan. But there are not sufficient data to develop this hypothesis. A relevant case is that of Tecuantepec, lacking in the Codex Mendoza but listed together with Xoconochco in section 8 of the "Memorial de Tlacopan." According to a colonial inquiry, Tecuantepec belonged to the "cabecera and summoning center" (*cabecera y llamamiento*) of Tlacopan, and Durán emphasizes the performance of the king of Tlacopan in one of the campaigns in the isthmus.[129] However, it is not probable that Tlacopan, with only one-fifth of the tribute of the Empire, would have many possessions of its own in the southern regions.

The differences between the sources might also be related to the specialized function that each of the three capitals performed in the government of the Empire. The military primacy of Tenochtitlan accords with the existence of the garrisons depicted in the Codex Mendoza. All the garrisons recorded in the "Memorial de Tlacopan" are in sections 7 and 8, which comprise the Tenochca sector, including Atlan, although it is geographically in the Tetzcoca sector. It is not clear, however, what would have been the particular activities of Tetzcoco and Tlacopan. There are no explicit reports of the functions of these two kingdoms other than the greater importance of Tetzcoco in the system of justice and the reputation of Nezahualcoyotl as a poet and builder;[130] nothing concrete is found about any special task of Tlacopan.[131]

However, the relative importance given to the payment of tribute in kind and to participation in the military organization provides a basis for explaining the different composition of the territorial units defined in the "Memorial de Tlacopan" and in the Tenochca sources. The Codex Mendoza registers separately the military garrisons and the provinces that paid tribute in kind. The Tetzcoca sources register the provinces in their own sector paying tribute in kind; they agree basically with the tributary provinces of the Codex Mendoza but provide no data about provinces with military obligations, and Atlan is not even mentioned. The "Memorial de Tlacopan" simply states that all the towns in the areas subject to the Empire paid tribute to all three imperial capitals and does not list the kind or quantity of the tribute. The information about the areas in the Tetzcoca sector (section 6) was probably provided by the authors of the Tetzcoca memorial. It is not known who provided the information about the Tenochca sector (sections 7 and 8), and the fact remains that these two sections are very different from the tributary provinces of the Codex Mendoza. It is clear, however, that the Tlacopan document lists towns not present in the tributary provinces of the Codex Mendoza that, according to other sources, did not pay tribute in kind but gave military support in men or supplies. It is therefore probable that the very different listings in the "Memorial de Tlacopan" take into account contributions other than tribute in kind, and this explains why the Memorial contains towns not listed in Codex Mendoza.

All the military districts of the Codex Mendoza are represented in the "Memorial de Tlacopan" except Atzaccan, and they are in the sections that embrace the southern, or Tenochca, sector of the Empire. Thus Atlan (7.1-25), Oztoman (7.4-1), Zozollan (7.2-43), Huaxyacac (7.4-6), and Xoconochco (8-6) are listed, but the districts that include more than one town are represented by only one of them. Quecholtenanco is missing, and its district is represented only by Cuauhtochco (7.2-5). Tetzapotitlan (of Atlan), Poctepec (of Oztoman), and Itzteyocan (of Quecholtenanco) are also missing. Other towns not in the Codex Mendoza but registered in the "Memorial de Tlacopan" are described in other sources as fortresses, military allies, or towns that gave provisions for war, as, for example, Quiahuiztlan, Teotitlan del Camino, or Petlatzinco. The fact that towns such as these did not give tribute in kind would be the reason for their not being included with the tributary provinces of the Codex Mendoza, while the "Memorial de Tlacopan" includes them because it lists both the towns paying tribute in kind and those giving other services. And it seems that, when dealing with those that gave provisions and military assistance to the imperial forces, the memorial is more complete because it lists allied towns, while the Codex Mendoza depicts only the military colonies.

Although Tenochtitlan directed the military undertakings of the alliance, the participation of the other two kings in the wars of conquest would have resulted in their rights to receive tribute from certain towns, which consequently were included in the lists of tributaries given by the sources from each capital. It was possible for each king to make conquests on his own, while others were made by the three kings together. This explains the distinction between Tetzcoco's exclusive rights to the tribute of the provinces won by Nezahualcoyotl in his first campaigns and the procedure concerning the tribute of the imperial provinces conquered by the three kings together, whose tribute was distributed among the three allies. However, those provinces of Nezahualcoyotl do not correspond exactly with Torquemada's eastern sector, although they are its most important provinces.[132]

The greater importance of a particular kingdom of the alliance in a given tributary province could also result from an individual king's feats in the conquest of that province, even though the others had also participated. The chronicles relate that Nezahualpilli distinguished himself in the conquest of Ahuilizapan, the king of Tlacopan in the campaign in the isthmus against Cuatzontlan and Xaltepec, and the king of Teotihuacan in the war with Xiquipilco.[133] But this might explain only the acquisition of individual lands or other honors; it does not coincide with Torquemada's tripartite division.

Each of the three parts of the Empire, for logistic reasons, must have had an important role in preparing for the expeditions against neighboring regions. Thus Cuauhchinanco, one of the Acolhua kingdoms, figured in the campaign against the Huaxteca.[134] Similarly, each one of the three great kingdoms could have played a special role in the administration of the cities in its sector.

Other possibilities can also be considered that might explain the different organization of the "Memorial de Tlacopan." A striking feature of this document is the content of the paragraphs comprising the southern sector, which list many more towns than the tributary provinces of the Codex Mendoza and embrace larger regions. It appears that various provinces in the Codex Mendoza had been put together in each single paragraph of the memorial. This might suggest that the paragraphs of the memorial represent a higher administrative level than that of the tributary provinces in the Codex Mendoza, but it is difficult to reconcile this idea with the overlaps that exist between the two sources.

Some of the overlapping might reflect the fact that certain towns paid tribute to various cabeceras at the same time, and each source mentions only one of them. There is only one good example: Cuauhxilotitlan is listed in the Codex Mendoza and the "Memorial de Tlacopan" in different jurisdictions; in the former it is one of the towns in Coyolapan (which includes Huaxyacac), while in the memorial it is in paragraph 7.2, headed by Cozcatlan (which also includes Coaixtlahuacan). According to the relación geográfica of Cuauhxilotitlan, this town had three calpixques, one in Huaxyacac, another in Coaixtlahuacan, and a third who took tribute to Tenochtitlan.[135]

Another possible explanation of the overlaps is that at some time or another certain towns had been transferred from one province to another, and the sources discussed represent different periods in the history of the Empire. However, the historical moment represented, both in the Codex Mendoza and the "Memorial de Tlacopan," seems to be the same: the time of the Spanish Conquest. This is evident in that both documents were prepared for the Spanish Crown in order to report conditions at the time of contact. Thus, both sources incorporate some of the conquests of Moteuczoma Xocoyotzin; for example, Tlachquiauhco is in the Codex Mendoza and Yoloxonecuillan in the "Memorial de Tlacopan." Yet the paragraphs in section 7 of the "Memorial de Tlacopan" reflect to some extent different periods of imperial expansion. Paragraphs 7.2 and 7.3 cover the conquests of the first kings, especially Ilhuicamina and Axayacatl, in the Balsas Basin and the Mixteca, whereas paragraphs 7.1 and 7.4 include the later conquests of Ahuitzotl and Mo-teuczoma Xocoyotzin in the coastal areas of the Pacific and the Gulf, but this can be simply the consequence of the later conquest of those regions. The arrangement of the "Memorial de Tlacopan" is evidently regional; it does not seem possible that the order followed in enumerating the cities within each paragraph could be chron-ological, according to the year of each conquest.

It might also be the case that some of the areas included in the "Memorial de Tlacopan" that are missing in the Codex Mendoza and related documents—such as the central part of the Balsas Basin, Veracruz, and the Pacific coast—did not pay tribute during the years to which these sources refer, or even that those areas were never incorporated effectively into the tributary structure of the Empire. Naturally, it is always possible that some pages of the original source of the Codex Mendoza, the *Matrícula de tributos*, and the *Información de 1554* were lost.

One might think that the organization of the regional calpixcazgos was some-what different from that in Tenochtitlan for the storing of tribute, but, again, there are no reports to support this idea. The twenty calpixques listed in Sahagún were present in Tenochtitlan, but comparing them with the tributary provinces in the Codex Mendoza does not show the kind of difference evident in the "Memorial de Tlacopan."

Finally, it is also possible that the three sectors defined by Torquemada, rather than being a strict delimitation of territories, expressed a symbolic connection with the directions of the world related to the nature of the patron gods of the three capitals: Huitzilopochtli of Tenochtitlan, the god of the south; Tezcatlipoca of Tetzcoco, god of the north; and Otonteuctli of Tlacopan, god of the west. This may have been evident in the different ways the sectors of the Empire participated in the ceremonial organization, but the data assembled here are not sufficient to develop this idea.

In conclusion, there are several possible explanations for the differences be-tween the "Memorial de Tlacopan" and the documents of the other capitals of the alliance in regard to the conquered towns, but usually they agree with the concept of the tripartite division of the regions conquered by the Empire. Each of the cap-itals may have had tributary provinces under its exclusive control, although no specific information is available about exclusive tributaries of Tetzcoco or Tlaco-pan in the distant regions of the Empire. As a rule the tribute was sent to Tenochti-tlan, where Tetzcoco and Tlacopan were given their shares. Although each of the capitals would have most of its possessions in its corresponding sector, each would also have land in the sectors of the other two capitals. The documents proceeding from each capital concentrate their data on their own capital's possessions and on matters pertaining to their capital's role in the total organization of the Empire.

Within the core area, the Codex Mendoza and related sources describe only the tributary provinces of Tenochtitlan, both in its own domain and in those of Tetzcoco and Tlacopan. There is no question about this, since we know from other sources that they do not include the possessions of the other two capitals. In those cases for which we have the best information, as in Tlalhuic and Tolocan, it concerns only the possessions of Tenochtitlan, which were geographically separate from those of the other two capitals.

The Codex Mendoza enumerates all the tributary provinces of the three sectors, beyond the core area, in which Tenochtitlan, as the dominant power in the alliance, was the central point for receiving the tribute that was to be shared with the others. The primacy of Tenochtitlan in the military organization is apparent in the importance given in the Tenochca pictorial sources to the imperial garrisons, which are depicted on pages separate from those recording the provinces paying tribute in kind.

There is not enough information to be absolutely certain whether the tribute of the imperial provinces listed in the Codex Mendoza was only Tenochtitlan's share or included as well what was due to the other two capitals. The Tetzcoca sources enumerate the tributary provinces within Tetzcoco's sector and those beyond it that paid tribute to it, but with few details on the provinces of the other sectors. They do not list the province of Atlan, which, although located in the east, does not appear to have pertained to Tetzcoco.

The "Memorial de Tlacopan" presents first the domain of the Tepanec capital in the core area and then enumerates the towns that paid tribute to the three capitals. On the northeast sector it coincides for the most part with the Tetzcoca sources. On the southern sector the material is organized in a very different way from that of the Tenochca sources and includes towns that, according to other sources, gave only military service. This perhaps reflects the tasks incumbent on Tlacopan in the imperial organization. But in addition it will be seen that the paragraphs on the basin of the Balsas River and the Mixtecas include the regions conquered by the first Tenochan kings, while the rest, on the Gulf coast, the Pacific coast, and the isthmus, include the conquests of Ahuitzotl and Moteuczoma Xocoyotzin. In this way the historical criterion is combined with the geographic and tributary organization.

The next three chapters discuss all the areas paying tribute to the Triple Alliance. These tributary entities traditionally have been given the name of province; this term is kept here for the entities depicted in the Codex Mendoza, but the groups of towns in the "Memorial de Tlacopan" are identified by the number of the paragraph in which this source enumerates them.[136]

Our principal interest is in the general questions of territorial organization that have been outlined in earlier chapters, with emphasis on the territorial divisions and their administration. The extent of each tributary province is compared with the history of its conquest to see to what extent the organization of the tributary provinces is related to the regions subjugated in the military campaigns narrated in the chronicles and how this organization may have changed in the course of time.

There is no need for a complete discussion here of the nature and quantity of the tribute paid by each province, topics that require special attention and have been studied by many scholars.[137] Nor will I attempt a complete account of the Empire's conquests.[138] For each tributary province I have tried to identify the previous existence of indigenous political entities and their continuity under the Empire. As has already been pointed out, one cannot take the list of place names in a tributary province as a series of kingdoms, or even of political subdivisions, unless concrete case materials can be found to confirm it; they were simply towns that paid tribute or where tribute in kind was collected. We will also see what information is available on the imperial calpixques stationed in each province and what is known about population movements, especially the sending of colonists from the Basin, even though this primarily has to do with the question of fortresses and military garrisons, discussed later in chapter 12.

In defining the tributary provinces of the Empire I have followed the Codex Mendoza, giving the variants in the *Matrícula de tributos* and the *Información de 1554* when they add something of importance for the topics of this study. My special objective is to compare the materials of these Tenochca sources with those of Tetzcoco and Tlacopan.[139] When feasible, I combine the sources of the three capitals in order to discuss a given province, but I discuss the material of the "Memorial de Tlacopan" separately when it gives a very different territorial organization.

There is evidence that some tributary provinces included more towns than are registered in the Codex Mendoza and the *Matrícula de tributos*. For a few provinces the *Información de 1554* gives a greater number of towns than the pictorial codices.[140] The Tetzcoca and Tlacopan sources include more towns in the provinces of the Tetzcoca sector. Tochpan is the case best documented; each of the seven towns that the Codex Mendoza lists in that province was the cabecera of a whole series of towns, and the case of Tziuhcoac seems to have been similar.[141] In the southern sector the situation is more complicated; the "Memorial de Tlacopan" includes many towns not registered in the Codex Mendoza, but the division into regions is very different. Local sources sometimes have information on towns that sent their tribute to towns registered in the Codex Mendoza. Thus, Tixtla and Tzompanco, in Guerrero, sent theirs to Ohuapan, which was part of the tributary province of Tepecuacuilco; Tecuicuilco and Itztepexic, in the Sierra Juárez, paid tribute to Huaxyacac. The following chapters will make use of information in other sources, especially the *Relaciones geográficas*, on towns in the regions encompassed by each tributary province without implying that they were part of a province unless there are good reasons to do so. When these sources state that certain towns paid tribute to the Empire without naming the center for collecting their tribute, it could be in one or another of nearby tributary provinces or else the towns could form another province that is missing in the Codex Mendoza. This codex registers the provinces that sent to Tenochtitlan tribute in kind, but there were also other forms of local organization whose relation to the tributary provinces is not well documented. It could be a matter of tribute for local use and not for sending to Tenochtitlan.

In presenting the different tributary provinces, I have followed the order of the Codex Mendoza on the assumption that it is significant; the *Matrícula* and the *Información de 1554* follow the same order. The provinces with which the Codex Mendoza begins are not discussed in the following chapters, since as part of the component kingdoms of the Empire they have been treated in earlier chapters. What remain, therefore, are the provinces that paid tribute to the three capitals; they have been grouped by taking into account the sectors defined by Torquemada.

Following the pages on the central region of the Empire—from Tlatelolco (1) to Huaxtepec (5)—the Codex Mendoza presents the northwest region that, according to Torquemada, would make up the Tlacopaneca sector of the Empire; these are the provinces that go from Cuauhtitlan (6) to Xocotitlan (16). However, according to the "Memorial de Tlacopan," none of them was part of the territory that paid tribute to the three capitals or of the towns and estancias that paid tribute to Tlacopan. Some were within the Tlacopan kingdoms, and they have already been discussed as tributaries of Tenochtitlan in the core area; the status of the rest is more difficult to define. Chapter 9 assesses the situation in the whole northwest sector of the Empire.

The Codex Mendoza then goes on towards the south and takes in the Tenochca sector from Tlachco to Tochtepec and Xoconochco, returning then to the Gulf coast and continuing to the north to enter the Tetzcoca sector. The southern sector is the one most at variance with the "Memorial de Tlacopan." Chapter 10 describes this sector in accordance with a geographical division suggested by the lower number of overlaps between the memorial and the Tenochca sources, but the paragraphs of the "Memorial de Tlacopan" have to be discussed separately. Following the order of the Codex Mendoza, the province of Tochtepec is included in this sector, although the sources of Tetzcoco and Tlacopan group it with the Tetzcoca provinces.

The northeast sector is the topic of chapter 11. The coincidence among the sources of the three capitals is greater than in the southern sector, but a comparison of the sources shows that the delimitation of the tributary provinces that had a special connection to Tetzcoco does not adhere to the demarcation lines that

Torquemada gives, and paragraph 7.1 of the "Memorial de Tlacopan," geographically in the northeast, is discussed in this same chapter.

The identification of all the towns that constituted the tributary provinces has been a difficult but essential task for the interpretation of these entities in terms of their geographical distribution and their political characteristics. The material of the Codex Mendoza and of the Tetzcoca sources has been analyzed by Barlow and other writers, who have identified the greater part of the towns named.[142] I have made several new identifications for both the core area and the distant conquered areas. The "Memorial de Tlacopan" has never before been thoroughly studied; in this book almost all its toponyms have been identified, although a few are still to be located.[143]

Chapter 9

THE NORTHWESTERN SECTOR
OF THE EMPIRE

Following the provinces in the center of the Empire (Tlatelolco, Petlacalco, Acol-huacan, Cuauhnahuac, and Huaxtepec), the Codex Mendoza presents the rest of the provinces in a counterclockwise direction, beginning in the north, going on to the west and then the south, and finishing in the northeast with Tziuhcoac and Ox-itipan. Therefore, we shall begin with the northwest quadrant that, according to Torquemada, was the Tlacopanec sector of the Empire.

The provinces in question—in the order of the Codex Mendoza—are Cua-uhtitlan, Axocopan, Atotonilco de Tula, Hueypochtlan, Atotonilco el Grande, Xilotepec, Cuahuacan, Tolocan, Ocuillan, Malinalco, and Xocotitlan.[1] After these provinces comes Tlachco, which is definitely in the southern, Tenochca, sector.

It should be noted that the sections defined in the "Memorial de los pueblos de Tlacopan" as containing towns that were tributaries of all three capitals do not include any places within this northwestern area,[2] which it deals with only when listing the towns of Tlacopan and the kingdoms that were dependencies of the Tepanec capital. Some regions, such as Tolocan and Ixtlahuacan, appear in this document only as the towns of tenant farmers of Tlacopan. They are not listed among the Tlacopan kingdoms, nor are they included in the sections that list towns paying tribute to the three capitals. Farther south, Ocuillan and Malinalco are completely absent from the "Memorial de Tlacopan." This source suggests, there-fore, that in the northwest quadrant the towns that were not part of Tlacopan or of its kingdoms were the tributaries of one of the other two capitals, categories not included in this document. In this particular case they were obviously tributaries of Tenochtitlan.

Some of the tributary provinces in the Codex Mendoza listed above—Cuauhtitlan, Axocopan, Atotonilco [de Tula], Hueypochtlan, Xilotepec, and Cuahuacan—were situated within the dependent kingdoms of Tlacopan in such a way that their geographical distribution overlapped that of the kingdoms; those provinces, as has been shown, were the possessions held by Tenochtitlan within the Tlacopanec kingdoms. Some other provinces were outside of this category. In the eastern extremity, Atotonilco el Grande was partly in Tetzcoca territory, and in the southwest, which, according to Torquemada's formula, was the transition area from Tenochtitlan's sector to that of Tlacopan, were the provinces of Tolocan, Ocuillan, Malinalco, and Xocotitlan.

The sequence of these provinces in the Codex Mendoza goes primarily from the north towards the west and south, but not in a strictly geographical order. First, the codex registers a group of provinces established in the territory of the Tepanec kingdoms—Cuauhtitlan, Axocopan, Atotonilco de Tula, and Hueypochtlan— and then turns to the east to include Atotonilco el Grande, in Tetzcoca territory. It then turns west again to Xilotepec, which forms a second group with the provinces that follow in the south: Cuahuacan, Tolocan, Ocuillan, Malinalco, and Xocotitlan. This interruption of the sequence coincides with the distinction between towns conquered by different Tenochca kings. The first group was won by Moteuczoma Ilhuicamina; the last comprises the region where Axayacatl waged war. The division into provinces can be related to the wars that Tenochtitlan carried on in those regions.

The Tepanec Kingdoms and the Establishment of Tenochca Predominance in the West

The establishment of a group of kingdoms that were direct dependencies of Tlacopan dates from the very beginning of the Triple Alliance. These were the kingdoms of Tepanec ancestry that had comprised part of the previous regime led by Azcapotzalco. Although the sources do not give their names at that time, citing specifically only Mazahuacan, it seems that they were towns in the western part of the Basin.[3] Later, the Tlacopanec kingdoms included Xilotepec and two other towns, Tollan and Apazco, that were in the region north of the Basin called Teotlalpan. As part of the Tlacopan domain, these kingdoms have already been discussed, but during the century of the Empire's existence they were subject to vicissitudes that strengthened Tenochca power and must be reviewed here.

According to the lists of conquests, in those areas Itzcoatl vanquished several towns,[4] whose inclusion in these lists can be understood in the same light as the conquest of Tlacopan—that is, as part of the conflicts that took place during the formation of the Triple Alliance. Other towns in this region that were part of the three great kingdoms of the alliance are depicted as conquests of Moteuczoma Ilhuicamina: Hueypochtlan, Atotonilco de Tula, Axocopan, Tollan, Xilotepec, Itzcuincuitlapilco, and—farther east—Atotonilco el Grande.[5] Apparently the tripartite structure of the Empire was still taking shape. Basically this list coincides with the cabeceras of the tributary provinces that the Codex Mendoza gives for this region; one must assume that these provinces were established at that time. Politically Tollan and Xilotepec were cabeceras of dependent kingdoms of Tlacopan, but the others were only cabeceras of Tenochca calpixcazgos; Atotonilco de Tula, Axocopan, and Hueypochtlan were subject to the Tepanec kingdom of Apazco. So was Itzcuincuitlapilco, not listed in the Codex Mendoza, although the *itzcuicuitlapilcatl* is one of the twenty calpixques of the Empire that Sahagún lists.

The province of Atotonilco el Grande included territory in the Tetzcoca part of the Empire, notably so in the case of Tollantzinco, seat of one of the Acolhua kings, and Tzihuinquillocan, a town established by Nezahualcoyotl. However, the northern zone of this province does not seem to have been completely integrated into the Acolhua kingdom. Several towns had long been in effect the frontier of the Acolhuacan against the Chichimecs of Metztitlan.[6] During the Empire, Atotonilco el Grande maintained this frontier situation, and it was from there that Tizoc began his campaign against Metztitlan.[7] In the Codex Mendoza this province combines towns in the Acolhua kingdom of Tollantzinco with the towns farther north that would be the military frontier.

Three of Itzcoatl's sons were sent to rule towns that were within the Tlacopan domain—Xilotepec, Apan, and Atotonilco—apparently an indication of the early incorporation of those towns into the Empire under Tenochca predominance (see p. 102). The conquests of Moteuczoma Ilhuicamina thus show a first strengthening of Tenochca power in territories that may have entered into the Triple Alliance as the domain of Tlacopan; this can be compared with the acquisition by Ilhuicamina of the Tenochca provinces of Acolman and Atotonilco el Grande in the domain of Tetzcoco.

North of the Basin, the Teotlalpan comprises the provinces of Axocopan, Atotonilco de Tula, and Hueypochtla. The relaciones geográficas of some towns in this area report the submission of the Tepanecs to the Mexicas either at the end of the Tepanec predominance or during the reign of Itzcoatl.[8] The Cuauhtlalpan (Forest Land) was the mountainous area between the Basin of Mexico and the Valley of Toluca, approximately from Xilotepec to Ocuillan; the people who lived there were called Cuauhtlalpanecs, or *"serranos"* (mountain people). The towns of the Cuauhtlalpan and the Teotlalpan participated in the military undertakings of the Triple Alliance. During the reign of Moteuczoma Ilhuicamina the Cuauhtlalpanecs were mentioned among those who went on the Huaxyacac campaign,[9] and some Xiquipilcas went to settle in the new city;[10] the Cuauhtlalpanecs and Mazahuas were among those who went to the wars against Tlaxcallan.[11] Under Axayacatl, Otomi warriors from the Cuauhtlalpan went on the disastrous campaign against the Tarascans.[12]

Axayacatl started another period of intense military activity in the west, concentrating more towards the south. During the conflict with Moquihuix of Tlatelolco, the latter tried to organize the old kingdoms of the Tepanec regime against Tenochtitlan, sending ambassadors to Tollan, Apazco, Xilotepec, Chiappan, and Cuahuacan.[13] After the defeat of Tlatelolco, Axayacatl's campaign against Matlatzinco led to the conquest of a group of towns similar to the one that constituted the tributary province of Tolocan. Axayacatl was the great reorganizer of the political and tributary situation in that region, and it must have been during his reign that the province of Tolocan was established as it appears in the Codex Mendoza. The lists of his conquests also include Ocuillan, Tenancingo, Xocotitlan, and Xiquipilco.[14] Although part of this region may have become part of the Empire under Tlacopan as a component of the former empire of Azcapotzalco, Axayacatl reorganized and extended it so that it came under Tenochca predominance. Two years before the war with Matlatzinco, Axayacatl appointed the king of Malinalco, a clear demonstration of Tenochca dominance in that town,[15] and a daughter of Axayacatl married the ruler of Ocuillan, further evidence of the supremacy of Tenochtitlan.[16]

Durán tells us that in Axayacatl's time there were great disturbances among nearby towns, especially a war between Ocuillan and Cuauhnahuac that Ocuillan won, and adds that the people of Xiquipilco rebelled and "made war on their own brothers and neighbors."[17] However, Durán may have been mistaken about the victory of Ocuillan over Cuauhnahuac; in other sources Axayacatl conquered both of them.[18] These wars were part of Axayacatl's campaigns in the west, which went beyond the Valley of Toluca. Some of the conquered towns were adjacent to the Tarascans: Xilotepec, Xocotitlan, Malacatepec, Amatepec, and Cimatepec.[19]

Tizoc, the successor of Axayacatl, took to the war against Metztitlan "all the Otomi mountain people of Xocotitlan" and those of Matlatzinco.[20] For the installation of Tizoc, people came from Matlatzinco, Tolocan, Tzinacantepec, Tlacotepec, Calimayan, Tepemaxalco, and Teotenanco; from Malinalco and Ocuillan; and also from Coatepec, Capolhuac, Xalatlauhco, and Atlapolco.[21] The last group pertained to Tlacopan. All this suggests that these towns were part of the Empire; however, during his reign Tizoc conquered three towns in that same region: Toxico, Cillan, and Mazahuacan.[22]

In spite of the conquests of Axayacatl and Tizoc, the Empire did not succeed in securing its control over the whole region. For his inaugural celebration Ahuitzotl undertook a campaign against the "province" of Chiappan, "seven towns very powerful and large, all of mountain people"—Chiappan, Xilotepec, Xocotitlan, Cuauhuacan, Xiquipilco, Cillan, and Mazahuacan—"which province was somewhat rebellious and obeyed and served the Mexicas much against their will."[23] The participants in this war against Chiappan included, among others, the neighboring towns of the Valley of Toluca, previously conquered by Axayacatl, and all the mountain area of Malinalco and Ocuillan.[24]

Of the seven towns that had rebelled, Xilotepec, Xocotitlan, and Cuahuacan are cabeceras of tributary provinces in the Codex Mendoza. The other four—Chiappan, Xiquipilco, Mazahuacan, and Cillan—are not found among the provinces of this codex. As for the organization presented in the "Memorial de los pueblos de Tlacopan," only Xilotepec was a dependent kingdom of Tlacopan, and Cuahuacan was one of the towns of Tlacopan that had been given to Spaniards. Many of Tlacopan's possessions were in the same territory as the province of Cuahuacan in the Codex Mendoza. None of the five other towns appear in the "Memorial de Tlacopan," although some towns of tenant farmers of Tlacopan were in the area of Chiappan, Xiquipilco, and Ixtlahuacan.[25]

The seven towns that Ahuitzotl set out to conquer perhaps constituted a political entity. According to Durán, Chiappan and Xilotepec were the two principal towns, and Chiappan played a major role in this military campaign, which suggests that together with Xilotepec it ruled this group of seven cities.[26] It was an important town in the ethnic consciousness of the Otomis, for whom the place of origin of "all those who have been born" was certain caves near the town of Chiappan.[27] It is also a prominent toponym; Chiappantonco[28] and Hueychiappan (present-day Huichapan) were in the region of Xilotepec. A group of Otomis emigrated from Hueychiappan to Michoacan, perhaps as a consequence of Ahuitzotl's conquest.[29]

The kingdom of Xilotepec was on the frontier with the Chichimecs, and there were several garrisons in this area.[30] It extended as far as Cimapan, whose relación names Imetzxayac as king of Xilotepec.[31]

Cuahuacan was a Tepanec town with its own king before the formation of the Triple Alliance. After Ahuitzotl's conquest it lost importance and became subject to Tlacopan and cabecera of the Tenochca tributary province of the same name.

In the early documentation Mazahuacan is not given specifically as the name of a town or city; at times it seems to be the name of a region. According to Torquemada the "province" of Mazahuacan pertained to Tlacopan when the Triple Alliance was founded, but it is not listed in the "Memorial de Tlacopan." The name Mazahuacan is sometimes combined with Xocotitlan and Xiquipilco. Xocotitlan does not appear in the "Memorial de Tlacopan"; it had its own king and was a tributary province in the Codex Mendoza, as discussed below. Nor does Xiquipilco appear in the "Memorial de Tlacopan," but its cabecera was called Ahuazhuatepec, one of the towns of tenant farmers belonging to Tlacopan.

In the *Suma de visitas*, Cillan was an estancia of Xiquipilco; today Sila is a hamlet of Jiquipilco, and there is a ranch called San José Sila in Ixtlahuacan.[32]

After the conquest of these seven towns, the chronicles describe the imposition of tribute but say nothing about the fate of the local rulers or the naming of calpixques.

The Codex Telleriano-Remensis also records the conquest of Chiappan by Ahuitzotl in 9 Tecpatl 1488; the legend that accompanies the painting identifies it as Chiappan, next to Xilotepec.[33] In the same year it records the taking of Cozcacuauhtenanco, a town near Texopilco,[34] already conquered by Axayacatl.[35] Torquemada puts the conquest of Cozcacuauhtenanco in a later campaign by Ahuitzotl and says that the people of this town fled to Quauchpanco.[36] This is another name for Michoacan,[37] an indication that Cozcacuauhtenanco was one of several towns whose people settled among the Tarascans.

Ixtlilxochitl does not discuss this war against the seven towns headed by Chiappan. When he does mention Chiappan, he is undoubtedly referring to the present-day Chiapa de Corzo, in the state of Chiapas,[38] and possibly that is also its location in the lists of towns conquered by Ahuitzotl.[39] Nevertheless, when Durán and Tezozomoc relate the wars of the isthmus, they do not mention Chiappan (de Corzo), whose actual conquest cannot be confirmed. Several sources give detailed accounts of Ahuitzotl's wars, both in the Chiappan-Xilotepec region and in the isthmus, but they speak of Chiappan only in one or the other of the two campaigns. What is most probable is that the supposed conquest of Chiappan (de Corzo) was included by mistake because of the similarity of the names.

After Ahuitzotl's campaign against Chiappan, the northwest region remained under the control of the Empire and participated in its enterprises together with the kingdoms of the Basin.[40] Of the seven towns conquered by Ahuitzotl, at least three were ruled by a king in 1519: Imexayac in Xilotepec, Acxoyatl in Chiappan, and Ocelotzin in Xocotitlan.[41] There is no clear information about new conquests in that region during the reign of Moteuczoma Xocoyotzin.[42]

The Provinces in the Valley of Toluca and the Southern Part of the Cuauhtlalpan in the Codex Mendoza

The situation of the Valley of Toluca was somewhat unusual.[43] The historical information suggests that it would have been part of the old Azcapotzalco empire and probably pertained to Tlacopan when the Triple Alliance was established. Nevertheless, it had to be subjugated by Axayacatl. The "Memorial de Tlacopan" does not include any of the towns in this area among the dependent kingdoms of Tlacopan, and therefore it cannot be considered as one of them. The problem is whether the province of Tolocan as depicted in the Codex Mendoza paid tribute to the three capitals. If so, one would expect Tolocan to be listed in the "Memorial de Tlacopan" among the towns that paid tribute to all three capitals. It is not. Tolocan appears as one of Tlacopan's towns of tenant farmers, and other sources identify towns in the Tolocan area, some of which paid tribute to Tenochtitlan, others to Tlacopan, and still others to Tetzcoco. It is a good example of the type of organization, also identified in Chalco and Tlalhuic, in which the three capitals of the Empire held separate possessions. Following the conquests of Axayacatl there is very little information about kingdoms and local rulers. The *Anales de Cuauhtitlan,* in the list of kings who were ruling in 1519, names only Mazacoyotzin of Matlatzinco and Ocelotzin of Xocotitlan.[44] This contrasts with the situation in Tlalhuic and Chalco, for which there is ample information on the continuity of the local rulers under the Triple Alliance. All of this must have resulted from Axayacatl's reorganization of the region, and the province in the Codex Mendoza is surely the part that corresponded to Tenochtitlan, since, as will be seen, it includes the towns that Axayacatl assigned to his city, but not those that he granted to Tetzcoco and Tlacopan.

It is difficult to define the political entities of these regions as they were before the conquests of Axayacatl. Zorita gives a brief description of the organization of this area before Axayacatl and refers to the "valley of Matlalzinco and Ixtlabac" (Ixtlahuacan), or "the valley of Matlalcinco, of which Toluca and Malinalco are part," as one of the "provinces" where there were three rulers. He gives their titles in a single hierarchical line of promotion (from tlacochcalcatl to tlacatecatl and finally tlatoani) but is not precise concerning whether the three governed together in one capital or separately, in different cabeceras.[45]

According to the accounts of the imperial conquest, Tolocan and Matlatzinco were two parcialidades of a single polity that quarreled with the king of Tenantzinco, who, "as a loyal vassal," asked the king of Tenochtitlan for help. Durán names two kings, Chimalteuctli (or Chimaltzin) of Tolocan and Chalchiuhquiauh of Matlatzinco, but Tezozomoc refers to Chimalteuctli as king of Tolocan and its neighboring towns and also as king of Matlatzinco. Chimalpahin, on the other hand, names Chimalteuctli as king of Calixtlahuacan.[46] According to local sources, the old cabecera of the Matlatzincas before Axayacatl conquered and expelled them was Calixtlahuacan; most of the exiled Matlatzincas went from Tzinacantepec to Michoacan.[47] Once there, they established themselves in Charo, known during the sixteenth century by the Nahuatl name of Matlatzinco.[48]

As reported in the relación of Atlatlauhcan, this town, together with (Teo)tenanco, Calimayan, Tepemaxalco, Malinalco, Ocuillan, and Tenantzinco, had been conquered by Axayacatzin, while he was one of Moteuczoma's captains, who "released them from the power of a principal of Tenantzinco, who was a tyrant."[49]

The toponym Matlatzinco denotes the region of the Valley of Toluca; the gentile name Matlatzincatl is applied to its inhabitants, but it is also the name of the

Otomian language spoken there, in addition to Otomi, Mazahua, and Nahuatl.[50] Matlatzinco is sometimes used as the name of a particular town; at other times it seems to be a second name added to a toponym, perhaps to indicate the region in which it is located. Thus, in the page of conquests by Axayacatl in the Codex Mendoza the glyph of Tolocan is accompanied by that of Matlatzinco,[51] while in the Codex Telleriano-Remensis it is beside that of Xiquipilco.[52] Throughout the sixteenth century the word *Matlatzinco* was used for the region of the valley of the Lerma River and for the river itself,[53] but there were also towns located in Matlatzinco farther south, such as Temazcaltepec[54] and Zoquitzinco.[55]

In the Codex Mendoza, Tolocan is followed by the provinces of Ocuillan, Malinalco, and Xocotitlan. The last two could be the cabeceras of the other supreme rulers of Matlatzinco that Zorita mentions, if we consider Xocotitlan and Ixtlahuacan as a single region. None of the important towns in these provinces, such as Ocuillan, Tenantzinco, and Malinalco, are found among the dependent kingdoms of Tlacopan. Tonatiuhco, one of the towns of the province of Ocuillan, is listed in the "Memorial de Tlacopan" in paragraph 7.3, one of the paragraphs that contain towns in the southern, or Tenochca, sector that paid tribute to the three capitals. Therefore, Ocuillan and probably Malinalco were already outside the domain of the Tepanec capital and should be considered tributaries exclusively of Tenochtitlan or part of the Tenochca sector of the Empire. They are discussed here because they are associated with the Tolocan region in the few remarks that the chronicles make on the political situation that the Mexicas encountered when they conquered this region. In addition, in the Codex Mendoza they are between Tolocan and Xocotitlan, which places them in the northwest quadrant of the Empire. However, the historical connections of Malinalco and Ocuillan point towards Colhuacan and Xochimilco.[56] Malinalco played a prominent role in the early history of the Mexicas. Both cities participated in the activities of the Triple Alliance, along with the cities of the Basin, in the same way as did the kingdoms of the core area. They took part in the coronation of Tizoc,[57] during the reign of Ahuitzotl they fought in the war against Chiappan,[58] and they were present at the inauguration of the temple.[59] Ocuillan also sent settlers to Oztoman.[60]

The lists that follow give the names of the towns in each of the tributary provinces in the northwest region, which are shown on Map 9-1. A variant in the *Matrícula de Tributos* is shown in brackets.

TOLOCAN (CODEX MENDOZA, 33R)

1. Tuluca — Toluca de Lerdo, Mexico.
2. Calixtlahuacan — Calistlahuaca, barrio of Tolocan (SV, sec. 561). Calixtlahuaca in Toluca, Mexico.

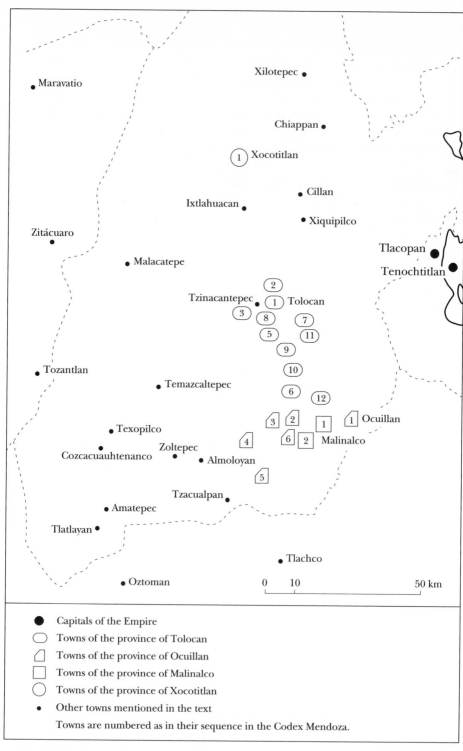

MAP 9–1. The tributary provinces of Tolocan, Ocuillan, Malinalco, and Xocotitlan

3. Xicaltepec   Jicaltepec in Toluca, Mexico.

4. Tepetlhuiacan   Not located.

5. Mitepec [Tlacotepec]   Mitepec and Tlacotepec could be alternative
readings of the same glyph, as either an arrow
(*mitl*) or a dart (*tlacotl*), but they are different
towns in the local documentation (Map from
AGN-HJ, 277, in Hernández 1952).
Santiago Tlacotepec in Toluca, Mexico.

6. Capulteopan   Capultenpan (*sic pro* Capulteupan), barrio of
Atlatlauhca (RG 6:47).

7. Metepec   Metepec (Hernández 1952:91, map from
AGN-HJ, 277).
Metepec, Mexico.

8. Cacalomaca   Cacalomaca (Hernández 1952:91, map from
AGN-HJ, 277).
Cacalomacán in Toluca, Mexico.

9. Caliymayan   Calimaya, bordering on Teotenanco
(RG 7:279).
Calimaya de Díaz González, Mexico.

10. Teotenanco   Teutenango (RG 7:277ff.).
Tenango de Arista in Tenango del Valle,
Mexico.

11. Tepemaxalco   Tepemaxalco, adjacent to Teotenanco
(RG 7:279).
San Lucas Tepemajalco in San Antonio de
la Isla, Mexico.

12. Çoquitzinco   Joquicingo, Mexico.

We have seen the conquest of this region by Axayacatl, the Matlatzincas exiled to Michoacan, the distribution of land to new settlers, and the granting of peasant towns to major cities of the Empire, that is, Tenochtitlan, Tlatelolco, Tetzcoco, Tlacopan, and Azcapotzalco. Axayacatl also designated certain places for himself or for his brother Ahuitzotl.[61] Some of the towns near Tolocan registered in this province of the Codex Mendoza—Calixtlahuacan, Mitepec, Metepec, Cacalomacan, and Calimayan—are among those granted to Tenochtitlan or to the Tenochca lords, but none of the towns granted to Tetzcoco and Tlacopan appear. As in Tolocan, the three capitals had tributaries in the southern part of the province, near Zoquitzinco, but in the north, in the Ixtlahuacan region where Tlacopan held three towns, none are in the Codex Mendoza. It is clear that each of the three capitals had its own calpixcazgo in this region. The possessions of Tlacopan in the Valley of Toluca are listed in section 5 of the "Memorial de Tlacopan." The possessions of Tetzcoco are reported in Ixtlilxochitl's account of Axayacatl's campaign against Matlatzinco, in which the other two allied kingdoms participated, and of the imposition of tribute to be paid to the three kingdoms. Nezahualpilli obtained towns for himself apart from those of the other two kingdoms and put in place his own steward, whose name is given (Yaotl). His share included towns or villages in the Valley of Toluca ("Maxtlacan, Coquitzinco [*sic*], and other towns"), from which he received as tribute each year a large quantity of fine cloaks of various types, gold jewels, ornaments, and insignia, plus the yield of a maize field in each town. The shares of the other two kings are briefly stated; that of the king of Mexico was equal to that of the king of Tetzcoco; the king of Tlacopan received "a certain part, that would be about a fifth."[62]

There is also a reference to the possessions of Nezahualpilli in Zoquitzinco in a report dated 1539 concerning the lands of Moteuczoma, prepared by his son Don Pedro Tlacahuepantzin and by Don Gabriel, son of Totoquihuatzin of Tlacopan. It states that Nezahualpilli, grandfather of Don Gabriel, owned part of the lands and commoners in the province of Matlatzinco called Zoquitzinco.[63] In the Memorial of Don Hernando Pimentel, "a certain part of Toluca" is in the list of towns that his ancestors won in battle and where they had tenant farmers and lands (see p. 59).

The colonial documentation describes the continuation of a local ruler in Tolocan and the persistent discord between him and new settlers from the Basin. Axayacatl took lands for himself and for Ahuitzotl and distributed plots of land to people who had come with him from Tlatelolco, Tetzcoco, Azcapotzalco, and Tlacopan. They cultivated the land to grow provisions for military campaigns and acknowledged Cachimaltzin, king of Tolocan, as the owner and answered his summons for labor services. Cachimaltzin and later his successor, Maçacoyotzin, believed that the land had been taken from them tyrannically and were at war with Axayacatl and later with Moteuczoma for more than four years. After Maçacoyotzin died, his successor was Tucoyotzin, who was the ruler of Tolocan when the Spanish came.[64]

Fifteen years before the arrival of Cortés, Moteuczoma Xocoyotzin also distributed lands in Tolocan, but it is not clear whether this was an administrative reorganization or the result of a new military intervention.[65]

In addition to Tlacopan, Cuauhtitlan—one of the Tlacopanec kingdoms—also held land in Matlatzinco, as in Chalco, which it acquired when land was distributed after Axayacatl's campaign.[66] The *Anales de Cuauhtitlan* report that the placing of boundary marks in the "eagle land" (*cuauhtlalli*) in Matlatzinco was accomplished in 5 Acatl 1471, with representatives of the four parts of Cuauhtitlan participating.[67]

Ocuillan (Codex Mendoza, 34r)

1.	Ocuilan	Oquila (SV, sec. 419).
		Ocuilan de Arteaga, Mexico.
2.	Tenantzinco	Tenançingo (SV, sec. 531).
		Tenancingo de Degollado, Mexico.
3.	Tequaloyan	Villa Guerrero, Mexico.
4.	Tonatiuhco	Tonatico, Mexico.
5.	Coatepec	One of the four cabeceras of Çaqualpa
		(*sic pro* Tzacualpan) (SV, sec. 109).
		Coatepec Harinas, Mexico.
6.	Cincozcac	Cincuzcatlan, estancia of Zumpahuacan
		(SV, sec. 101).

Ocuillan and Tenantzinco are counted among the towns conquered during the Matlatzinco campaign,[68] although Durán, in his account of this war, gives Tenantzinco as a "loyal vassal of the royal crown of Mexico" who asked Tenochtitlan for help against the ruler of Tolocan and fought on the side of the Mexicas.[69] Ocuillan's close connection with Tenochtitlan, as well as its subordination, is evident in Axayacatl's sending one of his daughters to marry the ruler of Ocuillan.[70]

Tonatiuhco appears in the "Memorial de Tlacopan" in the paragraph that includes the neighboring region of present-day Guerrero (7.3-5). Cuitlapilco, another of the cabeceras of Tzacualpan, is also found in this memorial (7.3-7).

Tzompahuacan, to which Cincozcac pertained, was a town of the tributary province of Malinalco, next on this list.

Malinalco (Codex Mendoza, 35r)

1.	Malinalco	Malinalco (SV, sec. 346).
		Malinalco, Mexico.
2.	Çompahuacan[Tzompanco]	Çumpaguacan (SV, sec. 101).
		Zumpahuacan, Mexico.

Although Malinalco is important in the traditions of the Mexica migration, information on its later history is very deficient. After the war with Tlatelolco and before the Matlatzinco campaign, Axayacatl made Citlalcoatzin the ruler of Malinalco;[71] there is no mention of a conquest of Malinalco, but this appointment of a ruler is probably related to those wars. Citlalcoatl was also the name of the leader of the Malinalcas when they left Chicomoztoc.[72] Several Tenochca princes had the same name. Although none of them is identified as king of Malinalco, it is possible that this is another example of a Tenochca prince installed as ruler of a dependent kingdom.[73]

The people of Tzompahuacan were "pure Mexicas, from the principal Indians of this city, head of their Empire."[74] This suggests either an ancient affinity with the Mexicas like that of Malinalco, or else a Mexica settlement during the imperial epoch.[75] Tzompanco, the variant in the *Matrícula de tributos*, can be explained as an alternate reading of the glyph, but there is no town of that name in this area.

Xocotitlan (Codex Mendoza, 35r)

1. Xocotitlan   Xocotitlan (SV, sec. 799).
                       Jocotitlan, Mexico.

Xocotitlan, like Tolocan, Ocuillan, and Malinalco, was probably a tributary province of Tenochtitlan only, since the sources of the other two allied capitals do not mention it among those that paid tribute to the Empire.

In the Codex Mendoza (35r) and in the *Matrícula de tributos* (plate 15) the provinces of Malinalco and Xocotitlan are on the same page, separated by a line. Both provinces are lacking in the *Información de 1554*. In their place—between Ocuillan and Tlachco, or between Tlachco and Tepecuacuilco—the tribute from Apan is described. This is a town that does not appear as cabecera of a tributary province in any other source. Present-day Apan, Hidalgo, is the only well-known town with this name, but it is very doubtful that it was the Apan in the *Información de 1554*.[76] There is sufficient evidence to affirm that this Apan is equivalent to the two provinces of Malinalco and Xocotitlan in the Codex Mendoza and in the *Matrícula*.

According to the *Información de 1554*, four other towns paid tribute along with Apan. In the *Matrícula* the Spanish commentary on the plate depicting Malinalco and Xocotitlan says that the tribute was paid by "the people of Malinalco, Zumpango [Tzompanco], Xocotitlan, and other towns depicted in the border." In its present condition the page has no such border with other towns depicted on it. The page interpreted by the witnesses must have had two more glyphs along with that of Xocotitlan on the right-hand side where the edge of the page is now very close to the pictures.[77] Perhaps when the codex was being bound the edge was cut off or a strip of amate with those towns on the border came loose. This means that the document explained by the witnesses in the *Información de 1554* contained the provinces of Malinalco (together with Tzompahuacan) and Xocotitlan—the same as in the Codex Mendoza and the *Matrícula*—but there must have been two more glyphs to make the total of five towns. One of these glyphs now lost was interpreted to be the cabecera called Apan, with which the four other towns paid tribute.[78]

The witnesses read the page as if it depicted only one province, as did the commentator in the Codex Mendoza (34v) and the one who wrote the legend cited above on plate 15 of the *Matrícula*.

The tribute as declared by the *Información de 1554* witnesses confirms that it included the tribute depicted as that of the provinces of Malinalco and Xocotitlan in both the pictorial codices. A comparison of the tribute paid by Apan with that paid by Malinalco and Xocotitlan makes it clear that Apan is the equivalent of those two provinces. Like Malinalco and Xocotitlan, Apan paid tribute only in cloaks, maize, and beans; it did not pay tribute in any other kind of clothing nor in warrior costumes or emblems, or any other product of the many that almost all the other provinces paid. This is a strong argument in favor of identifying Apan with those two provinces in the Codex Mendoza. It is also evident that the witnesses combined two provinces into one, for the quantity of tribute in grain is approximately double that which is indicated for other provinces. The *Información de 1554* counts such tribute in *fanegas*, with similar quantities in all the provinces. Almost all gave each year 4,100 (or 8,200) fanegas of maize and 4,100 of beans; some also gave 4,100 fanegas of chía and huauhtli. According to the witnesses, Apan gave 16,400 (or 16,300 or 16,100) fanegas of maize and 8,200 of beans, that is, double that of the provinces who paid the most.[79] No other province paid such a large quantity; only the sum of the tribute from two provinces could have resulted in a quantity for Apan so much larger than that of all the others. In the Codex Mendoza and the *Matrícula* the register of quantities of grains is more complex, but there also it is clear that the tribute paid by Malinalco and Xocotitlan added up to a total greater than normal payments.[80]

The toponym Apan does not occur in the Valley of Toluca and its environs; it may have been a town of little importance or an alternate name for another town better known under another name. What is most probable is that in the pictorial document submitted to the witnesses of the *Información de 1554* the glyph for Chiappan (present-day Chapa de Mota, Mexico) was like the one in the Codex Telleriano-Remensis and was read as Apan. This town and Xocotitlan are neighbors and are related in the history of Ahuitzotl's conquests in that region.[81]

In conclusion, the province of Apan in the *Información de 1554* corresponds to the two provinces of Malinalco and Xocotitlan. But these two provinces must be considered as separate entities, even though the early commentators of the pictorial codices put them together. The province of Xocotitlan included two other towns; one of them, given by the witnesses as Apan, was probably Chiappan. Xocotitlan is frequently mentioned among the towns that fought in the Empire's wars and participated in public works and the great ceremonies in Tenochtitlan. In 1519 a king named Ocelotzin ruled in Xocotitlan, and another named Acxoyatl ruled in Chiappan.[82]

The Frontier with Michoacan

The accounts of the Empire's conquests and some local documents indicate imperial control of towns along the frontier with Michoacan that are not included in any of the tributary provinces, and not enough information is available to determine to what political and tributary entity they pertained.

When the *Suma de visitas* was prepared, about 1548, Atlacomolco and Ixtlahuacan were adjacent to Tarascan towns. Ixtlahuacan was one of Tlacopan's towns of tenant farmers, but there are no early sources on Atlacomolco.[83] Farther south, facing the Tarascans of Zitácuaro, Malacatepec (present-day Villa Allende, Mexico) was conquered by Axayacatl during the campaign against Matlatzinco.[84]

The relación of Las Minas de Temazcaltepec records three cabeceras—Texcaltitlan, Texopilco, and Temazcaltepec—with numerous sujetos; they were in "the province that they say was formerly called Matalcinga," but there is no evidence of their being part of the tributary province of Tolocan.[85] They were conquered by Axayacatl and, later, "were governed by Indian governors that Moteuczoma chose from among them," who collected the tribute, punished those guilty of committing crimes, and organized the people for participating in the wars against the Tarascans who lived on the frontier of this region.[86] Cozcacuauhtenanco, a sujeto of Texopilco, was first conquered by Axayacatl and later retaken by Ahuitzotl; its king was sacrificed at the dedication of the temple of Huitzilopochtli.[87]

The relación of Las Minas de Zultepec (Zoltepec) has information on this town and also on Almoloyan, Amatepec, and Tlatlayan, saying that they were sujetos and tributaries of Mexico. Zoltepec had its own ruler, who named principals and tequitlatos to collect the tribute and assemble the people to go to war against the Tarascans.[88] Zoltepec and Tlatlayan (an estancia of Zoltepec in the sixteenth century) are listed among the conquests of Moteuczoma Xocoyotzin.[89] Amatepec, a conquest of Axayacatl,[90] was contiguous with the imperial garrison of Oztoman and with Cozamallan, which belonged to the Tarascan kingdom.[91]

A colonial lawsuit in 1562 between Amatepec and Texopilco over springs of saline water gives an idea of the situation of these towns facing Michoacan. The people of Amatepec, who had moved there from Zoltepec, Tepetitlan, and Tlamacaztepec, paid salt as tribute to Mexico. They were Mazahuas who had entered the territory of Texopilco, a Matlatzinca town, and although they were driven out, they came back, and the people of Texopilco asked for help from the Matlatzincas of Tolocan. To resolve this problem the king of Tenochtitlan, Ahuitzotl, sent his son Atlixcatzin, who determined the boundary between Amatepec and Texopilco. Several witnesses gave different dates for when this happened, from approximately 1478 to 1488. They reported the presence of calpixques who were in charge of collecting the tribute of salt for Moteuczoma. One of these calpixques was from Tenochtitlan, and another, from Tlacopan. Amatepec was near the kingdom of Michoacan; a witness from Tozantlan, a Tarascan town, declared that formerly they went to the salt pans to capture prisoners.[92]

The towns of this region that produced salt probably had some connection with the province of Ocuillan, which paid tribute in refined white salt that was exclusively for the rulers of Tenochtitlan.[93] However, in the "Memorial de los pueblos de Tlacopan" there are several towns in paragraph 7.3 (Tlachmalacac) that were situated in the area where today the states of Mexico and Guerrero share a boundary: Tonatiuhco (in the province of Ocuillan in the Codex Mendoza); Teoxahualco (in the province of Tlachco in the Codex Mendoza), formerly a subject of Amatepec; Almoloya, an estancia of Amatepec; and Cuitlapilco, in Tzacualpan. According to the "Memorial de Tlacopan" the towns in this paragraph paid tribute to the three capitals of the Empire; they occupy approximately the area of the present-day state of Guerrero and were part of the southern, or Tenochca, sector of the Empire. This region of Zoltepec and Amatepec may have been connected for certain services with the tributary province of Tlachco and with the fortress of Oztoman.

The frontier with Michoacan, farther south, is treated in connection with the provinces of Tepecuacuilco and Cihuatlan, which are discussed in the next chapter as part of the southern sector of the Empire.

Chapter 10

THE SOUTHERN SECTOR
OF THE EMPIRE

The southern sector of the Empire is described in the Tenochca sources and the "Memorial de los pueblos de Tlacopan" with very different regional organizations; the Tetzcoca sources have little information. I shall review the regional organization of this whole sector here, comparing the various sources, before describing the individual tributary provinces that comprise it.

In the Codex Mendoza the provinces that comprise the southern sector begin after Malinalco and Xocotitlan. First there are five pages that depict the seven provinces in large areas of the present-day state of Guerrero: Tlachco, Tepecuacuilco, Cihuatlan, Tlappan, Tlalcozauhtitlan, Quiauhteopan, and Yohualtepec. Then come two provinces more to the north—Chalco and Tepeyacac—and the sequence turns again towards the south and southeast with five more provinces made up of towns in the Mixteca, the valleys of Oaxaca, the Papaloapan Basin, and the isthmus—Coaixtlahuacan, Coyolapan, Tlachquiauhco, Tochtepec, and Xoconochco. The sequence then turns to the Gulf coast with two provinces, Cuauhtochco and Cuetlaxtlan, before going on to the region that forms the northeastern, or Tetzcoca, sector (see Table 4-4).

There are no Tetzcoca sources that treat systematically this southern sector of the Empire, which is completely lacking in Motolinía's "Memorial tetzcocano" and in the related part of the *Anales de Cuauhtitlan*.[1] It should be noted, however, that the Tetzcoca sources that do not include in their northeastern sector the provinces of Cuetlaxtlan and Cuauhtochco do consider Tochtepec to be part of it, although it is farther south. On the other hand, Atlan and Oxitipan, which geographically would be in the Tetzcoca sector, are not mentioned in the Acolhua sources. Atlan is in paragraph 7.1 of the "Memorial de Tlacopan," one of the paragraphs that list the southern sector, although it includes many towns on the Gulf coast, from Mictlancuauhtlan, near Medellin, to Tamiahua, in the north.

In contrast with the Tetzcoca sources, the "Memorial de Tlacopan" takes in the whole southern region of the Empire (sections 7 and 8). It agrees with Tetzcoca sources in that section 6, which corresponds to the northeastern sector, includes Tochtepec (6.3) and Chinantlan (6.6), but what is most striking is that the lists of towns in sections 7 and 8 depart markedly from the Tenochca sources. The towns are grouped into paragraphs in a very different way, and many of them are not present in the Tenochca sources. These sections include the coast of Veracruz (7.1), the Mixteca and adjacent regions (7.2), Guerrero (7.3), the center of Oaxaca with Oztoman and the Costa Chica (7.4), and the isthmus and Xoconochco (8). The composition of these paragraphs, therefore, is very different from that of the provinces in the Codex Mendoza.

In this chapter I discuss the relevant parts of the Tenochca sources, the "Memorial de los pueblos de Tlacopan," and Motolinía's "Memorial tetzcocano," either alternating or combining them, in order to present the data in a way that best permits a discussion of the similarities and differences among these sources. The provinces of Cuauhnahuac and Huaxtepec have already been presented as part of the core area; however, in the "Memorial de Tlacopan," Cuauhnahuac and Huaxtepec are included in paragraph 7.3 together with the towns in the area of present-day Guerrero. With this exception, in this chapter I present the material on the provinces of the southern sector according to the following plan:

First, I treat the seven provinces in the Codex Mendoza that occupy the middle part of the Balsas Basin and the Costa Grande: Tlachco, Tepecuacuilco, Cihuatlan, Tlappan, Tlalcozauhtitlan, Quiauhteopan, and Yohualtepec. Following them are the provinces of Chalco and Tepeyacac, keeping to the sequence of the Mendoza, although Chalco was closely connected with the kingdoms in the Basin. After this, I discuss paragraph 7.3 of the "Memorial de Tlacopan," headed by Tlachmalacac; it includes towns situated in the provinces in the Codex Mendoza treated before.

Next, I present the provinces located in the Mixteca and the valleys of Oaxaca—Coaixtlahuacan, Coyolapan, and Tlachquiauhco—following that with a discussion of the two paragraphs in the "Memorial de Tlacopan" that comprise regions included in those three provinces of the Mendoza but that extend beyond them. Paragraph 7.2, headed by Cozcatlan, comprises principally the Mixteca Alta and Baja but also many towns in La Cañada and as far as the coast of Veracruz, overlapping various provinces in the Codex Mendoza. Paragraph 7.4, which begins with Oztoman, primarily comprises the region of the central valleys of Oaxaca and coincides to a large extent with the province of Coyolapan in the Codex Mendoza, but it also includes the region that goes from Oztoman to the coast as well as part of the Costa Chica in Guerrero, which is not included in the Codex Mendoza.

Turning again to the sequence of Codex Mendoza, I discuss the next two provinces—Tochtepec and Xoconochco—that occupy the eastern limits of the Empire. The data on the province of Tochtepec in the Codex Mendoza are compared with those of the Tetzcoca sources and with the paragraphs on Tochtepec (6.3) and Chinantlan (6.6) in the "Memorial de Tlacopan." The data on the province of Xoconochco in the Codex Mendoza are treated together with section 8 of the "Memorial de Tlacopan," headed by Tototepec.

Finally, I deal with the provinces of Cuauhtochco and Cuetlaxtlan. These provinces have no approximate equivalent in the sources of Tetzcoco and Tlacopan; in the "Memorial de Tlacopan" they overlap with paragraphs 7.2 (Cozcatlan) treated above and 7.1 (Cempohuallan), which includes primarily towns along the entire Gulf coast and is therefore discussed in chapter 11, which treats of the northeastern sector.

The Provinces in the Balsas Basin
and the Costa Grande in the Codex Mendoza

Seven tributary provinces were situated between the Tarascan kingdom and the Mixteca Alta, most of them in the present-day state of Guerrero: Tlachco, Tepecuacuilco, Cihuatlan, Tlappan, Tlalcozauhtitlan, Quiauhteopan, and Yohualtepec. They are shown in three maps. Map 10-1 includes the provinces of Tlachco and Tepecuacuilco; Map 10-2, Cihuatlan; and Map 10-3, Tlappan, Tlalcozauhtitlan, Quiauhteopan, and Yohualtepe. The Codex Mendoza places them between Malinalco-Xocotitlan and Chalco-Tepeyacac before going on to Coaixtlahuacan. This sequence emphasizes the geographical cohesion of these provinces, which the comparison with the "Memorial de Tlacopan" corroborates.

TLACHCO (CODEX MENDOZA, 36R)

1. Tlachco	Tasco (SV, sec. 670).
	Taxco el Viejo in Taxco de Alarcón, Guerrero.
2. Acamilyxtlahuacan	Acamistlauaca (SV, sec. 37).
	Acamixtla, in Taxco de Alarcón, Guerrero.
3. Chontalcoatlan	Coatlan (SV, sec. 163).
	Chontalcuatlán, in Tetipac, Guerrero.
4. Teticpac	Teticpaque (SV, sec. 672).
	Tetipac, Guerrero.
5. Nochtepec	Nochtepeque (SV, sec. 410).
	Noxtepec, in Tetipac, Guerrero.
6. Teotliztacan	Gueyystaca (SV, sec. 273).
	Huixtac, in Taxco de Alarcón, Guerrero
	(Barlow 1949b: 23).

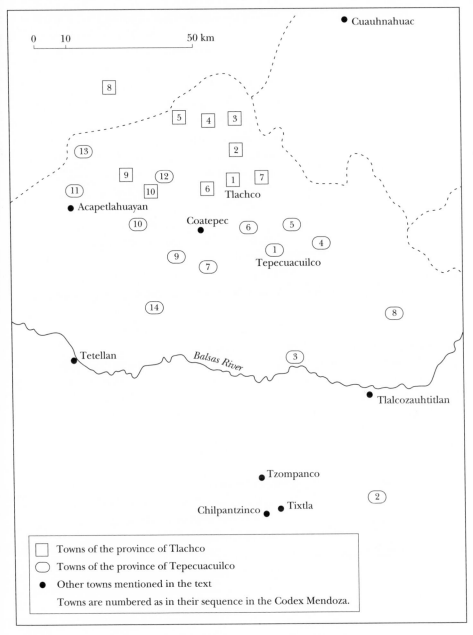

MAP 10–1. The tributary provinces of Tlachco and Tepecuacuilco

7. Tlamacazapan	Tamagaçapa, adjacent to Tlachco (SV, sec. 670). Tlamacazapa, in Taxco de Alarcón, Guerrero.
8. Tepexahualco	Teoxahualco ("Memorial de Tlacopan," 7.3-6). Teuxahualco, near the "province" of Tasco (Ramírez de Fuenleal in García Icazbalceta 1858, 2:176). Gueyxaualco, estancia of Amatepec (SV, sec. 38). Huyxahualco, sujeto of Zoltepec, bordering on Alahuiztlan (SV, sec. 7). San Pedro Hueyahualco in Sultepec, Mexico.
9. Tzicapuçalco	Çicapucalco (SV, sec. 162). Ixcapuzalco, in Pedro Ascensio Alquisiras, Guerrero.
10. Tetenanco	Tenango (SV, sec. 671; RG 7:118, 125). Tenanguillo, in Ixcateopan de Cuauhtemoc, Guerrero.

Itzcoatl undertook wars of conquest in this area, gaining control of several towns in the next province to be presented, Tepecuacuilco, but it was Moteuczoma Ilhuicamina who conquered (among many other towns in Guerrero) three in the province of Tlachco: Tlachco (1), Chontalcoatlan (3), and Teoxahualco (8).[2] Probably the establishment of the tributary province of Tlachco occurred at this time.

The Codex Mendoza list also coincides almost exactly with the eleven towns that comprise the jurisdiction of Tlachco, according to the relación geográfica of this town. The only difference is that in the latter the most distant towns, Tepexahualco (8) and Tzicapotzalco (9), are lacking, but on the other hand, Atzalan, Pilcaya, and Acuitlapan are included; instead of Tetenanco (10), the relación gives Tenango.[3]

The relación of Tlachco gives a brief report about the government of these towns. Moteuczoma and his ancestors established governors who ruled them and were constantly among the people. There was no governor for the entire province; each one governed only a cabecera with its estancias. When a governor died, the king of Tenochtitlan appointed another one in his place. Each governor dispensed justice according to their ways, redressing the injuries committed in cases of property; he also punished serious crimes, ordering the culprits to be stoned or punished in other ways. These towns paid tribute to the king of Tenochtitlan; all the people cultivated a large field, and the governors acting as stewards were in charge of sending its harvest to Moteuczoma. In addition, cloaks were given every twenty days.[4]

This description agrees with commentaries in the Codex Mendoza to the effect that the governors, appointed by the central government, combined judicial functions and the collection of tribute, but it does not explain the relation between the governor of the cabecera and those of each town. Nor does it allude to local rulers, although there are references in other documents to kings and lords. One version of the death of Tizoc attributes it to witches sent by the king of Tlachco, Maxtlaton, instigated by the king of Itztapalapan.[5]

Local rulers (señores) are also spoken of in a colonial lawsuit between Açala (Atzallan) and Teuliztaca (*sic*), or Hueiztaca, that confirms the composition of this tributary province. The ruler of Teotliztacan, called Tlacoatecutl, appointed as ruler of Atzallan his brother Colotl, who then took the name of Tecmani and marked the boundaries of the lands he had received 135 years before the lawsuit, that is, about 1438, which must be when this region fell under the power of the Triple Alliance. According to the evidence given by the witnesses from Atzallan, during the reign of Huehue Moteuczoma there was a controversy with Teotliztacan, and the king of Tenochtitlan sent two principals to divide the lands between them. Atzallan was the main town, where Moteuczoma's steward lived and tribute was collected. This document gives the names of nine tributary towns that are the same as those in the Codex Mendoza, except that Tepexahualco is lacking and Tetenango is written as Tenango.[6]

Tepecuacuilco   Codex Mendoza, 37r

1.	Tepequacuilco	Tepequacuilco (SV, sec. 764). Tepecoacuilco de Trujano, Guerrero.
2.	Chilapan	Chilapa (SV, sec. 236). Chilapa de Alvarez, Guerrero.
3.	Ohuapan	Ohuapan (RG 6:350). San Agustín Oapan, in Tepecoacuilco de Trujano, Guerrero.
4.	Huitzoco	Izuco (RG 6:354). Huitzuco de los Figueroa, Guerrero.
5.	Tlachmalacac	Taxmalaca (RG 6:352). Tlaxmalac, in Huitzuco de los Figueroa, Guerrero.
6.	Yoallan	Yguala (SV, sec. 336). Iguala de la Independencia, Guerrero.
7.	Cocolan	Cocula (SV, sec. 231). Cocula, Guerrero.
8.	Atenanco	Atenango (SV, sec. 90). Atenango del Río, Guerrero.
9.	Chilacachapan	[Missing in the *Matrícula de tributos*.] Chilacachapa, estancia of Cuetzallan (RG 6:293). Chilacachapa, in Cuetzala del Progreso, Guerrero.

10. Teloloapan	[Missing in the *Matrícula de tributos*.] Teloloapan (SV, sec. 544).
	Teloloapan, Guerrero.
11. Oztoman	Ostuma (SV, sec. 420). No longer exists as a town.
12. Ychcateopan	Ichcateupan (RG 6:262).
	Ixcateopan de Cuauhtemoc, Guerrero.
13. Alahuiztlan	Alahuiztlan (SV, sec. 7).
	Alahuiztlan, in Teloloapan, Guerrero.
14. Cueçalan	Cuezala (RG 6:314).
	Cuetzala del Progreso, Guerrero.

In the *Matrícula de tributos* there is a strip of paper covering the space that the glyphs of Chilacachapan and Teloloapan would have occupied. It may have been intended to cover the glyphs, or the scribe may have neglected to draw them.

The conquest of this region was begun under Itzcoatl,[7] but Moteuczoma Ilhuicamina also appears as the conqueror of Tepecuacuilco and many other towns in this tributary province as well as Tlachco, Tlalcozauhtitlan, Quiauhteopan, and Yohualtepec.[8] It may be that Ilhuicamina established those provinces as they are defined in the Codex Mendoza, yet Axayacatl also fought in this region,[9] and Ahuitzotl had to undertake an important campaign against Alahuiztlan (13), Teloloapan (10), and Oztoman (11). His victory led to the establishment of the fortress of Oztoman and the settlement of the three conquered cities by colonists from the Basin and neighboring areas. Most of them settled down in Oztoman and Alahuiztlan; others went to Teloloapan, "as a garrison for that town," which had not been so depopulated as the other two. In each town they were given land, houses, and provisions for a year until the harvest of the following year. Months later they elected a governor from among the principals who had gone with them. Ahuitzotl confirmed the election and sent the new governor a costly suit and insignia with which he gave him the rank of "caballero" (probably teuctli).[10] Tezozomoc relates that the governors of the new settlements were Mexica principals, chosen from Iztacalco, Popotlan, Coatlayaucan, and Acolnahuac, estancias of Tenochtitlan.[11] Oztoman was one of the principal frontier fortresses of the Empire, and various towns provisioned and garrisoned the fort; it is recorded in the Codex Mendoza and the *Matrícula de tributos* as a garrison separate from the tributary provinces. In addition, Oztoman was the cabecera of a group of towns in a paragraph (7.4) of the "Memorial de Tlacopan" that takes in the Costa Chica and the Valley of Oaxaca. This combination of towns must be connected with the conquests of Ahuitzotl in all those regions. He also conquered the Costa Grande, that is, the province of Cihuatlan, which comes after Tepecuacuilco in the Codex Mendoza.

The relaciones geográficas for the towns in this province confirm the status of tributaries for almost all of them, and record the considerable variation in local government and the kind of tribute they paid.[12]

The relación of Tepecuacuilco (1) states that the rulers of Tenochtitlan had a "presidio with people as a garrison who collected the tribute from the whole Cohuixco area, which was cloaks, cotton, maize and other things." Although the population was Chontal, many were Mexica immigrants; there was a local ruler.[13]

The ruler of Oztoman refused to pay the tribute that Ahuitzotl demanded and ordered that the Mexica messengers be killed. Defeated after a long struggle, he was killed by the Mexicas, and one of his relatives was appointed as his successor. Later, when Oztoman was attacked by the Tarascans and asked Axayaxatzin for help, he sent "a captain and some of his best men" with orders to settle there and construct a fort so that the men there would be a garrison against the people of Michoacan. The fort that the Mexicas constructed was "the most important fortress that the Mexicans had on all the borders with Michoacan." The people of Oztoman and all its towns helped them and gave provisions for the fort. Although subject to Tenochtitlan, "they always had a lord whom the natives acknowledged." The original town was on a fortified outcrop where the nobility lived. The fort constructed by the Mexicas was a league distant from this town, and next to the fort was the town of Acapetlahuayan, whose inhabitants were Mexicas, descendants of those "who were Moteuczoma's garrison people."[14] The relación gives many more details about the fortresses and the Mexica conquest, although it confuses the chronology of Axayacatl and Ahuitzotl. According to the people of Acapetlahuayan, the settlers that Ahuitzotl sent to the fort of Oztoman had no obligation other than guarding the fort as soldiers, and the neighboring Chontal towns gave them provisions; other goods were sent to them from Mexico.[15] At the time when the relación was written, Oztoman was a Chontal area, but there were also Mexicas in some towns who had been there since Moteuczoma's time, when they were a garrison at the fort against the Tarascans.[16]

Totoltepec, another Chontal town, had its own ruler when Axayacatl conquered it. They were not required to pay tribute, because they were on the frontier with Michoacan and supported the soldiers of the Oztoman fort. At certain times during the year they sent presents to Tenochtitlan, consisting of cloaks, green stones, and copper.[17]

Alahuiztlan (13), a Chontal town, was governed by its own ruler. Formerly it had been at war with Tzicapotzalco and Tlatlayan until it became subject to Tenochtitlan and began to be at war with Michoacan, going to the Oztoman fort with "provisions and weapons and assistance." There was another fort in Iztapan, a sujeto of Alahuiztlan, where there were *salinas* "to guard the salt from the Tarascans."[18]

In Teloloapan (10) Nahuatl-speaking people lived, in separate barrios, along with the older populations, which were Ixcuca and Chontal. There had been a

Chontal ruler whom the people supplied with everything he needed. When Itz-coatl sent envoys to tell the people to pay tribute to him and be his vassals, the town surrendered immediately and paid tribute to him "and all the other kings of Mexico." They served in the war against Michoacan, taking their weapons with them to the fort at Oztoman when they were summoned.[19]

The original population of the Cuezallan (14) region was Chontal, and they survived in two estancias subject to the town of Cuezallan. This town, with other estancias, was inhabited by Mexicas who had left Michoacan at the same time as those who went on to found Tenochtitlan. They lived in peace until the people of Tenantzinco and Cocollan (7) demanded tribute and they refused to pay it. In a war with Coatepec they lost many men, and they asked Huehue Moteuczoma for help; he sent sufficient men to vanquish Coatepec and then sent a principal to Cuezallan as governor. Since then they were sujetos of Tenochtitlan, paid tribute, and carried on wars with the Chontal people of the two neighboring estancias, which they subjugated.[20]

Cocollan (7) was divided into two barrios, one of Mexicas and the other of the native Cohuixcas; there were also some Matlatzincas.[21] Probably the Mexicas were recent immigrants, while the Cohuixcas were the oldest Nahuatl-speaking inhabitants. The towns of Mayanallan and Ohuapan were also said to be Cohuixca.[22]

The people of Yohuallan, or Yoallan (6), were "of the Chontal or Tuxtec nation"; there were rich people among them called merchants (*pochteca*) and some principals. They had the rites and customs of the Mexicas and were vassals of Moteuczoma.[23] In Tlachmalacac (5) a grandson of the "natural lord" was still living when the relación was written.[24]

For some towns in this region the *Relaciones geográficas* say nothing about submitting to the Empire. One of these is Ichcateopan (12), although it is found in the Codex Mendoza. The people were Chontal and had their own local ruler; they carried on wars with Tlachco, Tzicapotzalco, and Nochtepec "because they wanted to conquer them."[25] Similarly, the Mazatec-speaking people of Tzicapotzalco had a ruler of their own and fought with Alahuiztlan (13) and Ichcateopan (12).[26] The Chontal of Coatepec had their own ruler and carried on wars with Yohuallan, Cocollan, Cuezallan, and Teloloapan; there is no mention of Mexica domination in these towns, either.[27]

The towns of this province depicted in the Codex Mendoza are north of the Balsas River, with the exception of Chilapan (2). Other sources say more about this town and its region. In the *Relaciones geográficas*, Chilapan as well as its neighbor Tixtla (together with its sujeto Mochitlan) were founded by people sent by Moteuczoma Ilhuicamina; their obligation was to cultivate fields and take part in the war against the Yopis of the frontier. The people of Tzompanco gave the same services and also contributed slaves from among the prisoners of war they captured in battle.[28] It appears that the responsibilities of these towns were primarily military on the Yopi frontier. One of Chilapan's sujetos was Quecholtenanco, which Barlow identified with the garrison of the same name on folio 17v in the Codex Mendoza. I prefer to locate it in the Cuauhtochco region, although these relaciones show that on this frontier there were also towns that gave military service.[29]

There is some additional information on the region adjacent to Chilapan in a colonial lawsuit, in 1537, on whether Chilpantzinco was a sujeto of Tzompanco or of Tixtla. The suit names some local leaders, and it is said that each town was an independent entity, and "even though the entire province and its towns took their tribute to the two head towns named and to the calpixques who were there, this does not mean that they were sujetos of those towns but that they brought their tribute to the calpixques [who were there] for Monteuczoma and not as sujetos of those two towns."[30] Some of Moteuczoma's calpixques resided in Tepecuacuilco (1) and others in Ohuapan (3).[31] Tixtla and Tzompanco gave their tribute to Ohuapan; these towns are not included in the Codex Mendoza list. Among the witnesses there are some former calpixques, one of whom, a native of Mexico, states that before the Spanish came, "he resided about four years in Tixtla and Oapan [sic] as calpisque with another calpisque by order of Moteuczoma."[32] There were other witnesses from that area. One, a native of Huitzuco, declared that "in Monteçuma's time about thirty years ago more or less, by order of the calpixques that Monteçuma had put in Tepecuacuilco, this witness went to the said cabecera of Zumpango so that they could collect the tribute." Another witness, a principal from Yohuallan, also said that he went many times to Tzompanco by order of the calpixques that Moteuczoma had in Tepecuacuilco.[33]

The region included in the province of Tepecuacuilco was an ethnic and political mosaic with no original unity. Politically, there were different degrees of subjection; the local rulers continued as such, but in some towns there was strong political activity by the Mexica calpixques. In regard to tribute, the Codex Mendoza records the payment of maize, and some of the relaciones confirm this. Given the distance from Tenochtitlan, this tribute would be for local needs. In strategic areas, such as Tepeyacac and Huaxyacac, where there were fortresses and garrisons, maize was also given as tribute. For military matters there were two distinct regions, one of which served Oztoman and the other the Yopi frontier. The Empire's colonists were primarily concerned with organizing the struggle against the kingdom of Michoacan, but the local wars continued, and some towns remained half independent.

In the towns of this province several languages were spoken, some of them now totally unknown.[34] Nahuatl-speaking people were called Cohuixcas and the region Cohuixco; their dialect is described in the relación as corrupt Nahuatl. In some towns, such as Cocollan, there were both Cohuixcas and Mexicas. The region called Cohuixco comprised the Nahua towns of the provinces of Tlachco and Tepecuacuilco and others farther east such as Tlalcozauhtitlan, Olinallan, and Cualac.³⁵

The provinces in the Codex Mendoza leave a gap between Tepecuacuilco, which in its southwestern part does not extend south of the Balsas River, and Cihuatlan, which occupies the Costa Grande. The *Relaciones geográficas* provide information on this region of the Sierra Madre del Sur, and the "Memorial de Tlacopan," in paragraph 7.4, headed by Oztoman, includes Cocollan and a couple of towns northwest of Acapolco. All this material will be reviewed later in connection with paragraph 7.4.

CIHUATLAN (CODEX MENDOZA, 38R)

1.	Cihuatlan	Not located.
2.	Colima	Not located.
3.	Panotlan	Panutla or Pamutla (SV, secs. 900, 901, 902). Cf. Barlow 1949b: 11.
4.	Nochcoc	Nuzco (SV, sec. 903). Nuxco, in Tecpan de Galeana, Guerrero.
5.	Yztapan	Ystapa (SV, sec. 879 or 892; Barlow 1949b: 11–12).
6.	Petlatlan	Petatan (SV, sec. 896). Petatlán, Guerrero.
7.	Xihuacan	Xiguaca (SV, sec. 895; Barlow 1949b: 11).
8.	Apancalecan	Atenchancaleca (SV, sec. 854); or Echancaleca (SV, sec. 638). Barlow 1949b: 10.
9.	Coçohuipilecan	Not located.
10.	Coyucac	Coyuca (SV, sec. 900). Coyuquilla, in Petatlan, Guerrero (Barlow 1949b: 11)
11.	Çacatulan	Çacatula (SV, sec. 858). Zacatula, in La Unión, Guerrero.
12.	Xolochiuhyan	Solochuca (SV, sec. 898). Joluchuca, in Petatlán, Guerrero.

In the *Matrícula de tributos*, Xolochiuhyan appears as the sixth town after Yztapan; the towns that follow are in the same order as in the Codex Mendoza.

Imperial dominion of this province is reported in the Tenochca sources on tribute, in the lists of conquests, and in colonial documentation, but the Tenochca historical chronicles do not relate its conquest; the only account is that of Ixtlilxochitl. The "Memorial de Tlacopan" does not include it among the tributaries of the Empire.

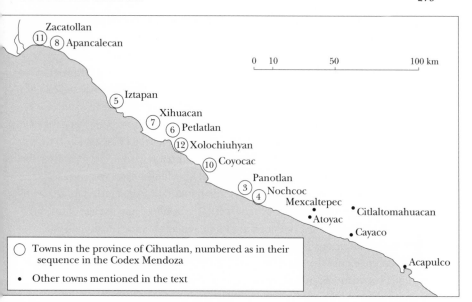

MAP 10–2. The tributary province of Cihuatlan

The exact location of these towns is difficult to determine (see Map 10-2). The name Cihuatlan suggests the present-day Zihuatanejo, but an old list of towns in the area of Zacatollan contains four possible locations.[36] Colima cannot be identified at all. Its glyph is an arm with water at the shoulder, which suggests reading it as Acolman or some other toponym with Acol. There is no doubt, however, that this province took in the Costa Grande, approximately from Zacatollan to Nochcoc. The relación geográfica of Zacatula (Zacatollan) gives a somewhat different picture. It describes the area from Cayaco, west of Acapolco, to Zacatollan and beyond the mouth of the Balsas to Motines. Moteuczoma had subjugated "the towns from Cayaco to Suluchuca [*sic*], where he had his frontier." Each of the other towns in this region was governed by its own "captain"; there was no single ruler over all of them. The account of the relación of Zacatula thus suggests a smaller extent of this tributary province than is given in the Codex Mendoza; perhaps Xolochiuhyan was a major stronghold and Zacatollan the advance point disputed by the Tarascans. Cayaco was between the present-day towns of Tecpan and Coyuca de Benítez. Farther north was Citlaltomahuacan, listed in the "Memorial de Tlacopan." Near Cayaco was Mexcaltepec, one of whose sujetos was Atoyac, present-day Atoyac de Alvarez.[37] Torquemada describes a large Cuitlatec "province" that extended about eighty leagues from west to east and included many towns. The largest was Mexcaltepec with 150 thousand householders (*vecinos*); it was the head (cabeza) of all these towns.[38] It is doubtful, however, that this could be interpreted as a large political unit at the time of the Empire.

The connection of this tributary province with Oztóman and the province of Tepecuacuilco, as well as with the Costa Chica east of Acapolco, is discussed later in connection with paragraph 7.4 of the "Memorial de Tlacopan."

The historical chronicles say very little about the conquest of this province. Some towns figure among the conquests of Ahuitzotl, as does Acapolco, which is not in the list of tributaries in this province.[39] Probably they were won after the Oztoman fortress was established. Ixtlilxochitl is the only writer who describes the conquest of Zacatollan at the time of Nezahualpilli and Ahuitzotl. The leader of the campaign was a certain Teuhchimaltzin, "of the house and lineage of the Tetzcoca kings," who killed the ruler of Zacatollan, named Yopicatl Acatonal, when he was inebriated during a ceremony. The people of Zacatollan gave their obedience to Nezahualpilli, and the son of the dead king became his successor.[40]

Four provinces occupied the area of present-day eastern Guerrero and adjoining regions of Oaxaca—Tlappan, Tlalcoçauhtitlan, Quiauhteopan, and Yohualtepec; they are shown on Map 10-3.

TLAPPAN   CODEX MENDOZA, 39R

1.	Tlapan [Tlauhpan]	Tlapa and Tlachinola (SV, sec. 725).
		Tlachinola or Tlapa (RO, 97).
		Tlapa de Comonfort, Guerrero.
2.	Xocotla	Jocutla, estancia of Tlapa (RO, 98).
3.	Ychcateopan	Ychacatempa (SV, sec. 322; RO, 103). Ixcateopan,
		in Alpoyeca, Guerrero.
4.	Amaxac	Atlimajac (SV, sec. 82). Atlemaxac (RO, 101).
		Atlamajac, in Tlapa de Comonfort, Guerrero.
5.	Ahuacatla	Ahuacatitlan, a town of Atlemaxac (RO, 101).
		Ahuacatitlan, in Tlalixtaquilla, Guerrero;
		or Ahuacatlán, in Olinalá, Guerrero.
6.	Acocozpan	Alcozauhca, a town of Atlemaxac (RO, 102).
		Alcozauca de Guerrero, Guerrero. Alcozauhcan
		and Acocozpan both mean "yellow water."
7.	Yoalan	Ygualan (SV, sec. 323; RO, 102).
		Igualita, in Xalpatlahuac, Guerrero.
8.	Ocoapan	Ocuapa, in Copanatoyac, Guerrero.
9.	Huitzamola	Huitzaxola, estancia of Cuitlapa (RO, 107).
		Huitzapula, in Atlixtac, Guerrero.

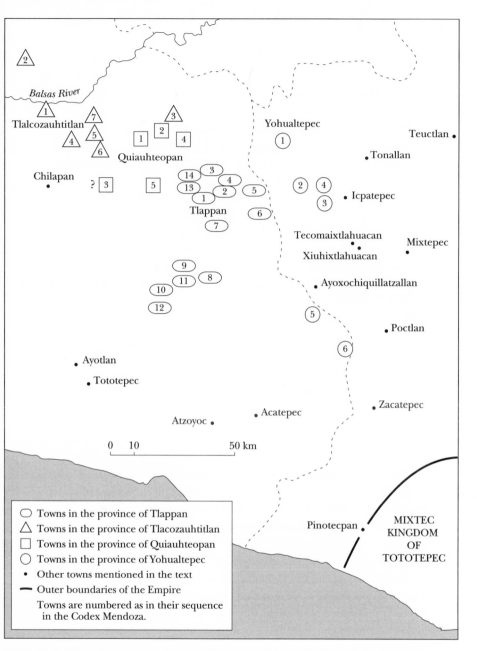

MAP 10–3. The tributary provinces of Tlappan, Tlalcozauhtitlan, Quiauhteopan, and Yohualtepec

10. Acuitlapan	Cuitlapa (SV, sec. 217; RO, 106). Teocuitlapa, in Atlixtac, Guerrero.
11. Malinaltepec	Estancia of Tlapa (RO, 98). Malinaltepec, Guerrero.
12. Totomixtlahuacan	Totomistlauacan (SV, sec. 726; RO, 106). Totomixtlahuaca, in Tlacoapa, Guerrero.
13. Tetenanco	Tenango, sujeto of Tlachinola (SV, sec. 727; RO, 104). Tenango Tepexi, in Tlapa de Comonfort, Guerrero.
14. Chipetlan	Chipetlan, sujeto of Tlachinola (SV, sec. 218; RO, 104). Chiepetlan, in Tlapa de Comonfort, Guerrero.

The province of Tlappan (Tlauhpan in the *Matrícula de tributos*) seems to have been a political unit of considerable size (see Map 10-3). Its extent can be traced fairly well by means of the data in the *Suma de Visitas* and the detailed enumeration of cabeceras and estancias in the 1571 *Relación de los obispados*. Both sources associate the name of Tlachinollan with Tlappan, but it is not clear whether this was a second name of Tlappan or the name of another cabecera of this province.[41] The above list notes that some towns were sujetos of Tlachinollan.

In addition to the cabeceras included in this province of the Codex Mendoza, there were those of Atliztaca, Caltitlan, Petlacallan, and Atzoyoc;[42] the last one—on the coastal plain—was the most distant. The province as depicted in the Codex Mendoza is completely in the mountains; Dehouve has recently solved some problems of location.[43]

The historical data are very few but do provide some evidence of indigenous rulers. The gentile name Tlappaneca was applied both to Nahuatl speakers, who were Cohuixcas, and to those who spoke Yopi.[44] Some of the Nahuatl-speaking inhabitants were recent immigrants from Xochimilco.[45]

Moteuczoma Ilhuicamina conquered a large part of what is now the state of Guerrero in the area that became the tributary provinces of Tlachco, Tlalcozauhtitlan, Quiauhteopan, and Yohualtepec, but the conquest of Tlappan is recorded for the first time in the lists of Tizoc and Ahuitzotl.

Among Ahuitzotl's conquests there was also Acatl iyacac, or Acatepec. This is a frequent toponym; identifying it with the present-day Acatepec, Guerrero, would indicate that the conquest of Tlappan continued toward the Pacific coast to the region included in paragraph 7.4 of the "Memorial de Tlacopan."[46]

It is not certain that Moteuczoma Xocoyotzin made further conquests in the Tlappan region. The *Anales de Tlatelolco* put Tlachinollan—the other name of Tlappan—among his conquests, but there are other possible identifications.[47]

Other reports attest to the presence of the Empire along the Costa Chica, in what was, perhaps, an extension of this province. Near Atzoyoc there was a town of Tlappanec speakers called Ayotlan (present-day Ayutla de los Libres, Guerrero) that paid tribute to Moteuczoma; not far away was Tototepec, a town of "Mexicas who were there as a garrison that Moteuczoma used to have."[48] This area is the same as the towns in paragraph 7.4 in the "Memorial de Tlacopan," which is discussed below. One of the campaigns of conquest passed through Xaltianquizco, near Acapolco, but extending the Empire to the Pacific coast could also have been carried out from Tlappan, since Atzoyoc was one of the cabeceras of Tlappan Tlachinollan,[49] or else from Ayoxochiquillatzallan and Xicayan in the province of Yohualtepec.

TLALCOZAUHTITLAN (CODEX MENDOZA, 40r)

1. Tlalcoçauhtitlan   Tlalcuçautitlan (SV, sec. 794).
       Tlacozotitlan, in Copalillo, Guerrero.
2. Tolimani   Tulimán, in Huitzuco de los Figueroa, Guerrero.
3. Quauhtecomacinco   Quauhtecontzinco, sujeto of Olinala
       (PNE 5:210).
       Cuateconcingo, in Cualac, Guerrero.
4. Ychcatlan   Ychcatlan, estancia of Tlalcozauhtitlan
       (PNE 5:250).
       Ixcatla, in Zitlala, Guerrero.
5. Tepoztitlan   Tepoztlan, in Ahuacuotzingo, Guerrero.
6. Ahuacicinco   Ahuacuotzingo, Guerrero.
7. Mitzinco   Mictzinco, estancia of Tlapa (RO, 98).
       Mitlancingo, in Ahuacuotzingo, Guerrero.
8. Çacatla   Not located.

Tlalcozauhtitlan seems to be the only important town included in this province (see Map 10-3); the rest are of a lower category. It was conquered at the time of Moteuczoma Ilhuicamina.[50]

It is worth noting that Ixtlilxochitl includes this conquest among those he attributes to Nezahualcoyotl. It might seem possible that the information he gives about the steward and the tribute goods of Tlalcozauhtitlan refers to Tlatlauhquitepec, a well-known province in the northeastern sector conquered at the same time, but the tribute goods—colored trays, copal, bowls and decorated gourds, and *tlacuilolquahuitl* (tinctoreal wood)—are products of the Balsas Basin. The steward appointed by Nezahualcoyotl was called Huitziltecuh, a name that perhaps alludes to Huitziltepec, a town near Tlalcozauhtitlan.[51] In the Memorial of Don Hernando Pimentel, Tlalcozauhtitlan closes the list of towns that his ancestors won in battle where they had tenants and lands. It appears then, that Tetzcoco, at least in Nezahualcoyotl's time, had received a share of the imperial conquests in this area. Perhaps, as in Cuauhnahuac, conquered immediately before, Tetzcoco acquired possessions in this region separate from those of Tenochtitlan. Tlalcozauhtitlan was one of the towns represented at the installation of Tizoc.[52]

QUIAUHTEOPAN (CODEX MENDOZA, 40R)

1. Quiauhteopan	Sujeto of Olinala, at three leagues of distance (PNE 5:210).
2. Olinalan	Olinala (SV, sec. 437).
	Olinalá, Guerrero.
3. Quauhtecomatla	(?) Tecomatlan, one of the cabeceras subject to Tlalcozauhtitlan (PNE 5:251).
4. Qualac	Sujeto of Olinala (PNE 5:210).
	Cualac, Guerrero.
5. Ychcatla	Estancia of Tenango, one of the cabeceras of Tlappan (RO:104).
	(?) Ixcatla, in Chilapa de Alvarez, Guerrero.
6. Xala	Tequisquitlan, in Scholes and Adams 1957:48.
	Not located.

The precise location of some of these towns is difficult to establish (see Map 10-3). Quiauhteopan itself is reported to be only three leagues from Olinallan, but the orientation is not given. Barlow suggested that Cuauhtecomatlan could be identified as the cabecera of Tlalcozauhtitlan called Tecomatlan, which he located seven leagues northeast of Chilapan.[53] Ichcatlan could be the estancia of Tenanco listed above, but its exact location is not known. It was eighteen leagues from Tlappan but—as with Quiauhteopan—we are not told in what direction; probably it was west of Tlappan, since that was the location of Tenanco, of which it was a sujeto.

There are few references to the conquest of this region, but Quiauhteopan is in the list of conquests of Moteuczoma Ilhuicamina together with Tlalcozauhtitlan and towns in the province of Tepecuacuilco.[54] Olinallan was represented at the installation of Tizoc, along with other towns subject to the Empire.[55]

YOHUALTEPEC (CODEX MENDOZA, 40R)

1. Yoaltepec	San Juan Igualtepec, Oaxaca.
2. Ehuacalco	Caleuallan, according to Paso y Troncoso (PNE 5:238).
	Calihualá, Oaxaca.

3. Tzilacaapan   Silacayoapan, Oaxaca.

4. Patlanalan   Patanala, sujeto of Tonala (PNE 5:238).

                       Santiago Patlanalá, in Silacayoapan, Oaxaca.

5. Yxicayan   Xicayan de Tovar (SV, sec. 810; RG 2:306; RO, 65).

                       Jicayán de Tovar, in Tlacachistlahuaca, Guerrero.

6. Ichcaatoyac   Yzcatoyaque, adjacent to Zacatepec and Xicayan

                       (SV, sec. 304). Also called Atoiocinapa (ENE 9:17).

                       Ayucinapa [Ayotzinapan], in the "province" of

                       Amusgos (RO, 65, 86; RG 2:306; 3:282).

The first four towns are in the Mixteca Baja, and the people spoke Mixtec. Xicayan and Ichcaatoyac (Ayotzinapan) spoke Amusgo, a language also spoken in other towns farther south (see Map 10-3). Little is known of the conquest of these towns. Yohualtepec is listed among the conquests of Moteuczoma Ilhuicamina and Nezahualcoyotl.[56] Other towns conquered by Moteuczoma Xocoyotzin can also be identified in these areas.

One of the towns in the Mixteca Baja, Patlanallan (4) was a sujeto of Tonallan, a town in paragraph 7.3 of the "Memorial de los pueblos de Tlacopan." In the same area the people of Icpatepec (Nieves Ixpantepec, Oaxaca) had been conquered by Moteuczoma and paid him tribute in green feathers, gold dust, and green stones. This they obtained by going elsewhere to trade, to towns more than thirty leagues distant, and then they delivered the tribute to the "captains" that Moteuczoma kept for that purpose in Teutla (*sic*).[57] This town is probably the present-day Santa María Tutla in San Andrés Dinicuiti (in the district of Huajuapan) whose Mixtec name—Yucuyaa or Ñuuhuiya, "hill or town of the lord"—would be Teuctlan or Teuctepec in Nahuatl.[58] Teuctepec is mentioned in several sources as conquered by Moteuczoma Xocoyotzin; the captives were sacrificed at the new fire ceremony of 1507.[59]

Another conquest of Moteuczoma Xocoyotzin that was probably in this area is Nopallan, which appears in the lists of conquests. This is a very frequent toponym, and consequently it is difficult to decide which was the conquered town. According to Durán and Tezozomoc, Nopallan together with Icpatepec were rebel "provinces" defeated by Moteuczoma Xocoyotzin. This places them in the Mixteca, where there is both an Icpatepec and a Nopallan.[60]

The relación geográfica for Justlahuaca (Xiuhixtlahuacan, present-day Santiago Juxtlahuaca, Oaxaca) reports on several towns in the Mixteca and Amuzgo regions of this province. Xicayan (5) is the only one included in this list in the Codex Mendoza; the others are Xiuhixtlahuacan, Tecomaztlahuacan (San Sebastián Tecomaxtlahuaca, Oaxaca), Mixtepec (San Juan Mixtepec, Oaxaca), Poctlan (Putla de Guerrero, Oaxaca), Zacatepec (Santa María Zacatepec), and Ayoxochiquillatzallan (Zochiquilazala, in Santiago Juxtlahuaca, Oaxaca). In all of these there were local rulers.[61]

Xiuhixtlahuacan and Tecomaixtlahuacan had no rulers other than their own caciques, although the people of Tecomaixtlahuacan sometimes "contributed" presents of chalchihuites to Moteuczoma; on two occasions they were at war with the Mexicas, whom they defeated.[62] Mixtepec was not subject to the Empire; the people recognized the ruler of Tlachquiauhco, to whom they paid tribute. They gave nothing to Moteuczoma and assisted Tlachquiauhco when it was at war with the Mexicas.[63] This must have been the situation before Tlachquiauhco was conquered by Moteuczoma Xocoyotzin.

In regard to the Amusgo towns, the people of Xicayan (5) "carried on wars with the Mexicas and the natives of this town were the victors. Having seen this, Moteuczoma had a great regard for them and always sent some Mexica noblemen to be with them in the town. This was understood to mean that Moteuczoma wanted to have some vassalage over them." Xicayan was governed by its own ruler, but Moteuczoma sent four Mexica principals there "to protect the town," and when the ruler had to punish some crime, he followed their advice. The people paid tribute to Tenochtitlan in cloaks and chile.[64]

The Mixtec name of Xicayan, Ñuudzavui, means place of rain, or of Tlaloc.[65] Therefore it can be identified with the town conquered by the last Tenochca kings that is called Iztactlalocan in the lists of Ahuitzotl's conquests,[66] while in Moteuczoma's lists it is Iztactlalocan in the Codex Mendoza but Tlalotepec or Quiauhtepec in other sources.[67]

Ayoxochiquillatzallan, where both Mixtec and Amusgo were spoken, had its own ruler, but the people took tribute to Moteuczoma in the form of gold dust. "They did not contribute anything else because Moteuczoma had people in this town as a garrison ready for war and these Mexicas ate the turkeys, deer, rabbits, and maize that they [this town] had to give to Moteuczoma; and thus they did not take to him any more tribute than the gold dust." They were governed by the local ruler, but for the punishment of crimes, "he accepted the opinion and advice of the Mexicas who were there as a garrison for Moteuczoma." In time of war, "when Moteuczoma summoned him, the ruler sent the men of the garrison who were there and he himself stayed [in his town]."[68]

This province of Yohualtepec may have been the point of departure for the Empire's penetration to the Costa Chica, where they encountered the Mixtec kingdom of Tototepec. Torquemada relates the conquest of Iztactlalocan with that of other nearby towns,[69] one of which—Cihuapohualoyan—is included in paragraph 7.4 of the "Memorial de Tlacopan."

Poctlan was a Mixtec realm on the lowlands. According to its relación geográfica the people had their own ruler to whom they paid tribute, and they gave nothing to Moteuczoma; they carried on wars with the Mexicas and with Tototoepec.[70] Durán includes Poctlan among the towns conquered by the Mexicas. However, he might be referring not to this town in the Mixteca but to the Poctla in the province of Tochtepec.[71]

The people of Zacatepec were Amusgos; they were governed by their own ruler and answered to no one else. They fought with the Mexicas and with the people of Tototepec;[72] nevertheless, Zacatepec appears in the Codex Mendoza among the conquests of Moteuczoma Xocoyotzin.

The Province of Chalco in the Codex Mendoza

Chalco is one of the regions where the three capitals of the Empire held lands separately. Before the Triple Alliance was formed the people of Chalco warred with the Tepanecs of Azcapotzalco and their Mexica allies. The first kings of the Triple Alliance continued these wars, which culminated with the conquest accomplished by Moteuczoma Ilhuicamina; under later kings there were important changes in the regime imposed by the Empire.

In addition to the separate possessions of each capital of the alliance, the Codex Mendoza contains a tributary province of Chalco that includes the following towns (shown in Map 10-4):

CHALCO (CODEX MENDOZA, 41R)

1.	Chalco	Chalco, Mexico, or Tlalmanalco, Mexico.
2.	Tecmilco	Tequimilco, estancia of Tenango Tepopula in 1594 (Colín 1967: sec. 1866). Hacienda San Miguel Tequimilco (Colín 1966: secs. 566, 567). Situated between Juchitepec and Santiago Tepopula (García Mora 1981:223 and fig. 1).
3.	Tepuztlan	Santiago Tepoztlan, sujeto of Tlatelolco, congregated in Tenango (AGI, Mexico 665, 2d cuaderno, fol. 117).
4.	Xocoyoltepec	Land of the kings of Tenochtitlan from the time of Axayacatl (Chimalpahin 1889:144–45). Rancho Xocoyotepec, between Pahuacan and Zoyatzinco (García Mora 1981: fig. 1).
5.	Malinaltepec	Land of Moteuczoma Xocoyotzin in Tlalmanalco (Chimalpahin 1889:178, 180).
6.	Quauxumulco	Sujeto of Tlalmanalco (RG 6:161).

Given its position in the sequence of the Codex Mendoza, this province could be considered as one of those that paid tribute to the three capitals of the Empire and whose tribute was taken to Tenochtitlan to be divided there. However, Chalco

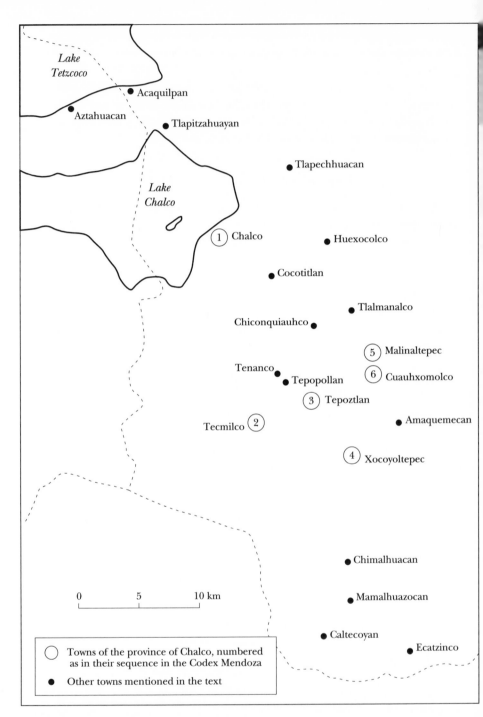

MAP 10–4. The tributary province of Chalco

is not found among the towns that, according to the "Memorial de Tlacopan," paid tribute to the three capitals. The sources from Tlacopan and Tetzcoco sources inform us only about the separate possessions of these two capitals in Chalca territory; other towns in Chalco are included in the Codex Mendoza in the provinces of Citlaltepec and Petlacalco and can be taken to be private possessions of Tenochtitlan. But if this province of Chalco was a tributary exclusively of Tenochtitlan, we would expect to find it among the first listed in the Codex Mendoza, together with those of Acolhuacan, Tlalhuic, and the provinces in the Tlacopan kingdoms.

The conflicts between Tenochtitlan and Chalco began when the former was part of the Tepanec empire. At the beginning of the Triple Alliance, Chalco is given as a conquest of Itzcoatl and Nezahualcoyotl,[73] but it was not incorporated into the Empire until the time of Moteuczoma Ilhuicamina, after a war that lasted twenty years.[74] As a consequence of this war, the lands of Chalco were divided among the three capitals of the Empire. Torquemada relates that once the conquest had been achieved, boundary marks were set in all the lands of Chalco, and they were divided among Mexicas, Tetzcocas and Tepanecs. The kings took for themselves the lands that looked best and gave many plots to the captains and noblemen; "there was no person of importance who did not share in this." Even in Torquemada's time there were many people in Tenochtitlan and Tlatelolco who farmed land in Chalco they had inherited from their fathers, who had received it in the land distribution that took place after the war finally ended.[75]

Tezozomoc enumerates various towns that the conquerors took over: Aztahuacan, Acaquilpan, Tlapitzahuayan, Tlapechhuacan, Cocotitlan, Ahuatepan, Huexocolco, and Tepopollan.[76] We know from other sources that some of these towns were part of the possessions of the cities of the Triple Alliance. Acaquilpan, on the south shore of the lake, was one of the towns where several Tenochca cities held land, and there was a Tepepulan in the tributary province of Petlacalco. Tlapechhuacan was in the Tetzcoca calpixcazgo established by Nezahualcoyotl in Tetitlan. None of the towns named by Tezozomoc is found among the possessions of Tlacopan in Chalco, but it is quite possible that Tezozomoc recorded only the Tenochca acquisitions.

Moteuczoma Ilhuicamina's conquests included all the kingdoms of Chalco. The Codex Mendoza lists Tenanco, Chiconquiauhco, and Mamalhuaztepec in addition to Chalco.[77] After their defeat by the Mexicas, the principal lords of the different cabeceras fled to Huexotzinco.[78] The conquered towns ceded lands to the Mexicas and promised to give materials and labor for construction, transportation, and provisions for their wars.[79] There were then no longer kings in Chalco, but nobles of local dynasties were left in charge of the government.[80] From that time on, Chalco took part in the activities of the Empire in the great public works and military expeditions together with the other kingdoms of the alliance, with Xochimilco, and with the towns of the Cuauhtlalpan.[81]

The chronicles mention new appropriations of land by Axayacatl in Amaquemecan, where the lots (*yntonal*) designated for the kings of Tenochtitlan were named Xocoyoltepec and Oztoticpac; because of the death of Axayacatl it was Tizoc who made use of them.[82] Later, Moteuczoma Xocoyotzin marked the boundaries of lands in Malinaltepec when he took control of the lands in Tlalmanalco.[83]

The territorial acquisitions under Ilhuicamina were probably those that formed part of the calpixcazgos of Petlacalco in Tenochtitlan and of Tetitlan in Tetzcoco, administered together with other possessions that these capitals held outside of Chalco. The later acquisitions of Xocoyoltepec and Malinaltepec are found among the towns in the tributary province of Chalco in the Codex Mendoza. Part of Xocoyoltepec, where Axayacatl took lands for himself, belonged to Tlacopan (see p. 200).

In the southernmost part of Chalco there were towns with military obligations on the frontier with Huexotzinco. In Caltecoyan and Ecatzinco the kings of Teotihuacan and Tepetlaoztoc held "war lands."[84]

Archaeological research in the rural areas of Chalco has demonstrated an increase of the population during the late pre-Spanish period, especially in the region of Tenanco and Tepopollan, where there had been the greatest occupation of land and establishment of colonists by the three powers of the Empire.[85]

In the principal cabeceras of Chalco, Tizoc and Ahuitzotl appointed kings from the traditional local dynasties.[86] The new Chalca rulers went to Tenochtitlan for the four-day fast that preceded the ceremony of installation.[87] Several matrimonial alliances between the Tenochca and Chalca dynasties were arranged, conforming to the norms that Tenochtitlan and Tetzcoco followed with their subject kings. Tlilpotonqui, cihuacoatl of Tenochtitlan, married two Chalca princesses. One of them came from Tecuanipan Huitzoco in Amaquemecan, where her son Miccacalcatl later became king. Tlilpotonqui's other wife was from Acxotlan Cihuateopan in Tlalmanalco. A daughter of this union went to Chalco to marry Quetzalmazatzin, *chichimecateuctli* of Itztlacozauhcan in Amaquemecan; their son was the next chichimecateuctli.[88] Moteuczoma Xocoyotzin sent a daughter to be the wife of Necuametzin, the teohuateuctli of Opochhuacan in Tlalmanalco; she was accompanied by two barrios (*tlaxilacaltin*) of Otomis to serve her.[89]

Fray Domingo de la Anunciación gives a brief history of the tribute Chalco paid to the kings of Tenochtitlan. When the people of Chalco were conquered during the reign of Moteuczoma Ilhuicamina, "he did not ask them for tribute while he lived because he wanted to have them more as friends than as vassals." In the time of his successor, Axayacatl, the people began to pay tribute but were required only to till for the king two plots of land four hundred measures long and eighty wide, "and they did not send him any other tribute except that they helped him to conquer some other provinces." During the reigns of Tizoc and Ahuitzotl, the requirements were the same as before "and nothing else; rather, all these kings gave the lords of Chalco gold jewels and precious cloaks and magnificent and valuable suits of armor." Moteuczoma Xocoyotzin, however, imposed new kinds of tribute or obligations, requiring them to go to Mexico two or three times a year to the dances and festivals held there; to assist in conquering "provinces" two or three times a year when necessary; and to take building material—stone, sand, and wood—to Mexico two or three times a year, with the stipulation that they took it only as far as the canoe landing place five leagues away. In addition, Moteuczoma required them to give him "the same tribute in maize as to the kings his predecessors; however when the rulers and principals went to these festivals, Moteuczoma gave them many gifts of clothing, and precious jewels, and food such as cacao and turkeys as was customary among the lords."[90]

This description is obviously a simplification, but it shows clearly the greater control exercised by Moteuczoma Xocoyotzin, the nature of the tribute and the compensatory gifts to the subject lords to maintain their friendship, and also the importance of Chalco's participation in the ceremonies, wars, and public works typical of the kingdoms and sujetos of the Basin. Fray Domingo says nothing about the donations of land to the victorious kingdoms, and the reference to the fields cultivated in "this cabecera" probably has to do only with Chimalhuacan.

In conclusion, following the defeat of the Chalcas by Ilhuicamina, there was a distribution of land to the three capitals of the alliance, and although the government remained in the hands of nobles of the local dynasties, there were no longer kings in Chalco. Later, the Tenochcas installed members of their ancient dynasties as kings of the principal cabeceras of Chalco, and matrimonial alliances were established of the type that the royal lineage of Tenochtitlan maintained with its subordinate kings. Chalco, then, occupied a situation similar to that of the dependent kingdoms of Tenochtitlan, contributing military contingents and participating in the public works of Tenochtitlan. As the Codex Mendoza demonstrates, Chalco, like the other tributary provinces of the Basin, was an important provider of subsistence goods.[91]

The Province of Tepeyacac in the Codex Mendoza

TEPEYACAC (CODEX MENDOZA, 42R)

1. Tepeacac	Tepeaca (SV, sec. 532).
	Tepeaca, Puebla.
2. Quechulac	Cachula (SV, sec. 118).
	Quecholac, Puebla.

3. Tecamachalco   Tecamachalco (SV, sec. 519).
                           Tecamachalco, Puebla.
4. Acatzinco   Acaçingo, estancia of Tepeaca (SV, sec. 532).
                           Acatzingo de Hidalgo, Puebla.
5. Tecalco   Tecalco (SV, sec. 543).
                           Tecali de Herrera, Puebla.
6. Ycçochinanco   Zuchinango, sujeto of Acatzinco
                           (Martínez 1984b: 236). San Geronimo
                           Ycçochinanco (Book of baptisms for 1614,
                           Archivo parroquial, Acatzingo).
7. Quauhtinchan   Guatinchan (SV, sec. 257).
                           Cuauhtinchan, Puebla.
8. Chietlan   Chietla (SV, sec. 108).
                           Chietla, Puebla.
9. Quatlatlauhcan   Guatlatlauca (SV, sec. 261).
                           Quatlatauca (RG 5:201).[92]
                           Huatlatlauca, Puebla.
10. Tepexic   Tepexi de Rodríguez, Puebla.
11. Ytzucan   Yçucar (SV, sec. 292).
                           Izúcar de Matamoros, Puebla.
12. Quauhquechulan   Guacachula (SV, sec. 260).
                           Huaquechula, Puebla.
13. Teonochtitlan   Teunuchtitlan, listed with Tepexuxuma
                           (SV, sec. 540).
14. Teopantlan   Teupantlan (SV, sec. 559).
                           Teopantlan, Puebla.
15. Huehuetlan   Gueguetlan (SV, sec. 259).
                           Santo Domingo Huehuetlán, Puebla;
                           or Huehuetlán el Chico, Puebla.
16. Tetenanco   Tenango, adjacent to Teupantlan (SV, sec. 559).
                           San Sebastián Tenango, in Teopantlan, Puebla.
                           (There is also a Santiago Tenango in the municipio
                           of General Felipe Angeles, Puebla.)
17. Coatzinco   Coaçingo (SV, sec. 120).
                           Coatzingo, Puebla.
18. Epatlan   Epatlan (SV, sec. 248).
                           San Juan Epatlán, in Epatlán, Puebla.
19. Nacochtlan   Nacuchtlan (SV, sec. 399).
                           Santa Ana Necoxtla, in Epatlan, Puebla.

20. Chiltecpintlan	Bordering upon Totomihuacan (HTCh, sec. 287). Chiltepin, in the jurisdiction of Acatlán (Méndez Martínez 1979, sec. 784). Located south of the Petlacingo River (map of the state of Puebla, Comisión Geográfica-Exploradora, 1908).
21. Oztotlapechco	(?) Oztoyahualco, on the border of Totomihuacan, close to Chiltecpintlan (HTCh, sec. 287).
22. Atezcahuacan	Atezcac, bordering on Cuauhtinchan (HTCh, sec. 298). San Martín Atexcal, in Atexcal, Puebla.

This province (shown on Map 10-5) includes several indigenous polities: the kingdoms founded by the Cuauhtinchan Chichimec, that is, Cuauhtinchan (7), Tepeyacac (1), Tecalco (5), Quecholac (2), and Tecamachalco (3), the last two with an important Popoloca population; Itzocan (11) and other towns of Coatlalpanecs of Nonoalca ancestry, Teonochtitlan (13), Teopantlan (14), and Epatlan (18);[93] Cuauhquechollan (12) on the frontier with Huexotzinco; and, towards the Mixteca, the Popoloca señorío of Tepexic (10).

Tepeyacac was conquered by Moteuczoma Ilhuicamina. The defeated rulers were taken to Tenochtitlan, and after hearing the king's orders concerning their future obligations—to guarantee safe passage through their lands to all foreigners, especially the merchants, and establish a great market in the city of Tepeyacac—they returned to their land with a governor, a noble named Coacuech, whom they were to obey and treat as the king's representative. The governor was charged with making sure that the orders given to their leaders were obeyed and with collecting the royal tribute, to be sent to the Tenochca king every eighty days. From that time on, the rulers of Tenochtitlan had a Mexica steward in each town to collect the tribute. Tepeyacac became an important commercial center, and new inhabitants from Cholollan and the Basin were settled in various towns in the region.[94]

Torquemada indicates that Ilhuicamina's campaign against Tepeyacac was in response to a rebellion by the people of Tepeyacac, who, although already tributaries of the Empire, withdrew their obedience.[95] There are no clear reports of an earlier conquest,[96] but the Tepeyacac region had been part of the Tepanec political system under Azcapotzalco. The *Historia tolteca-chichimeca* records the conquest of Cuauhtinchan (7) by Tlatelolco, and there were matrimonial alliances between the Tepanec dynasty and the rulers of that region; this connection may have continued after the formation of the Triple Alliance.[97]

Together with Tepeyacac, Ilhuicamina conquered other nearby towns; therefore, this region must have been constituted as a tributary province at that time.[98]

MAP 10–5. The tributary province of Tepeyacac

The conquest of Tepeyacac and Tecalco is also attributed to Axayacatl before he became king; later he ordered the redistribution of lands and determined the boundaries between the kingdoms of the region.[99]

Tepeyacac became the center for the expansion of the Triple Alliance towards the Gulf coast and Oaxaca. It was also of military importance in the wars against the tramontane kingdoms. In addition to paying tribute in kind, Tepeyacac gave prisoners of war and weapons. The accounts of the inauguration of the temple under Ahuitzotl emphasize the importance of Tepeyacac and of Cuauhquechollan (12) and its sujetos as providers of captives (see p. 418). The maize this province gave as tribute probably was for maintaining the local forts and armies passing through. It also gave pinolli, the usual provision for military expeditions.[100] Durán reports that Cuauhquechollan (12) ruled six towns, which are not recorded in the Codex Mendoza: Acapetlahuacan (next to Atlixco, Puebla), Atzitzihuacan, Yaote-huacan, Hueyapan, Tetellan, and Tlamimilolpan. These towns reported to Cua-uhquechollan with the royal tribute and, when needed, with men for war.[101] Hueyapan and Tetellan, according to their relación geográfica, were "like a fron-tier against other provinces."[102] Elsewhere in his *Historia*, Durán explains that Cuauhquechollan and Atzitzihuacan "were the frontiers where there were gar-risons of men from Mexico."[103] North of Atzitzihuacan was the easternmost Xochi-milca town—Ocopetlayocan, also called Tochmilco (Tochimilco, Puebla)—which obeyed Moteuczoma but did not pay him any tribute, "because he had them in this land as a fortress and frontier [against] those that were not subject to him."[104]

The local rulers maintained their importance through the whole period of Tenochca predominance. The three lords of Tepeyacac "did not acknowledge Motecuhzoma as superior . . . ; they considered him only as a friend and ally for the wars that Mexico waged against Tlaxcallan and Huexotzinco."[105] In Teca-machalco (3) the king ruling there in 1519 was a son of the previous ruler and a Tenochca princess, a daughter of Axayacatl.[106] In this whole region the impor-tance of the indigenous nobility continued throughout the early colonial period.[107]

Coatzinco (17) is described in the relación geográfica of Ahuatlan, which agrees substantially with the Codex Mendoza in that they were "vassals" of Moteuczoma, whom they served and to whom they gave as tribute shields made of canes, blades for spears, lime, bows, and arrows. They carried on wars with Tlaxcallan, Huex-otzinco, Cholollan, and Totomihuacan. This relación gives similar data on other towns not included in the Codex Mendoza but which were probably part of the same province. Coatzinco had formerly been subject to one of these, Zoyatitlana-pan. Others were Ahuatlan and its former sujeto, Texalocan. Information on the latter is more detailed. Although vassals of Moteuczoma, the people of Texalocan gave nothing other than men to wage war against Totomihuacan, Cholollan, Hue-xotzinco, and the "province" of Couixco, capturing people whom they gave to

Moteuczoma for sacrifice. Their ruler was established by Moteuczoma, and "as far as they remember, one was named Tzipain tlacochcalcatl and the other Acolnahuacatl tlacatecatl." The rulers punished crimes, but their titles also suggest military activities, for they are the same as the titles of the governors of the military colonies.[108]

In Epatlan (18) there were two barrios: Mexicapan and Xochimilcapan. Their names suggest that they were settled by people from the Basin.[109]

Tepexic (10) was a kingdom where Popoloca was spoken. Its king had married a daughter of Moteuczoma Ilhuicamina, and their son was ruling when the Spaniards arrived.[110] Probably Tepexic became part of the Empire under Ilhuicamina, who conquered Tepeyacac and Coaixtlahuacan, but the only report of a conquest that we have states that the king of Tepexic was vanquished in 11 Acatl 1503 because he had defeated the king of Cuauhtlatlauhcan;[111] this may have been a quarrel between kingdoms that were already part of the Empire. A land grant said to have been made in 1533 conceded lands to the principals of Tepexic, who claimed to be descendants of the Tenochcas, Tlatelolcas, and Tepanecs who had settled many estancias in the district of Tepexic. Perhaps the marriage mentioned above was accompanied by the arrival of settlers from the Basin.[112]

Atezcahuacan (22) was conquered by Moteuczoma Ilhuicamina in 8 Calli 1461,[113] and it also appears in the lists of conquests by Tizoc.[114] It has been identified with the present-day Atezcal, which in the early documentation is written Atezcac or Atezca, and was a dependency of Tepexic.[115]

The southernmost towns of this province—Chiltecpintlan, Oztotlapechco, and Atezcahuacan—reached to what had been the old boundaries of the Totomihuaques, whose territory later became the realm of Cuauhtinchan and Tepeyacac. Thus, Ahuatlan and Acatlan, reported as subject to the Empire in the *Relaciones geográficas*, were surrounded by the towns of this province and may have been closely connected with it; their contributions in military service and supplies agree with those of Tepeyacac. On the other hand, the "Memorial de los pueblos de Tlacopan," the *Relaciones geográficas*, and the lists of towns that were represented in Tenochtitlan for the great ceremonies also list as allies or tributaries of the Empire several towns south of this province, such as Piaztlan and Chiauhtlan, but without indicating whether they were part of a tributary province.[116] All these towns are discussed in the following section dealing with paragraph 7.3 of the "Memorial de Tlacopan."

The extent of this province toward the north may have been greater than is indicated by the towns listed in the Codex Mendoza. In the colonial period, the jurisdiction of Tepeyacac extended to the east and north as far as the boundaries with Teohuacan, Acoltzinco, Quimichtlan, Xalatzinco, Tzauctlan, Iztaquimaxtitlan, and Tlaxcallan.[117] This may well have been the situation during the Empire.

Paragraph 7.3 in the "Memorial de Tlacopan,"
Headed by Tlachmalacac

Paragraph 7.3 includes towns in the Balsas Basin and basically coincides with the provinces in the Codex Mendoza in the same area. The first of the three columns in Table 10-1 lists the towns in the "Memorial de Tlacopan," the second notes the towns that are also listed in the Codex Mendoza, and the third gives its identification. Map 10-6 includes the towns in paragraph 7.3 and also other towns cited in the discussion. The provinces in the Codex Mendoza situated in the same region are shown in Maps 5-5, 9-1, 10-1, 10-3, and 10-5.

As Table 10-1 indicates, paragraph 7.3 in the "Memorial de Tlacopan" includes towns listed in various provinces in the Codex Mendoza. The principal group comprises seven towns of Tepecuacuilco, including the cabecera. Another town—Coçollan—could be Cocollan, the second town listed in Tepecuacuilco, but it is preferable to identify Cocollan with the same toponym in the paragraph headed by Oztoman (7.4-2). The towns in paragraph 7.3 are in geographical order; therefore, the Coçollan of this list is probably an unidentified town between Tonallan (15) and Chilapan (16). This paragraph of Tlachmalacac also includes Tlachco (9), with two other towns in its province (4 and 6), and also the cabeceras of the provinces of Cuauhnahuac (19), Huaxtepec (20), Tlappan (18), and Yohualtepec (14), but with no other towns in these provinces. It also includes Tonatiuhco (5), of the province of Ocuillan, and two towns—Cuauhquechollan (21) and Itzocan (22)— from the western part of the province of Tepeyacac.

The few towns not listed in the Codex Mendoza are in neighboring regions. Cuitlapilco (7) and Atlmolonyan (8) are near Tlachco and Tonatiuhco. Cuauhmochtitlan (13) and Chiauhtlan (23) occupy the intermediate area between the province of Tepecuacuilco and the towns in the province of Tepeyacac that are also listed in this paragraph of the "Memorial de Tlacopan." Tonallan (15) is in the region that makes up the province of Yohualtepec.

In contrast with other parts of the "Memorial de Tlacopan," there are no overlaps in paragraph 7.3 with the provinces of the Codex Mendoza, although the Codex Mendoza provinces, some of whose towns are listed in this paragraph, include many more towns that are not listed in other paragraphs of the memorial.[118] Therefore, this paragraph of the "Memorial de Tlacopan" can be seen as a short summary (although with some other towns added) of a whole group of provinces depicted in the Codex Mendoza.

Missing in this paragraph of the "Memorial de Tlacopan" are some important towns listed in the Codex Mendoza that one would expect to find here as well. The province of Cihuatlan on the Costa Grande is not included, nor is the important town and fortress of Oztoman, which heads paragraph 7.4 in the memorial.[119] Also

TABLE 10-1.

Paragraph 7.3 in the "Memorial de Tlacopan," Headed by Tlachmalacac

"Memorial de Tlacopan"*	Codex Mendoza[†]	Identification[‡]
1. Tlachmalacac	Tlachmalacac (Tepecuacuilco, 5)	Tlaxmalac, in Huitzuco de los Figueroa, Guerrero.
2. Tepequacuilco	Tepecuacuilco (Tepecuacuilco, 1)	Tepecoacuilco de Trujano, Guerrero.
3. Youallan	Yoallan (Tepecuacuilco, 6)	Iguala de la Independencia, Guerrero.
4. Nochtepec	Nochtepec (Tlachco, 5)	Noxtepec, in Tetipac, Guerrero.
5. Tonatiuhco	Tonatiuhco (Ocuillan, 4)	Tonatico, Mexico.
6. Teoxaualco	Tepexahualco (Tlachco, 8)	San Pedro Hueyahualco, in Sultepec, Mexico.
7. Cuitlapilco		One of the cabeceras of Zacualpa (SV, sec.109). Acuitlapilco, in Coatepec Harinas, Mexico.
8. Atl molonyan		Almoloya, estancia of Amatepec (SV, sec. 34). Almoloya de Alquisiras, Mexico, or Almolonga, sujeto of Tutultepeque (RG 6:327). Almoloya, in Arcelia, Guerrero.
9. Tlachco	Tlachco (Tlachco, 1)	Taxco el Viejo in Taxco de Alarcón, Guerrero.
10. Telolopan	Teloloapan (Tepecuacuilco, 10)	Teloloapan, Guerrero.
11. Cuecallan [sic]	Cueçalan (Tepecuacuilco, 14)	Cuetzala del Progreso, Guerrero.
12. Ohuapan	Ohuapan (Tepecuacuilco, 3)	San Agustín Oapan, in Tepecoacuilco de Trujano, Guerrero.
13. Quammochititlan		Quamochtitlan (SV, sec. 485). Huamuxtitlan, Guerrero.
14. Youaltepec	Yoaltepec (Yohualtepec, 1)	San Juan Igualtepec, Oaxaca.
15. Tonallan		Tonala (SV, sec. 753; RG 2:290, 297, 299). Santo Domingo Tonala, Oaxaca.
16. Coçollan [sic]		Not identified. Cf. 7.4-2, 7.2-35, and 7.2-43.
17. Chilapan	Chilapan (Tepecuacuilco, 2)	Chilapa de Alvarez, Guerrero.
18. Tlappan	Tlapan (Tlapan, 1)	Tlapa de Comonfort, Guerrero.
19. Quauhnahuac	Cuauhnahuac (Cuauhnahuac, 1)	Cuernavaca, Morelos.
20. Vaxtepec	Huaxtepec (Huaxtepec, 1)	Oaxtepec, Morelos.

Table 10-1 continued

"Memorial de Tlacopan"*	Codex Mendoza†	Identification‡
21. Quauhquechollan	Quauhquechulan (Tepeyacac, 12)	Huaquechula, Puebla.
22. Itztzocan	Ytzucan (Tepeyacac, 11)	Izúcar de Matamoros, Puebla.
23. Chiyauhtla		Chiauhtla de la Sal, Puebla.

*Towns are numbered according to their sequence in the list (Zimmermann 1970:8).
†Names of the towns in the Codex Mendoza followed in parentheses by the name of the province in which each is located and its place in the sequence of towns as depicted in the codex.
‡In general, only the present-day name and location are given; more complete information on each tributary province has been given in the previous sections in each of the tributary provinces.

missing are towns on the Costa Chica that, according to local sources, pertained to the Empire and could have been extensions of the provinces of Tlappan or Yohualtepec; this coastal region is included in the paragraph headed by Oztoman. Two other provinces in the Codex Mendoza—Tlalcozauhtitlan and Quiauhteopan—are not included, although they fall within the territory encompassed by paragraph 7.3.

Also absent from this paragraph is Piaztlan, which Durán and Tezozomoc, in their lists of towns that were represented in Tenochtitlan during the great celebrations, associate with Chiauhtlan, Tlappan, and other towns of the Cohuixca region. In the relación geográfica of Piaztlan it is said that this town was in the "province" of Totollan, or of the Totoltecs, who spoke Nahuatl and were different from the neighboring Mixtecs of Acatlan and Chillan.[120] Piaztlan was conquered by Nezahualcoyotl and Moteuczoma Ilhuicamina.[121] As tribute it paid each year large amounts of salt and wax, and in addition, when the imperial armies passed by on the way to conquer distant areas, Piaztlan supplied them with flint-edged swords, round shields, and arrows and also food.[122] Piaztlan and Chiauhtlan were also close to Itzocan, in the tributary province of Tepeyacac, which was an important stopping place on the road to the Mixteca and Huaxyacac; their services to the Empire might have been coordinated by the imperial officials of that province.

Some towns in this paragraph are close to the Tarascan frontier, but the frontier towns about which the *Relaciones geográficas* and other documents give information are not in the list. Other paragraphs in the "Memorial de Tlacopan" include towns not listed in the Codex Mendoza that according to local sources were allies of the Empire or gave only military service; in this paragraph there are no such cases.

If we try to interpret the differences between these sources in terms of the period in which these regions were incorporated into the Empire, it can be said that

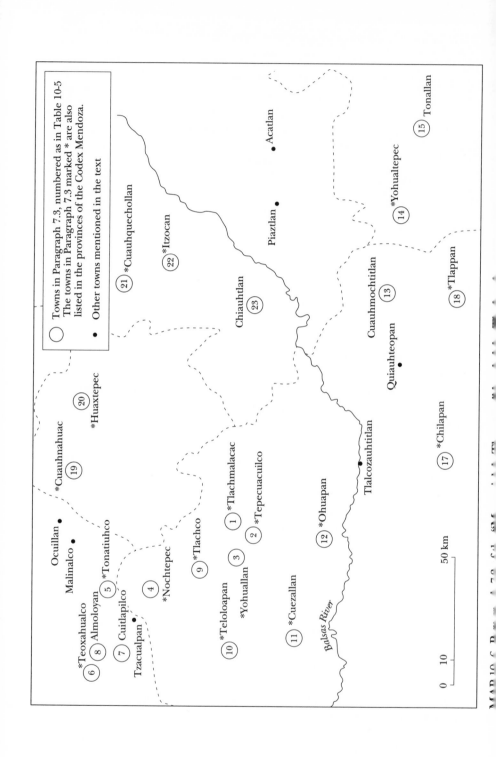

MAP 10.6. Provinces of the Codex Mendoza.

this paragraph of the "Memorial de Tlacopan" comprises towns in the areas conquered up to the reign of Moteuczoma Ilhuicamina, although it also includes
Tlappan, conquered by Ahuitzotl. It does not include the conquests of Ahuitzotl
and Moteuczoma Xocoyotzin on the Costa Chica, which are together with Oztoman in paragraph 7.4. Nevertheless, this historical explanation is not enough to
understand the composition of other lists in the "Memorial de Tlacopan."

It is odd to find Cuauhnahuac and Huaxtepec in this paragraph, which is said
to contain the towns that paid tribute to the alliance and whose tribute was divided among the three capitals. Some towns in those two provinces are already included in the "Memorial de Tlacopan" (section 5) among the estancias that paid
tribute to Tlacopan. Perhaps the presence of these two towns in this paragraph
represents obligations different from those of the other towns in that same region,
which have already been discussed in regard to the possessions that each one of the
three capitals of the alliance had in Tlalhuic. One function that associates them
with this wide area is the role of the stewards of Cuauhnahuac and Huaxtepec who
were charged with providing lodging for visitors from Yopitzinco during the installation of Ahuitzotl.[123]

The Provinces in the Mixteca and the
Valley of Oaxaca in the Codex Mendoza

Three tributary provinces in the southern sector occupy approximately the same
area as the present-day state of Oaxaca and can be compared with two sections
of the "Memorial de Tlacopan." These provinces—Coaixtlahuacan, Coyolapan,
and Tlachquiauhco—are discussed below and are represented in Maps 10-7 (Coaixtlahuacan and Tlachquiauhco) and 10-8 (Coyolapan). They will then be compared with paragraphs 7.2 (Cozcatlan) and 7.4 (Oztoman) in the "Memorial de
Tlacopan."

COAIXTLAHUACAN (CODEX MENDOZA, 43R)

1.	Coayxtlahuacan	Cuestlauaca, bordering on Texupa (SV, sec. 567).
		San Juan Bautista Coixtlahuaca, Oaxaca.
2.	Texopan	Texupa (SV, sec. 567).
		Santiago Tejupan, Oaxaca.
3.	Tamaçolapan	Tamaçulapa (SV, sec. 658).
		Tamazulapan del Progreso, Oaxaca.
4.	Yancuitlan	Yanguitlan (SV, sec. 308).
		Santo Domingo Yanhuitlán, Oaxaca.

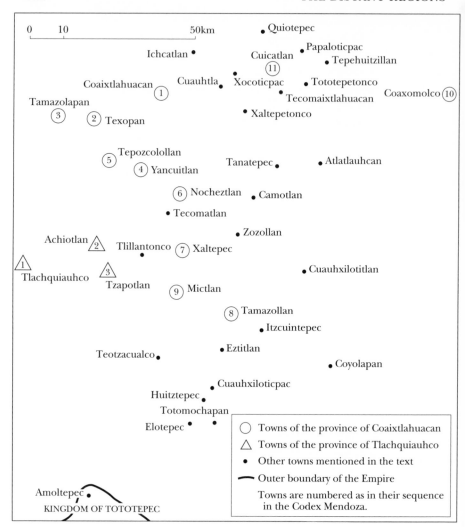

MAP 10–7. The tributary provinces of Coaixtlahuacan and Tlachquiauhco

5. Tepuzcululan   Tapazcolula (SV, sec. 654).
                     San Pedro y San Pablo Teposcolula, Oaxaca.
6. Nochiztlan   Nochistlan (SV, sec. 408).
                     Asunción Nochixtlán, Oaxaca.
7. Xaltepec   Xaltepeque (SV, sec. 836).
                     Magdalena Jaltepec, Oaxaca.

8. Tamaçolan	Tamaçola (SV, sec. 757).
	San Juan Tamazola, Oaxaca.
9. Mictlan	Mitlantongo (SV, sec. 395). Santiago Mitlatongo,
	in Asunción Nochixtlán, Oaxaca.
10. Coaxomulco	Santiago Cuasimulco, in San Juan Quiotepec,
	Oaxaca.
11. Cuicatlan	Cuycatlan (SV, sec. 227).
	San Juan Bautista Cuicatlán, Oaxaca.

The tributary province of Coaixtlahuacan includes a large part of the Mixteca Alta, Cuicatlan (11) in La Cañada, and in the distant mountain Chinantec region, Coaxomulco (10).

The conquest of Coaixtlahuacan in the Mixteca Alta, one of the most important by Moteuczoma Ilhuicamina, initiated the presence of the alliance in Oaxaca. The war began because the people of Coaixtlahuacan had murdered merchants from the cities of the Basin. After the victory, Tlacaelel, with the king's advice, sent a viceroy named Cuauhxochitl to Coaixtlahuacan to be in charge of that province and of the royal tribute. The viceroy went in person from Coaixtlahuacan to Tenochtitlan every eighty days to bring the tribute to the king, who gave him splendid gifts.[124] Tezozomoc adds that there was a steward in Tenochtitlan for the tribute from Coaixtlahuacan and another in the towns of the province.[125]

Torquemada also gives a detailed account of this war. Atonal, the ruler of Coaixtlahuacan, in his struggle against the Empire received a contingent of Tlaxcaltecs and Huexotzincas with whom he planned to attack the people of Tlachquiauhco, "who were close by and were on the side of the Mexicas, and they were to be killed along with the Mexicas who were there as a garrison." After their defeat, the ruler of Tlachquiauhco sent the news to Moteuczoma, who deferred his campaign until the following year, when the three kings of the Empire conquered Coaixtlahuacan and its allies. Defeated, Atonal "submitted to Motecuhzoma and became his vassal (*feudatario*)." The Mexicas returned home, leaving the "provinces" of Coaixtlahuacan, Tochtepec, Teuhzolzapotla, Tototlan, Tlatlactetelco, Chinantlan, and Cuauhnochco (*sic pro* Cuauhtochco) vanquished and subject to Moteuczoma. Later, Coaixtlahuacan and these other towns rebelled against Atonal, killed him together with the Tlaxcaltecas and Huexotzincas who had remained among them, and offered then to become tributaries of the king of Tenochtitlan. The following year, the three kings of the Empire conquered Cozamaloapan, and a year later Cuauhtochco, whose people had killed certain Mexicas.[126]

The Codex Mendoza depicts the death of Atonal beside the glyph of his conquered city, which is exceptional in the pages of this codex dealing with the conquests.[127] In the *Anales de Cuauhtitlan* it is said that the widow of Atonal acted as steward (cihuacalpixqui).[128] Coaixtlahuacan was the capital of a powerful state; some of the towns included in this conquest had perhaps been its tributaries.[129] This conquest opened the way for the Mexicas to go farther, into more distant regions that had had political and commercial relations with Coaixtlahuacan. The towns conquered at the same time as Coaixtlahuacan, according to Torquemada, are located in the provinces of Tochtepec, Cuetlaxtlan, and Cuauhtochco, which had also received help from the Tlaxcaltecs and were conquered by Ilhuicamina.

In the relación of Atlatlauhca, Coaixtlahuacan is described as "military borderland,"[130] and a source from Tecomatlan states that it had a Mexica garrison.[131] In Durán's account of the dedication of the temple in the reign of Ahuitzotl, he refers to Coaixtlahuacan as a metropolis of the entire Mixtec "province" and does not allude to more distant towns.[132] All this suggests that it became the military center for the conquests that followed farther south, and only later did Zozollan and Huaxyacac become the principal imperial fortresses. Tizoc, Ahuitzotl, and especially Moteuczoma Xocoyotzin won many towns in Oaxaca, including some in the region embraced by this tributary province of Coaixtlahuacan, indicating that there had not been an effective conquest.[133]

The "Memorial de los pueblos de Tlacopan" includes in paragraph 7.2 several of these towns in the Mixteca, together with others not in the Codex Mendoza; this will be discussed later. The *Relaciones geográficas* also provide material that considerably increases our knowledge of the extent of the Empire. Some treat of the same towns as the Codex Mendoza; others describe towns not listed in this codex but nevertheless subject to the Empire. On the other hand, there were towns in the same area that had kept their independence. The following data are from the most informative reports.

In the Mixteca Alta, Texopan (2) gave as tribute to Moteuczoma slaves, parrot feathers, and a small quantity of cochineal; to their own ruler they gave copal and other things necessary for their rituals.[134]

The people of Tamazollan (8) declared that their ruler always had friendly relations with Moteuczoma, and "when asked whether they paid parias or tribute, said no, that they only helped each other as friends by providing soldiers."[135]

Yancuitlan (4) was another conquest by Ilhuicamina, who also plotted the death by treachery of its ruler. Once it was overcome, the town gave as tribute green feathers, chalchihuites, and cochineal and also cultivated certain fields, all of this for "the king's garrisons."[136] The conquest of Yancuitlan is also attributed to Tizoc.[137]

The relación of Nocheztlan (6) mentions war with Mexico, although it also says that the people paid tribute to Moteuczoma. Probably this was a remembrance of the situation before the Mexica conquest, or it may refer to the rebellions after Ilhuicamina's first conquests.[138]

Between the provinces of Coaixtlahuacan and Tlachquiauhco there was an im-

portant Mixtec kingdom—Tlillantonco (present-day Santiago Tilantongo, Oaxaca)—
for which there is information in a relación geográfica that also describes Mictlantonco. It is not said that either of these two towns was subject to the Empire, but
nevertheless Mictlantonco, or Mictlan (9), is listed in the tributary province of
Coaixtlahuacan. Tlillantonco had many subject towns and warred with Tepozcolollan (5) and with the Tzapotecs.[139] The people of Mictlantonco declared themselves to be vassals of their own rulers and said that "they made war on each other
in the Mixtec area, most frequently with Tlachquiauhco and Tototepec."[140]

The people of Teotzacualco (San Pedro Teozacoalco, Oaxaca) were ruled by
their own natural lord, whom they had brought from Tlillantonco. Shortly before
the Spanish arrived, they agreed to become subject to Moteuczoma and gave him
as tribute chalchihuites, feathers, and cloaks of cotton and hennequen, and in addition they cultivated for him fields of maize, beans, chía, and cotton, "all of which
was expended by the soldiers they had as a garrison in this town."[141] Barlow puts
Teotzacualco in the tributary province of Coyolapan, but given its geographical
situation it is more probable that, like Mictlantonco and Tamazollan, it was in the
tributary province of Coaixtlahuacan. Farther south, Amoltepec was subject to
the Mixtec king of Tototepec and helped him in his wars against the Mexicas.[142]

A colonial lawsuit between Tecomatlan (San Miguel Tecomatlan, Oaxaca)
and Nocheztlan (6) informs us that Tecomatlan had its own ruler and took its tribute to the Mexicas that Moteuczoma had stationed in the town of Coaixtlahuacan,
or, according to another statement, "to the captains and men that Moteuczuma
had put there to collect the tribute of that whole province." Tecomatlan was a subject of Yancuitlan (4) and as such paid tribute to Coaixtlahuacan.[143] This is another concrete case that shows that the towns in the Codex Mendoza had dependencies of their own that participated in paying tribute.

The last two towns in this province, Coaxomulco (10) and Cuicatlan (11), bring
us to the extreme northeast. The "Memorial de Tlacopan" includes several towns
in the area between the Mixteca and these two towns, thus filling in the empty
space that the Codex Mendoza leaves between them; the *Relaciones geográficas* provide more information.

Cuicatlan, the center of the Cuicatec region, had its own ruler, called in Nahuatl Tecuanteuctli, who surrendered to the Mexicas. Before Moteuczoma subjugated this town, it was at war with its neighbor Quiotepec, each trying to take the
other's land and capture prisoners for sacrifice. All this stopped when Moteuczoma
sent his armies and most of the towns surrendered without a fight. The people of
Cuicatlan still recognized no authority other than Tecuanteuctli, but "so that their
ruler could pay tribute to Moteuczoma, whose subject he was, they searched for
feathers, gold, [and precious] stones." These objects were considered as a kind of
tribute or parias, sent by their ruler to Moteuczoma. In addition the people gave to

Moteuczoma's tribute collectors "cloaks, food, and other presents" and from time to time sent fruit to the men in Moteuczoma's garrisons in the Mixteca.[144]

There is information in other relaciones on the area between the cabecera of Coaixtlahuacan and Cuicatlan. Cuautla, a Mixtec-speaking town, had its own ruler to whom the people paid tribute, but it is also said that they were governed by an official placed by Moteuczoma in Coaixtlahuacan, to whom they took the tribute for the Tenochca king. They carried on a war with Tlachquiauhco, one of the last conquests by Moteuczoma Xocoyotzin.[145] The relación of Cuauhtla reports on various other towns. Xocoticpac, also Mixtec, was subject to the ruler of Coaixtlahuacan, to whom the people took feathers for Moteuczoma.[146] The Mixtecs of Xaltepetonco declared that they warred with Xaltepec, one of the towns of the province of Coaixtlahuacan according to the Codex Mendoza.[147] The people of Tototepetonco, a Cuicatec-speaking town, were ruled by their natural lord, to whom they paid tribute. He was Moteuczoma's captain and sent his people to war.[148] Tanatepec, also Cuicatec, had a natural lord who resided in Tlillantonco, and received no tribute other than assistance when called upon for war against the "province" of Chinantlan.[149]

Cuicatlan (11) is the only Cuicatec kingdom registered in this province in the Codex Mendoza, but several others are listed in the "Memorial de los pueblos de Tlacopan," the most important being Quiotepec, Tecomahuacan, Papaloticpan, and Atlatlauhcan (see below in the section on paragraph 7.2).

The relación of Atlatlauhca connects this town with Coaixtlahuacan. Moteuczoma conquered it "by force of arms." The tribute the town paid—cochineal, cotton cloaks, feathers, and chalchihuites—was obtained from other towns in exchange for small cloaks or blankets. It was collected by two calpixques sent by Moteuczoma, who took it to Coaixtlahuacan, where he had placed a garrison on the frontier. When Moteuczoma's captains ordered the people of Atlatlauhcan to send soldiers for other campaigns of conquest, they did so, but other than that, neither Moteuczoma nor any of his people intervened, leaving all authority to the natural lords in each town.[150]

Another relación treats of Ichcatlan, Quiotepec, and Tecomahuacan. Ichcatlan, Chochon-speaking, originally had its own ruler. Moteuczoma defeated him, deprived him of his rulership, and appointed a governor, but he ordered that the native ruler be supported with half of the tribute goods.[151] Quiotepec, a Cuicatec town,[152] was always subject to Moteuczoma, to whom they paid as tribute gold discs and small blankets; they waged war with Moteuczoma's enemies.[153] Tecomahuacan, where the language spoken was that "of the Pinoles," was also subject to Moteuczoma and was governed by its own natural lord.[154]

The relación of Papaloticpac reports on several Cuicatec kingdoms. In Papaloticpac "only their natural lord was obeyed and respected by the natives and he governed and commanded them." Formerly they were at war with all the towns in the surrounding area, but this ended when the Mexicas subjugated them. The people paid tribute in gold dust to their own ruler, who gave it to Moteuczoma; they also took provisions to the garrisons where Moteuczuma kept military forces.[155] Tepeucila (Tepehuitzillan) also had a natural lord subject to Moteuczoma, whom they served and gave as tribute cloaks and tiger skins that they bought in other towns in the district, and also some feathers. Formerly they had been at war with all the towns in their district, solely to capture prisoners for sacrificing.[156]

Cuauhxilotitlan is a special case. In the Codex Mendoza it is part of the province of Coyolapan, but according to its relación (as Guaxilotitlan) it also sent tribute to Coaixtlahuacan.[157] The town may well have had different obligations to each of the two tributary provinces with which it was connected; it is also possible that its attribution to a certain province could have been changed.

The region of the towns that the Spanish called Peñoles was subjugated by the Empire. There were six cabeceras: Itzcuintepec, Eztitlan, Cuauhxiloticpac, and Huitztepec, which were Mixtec, and Totomochapan and Elotepec, both Tzapotec. According to their relación geográfica, these Peñoles towns belonged to Moteuczoma, to whom they gave as tribute gold and cotton cloaks. They were formerly governed by their natural lords, who were subject to Moteuczoma. At times they skirmished with the people of the Tototepec kingdom, which was not subject to Moteuczoma.[158] The available data do not indicate which tributary province these towns might have been part of. Barlow adds them to Coyolapan;[159] they could just as well have pertained to Coaixtlahuacan. Itzcuintepec is found in the lists of conquests by Moteuczoma Xocoyotzin.[160]

During the reign of the last Tenochca sovereign, Yancuitlan and Zozollan rebelled and were then vanquished in a new campaign.[161] Torquemada describes this war as an extensive conspiracy by the rulers of the Mixteca and Tecuantepec. The leaders of the rebellion were the kings of Coaixtlahuacan, the principal center of the Empire in the Mixteca, and of Zozollan, already conquered by Ahuitzotl.[162] The king of Coaixtlahuacan invited many of the neighboring rulers, and also the Mexicas of Huaxyacac and other areas, to a great feast. When the Mexicas were returning home, the king of Zozollan set up an ambush in which they were all killed. In the war that followed, the Empire defeated the allied Mixtec rulers, including the king of Tototepec, in a great battle near Zozollan. Several of the conspirators were captured, among them the king of Coaixtlahuacan, who was sacrificed. A brother of the defeated ruler, who had gone over to the Empire's side, was installed as his successor.[163] Probably it was this war that led to the establishment of the military colony in Zozollan.

Cortés speaks of eight towns of the province of Coaixtlahuacan that came to

Itzocan to surrender, promising that four other towns would come later. These twelve towns were probably the same eleven listed in Codex Mendoza plus Zozollan, which Cortés also mentions as one of the towns where he had sent Spaniards searching for gold.[164] It is not known whether this means that the local imperial organization was submitting or that the Mixtec towns were turning against the Empire. According to one account, when the Spanish arrived, the Mixteca had rebelled against the Mexicas in the garrison at Coaixtlahuacan and had killed many of them. Routed by the rebels, the survivors fled to the Mexica garrison of Huaxyacac, where they were surrounded by the Mixteca until the Spanish came, at which time they surrendered peacefully and thus were saved from certain death.[165]

In conclusion, in the Mixteca there were a number of indigenous political units in which the local rulers kept their authority although they paid tribute to the Empire. Some of the relaciones geográficas concede little importance to what was rendered to the Empire; others speak of military assistance. In general the relaciones say little that would indicate direct interference by the imperial calpixques in the production of the goods to be given as tribute; they are frequently luxury objects defined as parias or as gifts. This was an unstable situation, and the Empire did not succeed in establishing its dominion solidly.[166] This failure explains the need for the many campaigns of Moteuczoma Xocoyotzin in this region and the rebellions on the eve of the Spanish conquest.

COYOLAPAN (CODEX MENDOZA, 44R)

1. Coyolapan	Cuilapan or Cuyolapan (RG 2:177).
	Cuilapan de Guerrero, Oaxaca.
2. Etlan	Etla (RG 2:213-16).
	San Pedro y San Pablo Etla, Oaxaca.
3. Quauxilotitlan	Guaxilotitlan (RG 2:213).
	San Pablo Huitzo, Oaxaca (Gerhard 1986:147–48).
4. Guaxaca	Guaxaca (RG 2:33). Oaxaca, Oaxaca.
5. Camotlan	Camotlán, near present-day San Francisco del Mar, Oaxaca (RG 3:112, 118, 127 and map); or Camotlan (SV, sec. 223), Santiago Camotlán, Oaxaca (in Villa Alta district); or Santiago Camotlán, in Asunción Nochixtlán, Oaxaca; or San Lucas Camotlán, Oaxaca (Mixe district).
6. Teocuitlatlan	The glyph should be read as Teocuitlapacoyan. Tacolabacoya (RG 2:269). Santa Ana Tlapacoyan, Oaxaca.

7. Quatzontepec	The glyph should be read as Tepecuatzontlan. Tepeguazontlan, in the area of present-day San Dionisio del Mar, Oaxaca (RG 3:112, 127 and map).
8. Octlan	Ocotlan (SV, sec. 440). Ocotlán de Morelos, Oaxaca.
9. Teticpac	Teticpac or Teticpaque (RG 3:169). Magdalena Teitipac, Oaxaca; or San Sebastián Teitipac, Oaxaca.
10. Tlalcuechahuayan	Tlalcuchaguaya (SV, sec. 644). Tlacochahuaya de Morelos, Oaxaca.
11. Macuilxochic	Macuilsuchil (SV, sec. 348). San Mateo Macuilxóchitl, in Tlacochahuaya de Morelos, Oaxaca.

This tributary province lies in the central valleys of present-day Oaxaca, with an extension towards the isthmus (see Map 10-8). The most important towns are well known, but a new identification of one or two towns must be emphasized: Cuatzontepec (7) (Tepecuatzontlan) was on the isthmus, and there is a strong probability that Camotlan (5) was also in the same area.

The accounts of the conquest of Huaxyacac (4) put it in the reign of Moteuczoma Ilhuicamina. The war had been provoked by the death, at the hands of the people of Huaxyacac, of royal envoys and merchants who were returning from Coatzacualco with gifts for the king of Tenochtitlan.[167] This was not a delivery of tribute but rather the return of a political-commercial expedition such as the one described in the reign of Ahuitzotl to Xicallanco.[168] Huaxyacac and its inhabitants were destroyed and the Mexicas founded a new city with settlers from the three imperial capitals and also from Xochimilco, Chalco, Tlalhuic, and Mazahuacan. Moteuczoma appointed a cousin of his as viceroy, with orders to organize the city so that each group of settlers, such as Mexicas and Tetzcocas, would be in their own barrio. As chiefs and lesser officials the viceroy was to choose the oldest and the most deserving individuals, and the city was to be governed in the same way as the city of Mexico.[169]

However, these deeds are attributed to Moteuczoma Ilhuicamina only in sources from the Tenochca tradition. No other conquests in this area are clearly documented in the accounts of this campaign, which do not report clearly the conquest of any other town during this campaign. Durán relates that after the conquest of Huaxyacac, the Mexicas sent messengers to Coyolapan and other towns in the area advising them to live in peace and warning them that any act of treason would bring upon them the same punishment as that given to the people of Huaxyacac. The Mixtecs and Tzapotecs surrendered, saying they were content and ready to

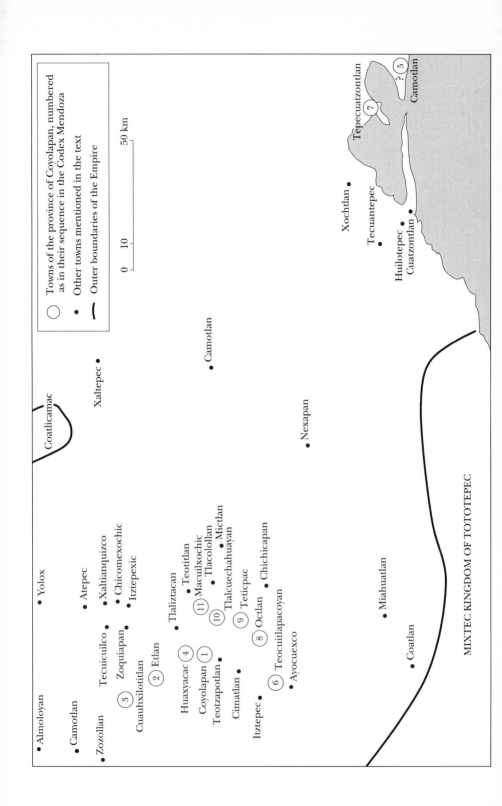

Towns of the province of Coyolapan, numbered as in their sequence in the Codex Mendoza

Other towns mentioned in the text

Outer boundaries of the Empire

0   10   50 km

Almoloyan

Camotlan

Zozollan

Tecuiculco

Zoquiapan

Cuauhxilotitlan

③

Yolox

Atepec

Xaltianquizco

Chicomexochic

Itztepexic

Coatlicamac

Xaltepec

Camotlan

Tlaliztacan

Teotitlan

Maculxochic

Tlacolollan

Mictlan

Tlalcuechahuayan

Teticpac

Octlan   Chichicapan

Teocuitlapacoyan

Ayocuexco

Nexapan

Huaxyacac ④

Coyolapan ①

Teotzapotlan

Cimatlan

Itztepec

⑧

⑥

Etlan ②

⑪

⑩

⑨

Xochtlan

Tecuantepec

Huilotepec

Cuatzontlan

Tepecuatzontlan

⑦

? 5

Camotlan

Miahuatlan

Coatlan

MIXTEC KINGDOM OF TOTOTEPEC

serve and obey the Mexicas as their lords; the army then returned to Tenochtitlan with their captives.[170] In Tezozomoc's account of this episode almost all the natives of Huaxyacac were killed, and the Mexicas took as prisoners only the Tzapotecs, the people of Otlatlan, and the Miahuatecs. They threatened the Mixtecs with death to all if they repeated the cruel treatment of the Mexicas by the people of Huaxyacac.[171] Probably the Mixtecs and Tzapotecs mentioned were, respectively, from Coyolapan and Teotzapotlan (present-day Zaachila). The Miahuatecs would be from Miahuatlan in the southern part of the valley; Otlatlan is difficult to identify.[172] The "Relación de la genealogía y linaje" also credits Moteuczoma Ilhuicamina with the conquest of Huaxyacac, together with that of Tecuantepec.[173]

Other sources, which say nothing about Huaxyacac, put the conquests of towns in that region in the reign of Ahuitzotl, who conquered Teotzapotlan, Coyolapan (1), and Mictlan in the valley, and Tecuantepec and Xochtlan (Juchitán) in the isthmus. Later, Moteuczoma Xocoyotzin fought in various regions of Oaxaca, with already established centers of power as points of departure. In the regions that interest us here, he is credited with the conquest of Mictlan in the valley and Cuatzontlan and Huilotepec in the isthmus.[174]

The center of imperial power was established in Huaxyacac (4), which appears on the page depicting garrisons in the Codex Mendoza, but the cabecera of the tributary province was Coyolapan (1). There is no problem in locating all the towns listed in the central valleys. The *Relaciones geográficas* provide information on several of them:

Coyolapan (1) was settled by Mixtecs who came from Almoloyan; they subjugated the Tzapotecs of the valleys, and as a result of these conquests, the people of Teotzapotlan fled to Tecuantepec.[175]

Cuauhxilotitlan (3) had a mixed population of Mixtecs and Tzapotecs. They were governed by their own natural lord but were also subject to Moteuczoma, to whom they paid tribute consisting of clothing, copper crowns, bluebirds (*xiuhtototl*), and maize. There were three calpixques to collect the tribute, one each in Huaxyacac, Cuauhxilotitlan, and Coaixtlahuacan. The calpixque of Cuauhxilotitlan sent maize and cloaks to Coaixtlahuacan, and the rest was taken to Tenochtitlan, to Moteuczoma himself. They carried on wars with Tecuicuilco, Coatlan, Miahuatlan, Chichicapan, and Nexapan; for that purpose they joined forces with the people of Huaxyacac (4), Coyolapan (10, and Etlan (2) and with warriors who came from Tenochtitlan.[176]

The location of Camotlan (5) on the isthmus is discussed below. If it was the Camotlan near Nocheztlan, as Barlow thought, it would be close to other Mixtec towns under the Empire. It is near Almoloyan, the place of origin of the Mixtecs of Coyolapan, and also near Zozollan, an important garrison town of the Empire. It is not known whether Zozollan had a special relationship with any of the tributary provinces. This Camotlan is also near Cuauhxilotitlan (3), which sent part of its tribute to Coaixtlahuacan even though it is in this same province of Coyolapan. In the mountains west of the valley, the Peñoles towns discussed in connection with Coaixtlahuacan could also have been part of this province as dependencies of the neighboring Coyolapan.

The glyph for Teocuitlatlan (6) in the Codex Mendoza is an arm that holds gold and water in its hand.[177] This must be understood to mean "gold washing," that is, Teocuitlapacoyan, without any doubt the present-day Santa Ana Tlapacoyan, Oaxaca.[178]

Octlan (8) is usually identified with Ocotlan, Oaxaca, although this name means "place of the pine tree (ocotl)". The glyph in the Codex Mendoza is a bowl with pulque (octli), which agrees with the spelling Octlan.[179]

The relación of Teticpac (9) gives slight importance to its subjection to the Empire. Its ruler was the king of Teotzapotlan, and later, Moteuczoma. The town's tribute to both consisted of hens, hares, rabbits, deer, and honey. When ordered by the ruler of Teotzapotlan, it made war on the people of the mountains.[180]

Macuilxochic (11) is described (together with Teotitlan del Valle) in a relación geográfica that does not mention its subjection to Tenochtitlan. Their ruler was the king of Teotzapotlan, to whom they gave no tribute other than to provide men and weapons for the war against Mictlan and other towns. They were governed by a principal installed by the king of Teotzapotlan.[181]

In the area of the central valleys there were important towns that are not listed in the Codex Mendoza and that local sources do not refer to as sujetos of the Empire, especially the Tzapotec capital, Teotzapotlan. Shortly before the arrival of the Spaniards, Teotzapotlan fought with Tototepec and Tlachquiauhco, both of them independent and bellicose, and with the forces of Moteuczoma. When the Spaniards came, Moteuczoma had a garrison near Huaxyacac on a hill called Acatepec. The local people said he had put it there out of friendship and without a battle, as a stopping place on the road to Tecuantepec and Guatemala. They paid no tribute to the Mexicas except out of friendship, and the king of Teotzapotlan continued as absolute ruler.[182]

As has been said, according to the relación of Coyolapan the people of Teotzapotlan went to Tecuantepec when the Mixtecs had conquered them, before the arrival of the Mexicas, but this must be understood as referring to a branch of the ruling dynasty and not the migration of all the people of the town. Teotzapotlan kept its power over other kingdoms in the valley.

Tlaliztacan was subject to Teotzapotlan, to which it paid tribute and served by going to war against neighboring towns in the mountains.[183] However, the "Memorial de Tlacopan" includes Tlaliztacan (7.4-7) among tributaries of the Empire.

The relación of Iztepec (Itztepec) also describes Tacolabacoya (*sic*), Ayocuexco, and two Tepecimatlans (Santa María Magdalena and San Bernardo). It says little about the pre-Spanish political situation, but Tacolabacoya can be identified with Teocuitlapacoyan, the Teocuitlatla (6) in the Codex Mendoza. Cimatlan appears in the "Memorial de Tlacopan" (7.4-11). Itztepec was governed by their natural lord, whose officials were stewards, who collected what was necessary for the palace, and tequitlatoque, who were in charge of the villages.[184]

The relación of Macuilxochic and Teotitlan del Valle gives both towns as former sujetos of Teotzapotlan; the information on Macuilxochic (11) has been cited above. The report on Teotitlan says that they were governed by their natural lord. Formerly they served and paid tribute to the king of Teotzapotlan and later to the king of Tecuantepec; after that they served and paid tribute to the Mixtec town of Cuilapan, that is, Coyolapan, the cabecera of this tributary province; nevertheless, the relación states that they fought with the Mexicas whom Moteuczoma sent to this area as a garrison.[185] Teotitlan is probably the same town as Teotitlantzinco in the "Memorial de Tlacopan" (7.4-3).

Mictlan and Tlacolollan also had their own local rulers subject to the king of Teotzapotlan. The people of Tlacolollan said that they paid their ruler no tribute other than to serve him in the war against the Mixe and against Mictlan.[186] The people of Mictlan paid tribute to the king of Teotzapotlan for only a few years; they went there to plant a maize field and gave him hens and honey. Formerly they warred with Tototepec and then with the Mexicas that Moteuczoma sent to wage war.[187]

Some towns in the mountains north of the Valley of Oaxaca that are not included in this province in the Codex Mendoza paid tribute to Huaxyacac. The relación of Itztepexic describes a complex situation: The people had their own rulers, who came from Yolox, and they entered into some kind of alliance with Teotzapotlan, Coyolapan, Huaxyacac, Chicomexochic, Tecuicuilco, and others until the Mexicas subdued them two hundred years before (that is, about 1380). After the Mexicas, they were subjugated by the Mixtecs of Tototepec, Achiotlan, and Tlachquiauhco and began to pay tribute both to the Mexicas in Huaxyacac and to the Mixtecs. They gave base gold, green feathers, which they obtained in Xoconochco, deer, maize, and firewood; they also provided personal services to the Mexicas of Huaxyacac. They fought with Chinantlan, Chicomexochitl, Zoquiapan, "and other neighboring towns for no reason but just for exercise."[188]

Tecuicuilco was another mountain town that paid tribute to Huaxyacac. The relación of this town also treats of Atepec, Zoquiapan, and Xaltianquizco. These towns recognized the authority of Moteuczoma, who had conquered them about twelve or twenty years before the arrival of the Spanish. Their tribute was green feathers and green stones that they obtained by trading small cloaks (*mantillas*);

they also sent soldiers when Moteuczoma's captains asked for them. Two of Moteuczoma's stewards resided in the province of Huaxyacac and came to collect the tribute and send it to Tenochtitlan. Local government was in the hands of the natural lords in each town.[189] Two of these towns appear as tributaries of the Empire in the "Memorial de Tlacopan," but in different subdivisions: Tecuicuilco (7.2-61) is listed in the paragraph headed by Cozcatlan that included Coyolapan but not Huaxyacac, while Atepec (6.6-11) is included in the paragraph headed by Chinantlan. Both Atepec and Xaltianquizco were conquered by Moteuczoma Xocoyotzin.[190]

Two towns in the province of Coyolapan, Cuatzontepec (7) and Camotlan (5), can be located in the isthmus; the latter is more problematical. The glyph for Cuatzontepec contains the elements for mountain (*tepetl*), skein (*cuatzomitl*), and teeth (*tlantli*), which can be read as Tepecuatzontlan. In the isthmus there were both a Tepecuatzontlan and a Cuatzontlan, the latter to the east of the mouth of the Tecuantepec River, the present-day San Mateo del Mar; Tepecuatzontlan was on the site of present-day San Dionisio del Mar.[191] The accounts of the conquest of Huaxyacac and of later campaigns also name Tecuantepec and other towns in the isthmus among the conquests of the Mexicas. The conquest of Cuatzontlan is recorded, along with that of Xaltepec, in the reign of Moteuczoma Xocoyotzin.[192] There is nothing odd in finding tributary towns there also, although it is questionable whether Moteuczoma Ilhuicamina's conquests reached as far as Tecuantepec. The tributary towns in the isthmus were probably added to the tributary province of Coyolapan after the conquests of later kings.

Camotlan (5) is a toponym too frequent to allow us to be sure of its ascription. Its location in the Huave region of the isthmus is reinforced by the presence of Tepecuatzontlan in that area, and it has been placed there in Map 10-8. However, the conquests of Moteuczoma Xocoyotzin include several towns in the mountains, so it is possible that the Camotlan listed in this province was the one in the Mixe district or another in the district of Villa Alta. It has already been noted that it could be identified with a town near Nocheztlan. For the present, nothing can be considered certain about the location of this Camotlan.

The extension of the province of Coyolapan to the isthmus makes sense, since there were conquests by the Empire in that region. Nevertheless, Tecuantepec does not appear in the Codex Mendoza, although it does in the "Memorial de Tlacopan," which in its last section includes both Xoconochco and Tecuantepec as well as other towns of the isthmus.

In the vicinity of this tributary province there are various towns subject to the Empire but not registered in the Codex Mendoza. They are discussed together with the paragraphs of the "Memorial de Tlacopan" that include them.[193]

The situation of Coyolapan province was similar to that of Coaixtlahuacan:

The presence of the Empire was assured in the colony established in Huaxyacac, but imperial control was not uniformly implanted throughout the whole region. Several independent towns remained, and the Empire's military domination was not secure. The old Tzapotec kingdom of Teotzapotlan survived as part of the local political organization underlying the imperial tributary province. Some of its dependent towns, such as Mictlan, Tlacolollan, and, farther south, Chichicapan, did not acknowledge the Empire; others, such as Teticpac, Macuilxochic, Tlaliztacan, and Teotitlan del Valle, paid tribute to the Empire but kept some kind of allegiance to Teotzapotlan.[194] The tribute sent to Tenochtitlan consisted of luxury objects obtained partly through long-distance trading; the tribute in maize was probably intended for the garrison of Huaxyacac and other local expenses.

TLACHQUIAUHCO (CODEX MENDOZA, 45R)

1. Tlachquiauco   Tlaxiaco (SV, sec. 754).
                   Santa María Asunción Tlaxiaco, Oaxaca.
2. Achiotlan   Achiutla (SV, sec. 33).
                   San Miguel Achiutla, Oaxaca.
3. Çapotlan   Çapotitlan, barrio of Malinaltepec (SV, sec. 364).

This province is represented with the province of Coaixtlahuacan in Map 10-7. There is a reference to Tlachquiauhco in Torquemada's account of Ilhuicamina's war against Coaixtlahuacan. At that time Malinaltzin, king of Tlachquiauhco, informed Tenochtitlan that the people of Coaixtlahuacan had attacked his city, killing his people and the Mexicas who were there as a garrison. But, as Jiménez Moreno points out, it is doubtful that the Mexicas would have acquired Tlachquiauhco at that time; probably it was only a temporary alliance against Coaixtlahuacan.[195]

Neither Tlachquiauhco nor Achiotlan appears among the conquests of the Tenochca kings who preceded the second Moteuczoma, nor are they listed in the "Memorial de Tlacopan." In several sources Moteuczoma Xocoyotzin is credited with the conquest of these two towns and of nearby Malinaltepec (present-day San Bartolomé Yucuañe), which probably was conquered at the same time,[196] the reason why one of its barrios, Tzapotlan (3) (Tzapotitlan) appears in this province.

Tlachquiauhco was the goal of an important campaign by Moteuczoma Xocoyotzin. According to the chronicles of Durán and Tezozomoc, it was provoked by Tlachquiauhco's attack on people who traveled within its boundaries when taking tribute to Tenochtitlan. These were, according to Durán, people from Coaixtlahuacan and the Mexica calpixques with them; Tezozomoc says the same, but adds people from the Tierra Caliente and Huaxyacac. The victorious Mexicas imposed tribute payments on Tlachquiauhco and the obligation to provide food and lodging to those who passed through there with the tribute from the coast, Huaxyacac, and Tecuantepec. In Tlachquiauhco they left "collectors and a Mexica principal to keep them as subjects and rule over them." In other words, the tributary province of Tlachquiauhco was established at that time.[197]

Torquemada's account is different; he attributes the Mexica attack to Moteuczoma Xocoyotzin's having asked Malinal, king of Tlachquiauhco, for a *tlapalizquixochitl* tree. The infuriated king refused, insisting that his land extended to "the smoking volcano." Moteuczoma's response was war; he killed Malinal and appropriated not only his gardens but also his towns, and on the way back to Tenochtitlan he conquered the people of Achiotlan.[198] Tlachquiauhco is not quite on the route from Coaixtlahuacan to Tenochtitlan, but its zone of influence must have been extensive if, as King Malinal alleged, his boundaries went as far as Popocatepetl. Achiotlan and Malinaltepec were perhaps its allies.[199] In Tezozomoc's account, the army of the Empire came to the boundaries of Tlachquiauhco in Acotepec (*sic*), a town that is not easily identified.[200]

The towns in this province are not listed in the "Memorial de Tlacopan." Perhaps, as a late conquest of Moteuczoma Xocoyotzin, then at the peak of his power, this province belonged exclusively to Tenochtitlan.

Paragraph 7.2 in the "Memorial de Tlacopan," Headed by Cozcatlan

Paragraph 7.2 is the most extensive of all the paragraphs in the "Memorial de Tlacopan." Most of its many towns are clustered in the Mixteca Alta and Baja, in the valley of the Río Salado, and in La Cañada; others are in the area of Cuauhtochco and Cuetlaxtlan or along the lower Papaloapan River. Between these two groups there is an empty space that to a large extent corresponds to the tributary province of Tochtepec. Table 10-2 lists all the towns in paragraph 7.2, and Map 10-9 represents them together with other towns mentioned in the following discussion.

As can be seen in the table, a number of towns are listed in one or another of five tributary provinces in the Codex Mendoza. There are five towns in Coaixtlahuacan, four in Tochtepec, three in Coyolapan, two (or three) in Cuauhtochco, and two in Cuetlaxtlan. Many other towns not in the Codex Mendoza are within the territory encompassed by these five provinces. There are also many important towns in the Mixteca Baja and the valley of the Río Salado, in areas that are completely absent in the Codex Mendoza. This paragraph of the "Memorial de Tlacopan" is the only one that includes towns in the Codex Mendoza provinces of Coaixtlahuacan and Cuauhtochco. Several towns of three other Codex Mendoza provinces—Cuetlaxtlan, Coyolapan, and Tochtepec—including the cabeceras of the first two, are listed in paragraph 7.2, but these provinces also overlap with

TABLE 10-2.

Paragraph 7.2 in the "Memorial de Tlacopan," Headed by Cozcatlan

"Memorial de Tlacopan"*	Codex Mendoza†	Identification
1. Cozcatlan		Cuzcatlan (SV, sec. 127; RG 5:93ff.). Coxcatlan, Puebla.
2. Teteltitlan		Teteltitlan, in Tepexic (Jäcklein 1978:191, 250, 262). San Lucas Teteletitlan, in Atexcal, Puebla.
3. Maçateopan		Mazateopan, estancia of Cozcatlan (RG 5:98). Mazateopan in San Sebastián Tlacotepec, Puebla.
4. Petlaapan		Petlapa, estancia of Cozcatlan (RG 5:99). Petlapa in San Sebastián Tlacotepec, Puebla.
5. Quauhtochco	Cuauhtochco (Cuauhtochco, 1)	Huatusco, Veracruz.
6. Tlatlac tetelco	Quauhtetelco (Cuauhtochco, 6)	Tlatlatelco (SV, sec. 843). Cuauhtetelco in the Mendoza (Gerhard 1986:85–86).
7. Matlatlan		Matlatlan (SV, sec. 350). Maltrata, Veracruz.
8. Tenexapan		(?) Tenejapan, in Huatusco, Veracruz (RO, 16) A frequent toponym in Veracruz; there are also Tenejapa de Mata, San Andrés Tenejapa, and others.
9. Teouacan		Teguacan (SV, sec. 510). Tehuacan, Puebla.
10. Tzaputitlan		Çapotitlan (SV, sec. 130; PNE 5:223). Zapotitlan, Puebla.
11. Eztepec		(?) Santa Ana Yeztepec, estancia of Tecuicuilco, Oaxaca. (RG 3: map following p. 94; the transcription on the verso is erroneous).
12. Chillan		Chila (RG 5:42). Present-day Chila, Puebla, or San Gabriel Chilac, Puebla, or Chila de la Sal, Puebla.
13. Tepexic		Tepexic, estancia of Petlatzinco (RG 5:32, 47). Tepejillo, in Petlalcingo, Puebla.

Table 10-2 continued

"Memorial de Tlacopan"*	Codex Mendoza†	Identification
14. Petlatzinco		Petalcingo (SV, sec. 447; RG 5:47). Petlalcingo, Puebla.
15. Acatepec		Acatepeque, sujeto of Tzapotitlan (PNE 5:224). Acatepec, in Caltepec, Puebla.
16. Atzompan		Azumba, sujeto of Tzapotitla (PNE 5:224). San Pedro Atzumba, in Zapotitlan, Puebla.
17. Caltzintenco		(?) In the Mixteca, under the influence of Tzapotitlan (Gerhard 1986:268).
18. Metzontlan		Mezontla, sujeto of Tzapotitla (PNE 5:224) Los Reyes Metzontla, in Zapotitlan, Puebla.
19. Axalpan		Ajalpan, Puebla.
20. Pochotitlan		Not identified.
21. Axocopan		Axocapan, in Guatusco (Gerhard 1986:85–86). Axocoapan, Veracruz.
22. Tlaliztacan		Santa María Tlalixtac, Oaxaca, in the district of Cuicatlán.
23. Miyauatlan		San José Miahuatlan, Puebla.
24. Teotitlan		Teutitlan (SV, sec. 508; RG 3:195). Teotitlan del Camino, Oaxaca.
25. Ohuatlan		(?) Guautla, sujeto of Teotitlan (RG 3:197–98). Huautla de Jiménez, Oaxaca.
26. Tenanco		Tenango, sujeto of Teotitlan (RG 3:197–98). San José Tenango, Oaxaca.
27. Maçatlan		Sujeto of Teotitlan (RG 3:197–98). Mazatlán de Flores, Oaxaca.
28. Tecolotlan		Tecolutla, sujeto of Teotitlan (RG 3:197–98). Tecolutlan or Los Kúes (Ciudad Real 1976, 1:165). San Juan Los Cúes, Oaxaca.
29. Nanauaticpac		Nanautipac (SV, sec. 401), sujeto of Teotitlan (RG 3:197–98). San Antonio Nanahuatipan, Oaxaca.

Table 10-2 continued

"Memorial de Tlacopan"*	Codex Mendoza†	Identification
30. Nextepec		Nextepec (SV, sec. 400). Sujeto of Teotitlan (RG 3:197–98).
31. Quiyotepec		Quiotepeque (SV, sec. 478; RG 2:235). Santiago Quiotepec, in San Juan Bautista Cuicatlán, Oaxaca.
32. Tecciztepec		Sujeto of Quiotepec (RG 2:236).
33. Coyollan		Sujeto of Quiotepec (RG 2:236). San Juan Coyula, in San Juan Bautista Cuicatlán, Oaxaca.
34. Etlantonco		Etlantongo (SV, sec. 249; RG 2:366). San Mateo Etlatongo, Oaxaca.
35. Coçollan *(sic)*		Çocola *(sic)* estancia of Tecomahuaca (SV, sec. 760). Coçolan (RG 2: maps following pp. 226, 236).
36. Nacaztlan		(?) Hasta, estancia of Tecomahuaca (SV, sec. 760). Aztatl (RG 2: maps following pp. 226, 236).
37. Tecomauacan		Tecomauaca (SV, sec. 760; RG 2:236). Santa María Tecomavaca, Oaxaca.
38. Pochotepec		Estancia of Tecomahuacan (SV, sec. 760). Pochotepec, in Mazatlán de Flores, Oaxaca.
39. Cuicatlan	Cuicatlan (Coayxtlahuacan, 11)	San Juan Bautista Cuicatlan, Oaxaca.
40. Ichcatlan		Ixcatlan (RG 2:227) Santa María Ixcatlan, Oaxaca. Cf. Ichcatlan in paragraph 6.3-20.
41. Papaloticpac		Papaloticpac (SV, sec. 475; RG 3:27). Concepción Pápalo, Oaxaca.
42. Atl ypitzauayan		Alpitzahua (RG 2:48). Alpitzauac or Don Dominguillo (Ciudad Real 1976, 1:166). Santiago Dominguillo, in San Juan B. Cuicatlan, Oaxaca.
43. Coçollan *(sic)*		Çoçola (SV, sec. 150). San Jerónimo Sosola, Oaxaca.

Table 10-2 continued

"Memorial de Tlacopan"*	Codex Mendoza†	Identification
44. Apouallan		Apuala (SV, sec. 86; RG 2:213). Santiago Apoala, Oaxaca.
45. Quatlauiztlan		Cotlahuixtla (RG 2:156). San Francisco Cotahuixtla in Santiago Nacaltepec, Oaxaca.
46. Quauhxilotitlan	Quauhxilotitlan (Coyolapan, 3)	San Pablo Huitzo, Oaxaca.
47. Atl tlatlacan		Atlatlauca (SV, sec. 87; RG 2:47). San Juan Atlatlauca, Oaxaca.
48. Nanacatepec		Nanalcatepec (RG 2:156, 214). Santiago Nacaltepec, Oaxaca.
49. Hapazco		Yapazco (SV, sec. 86). Subject to Guaxilotitlan (RG 2:213). Magdalena Apasco, Oaxaca.
50. Tlacpac		Not identified.
51. Cuetlaxtlan	Cuetlaxtlan (Cuetlaxtlan, 1)	Cotaxtla, Veracruz.
52. Teociyoc	Teoçiocan (Cuetlaxtlan, 6)	Tlalixcoya, Veracruz.
53. Tlacotlalpan	Tlacotlalpan (Tochtepec, 22)	Tlacotlalpa, Veracruz.
54. Coçamaloapan	Coçamaloapan (Tochtepec, 4)	Cozamaloapan, Veracruz.
55. Matlaquetzaloyan		Not identified.
56. Toztlan	Toztla (Tochtepec, 21)	San Andrés Tuxtla, Veracruz.
57. Copilco		Not identified. See the text concerning this town.
58. Couaixtlauacan	Coayxtlahuacan (Coayxtlahuacan, 1)	San Juan Bautista Coixtlahuaca, Oaxaca.
59. Tepeuitzillan		Tepeuçila (SV, sec. 765; RG 3:33). Tepeucila, Oaxaca.

Table 10-2 continued

"Memorial de Tlacopan"*	Codex Mendoza[†]	Identification
60. Teotilillan	Teotililan (Tochtepec, 9)	San Pedro Teutila, Oaxaca.
61. Tecuicuilco		Tecuquilco (SV, sec. 646; RG 3:87). Teococuilco, Oaxaca.
62. Comaltianquizco		Estancia of Papaloticpac (RG 3:28).
63. Tecomatepec		Tecomaltepec (SV, sec. 769). San Juan Tecomaltepec, east of Teotlillan (Gerhard 1986:310; Weitlaner y Castro 1954:190 [map], 196).
64. Tototlan		(?) Santa Cruz Tepetotutla in San Felipe Usila, Oaxaca, or possibly Totutla, Veracruz (Tototlan in Cuauhtochco, 3).
65. Vitzillan		Vcila (SV, sec. 793; RG 3:232). San Felipe Ucila, Oaxaca.
66. Yancuitlan	Yancuitlan (Coayxtlahuacan, 4)	Santo Domingo Yanhuitlan, Oaxaca.
67. Nocheztlan	Nochiztlan (Coayxtlahuacan, 6)	Asunción Nochiztlan, Oaxaca.
68. Tepozcolotlan	Tepuzcululan (Coayxtlahuacan, 5)	San Pedro y San Pablo Tepozcolula, Oaxaca.
69. Etlan	Etlan (Coyolapan, 2)	San Pedro y San Pablo Etla, Oaxaca.
70. Coyolapan	(Coyolapan, 1)	Cuilapan de Guerrero, Oaxaca. or San Francisco Coyolapa, subject to Nanahuaticpac (RG 3:197). Cf. 6.6-6

*Towns are numbered according to their sequence in the list (Zimmermann 1970:8).
[†]Names of the towns in the Codex Mendoza are followed in parentheses by the name of the province in which each is located and its place in the sequence of towns as depicted in the codex.

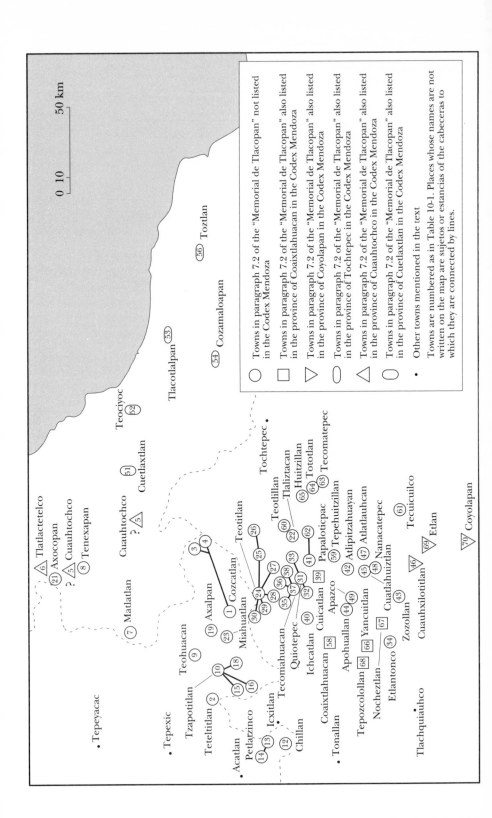

Towns in paragraph 7.2 of the "Memorial de Tlacopan" not listed in the Codex Mendoza

Towns in paragraph 7.2 of the "Memorial de Tlacopan" also listed in the province of Coaixtlahuacan in the Codex Mendoza

Towns in paragraph 7.2 of the "Memorial de Tlacopan" also listed in the province of Coyolapan in the Codex Mendoza

Towns in paragraph 7.2 of the "Memorial de Tlacopan" also listed in the province of Tochtepec in the Codex Mendoza

Towns in paragraph 7.2 of the "Memorial de Tlacopan" also listed in the province of Cuauhtochco in the Codex Mendoza

Towns in paragraph 7.2 of the "Memorial de Tlacopan" also listed in the province of Cuetlaxtlan in the Codex Mendoza

Other towns mentioned in the text

Towns are numbered as in Table 10-1. Places whose names are not written on the map are sujetos or estancias of the cabeceras to which they are connected by lines.

other paragraphs in the "Memorial de Tlacopan": Tochtepec is represented in paragraph 6.3 (Tochtepec), Cuetlaxtlan in 7.1 (Cempohuallan), and Coyolapan in 7.4 (Oztoman).

Local sources, especially the relaciones geográficas, describe some of these towns and neighboring areas as subject to the Empire, but only exceptionally do they give the name of the cabecera to which the town brought its tribute. These data have been cited above in the discussion of each of the provinces in the Codex Mendoza.

In the Codex Mendoza, towns in the Mixteca Alta are included in the provinces of Coaixtlahuacan and Tlachquiauhco. In paragraph 7.2 of the "Memorial de Tlacopan" there are four towns, Coaixtlahuacan (58), Yancuitlan (66), Nocheztlan (67), and Tepozcolollan (68), all of them in the province of Coaixtlahuacan; Tlachquiauhco is not included in the "Memorial de Tlacopan." There are also several towns in this paragraph that are in the same region although they are absent in the Codex Mendoza: Etlantonco (34), Ichcatlan (40), Zozollan (43), Apohuallan (44), and Apazco (49).

Cuicatlan (39) is also in the province of Coaixtlahuacan; it is the only Cuicatec town present in Codex Mendoza. The "Memorial de Tlacopan" lists many more Cuicatec towns: Quiotepec (31) with two sujetos (32 and 33), Tecomahuacan (37) with three estancias (35, 36, and 38), Papaloticpac (41) with one estancia (62), Atlapitzahuayan (42), Cuatlahuiztlan (45), Atlatlauhcan (47), Nanacatepec (48), and Tepehuitzillan (59). Some of these towns are also described in the relaciones geográficas and have been discussed in the section on Coaixtlahuacan.

Towns from the Cuauhtochco province in the Codex Mendoza that are included in this paragraph are Cuauhtochco itself (5), Tlatlactetelco (6), and perhaps Tototlan (64). Other towns in the same region are Matlatlan (7), situated near Ahuilizapan—which is in the province of Cuauhtochco—Tenexapan (8), and Axocopan (21).

Areas adjacent to the above regions—the valley of the Río Salado, and the Mixteca Baja—are well represented in this paragraph. The list begins with the valley of the Salado, which is the area where the Nonoalcas settled after they left Tollan.[201] It includes Cozcatlan (1), Teohuacan (9), Axalpan (19), Miahuatlan (23), and Teotitlan (del Camino, 24), towns that rarely figure among the conquests of the Empire. Only Muñoz Camargo gives as conquered Teohuacan, Cozcatlan, and Teotitlan,[202] while Ixtlilxochitl names Teohuacan as a conquest of Nezahualcoyotl.[203] None of these towns are included in the provinces of the Codex Mendoza.

Cozcatlan, which begins the list in this paragraph, is not cited in any source as a town of importance in the imperial organization and does not appear in the lists of conquests. However, an allusion in Tezozomoc indicates that there were settlers from the Basin of Mexico there, just as in Huaxyacac and Yancuitlan.[204] This could explain why it appears in the "Memorial de Tlacopan" as the cabecera of the towns in this paragraph. In addition to Cozcatlan, two of its estancias, Maza-teopan (3) and Petlaapan (4), are listed.

The relación geográfica of Teotitlan del Camino (24) states that "they were a commonwealth all by themselves, allied with Montezuma; they did not pay him anything."[205] Among its sujetos were Ohuatlan (25), Tenanco (26), Mazatlan (27), Tecolotlan (28), Nanahuaticpac (29), and Nextepec (30), which come after Teoti-tlan in this list.

The towns in the Mixteca Baja included in this paragraph are Tzapotitlan (10), with its sujetos Acatepec (15), Atzompan (16), and Metzontlan (18); Chillan (12); and Petlatzinco (14). The last two towns are described in the relación geo-gráfica of Acatlan, which gives important information on various towns. This ma-terial is therefore presented here.[206]

The relación of Chillan states that it was subject to the Empire, but it neither paid tribute to the king of Tenochtitlan nor recognized his position in any way ex-cept that the rulers of Chillan, when they so pleased, sent presents of gold jewels and cloaks to the king, who sent them presents in return.[207]

Petlatzinco, according to its relación, was also subject to the Empire but paid no tribute except that it was obliged to give provisions to the imperial armies that went through the town; it also provided some warriors, but nothing else.[208]

Other towns described in the relación geográfica of Acatlan, but which are lacking in the Codex Mendoza and the "Memorial de Tlacopan," are Acatlan it-self, Icxitlan, and Piaztlan. Acatlan and Piaztlan were conquered by Nezahual-coyotl and Moteuczoma Ilhuicamina.[209] The town of Acatlan was said to have been settled by "a son of a king of Mexico" who had subjugated the surrounding territory as far as Tototepec. Since their leaders were descendants of "the royal blood of the kings of Mexico," the town paid no tribute, but in recognition of the king of Tenochtitlan as their "supreme lord," when his armies passed through they were given provisions and weapons, and for this purpose there was a special store-house in the town. Now and then when the lords of Acatlan sent cloaks and the skins of hares and rabbits as gifts to the king of Tenochtitlan, he sent in return "gifts of cloaks and other things made in Mexico." The town was also required to keep two noblemen, with their wives, in the royal palace of Tenochtitlan in the king's service. They were replaced every eighty days and took with them from Acatlan whatever they needed for themselves.[210]

The people of Icxitlan, although subject to Tenochtitlan, gave no tribute other than gifts of feathers, precious stones, and live snakes to feed the birds in the king's collection. They also provided food and weapons to the Mexica warriors who passed through there, and some people of the town went with them.[211]

Chillan carried on wars with Petlatzinco, Atoyac, and Tonallan; Petlatzinco fought with Tecciztepec and Acatlan; Acatlan was at war with Itzocan and Tepeyacac; and Piaztlan fought with Tepexic and Acatlan.[212] All these towns, subject in one way or another to Tenochtitlan, fought one another. Probably imperial dominion was not total, but limited to the obligations specified in these reports.

In this same region are found the southernmost towns in the province of Tepeyacac in the Codex Mendoza, although none of them are listed in this paragraph of the "Memorial de Tlacopan." As is shown in Table 10-2, only a few towns in this paragraph are found in the other provinces of the Codex Mendoza (Coyolapan, Tochtepec, and Cuetlaxtlan) with which it overlaps.

The three towns in Coyolapan are the cabecera (70), Etlan (69), and Cuauhxilotitlan (46), all three Mixtec towns, which occupy the northernmost part of this tributary province. We have seen that Cuauhxilotitlan also took tribute to Coaixtlahuacan. Tecuicuilco (61), in the Tzapotec mountains, although not registered in the Codex Mendoza is also connected with the province of Coyolapan, since it paid tribute to Huaxyacac, located in that province.[213]

The four towns in Tochtepec are in two different parts of the province: Tlacotlalpan (53), Cozamaloapan (54), and Toztlan (56) are on the Gulf coast, and Teotlillan (60) is in the mountains between La Cañada and the Chinantec area. The sequence of the list suggests that Tepehuitzillan (59), Comaltianquizco (62), Tecomatepec (63), and Huitzillan (65) had been associated with Teotlillan. Tlaliztacan (22) is in the same area if the proposed identification is valid. Copilco (57) was perhaps an extension of the group of towns on the coast. Although it is far away, in Tabasco, it is near Chilapan, which is said to have belonged to Tetzcoco.[214] The two towns in this paragraph that are also in the province of Cuetlaxtlan in the Codex Mendoza are the cabecera (51) and Teociyoc (52).

In comparison with the Codex Mendoza and other Tenochca sources, this paragraph in the "Memorial de Tlacopan" expands the area dominated by the Triple Alliance considerably. It is noteworthy that in the region that is missing completely in the Codex Mendoza—the Mixteca Baja and the Tehuacan Valley—there are several towns that were said to be allies of the Empire or that gave no tribute other than provisions for the armies as they passed by and military assistance. As has been said, if these towns did not send tribute in kind to Tenochtitlan, this could explain why they are not registered in the Codex Mendoza. On the other hand, important towns listed in the Codex Mendoza, such as Tlachquiauhco and Achiotlan, are not included in the "Memorial de Tlacopan," nor is Teotzacualco, whose relación geográfica gives it as a tributary of the Empire. Perhaps these towns paid tribute exclusively to Tenochtitlan and not to the three capitals of the Empire.

Thus, paragraph 7.2 is not the sum of several provinces in the Codex Mendoza, as was the case of paragraph 7.3 (Tlachmalacac). It is an amplification of the provinces of Coaixtlahuacan and Cuauhtochco in the Codex Mendoza by the addition of towns in Coyolapan, Cuetlaxtlan and Tochtepec. This suggests that it corresponds to the conquests of Moteuczoma Ilhuicamina. These towns may have been part of the defeated empire of Coaixtlahuacan and came under the power of the Triple Alliance at the same time.

Paragraph 7.4 in the "Memorial de Tlacopan," Headed by Oztoman

The towns in paragraph 7.4 are in various unconnected areas. The towns in the central valleys of present-day Oaxaca form the principal nucleus, immediately recognizable. However, Oztoman, which heads the list, is the town and fortress on the frontier with Michoacan, and several other towns are on the coast of present-day Guerrero, from the vicinity of Acapolco to the frontier with the Mixtec kingdom of Tototepec in southern Oaxaca. Table 10-3 lists the towns in paragraph 7.4 of the "Memorial de Tlacopan." Map 10-10 contains all of these towns that have been identified and some others mentioned in the discussion; the relevant provinces in the Codex Mendoza are shown in Maps 10-1, 10-7, and 10-8.

In this paragraph two towns are listed that also appear in the tributary province of Tepecuacuilco and five in that of Coyolapan. All the other towns that have been identified are south of the Balsas River in areas not registered in the Codex Mendoza. That leaves three towns not yet identified. Çomatlan (4) is not a known toponym.[215] Tloapan (12) is a correct Nahuatl name ("Sparrow-hawk River"), but it has not been identified; it is also in the list of conquests by Moteuczoma Xocoyotzin in Sahagún.[216] The toponym Xicochimalco (18) is known only in Veracruz. Here it probably denotes another town with the same name, perhaps the Xicochimalco conquered by Ahuitzotl, since it is listed with towns in Pacific coastal areas.[217]

Although they occupy a very large and discontinuous area, the towns listed in paragraph 7.4, like some others in the "Memorial de Tlacopan," are in general arranged geographically, but with some inconsistencies. Starting from Oztoman in the west, the list changes course to the central valleys of Oaxaca and then turns back to the west, ending on the coast of Guerrero. However, there is one town in the west—Ciuapoualoyan (10)—listed among the towns in the valleys, and there are three others not identified. With the possible exception of Huaxyacac, paragraph 7.4 comprises conquests by Ahuitzotl and Moteuczoma Xocoyotzin incorporated into the Empire later than the regions represented in paragraphs 7.2 and 7.3.

In addition to conquering Oztoman and establishing a garrison there, Ahuitzotl went on to the Pacific coast, the area of the tributary province of Cihuatlan, conquered Tlappan, and consolidated imperial power in the Valley of Oaxaca. These conquests would be the base from which to continue the war against Yopitzinco and the towns on the Pacific coast listed in this paragraph of the

"Memorial de Tlacopan." Later, Moteuczoma Xocoyotzin made new conquests in areas already penetrated by Ahuitzotl.

The *Relaciones geográficas* and the lists of conquests of the Tenochca kings provide additional information on the towns listed in this paragraph that are not found in the Codex Mendoza and on some others in their vicinity. The following information is from reports on the regions where towns have been identified: Oztoman, the mountain area south of the Balsas toward Acapulco, the Costa Chica, and the central valleys of Oaxaca.

Oztoman is a toponym seldom found, and there is no evidence that it existed in Oaxaca;[218] it must be the name of the town and fortress on the Tarascan frontier. It is very far from most of the other towns, and one would expect to find it in paragraph 7.3 (Tlachmalacac), which includes the tributary province of Tepecuacuilco, within which Oztoman is listed in the Codex Mendoza. Nevertheless, the presence in this paragraph of other towns in Guerrero supports the proposed location. This is one more example of overlapping between the territorial units of the "Memorial de Tlacopan" and those of the Codex Mendoza.

The location of Coçollan (2) is somewhat doubtful, because the use of the cedilla is sometimes erroneous in this document. I take it to be Cocollan (Cocula, Guerrero), near Oztoman.[219]

South of the Balsas, in the mountainous region northwest of Acapolco, there is a town called Citlaltomahuacan that was subject to the Empire and paid tribute in slaves, cloaks, and gold dust.[220] It can be identified with the Tlatomahuacan (16) in this paragraph.[221] Farther south, the location given for Xaltianquizco (17) agrees with that of other towns in this paragraph that are on the Pacific coast.[222] Between these two towns and Oztoman lies the mountainous region south of the Balsas and north of the province of Cihuatlan and Acapolco, about which the *Relaciones geográficas* provide information.

Tetellan, on the bank of the Balsas River, was one of several Cuitlateca towns that formerly never had a ruler, although there were principals among them whom they respected to some extent, "more in time of war, because they were captains." When Ahuitzotl threatened them, they surrendered peacefully, and from then on the rulers of Tenochtitlan had a governor in the town who, together with two or three principals, natives of the town, served as judges and settled disputes. The town gave no tribute to the kings of Tenochtitlan, but served them in the war against Michoacan and against the towns of Axochitlan, Tlacotepec, and Totollan.[223] The ruler of Michoacan kept a garrison in Acaxochitlan, on the frontier with Tetellan and Calpollalcopolco, which belonged to Moteuczoma.[224]

Farther south, the Tepoztec-speaking people of Tlacotepec were ruled by their own king until Moteuczoma conquered them and sent a captain with men to establish a garrison and to rule both as governor and as steward to collect the trib-

TABLE 10-3.

Paragraph 7.4 of the "Memorial de Tlacopan," Headed by Oztoman

"Memorial de Tlacopan"*	Codex Mendoza†	Identification
1. Oztoman	Oztoman (Tepecuacuilco, 11)	Oztoman, in Guerrero.
2. Coçollan	Cocolan (Tepecuacuilco, 7)	(?) Cocula, Guerrero. Cf. 7.2-35, 72.-33, 7.3-16.
3. Teotitlantzinco		Teutitlan (RG 2:333). Teotitlan del Valle, Oaxaca.
4. Çomatlan		Not identified.
5. Octlan	Octlan (Coyolapan, 8)	Ocotlan de Morelos, Oaxaca.
6. Vaxxacac	Guaxaca (Coyolapan, 4)	Oaxaca, Oaxaca.
7. Tlaliztacan		Talistaca (SV, sec. 846; RG 3:73). Tlalixtac de Cabrera, Oaxaca.
8. Teticpac	Teticpac (Coyolapan, 9)	Magdalena Teitipac, Oaxaca.
9. Couatlan		Coatlan (SV, sec. 849; RG 2:81). San Sebastian Coatlan, Oaxaca.
10. Ciuapoualoyan		Cihuapaloya, in Cuautepec, Guerrero.
11. Çimatlan		Çimatlan (SV, sec. 230; RG 2:269, 270). Zimatlan de Alvarez, Oaxaca.
12. Tloapan		Not identified.
13. Macuilxochitlan	Macuilxochic (Coyolapan, 11)	San Mateo Macuilxóchitl, in Tlacochahuaya de Morelos, Oaxaca.
14. Tlacuechauayan	Tlalcuechahuayan (Coyolapan, 10)	Tlacochahuaya de Morelos, Oaxaca.
15. Miyauatlan		Miaguatlan (SV, sec. 851; RG 2:73). Miahuatlan de Porfirio Díaz, Oaxaca.

Table 10-3 continued

"Memorial de Tlacopan"* Codex Mendoza†	Identification
16. Tlatomauacan	Citlaltomahua or Citlaltomahuacan, northwest of Acapolco (RG 6:109–22).
17. Xaltianquizco	Xaltianquizco, estancia of Zalzapotla [Xaltzapotlan] (DA, 149). Xaltianguis, in Acapulco de Juárez, Guerrero.
18. Xicochimalco	Not identified.
19. Ayotlan	Ayutla (SV, sec. 28; RG 3:284, 286, 288). Ayutla de los Libres, Guerrero.

*Towns are numbered according to their sequence in the list (Zimmermann 1970:8).
†Names of the towns in the Codex Mendoza are followed in parentheses by the name of the province in which each is located and its place in the sequence of towns as depicted in the codex.

ute. Traditionally, Tlacotepec had waged war with towns along the coast—Tecpan, Acamalotla, Temazcaltepec, and others. At times Tlacotepec asked the Mexicas for help against the others; at other times, if the Mexicas had offended them, they allied themselves with the coastal people against the Mexicas.[225] Torquemada reports that in the eleventh year of the reign of Moteuczoma Xocoyotzin the Yopitzinca rebelled and tried to kill by treachery all the Mexicas in the garrison of Tlacotepec; they failed in the attempt and lost two hundred warriors, who were taken prisoner.[226] Tlacotepec is listed as a conquest of Ahuitzotl; it could be the town that concerns us here, but the toponym is so frequent that nothing can be taken as certain.[227]

In Otlatlan (Utatlan), also a Tepoztec-speaking town, there was no remembrance of anyone who had formerly been their ruler; they surrendered peacefully to Moteuczoma when they saw that he had subjugated neighboring towns and paid tribute to him in cloaks. They carried on wars with Tlacotepec and Tetellan.[228]

Tlacotepec, Otlatlan, and Citlaltomahuacan probably mark the route of the imperial armies to the Pacific coast, both towards the province of Cihuatlan and to the east, by way of Xaltianquizco, to Acapolco and the Costa Chica.

Acapolco and the Yopi region were near Xaltianquizco (17). Acapolco was conquered by Ahuitzotl, along with several other coastal towns,[229] although none of them are listed in the sources on tribute. Yopitzinco was never conquered; it is not clear whether the toponym denotes only a region or also a specific town.[230]

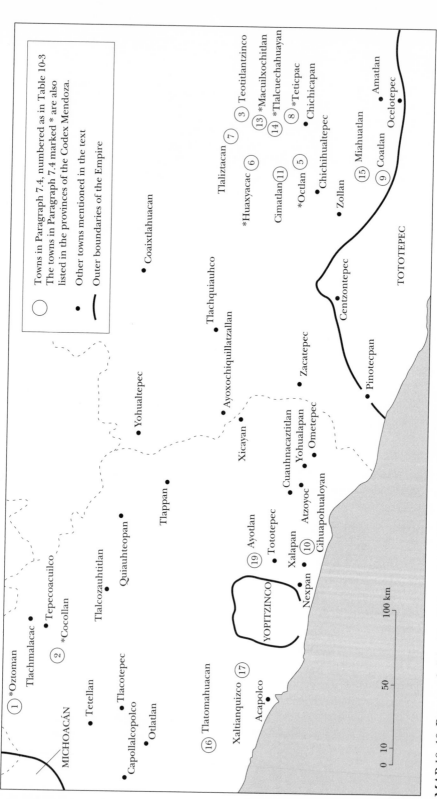

MAP 10–10. Paragraph 7.4 of the "Memorial de Tlacopan," headed by Oztoman

The extent of the territory of the independent Yopis was less than that which Barlow indicates in his map of the Empire:[231] probably it was not a hindrance to the Mexicas on their way from Xaltianquizco and Acapolco to the Costa Chica.[232] Yopitzinco, Acapolco, and Acatepec are named among the towns not subjugated by the Empire,[233] although the conquests reviewed here took place in those areas. Acatepec, or Acatl iyacac, is perhaps the Acatepec located in Ometepec, Guerrero, and it is also listed as conquered by Ahuitzotl. The toponym Acatepec occurs frequently, but this identification is supported by its place in the lists of conquests together with the coastal towns.[234]

East of Acapolco and Yopitzinco, the Costa Chica of Guerrero is represented in paragraph 7.4, although it is completely absent in the Codex Mendoza. Among the towns in this area Ayotlan (19) is identified in the table with the present-day Ayutla de los Libres, Guerrero.[235] This identification is strengthened by the fact that this town was subject to the Empire and that the Nahuatl-speaking inhabitants of its neighbor, Tototepec, were Mexicas sent there to man Moteuczoma's garrison.[236] Ayotlan had several maritime towns as sujetos, all of which paid to Moteuczoma gold, gourds, deer skins, fish, cotton, and jaguar skins,[237] products comparable to those paid by several distant provinces, but without the grain and cloaks that were given by Coyolapan.

Cihuapohualoyan (10) was conquered by Moteuczoma Xocoyotzin. According to Torquemada, in the thirteenth year of the reign of Moteuczoma (that is, 1514) the Mexicas went forth against Cihuapohualoyan and Cuezcomaixtlahuacan; they razed the first of these two, but the people of Cuezcomaixtlahuacan fled and fortified themselves in a town called Quetzaltepec. Two years later the three kings of the alliance made war against Quetzaltepec and Iztactlalocan, vanquished them, and made them subject to the Empire.[238] The lists of conquests of Moteuczoma Xocoyotzin give neither locations nor dates for the battles in these towns,[239] but Torquemada's account suggests that they were all in the same area. Barlow identified Cuezcomaixtlahuacan as a sujeto of Yohualapan (Igualapa, Guerrero); from this he deduced that the other towns, conquered at the same time, must have been nearby.[240] In addition, Cihuapohualoyan occurs in modern toponyms of the area, and Iztactlalocan could be another name for Xicayan de Tovar, which is—more towards the interior—in the province of Yohualtepec in the Codex Mendoza (see p. 282).

The sources that register the conquest of Quetzaltepec do not indicate exactly where it was, but the chronicles of Durán and Tezozomoc give in some detail an account of the campaign against Quetzaltepec and Tototepec, which formed a political unit or, at least, were allied against the Mexicas.[241] The identification of these towns has led to varying interpretations.[242] In the Codex Teleriano-Remensis it is said that in the year 8 Calli 1513, "the Mexicas subjugated Tototepec, a province eighty leagues from Mexico near the south sea."[243] However, the identification is only approximate, since it is not said whether the reference is to the Mixtec kingdom on the coast or to the Tototepec near Ayotlan, where there was a Mexica garrison, or to some other town with the same name. Ahuitzotl also vanquished a town called Tototepec, according to the lists of conquests, which probably was the Tototepec near Ayotlan, since Ahuitzotl also conquered Acapulco. His other conquests in this area are discussed below.[244]

In the accounts of Durán and Tezozomoc the imperial armies, before reaching Tototepec and Quetzaltepec, met to replenish their supplies at Xaltianquizco, which must be the town, near Acapolco, included in paragraph 7.4.[245] This suggests again the Tototepec near Ayotlan. Quetzaltepec and Tototepec were near each other, alongside the Quetzalatl River.[246] Quetzaltepec was fortified, and the allied armies had to make ladders for their assault.[247] During the struggle most of the people of Tototepec perished; only women and children were left alive, and the victors took all those who had fled as captives. The people of Quetzaltepec fought furiously but finally had to surrender, offering to pay tribute. Nothing is said about the local rulers or the naming of calpixques. The Codex of Azoyú, which treats of this region, registers the conquest of this Tototepec in the years 1503 to 1509.[248] The capital of the Mixtec kingdom on the coast (present-day San Pedro Tututepec, Oaxaca) was much farther away and was never conquered.[249]

There is no Quetzaltepec to be found near the proposed Tototepec; the well-known town of that name is in the Mixe area, the present-day San Miguel Quetzaltepec, Oaxaca. However, on the coast there is a Quetzalapan that might be its equivalent, given that in the chronicles the association of the town with the Quetzalatl River is evident. The river today called Quetzala flows down from the mountains to join the Río Grande, which disembogues in the area of the sandbar of Tecoanapa.[250] On its eastern side is Quetzalapan, former dependency of Igualapa,[251] today in Azoyú, Guerrero. According to these identifications Tototepec and Quetzaltepec would be relatively near each other, not so much as the accounts in the chronicles suggest but within an acceptable distance, given the slight geographical precision that these sources usually have.[252]

Although these reports place Quetzaltepec and Tototepec in the same area, the position of these two towns in the lists of conquests poses several problems of identification that the tribute documents do not solve.[253] Quetzaltepec is not listed in the provinces of the Codex Mendoza or in the "Memorial de Tlacopan," but there are several towns called Tototepec besides the one near Ayutla de los Libres. The Codex Mendoza lists a Tototepec in the tributary province of Tochtepec, and in the "Memorial de Tlacopan," Tototepec is the town that heads section 8, which comprises Tecuantepec and Xoconochco. The problem of the location of Quetzaltepec also requires, therefore, the identification of these other two Tototepecs, a problem that will be raised again later in connection with section 8 of the "Memorial de Tlacopan."

Ahuitzotl conquered many towns on the Pacific coast. Some towns on the lists of his conquests can be located in the region of the coast of Guerrero included in this paragraph (7.4) of the "Memorial de Tlacopan," but the *Relaciones geográficas* provide very little information. Later, Moteuczoma Xocoyotzin also carried out numerous conquests in Oaxaca. We have already seen the information relative to Tototepec, Quetzaltepec, and Cuezcomaixtlahuacan. Some other conquered towns may also have been part of this region. The best known of the towns conquered by Ahuitzotl is Acapolco, and there are no problems concerning its location. But in the lists of conquests there are some frequently encountered toponyms, and it is not always possible to be sure that they are the names of towns in this region. Another possible conquest of Ahuitzotl in this area is Tepechiapan, which is registered in the list of the Codex Mendoza but has not been identified satisfactorily. Other versions of the lists of conquests give in its place Nexpan or Xalapan, both situated on the coast of present-day Guerrero east of Acapolco. The relación geográfica of that region confirms the dominion of the Empire.[254] There is some doubt about the identification of Cuauhnacaztitlan, or Cuauhnacaztlan, which could be Guanacastitlan in San Luis Acatlán, Guerrero.[255]

Approximately half the towns in paragraph 7.4 are in the central valleys of Oaxaca and basically coincide with the province of Coyolapan in the Codex Mendoza. Five of the eleven towns in that province are in this paragraph: Octlan (5), Huaxyacac (6), Teticpan (8), Macuilxochic (13), and Tlacuechahuayan (14). Five others are listed that are not included in the Codex Mendoza: Teotitlan del Valle (3), Tlaliztacan (7), Coatlan (9), Cimatlan (11), and Miahuatlan (15). The last three extend more towards the southern part of the valleys than the towns in the tributary province of Coyolapan. On the other hand, Coyolapan itself, Etlan, and Quauhxillotitlan are not included here; in the "Memorial de Tlacopan" these towns are in paragraph 7.2, and all three are in the northern part of the province, inhabited by Mixtecs. The only towns in the province of Coyolapan in the Codex Mendoza that are not in the "Memorial de Tlacopan" are Teocuitlatlan, Cuatzontepec, and Camotlan.

The Valley of Oaxaca has been discussed, with additional material from other sources, when dealing with the province of Coyolapan in the Codex Mendoza. What follows here is information from the *Relaciones geográficas* on the towns in the southernmost part of the valleys not listed in the province of Coyolapan.

There is a relación that comprises Chichicapan, Amatlan, Miahuatlan, Coatlan, and Ocelotepec.[256] Miahuatlan (15) had its own ruler and was constantly at war with Coatlan and Ocelotepec until Moteuczoma sent governors for all these towns to arrange a peaceful settlement. As recognition of his authority, they gave him gold dust and jewelry.[257]

The people of Coatlan (9) had a ruler named Coatzin for many years until he offended them in some way and they rebelled against him. The principals sent parias to Moteuczoma, who took them under his protection and sent captains and soldiers to defend them against their enemies, for they were continually at war with the kingdom of Tototepec. Coatlan paid tribute to Moteuczoma in gold dust and cloaks, and he in turn took care to send men for the garrison there. The cacique Coatzin must have continued in place under Mexica dominion, for it is said that after the Spanish Conquest he was killed by the Spaniards for not bringing all the tribute that was due.[258] The historical chronicles allude to Coatlan only in the account of Moteuczoma Xocoyotzin's war against the people of Teuctepec, "who were confederated with Coatlan."[259] This might be a misunderstanding resulting from the fact that the captives of Teuctepec were sacrificed at the inauguration of the temple called Coatlan.[260]

Ocelotepec, in addition to having its own ruler, was subject to Moteuczoma. They gave him tribute of gold dust, cloaks, and cochineal, and he sent them other goods of greater value such as cloaks, sandals, and multicolored feathers that were highly esteemed. The people of Ocelotepec carried on wars with Mixes and Chontals, and when they captured a goodly number of prisoners, they sent some to Moteuczoma and sacrificed the rest.[261]

The other two towns covered in this relación are not described as subject to Moteuczoma. The people of Chichicapan were ruled by the king of Teotzapotlan, who was the "universal lord" of all Tzapotecs. The Mixtec were at war with them when the Spanish arrived, and only then did they all join together to help Moteuczoma.[262] The people of Amatlan had a ruler of their own, and they used to be at war with the men of Moteuczoma's garrison in Huaxyacac; they never fought with the other neighboring towns.[263]

The lists of Moteuczoma Xocoyotzin's conquests include towns in the southern part of the valleys, such as Çollan (Sola de Vega, Oaxaca) and Centzontepec (Santa Cruz Zenzontepec, Oaxaca). Perhaps some others, not well identified, should be considered here, as, for example, Chichihualtatacallan (possibly Santa María Chichihualtepec, Oaxaca) and Itzcuintepec, which could be one of the Peñoles towns.[264]

Paragraph 7.4 also makes clear the need to examine the frontiers of the Empire with the Mixtec kingdom of Tototepec south of the central valleys, in the isthmus, and in the Costa Chica.[265] According to the relación of Cuahuitlan, which also treats of Pinotecpan, Potutla, and Icpatepec, these towns were formerly subject to Moteuczoma, "although some say [they were subject] to the king of Tototepec," a statement that is not very useful for defining the boundaries of these two polities.[266] Coatolco (Guatulco) and the area around it pertained to the Mixtec kingdom of Tototepec, and there is no indication that it had been part of the Empire,[267] although there is a report that Coatolco and Tecuantepec were conquered by Axayacatl before the expansion towards the Pacific carried out by Ahuitzotl.[268] Nopallan was another town where Moteuczoma Xocoyotzin waged war; it could be the one on the coast (Santos Reyes Nopala, Oaxaca), but this toponym also occurs in the Mixteca.[269]

Paragraph 7.4 in the "Memorial de Tlacopan" confirms the information in the chronicles and the lists of conquests that record the incorporation into the Empire of the Costa Chica of Guerrero. It is an excellent example of towns in the "Memorial de Tlacopan" that are not found in the Codex Mendoza. As in other cases, it is probable that these towns are not recorded in the Codex Mendoza because the payment of tribute in kind was not their principal contribution. The presence of Tlatomahuacan and Xaltianquizco in this paragraph, together with data from the *Relaciones geográficas* on the same Tlatomahuacan (Citlaltomahuacan) and on Tlacotepec, fills the gap between the tributary province of Tepecuacuilco, the province of Cihuatlan, and the environs of Acapolco. More to the east, the towns in this paragraph and the relación of Ayoxochiquillatzallan illustrate the continuity of the provinces of Tlappan and of Yohualtepec (Xicayan) with the Empire's last conquests on the Costa Chica. Yopitzinco must have been a small, independent enclave that did not obstruct communication along the coast. On the Oaxaca coast there probably were incursions towards the Mixtec kingdom of Tototepec, but no lasting conquests.

The Province of Tochtepec in the Codex Mendoza and in the Sources from Tetzcoco and Tlacopan

The expansion towards the isthmus and the Maya countries took place along both the Gulf coast, from Cuextlaxtlan, and the Pacific coast, from Huaxyacac. This brings us to the provinces of Tochtepec and Xoconochco. For both provinces there is information in sources from the other capitals of the Empire that will be discussed together with the data from Tenochca sources. The province of Tochtepec is lacking in the *Matrícula de Tributos*. In the Codex Mendoza, Tochtepec contains twenty-two towns; the sources from Tetzcoco and Tlacopan also describe this province and increase its extent considerably.

The conquest of Tochtepec is one of those that Ixtlilxochitl attributed to Nezahualcoyotl, together with the other two Kings, soon after the formation of the Empire. Nezahualcoyotl named a steward to collect the tribute from twelve towns, which he does not name, but they are listed in Motolinía's "Memorial tetzcocano" and in the corresponding section of the *Anales de Cuauhtitlan*. The latter source also enumerates the tribute in kind, similar to Ixtlilxochitl's description, although it does not mention services rendered.[270]

In the section of the "Memorial de Tlacopan" that lists the towns paying tribute to the three capitals there are several paragraphs that correspond to the northeastern, or Tetzcoca, sector of the Empire; they encompass a wider extent of the Tochtepec region than the Codex Mendoza and Motolinía's "Memorial tetzcocano." One of these paragraphs (6.3) is headed by Tochtepec. As in the Codex Mendoza, it contains twenty-two names, but many are different from those in the Codex Mendoza and in Motolinía. There is in addition a paragraph (6.6) headed by Chinantlan, a town that the Codex Mendoza puts within the province of Tochtepec. Some of the towns situated in Tochtepec according to the Codex Mendoza appear in paragraph 7.2 of the "Memorial de Tlacopan," headed by Cozcatlan, and one, Tototepec, is listed in section 8, although it might be a different town with the same name.

Table 10-4 presents data from all these sources. The first column presents the list of the Codex Mendoza; the second combines the lists from Motolinía's "Memorial tetzcocano" and the corresponding section of the *Anales de Cuauhtitlan;* for the most part the orthography is based on that of the *Anales.* The third, fourth, and fifth columns present the data from the "Memorial de Tlacopan." The third column shows paragraph 6.3 (Tochtepec); the fourth column, paragraph 6.6 (Chinantlan); and the fifth column gives the position, in other sections of the memorial, of the towns in the province of Tochtepec according to the Codex Mendoza that are not included in paragraphs 6.3 or 6.6. Map 10-11 represents this whole region.

Table 10-4 shows the coincidences and divergences in the sources. Of the twenty-two towns in the Codex Mendoza, five are also included in the lists of the Tetzcoca sources and in paragraph 6.3 of the "Memorial de Tlacopan." Of the towns that are lacking in the Tetzcoca sources, two (Tecpan Tzacualco and Ayotzintepec) are in the same paragraph, and five (one of uncertain identification) are in other sections of the memorial. Ten other towns are found only in the Codex Mendoza: Xayaco (2), Mixtlan (5), Michapan (6), Michtlan (8), Xicaltepec (10), Cuezcomatitlan (16), Teteutlan (18), Ixmatlatlan (19), Yaotlan (20), and Tlacotlalpan (22). They do not occupy a contiguous area but are in different parts of the province.

The Tetzcoca sources include seven towns missing in the Codex Mendoza; all are found in the "Memorial de Tlacopan" in paragraph 6.3 (Tochtepec), which contains seven more towns that are found only in this paragraph. Paragraph 6.6 (Chinantlan) in the "Memorial de Tlacopan" contains thirteen names, but only the first is in the Codex Mendoza; it seems to be an amplification of what in the codex is only one town.[271]

The locations of all these towns are shown in the following lists. The first contains the twenty-two towns in the Codex Mendoza list:

1. Tochtepec	Tuchtepeque (RG 2:101, 102; 3: 272). San Juan Bautista Tuxtepec, Veracruz.
2. Xayaco	Xayacatzintla, estancia of Chinantlan (RG 2:100).
3. Otlatitlan	Otlatitlan (SV, sec. 441). Otatitlán, Veracruz.
4. Coçamaloapan	Cuçamaluaua (SV, sec. 232; RG 5:333, no. 90 in the map). Cosamaloapan de Carpio, Veracruz.
5. Mixtlan	In the Río de Alvarado area (RG 5:334, 336, no.84 in the map. Cf. Gerhard 1986:87–89); or an early colonial town in Zongolica (Gerhard 1986:375), present-day Mixtla de Altamirano, Veracruz; or a town in Coatzacualco (RG 2:118 and 126, map).
6. Michapan	South of Tuztla (Río de Michapan [RG 5:292]). Michapan, a hamlet (ranchería) in Acayuca, Veracruz; or estancia of Chinantlan (RG 2:100).
7. Tecpan Tzacualco	Tequepançaqualco in the mountain Tzapotec area (SV, sec. 241). San Juan Tepanzacoalco, in San Pedro Yaneri, Oaxaca.
8. Michtlan	Not identified. The glyph does not contain the element for tooth (*tlan*); it could be read as Michuacan, in Coatzacualco (RG 2:19; Gerhard 1986:142).
9. Teotlilan	Teutila (SV, sec. 768). San Pedro Teutila, Oaxaca.
10. Xicaltepec	Xicaltepeque, bordered on Oxitlan (SV, sec. 422; RO, 67, 82).
11. Oxitlan	Oxitla (SV, sec. 422). San Lucas Ojitlán, Oaxaca.
12. Tzinacanoztoc	Zinacanoztoc (RG 5:335, no. 78 in map; LT, 109; RO, 67).
13. Tototepec	(?) Totoltepec between Tuztla and Catemaco (García Martínez 1969:138, map; Gerhard 1986:352); or (?) Tepeltotutla (RG 3:273; Cf. Barlow 1949b: 94). Santa Cruz Tepetotutla in San Felipe Usila, Oaxaca.
14. Chinantlan	Chinantla (RG 2:100). Valle Nacional, Oaxaca.

TABLE 10-4.

The Tributary Region of Tochtepec According to Different Sources

Codex Mendoza (46r)	Motolinía and Anales de Cuauhtitlan*	"Memorial de los pueblos de Tlacopan"†		
		para. 6.3	para. 6.6	paras. 7.2 and 8
1. Tochtepec	1. Tochtepec [12]	1. Tochtepec		
2. Xayaco				
3. Otlatitlan	2. Otlatitlan [11]	11. Hotlatitlan		
4. Coçamaloapan				7.2-54
5. Mixtlan‡				
6. Michapan				
7. Ayotzintepec§ (sic pro Tzacualco)		18. Tecpan§		
		19. Tzacualco		
8. Michtlan				
9. Teotilan				
10. Xicaltepec				7.2-60
11. Oxitlan	8. Oxitlan [5]	2. Hoxitlan		
12. Tzinacanoztoc	4. Tzinacanoztoc [9]	17. Tzinacanoztoc		
13. Tototepec				(?) 8-1
14. Chinantlan			1. Chinantlan	
15. Ayocintepec		8. Ayotzintepec		
16. Cuezcomatitlan				
17. Puctlan	9. Poctlan [4]	3. Poctlan		
18. Teteutlan				
19. Yxmatlatlan				
20. Yaotlan				
21. Toztlan				7.2-56
22. Tlacotlalpan				7.2-53
	12. Quecchollan[1]	6. Quechollan		
	11. Tlacoapan [2]	12. Tlacoapan		
	5. Zoyatepec [8]	13. Çoyatepec		

6. Tlequauhtla [7]	14. Tlequauhtla	2. Ayautlan
7. Ichcatlan [6]	20. Ichcatlan	3. Caltepec
3. Xalapan [10]	21. Xalapan	4. Texcalco
10. Chiltepec [3]	22. Chiltepec‖	5. Xocpalco
	4. Itztlan	6. Coyolapan‖
	5. Cuauhcuetzpaltepec	7. Nopallan
	7. Icpatepec	8. Mixitlan‡
	9. Tlaquatzintepec	9. Yolloxonecuillan
	10. Nexticpac	10. Ichtlan
	15. Miccaoztoc	11. Atepec
	16. Aticpac	12. Chiltepec‖
		13. Quetzalapan

*The numbers that precede the toponyms give the sequence in Motolinía (1971:396); the numbers that follow in square brackets that of the *Anales de Cuauhtitlan* (p. 65).

†Towns are numbered as in Zimmermann 1970:7–8.

‡Mixtlan in the Codex Mendoza and Mixitlan in the "Memorial de Tlacopan" have been considered to be different towns, but there is the possibility that they are the same place.

§In the Codex Mendoza the toponym Ayotzintepec appears twice in the legends, but the first is with a glyph (a pyramid on top of a mountain) that evidently should be read as Tzacualtepec or Tzacualco. It therefore corresponds to Tecpan Tzacualco, which, although listed as two different names in the "Memorial de Tlacopan," should be read as one. This is proved in the list of identifications that follows this table.

‖The toponyms marked with this symbol also appear in other sections of the "Memorial de Tlacopan." See the lists of locations that follow this table.

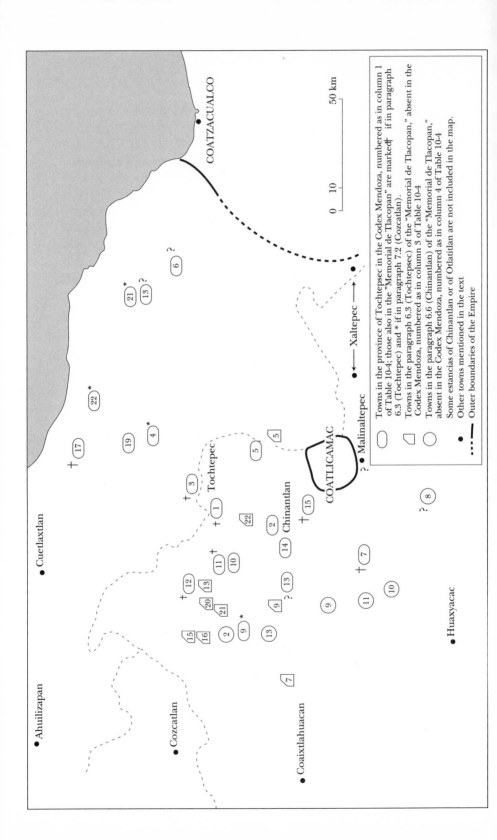

Towns in the province of Tochtepec in the Codex Mendoza, numbered as in column 1 of Table 10-4; those also in the "Memorial de Tlacopan" are marked† if in paragraph 6.3 (Tochtepec) and * if in paragraph 7.2 (Cozcatlan).

Towns in the paragraph 6.3 (Tochtepec) of the "Memorial de Tlacopan," absent in the Codex Mendoza, numbered as in column 3 of Table 10-4

Towns in the paragraph 6.6 (Chinantlan) of the "Memorial de Tlacopan," absent in the Codex Mendoza, numbered as in column 4 of Table 10-4

Some estancias of Chinantlan or of Otlatitlan are not included in the map.

Other towns mentioned in the text

Outer boundaries of the Empire

15.	Ayocintepec	Ayotzintepec, Oaxaca.
16.	Cuezcomatitlan	(?) Guazcomaltepec, in the mountain Tzapotec area (SV, sec. 283).
17.	Puctlan	Istayuca, also called Puctla, in Río de Alvarado (LT, 586). Puctla, in the lagoon of Río de Alvarado (PNE 5:236; ENE 14:87; Cf. RG 5:334, 336 and no. 85 in map; Gerhard 1986:87–89).
18.	Teteutlan	Not identified.
19.	Yxmatlatlan	Ixmatlahuacan, estancia of Puctlan (PNE 5:236; Gerhard 1986:87–89). Ixmatlahuacán, Veracruz.
20.	Yaotlan	Not identified.
21.	Toztlan	Tuztla (RG 5:290). San Andrés Tuxtla, Veracruz.
22.	Tlacotlalpan	Tlacotlalpa (RG 5:283). Tlacotalpan, Veracruz.

The next list gives the location of the seven towns in the Tetzcoca sources (Motolinía's "Memorial tetzcocano" and the *Anales de Cuauhtitlan*) and in the "Memorial de Tlacopan," paragraph 6.3. They are listed here in the order in which they appear in the "Memorial de Tlacopan."

6.	Quechollan	Estancia of Chinantlan (RG 2:100).
12.	Tlacoapan	Estancia of Otlatitlan (Gerhard 1986:89).
13.	Zoyatepec	Çoyatepeque (SV, sec. 125; RG 5:335 and no. 76 in map; RO, 67). San Miguel Soyaltepec, Oaxaca.
14.	Tlequauhtla	Tequachtla, bordered on Ichcatlan (SV, sec. 297).
20.	Ichcatlan	Ychcatlan (SV, sec. 297). San Pedro Ixcatlán, Oaxaca. Cf. Ichcatlan in 7.2-40.
21.	Xalapan	Xalapa (SV, sec. 802). San Felipe Xalapa de Díaz, Oaxaca.
22.	Chiltepec	San José Chiltepec, Oaxaca. Cf. Chiltepec in 6.6-12.

The following are the seven towns that appear only in paragraph 6.3 (Tochtepec) in the "Memorial de Tlacopan." The numbers are those of that list:

4.	Itztlan	In the Chinantec region (RO, 83).

5. Cuauhcuetzpaltepec   Guazpaltepec (Díaz del Castillo 1964:59, 362–63, 424; Motolinía 1971:229–30; Gerhard 1986:87, 376–77).
Guaxpala, hamlet of Playa Vicente, Veracruz.

7. Icpatepec   Icpaltepeque, estancia of Papaloticpac (RG 3:28).

9. Tlaquatzintepec   Tlaquacintepec (SV, sec. 770; RG 3:273).
San Juan Bautista Tlacoatzintepec, Oaxaca.

10. Nexticpac   Not identified.

15. Miccaoztoc   Mizcaoztoc (SV, sec. 349; Naicaosdoque [*sic*], RO, 83).

16. Aticpac   Aticpac (SV, sec. 16). Congregated with Tenango (San José Tenango, Oaxaca, Gerhard 1986:313).

And finally, below are listed the towns that, together with Chinantlan, comprise paragraph 6.6 in the "Memorial de Tlacopan." Only the first is also in the Codex Mendoza.

1. Chinantlan   Chinantla (RG 2, 99).
Valle Nacional, Oaxaca.

2. Ayautlan   Ayautla (RG 5:333, and no. 72 on the map).
Probably the Ayutla cited with Tepeapa, Putlanzingo, and Zinacanostoque (LT, 109).
San Bartolomé Ayautla, Oaxaca.

3. Caltepec   Caltepeque, estancia of Chinantlan (RG 2:100).

4. Texcalco   Tescalco, estancia of Chinantlan (RG 2:100).

5. Xocpalco   Not identified.

6. Coyolapan   (?) Sayolapan, estancia of Chinantlan (RG 2:100); or Zoyolapan, in Ayotzintepec, Oaxaca (cf. 7.2-70).

7. Nopallan   Nopala, estancia of Chinantlan (RG 2:100).

8. Mixitlan   (?) Mixe town (RO:67, 73).
Santa María Mixistlan de la Reforma, Oaxaca.

9. Yolloxonecuillan   Yoloxinequila (RO:67, 93); Los Yolos (RG 3:88).
San Pedro Yolox, Oaxaca.

10. Ichtlan   Ystlan (SV, sec. 302; RG 3:88).
Ixtlan de Juárez, Oaxaca.

11. Atepec   Atepeque (RG 3:88).
San Juan Atepec, Oaxaca.

12. Chiltepec   Not identified. Cf. 6.3-22.

13. Quetzalapan   Santiago Quetzalapa, in San Pedro Sochiapan,
                        Oaxaca.

In the Codex Mendoza the province of Tochtepec occupies the coast of Veracruz from the Alvarado River to the Tuxtlas and Coatzacualco. In the foothills
it includes primarily Mazatec and Chinantec towns, and in the highlands more
Chinantec towns and also Tzapotec. The sources of Tetzcoco and Tlacopan add
more names to these same regions. The towns in the mountains are easy to identify both in sixteenth-century sources and at the present time. On the coast there
are more problems because the area was so quickly depopulated only a few years
after the Spanish Conquest. Some towns require more extensive comments than
the identification given above.[272]

The identification of Tototepec (13) is difficult because it is a very frequent toponym, but nevertheless it is not found exactly in that form in this region. Two possible interpretations are given in the list that imply differences in the reading of the
glyph. Another problem is whether this toponym can be identified with the Tototepec in section 8 in the "Memorial de Tlacopan"; this question is discussed later
in connection with that section.

Chinantlan (14), present-day Valle Nacional, Oaxaca, is one of the towns the
Codex Mendoza lists in the province of Tochtepec, and it heads the list in paragraph 6.6 in the "Memorial de Tlacopan," which contains thirteen towns. Some
are estancias of Chinantlan or nearby towns, but others are in the highland area
of the Santo Domingo River: the Chinantec town of Yolox and the Tzapotec towns
of Ichtlan and Atepec. Farther away is the Mixe town of Mixitlan, if we accept this
identification.[273]

Chinantlan is said to have been subject to Moteuczoma,[274] but the accounts
of the Spanish Conquest say that it was independent, and its people welcomed the
two Spaniards that Cortés sent to them. Barlow considers these reports contradictory,[275] but the fact is that the name Chinantlan is applied to two different towns.
One is the town subject to the Empire described in its relación geográfica, and the
other is the town to which Cortés refers. The distinction is clear in a report on the
bishopric of Antequera, which enumerates two different groups of Chinantecs.
One included the Chinantlan described in the relación geográfica together with
other neighboring towns. The other group, also called Guatinicamames, was one
of the five nations in the region of Villa Alta.[276] These people are the ones described by Cortés when he writes of a "province" in which a language different
from Nahuatl was spoken, "which they call Tenis." Their ruler, Coatelicamat (*sic*),
was not subject to Moteuczoma. Cortés quotes from a letter written by one of the
Spaniards he had sent there, who reported that there were "seven cities of the
Tenez" and "Chinanta" was their cabecera.[277] The Guatinicamame towns of Villa

Alta, governed by Coatelicamat, probably Coatlicamac, were independent of Moteuczoma.[278] The town called Chinantlan in this region is not the same as the Chinantlan subject to the Empire and located in present-day Valle Nacional. The Guatinicamame towns were higher up in the mountains than Malinaltepec, a town of Bixana Tzapotecs subject to the Empire and located in the lowlands (Malinaltepec in Santiago Choapan, Oaxaca).[279] The domain of Coatlicamac, therefore, bordered on polities subject to the Empire, such as Malinaltepec, Cuauhcuetzpaltepec, and Xaltepec.

Chinantlan and Ayotzintepec (15) were probably two of the most important towns in the Tochtepec province. Sahagún lists the *ayotzintepecatl* as one of the twenty calpixques who guarded the insignias of war. He alludes elsewhere to the calpixques titled ayotzintepecatl and *chinantecatl*, who brought rabbit fur to Moteuczoma's palace when he was in the hands of the Spanish.[280]

Cuauhcuetzpaltepec (Guazpaltepec), where Chinantec was spoken,[281] is in paragraph 6.3 of the "Memorial de Tlacopan" and was one of the principal towns of the region. Díaz del Castillo, referring to Xaltepec, says that Guazpaltepeque was "the best thing there was in that province" because it was near the gold mines (placers). It seems to have been in the area of Playa Vicente and the Tesechoacán River.[282] He also says that the Mexica stewards who met Cortés were governors of the "provinces" of Cotustan (Cuetlaxtlan), Tustepeque (Tochtepec), Guazpaltepeque (Cuauhcuetzpaltepec), and Tatalteco (Tlatlactetelco).[283]

The "Memorial de Tlacopan" in paragraphs 6.3 and 6.6—to a larger extent than in paragraph 7.2—expands considerably the imperial presence in the mountain Tzapotec and Chinantec areas. Not all the area is covered, however. There is evidence to the effect that Coatlicamac was not subject to the Empire, and it is possible that some other areas about which no information is available were also independent. No towns are listed as tributaries among the Cajonos Tzapotecs. Mixitlan has been interpreted as present-day Mixistlan, but no other Mixe town has been identified as subject to the Empire. The areas of Tzapotec and Mixe population, called Las Zapotecas, strongly resisted the Spanish and probably had never been subject to the Triple Alliance. Farther south the route for the imperial campaigns from Huaxyacac to Tecuantepec went through Nexapan, but in this area of Tzapotec, Mixe, and Chontal populations some towns probably remained independent.

As in other cases, the comparison of the Codex Mendoza with the "Memorial de los pueblos de Tlacopan" shows a certain amount of overlapping among the regions they define. As has been pointed out, Cozamaloapan (4) and Toztlan (21) are listed in paragraph 7.2 of the memorial. If the Tototepec (13) in the province of Tochtepec is the same as that found in section 8 together with Tecuantepec and Xoconochco, this would show that the province of Tochtepec, in addition to its ties with towns in Oaxaca, was also connected with the isthmus and Xoconochco.

In the east, the province of Tochtepec bordered on Coatzacualco, which was independent, according to Moteuczoma himself, as Cortés tells the story.[284] This region must be the site of the fortress on the frontier of Coatzacoalco, which can be identified with the fortress of Atzaccan in the Codex Mendoza. In the identifications several toponyms have been noted of uncertain locations that are also found in Coatzacualco. There is no evidence to believe that this region was incorporated into the Empire, but it is possible that some towns were stages along the route of the merchants and envoys of the Empire towards Xicallanco.

Ixtlilxochitl attributes the conquest of several towns in this province to Nezahualcoyotl and Itzcoatl. Later, with Moteuczoma Ilhuicamina, Nezahualcoyotl conquered the provinces in the Balsas Basin and Cozamaloapan, another town in Tochtepec province. But it is more probable that the conquest of Tochtepec also took place during the reign of Ilhuicamina.[285] Torquemada names Tochtepec and Chinantlan, together with other towns in this province and in the provinces of Cuetlaxtlan and Cuauhtochco, among the towns subjugated by the Empire at the time of the conquest of Coaixtlahuacan. It is possible that these towns had been connected by tribute and commerce with Coaixtlahuacan and that the Triple Alliance assumed the preponderant role after their conquest.[286] No other source relates the conquest of Tochtepec; given its importance, this is unusual. Of later kings, Ahuitzotl conquered Chinantlan,[287] and Moteuczoma Xocoyotzin, Atepec and Yolloxonecuillan in the Tzapotec mountains.[288]

The relaciones of Chinantlan and Huitzillan (Ucila) give important information on the imperial presence in Tochtepec. In addition to noting the existence of a garrison, they explain the political and military functions of the Mexica governor and of the local indigenous caciques.

Chinantlan was a cabecera with a ruler of its own to whom several towns paid tribute. He, in turn, recognized the authority of Moteuczoma and with all his subjects paid tribute to Moteuczoma in gold and cacao:

> All the towns of Chinantlan, in war as in peace, answered to the summons of the lord of Chinantlan. Justice was provided by Moteuczoma who appointed two men as alcaldes, who visited the country and administered justice and did not allow people to be mistreated by the other lords. . . . In matters of great importance, such as carrying out justice on a principal personage and taking somebody's life, they reported to the Mexicas who resided in Tochtepec, where Moteuczoma had a very large garrison and the tribute from all the towns of this region was collected. And he had a court of justice from which came all the judges needed for all the towns of all the region held by Moteuczoma, as well as captains for the wars he waged against rebel towns or towns that Moteuczoma had not conquered. The procedure in the wars was that the lord of Chinantlan would assemble his men and deliver them to

the Mexica captain sent by Moteuczoma's government, who was acknowledged and obeyed as captain. They waged war against the towns that Moteuczoma ordered; before they became Moteuczoma's subjects they had been at war with all their neighbors.[289]

The people of Huitzillan obeyed Moteuczoma as their king, and to him they paid tribute and also sent every year a personal tribute of gifts: a round shield, gilded with much gold, a costly *quetzale* (crest) of feathers, and two necklaces of golden beads, one for Moteuczoma and another for his wife. They also gave regular tribute, as did all tributary provinces, to the imperial calpixqui, who resided in Tochtepec, consisting of gold, cacao, cotton, maize, chili, beans, cloaks, mats, and the many kinds of fruits grown there. Furthermore, they gave a similar tribute to their natural lord.[290]

There is little information on the local government of other towns in this province. It is said that in Tlacotlalpan (22) they were governed by a lord sent there by Moteuczoma to collect the tribute.[291] The people of Toztlan (21) had their own lord; later "they gave themselves in friendship" to Moteuczoma, who installed a calpixque as governor. They were at war with various groups who came from the Coatzacualco area.[292]

Tochtepec was an important center for commerce with the isthmus. Merchants from various Tenochca, Acolhua, and Tepanec cities in the Basin of Mexico traveled as far as Tochtepec. The merchants from Tenochtitlan, Tlatelolco, Cuauhtitlan, and Huitzilopochco, who had the right to trade in more distant lands, separated there, some going to Xicallanco and others to Xoconochco. In Tochtepec there were houses for the merchants of the Basin; when a merchant was preparing to participate in the festival of Panquetzaliztli, he traveled to Tochtepec to hold a ceremony and invite all the merchants who were there.[293] Among the merchants who traveled as far as Tochtepec were those of Tetzcoco, Huexotla, Coatlichan, and Otompan; their presence may explain the special participation of Tetzcoco in the conquest of Tochtepec and the naming of a steward. Since Tochtepec was on the road to Xicallanco, Ixtlilxochitl's statement that the "province" of Chilapan in Tabasco was subject to Tetzcoco may be relevant.[294]

The conquest of this region is recorded in Ixtlilxochitl and Torquemada; the Tenochca sources say nothing about it. Ixtlilxochitl states that Tochtepec was one of the provinces conquered by Nezahualcoyotl, who installed his own steward there.[295] This is another example—like those of Cuauhnahuac, Tlalcozauhtitlan, and Tolocan—of the provinces where Nezahualcoyotl installed his own steward and received all the tribute without dividing with the other kings, even though, according to Torquemada's formula, they were not within the Tetzcoca sector of the Empire. It could be argued that the province as presented in the Codex Mendoza was the dependency of Tenochtitlan; as described in the Tetzcoca sources it would pay tribute to the Acolhua capital, and as in the "Memorial de Tlacopan," to the Tepanec capital. However, it is more probable that the "Memorial de Tlacopan" registers more towns because it is not limited to the towns that sent tributes in goods to Tenochtitlan and also that the differences among the sources coming from the three capitals reflect changes over time in the disposition of the tribute from this region, especially the Tenochca preponderance achieved under the second Moteuczoma.

The Province of Xoconochco in the Codex Mendoza and in Section 8 of the "Memorial de Tlacopan," Headed by Tototepec

In the provinces of Coyolapan and Tochtepec, discussed above, there are towns that signal the entrance to the isthmus: Cuatzontlan (or Tepecuatzontlan) in Coyolapan, and Toztlan, Cuauhcuetzpaltepec, and perhaps Tototepec in Tochtepec. Section 8 of the "Memorial de Tlacopan" verifies completely the incorporation of many towns in the isthmus into the Empire. While in the Codex Mendoza the province of Xoconochco includes eight towns on the Chiapas coast, section 8 of the "Memorial de Tlacopan" lists eighteen towns, including, in addition to those of Xoconochco, several towns on the Isthmus of Tecuantepec. Table 10-5 presents the lists of these two sources, with the "Memorial de Tlacopan" in the first column because it contains more towns and encompasses a wider region. All the towns in the Codex Mendoza are also in the memorial. Those actually on the isthmus appear only at the beginning of the list in the "Memorial de Tlacopan." The towns on the coast of Xoconochco do not follow a well-defined direction in either of the lists.[296] This region is shown on Map 10-12.

The identification of some towns requires further comment. Tototepec (1) is such a frequent toponym that it is impossible to be certain of its identity. The problem is not only to identify the right Tototepec in the colonial or modern toponymy, but also to ascertain the relation between the two Tototepecs of the documents on tributary towns and the Tototepecs of the chronicles and lists of conquests. If we look for Tototepec in the area north of the isthmus, it could be the one included in the province of Tochtepec and would then be near Xaltepec, which comes next in this list. But as we have seen, the location of that Tototepec is uncertain. Farther south in the region of Tecuantepec there are other names with which it might have been confused through an erroneous reading of the glyph. Barlow identifies the Tototepec conquered by Ahuitzotl with Santa María Totolapilla, Oaxaca, near the Tehuantepec River.[297] Another possibility is the present-day San Pedro Huilotepec, Oaxaca, beside the mouth of the Tehuantepec, which would be the town conquered by Moteuczoma that the Codex Mendoza lists as Huilotepec and the

TABLE 10-5.

The Province of Xoconochco in the Codex Mendoza
and Section 8 of the "Memorial de Tlacopan," Headed by Tototepec

"Memorial de Tlacopan" (sec. 8)	Codex Mendoza (47r)	Identification
1. Tototepec	(?) Tototepec (Tochtepec, 13)	
2. Xaltepec		Xaltepeque (SV, sec.832). San Juan Jaltepec, Oaxaca, or Jaltepec de Candayoc, Oaxaca.
3. Tequantepec		Tequantepec (RG 3:107; SV, sec.780) Santo Domingo Tehuantepec, Oaxaca.
4. Xochtlan		Suchitan (RG 3:112). Juchitán, Oaxaca.
5. Amaxtlan		Not located.
6. Xoconochco	1. Xoconochco	Soconusco (SV, sec.501). Soconusco, in Acapetlagua, Chiapas.
7. Ayotlan	2. Ayotlan	Ayutla, Guatemala.
8. Veuetlan	8. Huehuetlan	Huehuetán, Chiapas.
9. Vitztlan	6. Viztlan	Huixtla, Chiapas.
10. Coyouacan	3. Coyoacan	Town in the visita of Ayotlan in the sixteenth century (RG 1:178).
11. Xolotlan		Not located. One of the towns conquered with Tecuantepec (Tezozomoc 1975:528).
12. Maçatlan	5. Maçatlan	Mazatlan (RG 1:178). Mazatán, Chiapas.
13. Miyauatlan		Not located.
14. Yacacoyauacan		Acacoyahua, Chiapas.
15. Totoncalco		(?) Tonalá, Chiapas.
16. Acapetlauacan	7. Acapetlatlan	Acapetagua, Chiapas.
17. Mapachtepec	4. Mapachtepec	Mapastepec, Chiapas.
18. Atlan		Not located.
19. Omitlan		Not located.

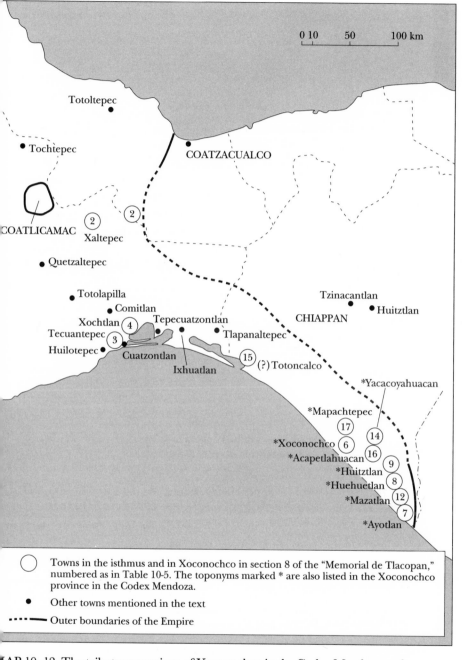

Scale: 0 10   50   100 km

Towns labeled on map:

Totoltepec

Tochtepec

COATZACUALCO

COATLICAMAC

② Xaltepec   ②

Quetzaltepec

Totolapilla

Comitlan

Xochtlan   ④   Tepecuatzontlan

Tecuantepec   ③

Huilotepec   Cuatzontlan

Ixhuatlan

Tlapanaltepec

Tzinacantlan   Huiztlan

CHIAPPAN

⑮ (?) Totoncalco

*Yacacoyahuacan

*Mapachtepec

⑰   ⑭

*Xoconochco ⑥   ⑯

*Acapetlahuacan   ⑨

*Huitztlan   ⑧

*Huehuetlan   ⑫

*Mazatlan   ⑦

*Ayotlan

Legend:

○ Towns in the isthmus and in Xoconochco in section 8 of the "Memorial de Tlacopan," numbered as in Table 10-5. The toponyms marked * are also listed in the Xoconochco province in the Codex Mendoza.

● Other towns mentioned in the text

- - - ▬ Outer boundaries of the Empire

MAP 10–12. The tributary province of Xoconochco in the Codex Mendoza and section 8 of the "Memorial de Tlacopan," headed by Tototepec

Anales de Cuauhtitlan as Tototepec.[298] Either one could be the Tototepec in this list of the "Memorial de Tlacopan."

Xaltepec (2) in earlier times was probably an independent polity. The *Suma de visitas* situates it in the mountain Tzapotec area ("en los Çapotecas"), twenty-five leagues from Villa Alta in the flatlands of jungle and wide rivers; it was also rich in gold. At that time it was subject to Manacatepeque (*sic*) or Malinaltepec in the same region, twelve leagues from Villa Alta.[299] The map in the relación of Coatzacualco puts Xaltepeque next to the confluence of what must be the Jaltepec River and the Coatzacualco, but Xaltepec is not among the towns of Coatzacualco listed in this relación.[300] Nowadays the name Jaltepec is found in two towns of the region: San Juan Jaltepec in Santiago Yaveo, Oaxaca (district of Choapan), and Jaltepec de Candayoc in San Juan Cotzocon, Oaxaca (Mixe district). Probably their common name derives from the name of an older and wider entity. Maps 10-11 and 10-12 show both the location given by the relación of Coatzacualco and that of present-day San Juan Jaltepec.

The exact location of Xoconochco (6) is not well documented. An old list of towns puts it between Acapetlahua and Mapachtepec.[301]

Maçatlan (12) in the Codex Mendoza must be the present-day Mazatán, Chiapas, but it is a very frequent toponym. In the isthmus there are two other Mazatláns, one the Mixe town of San Juan Mazatlán, Oaxaca, and the other the present-day Morro de Mazatán, in Santo Domingo Tehuantepec, Oaxaca.[302]

Miyauatlan (13) is probably the Miahuatlan, mentioned by the chronicles of the imperial conquests in the isthmus, that must have been near Tecuantepec or Xoconochco.[303]

The identification of Totoncalco (15) is not certain. Tonallan (Tonalá, Chiapas) was one of the three cabeceras of Xoconochco, mentioned below. The last two towns—Atlan (18) and Omitlan (19)—have not been identified. The two sources that mention them give them together as if they were a unit.[304]

It is difficult to determine the underlying political organization. To begin with, there was the Tzapotec kingdom of Tecuantepec, established by the dynasty of Teotzapotlan, whose ruler maintained his importance in spite of the imperial intrusion. Some of the towns in the region were subject to him, but it is not clear to what extent the older Huave and Mixe-Zoque towns remained independent.

The province of Xoconochco, at the time of the *Suma de visitas,* bordered on Tecuantepec and the governorship of Guatemala and was divided into three cabeceras: Soconusco, Tonalá, and Ahuehuetlan. The location of the town of Xoconochco is not given.[305] A relación of the bishopric of Guatemala gives Ocelocalco, Mapaztepeque, Tictepeque, Tonalá, and Tlapanatepeque as visita towns of Soconusco. If this reflects the pre-Spanish situation, Xoconochco would have extended as far as the Zoque town of San Pedro Tapanatepec, Oaxaca. In the same relación are described two other towns, Tustla and Huehuetlan, which were in the province of Xoconochco. Tustla had within its visita Copulco, Mazatlan, Cacahuatan, Etacalapa, Ilamapa, and Tlapachula; Huehuetlan had in its visita Cuilco and Tuzantlan. The relación also describes Ayutla, whose visita comprised Nahuatlan, Coyoacan, Chacalapa, Apacapa, and Tilapa.[306]

The linguistic picture of the Xoconochco region was complex. In addition to the local languages—Zoquean or Mayance—a variety of Nahuatl was spoken, but we do not know if it was the lingua franca used by speakers of the local languages or the native language of a population previous to the expansion of the Triple Alliance.[307]

The first mention of an expedition against Tecuantepec, which also went as far as Coatolco, is found in accounts of the inaugural campaign of Axayacatl. This is an isolated bit of information that is not confirmed in other sources; if it is true, we do not know what consequences it might have had, if any.[308]

Before there were conquests in the region of the isthmus, there were commercial relations and exchanges of gifts between the rulers of Tenochtitlan and those of Anahuac. The account of the conquest of Huaxyacac explains that the origin of the conflict was an attack by this town against merchants who had gone to Coatzacoalco and were returning with gifts to Tenochtitlan.[309] Sahagún relates that later, in the reign of Ahuitzotl, merchants who went to Anahuac Ayotlan, that is, the coast of Xoconochco, were detained for years in Cuauhtenanco, where they were under attack by the people of several large towns: Tecuantepec, Izhuatlan, Xochtlan, Amaxtlan, Cuatzontlan, Atlan, Omitlan, and Mapachtepec.[310] Five of these towns are included in the "Memorial de Tlacopan" and have been identified above. Cuatzontlan and Izhuatlan, are also located in the region of Tehuantepec. The latter is the present-day San Francisco Ixhuatlan, Oaxaca; Cuatzontlan, which is related to one of the towns in the province of Coyolapan in the Codex Mendoza, is the present-day San Mateo del Mar, Oaxaca.[311]

Tecuantepec is spoken of in connection with the conquest of Huaxyacac by Ilhuicamina,[312] but the first campaign recorded in the chronicles was the one undertaken by Ahuitzotl after the conquest of Oztoman. Other towns were conquered in addition to Tecuantepec: Izhuatlan, Otlatlan, Xochtlan, Amaxtlan, Xolotla, and Miahuatlan.[313] In another expedition Ahuitzotl marched against Xoconochco, which had mistreated the people of Tecuantepec because they had surrendered to Tenochtitlan, robbed the neighboring towns, and also attacked the imperial merchants. This campaign penetrated to the most distant part of the province, and the Mexicas took possession of Xoconochco, Xolotla, Mazatlan, and Ayotlan.[314] The lists of the conquests of Ahuitzotl also include a Tototepec that has not been identified with certainty.[315]

To state precisely which towns in the isthmus were conquered by Moteuc-

zoma Xocoyotzin is difficult. The location of some toponyms lends itself to different interpretations, and the accounts of the route followed in the military campaigns are equally confused. Both Durán and Tezozomoc describe a first campaign
against Xaltepec and Cuatzontlan. This Xaltepec could be the one in the Mixteca
and not the one in the isthmus, because Durán mentions Xaltepec together with
Icpatepec, but the latter has been mistaken for Cuatzontlan, which in both sources
is the other town conquered in this campaign. It is also said that, with the conquest
completed and Moteuczoma present in the destroyed Xaltepec, the Mihuatecs and
Izhuatecs from the coast of Tecuantepec came to serve him.[316] One must conclude
that the conquered town was the Xaltepec on the isthmus and that at the same
time the understanding with Tecuantepec and the other towns nearby was renewed.

We have seen that the Tototepec conquered by Moteuczoma, according to
Durán and Tezozomoc, can be identified with the Tototepec near the present-day
Ayutla de los Libres, Guerrero. The lists of conquests attribute to this king the tak-
ing of a town that the *Anales de Cuauhtitlan* calls Tototepec and the Codex Mendoza,
Huilotepec.[317] Barlow believed that Huilotepec was a misinterpretation of the glyph,
which had been read as *huilotl* (dove) instead of *tototl* (bird),[318] but the opposite is also
possible, in which case Huilotepec would be indeed the town referred to near
Tecuantepec.

The conquest of Tecuantepec is told in several sources, and there is no question that the imperial forces went that far; what we cannot be sure of is how effective was that war of conquest.[319] The report in the relación geográfica of Tecuantepec denies that this town was ever subject to the Empire. The king of Tecuantepec
and Xalapan was later called Don Juan Cortés, "whom the natives acknowledged
as their natural lord to whom they came with tribute and presents." The report
adds that the principal wars they fought were with Moteuczoma, who sent a large
army to Tecuantepec, but the natives successfully defended themselves against the
Mexicas, killing so many that they made a wall with their skulls on a mountain two
leagues northwest of Tecuantepec. Moteuczoma's forces were never able to subju-
gate the people of this "province," and after this war the Mexicas who survived
moved on to Xoconochco and Guatemala.[320]

In Durán's history, after Moteuczoma Xocoyotzin conquered Xaltepec, the
people of Tecuantepec came to welcome him and offered him grand presents. When
they asked for one of his daughters for the heir to their kingdom, Moteuczoma
agreed, and a princess was later sent from Tenochtitlan. The new ruler of Tecuantepec, once married and with an heir, no longer acknowledged Moteuczoma as his
superior, considering himself as great a ruler as the king of Mexico. Moteuczoma
then prepared an ambush, with ten thousand Mexicas hidden within Tecuantepec.
The queen revealed the plot to her husband, who ordered the death of all foreigners who had entered his kingdom. This tradition is probably related to the infor-

mation given above from the relación and has been passed on in several histories of Oaxaca.[321]

Thus, there were several campaigns to the isthmus and Xoconochco. The most important were those of Ahuitzotl, the first to Tecuantepec and the second to Xoconochco. Later, Moteuczoma conquered Xaltepec and Cuatzontlan. The tributary province of Xoconochco and the frontier fortress situated there undoubtedly resulted from Ahuitzotl's second campaign. One of these wars of conquest probably added Cuatzontlan to the province of Coyolapan. Nothing can be accepted as certain, but it is clear that the "Memorial de Tlacopan" includes towns, in paragraph 6.3 (Tochtepec) and especially in section 8, that correspond to the conquests of Ahuitzotl and Moteuczoma in the isthmus. As is the case of the towns of Teotitlan del Camino and the Mixteca Baja, which are in the "Memorial de Tlacopan" but not in the Codex Mendoza, they are towns of strategic importance that probably did not give tribute in kind—that is why they are not depicted in the Codex Mendoza—but provided free passage, provisions, and perhaps military assistance to the armies and merchants of the Empire. Tecuantepec kept its own king, and there is no evidence that the town paid tribute in kind; it may have been considered an ally rather than a tributary. The situation is comparable to that of Zaachila (Teotzapotlan), the Tzapotec capital, which did not have a Mexica calpixque even though it was surrounded by tributaries of the Empire. In the Codex Mendoza, according to the interpretation proposed above for the province of Coyolapan, the imperial calpixques of the isthmus would have been in the Huave towns on the coast.

Tecuantepec is the only town in the Tenochca sector of the Empire that any source identifies as pertaining to Tlacopan.[322] It is significant, therefore, that it appears in the "Memorial de Tlacopan" and not in the Codex Mendoza. The explanation lies in the important role of Tlacopan in Moteuczoma Xocoyotzin's campaign against Cuatzontlan and Xaltepec. According to Durán, the king of Tlacopan participated in this war and is mentioned in the history, unlike the king of Tetzcoco. The king of Tlacopan went personally to this war because he was a newly elected king, and it was essential for him to gain honor and demonstrate his valor.[323]

According to the accounts of the military campaigns, the route from the center of the Empire to Tecuantepec and Xoconochco started from Huaxyacac, and the extension of the province of Coyolapan to the isthmus confirms that connection. Later expansion into Xoconochco seems to have relied on the alliance with Tecuantepec. But there may have been another road to the isthmus from the north, since the tributary towns beyond Tochtepec include Cuauhcuetzpaltepec and Xaltepec. Just as one group of merchants went from Tochtepec to Xicallanco and another to Anahuac Ayotlan (Xoconochco), the armies and tribute collectors of the Triple Alliance could have taken the same routes.

Isolated data about advances by the Mexicas beyond the towns listed in the Codex Mendoza and the "Memorial de Tlacopan" demonstrate how the Empire's influence was extended along the Gulf coast towards Yucatan. It is said that in Xicallanco and Cimatlan there were Mexica garrisons and that Chilapan was subject to Tetzcoco.[324]

There is no good documentation on conquests in the interior of Chiapas. The kingdom of Chiappan, never subjugated, closed the way to imperial expansion.[325] Díaz del Castillo relates that the garrison of Xoconochco was to protect the way to Guatemala and Chiappan.[326] The Chiappanecs settled people taken from their nearby enemies to work in their fields, forced the Zoque towns to pay tribute to them, and made war on a Mexica garrison in Tzinacantlan.[327]

In earlier times merchants from the Basin traveled to Tzinacantlan in disguise (*nahualoztomeca*) because entrance to the town was forbidden to them.[328] Later, Tzinacantlan and Huitztlan were listed among the conquests of Moteuczoma. The latter might be a town in the highlands or else the town of the same name in Xoconochco, which would have been the base for the expedition to Tzinacantlan.[329] Another possible route to Tzinacantlan would go from Tochtepec through the northern Zoque towns that could be identified with other conquered towns such as Pantepec and Tecpatlan.[330] However, the location of these conquests in the Zoque region is not certain, because the same toponyms exist in other regions, and there are no sources that confirm one or another identification. Pantepec and Tecpatlan are probably towns in the northern Gulf region.[331] Comitlan, conquered by Ahuitzotl, must be San Pedro Comitancillo, Oaxaca, near Tecuantepec, not Comitán, Chiapas.[332]

All this poses the question of the nature of the relation between the Empire and Coatzacualco, which was on the communication route from Tochtepec towards Xicallanco and Xoconochco. In the reign of Ahuitzotl, Coatzacualco was one of the towns, such as Xicallanco and Cimatlan, that traded with Tenochtitlan,[333] but the political situation may have changed under Moteuczoma Xocoyotzin. One problem is that the toponyms in Coatzacualco include several names that are found in the lists of towns that paid tribute or that were conquered by the Mexicas, although generally they can be identified in regions closer to Tochtepec or Tecuantepec.[334] Moteuczoma told the Spanish that Coatzacualco was not subject to his rule and that he had a garrison on the frontier.[335] According to the oral tradition, the population of Cosoleacaque, Veracruz, descends from Mexica warriors of the garrison.[336]

There is no documentation on conquests by the Empire in Coatzacualco.[337] It is possible that there were stations for the provisioning and protection of trading expeditions, but in general the situation of Coatzacualco was different from that of Xoconochco, where many towns were incorporated into the tributary system of the Empire, as the Codex Mendoza and "Memorial de Tlacopan" bear witness.

The people of Xoconochco offered assistance to the Mexicas for their march against Guatemala, but there is no certain evidence that such a conquest was attempted.[338] Guatemalan sources that describe Quiché conquests reaching as far as Ayotlan may refer to the time of King Quicab;[339] the situation must have changed when his kingdom disintegrated before the arrival of the Mexicas at Xoconochco. Later, in 1510, an embassy from Moteuczoma to the Cakchiquels has been recorded, and also the payment of tribute by the Quichés to Moteuczoma, "who was in Tlaxcala." [340] Another report extends the activities of the Mexicas as far as Verapaz, Honduras, and Nicaragua;[341] they may have been commercial expeditions.

The Provinces in the South Coast of the Gulf in Codex Mendoza

The southern sector includes two provinces in the coastal area of the Gulf of Mexico, Cuauhtochco and Cuetlaxtlan, for which the Tetzcoca sources give no information. In the "Memorial de Tlacopan" they overlap the paragraphs headed by Cozcatlan (7.2) and Cempohuallan (7.1). I discuss the two provinces below according to information in Tenochca sources, and I make a comparison with the "Memorial de Tlacopan."

These two tributary provinces were conquered by Moteuczoma Ilhuicamina; the wars of conquest and the assigning of calpixques can be discussed at the same time for both provinces. The location of some of the towns is difficult to state precisely; this region of the coast was depopulated quickly after the Spanish Conquest, and the inhabitants of some towns were moved to distant towns. Both provinces are shown in Map 10-13. In the following list a place name in square brackets is a variant form in the *Matrícula de tributos*.

CUAUHTOCHCO (CODEX MENDOZA, 48R)

1.	Quauhtochco	San Antonio Guatusco, present-day Huatusco de Chicuéllar, Veracruz; or the former Santiago Guatusco in the Córdoba area.
2.	Teuhçoltzapotlan	Tezultzapotla, also called Guatusco (LT, 483).
3.	Tototlan [Toztlan]	Totutla, bordered on Zongolica (SV, sec. 843). Totutla, Veracruz.
4.	Tuchçonco	Tuchzonco (RG 5:335 and map). Tozongo, in Coscomatepec, Veracruz.

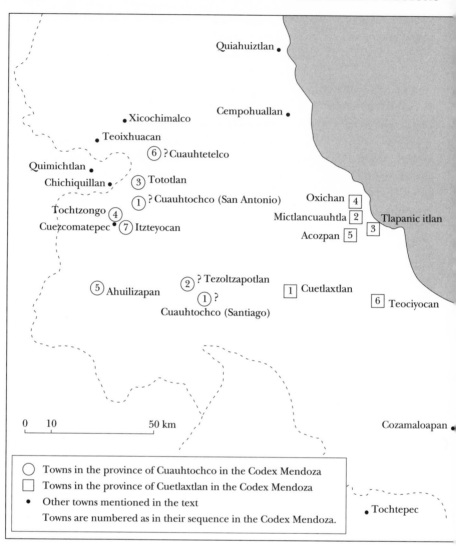

MAP 10–13. The tributary provinces of Cuauhtochco and Cuetlaxtlan

5. Ahuilizapan	Oliçaua (SV, sec. 423).
	Orizaba, Veracruz.
6. Quauhtetelco	Gerhard (1986:85) identifies it with Tlatlatetelco.
	(?) Tlatlatelco, bordering on Zongolica
	(SV, sec. 843). (?) Tlaltetela, in Axocoapan,
	Veracruz.

7. Ytzteyocan   Histehuca (RG 5:334 and map).
                       Formerly a sujeto of Cuezcomatepec, present-day
                       Juventino Rosas, in Coscomatepec, Veracruz.
                       (Barlow 1949b: 90 nn. 17, 18).

Colonial sources register two towns named Guatusco: San Antonio and Santiago. As Gerhard points out, the history of toponyms in San Antonio Cuauhtochco (Guatusco) is most confusing,[342] and the same can be said for other towns in this province. Although with different names, San Antonio Guatusco was established in the present location of Huatusco de Chicuéllar, Veracruz, and Santiago Guatusco much more to the southeast in the lowland region of Carrillo Puerto, Veracruz.[343] The archaeological site of Santiago Guatusco, explored by Medellín, is from the Mexica period, but it is not certain that it is the same town that is registered in the Codex Mendoza.[344] The *Libro de las tasaciones* mentions in this area a town called Cachultenango that probably should be identified with the imperial garrison of Quecholtetenanco, registered in the Codex Mendoza together with Cuauhtochco and Itzteyocan.[345]

Teuhzoltzapotla (2), in the Codex Mendoza list, should be read as Tezoltzapotlan according to the glyph (stone-quail-zapote), which is how it is written in other sources. In the *Libro de las tasaciones* there is an entry titled "Tezulzapotlan, by another name Guatusco, Istaiuca, in the province of Guazaqualco [*sic*] bishopric of Guaxaca,"[346] but this entry has been crossed out, perhaps because the error of putting it in Coatzacualco had been noted. In a relación of the towns that paid tribute to the Crown, which must have had a source in common with the *Libro de las tasaciones,* there is an article on "Guatusco, Porotrone, Ysteyuca and Teculcapotla, district of the Alvarado River."[347] Porotrone is obviously an erroneous reading of "por otro n[ombr]e" (by another name). Thus, there appear to be two locations for Cuauhtochco, and in addition it could be a second name of Tezoltzapotlan and Itzteyocan. These two towns must have been in the lowland area, since they both were required to give four loads of cacao every eighty days and to cultivate a field of cotton.[348] In 1560 both were dependencies of Santiago Cuauhtochco.[349]

Instead of Tototlan (3), the *Matrícula* gives Toztlan, which can be an alternative reading of the same glyph. Gerhard identifies Cuauhtetelco (6) with Tlatlactetelco and locates it north of Huatusco. This toponym, spelled in various ways, is used to describe a whole region. Francisco de Aguilar describes Tlatlatelco as a large "province" that "could have more than twenty thousand houses." In his enumeration of the coastal "provinces" he begins with Coatzacualco, with eighty thousand houses, and continues with another almost as large that he does not name but which must correspond to Tochtepec and Cuauhcuetzpaltepec (Guazpaltepec). Later he lists Tlatlatelco and continues with the "province" of Secotuxco [*sic*],

perhaps Cuauhtochco, "full of people." Then comes, "lower down the coast," Tla-
paniquito Cotaxtla (that is, Tlapanic itlan, Cuetlaxtlan), "provinces with many
people," and finally Sempoal (Cempohuallan), "which in its urban area had twenty
thousand houses." Clearly Tlatlatetelco was an important region, but the exact location of its old cabecera is not well documented.[350] In the map that accompanies
the relación of Veracruz, Tatalelco (*sic*) is north of the Alvarado River and south
of the Medellín River, with Acatepec to the northwest and Petlatzinco and Cuetlaxtlan to the southeast.[351]

The people of Cuezcomatepec, geographically in the Cuauhtochco region,
perhaps came from the Basin of Mexico, because they spoke "perfect Mexican language." The toponym is explained as "town of maize bins." Moteuczoma had
many of them there, since the cold, dry air preserved the maize in storage for times
of famine.[352]

Cuauhtochco seems to have been the name of a whole province and the second
name of some of its towns. In colonial times it was part of the names of two towns,
San Antonio and Santiago. This makes it impossible to know the exact location of
pre-Spanish Cuauhtochco. Santiago Cuauhtochco was very close to Cuetlaxtlan.
Probably this province of Cuauhtochco occupied the area from the edge of the
coastal plain to the highlands, while Cuetlaxtlan was entirely on the coastal plain,
including towns from Cotaxtla (Cuetlaxtlan) to present-day Medellín.

CUETLAXTLAN (CODEX MENDOZA, 49R)

1. Cuetlaxtlan	Cotaxtla, Cutlaxta (RG 5:315, 333). Cotaxtla, Veracruz.
2. Mictlanquauhtla	Mitanquauhtla (RG 5:289, 334, 336). Half a league from the mouth of the Medellín River (Barlow 1949b: 91).
3. Tlapanic ytlan	Tlapaniquito on the coast near Cuetlaxtlan (Aguilar 1938:97). Congregated in Medellín (Gerhard 1986:371).
4. Oxichan	Congregated in Medellín (Gerhard 1986:371).
5. Acozpan	Alcozahua, congregated in Medellín (Gerhard 1986:371).
6. Teociocan	Teociniocan (Sahagún 1975: book 12, chap. 2). Tezayuca, also called Taliscoya (LT, 468). Tlalixcoya, Veracruz.

The conquest of the Cuauhtochco and Cuetlaxtlan region began with Moteuczoma Ilhuicamina's first campaign against Ahuilizapan, Cempohuallan, Cuetl-

axtlan, and Cuauhtochco in response to the murder of royal envoys sent to request certain products of the coastal waters. All the merchants and others then in the area were also killed. After a fierce battle the lords of Cuetlaxtlan and of the other cities that fought with them surrendered and promised to send tribute of great value to Mexico. On returning from this conquest, Moteuczoma ordered that a governor should be sent to Cuetlaxtlan to see that the tribute was collected every eighty days and "to keep the province of Cuetlaxtlan subjugated." The governor, named Pinotl, was welcomed by the people, and the tribute was brought to him as ordered and sent to Tenochtitlan.[353]

Shortly thereafter, Cuetlaxtlan rebelled again, murdered the governor, and then massacred in a brutal way the envoys sent to investigate the delay in bringing the tribute as required. The Mexicas resumed the war; the commoners deserted their lords, who were subsequently put to death by executioners sent from Tenochtitlan.[354] The Mexicas then spoke to the people, emphasizing the vengeance they had just seen taken on those who had caused so many deaths.[355]

The commoners were pleased with the punishment their lords had received "and then elected new lords. And at the same time they were given a Mexica governor who was to maintain justice for the people and protect them, and collect the tribute and send it to Mexico. With this the executioners returned to Tenochtitlan and told their king . . . that all was quiet and peaceful and new lords in place, very much by the will of the community, and at the same time a new Mexica governor with the same name as the one who had been killed." Tezozomoc described the new governor as "a kinsman and brother of King Moteuczoma, a principal [named] Pinotototl," with whom the people were quite content.[356]

According to Torquemada, "the Cuetlaxteca were given Mexica governors and a fort [presidio] manned by Mexicas was established; thus they were deprived of their sovereignty and made vassals of Mexico."[357] The relación of Cuetlaxtlan states that they were governed by a calpixque named Tentiltzin appointed by Moteuczoma to collect the tribute and send it to Mexico.[358]

The chronicles of Durán and Tezozomoc also allude to the conquest of Cuetlaxtlan by Moteuczoma Ilhuicamina in connection with the creation of the king's garden in Huaxtepec. Envoys were sent to Cuetlaxtlan to request all the different kinds of plants that flourish there on the coast and workers to plant them in the new garden. Pinotl, the governor sent there after the second conquest, saw to it that these orders were carried out immediately.[359]

There is very little information on the local rulers of this region except that, as we have seen, after the execution of the defeated kings the people elected new rulers, and the Mexicas appointed a governor.

The province of Cuetlaxtlan is the region where imperial officials had their first encounter with the Spaniards; they were the principal steward (huey calpixqui) Cuetlaxtecatl Pinotl, the calpixques of Mictlancuauhtla and Teociniocan, and some lesser officials (*teyacanque*). One of these was called Tentlil, undoubtedly the same name that the relación gives for Moteuczoma's steward.[360] The names of the calpixques of this province, which are mentioned in several sources, always allude to people of foreign ethnic affiliation, such as Pinotl (plural, Pinome) and Tenitl (plural, Tenime).[361]

In this region the Spaniards were met by the local officials of the Empire. This contrasts with the situation in Cempohuallan, where the Spaniards went to the local ruler and the imperial tribute collectors are described as later visitors. It is no accident that Cuetlaxtlan is an important province in the Codex Mendoza, while Cempohuallan is absent, although it is the first town in paragraph 7.1. of the "Memorial de Tlacopan."

Several more towns in this general area are said to have been subjugated in these campaigns.[362] Tezozomoc defines the conquered region as all the towns on the Gulf coast, from Chalchiuhcueyecan (Veracruz) to Cuetlaxtlan, but it also included towns in the highlands. Chichiquillan, Teoixhuacan, Quimichtlan, and Tzauctla are north of the Pico de Orizaba;[363] their intervention in this war was probably related to Tlaxcallan's participation on the side of the coastal peoples. The towns of Tlatectla, near present-day La Antigua,[364] and Oceloapan, whose ruins are near Puente Nacional, Veracruz, are on the coast.[365] Another town, Macuilxochitlan, is of doubtful identification.[366] There are also references to Quiahuiztlan[367] and, as in the reports given above, to Cempohuallan, the Totonac and Huaxtec towns, and Cuextlan. It appears at times that this last name is used as a general term for the coastal region.[368] Paragraph 7.1 in the "Memorial de Tlacopan" comprises precisely this entire area, from Cuetlaxtlan to Pánuco.

Torquemada describes another campaign, after the war against Coaixtlahuacan, in which the following were conquered: Tochtepec, Tezoltzapotla, Tototla, Tlatlactetelco, Chinantlan, and Cuauhnochco (*sic*). In the following year, Cozamaloapan and Cuauhtochco also fell.[369] Ixtlilxochitl, writing from the Tetzcoca point of view, does not give details on these conquests; he puts Cuauhtochco and Cuetlaxtlan among the provinces won by the three kings of the alliance, not among those conquered by Nezahualcoyotl, in which he installed his stewards.[370]

In their accounts of the wars of Ilhuicamina and Nezahualcoyotl, both Ixtlilxochitl and Torquemada give a list of towns conquered later, within a year, that comprised several regions. Among them are Coxolitlan (now in Acultzingo, Veracruz) and Otlaquiquiztlan, which was formerly in Cuauhtochco.[371]

Cuetlaxtlan and Ahuilizapan appear again among the conquests of Axayacatl.[372] The report that Nezahualpilli, in 1481, conquered Ahuilizapan, Tototlan, Oztoticpac, and other towns on the Gulf coast must refer to this campaign. The king himself took part in the battle and celebrated the occasion by giving the name

of Ahuilizapan to a pond in his gardens.[373] According to Ixtlilxochitl, Nezahualpilli continued this war in 1485, taking Nauhtlan and the coast as far as Pánuco.[374]
The conquest of Ahuilizapan is told again later together with that of Xicochimalco
in 1493.[375]

The provinces of Cuetlaxtlan and Cuauhtochco complemented each other in
the tribute they paid. Cuauhtochco gave cotton, as raw material, and simple cloaks;
Cuetlaxtlan paid only luxury objects: embroidered cloaks, feathers, chalchihuites,
and lip plugs.[376]

Cuetlaxtlan is one of the places to which the Mexicas transferred populations.
The relación geográfica of the city of Veracruz names neighboring towns such as
Xamloluco (*sic pro* Xalcomolco), Espiche, and Cotaxtla and adds they were inhabited by people that the Mexica rulers had moved from other towns and forced to
live in this frontier area, although the malignancy of the climate was well known.
For the security of these "forced people," and to keep peace in the area, the Mexicas had "two fortresses and presidios with their garrisons and warriors"; one was
Cotaxtla (Cuetlaxtlan), five leagues from the city, and the other Otopa, eight leagues
distant.[377]

Commenting on the unhealthiness of the coast, Herrera notes that although
the coastal area was uninhabited in his day, because of disease, it was well populated in Moteuczoma's time. In view of the high death rate and scarcity of people
caused by epidemics, Moteuczoma "would transport 8,000 families from Mexico
and other large towns to settle in areas depopulated by disease, giving the people
houses and land, and making them free from tribute payments for a number of
years. Thus he could repopulate the coast whenever necessary, with people who
would not be needed in the towns from which he had taken them."[378]

The cabeceras of Cuauhtochco and Cuetlaxtlan are both included in paragraph 7.2 in the "Memorial de Tlacopan," centered on the Mixteca. Two towns in
Cuetlaxtlan are in paragraph 7.1 of the memorial, which covers the Gulf coast as
far as the Huaxteca; this is discussed in the next chapter, on the northeastern sector.

Chapter 11

THE NORTHEASTERN SECTOR OF THE EMPIRE

In Torquemada's formula, the Tetzcoca sector consisted of the northeastern quarter of the Empire. The Tetzcoca sources agree. Pomar, in his relación of Tetzcoco, states that the Acolhua kingdom reached as far as the Gulf coast and included many towns and "provinces" from the Gulf to the Pacific, encompassing—on the eastern side—everything except Tlaxcallan and Huexotzinco.[1]

The other Tetzcoca sources describe in more detail some of the provinces in that area in a way that indicates a close connection with Tetzcoco. In Ixtlilxochitl's account, once the Triple Alliance was established, Nezahualcoyotl conquered a number of provinces, in each of which he placed a steward, and Ixtlilxochitl lists the tribute given. He contrasts this with the provinces conquered jointly by all three kings, whose tribute was sent to Tenochtitlan even though all three capitals received a share of revenue. Of the provinces established by Nezahualcoyotl, Tochpan and Tziuhcoac are in the northeast, but Tochtepec is in the southeast and Tlalcozauhtitlan to the south, in the Balsas Basin. Ixtlilxochitl also reports the conquest of Mazahuacan and Tlapacoyan but does not name the calpixques or the tribute paid; he says these two towns were conquered by the three kings and were treated as others they had already conquered. In this passage the neighboring province of Tlatlauhquitepec is not mentioned.[2]

Motolinía's "Memorial tetzcocano" and its variant in the *Anales de Cuauhtitlan* also list several tributary provinces in the northeast, giving more details about the towns they included than the Tenochca sources. This suggests that Tetzcoco was more concerned with these regions than Tenochtitlan, probably because of its preponderance there.[3] The fact that the Tenochca chronicles devote very little space to the conquest of those regions and the installing of calpixcazgos leads to the same conclusion. Ixtlilxochitl's sources must have been the same as those of these other Tetzcoca documents. It is significant that Tlapacoyan and Tlatlauhquitepec, about which he gives no details as to the calpixques and the tribute paid, are included (without the names of their dependencies) within the paragraph about Tziuhcoac in Motolinía and in the *Anales de Cuauhtitlan*. Some copying errors may have been responsible for these differences and gaps of information. The "Memorial de los pueblos de Tlacopan," which probably derived its information from the Tetzcoca memorial prepared at the same time, is more thorough about this region. In section 6 the "Memorial de Tlacopan" arranges all the tributary towns of the northeastern sector into six paragraphs headed by Tochpan (6.1), Tziuhcoac (6.2), Tochtepec (6.3), Tlapacoyan (6.4), Tlatlauhquitepec (6.5), and Chinantlan (6.6); the last paragraph is in effect an amplification of the province of Tochtepec in the Codex Mendoza, which includes Chinantlan as only one of several towns.

All these data show a certain lack of agreement with a strict application of Torquemada's formula. Tlapacoyan, Tlatlauhquitepec, Tochpan, and Tziuhcoac certainly embrace an area that would coincide with Torquemada's northeastern sector, but other areas described as part of Nezahualcoyotl's early conquests are outside the northeastern quarter. Tochtepec, in the southeast, should have gone to Tenochtitlan. Perhaps this is an example of the greater importance of Tetzcoco in the first period of imperial expansion. Mazahuacan and Tlalcozauhtitlan obviously are not part of the northeastern sector; like parts of Tlalhuic, they were Tetzcoco's share in the other two sectors of the Empire.[4] On the other hand, the Tenochca sources contain two tributary provinces in the northeast, Atlan and Oxitipan, while the "Memorial de Tlacopan" has a paragraph (7.1) within the southern sector that combines towns in Cuetlaxtlan with many others on the coast, towards the north and as far as Tamiahua, which according to Torquemada's scheme would fall within the Tetzcoca sector. These were conquests of a later period that—although they took place in the northeast—fell under the predominance of Tenochtitlan.

The different sections of this chapter describe the provinces of the northeastern sector included in the Codex Mendoza, following the order of this source. First are two provinces in the area now called the Sierra de Puebla—Tlapacoyan and Tlatlauhquitepec. For these two provinces, in addition to the Codex Mendoza there is good information in the "Memorial de Tlacopan"; here the data from both sources will be combined. In the coastal lowlands and the Huaxteca there are three provinces—Tochpan, Atlan, and Tziuhcoac. For Tochpan and Tziuhcoac there are long lists of their towns in the memorials of Tetzcoco and Tlacopan which add to the information in the Codex Mendoza. For Atlan, as a province, there is only the data in the Codex Mendoza, although the two towns in this province also appear in paragraph 7.1 of the "Memorial de Tlacopan." Oxitipan is spoken of as a tributary province only in the Tenochca sources. The chapter ends with a discussion of paragraph 7.1 of the "Memorial de Tlacopan."

The Provinces in the Sierra in the Codex Mendoza
and in the Sources from Tetzcoco and Tlacopan

TLAPACOYAN

The Tetzcoca sources include Tlapacoyan among the provinces that paid tribute to the three capitals in the Tetzcoca sector but do not name its dependencies. Table 11-1 presents the lists of the Codex Mendoza and the "Memorial de Tlacopan." Map 11-1 shows both Tlapacoyan and Tlatlauhquitepec.

The province of Tlapacoyan was immediately east of the Acolhua kingdom of Cuauhchinanco, but the location of some towns is uncertain because the same toponyms are used for more than one town and because there are slight differences in the names on these lists and those that are suggested as their equivalents. Even the location of Tlapacoyan is subject to doubt.[5]

Barlow identified Acazacatla (7) with the well-known town of Zacatlan in Puebla, but Acazacata north of Zautla, Puebla, is preferable.[6] This location is somewhat distant from Tlapacoyan, but the towns that the "Memorial de Tlacopan" adds to this province also show a more southern extension than does the Codex Mendoza, into the area of several important polities bordering on Tlaxcallan, such as Tzauctlan and Iztaquimaxtitlan, and the memorial also adds the more distant Quimichtlan.[7] Another town, Tecolcuauhtla, cannot be located exactly, but the maps of the *Historia Tolteca-Chichimeca* place it on the northern boundaries of Cuauhtinchan, perhaps not too far from Quimichtlan.

Tzauctlan (modern Zautla, Puebla) is the first town in the highland plateau reached by Cortés on his route from Cempohuallan and Xalapan. From Xicochimalco he crossed a mountain pass, stopped at Teoixhuacan, and after three days of traversing cold desert areas crossed another pass and came to Tzauctlan and then to Iztaquimaxtitlan, from whence he continued towards Tlaxcallan.[8] The rulers of both towns acknowledged their subordination to Moteuczoma. Iztaquimaxtitlan had an important fortress. Cortés reports a population of five to six thousand householders (*vecinos*); López de Gómara says that Moteuczoma had five thousand soldiers in the garrison and posts of men in relay stations on the way to Mexico.[9] Tzauctlan appears with Quimichtlan—which the "Memorial de Tlacopan" puts in this province—and other towns farther south among the towns that were subjugated when Cuauhtochco and Cuetlaxtlan were conquered.

Zacatlan, also known as Tenamitec, was an early center of the Totonacs from which they expanded all the way to Cempohuallan. Later immigrants were Olmecs and Chichimecs from Tlaxcallan.[10] Zacatlan is named various times together with Tlaxcallan among the enemies of the Triple Alliance,[11] but later it is mentioned as being on the Empire's side. Torquemada reports the payment of tribute to Tenoch-

TABLE 11-1.

The Province of Tlapacoyan According to the
Codex Mendoza and the "Memorial de Tlacopan"

Codex Mendoza (50r)	"Memorial de Tlacopan" (para 6.4)	Identification
1. Tlapacoyan	1. Tlapacoyan	Tlapacoya, Puebla.
2. Xiloxochitlan	2. Xiloxochitlan	Eloxochitlán, in Zacatlán de las Manzanas, Puebla. Another Eloxochitlan was a sujeto of Chicahuaxtla when the latter was separated from Huauchinango in 1712 (García Martínez 1987:367, 375 n. 7).
3. Xochiquauhtitlan	10. Xochiquauhtla	Xochicuauhtla, estancia of Xuxupango (PNE 5:218). Xochicuautla, in Ahuacatlán, Puebla.
4. Tuchtlan		Estancia of Hueytlalpan (RG 5:154). Tuxtla, in Zapotitlan de Méndez, Puebla.
5. Coapan	8. Couapan	Cuapan, south of Huitzillan, Puebla, in the Carta General del Estado de Puebla, Comisión Geográfica Exploradora, 1908.
6. Aztaapan	4. Aztaapan	Not identified.
7. Acaçacatla		Acatzacata, in Zautla, Puebla.
	3. Tecolquauhtla	On boundary of Cuauhtinchan (HTCh, 129, 203)
	5. Vitzitziltepec	Huitziltepec in Cuyoaco, Puebla.
	6. Mexcaltepec	Mexcaltepec in Iztacamaxtitlan, Puebla.
	7. Tlapeualtepec	Not identified.
	9. Amatzcalapan	Not identified.
	11. Quimichtlan	Quimixlán, Puebla.
	12. Tlaquilpan	Once a sujeto of Ahuacatlán (García Martínez 1987:373).

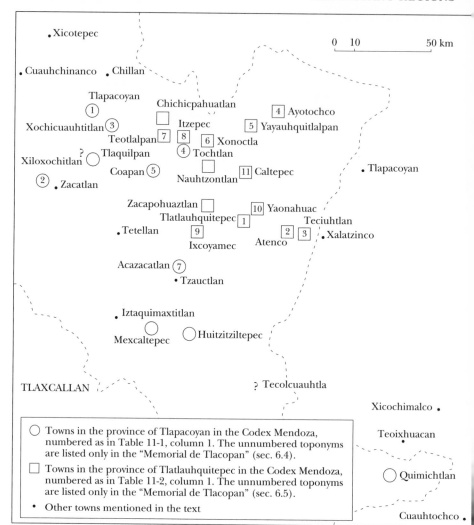

MAP 11–1. The tributary provinces of Tlapacoyan and Tlatlauhquitepec

titlan, although the local dynasty remained in power.[12] When Tizoc undertook a campaign against Metztitlan, messengers went to Zacatlan "so that they would be prepared"; under Moteuczoma Xocoyotzin, Zacatlan also fought against Tlaxcallan.[13] Yet there are no references to the conquest of Zacatlan, and, according to their relación geográfica, the people of Zacatlan were subject to no one; they were free and did not pay tribute as other towns did, except that when they wished to send a present to Moteuczoma, they did so and nothing else. They were at war with Tlaxcallan, and Moteuczoma helped them.[14]

Something similar is said about the people of nearby Tetellan. They were governed by their own ruler, carried on wars with Zacatlan and Tlaxcallan, "and the king of Mexico favored them with shields and other offensive weapons."[15]

In Moteuczoma Xocoyotzin's campaign against Tlaxcallan, several towns from this area participated: Zacatlan, Tozapan, Tetellan, Iztaquimaxtitlan, and Tzauctlan.[16] This region on the northern Tlaxcallan frontier does not hold an important place in the accounts and lists of conquered towns, but its people did fight on the Empire's side against Tlaxcallan, and although none of the cabeceras appear in the lists of tributary towns, some of their lesser settlements do. This is a sharp contrast with the early and important role of Tepeyacac in the southern borders against the tramontane kingdoms. It is probable that Zacatlan, Tetellan, Tzauctlan, and Iztaquimaxtitlan were primarily military allies of the Empire rather than suppliers of tribute goods.

TLATLAUHQUITEPEC

Tlatlauhquitepec, like Tlapacoyan, is described in both the Tenochca sources and the "Memorial de Tlacopan." Table 11-2 puts together the data from these sources; Map 11-1 shows Tlatlauhquitepec together with Tlapacoyan.

The conquest of Tlatlauhquitepec by Nezahualcoyotl and Moteuczoma Ilhuicamina is mentioned briefly in the histories, with no information on local rulers or the installation of an imperial calpixque.[17]

The relación of Xonotla (6) confirms that they paid tribute to Tenochtitlan and states that they had their own ruler.[18] The relación of Hueytlalpan or Teotlalpan (7) says they had a governor installed by Moteuczoma, to whom they paid tribute.[19]

A viceregal order of 1548 reports that Hueytamalco, later a subject of Teciuhtlan (3), had been an independent town with its own ruler, and the people gave their tribute to the calpixque of Tlatlauhquitepec, called Tlacuchi.[20]

The Provinces in the North Coast of the Gulf in the Codex Mendoza and in the Sources from Tetzcoco and Tlacopan

Two tributary provinces on the north coast of the Gulf of Mexico are well documented in the Tetzcoca sources: Tochpan, which comprised the Totonac region of the coast, and Tziuhcoac in the Huaxteca region. The inhabitants of both also included people who spoke Nahuatl. Two other provinces—Atlan and Oxitipan—were farther inland; they are not described in the Tetzcoca sources. Map 11-2 illustrates these four provinces.

TABLE 11-2.
The Province of Tlatlauhquitepec According to the
Codex Mendoza and the "Memorial de Tlacopan"

Codex Mendoza (51r)	"Memorial de Tlacopan" (para 6.5)	Identification
1. Tlatlauhquitepec	1. Tlatlauhquitepec	Tlatlauquitepeque (SV, sec. 522). Tlatlauquitepec, Puebla.
2. Atenco	2. Atempan	Atempa (SV, sec. 13). Atempan, Puebla.
3. Teciutlan	3. Teciuhtlan	Tocintlan (SV, sec. 520). Teziutlán, Puebla.
4. Ayutuchco		Ayotuchco, sujeto of Xonotla (RG 5:394). Ayotoxco de Guerrero, Puebla.
5. Yayauquitlalpa		Yayauquitlapan, estancia of Tlatlauhquitepec (SV, sec. 522). (?) Yancuitlalpan, in Cuetzalan del Progreso, Puebla.
6. Xonoctla		Xonotla (RG 5:381). Jonotla, Puebla.
7. Teotlalpan		Teutalpa or Guetlalpa (RG 5:151). Hueytlalpan, Puebla.
8. Ytztepec		Iztepec, sujeto of Hueytlalpan (RG 5:154). Ixtepec, Puebla.
9. Yxcoyamec	8. Ixcuiyamec	Ycuyomec, estancia of Tlatlauhquitepec (SV, sec. 522).
10. Yaonahuac		Yaonahuac, Puebla.
11. Caltepec		Calatepec in Cuetzalan del Progreso, Puebla.
	4. Pololtenco	Not identified.
	5. Potzalco	Not identified.
	6. Chichicpauatlan	Chichicpahuatlan, sujeto of Hueytlalpan (RG 5:154). Chipahuatlan, in Olintla, Puebla.
	7. Nauhtzontlan	Naozontlan, estancia of Tlatlauhquitepec (SV, sec. 522). Nauzontla, Puebla.
	9. Çacapouaztlan	Çacapuastla, estancia of Tlatlauhquitepec (SV, sec. 522). Zacapoaxtla, Puebla.
	10. Oztouacan	Oztocan, estancia of Tlatlauhquitepec (SV, sec. 522).

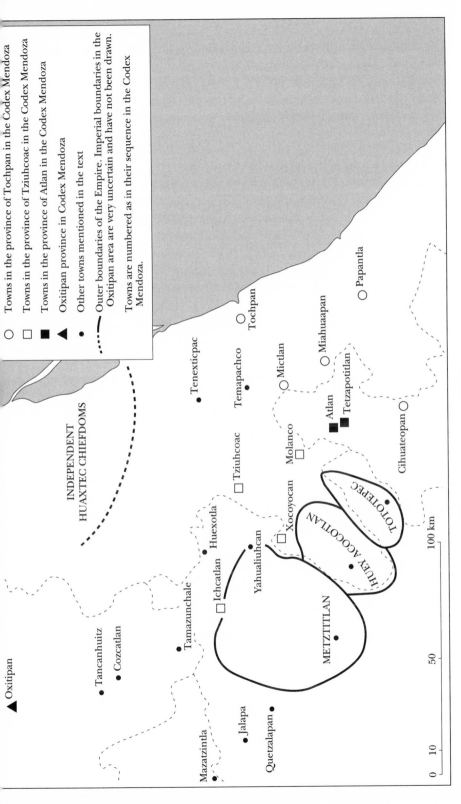

MAP 11–2. The tributary provinces of Tochpan, Atlan, Tziuhcoac, and Oxitipan

Legend:

○ Towns in the province of Tochpan in the Codex Mendoza

□ Towns in the province of Tziuhcoac in the Codex Mendoza

■ Towns in the province of Atlan in the Codex Mendoza

▲ Oxitipan province in Codex Mendoza

● Other towns mentioned in the text

⸱⸱⸱ Outer boundaries of the Empire. Imperial boundaries in the Oxitipan area are very uncertain and have not been drawn.

Towns are numbered as in their sequence in the Codex Mendoza.

▲ Oxitipan

INDEPENDENT HUAXTEC CHIEFDOMS

Mazatzintla

Jalapa

Quetzalapan

Tamazunchale

Tancanhuitz

Cozcatlan

Ichcatlan

Huexotla

Yahualiuhcan

METZTITLAN

Xocoyocan

Tenexticpac

Tziuhcoac

HUEY ACOCOTLAN

TOTOTEPEC

Molanco

Temapachco

Mictlan

Atlan

Tetzapotitlan

Miahuaapan

Cihuateopan

Tochpan

Papantla

0 10 50 100 km

The accounts of the conquests in this region usually combine towns in the territories of Tochpan and Tziuhcoac. It is noteworthy also that the two provinces complement each other as to tribute; Tochpan gave a large quantity of cotton, while Tziuhcoac gave elegant clothing and luxury objects.[21]

Compared with the wars of conquest in other regions, those in the north coast of the Gulf are given little attention in the chronicles. The Huaxteca was extremely fragmented politically,[22] and the Empire did not have to contend with powerful political entities there, as was the case in other areas. There is almost no mention of local kings or the naming of imperial calpixques. The conquests could not have been very lasting, for the same place names are repeated in the lists of conquests of several kings. Conquest and imperial dominion seem to have been more effective in parts of the Sierra de Puebla, close to the easternmost dependent kingdoms of Tetzcoco and in the province of Tochpan.[23]

The conquest of the coast began in the reign of Nezahualcoyotl, perhaps before the inauguration of Moteuczoma Ilhuicamina, although the Tenochca sources do not attribute the wars in these regions to Itzcoatl. Ixtlilxochitl relates that Nezahualcoyotl conquered the provinces of Tochpan and Tziuhcoac and installed his own stewards there.[24] The Tenochca sources credit Ilhuicamina with the conquest of Tziuhcoac, Tochpan, and Tamapachco.[25]

Subsequently, other kings waged war on the north coast, but there is no information on the effectiveness of their conquests or on local political conditions.[26] Axayacatl vanquished, among others, Tetzapotitlan, Miquetlan, Tochpan, and Tenexticpac. Tizoc undertook a campaign against Metztitlan, assisted by the Huaxtecs, and won Miquetlan and Tamapachco.[27] Ahuitzotl made war on Tziuhcoac, Tozapan, and Tamapachco, which had revolted.[28] This may be the same campaign referred to in the report that Nezahualpilli of Tetzcoco conquered, in 1486, Nauhtlan and all of the coast as far as Pánuco, and later Tziuhcoac, which had rebelled.[29] According to another source, Ahuitzotl undertook a campaign in the fourth year of his reign in which King Chimalpopoca of Tlacopan conquered Cuextlan.[30] Some other conquests, such as that of Miquetlan, are attributed to Moteuczoma Xocoyotzin, but these amount to nothing in comparison with his wars in Oaxaca.

For this region, therefore, the best information on securing the imperial dominion is in the Tetzcoca sources on the establishment of the provinces of Tlapacoyan, Tlatlauhquitepec, Tochpan, and Tziuhcoac. Later conquests took place when Tetzcoco had lost the position of strength it had under Nezahualcoyotl. Although the conquest of Nauhtlan is attributed to Nezahualpilli, this town is listed as a tributary only in the "Memorial de Tlacopan," which puts it in paragraph 7.1 (Cempohuallan) in the Tenochca sector. The conquest of Atlan (or Pantepec) and Tetzapotitlan are also attributed to Tenochca kings and are listed in the same paragraph of the memorial. Nothing is known about the conquest of Oxitipan.

Tochpan (Codex Mendoza, 52r)

1.	Tuchpa	Tuspa or Tomilco (SV, sec. 525). Tuxpan, Veracruz.
2.	Tlaltiçapan	Not identified.
3.	Cihuanteopan	Zihuateutla, Puebla.
4.	Papantla	Papantla (SV, sec. 449).
		Papantla de Olarte, Veracruz.
5.	Ocelotepec	Not identified.
6.	Miahuaapan	Miahuapan, in Tihuatlan, Veracruz.
7.	Mictlan	Mequetlan, in Teayo, Veracruz.

The glyph for Mictlan, both in the Codex Mendoza and the *Matrícula de tributos*, consists of a bean on the head of a funeral bundle, suggesting the toponym Miquetlan.[31] This is how it is written in the Tetzcoco and Tlacopan sources, as shown in Table 11-3. Tlaltizapan and Ocelotepec have not been located.[32]

In the Tenochca sources the province of Tochpan consists of only the seven towns listed above, but the Tetzcoca sources and the "Memorial de Tlacopan" list many more towns in this province (Table 11-3 compiles all these data). The great province of Tochpan, says Ixtlilxochitl, was divided into seven provinces that all together contain sixty-eight towns subject to them;[33] here these subdivisions will be called subprovinces. In the same way, Motolinía's "Memorial tetzcocano" states that the tribute of those sixty-eight towns was collected in certain principal towns where there were stewards from Mexico, Tetzcoco, and Tlacopan, who divided the tribute into three parts.[34]

Motolinía and Ixtlilxochitl agree that the province of Tochpan contained sixty-eight towns, but only Motolinía gives the names of all of them. The first three are incomplete and badly written, but they do add up to sixty-eight according to the interpretation proposed in Table 11-3. In the *Anales de Cuauhtitlan* there are seventy-two towns in Tochpan arranged in eight groups, each marked with a paragraph symbol at the beginning.[35] The first seven groups coincide with the lists for this province in Motolinía's "Memorial tetzcocano" and the "Memorial de Tlacopan." In Table 11-3 I have labeled them with the letters *A* to *G*. The eighth group contains five towns—Tlamacaztlan (68), Xochititlan (69), Mollanco (70), Xollan (71), and Teuctonallan (72)—that in the "Memorial de Tlacopan" are part of the province of Tziuhcoac. Motolinía's memorial counts them among the thirty-three towns in a paragraph that comprises the provinces of Tlatlauhquitepec, Tlapacoyan, and Tziuhcoac. Consequently, these five towns should be considered part of the province of Tziuhcoac and are included as such in Table 11-4.

It is clear that the seven towns listed in the Codex Mendoza correspond to seven paragraphs (*A* to *G*) in the *Anales de Cuauhtitlan*, to the seven subprovinces of Ixtlilxochitl, and to the "principal towns" of Motolinía. The seven towns in the

TABLE 11-3.   The Towns of Tochpan

Codex Mendoza (52r)	Motolinía*	Anales de Cuauhtitlan†	"Memorial de Tlacopan"‡	Suma de visitas§
1. Tuchpa	2. ochpantlan	C38. Tochpan	1. Tochpan	
	1. Coscaquahg-	37. Cozcaquauhtlan	61. Cozcaquauhtlan	
	3. Te . . .	36. Tochmilco	62. Tochmilco	T
	4. Tlazouallan	35. Tlaçohuallan	63. Tlaçouallan	
	5. Mazatlan	34. Maçatlan	64. Maçatlan	T
	6. Yyactecuicitla	33. Iyactecuiçotlan	54. Hiyactecuicitlan	
	7. Xochiquantla	32. Xochiquentlan	65. Xochiquentlan	
	8. Chiconcohuac	31. Chiconcoac	47. Chiconcouac	
	9. Quahucihacapan	30. Quauhtlaacapan	46. Quauhtlaapan	
	10. Ichcape	29. Ichcapetlacotla	45. Ichcapetlacotla	
	15. Amazcallapan	28. Amatzcallapan	66. Amatzcalapan	
	6. Tlatolloyan	¶27. Tlatolloyan	38. Tlatoloyan	
2. Tlaltiçapan	17. Tizapan	B26. Tiçapan	5. Tiçapan	T
	18. Ollan	25. Ollan	59. Ollan	
	19. Yxuac	24. Chiucnahuac	53. Chiucnahuac	
	20. Teotitlan	23. Teotitlan	52. Teotitlan	
	21. Yrzmatlan	22. Itzmatla	12. Itzmatlan	
	22. Tlacoxuchitla	21. Tlacoxochitla	3. Tlacoxochitlan	T
	23. Panzotlan	20. Pantzontlan	56. Paççotlan	
	24. Citlapoua	19. Citlalpollan	57. Citlapullan	
	25. Chinameca	18. Chinamecan	55. Chinamecan	
	26. Quahuzaputitlan	17. Quauhtzapotitlan	58. Quauhtzapotitlan	
	27. Teteltitlan	¶16. Teteltitlan	60. Tetltitlan	
3. Cihuanteopan	28. Ciuateopan	A15. Çihuateotitlan	8. Ciuateopan	P
	29. Couaapan	14. Coaapan	15. Couaapan	
	30. Tepetlapan	13. Tepetlapan		
	31. Cuaxipeztecomatlan	12. Quaxipetztenantlan		
	32. Maca apan	11. Maçaapan	13. Maçaapan	
	33. Tocolotlan	10. Tecolotlan	26. Tecolotlan	P
	34. Ometlan	9. Ometlan	27. Ometlan	
	35. Cemazac	8. Çemaçac	28. Cemaçac	
	36. Ytzmatlan	7. Itzmatla	12. Itzmatlan	
	37. Atlxoxohuya	6. Atlxoxouhcan	25. Atlxoxouhyan	
	38. Ytzcuinco	5. Yeyytzcuintlan	11. Eiytzcuinco	
	39. Tlapolhuitlan	4. Tlapollitlan	30. Tlapolintlan	
	40. Tozpatlan	3. Tozpantlan	31. Tozpantlan	
	41. Yxicayan	2. Ixicayan	2. Hixicayan	P
	42. Aternan	¶1. Aternan	14. Ateman	

4. Papantla	43. Papantla	G 67. Papantla	16. Papantla	
	44. Pouazantlan	66. Pohuaçanco	32. Pouaçantlan	P
	45. Tozpotonco	65. Tozpotonco	21. Tozhiuitlan	
	46. Omacatlan	64. Omacatlan	24. Omacatlan	
	47. Viloc	63. Huiloc	19. Viloc	
	48. Coahucalco	62. Quauhcalco	20. Quauhcalco	P
	49. Quezalcouatonco	60. Quetzalcoatonco	22. Quetzalcouatonco	
	50. Couatlachco	61. Cohuatlachco	23. Tlachcouac	
	51. Tollapan	59. Tollapan	18. Tolapan	
	52. Quahuzapotla	58. Quauhtzapotla	—	
	53. Xochmitlan	57. Xochimilco	34. Xochmitlan	
	54. Coyochicimalco	56. Coyochimalco	33. Coyochimalco	
	55. Pollotlan	55. Pollotlan	29. Polotlan	
	56. Yeztecatlan	¶ 54. Eztecatlan	10. Eztecatlan	
5. Ocelotepec	57. Ocelotepec	F 53. Ocelotepec	41. Ocelotepec	
	58. Tecomaapan		9. Tecomaapan	
	59. Quahucallapan	52. Quauhcallapan	17. Quauhcalapan	
	60. Patoltetipan	50. Patoltetitlan	43. Patoltetipan	
	61. Ayotepec	51. Ayotepec	44. Ayotepec	
	62. Miztontla	49. Miztontlan	48. Miztontlan	T
	63. Totoluacan	¶ 48. Totollocan	42. Totolhuacan	
6. Miahuapan	64. Miyauaapan	E 47. Miyahuaapan	39. Miyauaapan	
	65. Tetlmocincapa	46. Tetlmopaccan	40. Tetlmopaccan	
	66. Tecomaapa	45. Tecomaapan	37. Tecomaapan	
	67. Apachiquahutle	¶ 44. Apachiquauhtla	36. Apachiquauhtla	
7. Mictlan	68. Micquetlan	D 43. Micquetlan	35. Micquetlan	
	11. Telpuztecca	42. Tetlpozteccan	49. Tetlpuzteccan	
	12. Quaxipeztecomatla	41. Quaxipetztecomatlan	4. Quaxipetztecomatlan	
	13. Mayotlan	40. Moyotlan	6. Moyotlan	
	14. Sauicilco	¶ 39. Ahuitzilco	7. Avitzilco	
			50. Tapoco	
			51. Tencoyotlan	

*Motolinía 1971:395. The document gives Coscaquauhgochpantlan as the name of the first town; this must be a mistaken reading that combines two names—Cozcaquauhtlan Tochpa—but in the wrong order, contrary to the order of the list.

†AC, 65.

‡Paragraph 6.1. Towns are numbered as in Zimmermann 1970:6.

§SV, 449, 525. *T* signifies Estancia of Tochpan. *P* signifies Estancia of Papantlan.

Codex Mendoza were the cabeceras and coincide with the last toponym of each paragraph in the *Anales de Cuauhtitlan*. The "Memorial de Tlacopan," in paragraph 6.1, lists sixty-six towns that are almost exactly the same names given in Motolinía and the *Anales de Cuauhtitlan*, but the order is entirely different, there is no indication of the criterion followed in ordering the place names in the list, and the names are not grouped into subprovinces.

In Table 11-3 the first column contains the towns depicted in the Codex Mendoza; the second gives Motolinía's list, which follows the same order as the Codex Mendoza and gives the names of the sixty-eight towns. The third column gives the list in the *Anales de Cuauhtitlan*, whose orthography is much better than that of Motolinía. The toponyms in this list follow an order that is the opposite of that in the Codex Mendoza. As pointed out above, in the *Anales de Cuauhtitlan* the toponyms are arranged in seven groups, each one preceded by a paragraph symbol. In the table this symbol is placed before the first toponym in each group, and the letters that identify them for this discussion are also added beside the names of the seven towns of the province depicted in the Codex Mendoza. The table does not include the last paragraph, since the five towns it includes pertain to the province of Tziuhcoac.

The fourth column gives the names in paragraph 6.1 in the "Memorial de Tlacopan"; in the fifth column some of these are identified, following the *Suma de visitas*, as estancias of Papantlan or of Tochpan.

The table is in two parts. The first presents the subprovinces of Tochpan, Tlaltizapan, and Cihuateopan, and the second, those of Papantlan, Ocelotepec, Miahuapan, and Mictlan (Micquetlan). The differences in the order of the toponyms between Motolinía's "Memorial tetzcocano" and the *Anales de Cuauhtitlan* can be understood if we assume the material came from a pictorial document in which the names or glyphs were arranged in two parts as in the table. The amanuenses of those two sources would have read first the first part and then the second, but with the scribe of Motolinía's "Memorial tetzcocano" reading in one direction and the scribe of the *Anales* in the opposite direction. Some towns (Ahuitzilco, Moyotlan, Quaxipetztecomatlan, and Tetlpozteccan in the spelling of the *Anales de Cuauhtitlan*) are listed with Micquetlan in the *Anales de Cuauhtitlan* but with Tochpan in Motolinía. This means probably that in the original painting those towns were depicted close to the cabeceras of both provinces so that either reading would be possible. Since the *Anales de Cuauhtitlan* seems more reliable in the naming of the towns, they have been placed in the table within Micquetlan. The order of the toponyms, totally different in the "Memorial de Tlacopan," indicates that this document must have been based on another original, or else that it was read in accordance with a different criterion.[36]

In comparison with the *Anales de Cuauhtitlan*, the towns numbered 11 to 14 in Motolinía are misplaced; they have therefore been put in the subprovince of Micquetlan.

There are other minor differences in the sequence in which the toponyms are listed. In two cases, adjoining toponyms in the *Anales de Cuauhtitlan* are listed in the same order as in Motolinía instead of the opposite, as in the rest of the document. Compare 3 and 4 and 36, 37, and 38 in the *Anales de Cuauhtitlan* with 39 and 40 and 1, 2, and 3 in Motolinía.

Further comparison of the lists shows the following differences:

Cuaxipeztecomatlan is listed twice in Motolinía (31 and 12); in the second case it agrees with the *Anales de Cuauhtitlan* and the "Memorial de Tlacopan," but in the first the *Anales de Cuauhtitlan* writes the name Cuaxipetztenantlan and the "Memorial de Tlacopan" does not give any name.

Tapoco and Tencoyotlan, numbers 50 and 51 in the "Memorial de Tlacopan," do not correspond with anything in the other sources. Since the "Memorial de Tlacopan" follows a different order, it is not possible to know to which of the seven subprovinces they might pertain. Perhaps they are the equivalent of two of the three towns in the other two sources that have no identical correspondent in the "Memorial de Tlacopan"; in the table they are placed separately at the end.

In the "Memorial de Tlacopan" two towns are lacking: Tepetlapa (30 in Motolinía, 13 in the *Anales de Cuauhtitlan*) and Cuauhtzapotla (52 in Motolinía, 58 in the *Anales*).

Itzmatlan appears twice in Motolinía (21, 36) and in the *Anales de Cuauhtitlan* (22, 7), but only once in the "Memorial de Tlacopan" (12).

Tecomaapan is listed twice in Motolinía (66, 58) and in the "Memorial de Tlacopan" (9, 37), but only once in the *Anales de Cuauhtitlan* (45); the place it would have occupied would be between numbers 52 and 53.

The list of the towns of Tochpan in the Codex Mendoza, with which this discussion began, includes the location of these towns. It is much more difficult to identify the many towns listed in the other sources and shown in Table 11-3, but the description of Tochpan and Papantlan in the *Suma de visitas* gives us a basis for understanding the division of this province in two parts. The entry on Papantlan states that Papantlan and Tuspa (*sic pro* Tochpan) or Tomilco form "a single unit [tierra]; they are fourteen leagues from each other, but they have no dividing boundaries and their estancias are intermingled." Papantlan had fourteen estancias, although the following fifteen names are given: Coalitlan, Coatlan, Puçantla, Tanamastepeque, Ayotlan, Guacalco, Yztipa, Tacolutla, Quaotlan, Coapan, Papalotla, Tenuxtepeque, Macotla, Xicayan, and Çoquitla. The entry on "Tuspa or Tomilco" says that the town was depopulated, and the natives went to the estancia of Tomilco. There were eleven estancias: Tomilco, Tigotlan, Tlacosuchitlan, Vla, Achitlan, Moçotla, Xoloçingo, Chicomeacalco, Miztontla, Açeçeca, and Coyola; the entry adds, "The lands of this town are mixed with the town of Papantla; there is no division."[37]

The two parts in which all the settlements of this province are grouped in the sources from Tetzcoco and Tlacopan might coincide with the domains of Toch-pan and Papantlan, since each of the two parts is headed by one of these towns. However, the ascription of some settlements to one or another of the two cabeceras in the *Suma de visitas* does not quite agree with this interpretation. In the identi-fications that follow, the numbers given are those of the towns of the province, con-forming to the numbers of Motolinía's "Memorial tetzcocano" in the first column of the table; the spelling has been standardized.

In the subprovince of Tochpan, Tochmilco (3) and Mazaztlan (5) were es-tancias of Tochpan. There is still a trace of Tochmilco in the local toponymy; the Cerro de Tumilco is located in the municipio of Tuxpan, Veracruz, where one also finds Chiconcoa, which corresponds to Chiconcohuac (8).

In the subprovince of Tlaltizapan, Ollan (18) and Tlacoxochitla (22) were es-tancias of Tochpan.

In the subprovince of Cihuateopan, three towns on the list were estancias of Papantlan: Cohuaapan (29), Tecolotlan (33), and Ixicayan (41).

In the subprovince of Papantlan, Pohuazantlan (44) and Cuauhcalco (48) were estancias of Papantlan itself. Tollapan (51) might be Tulapilla in the area of the municipio of Coyutla, Veracruz.[38] Present-day Polutla in the municipio of Pa-pantla corresponds to Pollotlan (58) of this subprovince.

In the subprovince of Ocelotepec, Miztontlan (62) was an estancia of Tochpan.

No town in the subprovinces of Miahuapan and Mictlan (or Miquetlan) has been identified.

Given the large number of towns, those that have been located are very few, but they suggest that the subprovinces of Tochpan, Tlaltizapan, and Ocelotepec contained the estancias of the town of Tochpan, according to the *Suma de visitas*, while Cihuateopan and Papantlan had those of Papantlan. Nothing can be said about the other two subprovinces. Since the two cabeceras of Tochpan and Pa-pantlan did not have defined boundaries, and their estancias were intermingled, the subprovinces were not continuous territorial units but were dispersed, held to-gether by their common dependency to a cabecera (and subcabecera). The differ-ence between the sequences of the two lists not only could be the result of different ways of reading the same pictograph, but also could reflect different ways of com-bining the geographical location with their relationship with one or another of the two cabeceras. A better location of these towns would be necessary for a clearer interpretation.

The relación geográfica of Papantlan is very deficient in information on the political organization. It is said that formerly the people of Papantlan were not subjects of the king of Mexico but were at war with him and defended their lands until, exhausted, they surrendered peacefully to Moteuczoma. From then on they had "a governor placed by Montezuma who kept them in peace."[39]

Atlan (Codex Mendoza, 53r)

1. Atlan   Atlan "that by another name is called Pantepec" (LT, 76).
Pantepec, Puebla.
2. Teçapotitlan   In the Huaxteca, on the road to Pánuco (LT, 474).
Valpopocotla (*sic*), also called Tezapotitlan (ENE 8:160). Uzilpopotla (LT, 229).

The province of Atlan is found only in the Tenochca sources. The two towns that it contains are the same that form a military district that can be identified with the one situated on the Pánuco frontier. One can assume that both the military governors and the calpixques resided in these two towns.

The *Libro de las tasaciones* cites the two towns of this province as part of the corregimiento of Metateyuca (*sic pro* Metlateyocan).[40] It also gives Atlan and Pantepec as synonyms, although in the "Memorial de Tlacopan" and the Codex Mendoza they are different towns.[41] Pantepec was one of the towns bordering on Tziuhcoac;[42] it can be located in the town and municipio of the same name. Tetzapotitlan disappeared at the end of the seventeenth century. The name Huitzilpopocatlan may have survived in the hamlet called Huitzilac in the municipio Francisco Z. Mena, Puebla (Metlaltoyuca).[43]

The province of Atlan was, therefore, near the domains of Tetzcoco in the Sierra de Puebla that comprised the kingdoms of Cuauhchinanco, Xicotepec, and Pahuatlan, plus Tlacuiloltepec and Papaloticpac. However, the Tetzcoca sources have no reports on it. In the "Memorial de Tlacopan" it is listed in paragraph 7.1, headed by Cempohuallan, which appears to be the part of the Gulf coast that came into the Tenochca sector.

Axayacatl is credited with the conquest of Tetzapotitlan together with other towns of the region.[44] Later, Ahuitzotl reconquered it during his campaign against Tziuhcoac.[45] Pantepec was a conquest of Moteuczoma Xocoyotzin.[46] The fact that Pantepec appears only in reference to the reign of Moteuczoma suggests, again, that the establishment of that military district and tributary province came after the creation of the provinces of Tochpan and Tziuhcoac and represents the Tenochca intrusion into the area where formerly Tetzcoco had prevailed.

Tziuhcoac (Codex Mendoza, 54r)

1. Çtzicoac   Cicoaque (SV, sec. 135). In the vicinity of Chicontepec, Veracruz.
2. Molanco   Molango, in Ixhuatlán de Madero, Veracruz.

    3. Cozcatecutlan   Not identified.

    4. Ychcatlan   (?) Ixcatlán, in Huejotla, Hidalgo.

    5. Xocoyocan   Xococapa, in Ilamatlán, Veracruz.

The meaning of the toponym Tziuhcoac is not certain. Some modern writers prefer to correct it to Xiuhcoac, but the sources both in Nahuatl and in Spanish almost always give Tziuhcoac or equivalent spellings. There is no adequate reason to discard the traditional name.[47]

The province of Tziuhcoac is described, as is Tochpan, in the sources from the three capitals of the Empire. The Tetzcoca sources and the "Memorial de Tlacopan" give many more toponyms, thus facilitating the location of this province.

Motolinía's "Memorial tetzcocano" includes Tziuhcoac and its dependencies in one of the lists of towns whose tribute was divided among the three capitals. It says that there were thirty-three towns, but not all the towns named are dependencies of Tziuhcoac. The list begins with Tlatlauhquitepec and Tlapacoyan, which are separate tributary provinces, discussed above; then follow the towns that, as is seen in other sources, were the ones that comprised the tributary province of Tziuhcoac.

The *Anales de Cuauhtitlan* give the same towns as Motolinía's "Memorial tetzcocano" but in the opposite order. At the end of the list, after Tziuhcoac, come Macuextlan, Tlapacoyan, and Tlatlauhquitepec. The last two are the cabeceras of two other provinces. Macuextlan has no correspondent in the other sources; it is doubtful that it was part of Tziuhcoac, and it is not considered in the discussion.[48]

Table 11-4 puts together the names of all the towns in the province of Tziuhcoac mentioned in the sources.[49] The first column gives the five names in the Codex Mendoza; the second, those in Motolinía's "Memorial tetzcocano," which is used to organize the table as a whole. The third column contains the towns of this province that in the *Anales de Cuauhtitlan* are in the paragraph that includes most of Tziuhcoac. Column three also includes a few towns from the end of the paragraph that comprises the province of Tochpan, since these towns are part of Tziuhcoac in both Motolinía's "Memorial tetzcocano" and the "Memorial de Tlacopan"; they are placed at the end of this column and are numbered, in square brackets, according to their order in that paragraph. The list from the "Memorial de Tlacopan" (6.2) is in the fourth column. As is the case with Tochpan, this list is almost the same as in the Tetzcoca sources, but in a very different order. Moreover, it includes three more towns that do not occur in the other sources; they are put at the end of the column, apart from the five subprovinces.

The towns compiled in Table 11-4 are difficult to locate, but they help to define the territory of the province better than do the five towns in the Codex Mendoza. The identifications that follow are of towns for which there is information, numbered according to the order of Motolinía's memorial. Occasionally the spelling is corrected according to the other sources.

TABLE 11-4.

The Towns of Tziuhcoac

Codex Mendoza (54r)	Motolinía*	Anales de Cuauhtitlan[†]	"Memorial de Tlacopan" (sec. 6.2)[‡]
1. çtzicoac	1. Cihucouac	26. Tziuhcohuac	1. Tziuhcohuac
	2. Tlacotepetl	25. Tlacotepec	10. Tlacotepec
	3. Civatla	24. Çihuatlan	27. Çihuatlan
	4. Cozoquitla	22. Coçoquentlan	29. Conçoquitla
4. Ychcatlan	5. Tlapalichcatlan	23. Tlapalychcatla	28. Tlapalichcatlan
	6. Tamaoc	21. Tamaoc	30. Tamac
	7. Tonalla	20. Tonallan	23. Tonallan
	8. Quechicolihuacan	19. Quachicol	22. Quechicol
	9. Palzoquitla	18. Palçoquitla	8. Palçoquitla
	10. Xicalanco	17. Xicallanco	21. Xicalanco
	11. Tacatlan	16. Tecatlan	20. Tacatlan
	12. Ayacachtepec	15. Ayacachtepec	25. Ayacachtepec
3. Cozcatecutlan	13. Cozcatecutlan	14. Cozcatecotlan	24. Cozcatecutlan
	14. Avatla	13. Ahuatlan	19. Ahuatlan
	15. Xochimilco	12. Xochimilco	18. Xochmilco
	16. Zocotetlan	11. Cocotetlan	17. Tzocotetlan
	17. Tezquizapan	10. Tecçizapan	26. Teccizapan
	18. Teonochtlan	9. Teonochtlan	16. Teonochtlan
	19. Chicontepec	8. Chicontepec	13. Chicontepec
	20. Chamolla	7. Chamollan	12. Chamollan
	21. Teoquauhtla	6. Teoquauhtla	31. Teoquauhtlan
	22. Tamazolla	5. Tamacollan	32. Tamaçollan
5. Xocoyocan	23. Xocacapan	4. Xococapan	7. Xococapan
	24. Tanchol	3. Tanchol	6. Tanchol
2. Molanco	25. Tecpan Mollanco	2. Tecpan Mollanco	3.–4. Tecpan Mollanco
	26. Tlilzapoapan	1. Tliltzapoapan	5. Tliltzapoapan
	27. Tecatonalla	[72] Teuctonallan	33. Tecutonallan
	28. Xolla	[71] Xollan	2. Xollan
	29. Mollanco	[70] Mollanco	34. Mollanco
	30. Xochitlan	[69] Xochititlan	35. Xochitlan
	31. Tlamacaztlan	[68] Tlamacaztlan	9. Tlamacaztlan
			11. Vitzilquiyauiztlan
			14. Teoquauhtitlan
			15. Tamaçolinco

*Motolinía 1971:396. In the numbering of the towns, Tlatlauhquitepec and Tlapacoyan are not included, since they are separate provinces in all the other sources.

[†]AC, 64 and 65. The numbers begin with Tliltzapoapan, which is the first town of this province on p. 64 after the towns of what in Motolinía are tenants of Tetzcoco. Tecpan Mollanco is written as one word in the manuscript. The towns in square brackets are those listed after the towns of Tochpan on p. 65.

[‡]Numbered in the sequence of the manuscipt as in Zimmermann 1971:6.

Tziuhcoac (1), according to the *Suma de visitas,* took in a large territory twelve leagues square bordering on Huaotlan (Huautla, Hidalgo), Agualican (Yahualica, Hidalgo), Guayacocotlan (Hueyacocotla, Veracruz), Tututepec (San Bartolo Tutotepec, Hidalgo), Pantepec, Chilpopocatlan, Tuçapan, and Tenextiquipan. The entry on Tochpan also names Tziuhcoac as contiguous. Therefore, the extent of Tziuhcoac is sufficiently well defined towards the west but less clearly towards the north and the coast. The *Suma de visitas* also names two visitas of Tziuhcoac that are listed in the table: Ahuatlan (14) and Tliltzapoapan (26).[50] Chicontepec, Veracruz, has been suggested as the location of the cabecera of Tziuhcoac, but, as Table 11-4 indicates, Tziuhcoac (1) and Chicontepec (19) were different towns. Other suggested locations are Montes de Oca, near Tuxpan, in Temapache, Veracruz, and the archaeological site of Cacahuatenco, on the confluence of the Pantepec and Vinasco Rivers.[51]

Tlacotepec (2) could be the Tlacotepec in Huayacocotla, Veracruz, or the one in Huejutla, Hidalgo.

Ichcatlan, or Tlapalichcatlan, (5) could be one of two towns named Ixcatlán, one in Huejutla, Hidalgo, and the other in Molango, Hidalgo. The first is more suitable, because the second is far into the interior of the territory of Metztitlan, which never became subject to the Triple Alliance.

Tamaoc (6) may correspond to Tamaya, a toponym found in Chicontepec, Veracruz, and in Benito Juárez, Veracruz. In Hidalgo the municipio of Huauhtla contains Tlamaya and Tamoyon.

Palzoquitla (9) could be Palzoquitempa in Benito Juárez, Veracruz, or Palzoquico in Huejutla, Hidalgo, but toponyms with *zoquitl* (mud) are too numerous in this region.

Xicallanco (10) can be found today with the same name in Chicontepec, Veracruz.

Ayacachtepec (12) is, perhaps, Ayacaxtle in Chicontepec, Veracruz.

Cozcatecutlan (13) is given on the table as not identified. Barlow suggested that it had been where the present-day Coxcatlan now is, near Tancanhuitz in San Luis Potosí and therefore near Oxitipan. However, Table 11-4 suggests that it was in the same subprovince as Chicontepec and other nearby towns.[52]

Ahuatlan (14) was an estancia of Tziuhcoac.[53] Today there is an Ahuatlan in Chicontepec, Veracruz.

Xochimilco (15) could be the town with the same name in Ixhuatlán de Madero, Veracruz.

Tezquizapan (17) is perhaps the same as Teccizapa in Chicontepec, Veracruz.

Chicontepec (19) is the already mentioned Chicontepec, Veracruz.

Chamollan (20) is the same as present-day Chamola in Chicontepec, Veracruz.

Teocuauhtla (21) could be one of several similar present-day toponyms: Teocuayo in Chicontepec, Veracruz; Teocuatitlan in Huejutla, Hidalgo; or Hueycu-atitla in Benito Juárez, Veracruz.

Tamazollan (22) is probably Tlamazolcingo, congregated in Chicontepec in 1592.[54]

Xococapan (23) is today the name (spelled Xococapa) of a town in Ilamatlán, Veracruz. The comparison of the Codex Mendoza and the other sources as in Table 11-4 suggests that it was the same town as the Xocoyocan in the Codex Mendoza.

Tecpan Mollanco (25) must be present-day Molango in Ixhuatlán de Madero, Veracruz, since the Molango in the state of Hidalgo pertained to Metztitlan.[55] Tecpan Mollanco is a single town. In the *Anales de Cuauhtitlan* it is written as one name; in Motolinía it must be counted as one word to achieve the total of thirty-three towns, as stated in the document.

Tliltzapoapan (26) was an estancia of Tziuhcoac called Tilçipojapan in the *Suma de visitas*. Davies puts Tlilzapoapan in Ixhuatlan de Madero, Veracruz, according to the 1960 census. The 1950 census registers Tzilzacuapan.[56]

The province of Tziuhcoac was beyond the independent kingdom of Metztitlan, which had in Yahualiuhcan a frontier fortress against the Huaxteca,[57] and also beyond Tototepec and Hueyacocotla, which were also independent.[58] To the east it was contiguous with Tochpan, that is, with the province of the same name that included Papantlan. The nucleus of the province of Tziuhcoac is found in the region of Chicontepec. The northern limit cannot be well defined with the information available. The conquest of Tamapachco (Temapache, Veracruz) and Tenexticpac, and the more northern towns in paragraph 7.1 in the "Memorial de Tlaco-pan," mark the most distant towns conquered by the Triple Alliance on the Gulf coast.[59] The imperial boundary shown in Map 11-2 is only tentative.

Ixtlilxochitl relates the conquest of Tziuhcoac by Nezahualcoyotl together with that of Tochpan and states that he put a steward named Yaotl in the province of Tziuhcoac to collect the annual tribute payments. Ixtlilxochitl gives the list of tribute goods but not a list of towns included in the province.[60]

OXITIPAN (CODEX MENDOZA, 55R)

1. Oxitipan   Ojitipa de Mirador, in Tancanhuitz, San Luis Potosí.[61]

This province is not in the *Matrícula de tributos*. It consists of only one town, Ox-itipan, at a considerable distance from the nearest provinces and north of the independent kingdom of Metztitlan. It was also among the sujetos of the old kingdom of Xaltocan, which extended as far as Metztitlan.[62]

The very distant location of Oxitipan poses the question of whether the Empire's communication route to this town went through Tziuhcoac or started from Cimapan, a subject of Xilotepec. The latter is suggested by the route of Moteuczoma Xocoyotzin's campaign to the Huaxteca: "His armies went out through Chichimec country, entered the Huaxteca, and defeated the people of Quatzalapan."[63] Later, when Cacama was king of Tetzcoco, the three kings of the alliance went to "the Chichimecs and the lands of Mazatzintla and the Metztitecs came to meet them there, who were on the side of Ixtlilxochitl," that is, the brother of Cacama, who, with assistance from Metztitlan, had taken possession of the northern part of the domains of the Acolhua kingdom.[64] Quatzalapan must be a copying error for Quetzalapan, now an ejido in Jacala, Hidalgo. There is also mention of a river called Quetzalatl, near Metztitlan, in regard to Tizoc's campaign against that kingdom.[65] Mazatzintla still exists, in Querétaro, southeast of Jalpan.[66] It is clear, then, that they followed a route—through Chichimec territory west and north of Metztitlan—that from Cimapan would go to the Huaxteca in the direction of Tamazunchale and Tancanhuitz. Perhaps the establishing of this province of Oxitipan is related to the campaigns of Moteuczoma Xocoyotzin. We do not know if that route was taken earlier when Tziuhcoac was conquered; if it was, then it might justify the identification of Cozcateuctlan in the province of Tziuhcoac with the Cozcatlan near Tancanhuitz. The Empire's boundaries in this area cannot be defined from the available information and are not marked in Map 11-2.

Paragraph 7.1 in the "Memorial de Tlacopan," Headed by Cempohuallan

Paragraph 7.1 in the "Memorial de Tlacopan" includes a large part of the coastal zone that is almost entirely lacking in the Codex Mendoza, although some towns are also listed in the provinces of the Codex Mendoza, in both the southern and the northeastern sectors. Table 11-5 lists all the towns in paragraph 7.1, and Map 11-3 contains all of these towns that have been identified. Maps 10-13, 11-1, and 11-2 represent the provinces in the Codex Mendoza that are in the same region.

There are very few correlations with the Codex Mendoza: two towns in Cuetlaxtlan, Tlapanic itlan (6) and Mictlancuauhtla (7), mentioned as the area where the Spaniards disembarked, and Atlan (25), the cabecera of both a tributary province and a military district. If the identification of Tlilapan (3) is correct, it would be within the area occupied by the province of Cuauhtochco. Other doubtful identifications (30 and 35) might also be in this area. The rest of this paragraph contains towns along the coast and contiguous regions, from the two towns in Cuetlaxtlan (6 and 7) to Cempohuallan (1), Quiahuiztlan (17), Nauhtlan (9), and as far as Tamiahua (22). This paragraph does not include towns in the provinces of

TABLE 11-5.
Paragraph 7.1 in the "Memorial de Tlacopan," Headed by Cempohuallan

"Memorial de Tlacopan"*	Codex Mendoza[†]	Identification
1. Cempouallan		Cempoala (RG 5:314, 333, 336; RO, 12). José Cardel, Veracruz.
2. Ytzcalpan		Yzcalpa (RG 5:315, 334, 336). La Rinconada, Veracruz.
3. Tlilapan		Tlilapan, Veracruz, or Tilapa in Totutla, Veracruz.
4. Hamolapan		Not identified.
5. Xalapan		Xalapa (RG 5:343). Jalapa, Veracruz.
6. Tlapanic ytlan	Tlapanic ytlan (Cuetlaxtlan, 3)	In the area of Medellín, Veracruz.
7. Mictlanquauhtla	Mictlanquauhtla (Cuetlaxtlan, 2)	In the area of Medellín, Veracruz.
8. Vitzilapan		This is also the name of the river near the city of Veracruz (RG 5:313, 319, 363).
9. Nauhtlan		Estancia of Mizantla (LT, 429; RG 5:190). Nautla, Veracruz.
10. Nauhaxochco		Not identified.
11. Ichcaichquauhtla		Not identified.
12. Tetl iyacac		Not identified.
13. Tlatoloyan		Not identified.
14. Quiyauhapan		Not identified.
15. Xocotla (Cf. 35)		Xocutla, seventeen leagues from La Villa de Pánuco; bordered on Tantoyetle and Moyutla (SV, sec. 805). Jocutla in Tantoyuca, Veracruz.
16. Tepetzalan		Tepecelan or Topocelan (RG 5:334, 335; 19 or 12 in the map).
17. Quiyauiztlan		Half a league north of La Antigua, Veracruz. (Díaz del Castillo 1964:75).
18. Tenexticpac		Tenestequipaque on the north coast (ENE 9:31). Bordered on Tziuhcoac, Tochpan, and Tamiahua (SV, secs. 135, 525, 530). Cf. H. Cortés 1973:191. See Kelly and Palerm 1952:274 n. 49.
19. Tlacuilollan		Tlaculula. (RG 5:351, pictograph). Tlacolulan, Veracruz.
20. Techochola		Not identified.
21. Moyotlan		Moyutla, bordered on Xocotla and Tamasonchal (SV, secs. 358, 616). Two leagues from Metatepec (Tantoyuca) (Gerhard 1986:221).

Table 11-5 continued

"Memorial de Tlacopan"*	Codex Mendoza†	Identification
22. Tamiyaua		Tamiagua, on the boundary of Pánuco (SV, sec. 930). Tamiahua, Veracruz.
23. Tancochtlan		(?) Tancuche, bordered on Tanpache and Tamaloluco (SV, sec. 606).
24. Metlateyocan		Metateyuca, bordered on Tuçapan (SV, sec. 526). Metlalteyuca, Puebla.
25. Atlan	Atlan (Atlan, 1)	In the corregimiento of Metlateyuca (LT, 76).
26. Poxaquatlan		(?) Puxutlan in the corregimiento of Metlateyuca (LT, 76).
27. Pantepec		Pantepec (RO, 4). Listed with Metlateyuca and Tezapotitla (LT, 233). Pantepec, Puebla.
28. Mecapalapan		Mecapalapan, in Pantepec, Puebla.
29. Ichcatepec		Ixcatepec, Veracruz.
30. Tecolotlan		San Mateo Tecolotlan, in Pauatlan (PNE 5:279), or Puerto de Tecolutla, (RG 5:179), estancia of Papantla, (SV, sec. 449). or Tecolotla, in Tomatlan, Veracruz.
31. Vitzilpopocatlan		Chilpupucatlan, bordered on Tuspa, Tututepeque, Tuçapan and Çicoaque (SV, sec. 134). In the area of Metlateyuca (LT, 230). 3 leagues east of Ameluca. (RO, 4). (Ameluca, in Pantepec, Puebla)
32. Chauichtlan		Not identified.
33. Teocaltepec		Not identified.
34. Quachiapan		Not identified.
35. Xocotlan (Cf. 15)		Jocutla, listed with Tlacocoauntla and Etlatozca, near Xalapa, on the road to Veracruz (LT, 502), Xocotla, in Tlalnehuayocan, Veracruz, or San Nicolás Xocotlan, in Tlacuiloltepec CPNE 5:283), or Xocotla, in Coscomatepec, Veracruz, or Xocotla, in Huatusco, Veracruz.
36. Cuetlaxco		Not identified.
37. Miyauatlan		Miahuatlan (RG 5:334, 359, 373). Miahuatlán, Veracruz.
38. Tonatiuhco		Tonatico, bordered on Tuçapan, Tenanpulco, and Tlatlauquitepeque (SV, sec. 529). Cabecera in Hueytlalpan (RG 5:166). Moved to Zozocolco, Veracruz (Gerhard 1986:225).

Table 11-5 continued

"Memorial de Tlacopan"* Codex Mendoza†	Identification
39. Mexcaltzinco	Mexcalcingo (SV, sec. 351). Seven leagues west of Misantla (RG 5:189). On border of Tocintla [Teziuhtlan] (SV, sec. 520) Azalamexcalcingo (RO, 10) Mexcalzingo, Azamexcalzingo, or Azcalamexcalcingo (LT, 225–26).
40. Tlauitomizco	Not identified.
41. Teucxochco	Not identified.
42. Palachico	Not identified.
43. Achachalintlan	Achachalintla or Achichilintla, bordered on Chila and Toçapan (SV, secs. 136, 526). Achachalintla (RO, 7). Chichilintla, in Coyutla, Veracruz.
44. Quetzalcouac	Queçalcoaque or Quecalcoatl, bordered on Toçapan and Tlapotongo (SV, secs. 526, 528). Eight leagues south of Papantla (RG 5:175).
45. Centochco	Zetusco, in the corregimiento of Xonotla (LT, 217).
46. Tenampolco	Tenanpulco (SV, sec. 527; RG 5:155). Tenampulco, Puebla.
47. Machanco	Not identified.
48. Toçapan	Tuçapan (SV, sec. 526). San Diego Tuzapan, in Venustiano Carranza, Puebla.
49. Vilopulco	Not identified.
50. Nexquauhtla	Not identified.
51. Totolapan	Totolapan, in Actopan, Veracruz.
52. Xomiloc	Not identified.
53. Ocelotlan	Estancia of Achachalintlan (AGI, Justicia 144-3).
54. Tlaquaquilotlan	Not identified.
55. Xoxouhtlan	Xoxotla, in Tlacolulan, Veracruz.
56. Avatzitzitlan	Not identified.
57. Ayomolla	Not identified.
58. Chiqualotlan	(?) Chicualoque, in Coyutla, Veracruz.

*Numbered as in Zimmermann 1970:7
†Names of the towns in the Codex Mendoza followed in parentheses by the name of the province in which each is located and its place in the sequence of towns as depicted in the codex.

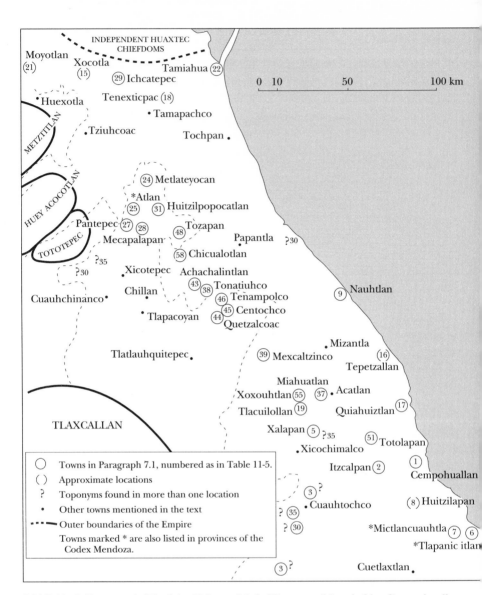

MAP 11–3. Paragraph 7.1 of the "Memorial de Tlacopan," headed by Cempohuallan

Tlapacoyan, Tlatlauhquitepec, Tochpan, and Tziuhcoac in the Tetzcoca sector. It includes, on the contrary, what those provinces do not.

The Totonac area of central Veracruz is one of the main areas covered by this paragraph. Its conquest, in general terms, is also reported by the Tlaxcallan historian Muñoz Camargo, who says that the Tenochcas conquered the entire Totonacapan and the provinces of the Tohueyos (that is, Huaxtecs), Xalapan, Nauhtlan, Mexcaltzinco, and others just to prevent access to the Tlaxcallans and to impede the trade they carried on in those areas.[67]

Cempohuallan (1) and Quiahuiztlan (17) are mentioned briefly as conquered by Moteuczoma Ilhuicamina at the same time as Cuetlaxtlan. But later, Axayacatl invited the kings of Cempohuallan and Quiahuiztlan, "who had not yet been conquered," to the Tlacaxipehualiztli celebration after his conquest of the Matlatzincas.[68] Nothing is known about Cempohuallan as an administrative center of the Empire. The first reports of the Spanish tell of a local ruler and the visit by Moteuczoma's tribute collectors, but there is no evidence about the presence of permanent officials of the Empire.

As pointed out in the discussion of Cuauhtochco, Aguilar in his account of the "provinces" of the Gulf coastlands described Cempohuallan as an important province with twenty thousand houses in its urban area, but he says nothing about the area farther north. Of the town of Cempohuallan and all the adjoining area towards the north and the mountains, Cortés writes that it included about fifty thousand men of war and fifty towns and strongholds; they had become subject to Moteuczoma only recently and by force. When the Spaniards left Cempohuallan, they traveled three days through the territory (tierra y señorío) of this town until they reached Xalapan, and one day later they came to Xicochimalco, which belonged to Moteuczoma.[69] Díaz del Castillo speaks instead of thirty Totonac towns in the mountains that rebelled and became friendly towards the Spanish.[70]

The *Anales de Cuauhtitlan*, in the list of the kings who were ruling in 1519, name Tlacochcalcatl of Cempohuallan and Cohuatlpopoca of Nauhtlan (9).[71] Ixtlilxochitl states that Cuauhpopocatzin was "lord of Coyoacan, one of the great lords of the Empire," who resided in Nauhtlan and had under his charge the government of the coast.[72] He was the lord whom Cortés ordered to be burnt to death as responsible for the death of Juan de Escalante, who had stayed in La Antigua when Cortés departed on the way to Tenochtitlan.[73] This would indicate that the king of a city in the Basin of Mexico was put in charge of governing one of the subjugated towns. But there might have been confusion in identifying the kings of Coyoacan and Nauhtlan, since the latter is named Cohuatlpopoca in the *Anales de Cuauhtitlan*.

Another ruler of this region governed Quiahuiztlan (17); Tezozomoc refers to him in relating the conquest of Cuetlaxtlan.[74] Quiahuiztlan is described as a fortress, but it does not seem to have been an imperial garrison, but rather a Totonac town.[75] In contrast, nearby Tizapantzinco was an imperial fortress with a Mexica garrison.[76]

This paragraph of the "Memorial de Tlacopan" also includes towns not found in the Codex Mendoza that were probably part of the Totonac towns alluded to in the first reports of the Spanish conquerors, such as Xalapan (5), Tlacuilollan (19), and Miahuatlan (37), said to be subject to the Empire in the relación geográfica of Xalapan.[77] In this relación other towns are also said to be subject to Moteuczoma but are not listed in either the Codex Mendoza or the "Memorial de Tlacopan."[78] One of them, Acatlan, declared that Moteuczoma kept a governor and a garrison there "only for the security of the district."[79] As for another of these towns—Xicochimalco—the very brief report says nothing about its relations with the Empire. The Spanish stopped there on the road from Veracruz to Tlaxcallan. Cortés describes it as a "very strong" town subject to Moteuczoma, but Díaz del Castillo says that the people were friends of Cempohuallan and paid no tribute to Moteuczoma.[80] There is a Xicochimalco among the towns conquered by Ahuitzotl, but probably it is not this one.[81] One more town in the relación of Xalapan is Ixhuacan, the same as Teoixhuacan, which the Spaniards reached one day after Xicochimalco. Cortés described this town also as a fortress of Moteuczoma's; Díaz del Castillo says it did not pay him tribute.[82]

Of the towns described in the relación of Hueytlalpan, this town and Xoxouhpanco declared that they paid tribute and were under the command of a governor put there by Moteuczoma.[83] Other relaciones from this Totonac area describe more towns that paid tribute to Moteuczoma. Matlatlan and Chillan paid in cloaks.[84] Mizantla gave liquidambar.[85]

Several towns of paragraph 7.1 are in the area between the provinces of Tlapacoyan and Tlatlauhquitepec on one side and Tochpan on the other: Tonatiuhco (38), Mexcaltzinco (39), Achachalintlan (43), Quetzalcoac (44), Centochco (45), Tenampolco (46), and Tozapan (48).

The location of Tozapan is of some interest. Motolinía reports that the domain of Tetzcoco comprised fifteen provinces and extended as far as Tozapan, but he does not state clearly whether Tozapan is included or not.[86] Paragraph 7.1 suggests that it was not, but was part of a region, under Tenochca supremacy, intermingled with the imperial provinces of the Tetzcoca sector. The *Suma de visitas* gives the following towns as bordering on Tozapan: Quetzalcoac (44), Achichilintlan (43), Tlapotonco, Tonatiuhco (38), Chillan, Cuauhchinanco, Xicotepec, and Metlateyocan (24). Chilpopocatlan, or Huitzilpopocatlan (31), and Tziuhcoac were also adjacent to it.[87] In other words, Tozapan was surrounded by two Acolhua kingdoms (Cuauhchinanco and Xicotepec), a tributary province in the Tetzcoca sector (Tziuhcoac), and other towns, some of them also included in this paragraph of the "Memorial de Tlacopan" but not in the provinces of the Codex Mendoza. It seems, then, that Tozapan was—like most of this paragraph—a Tenochca intrusion into regions initially organized as imperial provinces of the Tetzcoca sector. The conquest of Tozapan is attributed to Ahuitzotl in a campaign directed against this town, Tziuhcoac, and Tamapachco.[88]

Further north, paragraph 7.1 includes Atlan (25), a tributary province in the northeast sector mentioned only in the Tenochca sources, and the neighboring Pantepec (27), Huitzilpopocatlan (31), and Metlateyocan (24). North of these towns was the tributary province of Tziuhcoac, none of whose towns are included in this paragraph.

Some towns in this paragraph are located to the north of Tziuhcoac, such as Moyotla (21), Xocotla (15), Ichcatepec (29), Tenexticpac (18), and Tamiahua (22). All this extends the frontier of the Empire farther than that indicated in the Codex Mendoza.

Huexotla (present day Huejutla, Hidalgo) was an important town on the northern frontier of independent Metztitlan. Its political status is not clear. Huexotla's relación geográfica does not say anything about its relation to the Empire. There is only one report stating that it was punished by Moteuczoma Xocoyotzin because it had rebelled and killed stewards bringing tribute to Tenochtitlan and Tetzcoco; it is not said which town was sending the tribute, nor is the punishment described.[89]

This paragraph of the "Memorial de Tlacopan" enlarges the domains of the Tenochca sector from the Cuetlaxtlan region towards the north, principally on the coast and between the provinces of the Tetzcoca sector. The expansion would have taken place after the creation of those provinces during the reign of Nezahualcoyotl, probably during the campaigns of Ahuitzotl and the second Moteuczoma reviewed above, and must have resulted also in the establishment of the military district of Atlan, which appears in the Tenochca sources as a tributary province and as a military district.

Chapter 12

GARRISONS AND MILITARY COLONIES

The military organization of the Empire was based above all on the military service of the dependent kingdoms of each of the three capitals of the alliance that formed the core area of the Empire. In addition, certain territorial entities had specialized obligations of a military nature. In the Tenochca kingdom the group of towns in the Basin headed by Citlaltepec constituted a military district, from which came the principals sent to govern the colonies of Oztoman and Alahuiztlan. Tlatelolco contributed provisions for military campaigns and for this purpose may have been connected with the towns of Citlaltepec. The Tizayocan region, although considered part of the Acolhuacan, had military functions connected with Citlaltepec; the area is described as cuauhtlalpan (war land) in which meritorious warriors were probably given land.[1] Other towns under Tenochca control in the Acolhuacan may also have given military assistance in the expeditions to Metztitlan and the Huaxteca. Within Tetzcoco itself, Calpollalpan was a military post on the Tlaxcallan border. In the same way, the regions of Chalco and Cuauhtlalpan (the mountain range between the Basin and the Valley of Toluca) took part in military undertakings together with the kingdoms of the alliance. South of Chalco the towns of Xochimilca affiliation served on the frontier with Huexotzinco.[2] In the kingdom of Xilotepec there were garrisons on the frontier against the enemy Chichimecs.[3]

In the regions conquered by the Empire beyond the core area, several sources give as standard practice the establishment of garrisons or presidios and colonies of settlers from the Basin.[4] According to López de Gómara, Moteuczoma had a hundred large cities, capitals of as many provinces, from which he received tribute, where he had forts and garrisons.[5] The *Relaciones geográficas* frequently speak of imperial garrisons. Pomar relates that in all the conquered towns garrisons were established with people from the three capitals of the Empire,[6] and Muñoz Camargo explains that after conquering any kingdom or province "a garrison of Mexicas was established, and they were governed by Moteuczoma's calpixques and governors." He gives the meaning of calpixque as "governor of a stronghold or fortress," which differs from the usual definition.[7]

Nevertheless, Gorenstein and Davies question the existence of garrisons that could have been part of a permanent army of the Empire, basing their argument on the meaning of the word *garrison* in writings of that time. They cite the definition in the dictionary of Covarrubias (1610), "Guarnición de soldados, porque guardan y asseguran la fuerça o plaça donde están" (garrison of soldiers, because they guard and secure the fort or place where they are),[8] and they affirm that this does not imply a fortress occupied by soldiers of a permanent army.[9] It should be noted that the sources also use the term *presidio*. Covarrubias states: "Comúnmente llamamos presidio el castillo o fuerça donde ay gente de guarnición" (usually we call presidio the castle or fort where there are men as a garrison).[10] And the *Diccionario de Autoridades* gives the following:

> Guarnición. Se llama assimismo el Presidio de soldados, para defensa de alguna Plaza o castillo. [Presidio of soldiers for the defense of a place or castle.] . . .
>
> Presidio. la guarnición de soldados que se pone en las Plazas, Castillos y fortalezas, para su guarda y custodia. [Garrison of soldiers put in places, castles and forts for their protection and custody.]
>
> Presidio. Se toma también por la misma Ciudad. Fortaleza, que se puede guarnecer de soldados. [Also means the city itself. Fortress that can be garrisoned by soldiers.]

The chroniclers at times use *guarnición* or presidio for an armed force that defends a certain place temporarily, but also for the new military settlers assigned permanently for the defense of a territory. In order to define the organization of territorial entities with military functions, it is important to identify the procedures for recruiting and remunerating military personnel, especially in regard to their rights to land in the places where they were settled. The sources give enough information to identify the general characteristics of this system.

Although there was no permanent army in the modern sense of the word, the Empire could at any time call on armed forces made up of noblemen, youths from the telpochcalli, and commoners whose obligation was to serve in time of war. The centers for the organization and coordination of their activities were the halls of the palace called *tecpilcalli* (house of princes) and *cuauhcalli* (eagle house) where warriors of high rank assembled; the *cuicacalli* (house of songs) for the officials in charge of the youths (*telpochtlatoque*) and the telpochcalli, the youths' houses. The kinds of land tenure granted to nobles and meritorious warriors were in effect a system for maintaining military personnel of high rank.

In the conquered regions the same procedures were used through the establishment of colonists from the Basin who gave military service and by requiring similar service from the towns of the region. Some early sources describe these procedures in general terms. A report of the Augustinians states that "some towns only served as warriors and others maintained them."[11] Oviedo explains that the agricultural products from Moteuczoma's fields in the towns in which he had no garrison were taken to Tenochtitlan, but when there was a garrison in a town, his warriors consumed these products, and if the people did not cultivate special fields for the garrison, they still had the obligation of supporting the garrison and gave the warriors as well turkeys and any other necessary victuals.[12] As will be seen, the concrete case material from other sources supports this general statement.

Some modern writers have misused the term *mercenary* for those who gave military service. In ancient Mexico it was common practice for the different social segments that constituted a kingdom to carry out different functions within the social and political organization. There were towns whose contribution was principally military, just as others specialized in commerce or crafts and therefore gave tribute and service related to their specialization. That certain groups acted as military auxiliaries does not imply that they were hired to fight for pay; they were people who gave military service instead of tribute in kind. There are no believable data describing the hiring of soldiers, and if there were any who could be described as mercenaries, they were not of sufficient importance to leave any trace in the chronicles.[13]

People with military duties who were settled in strategic areas were not mercenary troops but military colonists, such as those who settled in Oztoman (see below).[14] Similarly, Tlaxcallan and Michoacan welcomed Otomis and Matlatzincas who were fleeing from the Mexicas and gave them land on their frontiers for defense against the Empire. There is a striking difference in the two procedures in that the latter groups of settlers were foreigners, while the Triple Alliance for the most part resettled peoples from the Basin. It is also said that Nezahualpilli ordered that the law be changed so that a warrior guilty of adultery would not be condemned to death but to "perpetual banishment to one of the frontiers and presidios held by the Empire."[15]

The best information on the military garrisons as a distinctive type of political-territorial entity is in the Codex Mendoza; the corresponding pages in the *Matrícula de tributos* have survived only in fragments, and therefore one must rely principally on the Codex Mendoza.[16] In the *Matrícula* the arrangement of the glyphs shows that some garrisons formed units or groups that always consist of a garrison with one or two governors and another town or towns for which there is no indication of their having governors. One can assume that the latter were under the command of the town with governors, thus constituting a military district. The geographic location of the different garrisons confirms the clustering shown in the *Matrícula*.

TABLE 12-1.

Distant Garrisons According to the Codex Mendoza			
17v		18r	
Cuauhtochco	Quecholtetenanco* *tlacatectli* (Mixcoatl)	Oztoman *tlacochcalcatl*† *tlacatecatl*	Atzaccan *tlacatectli* *tlacochtectli*
Huaxyacac *tlacatectli* *tlacochtectli*	Itzteyocan	Atlan *tlacochtectli*	Xoconochco *tezcacoacatl* (Omecuauh) *tlillancalqui* (Atl)‡
Zozollan *tlacatectli* *tlacochtectli*	Poctepec	Tetzapotitlan	

NOTE: This table includes place names and beneath them the titles of the governors, with the personal name, when given, within parentheses. The spelling has been normalized.

*There is no legend; the glyph should be read as Quecholtetenanco.

†*Tlacochcalcatl* is the reading of the glyph. The legend is written as *tlacochtectli*.

‡The legend is smudged. The glyph represents *atl* (water).

TABLE 12-2.

Distant Garrisons According to the *Matrícula de tributos*			
Plate 1		Plate 2	
		Atzaccan	Xoconochco
Huaxyacac	Zozollan	Tetzapotitlan	Atlan
Oztoman	Poctepec		

NOTE: Only place names are given in this table. The glyphs of the governors are almost entirely erased.

Tables 12-1 and 12-2 present the disposition of the distant garrisons as shown in the pages of the Codex Mendoza and the *Matrícula*. It is not clear in what order one should read the garrisons represented in these documents.[17] The Codex Mendoza contains all the garrisons but has evidently changed the arrangement of the original manuscript, as can be seen by Oztoman and Poctepec, which are not depicted together as in the *Matrícula* but appear on different pages. Perhaps, in copying the original, Oztoman was placed on folio 18r instead of 17v simply because there was no more space on the latter. These two pages of the open book have to be seen as a unit.[18] The three garrisons that are not included in the *Matrícula*— Quecholtetenanco, Cuauhtochco, and Itzteyocan—may have been depicted on the torn margin or on some page that has been lost. In discussing the garrisons the order followed is that suggested by the Codex Mendoza.

As the tables show, there was a total of seven military districts. This clustering is clearly indicated in the *Matrícula* by lines that separate them, and there is also a legend next to the governor of Atlan that says, "This one has these two towns," which are obviously Atlan and Tetzapotitlan. By combining the information from both codices it is evident that each district has one or two governors, depicted alongside the town that must be the cabecera. Three of these cabeceras are grouped with towns without governors: Quecholtetenanco together with Cuauhtochco and Itzteyocan, Oztoman with Poctepec, and Atlan with Tetzapotitlan. Huaxyacac, Zozollan, Atzaccan, and Xoconochco are alone, with no associated towns. The colonies and garrisons are shown on map 12-1.[19]

Quecholtetenanco,[20] Cuauhtochco, and Itzteyocan comprise a first military district that is lacking in the *Matrícula*. Cuauhtochco is obviously Huatusco in Veracruz, although it is not possible to know which of the two towns of this name is concerned here.[21] Itzteyocan is one of the towns in the tributary province of Cuauhtochco that is identified with a sujeto of Cuezcomatepec.[22] The location of Quecholtetenanco is more difficult. Barlow identifies it with Quechultenango, south of Chilapa in Guerrero, which would make sense, since it would then be on the frontier of the Yopis.[23] However, another identification that associates it with Cuauhtochco and Itzteyocan is more suitable. The *Libro de las tasaciones* mentions a Cachultenango in the "district of Tehuacan" that later disappears from colonial documentation.[24] In 1579 the surviving population was moved to Tomatlan, between Córdoba and Huatusco.[25] If one looks for Quecholtetenanco near Tehuacan, it is worth noting that Tezozomoc alludes to settlers from the Basin in Huaxyacac, Yanhuitlan, and Cozcatlan. If Quecholtetenanco was near this last town, it would be in the region of the Salado River, which enters the Alvarado River, and close to Tehuacan.[26] Cline identifies Cachultenango with a Cuacultenango in the map of the relación geográfica of Veracruz and situates it near Cuezcomatepec.[27] If we look for Quecholtetenanco in the low country, it could be the archaeological site near Santiago Guatusco in Carrillo Puerto, Veracruz; Medellín's exploration of this site shows that it has characteristics typical of the Mexica period.[28] Clavijero writes of the "old castle of Cuauhtochco," eight or nine leagues northeast of present-day Córdoba; it could be another town in this district.[29]

At any rate, the three towns—Quecholtetenanco, Cuauhtochco, and Itzteyocan—together comprise a military district and must have been depicted together in the *Matrícula*. The military governors of Quecholtetenanco would have had authority over Cuauhtochco and Itzteyocan as did the governor of Atlan over Tetzapotitlan. The Quecholtetenanco district is therefore located in the important region of Veracruz conquered by Moteuczoma Ilhuicamina that includes Cuetlaxtlan (Cotaxtla), Ahuilizapan (Orizaba), and Cuauhtochco.[30] The relación geográfica of Veracruz also speaks of "two presidios and fortresses with a garrison of war-

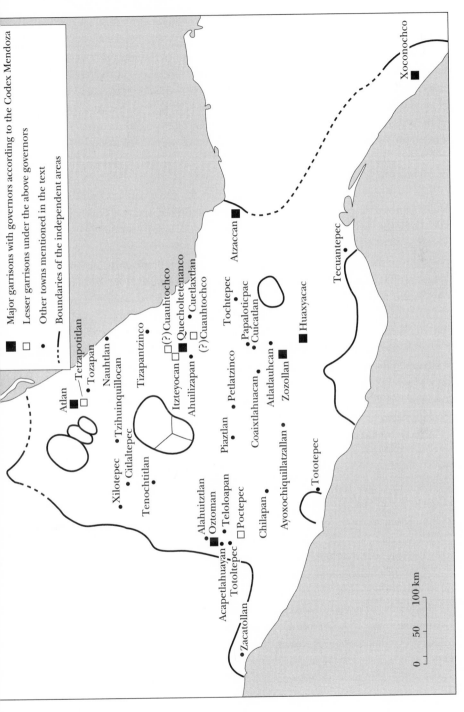

Legend:

■ Major garrisons with governors according to the Codex Mendoza
□ Lesser garrisons under the above governors
• Other towns mentioned in the text
–·–·– Boundaries of the independent areas

Xoconochco

Tetzapotitlan

Atlan
Tozapan
Nauhtlan
Xilotepec • Tzihuinquillocan
Citlaltepec
Tenochtitlan
Tizapantzinco
Cuauhtochco
Itzteyocan □(?)Quecholtetenanco
Ahuilizapan • Cuetlaxtlan
(?)Cuauhtochco
Atzaccan

Tochtepec
Papaloticpac
Piaztlan • Petlatzinco Cuicatlan
Coaixtlahuacan •
Atlatlauhcan •
Ayoxochiquillatzallan • Zozollan
Alahuiztlan Huaxyacac
Oztoman • Teloloapan
Poctepec
Chilapan
Tototepec

Acapetlahuayan
Tototepec
Zacatollan
Tecuantepec

0   50   100 km

MAP 12–1. The military garrisons

riors," one in Cuetlaxtlan and another in Otopa (eight leagues northeast of Veracruz).[31]

Oztoman and Poctepec are depicted in the lower part of the first existing page of the *Matrícula*. Although their glyphs are on different pages in the Codex Mendoza, in the *Matrícula* they are together and separated from Huaxyacac and Zozolan by a horizontal line, now very faint. The town of Oztoman was also included in the tributary province of Tepecuacuilco;[32] Poctepec was in the same region.[33] The conquest of these towns is attributed to Moteuczoma Ilhuicamina,[34] and that of Oztoman also to Axayacatl,[35] but the definitive conquest and the establishment of colonists took place under Ahuitzotl.[36]

In the upper part of the same page, Huaxyacac and Çoçolan (Zozollan), may have been separated by a vertical line, the beginning of which is barely perceptible. Each has two governors; they must have been two different military districts. Both are well-known towns. Huaxyacac, present-day Oaxaca, was settled by people from the Basin during the reign of Moteuczoma Ilhuicamina, following the conquest of Coaixtlahuacan and other towns in the Mixteca.[37] Zozollan (present-day Sosola in the Mixteca) was conquered later by Moteuczoma Xocoyotzin.[38]

Tetzapotitlan and Atlan are depicted in the lower part of the second page of the *Matrícula*, separated by a line from the glyphs of Atzaccan and Xoconochco. These, in turn, are separated by another line, which indicates that each one constituted a different military district. Atlan and Tetzapotitlan also formed a tributary province, situated in the extreme north of the state of Puebla in the Metlateyocan region. There are no data on the conquest or foundation of Atlan. Tetzapotitlan was taken first by Axayacatl and again later on by Ahuitzotl.[39]

Atzaccan has been identified in the past with an Atzacan near Córdoba, Veracruz.[40] It is better to situate it in the region of Coatzacualco. According to Sahagún the "provinces" of Atzaccan, Tepotzotan, and Tlaquilpan were "toward Honduras."[41] Tepotzotan is the Tepozuntlan of Coatzacualco,[42] and Tlaquilpan must be the same as Taquilapa, also in Coatzacualco.[43] Thus, Atzaccan is the garrison that Moteuczoma spoke of to Ordaz, when he told him that his rule did not reach as far as Coatzacualco, and that before arriving there, "he would encounter his garrisons of warriors that he had in the frontier."[44]

Although independent, Coatzacualco was visited by messengers from Moteuczoma Ilhuicamina, who obtained gifts for the temple of Huitzilopochtli and were killed by the people of Huaxyacac, thus provoking the conquest of that city.[45] During the reign of Ahuitzotl, Coatzacualco, Cimatan, and Xicallanco were the towns in Anahuac where the merchants exchanged gifts from the Tenochca king with the local rulers.[46] During this same reign, Coatzacualco is named among the towns of the isthmus (with Xoconochco, Chinantecatl, and Ayotecatl) that armed themselves against the Mexicas before the conquest of Xoconochco, but those towns are not listed among the conquered towns that were tributaries.[47] In this extensive frontier region the Empire may have established outposts, but without permanent political and military dominance. According to the relación of Santa María de la Victoria, Moteuczoma had two forts (*fuerzas*) in the "province" of Tabasco, one in Cimatlan and the other in Xicallanco;[48] the "province" of Chilapan, which Ixtlilxochitl states was subject to Tetzcoco, was between these two towns.[49]

Xoconochco was the town that gave its name to the whole coast of Soconusco. It was also the cabecera of a tributary province. It is in this region that the Empire reached its most extreme expansion.

Four of these military districts correspond to the garrisons that, according to Díaz del Castillo, were on the frontiers of the Empire. "The great Montezuma had many garrisons and captaincies of soldiers in all the provinces, that were always close to their border. He had one in Xoconochco to guard [the area] of Guatemala and Chiapa [Chiappan], another in [the area of] Coatzacualco, and another captaincy in [the area of] Michoacan, and another at the border of Pánuco, between Tuzapan and a town we named Almería, which is on the northern coast."[50]

That is to say, Xoconochco in Chiapas, Atzaccan in Coatzacualco, Atlan towards Pánuco,[51] and Oztoman facing Michoacan were the garrisons on the most distant frontiers of the Empire. The other three military districts were situated in the interior of the Empire. Zozolan and Huaxyacac, in regions not totally dominated by Mixtecs and Tzapotecs, also protected the road to the isthmus. Quecholtetenanco, together with Cuauhtochco and Itzteyocan, must have been of strategic importance in order to deny the Tlaxcaltecs access to the coast, where they had incited the people of Cuetlaxtlan to rebel against the Mexicas, and to secure the road to Tochtepec. Probably these were the most distant frontier garrisons before the expansion to the isthmus.

Quecholtetenanco and Atlan each had only one governor; the other districts had two each. The titles of the governors were not all the same and give an idea of their duties and social rank.[52]

Quecholtetenanco had a *tlacatectli* and Atlan a *tlacochtectli*. Huaxyacac, Zozollan, and Atzaccan each had a tlacatectli and a tlacochtectli. The glyph of a tlacatectli is a headband (*xiuhuitzolli*) that signifies teuctli; that of a tlacochtectli is a headband with a dart (*tlacochtli*). In the *Matrícula*, beside the head of the tlacochtectli of Atlan is the legend *tlacochcalan*; a line connects the legend to a glyph (a house with two darts crossed on the façade) that probably represents his residence. None of these governors has a distinctive hair style. The governors of the other two garrisons have very different characteristics. Oztoman has a tlacochcalcatl (although the legend mistakenly says tlacochtectli) and a tlacatecatl. The glyph of the tlacochcalcatl is a house with two darts above it (that is, *tlacochcalco*); his hair is in the style called *temillotl*, a knotted tuft of hair upright on the crown of the head.[53] The tlacatecatl also has the temillotl. In the third part of the Codex Mendoza (65r), a tlacochcalcatl is depicted with the same glyph and hair style, but in addition with feathers in his headdress and a lip plug.

These titles ending in -*tectli*[54] were held by generals of noble origins, while titles ending in -*tecatl* and -*calcatl* were given to generals of plebeian origins.[55] In the Codex Mendoza the temillotl is the hair style of four "brave men valiant in war and captains of the Mexica armies and men who carry out the duties of generals of the Mexica armies," and who held the titles of tlacochcalcatl, *tezcacoacatl, ticocyahuacatl*, and *tocuiltecatl*. All these individuals also had a plume of feathers in their hair and a lip plug.[56]

The two governors of Xoconochco were a tezcacoacatl and a tlillancalqui. The tezcacoacatl did not have a special hair style; his glyph is a snake. One of the four generals depicted on folio 65r has the same title but has a feathered headdress and a lip plug; the governor of Xoconochco does not. The glyph of the tlillancalqui is the temple called tlillancalco (house of darkness); his hair is long tied with string so that it falls over his back, as is typical of the achcacauhtin, officials of plebeian origin who have distinguished themselves in battle;[57] this tlillancalqui is the only one of the governors who wears this type of hair style. The third part of the Codex Mendoza represents the achcacauhtin in several scenes, always with the same hair style.[58]

Everything seems to indicate that in contrast to the governors of the other garrisons, the governors of Oztoman and Xoconochco were captains of plebeian origin. As is illustrated in Table 12-1, the Codex Mendoza gives the personal name of three governors, but they cannot be identified with individuals mentioned in other sources. The principals who went to Oztoman came from the military district of Citlaltepec,[59] in contrast to the high rank of the first governor of Huaxyacac, Atlazol, a cousin of Moteuczoma Ilhuicamina, who sent him there as viceroy. Atlazol was a son of Moteuczoma's uncle Ocelopan, killed in battle by the Chalcas, who was one of the Tenochca leaders who founded Tenochtitlan and gave their daughters to be wives of Acamapichtli.[60] Atlazol was therefore of illustrious ancestry although not of royal lineage. In any case, the governors of these districts held military titles and were of higher rank than the calpixques.

The attribution of administrative and military functions to the governors of the garrisons is found in the commentaries of the Codex Mendoza and some other sources, as for example, the relación geográfica of Tepecuacuilco, which speaks of a "presidio of garrison men who collected the tribute."[61]

It is clear that some towns contributed both military service and tribute in goods. In the core area Tlatelolco is depicted among the tributary provinces; it gave tribute in kind and labor for repairing the temple of Huitznahuac, but also in time of war gave provisions and participated in battle. The military governors of Tlatelolco held the titles of tlacateccatl and tlacochcalcatl, as did some of the governors of garrisons in the Codex Mendoza.[62] The military district in the Basin that comprised the eleven towns headed by Citlaltepec may also have given tribute in kind, since some of the towns in that district appear in other sources as tributaries.[63]

However, there were different officials for war and for collecting tribute. Military service is not shown on the pages depicting tribute that the calpixques collected, although the tributary province of Tepeyacac gave captives and canes to make weapons. The towns presented on the pages Codex Mendoza devoted to the garrison towns (17v 18r) are not depicted as paying tribute in kind, and the titles of their governors, as well as the reports from other sources on Oztoman and Huaxyacac, prove that they were military establishments. Some towns are found both in these pages and in those that depict tribute in kind, thus confirming the separation between tribute and military service. When the name of a town appears in the pages depicting the garrisons and also in those depicting provinces that paid tribute in kind, one can assume that the town contributed warriors (or, perhaps, provisions) to the military governors, and in addition paid tribute to be sent to Tenochtitlan; the latter may have been given by the indigenous population rather than by the military colonists.

The towns in the military districts that also appear in the tributary provinces are the following: Cuauhtochco, the cabecera of the tributary province that includes Itzteyocan; Atlan, which heads a province that also includes Tetzapotitlan; Xoconochco, also the cabecera of a province; Oztoman, in the province of Tepecuacuilco; and Huaxyacac, in the province of Coyolapan.[64] The garrison towns of Zozolan, Atzaccan, Quecholtetenanco, and Poctepec do not appear in any tributary province.

In addition to the information provided by the titles of their governors, the best material on the organization of the garrisons is found in the reports available on Oztoman and Huaxyacac. The data on the establishment of these colonies has been summarized above. Settlers from the Basin went to Huaxyacac with a governor from the Tenochca nobility.[65] Colonists from the Basin also went to the region of Oztoman, and the principals who governed were from the military district of Citlaltepec.[66]

The relación geográfica of Ichcateopan, whose jurisdiction included Oztoman, adds significant information on the organization of the military colonies. There were several towns in the region that gave military service and helped to provision the military. In the fort at Oztoman there were houses for the soldiers and their wives.[67] The inhabitants of nearby Acapetlahuayan were part of the group of Mexicas who manned the garrison at Oztoman; they paid no tribute and did nothing other than guard the fort as soldiers, "the reason why they did not pay tribute." All the nearby Chontal towns gave the necessary provisions, and whatever was not available in that area was sent to them from Mexico.[68]

In Teloloapan there were barrios of Mexicas, of Chontals, and of people who spoke Yscuca. They paid tribute and reported to the fort at Oztoman for a designated length of time when they were ordered to.[69] The Chontals of Alahuiztlan reported to the fort "with provisions, weapons and help when they were needed,"[70] and the people of Totoltepec did not take tribute to Mexico but instead provisioned the Mexicas at the Oztoman fort.[71]

To sum up, the garrison of Oztoman was made up of both recent colonists from the Basin and the indigenous people of that region; they all gave military service, guarding the fort in turns and participating in the wars. They gave no tribute in kind but were provisioned by other local tributaries with that particular responsibility and were sent from Mexico whatever they could not obtain in that region.

The data on Oztoman are the best available, but there are sufficient indications from other regions to believe that the picture presented was characteristic throughout the Empire. According to Torquemada, sending the soldiers' wives to the garrisons was common practice, which is in accord with the role of the soldiers as colonists. Referring to the Mexicas in Huaxyacac and other towns who were invited by the ruler of Coaixtlahuacan, he states that they came with their wives, and he adds that men who were stationed at the forts (presidios) "anywhere in these Indies used to take their wives with them, so that the kings could keep them there more securely."[72] Durán also speaks of military service by turns in his description of frontiers of the enemy kingdoms whose rulers were invited to the installation of Moteuczoma Xocoyotzin. These kingdoms had watchtowers and many men constantly on guard, "who were replaced every eighty days," under orders that no Mexican pass their boundaries without being interrogated or killed. The Mexicas had the same arrangement.[73]

Several sources mention the existence of forts or garrisons in addition to those depicted in the Codex Mendoza. It is also said that there were conquered or allied kingdoms with obligations of a military kind, although it is difficult to distinguish in these cases whether they were allies or tributaries who specialized in military service. All this enlarges the picture of the military organization of the Empire.

On some frontiers the kingdoms of the alliance confronted polities that were never conquered. The region north of the Basin pertaining to Tenochtitlan and Tetzcoco bordered upon Metztitlan, while the kingdom of Xilotepec had garrisons against the Chichimecs and bordered on part of the Tarascan frontier. But the most important enemies, and those closest to the center of the Empire, were the tramontane kingdoms of Tlaxcallan, Huexotzinco, and Chololan, adjacent to the kingdoms of the Acolhuacan and Chalco, within the Basin, and near subjugated towns or allies of the Empire on the other frontiers.

The Codex Mendoza does not depict any military district facing the tramontane kingdoms, but to the south Tepeyacac, together with other towns in its tributary province, constituted a center of military activity in the war against Huexotzinco and Cholollan. In addition to tribute in goods, Tepeyacac also contributed prisoners of war and weapons. Probably the tribute they gave in maize was used to maintain the garrisons of the region. The importance of the province of Tepeyacac in the military organization was probably a result of its being on the road that had to be taken for the campaigns to the southern part of the Gulf coast and the present-day state of Oaxaca. Some of the towns in this province had important military obligations. On the southern border of Huexotzinco, Ocopetlayocan (Tochmilco) and Cuauhquechollan with its six subject towns, including Hueyapan and Tetellan, are all described as frontier garrisons.[74] East of Itzocan, within the area of the province of Tepeyacac, were located Ahuatlan and its sujeto Texallocan, not recorded in the Codex Mendoza; they fought in the wars and gave captives to be sacrificed. Texallocan was governed by two officials appointed by Moteuczoma; their titles—tlacochcalcatl and tlacatecatl—indicate a military rank like that of the governors of the military districts in the Codex Mendoza.[75]

On the frontier north of Tlaxcallan there was no garrison or tributary province such as Tepeyacac that could serve as a center of the Empire's military activity. The starting points against the Tlaxcaltecs were two towns in the kingdom of Tetzcoco, Tepepolco and Calpollalpan, near the customary battlefields. Farther east there were several kingdoms, not usually described as tributaries, that took part in the various wars on the Empire's side. Tetellan (present-day Tetela de Ocampo) was governed by its own natural lord; it was at war with Zacatlan and Tlaxcallan, and the king of Tenochtitlan provided it with weapons. Zacatlan is sometimes named together with Tlaxcallan among the enemy towns of the Triple Alliance, but later it fought on the side of the Empire; the people did not pay tribute, although they gave presents to Moteuczoma. There was an important fortress in Iztaquimaxtitlan, but there is no good information on its political situation. It is not mentioned as a conquest of the Empire nor as a tributary and was probably an ally like Tetellan.[76]

Most of the towns where there were garrisons, according to local sources, were located in regions that had submitted to the Empire. Some were near the garrisons recorded in the Codex Mendoza and could have been connected with them in the military organization, but others were at a considerable distance.

In the northeast sector of the Empire were garrisons in the area of Tozapan and Mexcaltzinco that may have been connected with Atlan. Farther south, on the coastal plain, there was Tizapantzinco,[77] and, beyond Xalapan toward the Mesa

Central, Xicochimalco and Ixhuacan.[78] In accounts of the Spanish Conquest all three towns are described as fortresses. In nearby Acatlan, Moteuczoma had installed a governor and "a garrison and many weapons, only for the security of the region."[79] These towns do not appear in the Codex Mendoza. Perhaps they were connected with the military district that included Quecholtetenanco and Cuauhtochco, since the campaigns against the latter and Cuetlaxtlan went farther north and closed to Tlaxcallan the road to the coast.

Several towns along the roads to the southeast are described as allies or as sujetos that gave military provisions or service. The most notable example is Teotitlan del Camino, whose relación geográfica states that it was independent and allied with Moteuczoma but did not pay tribute. Nevertheless, Teotitlan and several of its sujetos are included in the "Memorial de los pueblos de Tlacopan."[80] Other towns in the Mixteca Baja recognized the authority of the Empire and gave military assistance. Acatlan's ruler was of Tenochca ancestry; the town did not pay tribute but did give provisions and weapons to the Mexica armies that passed through the town. Similarly, Petlatzinco and Piaztlan gave no tribute except provisions and warriors. Acatlan and Petlatzinco are not given as tributaries in the Codex Mendoza, but they are listed in the "Memorial de Tlacopan."[81]

In the Mixteca the Codex Mendoza depicts only the garrison of Zozollan. However, the relación of Atlatlauhcan states that the calpixques took their tribute to Coaixtlahuacan, where Moteuczoma had put warriors on the frontier. When Moteuczoma's captains required the people of Coaixtlahuacan to send men for other conquests, they did so.[82] In the Codex Mendoza Coaixtlahuacan is the cabecera of the tributary province of that name, and probably other reports from La Cañada allude to its garrison when referring to garrisons that are not named. Thus, Cuicatlan, in addition to tribute, sometimes sent fruit to the men in Moteuczuma's garrisons.[83] Nearby Papaloticpac also took provisions to the garrisons.[84]

On the Tarascan frontier the activity of Oztoman perhaps extended towards the north, where Zoltepec and Amatlan fought against the Tarascans, but it is not known whether they were coordinated with the garrisons depicted in the Codex Mendoza. Farther away, towards the south, the Cuitlatecs of Tetellan gave no tribute other than to serve in the wars against Michoacan and Axochitlan.[85] There are no reports on garrisons against the Tarascans in Zacatollan at the mouth of the Balsas.

In the Sierra Madre del Sur, north of the Costa Grande, Moteuczoma sent a captain, with a garrison, to govern Tlacotepec "as governor and steward" and collect the tribute to be taken to Mexico. Tlacotepec waged war on the towns of the coast (Tequepan, Acamalutla, Temazcaltepec, and others).[86] The Mexica garrison of Tlacotepec is also mentioned in regard to a rebellion by the Yopis during the reign of Moteuczoma Xocoyotzin.[87] Farther east and north of the Yopi region,

Tixtlan, Cuauhmochtitlan, Chilapan (in the province of Tepecuacuilco), and Tzompanco also fought against the Yopis.[88] These towns are not described as Mexica garrisons, but on the eastern frontier of the Yopis, Tototepec, near Ayotlan, was a garrison established there by Moteuczoma.[89] However, there is no information about a military district on this frontier comparable to what is depicted in the Codex Mendoza for other distant garrisons.[90] Along the coast of Guerrero and Oaxaca, the Empire's campaigns must have been undertaken from Oztoman, Tlappan, and Yohualtepec. In addition to Tototepec, near Ayotlan, there was a garrison of Mexicas in Ayoxochiquillatzallan facing the Mixtec kingdom of Tototepec on the coast.

In the Mixteca, north of the frontier with the kingdom of Tototepec, Teotzacualco cultivated fields for Moteuczoma and sent the produce to his garrison in the town.[91] It is not said whether these soldiers were from Tenochtitlan or were local people.

Tochtepec, according to the relación geográfica of Chinantlan, had a "very large garrison" where all the tribute was collected and where there was a court of justice for the towns of the area.[92] Clearly it had more administrative functions than the simple collection of tribute, but it does not appear to be the garrison that Bernal Díaz says was in the Coatzacualco area, which must be that of Atzaccan in the Codex Mendoza.

On the isthmus, Tecuantepec was on the road to Xoconochco and assisted Ahuitzotl's expedition, but there is no information about garrisons of warriors from the Basin.[93]

Almost all these towns are missing from the lists of tributaries in the Codex Mendoza, probably because their obligations were military, although not so well defined or so important as those of the garrisons in folios 17v–18r of the Codex Mendoza, and therefore they were not listed as such. Their incorporation into the imperial system may have been less secure than that of the others.

In conclusion, there were towns that gave both military service and tribute in kind, but the Codex Mendoza shows that the two types of contributions were recorded separately, and there was a distinction made between the governors of the garrisons and the calpixques.

Judging by their titles, the governors of the garrisons depicted in the Codex Mendoza were of a higher rank than the calpixques of the tributary provinces. What was the relationship between the military governors of the garrisons and the calpixques of the tributary provinces? Were these governors in charge of large territorial subdivisions that comprised several tributary provinces? There are no data to provide an answer to these questions, but it will be useful to compare the garrisons in the Codex Mendoza with the sections of the "Memorial de Tlacopan," since this document enumerates not only the towns that paid tribute in goods but also those that gave only military assistance. With the exception of Atzaccan, all the military districts of the Codex Mendoza are represented in the "Memorial de Tlacopan" by the garrison towns where the commanders resided except for Quecholtenango, which is missing, although Cuauhtochco—in the same district— is listed. All these towns are in the sections of the "Memorial de Tlacopan" that comprise the Tenochca sector of the Empire.

The preponderance of Tenochtitlan within the Empire, especially in military matters, explains the Tenochca control of the military garrisons. For this reason, although the northeast sector of the Empire comprised the Acolhua domain, the tributary province of Atlan, seat of one of the principal garrisons, is not included in the reports of the Tetzcoca sources.

The garrisons, or presidios, described in the sources can be defined more precisely as military colonies; that is, they were settlements established in strategic areas with the obligation of providing military service, and they received supplies from the tribute of other local people. Indeed, they were exempt from other types of tribute, and—even if they might have practiced some cultivation and other arts for their own sustenance—from the point of view of the imperial organization they are to be considered as specialists in warfare.

PART FOUR

The Territorial Entities within the Organization of the Empire

Chapter 13

THE ROLE OF THE TERRITORIAL ENTITIES IN THE IMPERIAL ENTERPRISES

The political-territorial entities of the Tenochca Empire have been discussed with emphasis on the sources—such as the Codex Mendoza and the memorials of Tetzcoco and Tlacopan—that are primarily catalogs of the kingdoms, towns, and provinces of the Empire. We have seen not only their geographical distribution but also their differences in terms of economic and political characteristics, thus making it possible to define the territorial structure of the Empire.

In contrast, Durán and Tezozomoc, the two principal narrators of Tenochca history, describe the expansion of the Empire as a series of conquests that modify local political organizations and impose the payment of tribute. They give important data on all the aspects already discussed of the territorial structure and the history of the conquests, and also on the extent of the Empire at various times, especially during the reigns of Tizoc and Ahuitzotl. But the most valuable contribution of these sources is their detailed documentation of the imperial organization as they recount the ways that the different territorial entities participated in each of the enterprises of the Empire that they describe. Therefore, the analysis of these chronicles will concentrate on the social and political activities of the Empire and determine which were the entities that performed them. It becomes clear that it was the kingdoms of the core area that provided contingents of soldiers to carry out military expeditions, the colonists sent to establish the garrisons of the Empire, the merchants who went out on commercial expeditions, the workers who contributed labor and material for public works, and the rulers and officials who attended the great political and the religious ceremonies.

The Participants in the Military Campaigns

When relating the conquests of the Empire the chronicles carefully identify the towns that provided warriors for the campaigns of conquest, especially those undertaken by the Tenochca kings, from Moteuczoma Ilhuicamina to Ahuitzotl. The repeated enumerations of the participants in the military campaigns show that it was always the same towns that sent their warriors to the field. The following brief accounts of the better-known campaigns illustrate this point.

Of all the military campaigns of Moteuczoma Ilhuicamina, the war with Tepeyacac led to the first great conquest eastwards beyond the Basin. The Tenochca rulers, in preparing for this campaign, sent messengers to Tetzcoco, Xochimilco, Colhuacan, Chalco, Cuitlahuac, Coyoacan, and Azcapotzalco to inform them that they should prepare for war. On this same occasion, according to Tezozomoc, Azcapotzalco, Tlacopan, Cuauhtitlan, Acolhuacan, Tetzcoco, Chalco, Colhuacan, Cuitlahuac, Mizquic, and Coyoacan sent provisions for the campaign.[1]

For the expedition against the Huaxteca, Ilhuicamina—according to Durán—asked his cihuacoatl Tlacaelel to send messengers to Tetzcoco, Tlacopan, Chalco, Xochimilco, and all the neighboring towns, including Coyoacan, Cuitlahuac, Colhuacan, and Mizquic. Tezozomoc adds to this list towns in the region to the west of the Basin: Tolocan, Xocotitlan, Xiquipilco, Mazahuacan, Tollan, and Tepexic.[2]

In Ilhuicamina's war against Coaixtlahuacan, provoked by the slaughter of merchants from the Basin, those who were informed first were the kings of Tetzcoco and Tlacopan; "war was then proclaimed throughout all the cities of Chalco, all the cities of Tetzcoco and Itztapalapan, Colhuacan, Mexicatzinco, Xochimilco, Huitzilopochco, Coyoacan, Tlacopan and Azcapotzalco with its whole province, Tollan [and] Matlazinco."[3] Tepeyacac and Tollantzinco, according to Tezozomoc, were also summoned, and the tramontane cities—Huexotzinco, Cholollan, Itzocan, Acatzinco, and Cuauhtinchan—were invited to participate in this war. Although not all of them were part of the Empire, their merchants also had been attacked in Coaixtlahuacan, and as Tlacaelel told Ilhuicamina, "Vengeance belongs to them as much as to us."[4]

When the "flower wars" against Tlaxcallan and other tramontane kingdoms were initiated, Ilhuicamina and Tlacaelel called upon the kings of Tetzcoco and Tlacopan, as well as the rulers of Chalco, Xochimilco, the Tierra Caliente, the entire Cuauhtlalpan, and Mazahuacan, to help in the struggle against Tlaxcallan. All of these—we are told—took part in all the flower wars that followed.[5]

For his ill-fated campaign against Michoacan, Axayacatl called on the kings of Tetzcoco and Tlacopan and the rulers of Chinampan, Chalco, and Tlalhuic.[6] The list of defeated survivors names Mexicas, Tetzcocas, Tepanecs, Chalcas, Xochimilcas, Chinampanecs, the Otomis of the Cuauhtlalpan, and the people from the Tierra Caliente.[7]

When Tizoc undertook a campaign against Metztitlan, according to Durán, he summoned Tetzcoco, Tlacopan, Chalco, Xochimilco, Tierra Caliente, the Cuauhtlalpan, and Matlatzinco.[8] Tezozomoc's account adds that messengers were sent to other towns of the Tierra Caliente as far as Tepeyacac and Tecamachalco and to all the mountain people, to the Otomis, to the Malinalcas, and to more distant towns such as Huaxyacac, Colima (*sic*), Tollantzinco, and Zacatlan. When Tizoc reached Atotonilco el Grande, its people joined his army, as did "the Otomis of Itzmiquilpan, and those of Atocpan, valiant Otomis," who probably were frontier settlers with military obligations.[9]

Ahuitzotl fought in the Huaxteca against Tziuhcoac, Tozapan, and Tamapachco, which had rebelled against him. He planned the campaign together with the kings of Tetzcoco and Tlacopan, and when war had been proclaimed, the armies of Mexico, Tetzcoco, the Tepanec region, Xochimilco, and Chalco went forth to battle. Once arrived at Cuauhchinanco, Ahuitzotl asked its king for soldiers and sent scouts from the three capitals plus others from Chalco, Xochimilco, and the Four Lords to reconnoiter the area.[10]

In Ahuitzotl's expedition against Oztoman, the participants were Tetzcoco, Tlacopan, the Four Lords, Cuitlahuac, Mizquic, Cuauhnahuac, Huaxtepec, Yacapichtlan, the "towns further down, called Coayxtlahuacan" (*sic pro* Cohuixco), others all the way to Tollantzinco and Metztitlan, and the people of the mountains of Tolocan, Malinalco, and Xiquipilco.[11]

In the war against Xoconochco, undertaken by Ahuitzotl, the king first ordered that all the "provinces" should pass in review so that he could see how many went from each one: "Thus went forth the men of the whole province of Tetzcoco, and of Tacuba [Tlacopan], and of Chalco, and of the Tierra Caliente, and of Xochimilco with all the Chinampan, and of the whole Cuauhtlalpan, each province separately arranged in companies with their captains, in an orderly fashion." The ruler of Tecuantepec, who had also been summoned to take part in this expedition, waited with his army for the others, in Huaxyacac.[12]

In all these accounts the first to be called upon were the kings of Tetzcoco and Tlacopan, and their armies always took part in the military campaigns. The dependent kingdoms of Tenochtitlan were also summoned: the Four Lords of Colhuacan and the Chinampanec cities of Xochimilco, Cuitlahuac, and Mizquic. The dependent kingdoms of Tetzcoco are not identified individually except for Cuauhchinanco, the point of departure towards the Huaxteca, but one can assume that they formed part of the contingents from the Acolhuacan. We also know that the king of Teotihuacan took part in Axayacatl's war against Xiquipilco. The dependent kingdoms of Tlacopan are sometimes identified, but often the text uses expressions such as "the Otomies" or "the mountain people" or "the Cuauhtlalpan." Some regions, such as Mazahuacan, Matlatzinco, and Tolocan, are frequently named; in one case Malinalco also appears. This indicates that Tenochtitlan was more active in organizing the participation of those western regions than it was in the domain of Tetzcoco. All this makes up what we have called the core area, comprising essentially the three groups of kingdoms, each under the great king of one of the three capitals of the Empire, but it also included Chalco, Tlalhuic, and Tolocan. For expeditions to more distant areas, towns outside the core area are also mentioned, although not systematically: in one case, Tepeyacac and Zacatlan, for the war against Metztitlan; in another, Tecuantepec, for the campaign against Xoconochco. These are cities that had already been conquered or had become allies and were neighbors of the enemies they went to attack.

The Settlers Sent to Conquered Territories

The conquest of new territories at times led to the sending of new settlers; there are two instances—Huaxyacac and Oztoman—in which it is told who they were.

Both chroniclers attribute the conquest of Huaxyacac to Moteuczoma Ilhuicamina and describe the establishment of a colony with settlers from the Basin. Ilhuicamina and Tlacaelel chose six principals to go with the Mexicas to settle in different parts of the town. According to Durán, when Tlacaelel planned this colonization, he proposed that six hundred married men from Mexico should go; that Nezahualcoyotl should provide sixty married men from his entire "province" and the king of Tlacopan the same number from his people; and that Xochimilco, Chalco, the Tierra Caliente, and the Mazahuas should provide what they could. When the plan was carried out, Moteuczoma sent his cousin Atlazol as viceroy of all those groups so that the new town would be ordered in such a way that each group—Mexicas, Tetzcocas, Tepanecs, and Xochimilcas—would be settled in its own barrio.[13]

Tezozomoc's account is somewhat confused, combining this colonization with those in other towns that he does not specify clearly. He tells first of the Mexicas who had been established in Chalco and then went to Huaxyacac to settle there, except for some who stayed in places along the road. The settlers included Mexicas, Tetzcocas, Tecpanecs (*sic*), Chalcas, Xiquipilcas, and others. He ends by saying that "to the coastlands of Huaxyacac went the people of Cuauhtochpan, the Tochtepecas and Teotlitlecas [*sic*], who went very content and happy."[14] In this case the coastlands obviously refer to the watershed of the Gulf. The first town, Cuauhtochpan, must be Cuauhtochco, and the second, Tochtepec; the third could be either Teotitlan (del Camino) or Teotlillan, both present in the "Memorial de los pueblos de Tlacopan" (7.2-24 and 7.2-60).

Tezozomoc alludes again to new military settlements apropos of the colonization of Oztoman. The kings who were planning it said they were going to imitate what Moteuczoma Ilhuicamina had done in his conquests: "We sent our vassals to the destruction of the lands and peoples of Huayxacac, Yancuitlan, Cozcatlan and the rest of those lands. They went everywhere and are now those who preside and multiply. They were all from these areas, Mexicas, Acolhuas, [the people from] Tlacopan, Azcapotzalco, Xochimilco, and Chalco. The same thing should be done now."[15]

Ahuitzotl ordered the settlement of three towns—Teloloapan, Oztoman, and Alahuiztlan. As a consequence of the war, half the population of Teloloapan had perished; the other two towns were destroyed with no one left alive. New settlers came from Mexico, both Tenochtitlan and Tlatelolco, from Tetzcoco and Tlacopan, and from all the neighboring regions. Messengers went to all the towns of Coatlapan (*sic pro* Cuauhtlalpan) and to Tlalhuic, Chalco, Xochimilco, Cuitlahuac, Mizquic, Colhuacan, Itztapalapan, Matlatzinco, Xilotepec, Chiappan, Mazahuacan, Xocotitlan, Cuahuacan, Cillan, and Ocuillan so that all of them would choose people to be sent as settlers. Then the principals of Mexico decided that the rulers of the three repopulated cities should be twenty married principals from the estancias of Iztacalco, Popotlan, Coatlayauhcan, and Acolnahuac.[16]

It is evident, then, that the cities in the core area who undertook the wars of conquest were those whose people were sent to repopulate the conquered regions.

The Participants in Public Works

All the principal kingdoms of the Basin played a role in public works. They provided skilled artisans, who were an important part of the urban population, as well as masses of laborers, and at the same time brought the necessary construction materials. The concrete cases in the chronicles of Durán and Tezozomoc confirm the general statements to this effect in the memorials of Tetzcoco and Tlacopan.

Perhaps the best example is the construction of the temple of Tenochtitlan during the reign of Moteuczoma Ilhuicamina. The king convoked the rulers of Tetzcoco, Xochimilco, Cuitlahuac, Mizquic, Colhuacan, Tlacopan, Azcapotzalco, and Coyoacan; explained the need for a new temple; and ordered them to have their vassals report to the work project with the necessary materials: heavy stone for cement, light stone for the building, lime, and wood. The rulers of Chalco were also asked to assist, but they refused, thus provoking the war that eventually ended with their defeat.[17] This war and several others delayed the construction of the temple. Finally, Moteuczoma, before the campaign against Huaxyacac, called together "all the lords of the provinces" and the kings of Tetzcoco and Tlacopan, told them that he wanted to finish the temple of Huitzilopochtli as soon as possible, and asked for their help; "the kings and lords of all the land" agreed. Moteuczoma told the king of Tetzcoco that he and his "province" were to take charge of the front of the building, and the king of Tlacopan and his kingdom would take the back. He charged Chalco with the right side and Xochimilco, with all the Chinampan, the left side. He also ordered that the Mazahuas, "who are the Otomi nation," that is, Chiappan, Xiquipilco, Xocotitlan, Cuahuacan, and Mazahuacan, "which are those called Cuacuatlaca [*sic*]" should bring sand and that those of the Tierra Caliente should bring lime.[18] At this time the Otomi region had already entered the Empire as part of the Tepanec kingdoms of Tlacopan; however, in this list it seems to be defined in a manner similar to the region that was conquered later (or reconquered) by Ahuitzotl.[19]

The cities of the Basin cooperated with the Mexicas in several hydraulic works.[20] Nezahualcoyotl's participation in the construction of the dike that separated Lake Tetzcoco from that of Mexico is well known. The best report on this is by Torquemada, who puts this event in the ninth year of the reign of Moteuczoma Ilhuicamina, when there was a great flood and the city was about to be inundated. The Tenochca king summoned Nezahualcoyotl, "who he knew was a man of great intelligence and inventiveness for anything"; they decided that the remedy was to construct a wall of wood and stone. They asked for help from the kings of Tlacopan, Colhuacan, Itztapalapan, and Tenayocan, all of whom—that is, the workers of whom—built the wall. The wooden stakes were brought by the "Tepanecs, Coyohuaques, Xochimilcas," and the stones were brought "from more than three or four leagues away."[21] In other words, the workers and the raw material came from cities in the Tepanec and Tenochca domains, which were closest to the site of the project. The role of Nezahualcoyotl, whose name is usually given to this dike, is in accord with his reputation as a great builder. He is also credited with the construction of the Tepeyacac causeway that entered the city of Mexico from the north and of the aqueduct that brought from Chapultepec the water that had previously entered the city through a ditch.[22]

Another example occurred in the reign of Ahuitzotl, when water was first brought to the city from the Acuecuexco spring in Coyoacan. Tetzcoco and its "province" brought both heavy and light stone, and the Tepanecs, heavy stone. Chalco came with sand, beams, and stakes for the foundation. The Xochimilcas came with instruments for digging up sod and canoes filled with dirt to close off the water; the people of the Tierra Caliente brought innumerable loads of lime. In addition to all these, the Otomis of Xilotepec and the Cuauhtlalpan were also on hand, but their contribution is not specified.[23]

An interesting case occurred, during the last years of Moteuczoma Xocoyotzin, who decided to have transported to Tenochtitlan a huge stone that would be used to make a *temalacatl* (a round stone for the gladiatorial sacrifice) for the temple of Huitzilopochtli. The chronicles give very detailed accounts of the attendant ceremonies and emphasize the supernatural behavior of the stone, which spoke to the laborers; they also tell who took part in transporting the great stone.

A suitably large stone had been located in Acolco Chalco; Moteuczoma ordered that men from Xochimilco, Cuitlahuac, and the cities of the Four Lords were to assemble with levers and ropes to bring the stone, but these workers were unable to move it. Moteuczoma requested help from the king of Tetzcoco, and with the men that he sent, the stone was dragged as far as Tlapechhuacan, but they could not move it beyond that. Durán relates that Moteuczoma then summoned the "province" of Cuautlalpan, "who are the Otomi." Tezozomoc states more specifically who came: "all the Tecpanecs, mountain people, Chiappan, Xilotepec, Xiquipilco, Cuauhtitlan, Mazahuacan." All of them took the stone as far as Tlapitzahuayan, and there Moteuczoma asked the king of Azcapotzalco for help. In the following days the workers succeeded in moving the stone to Techichco (in Iztapalapan), then to Tocititlan (at the entrance to the city of Mexico) and to the bridge of Xoloco, where all the beams broke and the stone sank into the water. Moteuczoma summoned all the divers of Xochimilco, Cuitlahuac, Mizquic, and Tlacochcalco, who were unable to find the stone; they saw only a path of water that led towards Chalco. The stone later appeared on the same spot from which it had been taken.[24]

The Merchants of the Empire who Traveled to the Isthmus

Beginning with the reign of Ahuitzotl, the merchants of the cities of the Basin took their trading expeditions to regions beyond the isthmus. Sahagún, in his *Historia general*, gives the best information about these merchants who traveled to the frontiers of the Empire. There were twelve cities with merchants of the rank called "bathers of people" (*tealtianime*), that is, purifiers of the victims they offered to be sacrificed. All these cities were component kingdoms of the three parts of the Empire. Five were in the Tenochca domain: Tenochtitlan, Tlatelolco, Chalco, Xochimilco, and Huitzilopochco. In the domain of Tetzcoco there were four, including the capital, plus Huexotla, Coatlichan, and Otompan. Three cities were in the Tepanec domain: Azcapotzalco, Mixcoac (pertaining to Coyoacan), and Cuauhtitlan. The merchants from these cities maintained a house in Tochtepec, the center of commercial operations in the region. Only merchants from some of the twelve cities went to the coast (Anahuac); they were the Mexicas of Tenochtitlan and Tlatelolco, together with their "companions" (*inuicalhuan*) from Cuauhtitlan and Huitzilopochco.[25] In other passages those who went to the coast were from these same four cities plus Azcapotzalco, also a provider of "companions."[26] It appears that only merchants from the Tenochca and Tepanec domains were allowed to go that far.

Many of the military expeditions related in the chronicles are justified as attacks on towns that had killed Mexica merchants. With this motive the authors specify the origins of the merchants who went to trade beyond the Basin. Durán and Tezozomoc differ slightly concerning the names of the cities from which the merchants departed, and they do not limit themselves to those who traveled as far as Tochtepec and the isthmus. It may be that their reports are not very exact, but they give an indication of what cities they came from. The war against Tepeyacac was undertaken because of the massacre of merchants from Mexico, Tetzcoco, Azcapotzalco, Colhuacan, Tlacopan, Coyoacan, Itztapalapan, Xochimilco, Cuitlahuac, Mizquic, Chalco, Toltitlan, Cuauhtitlan, and Tenayocan.[27] Among those whose death at Coaixtlahuacan provoked an attack by the Empire were merchants from Mexico, Azcapotzalco, Tlacopan, Toltitlan, Tetzcoco, Xochimilco, and Chalco.[28]

When Ahuitzotl undertook a campaign against Tecuantepec, the merchants who had been attacked were long-distance traders (*oztomeca*) from Mexico, Acolhuacan, Cuauhtitlan, Toltitlan, Tecpanecas, Tenayocan, Cuitlachtepec, Xochimilco, Cuitlahuac, Mizquic, and Chalco.[29] Although the list includes Acolhuacan, all the rest are from the Tenochca and Tlacopanec domains, confirming in a way Sahagún's report that these were the ones who went to the coast. Usually these enumerations of Tezozomoc and Durán concentrate on Tenochca and Tepanec cities; perhaps it is they who were most active in exterior trade. Also, the regions that they discuss—Tepeyacac, Coaixtlahuacan, and Tecuantepec—are in the southern, or Tenochca, sector of the Empire. But it is also possible that these chronicles name Tetzcoco as representing all the cities in its domain, while they give more details about the Tenochca and Tepanec domains, conforming to the point of view of these chronicles, which give the Tenochca version of history.

The Participants in Political and Religious Celebrations

Several accounts enumerate the territorial and political entities that participated in religious and political ceremonies. The most detailed description of a religious festival is that of the inauguration of the temple in the reign of Ahuitzotl, which will be presented below, but there are other examples. After Moteuczoma Ilhuicamina defeated the Huaxtecs, the festival of Tlacaxipehualiztli was celebrated in the recently finished temple. The king invited the rulers of Tetzcoco, Tlacopan, Chalco, Xochimilco, Tlalhuic, Cohuixco, Matlatzinco, and the Mazahuas; and "everyone they could from the surrounding area, so that they could come to see what that festival signifies and what is done in it." That is, they were the components of the Empire and the cities in the basin of the Balsas River whose conquest had begun in the time of Itzcoatl.[30]

Moteuczoma Xocoyotzin, after the war against Teuctepec,[31] celebrated the inauguration of the Coatlan temple with the sacrifice of the prisoners of war.[32] He invited foreign rulers and those of Tetzcoco and Tlacopan, and also the great lords of Mexico, the rulers of Chalco, Xochimilco, Colhuacan, Cuitlahuac, Mizquic, Itztapalapan, Mexicatzinco, Huitzilopochco, and the Tierra Caliente. Before the sacrifices, the king gave titles and insignia to the warriors of his kingdom who were from the cities named and who had distinguished themselves in the war. Then the kings of Tetzcoco and of Tlacopan did the same with their warriors. Here again, the participants in the ceremony illustrate the tripartite division of the Empire.[33]

The installation of a new king was another occasion in which the entities that comprised the Empire participated. In fact, the principal celebration was Tlacax-ipehualiztli, in which the prisoners captured in the first military campaign of the new king were sacrificed. The most detailed account is about the installation of Tizoc, which will be discussed below.

The descriptions of the funeral rites for the kings also illustrate the participation of the component cities of the Empire. At the death of Axayacatl, the first who came to give funeral orations and present gifts were the kings of Tetzcoco and Tla-copan. Then followed the kings of Chalco, Cuauhnahuac, Yauhtepec, Huaxtepec, Yacapichtlan, Tepoztlan, Xochimilco, Tepeyacac, and Cuetlaxtlan. That is, first the other two kings of the alliance, followed by the dependent kings of Tenochti-tlan, and in last place, the rulers of the principal conquests made outside the Basin. After all these, "entering secretly the retreat where Tlacaelel was," the rulers of Tlaxcallan, Huexotzinco, and Cholollan brought their offerings.[34]

At the funeral rites for Tizoc, the kings of Tetzcoco and Tlacopan came to dress the body of the deceased king. They were followed by the Chinampanecs and the people of Colhuacan, Cuitlahuac, Mizquic and Ayotzinco. Then came the rulers of the Coatlalpanecs, Cohuixco, the Mazahuas, the mountain people, and the Oto-mis; and then those of Cuauhnahuac, Yauhtepec, Huaxtepec, Tepoztlan, Yacap-ichtlan, and of Malinalco, Tolocan, Calimayan, Tenantzinco, Teotenanco, Tzina-cantepec, and Xocotitlan. Again, we have a list very similar to that of Axayacatl's funeral rites except that it enumerates in detail the towns of the Tolocan region that had been conquered (or reconquered) by Axayacatl and Tizoc.[35] The chron-icles give many more details on the funeral rites for Ahuitzotl, which will be dis-cussed below.

The following sections describe the events that best exemplify the participation of the territorial entities in the political and religious celebrations of the Em-pire. The lists of towns that participated in these activities make evident the extent of the Empire at the time when the events took place and at the same time provide important information on the territorial divisions. The data are presented in the form of comparative tables, with parallel passages from the two chronicles. The functions carried out by the different regions are examined and a comparison made with the territorial organization discussed in the preceding chapters. Since most towns have already been identified, there will be no need to document locations other than those of towns not already named.

The Installation of Tizoc

The installation of Tizoc took place when he returned from his campaign against Metztitlan. The chronicles of this event give a long enumeration of the component parts of the Empire at that time and thus provide a picture of the Empire's extent before the great expansion under Ahuitzotl.

In Durán's account, all the rulers of the Empire were invited—"the king of Tetzcoco, the king of Tlacopan, the lords of Chalco, of Xochimilco and of the whole Chinampan area, Colhuacan, Itztapalapan, Mexicatzinco, Huitzilopochco, all those from the Tierra Caliente, Cuauhtlalpan, Matlatzinco, Tolocan and the Coatlapa [*sic pro* Coatlalpan]. . . . They also sent messengers to all the towns where Tenochtitlan had stewards and governors, asking them to provide everything needed for this festivity and to come and be present for the ceremony."[36] Finally, Durán lists the stewards who brought the requested goods. Tezozomoc names only the kingdoms of Tetzcoco and Tlacopan and adds that messengers went to all the other towns, as far as the coast, to Cuetlaxtlan, Ahuilizapan and Cempohuallan; he then proceeds to list the principals and stewards who came to Tenochtitlan.[37]

Table 13-1 presents in parallel columns the place names provided by Durán and Tezozomoc in their lists of stewards, and a third column gives the province, from the Codex Mendoza, in which the town is located. Numbers have been added to identify each regional group.[38]

The order followed in the lists is clearly geographic, from the northeastern part of the Empire to the south and west, that is, clockwise, as in Sahagún's list of calpixques, although the groupings of towns are different.

The first group in the table comprises the tributary provinces of the northeastern sector, but it should be noted that Tezozomoc had previously mentioned messengers sent to Ahuilizapan and Cempohuallan, towns not included in the lists of stewards who reported to Tenochtitlan, nor does Durán mention them; probably they were included among those of Cuetlaxtlan.

The second group consists of the principal kingdoms of Tlalhuic. It is obviously a list of political units and does not coincide with the Codex Mendoza's division of this area into only two tributary provinces.

In the third group, Tezozomoc begins with Coaixtlahuacan, which would be the only town in Oaxaca on this list, but it must be an error for Cohuixco.[39] This is what the following toponyms suggest, all of them towns in the tributary provinces of Tlachco and Tepecuacuilco; several are represented in the Codex Mendoza. Of the remaining cities, Tepetlan is probably Tepetlapan, a sujeto of Cocollan,[40]

TABLE 13-1.

Towns Whose Stewards Were Present at Tizoc's Inauguration

Durán 1967, 2:307	Tezozomoc 1975:446	Codex Mendoza
1. Cuetlaxtlan	Cuetlaxtlan	Cuetlaxtlan
Tochtla	Tochpan	Tochpan
Tziuhcoac	Tziuhcoac	Tziuhcoac
and Tozapan	Tozapan	—
2. Cuauhnahuac	Cuauhnahuac	Cuauhnahuac
Yauhtepec	Yauhtepec	In Huaxtepec
Huaxtepec	Huaxtepec	Huaxtepec
Yacapichtlan	Yacapichtlan	In Huaxtepec
3. Couixco	Coaixtlahuacan (*sic*)	
Huitzoco	Huitzoco	In Tepecuacuilco
Tepecuacuilco	Tepecuacuilco	Tepecuacuilco
Tlachmalac	Tlachmalacac	In Tepecuacuilco
Yohuallan		In Tepecuacuilco
Tepetlan		—
Nochtepec	Nochtepec	In Tlachco
Teotliztac		In Tlachco
Tlachco	Tlachco,	Tlachco
Tzacualpan	Tzacualpan	—
Iztapan	Iztapan	—
4. The governors of	The artisans and stewards	
the Totoltecs	Toltecs	
Chiauhtlan	Chiauhtlan	—
Piaztlan	Piaztlan	—
Teotlala (sic)	Teotlalco	—
Cuitlatenanco	Cuitlatenanco	—
Cuauhapazco	Cuahuapazco	—
Xochhuehuetlan	Xochihuehuetlan	—
5. Olinallan	Olinallan	In Quiauhteopan
Tlalcozauhtitlan	Tlalcozauhtitlan	Tlalcozauhtitlan
6. Matlatzinco	Matlatzinco	—
Tolocan		Tolocan
Tzinacantepec		—
Tlacotepec	Tlacotepec	In Tolocan
Calimayan	Calimayan	In Tolocan
Tepemaxalco	Tepemaxalco	In Tolocan
Teotenanco.	Teotenanco	In Tolocan
	all their stewards	
7. Those of the Mountains:		
Malinalco	Malinalco	Malinalco
Ocuillan	Ocuillan	Ocuillan
Coatepec		In Ocuillan or in Cuahuacan
Capulhuac		—
Xalatlauhco,		Tlalatlauhco in Cuahuacan
Atlapulco		—

which is included in the Codex Mendoza. There are two others, Tzacualpan (Zacualpa, Mexico) and Iztapan (Ixtapan de la Sal, Mexico), whose presence in this context supports the association of that region with the tributary province of Tlachco rather than with the Valley of Toluca.

The fourth group includes towns in the Balsas Basin that are lacking in the Codex Mendoza. First on the list are the Totoltecs and a few towns, one of which is Piaztlan, whose relación geográfica places it in the "province" of the Totoltecs.[41] Tezozomoc's interpretation that they were Toltec artisans is clearly erroneous. Other towns in this group in addition to Piaztlan may have been Totoltec; the text is not clear on this point. Chiauhtlan (Chiautla de la Sal, Puebla) is found in the "Memorial de Tlacopan" (7.3-23). Teotlalco was a town with many estancias;[42] today it is the municipio of the same name in the state of Puebla near the boundary with Morelos. Cuitlatenanco is the same as Cuitlatenamic, which was in the region of Jolalpa, Puebla.[43] Xochihuehuetlan was an estancia of Cuauhmochtitlan,[44] a town that is also listed in the "Memorial de Tlacopan" (7.3-13); it is the present-day Xochihuehuetla, Guerrero. Cuauhapazco has not been located.

The towns of the fifth group, farther south, can be identified with two other tributary provinces in the Balsas Basin, Quiauhteopan and Tlalcozauhtitlan. Instead of naming the cabecera, both Durán and Tezozomoc list Olinalan, a major town in the province of Quiauhteopan, The sixth group coincides basically with the province of Tolocan in the Codex Mendoza. In the seventh, Malinalco and Ocuillan are provinces in the Codex Mendoza; Xalatlauhco was in the province of Cuahuacan, located in territory of Tlacopan; and Capolhuac and Atlappolco pertained to Tlacopan.[45]

To sum up, this enumeration begins with the northeastern, or Tetzcoca, sector and continues with the southern, or Tenochca; the latter takes up the greater part of the list. This southern sector comprises towns in Tlalhuic and Cohuixco. The latter corresponds to the tributary provinces in the Codex Mendoza headed by Tlachco, Tepecuacuilco, Quiauhteopan, and Tlalcozauhtitlan, and in addition, Piaztlan, and other towns that might also have been part of a Totoltec region. The Coatlalpan region is also mentioned among those whose rulers were invited to the installation, but it is missing from the list of stewards. In the Codex Mendoza, Tepeyacac is the cabecera of the province including the Coatlalpan towns, but probably Tepeyacac is not included here because it did not pay tribute in the kinds of goods that were required for the celebration. This contrasts with the important participation of Tepeyacac in the inauguration of the temple, for which it contributed captives to be sacrificed. The provinces of Cihuatlan and Tlappan of the Codex Mendoza are lacking here; they were conquered later by Ahuitzotl. What is more striking is the omission of towns in Oaxaca, Cuauhtochco, and Tochtepec, which at that time were the most distant areas subject to the Empire, since Xoconochco had not yet been conquered.

The list ends with the northwestern sector, represented by the region of Tolocan and several towns near Tlacopan. However, Chiappan and other towns nearby are missing; these were rebellious and were conquered by the next king, Ahuitzotl.[46] Also missing are the Tlacopanec kingdoms, the Acolhua kingdoms, and the Chinampanec kingdoms of Tenochtitlan. Obviously only tributaries of the Empire are included, since this is basically a list of stewards. The dependent kingdoms of the three capitals, whose rulers have been cited at the beginning of the account, are not listed.

Inauguration of the Great Temple

The inauguration of the great temple at the beginning of Ahuitzotl's reign is another occasion in which Durán and Tezozomoc enumerate the rulers that attended a ceremony taking place in Tenochtitlan. It is the best example of the manner in which the different territorial units of the Empire contributed to such a great political, military, and religious celebration. Both chronicles describe the participation of the various polities in two parts. First they describe the process of inviting the rulers to come to the festival with their captives, and then their arrival. Later they enumerate the stewards who brought the tribute. The towns in the first group comprise the kingdoms of the core area and the nearby regions that had important military obligations. The second group includes several of these towns but adds others from more distant areas and emphasizes the contribution of tribute in kind.

In recounting the invited rulers who brought their captives with them, the two chronicles follow a different order. Table 13-2 puts together the data from both, listing them according to the order followed by Tezozomoc. Durán agrees on the towns named but differs in the order in which he presents them. In the table, the material from each source is put in sections numbered according to the sequence in each author's account.[47]

Tezozomoc gives first place to the kings of Tetzcoco and Tlacopan, whom Ahuitzotl calls "the two kings our brothers." His second group and Durán's fifth contain the kingdoms that are direct dependencies of Tenochtitlan, that is, the Chinampanecs and the Four Lords. Tezozomoc also includes Chalco, although he repeats it later in his seventh group, while Durán names it only once in his third group.

The towns of the Cuauhtlalpan in Tezozomoc's third group and Durán's seventh were conquered by Ahuitzotl in his first campaign because they had rebelled.

TABLE 13-2.
Kings and Towns Summoned by Ahuitzotl to the Temple's Inauguration

Tezozomoc 1975:486	Durán 1967, 2:334–36
1. "The two kings our brothers" (i.e., Tetzcoco and Tlacopan)	8. Tetzcoco with its sujetos (see list in comments in text)
	9. Tlacopan with the lords of its province (not named)
2. Lords and principals from the Chinampanec towns: Colhuacan, Cuitlahuac, Mizquic, Chalco, Xochimilco, and the Four Lords	5. Xochimilco, Cuitlahuac, Mizquic The Four Lords of Colhuacan, Itztapalapan, Mexicatzinco, Huitzilopochco.
3. Coatlapan (sic pro Cuauhtlalpan), Xocotitlan, Mazahuacan, Xiquipilco, Cuahuacan, Chiappan, Xilotepec.	7. Mazahuacan, Xocotitlan, Xiquipilco, Cuahuacan, Cillan, Chiappan, Xilotepec.
4. Matlatzinco, Tzinacantepec, Calimayan, Tlacotepec, Tepemaxalco, Teotenanco, Zoquitzinco, Xochihuacan, Coatepec and Copalhuac (sic), with all the sujetos of Matlatzinco.	6. Tolocan, Matlatzinco, Calimayan, Tepemaxalco, Tlacotepec, Teotenanco, Metepec, Capolhuac, Xochiacan, Zoquitzinco, Tenantzinco, Malinalco, Ocuilan.
5. Tepeyacac, Cuauhtinchan, Tecaltzinco, Acatzinco, Oztoticpac, Tecamachalco, Quecholac	1. Tepeyacac with four sujetos: Cuauhtinchan, Tecalli, Acatzinco, Oztoticpac. Tecamachalco, Quecholac
6. Acapetlahuacan	2. Cuauhquechollan, with its six sujetos: Acapetlahuacan, Atzitzihuacan, Yaotehuacan, Hueyapan, Tetellan, Tlamimilolpan
7. Chalco	3. Chalco
8. Atlatlahuacan	4. Atlatlahuacan with seven cabeceras, of which only Tlayacapan and Totolapan are named

NOTE: Numbers refer to the sequence in which towns are mentioned in each source.

Xocotitlan, Cuahuacan, and Xilotepec are tributary provinces in the Codex Mendoza. Mazahuacan, Xiquipilco, and Chiappan play a role in accounts of the conquests; probably they had important military obligations, but they are also included among the tributaries of Tlacopan and Tenochtitlan.

The fourth group in Tezozomoc's sequence and the sixth in Durán's coincide to a large extent with the province of Tolocan in the Codex Mendoza. Tolocan, Calimayan, Tepemaxalxo, Tlacotepec (Mitepec), Teotenanco, Metepec, and Zoquitzinco constitute part of it. It is difficult to decide which towns are meant by Coatepec and Capulhuac, since these toponyms are found repeatedly in the region. Xochihuacan, or Xochiacan, must be the present-day San Juan Xochiaca in Tenancingo, Mexico.[48]

Durán also includes Malinalco and Ocuillan, cabeceras of provinces in the

Codex Mendoza, as well as Tenantzinco, which was in the province of Ocuillan. Tezozomoc mentions Malinalco when he speaks of the return of the ambassadors who had gone to invite the rulers of the towns listed. One group of these ambassadors "went by Malinalco as far as Metztitlan," which must refer to groups 3 and 4 in Tezozomoc. However, neither of the two sources includes towns in the direction of Metztitlan.

In Tezozomoc's groups 5 to 8 and Durán's 1 to 4, all the towns named, from Tepeyacac to Atlatlahuacan (Atlatlauhcan), can be seen as a unit made up of towns with special obligations to the Empire, principally military. The province of Tepeyacac, according to the Codex Mendoza, paid tribute in captives from the tramontane kingdoms. The cabecera of Tepeyacac appears in this list with its four subjects: Cuauhtinchan, Teccalli or Tecaltzinco (that is, Tecalco), and Acatzinco, which are in the Codex Mendoza, and Oztoticpac, which is not, although it is a well-known town.[49] Cuauhquechollan was also in Tepeyacac province; it is described in this list with six sujetos not mentioned in the Codex Mendoza. Atlatlauhcan, according to Durán, had seven subject cabeceras, of which he names only Tlayacapan and Totolapan. These three towns are in the province of Huaxtepec in the Codex Mendoza. Chalco, in this table, may refer to the kingdom of Chimalhuacan-Chalco, which, like the other Xochimilca towns in this area, would serve in the wars against Huexotzinco.

Our two sources differ not only in the order in which they list towns; they also combine the sending of ambassadors with the arrivals of the invited rulers in a somewhat different way. Tezozomoc as a rule follows the hierarchical order of the Triple Alliance. He begins with the two kings allied with Tenochtitlan and follows with the kingdoms that are direct dependencies of that city: Colhuacan with the Four Lords and Xochimilco with the Chinampanec kingdoms. Then he goes on to the Otomi towns of Cuauhtlalpan and those of Matlatzinco. All of these are mentioned in other lists (examined in this chapter) among the towns that participate in various undertakings together with the three capitals of the Empire. Only then is there a convocation "of all the neighboring rulers subject to Mexico Tenochtitlan." This includes towns in the region of Tepeyacac, Chalco, and Atlatlauhcan. When the ambassadors returned to Mexico, they gave an account of "how all twenty-eight towns with rulers were coming with their tribute and slaves." This must refer to groups 5 to 8, which are those situated in the southern part of the Basin, because immediately afterwards is the statement that "other messengers arrived who had gone by Malinalco as far as Metztitlan, which would be thirty-two towns more." These would have to be the towns in groups 3 and 4. As has been pointed out, the lists of towns do not include any near Metztitlan, but it is notable that Atocpan appears in the list of towns whose stewards brought tribute in kind, as shown in Table 13-3.

In Durán's account the embassy to Tepeyacac and Cuauhquechollan comes first. No doubt he emphasizes this region because it was the center of the military organization against the tramontane kingdoms and had the tributary obligation of providing captives, which is stressed in this first list of the rulers called upon to bring victims for sacrifice in the inauguration of the temple. In recounting the embassies, Durán notes that the ambassadors reported that they had gone to twenty towns, whose rulers had already arrived. This is said after enumerating the first five groups and therefore must refer to these, which take in the same regions as the twenty-eight of Tezozomoc. He then speaks of the ambassadors sent to the region of Tolocan and to Mazahuacan and other neighboring towns.

Durán ends his enumeration with the arrival, first, of the king of Tetzcoco with his sujetos and, finally, the king of Tlacopan with the lords of his "province." The components of the kingdom of Tlacopan are not identified, but there is a long list of the sujetos of Tetzcoco that includes the dependent kingdoms and many tributary towns. Durán states that on this day Nezahualpilli of Tetzcoco arrived with the rulers of towns subject to him, such as Huexotla, Coatlichan, Coatepec, Chimalhuacan, Itztapallocan, and, to the north, Tepetlaoztoc, Papalotlan, Totoltzinco, Tecciztlan, Tepechpan, Acolman, Chiucnauhtlan, Zacatzontitlan, Oztoyocan, Tecoac, Calpollalpan, Tlatzcayucan, Apan, Tepepolco, Tlallanapan, Tezoyocan, Otompan, Achilhilacachocan (*sic*), Tzacuallan, Cempohuallan, Huitzillan, Epazoyocan, Tollantzinco, Tlaquilpan, Tezontepec, Hueitihuacan, and all the other towns subject to Tetzcoco. He then makes a brief digression on the lesser importance of Tetzcoco in respect to Tenochtitlan.[50]

This list is much longer than is the norm in Durán's chronicle when he refers to the kingdoms of Tetzcoco and Tlacopan. It includes not only the kingdoms of the Acolhuacan but also other towns, some of them known as towns within the calpixcazgos of Tetzcoco or of the Tenochca tributary province of Acolman, and some others not included in either one. The importance of the tributaries of Tenochtitlan in this list is in accord with the statement in the relación geográfica of Cempohuallan that Ahuitzotl increased the demand for tribute from that region precisely at the time of the dedication of the temple.[51]

In these accounts of Durán and Tezozomoc the predominance of the core area is emphasized: that is, the three capitals with their dependent kingdoms together with the region of Tolocan in the west and the towns of the southeastern part of the Basin and of Tepeyacac, which were the military centers against the tramontane kingdoms and had the obligation of providing captives.

These towns can be related to the places where the captives were taken on the day of the ceremony in preparation for the sacrifices and to the temples where the great kings of the Empire and the priests, attired as gods, performed the sacrifices. Each king sacrificed the captives brought by his subjects and assembled at one of the three entrances to the city. According to Tezozomoc, the captives brought by the Acolhuacan were congregated in Coyonacazco, in the northern part of the city where the causeway from the north reached the city. The captives of Tlacopan were lined up in Mazatzintamalco on the causeway that entered the city from the west. The captives brought by the people of the Cuauhtlalpan and by the Chinampanecs came together in Acachinanco in the southern part of the city. King Ahuitzotl and the cihuacoatl Tlacaelel sacrificed in the great temple, the king of Tetzcoco in Yopico (in the barrio of Moyotla), and the king of Tlacopan in Huitznahuac (in Teopan).[52]

After the kings of the Empire had been convened, the enemy rulers of the tramontane kingdoms were invited and also those of Metztitlan, Michoacan, and Yopitzinco; they were lodged in a place where, without being seen, they could contemplate the ceremonies.

Finally, Ahuitzotl asked the petlacalcatl to bring tribute of clothing for the principals and rulers and ordered that the stewards of the provinces should come.[53] For the most part both Durán and Tezozomoc enumerate the towns, outside the core area, whose calpixques brought goods for the celebration. Tezozomoc finishes with a long list of jewelry, clothing, and other objects contributed by Cuetlaxtlan. Table 13-3 presents the lists of both writers.[54]

The marked difference between the two lists of participants in the inauguration of the temple relates to the nature of the tribute. The emphasis in the first list (Table 13-2) is on the prisoners of war to be sacrificed; in the second (Table 13-3) it is on luxury objects provided by provinces such as Tziuhcoac, Cuetlaxtlan, and Tochtepec, which—according to the Codex Mendoza—paid tribute principally in highly decorated clothing and jewels. Towns with military obligations, which were close to the center and brought captives to be sacrificed, are identified in detail, but the garrisons on distant frontiers are not named. In general, these lists confirm the information given in other sources concerning the extent of the Empire at that time.

The Funeral of Ahuitzotl

The funeral rites for Ahuitzotl are described with detailed enumerations of the rulers who came to this event. No new data are given about the extent of the Empire; the importance of these accounts lies in the fact that the places of origin of the participants coincide basically with the core area of the Empire. Durán's information is better, for he lists all these cities twice, first describing the arrival of the rulers who came to Tenochtitlan, then naming them again in relating the speeches and offerings that they made in the room where the deceased king lay. Table 13-4 presents these two lists together with the data from Tezozomoc.[55]

TABLE 13-3.

Towns Whose Stewards Brought Tribute to Mexico
for the Inauguration of the Temple

Durán 1967, 2:341	Tezozomoc 1975:494
The city of Mexico itself	Petlacalco
Xochimilco, Chinampan Chalco	the steward of Chinantla (*sic*)
Coaixtlahuacan, these were the Mixtecs,	Coaixtlahuacan
Tochpan Tochtepec Tziuhcoac Tlatlauhquitepec	Tochpan Tochtepec Tziuhcoac Tlatlauhquitepec
Tepeyacac Piaztlan Tlappan Tlalcozauhtitlan the Chiapanecs (Chiauhtlan?) Couixco, Tepecuacuilco Huitzoco, Yohuallan Tlaxtecas (Tlachco) Teotliltecas (Teotiztacan?), Nochtepec Tzacualpan	Tepeyacac Piaztlan Tlappan Tlalcozauhtitlan Chiauhtlan Cohuixco, Tepecuacuilco Teotiztacan, Nochtepec Tzacualpan
Tierra Caliente, namely: Cuauhnahuac, Yauhtepec, Huaxtepec, Yacapichtla	Cuauhnahuac, Yauhtepec Huaxtepec, Yacapichtla
Matlatzinco, Xocotecs (Xocotitlan) Xilotepec, Atocpan	Matlatzinco, Xocotitlan, Xilotepec, Atocpan
and other towns not mentioned.	Xochimilco with all the Chinampanecs, except Azcapotzalco, Coyoacan, Chalco, Cuauhtitlan, and others who came last.

NOTE: Durán often gives gentile names instead of place names. In the table they have been changed
into place names, except for a few followed by what I believe is the correct toponym in
parentheses. The spelling of toponyms has been standardized.

In these lists, as in several of the previous enumerations, we find the principal
kingdoms of the Tenochca group: Xochimilco, the cities of the Chinampan, and
the Four Lords. Tetzcoco appears as a unit, without citing its dependent kingdoms, as is usual in both these chronicles. The dependent kingdoms of Tlacopan
are included in Durán's second list: Xilotepec, Tepexic, Apazco, Tollan, Tepo-

tzotlan, Cuauhtitlan, and Toltitlan. In the same geographic sequence are named Tenayocan and Ecatepec, Tenochca kingdoms that do not appear in these lists with the same frequency as do the Four Lords and the Chinampanec cities. Also named by Durán are Xocotitlan, Chiappan, Xiquipilco, and Xilotepec with all the Cuauhtlalpan. These are towns ruled by kings and are usually mentioned as part of the core area of the Empire that fought in the wars and attended the great ceremonies. Similarly, the lords of Chalco are mentioned, but nothing is said about the Tolocan region, which usually participates with the preceding towns in other activities. Clearly the emphasis in this enumeration is on the cities with their own kings, thus explaining the inclusion of Apazco and Tollan, cabeceras of Tlacopanec kingdoms but not seats of calpixques.

TABLE 13-4.
Rulers Attending the Funeral of Ahuitzotl

Durán 1967, 2:392	Durán 1967, 2:393	Tezozomoc 1975:568–70
King Nezahualpilli	The king of Tetzcoco	The king of Acolhuacan
The king of Tlacopan	The king of Tlacopan	The king of the Tepanecs
The lords of Chalco	Chalco with all its rulers	Chalco
Xochimilco, with all those from Chinampan	Those from Chinampan, that is Xochimilco, Cuitlahuac, and Mizquic	Xochimilco and the Chinampanecs
Those of the Tierra Caliente (i.e. Tlalhuic)	Cuauhnahuac and all the kings of Tierra Caliente	
Xilotepec with all the Cuauhtlalpan, Otomi "province"	Matlatzinco with all the Cuauhtlalpan, Mazahuacan, and all the Otomis of Xocotitlan, Chiappan Xiquipilco, Xilotepec, Tepexic, Apazco, and Tollan	
	Tepotzotlan, Cuauhtitlan, and Toltitlan	
	Tenayocan and Ecatepec	
The Four Lords of Colhuacan, Itztapalapan, Mexicatzinco, and Huitzilopochco		
		Tlatelolco

NOTE: The spelling of toponyms has been standardized.

The lists of participants in the imperial undertakings, which Durán and Tezozomoc supply in abundance, complement the sources, such as the Codex Mendoza, that systematically enumerate all the components of the Empire. They also add important information on some of the conquered regions, such as Piaztlan and the cities south of the volcano that formed the frontier against Huexotzinco.

But the principal contribution of these sources is their confirmation of the distinction between the core area and the conquered regions, identifying the components of the core area and documenting the activities in which they took part. They made up the contingents of the campaigns of conquest, supplied labor for public works, and participated in the great ceremonies, in accord with the brief formula given in the memorials of Tetzcoco and Tlacopan on the contribution to the Empire of the dependent kingdoms of the three capitals. They also demonstrate the position of Chalco, Tlalhuic, and the Cuauhtlalpan, which joined the kingdoms of the core area in the military campaigns and had a fundamental role in bringing materials and masses of workers for public works projects.

Durán and Tezozomoc pay more attention to the Tenochca and Tlacopanec domains than to Tetzcoco, which usually appears as a unit, its component kingdoms and towns of peasants seldom named. These Tenochca chronicles verify the greater subordination of Tlacopan to Tenochtitlan, in accordance with the content of the "Memorial de Tlacopan," which on some points presents a fuller picture of the Tenochca sector than do the Tetzcoca sources.

The enumeration of the components of the Empire is based on local political units rather than tributary provinces, as in the Codex Mendoza, confirming the distinction between the underlying political organization and the tributary provinces established for the collection of tribute.

SUMMARY

The basic political-territorial entity in central Mexico—the altepetl (town or city)—comprised one or more civic and ceremonial centers, more or less compact, with temples and palaces where the governing estate resided and also a number of rural settlements in which peasant tributaries predominated. The altepetl was a political unit governed by a king, or tlatoani; as such, it was a tlatocayotl, the government of the tlatoani, the kingdom. At times the altepetl was an independent entity, but in general several *altepeme* were parts of larger political entities, of variable degrees of complexity, in which each one kept its own government. In these cases the king of the dominant city was called huey tlatoani, great king, and his city was a huey altepetl, great city. In modern historical literature such political units, comprising several kingdoms, are usually denominated empires.

The Tenochca Empire, under the supremacy of Tenochtitlan, was ruled by the alliance of three great kings, each dominant over a group of lesser kings of a common ethnic and dynastic affiliation. Hence the name Triple Alliance, by which this political entity is also known. Tenochtitlan was the capital of the Mexica and Colhua kingdoms, and Tetzcoco continued as the capital of the Acolhua-Chichimecs, while Tlacopan took the place of Azcapotzalco as the capital of the Tepanecs. These three cities and their dynasties had formed part of the preceding political regime, the Tepanec empire of Azcapotzalco. The new empire was based on principles of organization already present before it was formed, but it developed these principles to a higher degree of complexity than had been reached by the polities it replaced.

From the moment of its foundation the territorial structure of the alliance clearly exhibited two fundamental traits of Mesoamerican political organization, which characterize it throughout the various levels of its organization: the segmentation of political entities and the geographical intermingling of territories.

In this study segmentation signifies the subdivision of a larger political entity into lesser entities with their own social and territorial characteristics that participate as corporate units in the integration of the total structure. Segmentation is found at different levels of the structure: the kingdoms of an empire, the parcialidades of a city, the barrios of a parcialidad. The various segments are replicas of each other to the extent that they carry out the same functions, each within its territory, but also—and this is what is most important in order to characterize the structure as a whole—the segments specialize in tasks that contribute to the total organization, or they take turns in doing so, in such a way that the social division of labor, both in economic and political matters, is based on the territorial segments. The total structure is then an alliance or confederation of component segments.

The intermingling of territories signifies that the different social segments are represented in the territories of several or all of them. The principal ethnic parcialidades of central Mexico—such as the Colhuas, Mexicas, and Tepanecs in the Tenochca Empire—are found in all the kingdoms; the ethnic barrios—also connected with different ethnic elements and with specific professions and cults—are similarly found in various cities. Each of the parcialidades and barrios of a city held lands in several of the city's rural dependencies. All this constitutes a manner of sharing the resources of various areas and in different environments. It is moreover a mechanism of integration, not only economic but also social and political, thus counteracting the fragmentation of the different segments into independent societies.

The Core Area of the Empire

The three allied capitals with their dependent kingdoms—a total of about thirty—constituted the ruling element in the core area of the Empire, which also controlled adjacent areas under rulers of lesser rank with a numerous peasant population.

Before the Triple Alliance was established, the two Mexica cities—Tenochtitlan and Tlatelolco—when they were part of the Tepanec empire of Azcapotzalco ruled by Tezozomoc, played an important role in military enterprises; they were granted the tribute from some of the towns subjected by Azcapotzalco, with the result that there were tributaries of both Mexica cities in the Acolhuacan and in the Chinampanec area.

From the beginning, Tenochtitlan established itself as the controlling power of the Triple Alliance, whose armies were commanded by the Tenochca king. Acamapichtli, founder of the Tenochca dynasty, was of both Colhua and Mexica ancestry. Tenochtitlan was thus the capital of the cities of the old Colhua zone, that is, the cities of the Four Lords (nauhteuctin) of Colhuacan, Itztapalapan, Mexicatzinco, and Huitzilopochco in the area around Mount Huixachtecatl (present-day

Cerro de la Estrella) and the kingdoms of the Chinampanec region: Xochimilco, Cuitlahuac, and Mizquic.

Tetzcoco, seat of the dynasty of the Chichimecs of Xolotl, entered the Triple Alliance together with the other cities of the Acolhuacan. The principal cities in the center of the kingdom—Tetzcoco, Huexotla, and Coatlichan—situated in the piedmont, had sujetos in the mountains and along the lake shore. North of Tetzcoco were the cities of Chiauhtlan, Tezoyocan, Acolman, Tepechpan, Teotihuacan, and the farthest north, Chiucnauhtlan. Of the Acolhua cities in the Basin, Otompan was the farthest from the lake. Chimalhuacan was the only city in the southern part of the Acolhuacan; other towns, such as Coatepec, had lost importance when the alliance was formed. Outside the Basin, Tollantzinco, Cuauhchinanco, and Xicotepec were also part of the domain of Tetzcoco.

Tlacopan, which had been one of the cities of the Tepanec empire of Azcapotzalco, entered the Triple Alliance as the head of the Tepanec kingdoms that occupied the western part of the Basin and, farther away, the regions of the northwest. The principal kingdoms of the Tlacopanec domain were Coyoacan, Cuauhtitlan, Tollan, Apazco, and Xilotepec.

Beyond the original domains of the three founding kingdoms, certain areas were thoroughly integrated with the core area; they all had a numerous peasant population, some of it resettled by the kings of the Empire, and their rulers were of lesser rank. In the old Otomi kingdom of Xaltocan, defeated during the last years of the Tepanec empire, the Triple Alliance established its control and new settlers moved in. From that time on the new rulers of Xaltocan, descendants of the old local dynasty, took Tenochca wives, but the area had obligations towards both Tenochtitlan and Tetzcoco.

Tlalhuic was incorporated into the Empire from the beginning, and the three allied capitals had possessions there, each collecting tribute and administering justice in its own towns. Tenochtitlan held the two provinces headed in the Codex Mendoza by Cuauhnahuac and Huaxtepec; Tetzcoco had its own calpixcazgo, also headed by Cuauhnahuac; and Tlacopan had a group of estancias in the same region. Nevertheless, the possessions of each capital were different; only a few towns paid tribute to more than one of them.

In Chalco—defeated by Moteuczoma Ilhuicamina—the three kingdoms of the alliance obtained possessions that they incorporated into calpixcazgos that also included other settlements within their own domains. Consequently, the Tenochca provinces of Citlaltepec and Petlacalco contained a few towns in Chalco; the Tetzcoca calpixcazgo of Tetitlan included Tlapechhuacan; and Tlacopan combined tributary towns in Chalco and the Chinampanec region into one of its own tributary districts. There was also a tributary province of Chalco, registered in the Codex Mendoza, administered by Tenochtitlan. The native rulers of Chalco were at first deposed, but some of them were eventually restored and established marriage alliances with the Tenochca dynasty.

The region of Toluca was also thoroughly integrated into the core area. It may have been part of the Tlacopan kingdom from the beginning of the Empire; at least Mazahuacan was part of it. But the later conquest by Axayacatl brought about profound changes in that area. Many Matlatzincas emigrated to Michoacan; the Tenochca king distributed the lands they had abandoned and brought new settlers from the Basin. Few native rulers remained. The provinces of Tolocan and Xocotitlan in the Codex Mendoza were probably exclusively tributaries of Tenochtitlan, since the possessions of the other two capitals in that region are identified separately in other sources, and the "Memorial de los pueblos de Tlacopan" does not include these regions among those that paid tribute to the three capitals. Tlacopan had tributaries in Xiquipilco, Ixtlahuacan, Tolocan, and Zoquitzinco; Nezahualpilli of Tetzcoco established his own calpixcazgo in Tolocan, which also included lands in Zoquitzinco; but the greater part of the region paid tribute to Tenochtitlan.

Each of the three allied capitals had a special function in the central administration of the Empire. The preponderance of Tenochtitlan was largely a consequence of the role of its king as commander of the armies of the alliance. Tetzcoco had greater authority in the judicial organization and in public works. The role of Tlacopan is more difficult to determine. The "Memorial de Tlacopan" has more data on tributaries of the Triple Alliance than the Tetzcoca and Tenochca sources; possibly the list in the "Memorial de Tlacopan" of towns subject to the three capitals is connected with the functions of Tlacopan in the imperial organization. The administration of tribute and commerce may well have been part of its charge.

Whether jurisdiction over the subjugated regions and the responsibility for effecting political changes was divided is problematical. Data from Tlalhuic shows that each of the three capitals had jurisdiction in the towns from which it received tribute and sent judges to resolve local problems, but there is not enough information to permit a generalization about this procedure. When deciding on the need for a military campaign against a certain place, all three capitals sent their envoys in turn to persuade the inhabitants of the advantages of a peaceful surrender. The armies of the three capitals set forth together when war became necessary.

Within the core area the principal social, political, and economic distinction was that between the governing estate, concentrated in the cities, and the tributaries of its rural dependencies.

The cities were the principal seats of the nobility and of highly skilled craftsmen. The kings subordinate to each of the three great kings went to their capital city for the ceremonies of their installation and participated in the highest councils of the kingdom they were subject to. They also kept residences there. The dependent cities gave military assistance to their capital's king, and they were charged with certain special services and tribute, such as the construction and maintenance of temples and palaces. The rulers of these dependent kingdoms also took part in the great civic and religious ceremonies of the Empire, such as the funerals and installations of the kings and the great monthly religious festivals.

Each of the three great kingdoms that comprised the alliance was provisioned by the territories it held within the core area. The peasant communities, organized in calpixcazgos in the charge of calpixques, furnished the provisions needed for the royal palaces or gave specialized forms of labor, such as caring for the royal gardens and forests. Certain settlements in the rural area also had military duties, and the forms of land tenure granted to distinguished warriors prevailed in these areas. In Tetzcoco, and it is to be supposed in the other capitals, the calpixcazgos took turns in bringing the food needed for a certain part of the year; this system of turns was also used for supplying the palaces and temples with firewood.

In contrast with the concentration of cities along the lake shores, the settlements of tributary peasants predominated in the interior areas. In the Acolhua kingdom, the environs of Otompan were populated by peasants, as was the region north of the Cerro Gordo and, towards the northeast, Tepepolco and Calpollalpan. In the other two kingdoms of the alliance the northern part of the Basin, the mountains that separated it from the Valley of Toluca, and parts of the latter were peasant areas. In the northern part of the Basin there were also settlements with military obligations.

The Triple Alliance, therefore, had its economic base within the core area, made up of its component kingdoms. In the economic organization of the thirty-odd dependent kingdoms, their own calpixcazgos of peasants provided them with the necessities of daily life. Contrary to what has sometimes been said, the alliance was not a predatory organization that maintained itself by the tribute from conquered peoples. The core area that comprised the ruling center of the Empire was in the Basin of Mexico, especially in the southern half, and was the most productive region of Mesoamerica.

Segmentation and Factionalism in the Kingdoms of the Alliance

The segmentation that existed at all levels of the society is obvious in the tripartite composition of the alliance and in the several kingdoms within each of the three parts. Segmentation is also evident within the three capital cities and their dependent kingdoms, which were all subdivided into parcialidades or cabeceras, some of the latter also with their own rulers. These divisions were not only territorial; their inhabitants were also frequently of a particular ethnic origin. As a rule they were part of the groups that moved south after the fall of Tollan; they had distinct cultural traditions with their own patron gods and had belonged to the major political entities of the Basin before the foundation of the Triple Alliance. Thus, the various components of a given city had been settled at different periods of its history, and their leaders came from dynasties that had governed in other cities.

The nature of the segmentation that prevailed in Tetzcoco, and its connection with ethnic elements, is the best known. The reigning dynasty descended from the founders of the city—the Chichimecs of Xolotl—but the six parcialidades of the city were settled by groups that had been welcomed by the Chichimec kings: the Tlailotlaques and Chimalpanecs from Chalco and the four "nations"—Colhuas, Mexicas (or Mecitin), Tepanecs, and Huitznahuas—who came from Colhuacan. These groups were established in various cities of the Acolhuacan and participated in specific administrative tasks within the organization of the kingdom. Part of the peasant population were Otomis who had been given refuge when they fled from the old Xaltocan kingdom, defeated by the Tepanecs of Azcapotzalco.

The social segments of Tenochtitlan derived from the original calpollis that had migrated from Aztlan to Tollan and then to Mexico. In their names, which indicate their ethnic identity and in some cases their patron gods, the parcialidades of Tenochtitlan resemble those of the Acolhua towns and of Colhuacan. In Tlacopan, as in Azcapotzalco, there were parcialidades called Mexicapan and Tepanecapan, and the names of the barrios of both cities allude to patron gods and occupations that resemble those of the parcialidades of Colhuacan, Tenochtitlan, and Tetzcoco. Cuauhtitlan, of Chichimec origin, like Tetzcoco accepted as new settlers the four groups from Colhuacan, who established the division into four parcialidades.

The segmentation of the political entities, each with its own ruler and territory, was the basis of a political factionalism that broke out frequently during their history. The towns of a kingdom, or the parcialidades in which a city was divided, had inherited different cultural traditions, and at times their rulers came from previous dynasties and political regimes. The king of Tlatelolco, for example, descended from the Tepanec dynasty; in Azcapotzalco and in Tlacopan there were Mexica parcialidades. On occasion the parcialidades of a given kingdom were on opposing sides in the armed conflicts. During the war against Azcapotzalco, which concluded with the formation of the Triple Alliance, some of the cities of the Colhua group and of the Acolhuacan sided with the Tepanecs of Azcapotzalco. At the end of the war Nezahualcoyotl of Tetzcoco restored most of the rulers who had opposed him, but even after the Spanish Conquest, some of the Acolhua cities claimed to have been tyrannized by Tetzcoco and Tenochtitlan. On the other hand, during the war against Azcapotzalco, Tlacopan, a Tepanec city, secretly favored Tetzcoco and Tenochtitlan. The most important factional conflict during the Empire was the struggle against Axayacatl of Tenochtitlan, begun by Moquihuix of Tlatelolco, who tried in vain to obtain the help of the cities that had been part of the Tepanec regime.

The Intermingling of Territories within the Core Area

The intermingling of territories is well documented for the core area of the Empire. Each of the three capitals had tributaries not only in its own domain but also in those of the other two members of the alliance.

The tributaries of Tenochtitlan within its own domain constituted three provinces in the Codex Mendoza. One, headed by Citlaltepec, incorporated several towns in the Basin, almost all in the north and with primarily military obligations; another was Tlatelolco, and the third, Petlacalco, which included towns in the southern part of the Basin. But Tenochtitlan also had many tributary towns in the territory of the kingdoms of the Acolhuacan and of the Tlacopanec kingdoms. The tributary provinces of Acolman and of Atotonilco el Grande included towns in the region occupied by the Acolhua kingdoms. Within the area of the Tlacopanec kingdoms were the tributary provinces of Cuahuacan, in the territory of Tlacopan itself, and those of Cuauhtitlan, Atotonilco de Tula, Hueypochtlan, Axocopan, and Xilotepec, situated within the territory of the kingdoms of Cuauhtitlan, Tollan, Apazco, and Xilotepec but without being coterminous with them.

The tributaries of Tetzcoco within its own domain were organized in eight calpixcazgos in the Acolhuacan and another in Tollantzinco. But from the earliest days of the Empire, Nezahualcoyotl also received—until Moteuczoma Xocoyotzin suspended the privilege—what was called the tribute of the Chinampan, paid by various towns in the southern part of the Basin within the domains of Tenochtitlan and Tlacopan.

Tlacopan also had tributaries within its own domain in the southwestern part of the Basin and in the nearby mountains, with others more towards the north and in Matlatzinco. It also had tributaries in the Chinampanec region in the south, which was part of the Tenochca domain, in Tlalhuic, and in Chalco. However the extent of the lands of Tlacopan in the Tenochca domain was much less than the extensive possessions of Tenochtitlan in the Tlacopaneca domain.

Information on Tlalhuic, Tolocan, and Chalco demonstrates that in these regions each of the three allied capitals had its own tributary towns. There was thus an intermingling of territories similar to that which prevailed within the domains of the three kingdoms that founded the Empire.

Not only the three great kingdoms had possessions in the three parts of the alliance; their component kingdoms were also part of this system of intermingling territories. Teotihuacan and other Acolhua cities had lands in Tenochtitlan, Tlatelolco, and Ecatepec, while these Tenochca cities in turn had lands in the Acolhua cities. The king of Cuauhtitlan had lands in Chalco and Matlatzinco, while in the territory of Cuauhtitlan there were lands pertaining to several Tenochca and Tlacopanecan cities. In Tolocan, land was also given to new settlers from Azcapotzalco and Tlatelolco in addition to the three capitals of the Empire.

In the rural areas where the peasant towns predominated there were also lands of the king's relatives, of high officials, and of meritorious warriors. This was said to be the norm for the Acolhuacan. The lands of Moteuczoma and Ahuitzotl, whose location is the best known, were found throughout the whole core area. The lands of the other two kings of the Triple Alliance, as far as is known, were located within a less extensive region.

The Three Sectors of the Empire

Beyond the domains of the three allied kingdoms that constituted the core area, the Empire as a unit incorporated new territories that either submitted voluntarily or were conquered by force of arms. The tripartite division of the alliance was extended to these conquered regions.

Torquemada defines a division of the Empire into three sectors, each one associated with a geographical direction and each dominated by one of the three capitals. Approximately—defining the geographical areas from Tenochtitlan—Tetzcoco's portion was the northeastern quarter, Tlacopan's the northwestern quarter, and Tenochtitlan's the southern half. The Codex Mendoza, which lists all the tributary provinces of the Empire, does not present such a three-part division, but the sources from Tetzcoco and Tlacopan confirm it to a large extent. However, there are no reports to the effect that each of the sectors constituted a distinctive level in the administration of the Empire. Within each sector there were gradations in the imperial control of the subjugated regions.

On Tetzcoco we have Ixtlilxochitl's account of how Nezahualcoyotl conquered various regions, wherein he named calpixques and whose tribute he kept without sharing it with the other two kings of the Empire. These were the provinces of Tochpan, Tziuhcoac, Tlapacoyan, Tochtepec, and Tlalcozauhtitlan and Nezahualcoyotl's share of Cuauhnahuac. Motolinía's "Memorial tetzcocano" and the *Anales de Cuauhtitlan* enumerate those provinces and the towns that they included with more details than the Codex Mendoza, and this is in accord with their relation to Tetzcoco. But—in spite of what Ixtlilxochitl affirms—Motolinía and the *Anales de Cuauhtitlan* specify that they paid tribute to the three capitals.

The "Memorial de los pueblos de Tlacopan" distinguishes between (1) Tlacopan and its rural settlements, (2) the towns or estancias of Tlacopan's tributaries in other neighboring regions, (3) the kingdoms directly subordinate to Tlacopan, and (4) the subjects of the Empire that paid tribute to the three allied capitals. Those in the last group are enumerated in three sections subdivided into paragraphs. One of the sections includes Tochpan, Tziuhcoac, Tlapacoyan, Tlatlauhquitepec, Tochtepec, and Chinantlan, basically coinciding with the same list that Ixtlilxochitl gives as Nezahualcoyotl's conquests, whose tribute he kept for himself, and with the northeastern or Tetzcoca sector, according to Torquemada. The other two sections comprise the southern half, or Tenochca sector, of the Empire. The towns are grouped in paragraphs that do not coincide with the provinces of the Codex Mendoza but overlap with them; they are in the Balsas Basin, the Mixteca, the coast of Guerrero, the valleys of Oaxaca, the Gulf coast, and the Isthmus of Tecuantepec, together with Xoconochco.

These sources support the tripartite formula of Torquemada insofar as they make clear that there was a Tetzcoca sector of the Empire, but the extent of this sector is not defined with so close an adherence to the cardinal directions. It does not include the provinces of Atlan or Oxitipan but does include Tochtepec and Chinantlan (which in the Codex Mendoza is listed in the province of Tochtepec). Tlalcozauhtitlan, far from the northeastern sector, in the Balsas Basin, is given by Ixtlilxochitl as a possession of Tetzcoco, but it is a province in the Codex Mendoza and is not registered in the "Memorial de Tlacopan."

The "Memorial de Tlacopan" does not place any town that paid tribute to the three capitals in the northwestern sector of the Empire; in that sector it registers only the Tepanec kingdoms in the core area and the towns and estancias of Tlacopan in Matlatzinco. The tributary provinces of the Codex Mendoza in that same region must have been those that paid tribute to Tenochtitlan. This was the consequence of the reorganization that took place after the wars of Axayacatl against Matlatzinco and Ahuitzotl against Chiappan, but it may also reflect the subordination of Tlacopan to Tenochtitlan from the very beginning of the Empire.

In the regions conquered by the Empire the sector of Tenochtitlan comprised the whole southern half. The provinces in the Codex Mendoza that correspond to this sector are Tlachco, Tepecuacuilco, Cihuatlan, Tlappan, Tlalcozauhtitlan, Quiauhteopan, Yohualtepec, Chalco, Tepeyacac, Coaixtlahuacan, Coyolapan, Tlachquiauhco, Tochtepec, Xoconochco, Cuauhtochco, and Cuetlaxtlan. But, as pointed out above, in the Tetzcoca sources Tochtepec was part of the Tetzcoca sector. The "Memorial de Tlacopan" contains a section dedicated to the southern sector, but it is organized into paragraphs that are different from the provinces of the Codex Mendoza. It does not include Tochtepec, which is found among the paragraphs of the northeastern, or Tetzcoca, sector. Instead, it registers towns that augment the extension of the Tenochca sector in the Balsas Basin and in the Costa Chica, as well as in the isthmus, where Xaltepec and Tecuantepec are listed together with

Xoconochco. It also extends the Tenochca sector towards the north along the Gulf coast; the paragraph headed by Cempohuallan includes all the coast from Mictlan-cuauhtla to Tamiahua and also includes Atlan. It indicates, therefore, a Tenochca intrusion into the northeastern sector of Tetzcoco.

Political Organization of the Regions Subjugated by the Empire

In the subjugated regions there were different procedures for maintaining the authority of the Empire. In general there was a system of indirect government through the indigenous rulers, who kept their authority over the internal affairs of their kingdoms. At times the Empire forced changes at the highest level by replacing a defeated king with another member of his lineage or by reducing the power of some of the kings and local lords. Thus, the previous political system was allowed to continue, but with some degree of imperial control imposed upon it.

In the regions conquered by the Empire as a unit, the kings of the alliance established tributary provinces and named governors and calpixques in charge of collecting the tribute. This constituted a new level of territorial organization superimposed on the indigenous political organization. It can be compared to the manner in which the dependent kingdoms of the core area were discrete political and territorial units, different from the calpixcazgos established by each of the three capitals in those same territories.

In strategic areas the Empire also established garrisons or presidios and brought settlers from the Basin as military colonists, thus establishing yet another form of territorial organization different from the tributary system.

In addition to these procedures that placed permanent officials of the Empire in the conquered areas, envoys were sent from the capitals in the Basin to carry out special missions, such as to reorganize a conquered region, as was done in Tepeyacac and Cuetlaxtlan, or to resolve disputes over land between neighboring kingdoms. No separate territorial organization is reported in the sources for the functioning of these envoys. In some cases they were sent from Tenochtitlan, but in one case, in the Sierra de Puebla, they were sent also from the Acolhuacan and Tlacopan. Perhaps the division into three sectors that Torquemada describes was taken into account when dispatching these envoys. The judges sent to the towns of the Chinantec region came from the Tochtepec garrison; it is possible that a similar procedure was used in other regions.

For trading expeditions to the isthmus the center of operations was Tochtepec, where the merchants from the Basin maintained houses. There are references to trading outposts in Xicallanco and other places, but there are no other reports that would indicate a special territorial organization for the activities of the merchants.

The relative importance of the indigenous rulers and the imperial officials in the various subjugated areas illustrate gradations in the authority exercised by the Empire. The accounts of the arrival of the Spanish show the difference between the region of Veracruz, where they were welcomed by the calpixques of the tributary province of Cuetlaxtlan, and Cempohuallan, where the Spanish dealt directly with the cacique and the calpixques from the center were temporary visitors, not permanent residents.

In cases in which the polities voluntarily submitted, or gave a minimum of resistance, the polities incorporated into the Empire remained as allies of a sort with the responsibility of giving military help. Although they exchanged gifts with Tenochtitlan, these kingdoms do not appear in the tribute codices, and it is doubtful that the payment of tribute in kind was their principal contribution to the Empire. Examples of this situation are Tetellan, north of Tlaxcallan; Acatlan, in the Mixteca Baja; and Teotitlan del Camino. In some instances, as in Tecuantepec, a matrimonial alliance was arranged similar to those practiced among the dynasties of the Basin.

Some defeated kingdoms did pay tribute in luxury goods, at times called parias in the Spanish sources. They did not take part on a regular basis in the military enterprises of the Empire and were always disposed to rebellion, thus making new military interventions necessary to reaffirm their subjection. This was the situation in several of the indigenous kingdoms in Oaxaca.

In some kingdoms the local dynasties continued in charge of local government and also played an important role in the collection of tribute and in the military organization. An outstanding example is the situation in the kingdoms of the Tepeyacac region, where there were also matrimonial alliances with the Tenochca dynasty in Tecamachalco and Tepexic. However, they were not included among the dependent kingdoms that constituted the three parts of the alliance.

There were also cases of strong intervention by the Empire in local government, and the indigenous ruler had to consult with the imperial officials who resided in the kingdom. For example, in Chinantlan and other towns of the region, the local ruler governed, but the Mexica garrison in Tochtepec sent judges to the towns when necessary. In some cases, as in Cuetlaxtlan, there are references to local rulers, but their attributions are not described. In several towns in the Cohuixca region in Guerrero the only government mentioned is that of the governors or calpixques sent by the Empire, and nothing is said about whether there were local rulers. In all these cases the information available is inadequate.

The calpixcazgos or tributary provinces, as they are described in the Tenochca and Tetzcoca chronicles, were the result of a reorganization of the conquered regions, which imposed on the native polities a system for collecting the tribute demanded by the Empire, with calpixques chosen by·the victors to be in charge of the collection. The tributary provinces were, as a rule, different from the indigenous political-territorial units. At times a calpixcazgo coincided with the political entity, but the most frequent procedure was to combine several of the preexisting political units and not have all the tribute collection points coincide with the principal indigenous cabeceras. The importance of the local rulers varied from one town to another within a given province.

The Tributary Provinces and the Division of Tribute

The principal Tenochca sources—the tribute registers in the *Matrícula de tributos* and the Codex Mendoza—provide lists of tributary towns, but without any description of the underlying political organization in either the core area or the conquered regions. The registers give the kinds and quantities of tribute but do not indicate who would receive it or how it was divided among the three capitals. Other sources give general information on the distribution of tribute, but they are at times contradictory and in any case insufficient.

According to Zorita there were several ways of dividing the resources of the conquered regions. Each of the three capitals collected tribute from the conquered towns that had become subject to them. They also held other towns in common whose tribute they divided equally or into five parts, of which Tenochtitlan and Tetzcoco each were given two parts and Tlacopan only one. As Zorita does not give concrete examples, we do not know if he makes a distinction between the core area and the distant regions conquered in common, or if all the modalities he describes were found among the subjugated towns beyond the core area. As described above, Ixtlilxochitl gives specific data on the provinces conquered in the early days of the Empire, but his statement that Nezahualcoyotl took for himself all the tribute of the provinces that he conquered is contradicted by other sources, which relate that those same provinces of Tetzcoco paid tribute to the three capitals. This contradiction may be a result of changes that came about later. In any case there were two ways of distributing the lands and tribute of the conquered regions. In one, each capital took separately certain towns and collected all the tribute; in the other, the tribute was taken to Tenochtitlan and there part of it was given to the other two capitals. All the tribute registered in the Codex Mendoza was probably taken to Tenochtitlan. Of all this tribute, that from the provinces situated within the domains of the three capitals was exclusively for Tenochtitlan, since the Tetzcoca and Tlacopan sources register their possessions in those same regions. One can assume therefore that the tribute of Tlatelolco and Petlacalco in the Tenochca domain, of Acolman and Atotonilco el Grande in the Acolhuacan, and of Cuauhtitlan, Axocopan, Atotonilco de Tula, Hueypochtlan, Xilotepec, and Cuahuacan in the Tlacopan domain, was all for Tenochtitlan.

Probably the organization for collecting and distributing tribute was more complex than that described by any one of the sources, and it may be that all the reports we have are simplifications. For one thing, the numerical formulas on the distribution of tribute are also used for the division of territory. The towns in a given province were usually of different types—from cities with kings to small rural settlements—and their specific roles within the tribute system are not explained. In some cases we know that more towns belonged in a certain province than are listed in the standard sources. And it must also be admitted that the towns that were components of a province could have changed over time as a consequence of new conquests. Sometimes the recipient of the tribute changed, as in the case of the tribute from the Chinampan for Tetzcoco that Moteuczoma Xocoyotzin took back for himself.

The calpixques in charge of collecting the tribute came from the conqueror group, and the more important of them were of the nobility (pipiltin). There were at least two levels of calpixques, one consisting of those stationed in the cabeceras and a lower level of those assigned to the rest of the towns in the province. Also, it was probably general practice to have a second lower level of calpixques in settlements that were under each of the towns of the province, as is well documented for Tochpan and Tziuhcoac. In Cuetlaxtlan the official stationed in the cabecera was called huey calpixqui, and the officials of the other towns were simply calpixqui plus the toponym of the town. In addition, there were tlayacanque (headmen), whose functions are not specified. For a given province there were, in addition to the calpixques of towns in the province, others in Tenochtitlan in charge of the tribute that was brought there and the houses that the province had in the city.

The tribute in kind paid by the provinces consisted of products of the region, so several goods came from only certain provinces. The more distant regions gave luxury objects or raw materials such as cotton, in contrast with the foodstuffs that were a basic part of the tribute from the core area near the capitals of the Empire. Nevertheless, some towns in Oaxaca obtained goods needed for their tribute payments in neighboring marketplaces or in more distant regions. Other goods or special services supplied by certain provinces were military assistance or provisions for the garrisons or the imperial armies passing through.

Isolated data suggest that the provincial calpixques and the houses they kept in Tenochtitlan provided specialized services in the organization of the city. As one example, the rulers of Cempohuallan and Quiahuiztlan were lodged in the house of the Cuetlaxtlan calpixque for the celebration of Tlacaxipehualiztli that Axayacatl held after the campaign against Matlatzinco, and the calpixques of Cuauhnahuac and Huaxtepec lodged the Yopis in their houses during the festival for the installation of Ahuitzotl.

The Garrisons

Since participation in the many wars was one of the principal functions of the dependent kingdoms of each of the three imperial capitals, the territorial organization for military activities coincided with the political organization of the Triple Alliance. Each kingdom sent its contingents to fight in the military campaigns, and within their territory there were regions whose principal contribution was military service, as, for example, the military district headed by Citlaltepec in the northern part of the Basin and the region of Calpollalpan in Tetzcoco. In addition, Chalco, Tlalhuic, and the Otomi regions of the Valley of Toluca also participated in military expeditions together with the leading kingdoms of the alliance.

Some sources give as a general principle the establishment of imperial garrisons in the cabeceras of the tributary provinces, but there is not sufficient specific information on all of them to confirm this. The best reports show that there were well-defined territorial entities with military responsibilities that were different from the tributary provinces. Military colonies were established in strategic areas by settlers coming from the core area of the Empire, both in the midst of the conquered areas such as Huaxyacac and on its exterior frontiers. In these colonies the new settlers served in fortresses commanded by governors with military titles whose rank and duties were different from those of the calpixques. The towns of the region supplied provisions and—some of them—military service as well. Necessary goods that were not available in the region were sent from Mexico. As reported for Tochtepec, officials were sent from the garrisons to administer the towns in the region or to settle disputes.

The most important military colonies of the Empire are shown in the Codex Mendoza. They formed seven military districts: Quecholtetenanco (together with Cuauhtochco and Itzteyocan) between the highlands and the Gulf coast; Zozollan and Huaxyacac, in the central region of Oaxaca; and, on the four exterior frontiers, Atlan (with Tetzapotitlan) towards the Huaxteca, Oztoman (with Poctepec) facing Michoacan, Xoconochco on the Pacific coast of the isthmus, and Atzaccan on the Gulf coast towards Coatzacualco.

In local sources there are references to fortresses or garrisons located in other towns; the most important were Cuauhquechollan, south of Huexotzinco; Iztaquimaxtitlan, north of Tlaxcallan; Tototepec (near present-day Ayutla de los Libres, Guerrero) on the Costa Chica; Ayoxochiquillatzallan, in the southern Mixteca; and Tochtepec, on the way towards Coatzacualco and the isthmus.

Thus, there were important fortresses north and south of the tramontane kingdoms. Three of the major military districts were located in the center of the conquered areas, one beyond Tlaxcallan on the way to the coast and two in the center of imperial expansion within Oaxaca; four others were placed on the external frontiers of the Empire.

The Predominance of the Tenochca

Although the three capitals of the Empire all had separate possessions, each one in the domains of the others as well as in Tlalhuic, Chalco, and Tolocan, there is no doubt about the predominance of Tenochtitlan, whose possessions in the domains of the other two were much more extensive than those that they held in the Tenochca domain. Tetzcoco and Tlacopan had few possessions in each other's territory.

Above all, the preponderance of Tenochtitlan in relation to Tlacopan is most striking. In addition to the numerous possessions of Tenochtitlan in the region of the Tlacopanec kingdoms, it is significant that some Tepanec kingdoms were ruled by kings of the Tenochca dynasty, as, for example, Xilotepec, Tollan, Azcapotzalco, and Tiliuhcan Tlacopan. All of this suggests that Tlacopan was more dominated by Tenochtitlan than was Tetzcoco. According to one report, when the Empire was founded, Itzcoatl did not want to give Tlacopan the rank of ally, but the opinion of Nezahualcoyotl prevailed that it should be incorporated into the alliance as capital of the Tepanec kingdoms. It is reasonable to conclude that Tlacopan was in fact subordinate to Tenochtitlan from the beginning, and the Tenochca preponderance in the west of the Empire increased after Axayacatl's wars against Matlatzinco.

Tetzcoco and Tlacopan cooperated in the wars of the Empire under the direction of the Tenochca king and responded when needed for public works in the same way as did the cities of the Chinampanec area that were dependencies of Tenochtitlan. In this respect they occupied a subordinate position similar to that of the cities of the Colhua-Mexica domain. The Tenochca ascendancy compared with Tetzcoco is clear in the decision of Moteuczoma Xocoyotzin to suspend the tribute payment of the Chinampan that had been given to Tetzcoco; it is possible that similar changes took place in other regions of the Empire. The internal conflict of the Acolhuacan that broke out after the death of Nezahualpilli, with the subsequent division of the kingdom between two of his sons, opened the way to greater subordination of Tetzcoco under Tenochtitlan.

In the last years of the Empire the centralization under Tenochca predominance was increasing at the expense of the tripartite organization of the alliance. The segmentary structure continued, however, with the two other great kings and the thirty-odd lesser kings and the intermingling of territories in the core area. In the distant conquered areas native rulers were kept under a regime of indirect rule in different degrees of submission. Imperial control was maintained by the garrisons in the military colonies and by the resident officials and occasional envoys sent from the center.

Abbreviations

AGI	Archivo General de Indias, Seville
AGN	Archivo General de la Nación, Mexico City
AGN-HJ	Archivo General de la Nación, Hospital de Jesús, Mexico City
AH-INAH	Archivo Histórico, Instituto Nacional de Antropología e Historia, Mexico City
AC	*Anales de Cuauhtitlan*
ATl	*Anales de Tlatelolco*
CDI	*Colección de documentos inéditos . . . de Indias*
DA	*Descripción del arzobispado de México*
ENE	*Epistolario de Nueva España*
HMP	"Historia de los mexicanos por sus pinturas"
HTCh	*Historia tolteca-chichimeca*
LT	*Libro de las tasaciones*
OM	"Origen de los Mexicanos"
PNE	*Papeles de Nueva España*
RG	*Relaciones geográficas*
RGL	"Relación de la genealogía y linaje"
RO	*Relación de los obispados*
SV	*Suma de visitas*

Notes

CHAPTER 1

1. See, for example, Barlow 1949b: vol. 20 (1966) of the *Revista Mexicana de Estudios Antropológicos,* which is devoted to a symposium on "Los imperios prehispánicos en Mesoamérica" (p. 7); Gibson 1971:376; Davies 1987.

2. As an example, in Dibble's preface to *El Códice de Xicotepec: Estudio e interpretación* (1995:7) Aztecs are the people of Mexico Tenochtitlan and the people of Tetzcoco are Acolhuas.

3. Barlow 1990:213–19. First published in 1944.

4. The political situation of these two Otomi towns is not well documented. See Davies 1968: 56–65.

5. Aragón 1931. Orozco y Berra devoted two chapters of his *Historia antigua* (1960, 2:145–75) to geography. One, titled "Geografía: Imperio mexicano," treats of the region subject to Tenochtitlan but also the tramontane realms; the other chapter discusses Tlacopan, Tetzcoco, and various independent areas. The focus is geographical and ethnogeographical; it is not based on the Empire's conquests or the registers of tribute.

6. Barlow 1949b.

7. In this case *province* would be in Nahuatl *calpixcayotl,* the entity under a *calpixqui* (steward or tribute collector). See below on other uses of the word *province.*

8. Gibson 1956, 1964b, 1971. For finding the greater part of the places that belonged to the Empire, the following are also important: Kelly and Palerm 1952, Tschohl 1964, and Trautman 1968. Other more recent publications are Berdan 1980b, 1992; Gerhard 1986; Mohar 1987; Castillo 1991. More emphasis is given to organization in Hassig 1984, Rojas 1991, Hicks 1992, Kobayashi 1993, and Berdan et al. 1996. Davies 1980b and 1987 and Berdan et al. 1996 treat the Empire as a whole, emphasizing Tenochtitlan; they make very limited use of the sources from Tetzcoco and Tlacopan.

9. For the kingdom of Tetzcoco, see Corona 1973, Hicks 1982, and Offner 1983. For the kingdom of Tlacopan, see van Zantwijk 1969 and Pérez Rocha 1982.

10. His papers on the conquests of the Empire are collected in Barlow 1990.

11. Kelly and Palerm 1952:264–317. Many of their identifications are erroneous and have misled later scholars. Their knowledge of Nahuatl was deficient, and they identified toponyms on the basis of unfounded similarities in the names. Their paleography of some toponyms in Codex Mendoza is incorrect and did not take the glyphs into consideration. Most important, they wrongly interpreted all the towns of folios 17v–18r as conquests of Moteuczoma Xocoyotzin. More recently, Hassig (1988) discusses the military campaigns of the Empire.

12. Kelly and Palerm 1952:265.

13. Tschohl 1964.

14. See, for example, Hodge 1984, which discusses Amaquemecan, Cuauhtitlan, Coyoacan, and Teotihuacan. In a typology of worldwide applicability, Hassig (1984) distinguishes between territorial and hegemonic states, putting the Tenochca Empire in the second type. In this book it is not possible to cover all aspects of the political organization. The different degrees of domination presented here and, more concretely, the contrast between indirect rule through native rulers and functionaries sent by the Empire can be related to Hassig's categories (see chapter 8).

15. I have discussed segmentation in ancient Mexico in Carrasco 1971a: 363 and 1977:189–91. See also Kirchhoff 1963 and Ruhnau 1988:29–31. Compare the concept of segmentary state in Southall 1956:243–63 and 1988. The segments may be associated with ethnic or kin groups of the population or with dominant lineages, but this is not true in all cases. Segmentation should not be identified with the system of segmentary lineages that was developed for the analysis of stateless societies.

16. See Brumfield and Fox 1994 on factionalism in the New World, especially the chapters by van Zantwijk on the rivalry between two branches of the reigning dynasty of Tenochtitlan and by Hicks on the factional struggles in Tollan, Cuauhtitlan, and Tepeyacac.

17. The principal Nahuatl terms denoting social rank are discussed later in this chapter in the section on terminology. In Carrasco 1977 I propose using the concept of estate together with that of class to analyze pre-Spanish social stratification. Smith 1986 has defined the rulers (tlatoani) as a class on the basis of their economic exchanges and matrimonial unions.

18. References to Sahagún's *Historia general* give the book and chapter as well as the page number in the Anderson and Dibble edition, which includes the complete Nahuatl text of the Florentine Codex together with its English translation. The Spanish text, from the Porrúa edition (1969), is referred to only when it adds something to the Nahuatl.

19. Zorita presents some information from his own experience on Matlatzinco and Guatemala and copies extensively from known sources such as Motolinía, but above all he includes material given to him by Francisco de las Navas, which is what has made Zorita's book a basic source on the social organization of ancient Mexico. See Baudot 1977:452–61 and Carrasco 1994.

20. Durán 1967:2; Tezozomoc 1975.

21. Barlow 1990:13–32.

22. See, for example, Dyckerhoff 1970 on attire and funeral customs.

23. O'Gorman, in the introduction to his edition of Ixtlilxochitl, includes a section on the sources used by the chronicler (Ixtlilxochitl 1975–77, 1:47–85).

24. Ixtlilxochitl 1975–77, 1:382–84.

25. Barlow 1990:6.

26. Gibson (1956:13–14) and Trautmann (1968:65n. 1) used the "Pintura de México" to identify the extent of the kingdom of Tetzcoco and made comparisons with other sources. The Spanish edition of this book (Carrasco 1996:85–102) includes a detailed analysis of the "Pintura de México" in relation to all the other writings of Ixtlilxochitl.

27. The edition of Torquemada (1975–83) prepared by León-Portilla includes a study (6:93–266) of the sources of the Monarquía Indiana with a table that identifies the sources used for each chapter.

28. The Codex Chimalpopoca contains two documents in Nahuatl, the *Anales de Cuauhtitlan* and the *Leyenda de los Soles*, together with a report in Spanish on religion by Pedro Ponce. The two documents in Nahuatl have been translated by Lehmann (1938), Velázquez (1945), and Bierhorst (1992a, 1992b). Velázquez includes a facsimile of the manuscripts; Lehmann (1938) and Bierhorst (1992b) give a transcription of the Nahuatl text. See Bierhorst (1992a: 10–14) for the history of the manuscript and its editions. In this book I use in the references the abbreviation AC followed by the page number in the manuscript, which is noted in all three editions. As a rule I refer to specific editions only when there are differences in the translations.

29. The document related to Motolinía's "Memorial tetzcocano" is on pp. 64 and 65 of the manuscript (secs. 223–33 in Velázquez's edition). The list of kings is on pp. 63–64 (sec. 226 in Velázquez), and the lists of conquests are on pp. 65–68 (secs. 234–42 in Velázquez).

30. Barlow (1990:1–150) was the first to make a comparative study of these lists. On the relation between the five existing versions, see Tschohl 1989:207–15. For the conquests of Ahuitzotl and Moteuczoma Xocoyotzin, the best discussion is Tschohl 1964:43–158. A complete comparative study of all these lists has yet to be done.

31. The Codex Mendoza lists make up the first part of the codex (1r–16v). The list in the *Leyenda de los Soles* is incomplete in the manuscript of the Codex Chimalpopoca (see Velázquez 1945, p. 8 of facsimile), but Tschohl (1989:250–52) has completed it with the copy by Pichardo, and Bierhorst (1992a: 161–62; 1992b: 99–100) has incorporated this text in his edition.

32. The lists in AC are in pp. 65–68; those in ATl are in secs. 52–67. These sources also cite conquests in the sections organized as annals. The lists of Nazareo are in one of his letters (ENE 10:118–19; Zimmermann 1970:26–27).

33. A comparative study of these lists—already begun by Barlow (1990) and Tschohl (1964)—is beyond the limits of this book. In referring to these lists they will be treated as a unit called Lists of Con-

quests, citing only the first part of Codex Mendoza when there are no notable differences in the other lists and adding data from the others when there are important divergences. In some cases I will refer only to the data compiled in Kelly and Palerm 1952.

34. Sahagún 1954:1–4 (book 8, chap. 1).

35. Chapter 4, in the discussion of each tributary province, puts together and compares the data from all these sources. Chapter 8 compares the *Memorial de los pueblos de Tlacopan* with the Tenochca sources in regard to the organization of the regions that gave tribute to the three capitals of the Empire.

36. All citations of the *Relaciones geográficas* (RG) refer to the edition of Acuña (1982–88) which is complete and contains indexes. In a few cases it will be necessary to use Paso y Troncoso's edition (1905–1906). For locating towns on the Gulf coast there is the important study by H. Cline (1959) on the maps in the *Relación de Veracruz*. Acuña's edition includes the original maps and Cline's interpretive map; I refer to Cline's article only when it contains data not included in those maps. The *Relaciones* of Pomar and Muñoz Camargo have been given separate entries in the bibliography.

37. On the altepetl, especially in the colonial era, see García Martínez 1987:72–78; Lockhart 1992: chap. 2.

38. Sahagún 1969a: 79–82 (book 6, chap. 15).

39. Molina 1970: sub voce.

40. *Altepenanyotl* might have been coined by Molina to translate "Matriz de las ciudades, metropolis" in Nebrija's Spanish-Latin dictionary (1973, s.v.). Molina's Spanish-Nahuatl dictionary is based on this dictionary of Nebrija.

41. See chapter 6 on the "renters" of the Acolhua kingdom.

42. Also, the calpoleque (people of the wards, or barrios) were the hands and feet of those called *calmecactlaca* (people of the calmecac), *tepeuani* (conquerors), or Toltecs, who were the first to come to Cholollan. Some of these Chololtec calpoleque established themselves later on in other cities of the area (HTCh, secs. 11, 123, 266, 273, 337–38, and 396 and notes by Reyes García. Cf. Carrasco 1971b).

43. HTCh, sec. 265.

44. Vetancurt 1961, 1:329. For these problems, see Carrasco 1971a, Reyes García, et al. 1996, Ruhnau 1988, Schroeder 1991, Lockhart 1992.

45. Zimmermann 1960:21.

46. Ruhnau 1988:147. This use is frequent in colonial documents. Zorita (1941:84) uses tlatoque for those he calls "señores supremos" (supreme lords), that is, the kings.

47. Ixtlilxochitl 1975–77, 2:82.

48. Carrasco 1966.

49. Codex Mendoza, 68r.

50. Torquemada 1975–83, 4:332.

51. The most important are Ometeuctli, lord of the number two; Tlalteuctli, lord of the earth; Mictlanteuctli, lord of the place of the dead; Tlalocanteuctli, lord of Tlalocan (uncertain etymology), the god of rain; Xiuhteuctli, lord of the year; and Otonteuctli, lord Otomí.

52. Molina 1970 (s.v.): "Tetecuyo. amo de criados o de esclavos."

53. See Carrasco 1966, Prem 1974, Reyes García 1977, Martínez 1984a, Olivera 1978, Ruhnau 1988, Schroeder 1991, Lockhart 1992.

54. Durán 1971, 2:123: "casi como emperador y monarca de este nuevo mundo." Muriá (1973) discusses this, especially in chaps. 6, 8, 12, 13, and pp. 141–42.

55. Clavijero (1982:103) refers to "esta triple alianza" when describing the alliance of the three kings. Among scholars of ancient Mexico it has been used at least since Orozco y Berra (in a note to chap. 78 in his 1878 edition of Tezozomoc [1975:551]).

56. Ixtlilxochitl 1975–77, 2:146.

57. Chimalpahin 1958:6, 14, 15.

58. AC, 63.

59. Codex Osuna, 496r, 498v.

60. Durán 1971, 2:177, 182, 335, 336.

61. See above in the discussion of altepetl.

62. In Molina 1970: "cecentlayacapan. a cada barrio, o cada barrio." Chimalpahin uses this word (Ruhnau 1988:66ff.; Schroeder 1991:131–36).

63. Ramírez de Fuenleal in CDI 13:253–54.

CHAPTER 2

1. Gibson (1971:389) suggests that the concept of a Triple Alliance may have been an invention of colonial historiography. It is true that some sources use this concept as a way of exalting the importance of Tetzcoco or Tlacopan, but there is no reason to reject the importance of the tripartite structure. The alliance of three or more cities that made up the highest levels of the political structure was normal in Mesoamerica; the best known example is the League of Mayapan.

2. Motolinía 1971:414. This is from the well-known letter in which Motolinía criticizes Fray Bartolomé de Las Casas. Other data in this letter on pre-Spanish life are also found in his other works, but not this particular information, although the report in his *Memoriales*, cited below, seems to be a continuation of what he says in the letter.

3. Ibid., 337.

4. Ibid., 206, 322. Cf. Torquemada 1975–83, 4:71.

5. López de Gómara 1988:109. He also says (111) that "Moteuczoma had 100 large cities with their provinces." Cf. Cervantes de Salazar 1971, 1:321 and Torquemada 1975–83, 1:316.

6. Ixtlilxochitl 1975–77, 2:88. Cf. 1:445–46.

7. Ibid., 2:80 ff.

8. Ibid., 2:75, 79.

9. Durán 1967, 2:88–90, 105–23; Tezozomoc 1975:258–60, 272–81; AC, 46; Ixtlilxochitl 1975–77, 2:80–81.

10. See p. 44 on the entrance of Tlacopan into the alliance.

11. Ixtlilxochitl 1975–77, 2:89. The total number of kingdoms listed in the different sources comes to fifteen. Chapter 6 discusses these kingdoms in detail.

12. See chapter 7 on the dependent kingdoms of Tlacopan.

13. Barlow 1949b, especially pp. 33, 51, 73, and 87. Other writers follow basically the same division; they recognize the groups of Acolhua and Tepanec kingdoms, but not the group of kingdoms dependent on Tenochtitlan in the south of the Basin. Krickeberg (1952:265) follows Barlow's subdivisions, but in his last book (1961:55–57) he still speaks of the Empire as an alliance of three tribes, similar to the league of the Iroquois. Gibson (1964a: 9–22), in his chapter on the "tribes" that existed in the Basin, combines the ethnic divisions that preceded the Empire with political divisions. He indicates the existence of several kingdoms among the Tepanecs and Acolhuas, but gives a reduced area to the Mexicas, although he recognizes that under Moteuczoma Xocoyotzin, Mizquic, Cuitlahuac, and Colhuacan were in effect included in the Mexica area. His article on the Empire (1971) avoids this problem. Trautmann (1968:62–81 and fig. 6) assigns to Tlacopan and Tetzcoco a series of dependent kingdoms and tributary towns but limits Tenochtitlan to its island and adjacent lands, although he does note that the city obtained some estancias farther away; he considers Xochimilco, Colhuacan, and Cuitlahuac as separate entities. He gives a map (fig. 6) that shows Acolhuacan as a unit but indicates the boundaries of the various dependent kingdoms of Tlacopan. Hodge (1984:17, table 2-1) recognizes that the Empire was a union of three parts and describes Tenochtitlan, Tetzcoco, and Tlacopan as confederations, but she assigns to the Tenochca confederation only Tlatelolco, Ecatepec, and Azcapotzalco Mexicapan; she considers Colhuacan, Mizquic, Xochimilco, Cuitlahuac, and Chalco to be separate confederations. Prem (1989:48–49) considers the cities of the southern Basin as part of the Tenochca domain. Kobayashi (1993:68) notes that Tenochtitlan dominated the southern part of the Basin, but he does not discuss the status of the kingdoms in that zone. I first published the interpretation here given in Carrasco 1991. In a recent publication Hodge (1996) also recognizes the importance of the Tenochca domain.

14. See chapter 5 on the dependent kingdoms of Tenochtitlan.

15. Ixtlilxochitl 1975–77, 1:444. This formula is usually applied to the division of tribute among the three kingdoms; here it obviously refers to the division of territory (see chapter 8).

16. Torquemada 1975–83, 1:242. This report is included in his chapter on the kingdom of Tetzcoco, which suggests that it comes from a Tetzcoca source not identified. See the complete quotation on p. 233.

17. The Tenochca sources are less clear, although they do describe the division of tribute into three parts (Durán 2:122–23).

18. Durán 1967, 2:83, 101–102; Tezozomoc 1975:253–54, 271, 277.

19. Ixtlilxochitl 1975–77, 2:90 and the data on Teotihuacan given below in this section.

20. Ibid., 2:86–88, 187; Torquemada 1975–83, 1:242–43.

21. Durán 1967, 2:125–31.

22. Cf. Gibson 1971:385; Hicks 1984.

23. Tratado de Teotihuacan, 4v–5r.

24. Amply documented in the sources. See chapters 5 and 7.

25. See chapters 5, 6, and 7; also chapter 10 on Chalco and chapter 9 on Tolocan.

26. Motolinía 1971:395, in his "Memorial tetzcocano"; see also a document from Tlacopan (AGI, Justicia 1029, no. 10, fol. 10v). On these matters, see chapter 8.

27. Ixtlilxochitl 1975–77, 2:108.

28. Ibid., 2:187.

29. Landownership has been the object of very different interpretations. See Dyckerhoff and Prem 1978; Carrasco 1988:512–13. The lands of kings and nobles will be treated in another work in preparation.

30. Zavala 1938:70. See the complete quotation on p. 68.

31. Principal data in AGI, Patronato 181, ramo 8; 245, ramo 3. Pérez Rocha is preparing the edition of these documents.

32. Hernández Rodríguez 1988:104–10, 115–20.

33. See p. 59. Cf. p. 144 on the chamber (*recámara*) of the king of Tetzcoco according to Ixtlilxochitl.

34. Zimmermann 1970:1–4, 12–14, plates 34–35; Pérez Rocha 1982:87–93.

35. See section on Chalco in chapter 10.

36. Ixtlilxochitl 1975–77, 2:90 (quoted on p. 143), 108, 150–51 (quoted on p. 220); Zorita 1941: 91–92 (quoted on p. 226). Cf. Pomar in RG 8:53.

37. Ixtlilxochitl 1975–77, 1:449.

38. "Yn ic tetlalmacoc yn mac yn acxotlan calpixqui amo yn machiz mochiuh yn pipiltin" (AC, 60). Cf. Molina 1970 (s.v.): "nomachiz. está a mi cargo, o tengo yo el cuydado desso." See Bierhorst 1992a: 123.

39. This is comparable to the colonial situation, when the encomienda, especially in its later form, was a grant defined as the tribute coming from a given town, appraised and collected by royal officials.

40. Cf. Carrasco 1979; Hicks 1984, 1992.

41. Gibson (1964:263) notes the geographic extension and separation of the possessions of a single individual.

42. For example, in Tepechpan (AGN, Tierras 1871, exp. 17).

43. Gibson (1971:390–92). Note also the cases of Cuauhtitlan and Teotihuacan where various cities of the alliance had possessions.

44. There are several examples of towns that did not have defined boundaries or whose subject villages were intermingled with those of other towns. It was so in Tochpan and Papantla (SV, secs. 449, 525; see chapter 11), in Metztitlan (SV, sec. 355, on Malila; PNE 3:109, 111, on Ilamatlan and Atlihuezyan), in Cholula (SV, sec. 114), in Tepeyacac and Cuauhtinchan (SV, sec. 532), in Quecholac and Tecamachalco (SV, secs. 118, 201), in Itzocan and its barrios (SV, sec. 292), and in Chilpopocatla (SV, sec. 134).

45. Torquemada 1975–83, 1:127–28. The numbers of kingdoms and provinces cannot be accepted without question, because they come from plates V and VI of the Codex Xolotl in which all

those lords are depicted, and in spite of what Ixtlilxochitl says (1977, 1:321, 324–25), there is no indication that they were subject to Techotlalatzin (Dibble 1951:78, 84). It is not known where Torquemada got this information, which is not in Ixtlilxochitl, but there is no reason to reject the policy of population transfers and the creation of parcialidades. The manuscript Mexicain 254 of the Bibliothèque Nationale, Paris, fol. 7r–7v, has a description in Nahuatl similar to that of Torquemada that provides the Nahuatl terminology.

46. Cf. the concept of "composite peoples" in Kirchhoff 1979. As for the material aspect, intermingling provided each subgroup with access to the different natural resources of the territory under control, as in the case of Andean verticality. Cf. Carrasco 1979; Zamora 1979.

CHAPTER 3

1. Davies 1980a treats the history of the period between the end of Tollan and the Mexica predominance. The principal sources for the history of the Empire are the ones referred to in the preceding chapter. Among modern authors Davies (1980b and 1987) covers the general history of the Empire; Barlow (1990) and Kelly and Palerm (1952) catalog the conquests; and Hassig (1988) deals with military history and the campaigns of each Tenochca king.

2. Carrasco 1984b and n.d. treat the history of the Tepanec empire.

3. Codex Mendoza, 2r–v. On the fall of Colhuacan: RGL, 250–52; OM, 267–68; AC, 23–24, secs. 122–25; Ixtlilxochitl 1975–77, 1:303, 313–15, 320, 323; 2:36–37.

4. Ixtlilxochitl 1975–77, 1:346–47; 2:53.

5. Ibid., 2:82–88.

6. Ibid., 2:86–88. Torquemada (1975–83) knew and used the same Tetzcoca sources as Ixtlilxochitl, but according to his version of this event (1:242–43) there was no armed struggle; when Nezahualcoyotl's army went to Mexico, the Mexican lords came out humbly to make peace, and there were great festivals to celebrate the new alliance. Nor does he say anything about the Chinampan tribute.

7. Torquemada 1975–83, 1:200–201.

8. Durán 1967, 2:122–23. López de Gómara (1988:292) states that Itzcoatl had as companions (*acompañados*) in government Nezahualcoyotzin, king of Tetzcoco, and the king of Tlacopan. His use of the term *acompañados* recalls the Nahuatl *huicalli*. See p. 470n.131, on the ethnic groups of the Acolhuacan that were acompañados of the officials in the government of the kingdom.

9. AC, 47, 48.

10. Chimalpahin 1987:103, 109.

11. "Auh ça no yhcuac ypan in pehualloque yn acolhuaque tetzcuca; auh macihui pehualloque ca çan tlaco tonatiuh yn onmaca yaoyotl, ynic ceuh çan tlacualizpan; y hualcallaque yn tetzcuca; çan yehuatl quichichiuh y Neçahualcoyotzin ynic pehualloque, yehuantin tepeuhque yn mexica tenuhca" (Chimalpahin 1889:102). The text of the third relación contains some variants; instead of *quichichiuh*, "he arranged." he says *quichiuh*, "he did," (Chimalpahin 1987:114). The word that I translate as "they submitted" is *hualcallaque*. Literally it means "enter the house," but the context here and in other passages shows that it is equivalent to the expression in Molina (1970): "tetlancalaqui. el que se subjecta y somete a otro" (he who submits to someone else; s.v. *someter*), and to "tlacalaquia. ni, vel. non. acudir con la renta, o tributo, o meter algo dent[r]o de casa" (to bring rent or tribute or take something into the house).

12. RG 6:75.

13. Durán 1967, 2:125–31. See chapter 5 on the places acquired for Tenochtitlan in this war.

14. Chimalpahin 1889:96, 103, 105. As we have seen, according to Durán (1967, 2:122), Itzcoatl ordered that Tetzcoco should be the second kingdom of the area and Tlacopan the third.

15. RGL, 252.

16. Ixtlilxochitl 1975–77, 2:20. Cf. 1:543.

17. Chimalpahin 1889:98–105.

18. "Aun in yehuantin yn tlacopaneca ypan in yn xihuitl y hualmocauhque yn imac Mexicatl ynic tetlan hualcallaque yhuan colhuaque tetlan hualcallacque yn Mexico" (Chimalpahin 1987:111).

19. "Ypan 3 tochtli, hualcalacque Tenuchtitlan tlacopaneca, Tlacacuitlahua yhuan Aculnahuacatl Tzacualcatl, tlahtohuani Tlacopan" (Chimalpahin 1889:100–101).

20. AC, 46; Ixtlilxochitl 1975–77, 2:89.

21. Codex Mendoza, 5v–6r; AC, 66, sec. 237.

22. AC, 46.

23. After discussing Nezahualcoyotl's restitution of the Acolhua kings, Veytia (1944, 2:174) remarks that the same procedure was followed by Itzcoatl with the kings of Xochimilco, Mizquic, and Tenayocan.

24. Matrimonial alliances among the dynasties of the Triple Alliance are discussed in Carrasco 1984a.

25. Codex Mendoza, 6r; AC, 66.

26. Chimalpahin 1889:98, 100, 108. For the location of the last two places, see p. 102.

27. Codex Mendoza, 7v–8r.

28. Ibid., 8r; AC, 66; Ixtlilxochitl 1975–77, 2:108.

29. Codex Mendoza, 8r; AC, 66; Ixtlilxochitl 1975–77, 2:107; Durán 1967, 2:163–70.

30. Codex Mendoza, 7v (Coaixtlahuacan); Durán 1967, 2:177–203, 225–32; Ixtlilxochitl 1975–77, 2:107–108; Torquemada 1975–83, 1:221–25.

31. Codex Mendoza, 10r–v; AC, 67; Durán 1967, 2:253–93; Torquemada 1975–83, 1:243, 250–51.

32. Codex Mendoza, 12r; AC, 67; Durán 1967, 2:303–305; Torquemada 1975–83, 1:252.

33. Durán 1967, 2:318–21.

34. Codex Mendoza, 13r–v; AC, 67; Durán 1967, 2:347–62, 383–89; Torquemada 1975–83, 1:257–59, 263–65, 267.

35. Codex Mendoza, 15v–16v; AC, 67–68; Durán 1967, 2:417–31, 479–82; Torquemada 1975–83, 1:281, 285–87, 290, 293–96.

36. Ixtlilxochitl 1975–77, 2:185–89.

37. Ibid., 2:190–92.

CHAPTER 4

1. Published in ENE 14:118–22; Zimmermann 1970:5–8, facsimile in plates 6–8. The manuscript heading says only "Memorial de los pueblos." Zimmermann titles it "Memorial de Tlacopan." The ENE edition gives as the title "Memorial de los pueblos sujetos al señorío de Tlacupan, y de los que tributaban a México, Tezcuco y Tlacupan." I will call it "Memorial de los pueblos de Tlacopan" or simply "Memorial de Tlacopan" when there is no possibility for confusion.

2. Published without a title as part of Motolinía's *Memoriales* (1971:394–96).

3. AC, 64–65 (paragraphs 224–33 of Velázquez's translation). A version of this text was also published by Paso y Troncoso and Chimalpopoca Galicia in 1897, but recent editions of the AC are preferable. Ixtlilxochitl (1977, 2:89–90, 106–108) gives related material but presents it as part of the organization Nezahualcoyotl ordered of the Acolhua domain and of his first conquests; he does not list the towns of all the territorial units.

4. See p. 65 of the manuscript in the Velásquez edition; cf. Bierhorst 1992a: 134; 1992b: 80.

5. The "Memorial de Tlacopan" gives a total of 446 toponyms, of which 99 were in the Tlacopan core area and 347 towns that paid tribute to all three capitals. The latter are listed in eleven paragraphs grouped in three divisions (6, 7, and 8). See Table 4-1.

6. ENE 16:72.

7. Cf. Zimmermann 1970:vi, 1; Gibson 1964b: 136–43; Trautmann 1968:71–72.

8. "Documentos de Texcoco" 1903:9–10.

9. ENE 16:63–64.

10. "Documentos de Texcoco" 1903:10–11.

11. Several sources give the total number of towns that paid tribute to the Empire, but the numbers are not in agreement. The 123 towns could be connected with the 113 towns mentioned in Motolinía's "Memorial tetzcocano" that paid tribute to the three capitals in the provinces of Tochpan, Tziuhcoac, Tlapacoyan, Tlatlauhquitepec, and Tochtepec, which with the nine in the province of Cuauhnahuac would be 122, although this last province paid tribute only to Tetzcoco according to the memorial. Nor does the number 123 agree with the 160 that, according to a letter by Motolinía (1970:414), was the number of provinces or kingdoms subject to the three capitals. The "Memorial tetzcocano" lists a total of 152 places if we include also the kingdoms and towns of tenants subject to Tetzcoco. It is possible that there has been a mistake made in identifying these numbers as the category of towns that paid tribute to the three capitals. One hundred sixty was also the number of "aldeas y lugares" in the Acolhuacan that Nezahualcoyotl distributed to his children, relatives, and meritorious individuals (Ixtlilxochitl 2:90). The total number of the towns that paid tribute to the three capitals must have been much greater, since Motolinía's "Memorial" lists only the tributary provinces of the Tetzcoca sector. The "Memorial de Tlacopan" lists 347 towns paying tribute to all three capitals. The Codex Mendoza does not distinguish between the towns subject to Tenochtitlan and those that paid tribute to the three capitals. If we make this distinction on the basis of other sources, the tributary towns of the alliance (the provinces from Tlachco to Oxitipan) would be 229, which also does not agree with the numbers of the two other sources. It would be even higher if the provinces of Morelos and of the Valley of Toluca are counted among those paying tribute to the Empire as a whole. These divergences might result in part from the different ways of counting the subject towns according to their political category. Above all, the considerable difference between the "Memorial de Tlacopan" and the Codex Mendoza should be noted. This difference is best explained in the case of the provinces of Tochpan and Tziuhcoac, for which all the towns listed in the Codex Mendoza had in turn many sujetos enumerated in the Tetzcoca and Tlacopan sources.

12. See the introduction by O'Gorman to his edition of the works of Ixtlilxochitl (1977, 2:82).

13. From 1554 to 1557 there was no governor in Tenochtitlan; Don Esteban de Guzmán of Xochimilco acted as *juez de residencia*. From 1557 to 1563 the governor was once more a descendant of the old Tenochca dynasty, Don Cristóbal de Guzmán Cecepatic (Gibson 1964a: 169). The letter of 1562 was sent by Don Cristóbal de Guzman of Mexico, Don Hernando Pimentel of Tetzcoco, and Don Antonio Cortés of Tlacopan (Menegus 1991:251–54).

14. The six categories correspond to the paragraphs in O'Gorman's edition (pp. 394–96) as follows: 1 to pars. 803–804; 2 to pars. 805–806; 3 to par. 807; 4 to par. 808; 5 to par. 809; 6 to par. 860. In referring to this document and to the "Memorial de Tlacopan," the word *town* (pueblo) is used for all the different kinds of settlements, because that is the usage in both documents, but the descriptions quoted indicate clearly that one must distinguish between the cities with kings and the peasant settlements where there were tenants (renteros) of the kings.

15. See the complete quotation in p. 136.

16. See the complete quotation in p. 143.

17. At first glance the version in the AC seems to combine this list with the towns of tenants defined as the second category in Motolinía. However, in the manuscript of AC (p. 64, see transcription in Bierhorst 1992b: 79) one sees that with Tliltzapoapan a new paragraph begins on Tlatlauhquitepec, Tlapacoyan, and Tziuhcoac. All the toponyms in this new paragraph are separated by two short lines, which is not the case in the preceding paragraph that coincides with the towns of tenants. The translators have not observed this distinction and give the two groups of towns in one list (Velázquez 1945: sec. 226; Bierhorst 1992a: 131).

18. In the AC text (64–65), related to Motolinía's "Memorial tetzcocano," Cuauhnahuac and its towns make up the first group instead of the last. Cf. Ixtlilxochitl 1975–77, 2:106.

19. All the sections of the manuscript are preceded by a sign in the left margin of the page; the same sign is used at the beginning of each of the lists of places that comprise the paragraphs, even when there is only one list in the section (excepting the list in the first section). Zimmermann (1970:5–8), in

addition to numbering sections and paragraphs, adds small letters (from *a* to *m*) for each paragraph in sections 1 to 5 and capital letters (*A* to *L*) for sections 6 to 8. In this book references to the "Memorial de Tlacopan" will identify a place by giving the section, the paragraph, and the place it occupies in the list. For example, 6.4-2, indicates section 6, paragraph 4, second place in the list.

20. See the complete quotation in p. 185. Note that this memorial names the subjects of the dependent kingdoms, which is not done systematically for those of Tenochtitlan or Tetzcoco in any of the sources from those two capitals.

21. See the complete quotation in p. 196.

22. Such as towns in Tetzcoco and other kingdoms of the Basin, in Tollantzinco, in Tlalhuic (Morelos), and in Tochtepec (Ixtlilxochitl 1975–77, 2:90, 106–108).

23. Orozco y Berra 1960, 2:172–73. The note by Ramírez further states that "the original has neither date nor signature, but it is old and, it appears, the rough draft of the author. It belongs to the fragments of the museum of Boturini, conserved in the Museo, and is found listed in the second inventory, number 26, made by D. Patricio Antonio López on the 15th of July of 1745, and whose original exists in the Archive."

24. Ixtlilxochitl 1975–77, 2:107–108.

25. See p. 168. The Chinampan tribute given to Tetzcoco ended during the reign of Nezahualpilli.

26. RG 6:169–73; Durán 1967, 2:23.

27. Ixtlilxochitl 1975–77, 2:107.

28. References to the Codex Osuna will be given to the folio number of the 464–501 sequence in matters relating to the pictorial document, or to the page of the 1947 edition in matters relating to the text, the transcription, or the translation.

29. The handwriting is different from that of the rest of the codex, and there are differences in orthography, as, for example, that for Tlacuban, and at times *s* instead of *x*, as in *isquich* (cf. Tlacopan, *ixquich* in 501r).

30. The last two words are written clearly, but *quitl* does not make sense and must have been an error, which can be corrected to *yehuatl tequitl*, according to Castillo (Codex Osuna 1947:331), or as *yehua tequitl*.

31. Codex Osuna 1947:114–15.

32. Gibson 1964b. The town called Xilotzinco in the legend could also be read as Xilotepec, since the glyph does not contain the element *-tzinco*, usually designated by the lower half of a body. However, the hill depicted in the glyph does not have to be read as though the ending *-tepec* were part of the toponym, because this document uses it for almost all places, no doubt to indicate that they are towns (altepetl). If Xilotepec were depicted, its ruler would have the rank of tlatoani, which is not the case.

33. The places depicted in the Codex Osuna are arranged in three horizontal rows to be read from left to right across the two facing pages of 496v–497r and 497v–498r. This is how Robertson (1959:118–19) read it, but Gibson (1964b) reads it page by page, which changes the relation between the cabeceras and their sujetos. Reading the two open pages as a unit makes clear that the head at the left of the glyph of Atotonilco belongs with the teuctli glyph of Apazco in the previous page. In Carrasco 1996 (pp. 107, 283, 286) I erroneously said Atotonilco had two lords. The numbers to indicate the order of listing are used also in Tables 7-1 and 7-2, which include the data from the Codex Osuna in charting the territorial organization of the kingdom of Tlacopan.

34. In only one case do these sources list the conquests of the Tenochca in a brief retrospective remembrance at the time the history was written. (Durán 1967, 2:205; Tezozomoc 1975:249–50. They do not add much that is not better reported elsewhere. See Carrasco 1996:130–34 for a detailed discussion of this material.

35. The best facsimile editions are the 1980 edition of the *Matrícula de tributos* and, of the Codex Mendoza, the 1938 edition by Clark and the 1992 edition by Berdan and Anawalt. For a comparative study of both codices the most useful edition is that of the *Matrícula* by the Secretaría de Hacienda (1991), which presents both documents side by side. References are given to the folio numbers of the

documents so that any edition can be used. I have used principally the most accessible editions: for the Codex Mendoza the 1979 reprint of Galindo's edition of 1925, and for the *Matrícula*, that of Castillo Farreras (1974). In the introduction to his new edition of the *Matrícula*, Reyes García (n.d.) has developed several points similar to those discussed in this chapter.

36. The explanations in the Codex Mendoza and the *Información de 1554* do not use the word *provincia* but describe each tributary entity as a head town together with other towns. The *Información de 1554*, as a rule, names only the head town.

37. Zavala 1938:70. This document bears no date but seems to be from about 1547 (ibid., 61). The writer speaks of "provincias" but in a wider sense than that of tributary province.

38. For example, Barlow 1949; Molins Fábrega 1956; Castillo 1974, 1991; Berdan 1980, 1992; Mohar 1987.

39. On these problems, see Berdan 1992.

40. References from here on will be to the Codex Mendoza, except when the other sources have important variants or data not in that codex. All three have to be compared to know the nature and quantity of the tribute, but that is outside the scope of this study.

41. From the statement by the second witness (Scholes and Adams 1957:93–94). Statements by the other witnesses are almost exactly the same.

42. Barlow 1949b. Berdan (1980; 1992) and Mohar (1987) keep the order in the codices, but they do not use it to interpret the territorial organization. See also Vollmer (1972:61, 92–93). Reyes García (1979) keeps the order given in the sources and analyzes it in terms of the four directions of the world.

43. Boturini 1974:117.

44. Cf. Robertson (1959:73): "Close examination of the original by me showed no indication that the actual *Matrícula* represents a screenfold cut and bound into the Post-Conquest book form." In his forthcoming edition, Reyes García (n.d.) discusses the characteristics of the different pages of the codex.

45. Usually the leaves of the Codex Mendoza are numbered in the top right-hand corner of each recto, while the versos have no numbers. However, in some cases the number written on the recto of the following folio has also been written on the top left-hand corner of the preceding verso; this occurs on the versos of the folios preceding those marked 19, 20, 43, 44, 51, and 57 on the recto.

46. Kelly and Palerm (1952:313) consider the towns painted on these two folios as conquests of Moteuczoma Xocoyotzin, but they cannot be part of his conquests, of which there were forty-four according to the text on 14v (quoted below); all forty-four are depicted on 15r–16v.

47. Codex Mendoza, 15r.

48. In his final remarks the commentator of the Codex Mendoza excuses himself for not having had time to polish his diction, but he seems to have no doubts about his interpretation of the paintings; he states that "although the interpretations are rough, one has to take note only of the substance of their declarations, what the figures mean, which are well explained since the interpreter of them is a good speaker of Mexican [Nahuatl]" (71v).

49. Caso 1956; Gibson 1964a: 47–49, 372–76.

50. Tezozomoc 1975:253, 271, 277, 305. Cf. Durán 1967, 2:83, 101–102, 113–14, 151.

51. According to Krickeberg (1961:67) all the places on these pages were "Crown lands belonging to Moctezuma II," but he does not elaborate on this to explain the difference between the towns in the Basin and the distant places, nor to distinguish between the towns on these two pages and those registered in the other provinces in this codex where there were also lands of the crown.

52. Van Zantwijk 1967; Tezozomoc 1975:534.

53. Barlow (1949b: 130) suggests that the tribute not painted on 17v, which lists Citlaltepec, was perhaps included in the tribute depicted for Tlatelolco. The towns headed by Citlaltepec are not represented in any of the existing pages of the *Matrícula*.

54. Petlacalco was also the name of a site on the Tlacopan causeway (Sahagún 1975:68, 71 [book 12, chaps. 24, 25]).

55. Tezozomoc 1975:271, 276–77, 305.

56. Hicks 1984.

57. The Mendoza province of Chalco is discussed in chapter 10. For the separate possessions of the three capitals in Chalco, see pp. 109, on Tenochtitlan, 231 on Tetzcoco, and 200 on Tlacopan.

58. The situation of Chalco and of Tolocan lends itself to different interpretations; see the discussion of these provinces in pp. 283 and 255.

59. Sahagún 1954:51, 52 (book 8, chap. 17). This list is not in the Spanish version. The Nahuatl text is found in both the Florentine Codex and the Madrid manuscript. The names in the table follow the spelling of the Florentine Codex.

60. Caso 1956:12, 51. Torquemada (1975–83, 1:226) describes it as a barrio "out towards the woods of Chapultepec" in which King Moquihuix of Tlatelolco was given land when he married Axayacatl's sister. Probably it is the place where the Mexica went after their defeat in Chapultepec (Chimalpahin 1963:53–55; 1889:45; 1968:123). See also Zimmermann's comments (1960:51).

61. Colín 1966: secs. 707, 736, 1739; 1968: sec. 3873. Torquemada (1975–83, 1:226) refers to the hill of Tatlalo "which are the quarries of Aztacalco." This must be the hill called Tetalo in Temazcalapan (Colín 1967: sec. 1637). Aztacalco is one of the places around Xaltocan where Axayacatl had lands (Nazareo in ENE 10:120; Zimmermann 1970:27). The Tira de Tepechpan also represents parcels of land of this name in a painting that seems to depict a distribution of land. Noguez (1978, 2:12) identifies it with Santa María or San Francisco Aztacalco in the jurisdiction of San Cristóbal Ecatepec.

62. Reyes García (1979) uses the text of Sahagún's manuscript in the Real Academia de la Historia, Madrid.

63. Reyes García 1979:39.

64. Reyes García (1979:39) suggests identifying Aztacalco with Aztaquemecan in the same province of Acolhuacan.

65. Broda (1978:173) compiles the quantity of warrior garments and shields given by the different provinces of the Empire.

CHAPTER 5

1. Motolinía 1971:207, 211, 337; Sahagún 1969, 2:313; 1954:44 (book 8, chap. 14).

2. Torquemada 1975–83, 1:284. A concrete example is that of Cuitlatenamic, in the extreme southwest of Puebla near Morelos and Guerrero (see p. 414), which had land and houses in the barrio of Neccaltitlan in the parcialidad of San Juan (Moyotla) to lodge those who brought in the tribute (AGN, Tierras 34, exp. 4).

3. Sahagún 1951:165–80 (book 2, Appendix).

4. Caso 1956.

5. Codex de Ixhuatepec (Chavero 1901: plate 1) and Codex de Santa Isabel Tula (Peñafiel 1897: 9–10). Cf. Seler 1902–23, 2:57.

6. Caso 1956:13, 21–22.

7. Peñafiel 1897:49; Chimalpahin 1889:227. For the meanings of the word *calpolli*, see Carrasco 1971a; Reyes García, et al. (n.d.); Ruhnau 1988:20–21.

8. The list of temples in Sahagún (1951:165–180 [book 2, Appendix]) names seven calmecac: Tlillan, Mexico, Huitznahuac, Tetlanman, Tlamatzinco, Yopico, and Tzonmolco.

9. Van Zandwijk (1985) has discussed these matters. Another complication results from the establishment of the Spanish city in the center of Tenochtitlan so that colonial sources on the barrios of the city do not have information on the old urban center.

10. On the problems of provisioning the city, see Calnek 1974 and 1976; J. L. de Rojas 1986.

11. Zorita 1909:434, 435–36.

12. AGI, Mexico 282: Memoria de las cosas en que los indios principales y naturales de la ciudad de México pedimos y suplicamos a su mgt del rey don Felipe nuestro señor sea servido de mandarnos desagraviar, 13 marzo 1574. See full quotation in Carrasco 1996:148.

13. Gibson 1964a: 47, 438, 440. See p. 103–13 for more information on dependencies of Tenochtitlan in the Sierra de Guadalupe, the Tlacopan region, and the Chinampan area south of the city.

14. Lands held by kings and nobles as individuals are not discussed in this essay. Although there will be some allusions to the system of land tenure, this is a topic that requires a separate study.

15. Ixtlilxochitl 1975–77, 1:444 ("Compendio Histórico"); 1:376–77("Sumaria Relación"); 2:80 ("Historia Chichimeca").

16. Table 5-1 sums up the data on the Chinampan towns from the "Historia chichimeca" (Ixtlilxochitl, 2:87–88) and the "Compendio histórico" (1:446). See Table 6-9 on the towns that paid this tribute of the Chinampan.

17. Ixtlilxochitl 1975–77, 2:141.

18. Sahagún 1975:37 (book 12, chap. 14).

19. Chimalpahin 1958:5.

20. AC, 28, 49; Ixtlilxochitl 1975–77, 2:36.

21. Tezozomoc 1949:7, 337, 347.

22. Nazareo in ENE 10:121, 125; Zimmermann 1970:27, 29.

23. Ixtlilxochitl 1975–77, 2:89; Motolinía 1971:394.

24. Codex Mendoza, 69r.

25. AC, 46. Don Antonio Cortés, in a letter dated 1561, asked that he be granted Tenayocan, implying that it had belonged to him (ENE 16:73).

26. The affiliation of King Chimalpopoca, who governed Tenayocan during the reign of Moteuczoma Ilhuicamina, is not well documented (Torquemada 1975–83, 1:219, 224). Later kings who are known were princes of the Tenochca dynasty (Tezozomoc 1949:134, 138; Torquemada 1975–83, 5:229; Durán 1967, 2:516).

27. It may be significant that there are two towns called Chiconautla—Santo Tomás and Santa María—in the municipio of Ecatepec. Cf. Vetancurt 3:201. In the *Relación geográfica* Chiucnauhtlan is said to have had four barrios (RG 6:230).

28. The other council painted in Codex Mendoza in the lower level would be the *teccalco*, a tribunal composed of lords (teteuctin) but not kings (Sahagún 1954:41–42 [book 8, chap. 14]).

29. Carrasco 1984a.

30. Tezozomoc 1949:112, 131, 134, 136, 137, 164, 272, 300; Durán 1967, 2:516; Ixtlilxochitl 1975–77, 2:158; Chimalpahin 1889:107–108.

31. Durán 1967, 2:22, 227, 393.

32. Ibid., 114. This case is comparable to those of Coatlichan and Acolman in the Acolhuacan, whose defeated rulers were reinstated by Nezahualcoyotl.

33. Pérez Zevallos 1981:112–16; Ixtlilxochitl 1975–77, 1:411–12. On the enmity between Tecpan and Tepetenchi, see Torquemada 1975–83, 1:250.

34. AC, 61–62.

35. Durán 1967, 2:88–89, 514; HMP, 219.

36. Durán (1967, 2:22) lists all the Xochimilca towns in this area; RG 7:267.

37. López de Gómara 1988:292. See Smith (1986:78) for the genealogy. Cf. García Granados 1952–53, 3:413.

38. Codex Aubin, 38v. Seler (1902–23, 2:201–202) suggests that the glyph that the text of the codex reads as Xiloxochitepec is really Yauhtepec.

39. RG 6:186–88 (Tepoztlan), 201–203 (Huaxtepec), 216–18 (Yacapichtlan). See p. 211 on the concept of natural lord.

40. Codex Mendoza, 6r, 19r.

41. Ixtlilxochitl 1975–77, 2:177.

42. Carrasco 1984a: 77.

43. Chimalpahin 1889:107–08. In Tezozomoc (1949: sec. 193) the son of Itzcoatl who went to Xilotepec was called Mixcoatl; the other two are not mentioned. The city could be Atotonilco el Grande and not Atotonilco de Tula. The identification of Apan is problematic; perhaps it was Chiappan (see p. 261).

44. RG 8:138. Tolnacochtla is not found in the "Memorial de Tlacopan" among the cities that comprised the Tlacopan kingdoms, but it appears (spelled Tulnauehutla) in one of the colonial summonses of the towns that reported to Tlacopan for public works projects (see Table 7-2). Probably it was a town of a lesser political category, as in the similar case of Xaltocan.

45. Torquemada 1975–83, 1:258.

46. Codex Mendoza, 20r–v; AC, 61.

47. Durán 1967, 2:133–34, 156, 164, 196, 270, 442, 485. Cf. chapter 13.

48. RG 7:39.

49. Ibid., 45.

50. Ibid., 34.

51. Cuauhtlalpan, "Forest Land," is derived from *cuauhtli* (with short *a*), "tree, wood." It is the name given to the region, between the Basin and the Valley of Toluca, inhabited by the Otomis. It can also be the name of a town. It is different from Cuauhtlalpan, derived from *cuahuitl* (with long *a*) meaning "eagle land" and in a figurative sense "war land."

52. In some codices the glyph for Acalhuacan is a canoe placed as a sort of bridge across the river flowing from the north towards Lake Tetzcoco (Boehm de Lameiras 1986:304 n. 8). Ixtlilxochitl refers several times to this town as the frontier of Tetzcoco in the western part of the Basin, but he spells it Aculhuacan, probably because of a copying error (Ixtlilxochitl 1975–77, 1:330, 334, 378, 442, 543; 2:77, 84). Cf. Torquemada 1975–83, 1:192, and Tezozomoc 1949: sec. 52.

53. Vetancurt (1961, 3:186) says this was a visita of Tlatelolco. He describes it as "Santa Magdalena Coatlayauhcan, also known as Atepetlac, whose inhabitants belong to the government of Mexico, in the parcialidad of San Juan." However, Tezozomoc (1949:37–46), quoted below, gives these two toponyms as two different towns.

54. Perhaps it also included Ayotzinco, which formerly had four barrios—Tenochtitlan, Tlatelolco, Xochimilco, and Coyoacan—that probably were colonies of those cities, which gave them their names (Brinkman 1969: facsimile following p. 30).

55. Nazareo in ENE 10:125; Zimmermann 1970:29; AC, 49.

56. AC, 49. Toltepec is Tultepec, Mexico, and Tepeyacac must be the same as the subject town of Tlacopan identifiable as San Francisco Tenopalco, Mexico, northeast of Cuauhtitlan (see p. 202 on the tributaries of Tlacopan).

57. Gibson 1964a: 47, 374–75.

58. See chapter 4 for the comparison of these two pictorials.

59. Tezozomoc 1949:37–46. See Boehm de Lameiras (1986:376–77) for a table comparing the route of this migration according to various sources.

60. This point is made by Durán (1967, 2:29) and Tezozomoc (1975:224–25).

61. Barlow 1949b: 130. See below in the section on Tlatelolco.

62. Van Zantwijk 1967. See chapter 4 on the Codex Mendoza and chapter 12 on the garrisons.

63. RG 7:198.

64. Ibid., 199. On the military role of Citlaltepec, see also AC, 53–54.

65. On the borders between Tenochtitlan and Tetzcoco, see Ixtlilxochitl 1975–77, 2:84.

66. Peñafiel 1897 and Chavero 1901; AH-INAH, MS 210, pp. 228–30.

67. Codex Cozcatzin, 16v–17v.

68. AC, 54. See the quotation below in the section dealing with the tributary province of Acolman, where Tizayocan was located.

69. Chimalpahin 1889:101, 122.

70. Torquemada 1975–83, 1:218. In AC (p. 66) the death of Cuauhcoatl is attributed to Itzcoatl. Cf. HMP, 230, 237.

71. ATl, sec. 7, 259–74; Sahagún 1954:7 (book 8, chap. 2). See the pertinent observations of Litvak (1971). For more details and problems, see Barlow 1989 (pp. 31–57) and Monjarás-Ruiz 1991.

72. Tezozomoc 1975:396.

73. Colín 1966: sec. 1635. Carta de la República Mexicana a la 100 000ª, Secretaría de Estado y del Despacho de Fomento, Mexico City, 1909: leaf 19-I-(M).

74. Durán 1967, 2:264.

75. Durán 1967, 2:263–65; Tezozomoc 1975:394–97. According to the legend on the damaged page in the *Matrícula*, transmitted in the publication by Lorenzana, the temple they repaired was that of Tlatelolco, although the glyph also identifies it as Huitznahuac (Barlow 1989: plate 1, p. 113).

76. Barlow 1949b: 130. Also, on this page there is not enough room for the glyphs of the eleven cities (Barlow 1989:112ff.).

77. ATl, secs. 16, 17.

78. See what is said about Chiucnauhtla on p. 100.

79. Variant forms of the glyph of this town appear in the Codices Mendoza (province of the Acolhuacan), Xolotl, and Aubin (Noguez 1978, 1:47 and n. 116).

80. The glyph (water, road, and banner) agrees perfectly with the legend. There is no reason for identifying it with Ayapanco (as in Barlow 1949b: 132).

81. Tlaxoxiuhco, a similar name, is more frequent; it was a barrio of Tlatelolco (Vetancurt 1961, 3:185; Caso 1956:40), Mexicatzinco (AGN, Tierras 2809, exp. 3), and Colhuacan (S. Cline 1986:95).

82. Tezozomoc 1975:271, 277, 305.

83. Scholes and Adams 1957:29.

84. Durán 1967, 2:341.

85. Tezozomoc 1975:494. As in other cases, here Chinantlan is the Chinampan region in the southern part of the Basin.

86. AGN, Tierras 2809, exp. 4.

87. Codex Cozcatzin, 17r–v.

88. A document in the Codex Osuna (473r) lists ten barrios of Iztacalco: Acaquilpa, Aztahuacan, Nexticpac, Acolco, Zacatlamanco, Teteppilco, Zacahuitzco, Tepetlatzinco, Huehue——, and Chapol——. The last two names are incomplete because the document is torn.

89. Tezozomoc 1975:305.

90. AGI, Justicia 260, fol. 36ff. Cf. Ruiz Medrano 1991:246–48.

91. According to Arenas (1982:9), Ximilpan means "rainfall field."

92. AH-INAH, MS 211:230.

93. AGI, Mexico 95, ramo 1, no. 22.

94. Colín 1966: secs. 1508, 1602. See p. 369. There is another Xoconosco (Colín 1966: secs. 1307, 1319) today in Donato Guerra, Mexico.

95. This place is mentioned in connection with the war against Azcapotzalco, together with Nonoalco, Mazatzintamalco, and Popotlan (Durán 1967, 2:80; Tezozomoc 1975:240–41).

96. Colín 1966: sec. 1701. See p. 152.

97. Colín 1967: secs. 425, 2080.

98. See p. 154–61 on the two parts of the Acolhuacan.

99. Scholes and Adams 1957:31, 68. Barlow (1949b: 68) suggests that the cabecera was Coatlichan, but there is nothing in the glyphs or the legends to support this idea. Acolman and Coatlichan were the cabeceras of the Acolhuacan during the reign of Tezozomoc of Azcapotzalco (Ixtlilxochitl 1975–77, 1:344–45). In the Codex Mendoza, where the conquests of Huitzilihuitl are depicted (3v), slightly different glyphs are used for Acolman (water over the forearm) and Acolhuacan (water over the shoulder); the latter is next to the glyph for Tetzcoco and can be understood as the name of the region or as the surname of Tetzcoco. In the Codex Osuna (496r), next to the glyph for Acolhuacan is the name Tetzcoco. In the chronicles Acolhuacan is paired with Tetzcoco (Chimalpahin 1889:104, 133, 145, passim; AC, 63) or with Coatlichan (Chimalpahin 1950:16–17; 1987:111).

100. The reference to the kingdoms in Table 5-2 follows the order of the *Anales de Cuauhtitlan*; references to the towns of tenants in Table 6-4 are according to Motolinía.

101. Durán 1967, 2:335. See the complete quotation in p. 418, apropos of the dedication of the temple under Ahuitzotl.

102. Durán 1967, 2:336. Moteuczoma Xocoyotzin had patrimonial lands in this province in Acolman, Totolcingo, Ecatepec, and Quauhquemecan (AGI, Patronato 245, ramo 3, fols. 8v, 10r).

103. Tezozomoc 1975:282. Concerning this war, see p. 44.

104. RG 7:240–41. Tequisistlan is today a town in Tezoyuca, Mexico.

105. Zacatzontitlan is the first town on the route followed by the Chichimec founders of Quiahuiztlan on going from Tepetlaoztoc to Tlaxcallan (RG 4:274). It appears as San Cristóbal Zacatzontitlan in Colín 1967 (pars. 2019, 2034, 2279). Probably it is present-day San Cristóbal Zacacalco in Calpulalpan, Tlaxcala.

106. RG 6:83. Present-day Oztoyuca in Zempoala, Hidalgo.

107. This is a good Nahuatl toponym, derived from *tlatzcan*, "cypress." It is the same name as that of the mountain called Tlaxcajoca in Tlalmanalco (Colín 1967: sec. 2417), but it is not certain that Durán refers to this place.

108. Apan is also found in the "Pintura de México" (Ixtlilxochitl 1975–77, 1:384) between Calpollalpan and Tepepolco. Probably it was the unnamed sujeto of Tepepolco alluded to in the Memorial of Don Hernando Pimentel (see p. 59). For the Apan in the *Información de 1554*, identifiable in the province of Xocotitlan, see p. 260–61.

109. RG 6:75–76, 85. But according to this relación, Tzacuallan remained under Tetzcoco when Cempohuallan, Tlaquilpan, and Tecpilpan became part of the kingdom of Tenochtitlan.

110. Scholes and Adams 1957:31, 68.

111. Hicks (1984) studies the question of the intermingled domains of Tenochtitlan and Tetzcoco in Temazcalapan.

112. RG 6:75–76, 85.

113. Durán 1967, 2:125–31; Tezozomoc 1975:282–86. Tezozomoc (286) states that land was distributed to all the calpixques for the communities of Coyoacan, Xochimilco, Azcapotzalco, and Cuitlahuac.

114. RG 7:222, 225. There was another Tochatlauhco in Epazoyuca (RG 6:81, 83).

115. *Cuauhtlalli*, "eagle land," hence war land, seems to be the name for a type of military land tenure; Cuauhtlalpan is the region where there is such land. The distinction between cuauhtlalli and *yaotlalli* (enemy land, battle land) is not always made in this way.

116. AC, 54; Bierhorst 1992a: 112. The word *xoxotitimani* has been read in other ways. Velásquez (1945:107) reconstructed *xoxotlalotimani* as "the boundary marks have been drawn." Cf. Lehmann 1938:263.

117. Xaltocan was incorporated into the realm of Tetzcoco by Nezahualcoyotl (Ixtlilxochitl 1975–77, 2:89). See p. 145.

118. AGI, Justicia 134, no. 1; AGI, Indiferente 1084, fol. 276r.

119. In the same Tizayocan region, Huitzillan (2) was also in the province of Acolman. Tecaman, listed in the "Pintura de México" (Ixtlilxochitl 1975–77, 1:384) must be the Tecaman that was in the vicinity of Xaltocan (AC, 20, 28–29, 49). The modern name is Tecamac.

120. SV, sec. 515. The estancia called Tecalco must be the one bordering upon Tepechpan (SV, sec. 512).

121. Zavala 1989:37; Colín 1967: secs. 1540, 1541.

122. AGI, Patronato 245, ramo 3. Doña Isabel inherited the Tecalco of Ecatepec from Moteuczoma (8v); that of Acolman, from Ahuitzotl (15r).

123. This statement is made by Don Diego Huanitzin in a letter dated 1532, in which Tolcayocan and Acayocan are also given as subjects of Ecatepec (AGI, Mexico 95, ramo 1, no. 22).

124. Tezozomoc 1975:282–83. In this passage Tezozomoc writes Culhuacan instead of Acolhuacan.

125. RG 7:217–22. Gibson (1964a: 45–47) emphasizes this case and that of the estancias of Tenochtitlan and Tlatelolco in the northern part of the Basin. Cerro Gordo is the mountain to the north of Teotihuacan.

126. It is also relevant that the king of Tenochtitlan intervened, together with the king of Tetzcoco, in appointing the governors of Coatepec. See p. 145–46.

127. Zimmermann 1960:53, 55.

128. RG 6:75, 76, 85.

129. Ibid., 78. The *Relación de Epazoyocan* also names various ranks and titles of the local officials (RG 6:87).

130. ATl, sec. 118; Codex Osuna, 498r; HMP, 222. However, the *Información de 1554* is not consistent; one witness uses the name Atotoniltonco for Atotonilco de Tula and another for Atotonilco el Grande (Scholes and Adams 1957:38, 73). The distinction between the two places cannot always be discerned in the texts that give just Atotonilco, because the context does not make clear which one is meant.

131. Ixtlilxochitl 1975–77, 2:108. See p. 141–42.

132. Ixtlilxochitl 1975–77, 2:15.

133. Ibid., 1:318, 430.

134. Durán 1967, 2:303–304.

135. On the earlier importance of Cuahuacan, see AC, 21, 22, 30, 47–48, 63. See chapter 9 for the war with Chiappan.

136. Scholes and Adams 1957:36, 71.

137. AGN, Tierras 13, exp. 4:320r–323v.

138. The glyph is a bunch of green feathers grasped by a hand. The annotator read it as Quetzalmacan, but it can also be read as Quetzalhuacan, as in the similar glyph in the Matrícula de Huexotzinco (1974:627r, 730r). The hand can also denote possession (-uah); in the Codex Mendoza (29r) the glyph for Xicalhuacan is a hand holding a bowl (xicalli).

139. Chapter 7 covers the Tlacopan kingdoms and chapter 9 outlines the establishment of the preponderance of Tenochtitlan in the northwest sector of the Empire. The Codex Mendoza puts the province of Atotonilco el Grande, together with those that precede it, between Hueypochtlan and Xilotepec. However, it does not extend as far as the kingdoms in the Tlacopan sector, but was, at least partly, in the region of Tollantzinco, which was one of the kingdoms of Tetzcoco.

140. Cf. van Zantwijk 1969; Pérez Rocha 1982: map 1; Hicks 1992.

141. There are several studies on Morelos in the colonial period. Maldonado (1990) gives an overall picture and discusses all the connections with the pre-Spanish situation. The works of Smith (1986, 1987) combine historical and archaeological material. Gerhard (1970a) and Maldonado have identified in detail the towns of these two provinces. Here I give only the identifications with modern towns; references to early sources are given for towns that no longer exist or whose identification is uncertain.

142. Gerhard (1970a: 34) identifies it as the colonial Metla, near Tetelpa (now in Zacatepec, Morelos), but there were two Molotlas in Cuauhnahuac different from Metla, one of them in San Pedro Tecpan, one of the four cabeceras (AGN-HJ 290:1707v). In addition, the same toponym is found in other parts of the Xochimilca and Tlalhuica regions. There is one in Xochimilco (barrio of San Antonio Molotla [Vetancurt 1961, 3:155]), and another in Yautepec (Carrasco 1976:114; Hinz et al. 1983: xii–xiv; Martin 1985:59). There is also a Molotla among the possessions of Tlacopan in this region. See p. 201.

143. Itzteyocan was an estancia of tenants of Tlacopan. See p. 201.

144. Scholes and Adams 1957:33, 69.

145. For the extension of the Xochimilcas, see Durán 1967, 2:22. The gentile name tlalhuica is associated with Cuauhnahuac, but at times it is also applied to Xochimilca towns (Durán 1967, 2:23, 559; Tezozomoc 1975:276).

146. For Yacapichtla and the Tlalnahuac, see Nuevos documentos 1946:173–265; on Las Amilpas, AGN-HJ 282:2223v.

147. Durán 1967, 2:247–48; Tezozomoc 1975:370–72.

148. AGN-HJ 284:792v.

149. RG 6:198.

150. AGN-HJ 290:888r, 1036v, 1062v.

151. See p. 132 on the government of Huaxtepec and Yacapichtla.

152. AGN-HJ 284:792v. On the subjects of Tetzcoco in Tlalhuic, see p. 172–75, and on those of Tlacopan, p. 201.

153. RG 8:161.

154. Ibid., 7:267. The present-day towns are Tetela del Volcán, Morelos, and Hueyapan, in the same municipio. Nepopoalco is the old cabecera located next to Tetellan (7:265), not the one near Totolapan, Morelos.

155. Gerhard 1970b: 110.

CHAPTER 6

1. Gibson (1956) studied the territorial entities of the Acolhuacan and identified almost all the towns therein but without analyzing the different political categories. This material has also been studied by Trautmann (1968:62–69), Corona (1973), and Offner (1983).

2. According to Don Hernando Pimentel, the different towns that paid tribute to Tetzcoco had

their houses in the city (see p. 60). Ixtlilxochitl (1975–77, 2:96) states that "all the states and provinces had their offices for the tribute [*cargos de tributos*] inside the palace, and all the others had them outside in special houses devoted to this purpose."

3. Hicks 1982:231–32.

4. Ixtlilxochitl 1975–77, 2:89–90.

5. Ibid., 1:315, 402, 430; 2:32–35, 101.

6. Pomar 1986:50. The Codex Xolotl depicts the leaders of these settlers with glyphs of their personal names and of their gentile identity; it also depicts houses, that is, calpolli, with glyphs of their gentile toponyms (Dibble 1951:79, 80, and plate v).

7. Vetancurt 1961, 3:140–42.

8. The name that Vetancurt gives as Tecuilan (1961, 3:141) is present-day Tocuila in Texcoco, Mexico. He seems to have confused two towns called San Miguel, Tlaixpan in the mountains and Tocuillan on the shore.

9. See above, p. 136, 139. In 1582, Tezoyocan was a separate township even though it was a visita of Tetzcoco (Pomar 1986:47, 48). Some towns included in this visita (Cuanallan, Huitzilhuacan, and Tetitlan) are identified in other sources as barrios of Tetzcoco. In 1769, Cuanala had three barrios: San Lucas (Huitzilhuacan), (San Francisco) Zacanco, and San Mateo (Ixtlahuacan) (Colín 1968: sec. 3304). The other towns on Vetancurt's list can be taken as dependencies of Tezoyocan, especially San Sebastián Mexicapan, since there is another Mexicapan in Tetzcoco.

10. Cf. Hicks 1982: map 1. It extended even farther if we add the region of Calpollalpan, Mazapan, and Yahualiuhcan.

11. Acolman's southern border was contiguous with estancias of Tetzcoco, and Teotihuacan also shared boundaries with Tetzcoco (SV, secs. 19, 263).

12. Torquemada 1975–83, 4:332.

13. Hicks 1982:236.

14. Motolinía 1971:394. In this quotation I have changed the division into paragraphs in O'-Gorman's edition and omit the variant spellings of the toponyms, which he adds between brackets as in the corresponding text of the *Anales de Cuauhtitlan* published by Paso y Troncoso. I add some corrected spellings within brackets. See in p. 185 the definition of the corresponding category in the "Memorial de Tlacopan."

15. Ixtlilxochitl 1975–77, 2:89.

16. Aubin 1885, plate II.

17. Ixtlilxochitl 1975–77, 1:446; 2:106.

18. AC, 64.

19. Motolinía 1971:206, 322. See p. 384 concerning Tuzapan.

20. Torquemada 1975–83, 1:242. This is his version of the conflict between the two kings, but here he contradicts what he affirms elsewhere, to the effect that Itzcoatl maintained the dominance that Tenochtitlan had acquired over Tetzcoco. The two versions certainly represent two conflicting points of view, one Tenochca, the other Tetzcoca (see p. 43–44).

21. Ibid., 1:243. In this quotation it is not clear when Torquemada stops quoting Motolinía and resumes writing on his own. He seems to allude to the painting described in Motolinía's "Memorial tetzcocano," which he may have seen (cf. 3:243), but he may also continue quoting from Motolinía; not all of Motolinía's writings have survived.

22. Motolinía 1971:353.

23. Torquemada 1975–83, 4:71.

24. Ixtlilxochitl 1975–77, 2:94. Cf. Table 6-8. The number six also suggests the six parcialidades in which Tetzcoco was divided (Ixtlilxochitl 1975–77, 2:101).

25. Durán 1967, 2:335. See p. 415 in regard to the dedication of the temple during the reign of Ahuitzotl.

26. Ixtlilxochitl 1975–77, 2:89. See p. 157–58.

27. Durán 1967, 2:128, 225.

28. For example, Quinatzin, king of Tetzcoco, installed as the first king of Teotihuacan a son of the king of Huexotla (Guzmán 1938:92).

29. RG 6:160–62.

30. Guzmán 1938; Carrasco 1974; Münch 1976.

31. Ixtlilxochitl 1975–77, 2:89, 142.

32. Stresser-Péan 1995:23, 86, 88, 101, 111–13, 141–44, 149.

33. Ixtlilxochitl 1975–77, 2:88.

34. RG 7:226. The "Relación of Teotihuacan" relates that they paid cloaks and maguey leaves to Nezahualcoyotl and Moteuczoma, but earlier it said that these two kings divided among themselves the lands of Teotihuacan and Acolman. Therefore, the payments may have been only from these lands (7:235).

35. Ixtlilxochitl 1975–77, 2:89, 106. In the much shorter text in the "Compendio Histórico" (1:446), and in the "Pintura de México" (1:382), Pahuatlan is listed instead of Totonapan.

36. Ibid., 2:108. See p. 120–21, 154 on Tzihuinquillocan (present-day Singuilucan, Hidalgo).

37. Torquemada 1975–83, 1:232.

38. The case of La Sierra will be treated below in the discussion of the peasant villages and the rotation of tributaries.

39. Durán 1967, 2:328.

40. AGI, Justicia 179.

41. Motolinía 1971:394–95. In this quotation I make a division into paragraphs different from that used in O'Gorman's edition, and I do not add the toponyms as written by Paso y Troncoso. Instead, for some names I add between brackets the spelling used in this book. For the corresponding text in the "Memorial de Tlacopan," see p. 196.

42. AC, 64. AC writes Papalotla as Papallotla Tetzcoco, to be understood as meaning that Papalotlan pertained to or was in Tetzcoco.

43. Torquemada 1975–83, 1:232–33 (cf. 3:243). Elsewhere (4:334–35), Torquemada gives a general description of the provisioning of firewood, part of which is quoted in p. 225.

44. Ixtlilxochitl 1975–77, 2:89–90. In another passage (1:380) one sees that "mayordomo" is the same as "calpixque." Both terms will be translated as steward; calpixcazgo (calpixcayotl) was the jurisdiction of a calpixque.

45. Ibid., 1:380.

46. In Table 6-4 there is a comparison with the towns of tenants in Motolinía and the *Anales de Cuauhtitlan.*

47. Ixtlilxochitl 1975–77, 2:90–91. Torquemada (1975–83, 4:333, 334) also defines these lands as "of the lord's chamber" (de la recámara del señor). Veytia (1944, 2:178) calls them "land of the palace or the lord's chamber (tierra del palacio o cámara del señor).

48. Ixtlilxochitl 1975–77, 2:114. Atenco and Papalotlan were near the city but the other towns were not.

49. Ixtlilxochitl (1975–77, 2:90) gives tlatocamilli and tlatocatlalli as synonymous, and he also describes the *itonalyn tlacatl* (literally, "the lot of the man") as landplots of the king. In medieval terminology the term *realengo* was applied to crown lands under the administration of the king, but it cannot be determined whether they were merged with the family property of the king (P.L. in *Diccionario de historia de España,* s.v. realengo [1952, 2:976]). Covarrubias (s.v.) defines *recámara* as a room beyond the king's bedroom, or a room where the *camarero* (steward) keeps the king's clothes and jewels. The camarero carried out the functions of (1) chief waiter, (2) curator of the royal chamber and custodian of the royal treasure, (3) marshal, or chief of the stables, and (4) cup bearer in charge of the prince's wine cellar (L. G. de V. in *Diccionario de historia de España,* s.v. camarero [1952, 1:508])

50. Veytia 1944, 2:173.

51. Ixtlilxochitl 1975–77, 1:327, 330, 335, 436; 2:45, 64, 85.

52. RG 6:143.

53. ENE 10:124–25; Zimmermann 1970:29.

54. See p. 118–19 in regard to Tizayocan and Tecalco.

55. Ixtlilxochitl 1975–77, 1:325.

56. Ibid., 1975–77, 2:89–90. See below the discussion on the two parts of Acolhuacan.

57. Durán (1967, 2:335) gives a list of towns pertaining to Tetzcoco that does not distinguish between cities ruled by kings and towns of peasants. For this reason, and because it includes towns in the province of Acolman that paid tribute to Tenochtitlan, it is not included in this table. It also contains towns that are not among the tributaries of Tetzcoco nor among those of Acolman province; they have been discussed on p. 117. The towns that answered the summons (*llamamiento*) of Tetzcoco for public works in the colonial epoch coincided with the extent of the Tetzcoca domain. Gibson (1956: table 1), using all the available sources, compiles all the towns of the Acolhua domain, both kingdoms and towns, that were tributaries of Tetzcoco or Tenochtitlan.

58. Vetancurt 1961, 3:140–42. See the discussion of Tetzcoco's barrios at the beginning of this chapter.

59. Pomar 1986:47.

60. Calpollalpan is mentioned in several colonial sources as a direct dependency of Tetzcoco, which would be a continuation of the pre-Spanish situation. In relating the struggle against Maxtla of Azcapotzalco, Torquemada (1975–83, 1:188) states that Nezahualcoyotl went to Calpollalpan, "a town of his in the jurisdiction of Tetzcoco." A document dated 1533 describes it as "annex of the said city of Tezcuco" (*Cedulario Cortesiano* 1949:252). In 1567 it is described as "a small hamlet of . . . [Tetzcoco] that is called Calpulalpan" (AGI, Mexico 1089, Book C5, fol. 68r). In 1576, Mazapan, Calpulalpan, and Ahualulco (*sic pro* Yahualiuhcan?) were estancias of Tetzcoco and participated in its public works (Zavala y Castelo 1939–46, 1:108, 137). Tepepolco, according to its relación (RG 7:173), shared boundaries with "Calpulalpan, subject to Tetzcoco."

61. Ixtlilxochitl 1975–77, 2:114.

62. Pomar 1986:50.

63. This document is published in Horcasitas 1978:150–51.

64. Ixtlilxochitl 1975–77, 2:112. According to Muñoz Camargo (1984:274), these two towns were on the route of the Chichimecs, who founded Quiahuiztlan in Tlaxcallan—that is, Tepetlaoztoc, Zacatzontitlan, Teomulixco, Zultepec, Yahualiuhcan, Mazaapan, Quauhtepec, and Ocelotepec. This same writer (1978:93–94) places the Tlaxcallan boundary with Tetzcoco at the fort of Calnepalolco on the slopes of Mount Quauhtepec. In the eighteenth century Cuauhtepec was the hacienda of San Miguel Cuauhtepec (Quatepeque) in the partido of Hueyotlipan (González Sánchez 1969:58, 166, 170, 175). Trautmann (1981:22) identifies Ocelotepec with Mount Concepción on the northwestern side of the mesa of Españita. In the *Memorial de los indios de Tepetlaoztoc*, map 1 depicts Ocelotepec, Cuauhtepec, Yahualiuhcan, Mazaapan, and Zoltepec (Valle 1993:13–14).

65. See p. 148. Pomar (1986:50) writes of these towns in his *Relaciones* but does not locate them. Nezahualcoyotl passed through Yahualiuhcan, between Tepepolco and Calpollalpan, when fleeing from the Tepanecs (Ixtlilxochitl 1975–77, 2:71). Present-day Mazapan is a hacienda in the municipio of Calpulalpan, Tlaxcala.

66. Ixtlilxochitl 1975–77, 2:36.

67. Ibid., 1:384; 2:30, 74; RG 4:274.

68. Ixtlilxochitl 1975–77, 2:90. Atenco is also the name of other towns near the lake shore: San Bernardino in Huexotla and La Asunción de Atenco, a barrio of Chiauhtla (Vetancurt 1961, 3:141, 199, 222).

69. AGN, Vínculos 234; Hicks 1978.

70. The document states that the aforementioned estancia or barrio of Atengo was also called Atlixeliuhyan and that Atengo was the name of all eight estancias in the site (pago) of Atengo. (AGN, Vínculos 234:228v. Cf. 117r–v, quoted in Hicks 1978:136). For this reason the town that Vetancurt calls simply San Francisco Acuezcomac, is called in the lawsuit (60v) San Francisco Acuescomac Atenco, and a witness from the barrio of Santa María Magdalena (that is, Panoayan) declared that his barrio was also called Atengo.

71. AGN, Vínculos 234:117r–v; Hicks 1978:136–38.

72. AGN, Vínculos 234:167r–212r.

73. As has been noted above, Vetancurt confused two San Miguels, Tocuillan in Atenco and Tlaixpan in the mountains.

74. In 1769, San Lucas Huitzilhuacan, San Mateo Chipiltepec, and Zacanco were barrios of Cuanallan (Colín 1968: secs. 1196, 3304).

75. This is also identified (written Ixquipayaq) as a subject of Tetzcoco, where the people of Tepechpan went to get salt (RG 7:250).

76. RG 7:225–47.

77. AGN, Vínculos 234:46r, 48r, 53r, 58r, 63v, 65v, 69v, 74r, 75r, 81r, 260r.

78. RG 7:180–81.

79. Apan was a sujeto of Tepepolco (RG 7:173).

80. It was contiguous with Hueyotlipan (RG 7:173), and the nearby fields were a battlefield (Durán 1967, 1:34; 2:290). A more precise location of these fields puts them between Calpollalpan and Hueyotlipan; see the identification in p. 150 above. Nicholson (1972) has compiled the historical material on Tepepolco.

81. Ixtlilxochitl 1975–77, 1:293. This town took San Nicolás as its patron. Oztoticpac was also the name of a palace of Tetzcoco (1:363; 2:22, 223) and of an estancia of Tizayocan (DA, 54).

82. Ixtlilxochitl 1975–77, 1:437. Cf. Barlow 1949b: 68 n. 65.

83. Ixtlilxochitl 1975–77, 1:384. RG 7:225 and map. Cf. Gibson 1964a: 48.

84. RG 7:247. Cf. Coyoacac (Colín 1966: sec. 2633). Probably it is the same town as San Juan Cuybaca, Cuyac, or Cuyoaque in the jurisdiction of Otompan (Colín 1967: secs. 21, 1374, 1377).

85. Ixtlilxochitl 1975–77, 1:437. Cf. Barlow 1949b: 68 n. 65.

86. RG 6:140.

87. Durán (1967, 2:142, 485) places Tlapechhuacan on the Chalco frontier, on the road from the Basin to the Puebla region. The *Anales de Cuauhtitlan* (p. 10) mention it as a town through which the Toltecs passed towards Cholollan. Ixtlilxochitl (1975–77, 2:241) says that the Tetzmollocan road leads to Tlepehuacan (*sic*) at the foot of the mountains. On the Mapa de Santa Cruz, south of Coatepec there is a glyph in the shape of a platform which must correspond to Tlapechhuacan (León Portilla and Aguilera [glyph 8-29] take this to mean Cuauhtenanco).

88. RG 6:145–46.

89. Tezozomoc 1975:305. Tlapechhuacan is also listed in the "Pintura de México" (Ixtlilxochitl 1975–77, 1:384).

90. Tratado de Teotihuacan, 4r; Valle 1993:103.

91. Ixtlilxochitl 1975–77, 1:449; 2:96.

92. Tratado de Teotihuacan, 4r. Tlapechhuacan has been identified above. Ecatzinco is present-day Ecatzingo, Mexico. Caltecoyan is probably Tlaltecoyan in the municipio of Ozumba, Mexico. Caltecoyan appears on the map of the Valle de México 1943, published by the Secretaría de Agricultura y Fomento, between Nepantla (in Tepetlixpa, Mexico) and Tlalamac (in Atlautla, Mexico). The other towns have not been identified in the Chalco region.

93. Valle 1993:103.

94. Ixtlilxochitl 1975–77, 1:448–49; 2:142.

95. See p. 59. Chicualoapan is present-day Chicoloapa, Mexico.

96. RG 6:73–74.

97. Ixtlilxochitl 1975–77, 1:384; 3:90.

98. RG 6:92.

99. Ibid., 83.

100. Ixtlilxochitl 1975–77, 1:12, written Xezontepec.

101. This name is spelled in different ways in the sources; it is derived from achichilacachtli. Sahagún defines *ymaachichilacachtempilol* (1951:94 [book 2, chap. 27]) as lip plugs made of sea shells (1969b, 1:177). This town is named in several documents of the Viceroy Velasco from 1551 and 1552 published by Zavala (1982:43, 44, 112, 417, 421). One, from Cempohuallan, gives information on a visita to Achichilacayocan and is an order to the encomendero about tribute and cattle. Other orders given in this town deal with matters of Tepepolco. This suggests that it would be found in the region that extends from Cempohuallan to Tepepolco. Gerhard (1986:214) identifies it as Axapochco. If we look farther afield, a similar toponym is Achichilacachapa, an estancia of Chimalhuacan (RG 6:160).

102. RG 6:75.

103. For the possessions of Tenochtitlan in the domain of Tetzcoco, see p. 144–20, in which the question of local government in this region is also discussed. On the possessions of Tetzcoco according to a report by Durán (1967, 2:335), see p. 117.

104. Ixtlilxochitl 1975–77, 2:108.

105. Torquemada 1975–83, 1:232.

106. Ixtlilxochitl 1975–77, 2:108 (quoted above), 114.

107. Torquemada 1975–83, 1:232. Torquemada continues with the towns of La Sierra whose rulers served in Tetzcoco in matters touching on government and warfare. He then speaks of the stewards in the provinces paying tribute to all three capitals of the Empire.

108. Ixtlilxochitl 1975–77, 2:137.

109. Ibid., 114.

110. Ibid., 89.

111. Ibid., 1:380.

112. Ibid.; cf. 1:535.

113. Guzmán 1938:95; Tratado de Teotihuacan, 5r. Carochi (1983:57r) says that *millacatl* (farmer) derives from *milla* (sown field). Elsewhere the Nahuatl text says "milla tlalli" and the Spanish, "la tierra de la milpa" (Guzmán 1938:97; Tratado de Teotihuacan, 6v).

114. Carrasco 1989:54–56.

115. Gibson 1964:45–46.

116. Ixtlilxochitl 1975–77, 2:53. A colonial lawsuit confirms that Otompan and some of its sujetos had also at one time given their tribute to Huexotla (AGI, Justicia 134, no. 1).

117. For example, the lands of Doña Ana, daughter of Nezahualpilli (AGI, Mexico 203, ramo 2, no. 15, Probanza de Juan de Cuéllar). The tributaries of Tenochtitlan are discussed on p. 144–20.

118. Ixtlilxochitl 1975–77, 2:191–92. Torquemada (1975–83, 1:307), in relating this same event, states that Ixtlilxochitl wanted the dominion of the thirty-three "provinces" that lie towards the north. This recalls the thirty-three towns of one of the sections of Motolinía's "Memorial tetzcocano" (Motolinía 1971:395) that comprise the imperial tributary provinces of Tlapacoyan, Tlatlauhquitepec, and Tziuhcoac. Later, Torquemada (1975–83, 1:311) relates that Cacama assigned to his brother Coanacotzin thirty-three "provinces" in the southern part.

119. Ixtlilxochitl 1975–77, 1:484.

120. Durán's list (1967, 2:335) of Tetzcoco's possessions can also be seen as forming two halves. First he names Huexotlan, Coatlichan, Coatepec, Chimalhuacan, and Itztapallocan; then, "on the other side towards the north," all the rest. See p. 117.

121. Aubin 1885:74–106.

122. Ixtlilxochitl 1975–77, 2:94.

123. In the Florentine Codex, tlatoloyan and audiencia are used together in the Nahuatl text, which concerns a council that combines executive and judicial functions (Sahagún 1954:41 [book 8, chap. 14]).

124. Aubin 1885:99–100; Motolinía 1971:353.

125. For *temayecan* and related terms, see Carrasco 1989:126, 154–57.

126. The meaning of a glyph for the number 20 beside each fire is doubtful (Aubin 1885:87).

127. For the provisioning of firewood, see pp. 136 and 225.

128. See Tables 6-6 and 6-7.

129. Ixtlilxochitl 1975–77, 2:89. There is also the possibility that some of the toponymic glyphs of the torn edge were those of the other cities whose kings are depicted in the palace: Tollantzinco, Cuauhchinanco, and Xicotepec.

130. See Table 6-5. Gibson (1956) and Offner (1983:97–109) have discussed these problems.

131. Ixtlilxochitl 1975–77, 1:446 ("Compendio Histórico"), and 2:87–88 ("Historia Chichimeca"). The *Relación sucinta* and the *Sumaria relación* do not include lists of these towns in the Chinampan.

132. Caso 1956:14–15; Sahagún 1951:98 (book 2, chap. 27); 1959:64 (book 9, chap. 14); 1975:43,

85, 88 (book 12, chaps. 16, 30, 31). However, given the ambiguity of the word *barrio*, which can also be applied to a village or estancia distant from the city, this town could also be the Xoloc north of Xaltocan, which was an estancia of Tlatelolco in the sixteenth century (Gibson 1964a: 47).

133. Codex Mendoza, 17r; Tezozomoc 1975:283. Cf. Barlow 1949b: 130.

134. Ixtlilxochitl 1975–77, 1:433; 2:34. This author writes the name of the mountain as Huexochtecatl. In other sources the mountain is Huixachtecatl and the town (or temple) is Huixachtlan (Sahagún 1953:25, 27–28 [book 7, chap. 10]; Durán 1967, 2:453; AC, 60; Chimalpahin 1889:177). Tezozomoc (1949:38, 45–46) makes a distinction between Huixachtitlan north of Tepeyac and Huixachtlan on the Cerro de la Estrella. The map of Itztapalapan in AGN, Tierras 2809, exp. 4, also writes Huixachtlan. Perhaps Axoctitlan in the "Compendio Histórico" was a mistaken reading of Vixachtlan. The map in González Aparicio 1973 includes both places: Huizachtitlan for the town in the north and Huixachtitlan for the one on the Cerro de la Estrella.

135. Chimalpahin 1958:114.

136. Spelled Cuexomotitlan (Tezozomoc 1975:291) or Cuaxomoltitlan (Durán 1967, 2:137–38). In González Aparicio's map it is next to the Cerro de la Caldera.

137. It is the Cerro de la Caldera in the map of AGN, Tierras 2809, exp. 4. In the *Crónica Mexicayotl* (Tezozomoc 1949:45–46) it is written Tetlacuexomac, as one word, although there are obviously two places; Tetla must be one of the mountains called Totlaman and Teyo on the map of AGN.

138. Ixtlilxochitl 1975–77, 1:543; 2:84.

139. It is mentioned in the narration of the founding of Cuitlahuac by Iztac Mixcoatl (AC, 61–62) and in a document about the boundaries of Cuitlahuac (AH-INAH, Anales Antiguos de México y sus Contornos, 2:209). Ixtlilxochitl (1975–77, 1:543) states that Mount Quexamatl (*sic*) was on the boundary of Chalco and Cuitlahuac.

140. Also mentioned in the relation of Chicualoapan (RG 6:170).

141. See the map of González Aparicio 1973, square XE.

142. Colín 1966: secs. 682, 689, 794; Colín 1968: sec. 1293. There was also a barrio called Coacalco in Ecatepec (RG 6:229).

143. Sahagún 1981:189, 212–13 (book 2, Appendix); Torquemada 1975–83, 1:254. Cf. Ixtlilxochitl 1975–77, 1:549; 2:152.

144. Carrasco y Monjarás-Ruiz 1978:19, 165.

145. S. Cline 1986:56.

146. Colín 1968: secs. 281–85. There was an Aticpac on the border of Cuitlahuac that could be one of the preceding (AC, 62).

147. Ixtlilxochitl 1975–77, 2:87–88.

148. Ibid., 1:446.

149. Durán (1967, 2:335–36), in describing the presence of tenant farmers of Tenochtitlan in the Acolhuacan, also says that Tetzcoco did not pay tribute to Tenochtitlan in "cloaks nor jewels nor feathers nor foodstuffs, as other provinces did," but this does not agree with the data in the Codex Mendoza unless it means only that they did not pay as much tribute as the other provinces.

150. Tratado de Teotihuacan, 4v–5r.

151. Gibson 1964:264.

152. See p. 100 on the relation of Chiucnauhtlan to Tenochtitlan.

153. Ixtlilxochitl 1975–77, 2:187.

154. AGI, Patronato 245, ramo 3; Pérez-Rocha (n.d.).

155. Ixtlilxochitl 1975–77, 2:106–107. Tlacopan's part was a fifth of the total, since he says that the distribution was done as explained before, that is, in the 2/2/1 proportion described in 2:104.

156. Motolinía 1971:396; AC, 64.

157. Ixtlilxochitl 1975–77, 2:96.

158. Ibid., 114.

159. The same towns appear in his "Pintura de México" (ibid., 382, 446).

160. In SV, sec. 553, Tepapayeca (now in the municipio of Tlapanala, Puebla) had an estancia, Tepachao (*sic*), that could be the same as Tepechco or Tepexco.

161. PNE 5:269; it was still mentioned in the seventeenth century (Gerhard 1986:320).

162. See p. 59. Durán (1967, 2:473) alludes to one "of the best cities in the Marquesado" conquered by Tetzcoco and a tributary of Nezahualpilli, but does not give its name.

163. AC, 64.

164. AGN-HJ 284:2225–29.

CHAPTER 7

1. The territorial organization of Tlacopan has been studied by Gibson (1964b), van Zantwijk (1967), Trautmann (1968:69–77), and Pérez Rocha (1982), who have presented the most relevant data and established the location of almost all the towns concerned. See also Hicks 1992.

2. Pérez Rocha 1982:107.

3. Carrasco 1984:76–77.

4. As noted by Cervantes de Salazar (1971, 1:130), "the Mexican language, although corrupt because it is a mountain area where they speak it, Otomí, Guata, Mazaua, Chuchumé, and Chichimec." The reference to the Mexicano of the mountain country indicates that he is describing an area bigger than the city of Tlacopan. Guata or Quata is another name for Matlatzinca. Chichimec could be the language spoken by the hunting peoples on the frontier of Xilotepec or by the Chichimecs in certain towns northeast of the Basin, such as Pachyocan, Acayocan, Epazoyocan, Cempohuallan, Tepopolco, and Apan. Chuchumé must be Chocho, which is usually identified with the Popoloca spoken in Puebla, but this is one of the terms used for foreign languages and one can not be sure of this; in Teotihuacan there were also some Popolocas (Carrasco 1950:27–38).

5. The names of several barrios in Azcapotzalco are connected with temples, crafts, and commerce; they lend themselves to comparisons with Tenochtitlan rather than with those of Tlacopan (Pérez Rocha 1982:69, 107). The slave market was in Azcapotzalco, and its merchants were among those who could go to Tochtepec (Durán 1967, 1:64, 180–81; Sahagún 1959:45, 48–49 [book 9, chap. 10]). Moteuczoma's silversmiths also resided in Azcapotzalco (Díaz del Castillo 1964:157, 188, 191, 278).

6. Ixtlilxochitl 1975–77, 1:543; 2:84. Cf. Veytia 1944, 2:159.

7. Ixtlilxochitl 1975–77, 2:82.

8. AGI, Patronato 245, ramo 9.

9. Zimmermann 1970:4.

10. ENE 16:73.

11. AGI, Justicia 1029, no. 10. This is a report included in a petition of Don Antonio Cortés, cacique, and the other notables of the town of Tacuba about their town's being placed under the Crown. According to another document, some of the places were "estancias" that wanted to be removed from the government of Tlacopan in 1553: Ysquilucan, Hetepeque, Yautochco, Chimalpa, Tetleolican, and Mestitan (Newberry Library, Ayer MS 1121: fol. 276).

12. Gibson 1964b. See also the pertinent columns in Table 7-2.

13. Durán 1967, 2:273.

14. Carrasco y Monjarás-Ruiz 1978:144, 159.

15. AGI, Patronato 245, ramo 9.

16. AGI, Justicia 165, no. 2.

17. SV, sec. 245.

18. For the possessions of Tlacopan in Chalco, see below and chapter 10 for the tributary province of Chalco according to the Codex Mendoza.

19. Vetancurt 1961, 3:189. Cf. Tezozomoc 1975:142; Gibson 1964b: 142.

20. Gibson 1964b.

21. Ixtlilxochitl 1975–77, 2:88. In another passage (2:80) Ixtlilxochitl mentions seven Tepanec cities in the time of Maxtla. He relates that after the defeat of Azcapotzalco, the armies of Tetzcoco and Mexico kept on pillaging the remaining towns of the Tepanec kingdom, namely Tenayocan,

Tepanoayan, Toltitlan, Quauhtitlan, Xaltocan, Huitzilopochco and Colhuacan. But these were the towns that were under Azcapotzalco before the war, not those assigned later to Tlacopan. Cf. Ixtlilxochitl 1975–77, 1:376, 444.

22. Torquemada 1975–83, 1:201.

23. Gibson 1964b.

24. Motolinía 1970:206. See p. 30.

25. See van Zantwijk 1969.

26. Zimmermann 1970:5. The Spanish text is somewhat garbled and has been translated freely. It says literally: "Los pueblos que obedecian a Tlacupan que se juntauan aqui para las guerras y daqui los repartian los tributos y buscauan y trayan cal, piedra, y madera, petlatl, escudillas, platos, a todos y los demas, los materiales, son los siguientes, con los a ellos sus subjetos." Perhaps the intent was to say that the requirements for tribute and labor were distributed among all the towns where there were artisans, and the rest provided the necessary materials. Compare this with the longer definition, quoted above on p. 136, of the corresponding category in Motolinía's "Memorial tetzcocano." The "Memorial de Tlacopan" does not define the subordinate kings as sons-in-law of the sovereign of the capital, nor does it speak of firewood as part of the tribute.

27. Codex Osuna 1947:250v–53r. See Table 4-3.

28. AC, 63. According to this source there was a king in Xippacoyan Tollan.

29. Gibson 1964b. Note that in the quotation from Torquemada on p. 185, the former extent of the kingdom of Tlacopan is compared with the colonial labor draft for public works.

30. According to a report dated 1566 (AGI, Justicia 1029, no. 10). See Table 7-1.

31. The labor drafts of 1555 and 1556—like the "Memorial de Tlacopan" and the Codex Osuna— enumerate the towns according to their belonging to the kingdoms of Tlacopan, Coyoacan, Cuauhtitlan, Tollan, and Apazco, while the draft of 1563 follows a different order: Azcapotzalco, Cuauhtitlan, Apazco, Tlacopan, and Tollan.

32. Carrasco 1984b.

33. In the following discussion I standardize the spelling of the toponyms; the tables give the spellings of each document.

34. It is known that there were two kings in Azcapotzalco, one for each of those two parcialidades (Carrasco 1950:111).

35. Carrasco 1984b.

36. AC, 40, 47, 63; Chimalpahin 1889:97; Sahagún 1954:13 (book 8, chap. 4).

37. Ixtlilxochitl 1975–77, 2:145.

38. Durán 1967, 2:87, 88, 96.

39. Gerhard 1986:343.

40. Like the four lords of Colhuacan, Itztapalapan, Huitzilopochco, and Mexicatzinco in relation to Tenochtitlan.

41. AC, 21, 29, 46–47, 55, 64.

42. RG 6:231.

43. AC, 64.

44. Gerhard 1986:344.

45. RG 6:33, 37. In the map in this relación, the three rulers are painted seated on stools, and the legends give them the title of teuctli.

46. Gibson (1964b: 141) suggests that Tlaquepa could be Tlahuililpan. He identifies Tlacotepec with the town of that name south of Toluca, but it is too far away, and the towns in the Toluca region are not included in the labor drafts of Tlacopan.

47. AC, 64. This source does not list the twenty towns.

48. RG 8:133; Gerhard 1986:309.

49. RG 8:149–51.

50. Ibid., 133, 135.

51. Ibid., 138.

52. Ibid., 142, 146–47.

53. Ibid., 127–29. This statement could refer either to king Chimalpopoca of Tenochtitlan, during whose reign Axocopan was founded, or to king Chimalpopoca of Tlacopan, a contemporary of Ahuitzotl. According to Ixtlilxochitl (1977, 2:155), the latter participated in Ahuitzotl's conquest of Chiappan, but he seems to refer to Chiappan (de Corzo). See p. 251–52 on the conquest of the Otomi town of Chiappan (de Mota).

54. RG 6:62. See more on this case on p. 211, 214 about the concept of señor natural and the policy of keeping local rulers.

55. Tlauhtla also appears as a barrio (tlaxilacalli) of Xilotepec in the list of witnesses in the Codex Mariano Jiménez (1967). The plates are not numbered; the name appears on what would be plate 13, although from the context it is a continuation of plate 14.

56. RG 9:217–18.

57. Simpson 1934:47–56; Gerhard 1986:395.

58. RG 6:101–102. The present-day town is Zimapán, Hidalgo.

59. Durán 1967, 2:319. The same seven cities participated in the inauguration of the temple under Ahuitzotl (p. 335) and sent settlers to Oztoman and Alahuiztlan (p. 353).

60. Axayacatl was rescued by Quetzalmamalitzin, lord of Teotihuacan, in a battle that Ixtlilxochitl (1975–77, 2:144–45) places in Xiquipilco. But Chimalpahin writes that Axayacatl "defeated the people of Tepeticpac, the people of Tonalliymoquetzayan, the Mazahuas called Xiquipilcas" (quinpeuh yn Axayacatzin yn Tepeticpac tlaca y Tonalliymoquetza tlaca y maçahuaque in ye motenehua xiquipilca), and a marginal note says: "Quetzalmamalitzin helped Axayacatl in the war in Mazahuacan" (Quetzalmamalitzin nican quipalehui yaoc yn Axayacatzin yn Maçahuacan). (Chimalpahin 1987:138, 140. Cf. Chimalpahin 1889:134).

61. Sahagún 1961:183–84 (book 10, chap. 29).

62. AC, 64.

63. Durán 1967, 2:122. Chimalpahin (1889:158) uses Tlalhuactlipan as a synonym of Tlacopan when he names the towns that had captives to sacrifice at the dedication of the temple under Ahuitzotl.

64. Tezozomoc came to the throne in 8 Acatl in Tlalhuacpan, according to the Cuitlahuacas, and in 13 Acatl in Azcapotzalco (AC, 23–24).

65. Tepanoayan is the place where Huehue Ixtlilxochitl, father of Nezahualcoyotl, was killed (Ixtlilxochitl 1975–77, 1:438, 536); it is represented in the Codex Xolotl (Dibble 1951:96 and plate VII, A1).

66. Sahagún 1952:33 (book 3, chap. 13).

67. Torquemada 1975–83, 3:83–84; cf. Ixtlilxochitl 1975–77, 1:335, 437, 535; 2:42. For information on Mount Temacpatl, see Ixtlilxochitl 1975–77, 1:336; AC, 10, 19, 46.

68. Coaatl was one of the springs between Coyoacan and Huitzilopochco (Sahagún 1954:2 [book 8, chap. 1]) and was given this name in reference to Ahuitzotl's hydraulic work. Coaapan, perhaps the same place, was a ceremonial site (Sahagún 1981:187, 205). It is probably the present-day Coapan near the Estadio Azteca in Mexico City.

69. Acxotlan Calnahuac Cochtocan was in Chalco (Chimalpahin 1889:80). San Juan Coxtocan is today in the municipio of Tenango del Aire, Mexico.

70. Ixtlilxochitl 1975–77, 1:376; 2:80. The second reference suggests that Tepanoayan was a town conquered by Cuacuauhpitzahuac of Tlatelolco and Huitzilihuitl of Tenochtitlan, according to the ATl (secs. 4, 53), but in this source the conquests of Huizilihuitl are attributed to Acamapichtli. The Codex Mendoza (2r) gives Tenayocan as conquered along with Colhuacan, before the enthronement of Acamapichtli, but it does not record its conquest during the Empire.

71. AC, 63.

72. Chimalpahin 1889:196–97.

73. The sources written in Nahuatl contain several examples: According to Chimalpahin (1889:97), in 1428 the people of Azcapotzalco expelled Matlacxochitl from Tepanoayan; in another passage (1987:109, 110) he uses Tepanoayan Azcapotzalco as synonymous with "yn tepaneca yn azcapotzalca." There are more examples in the *Anales de Cuauhtitlan*: Tezozomoc invites Xaltemoctli of Cuauhtitlan to Tepanoayan in order to kill him (AC, 30); the Mexicas win war land (cuauhtlalli) in Tepanoayan (AC, 32, 47); Maxtla reigned in Tepanoayan when he had already been enthroned in Az-

capotzalco (AC, 40); the people of Cuauhtitlan paid tribute to Tepanoayan (AC, 41). In the *Crónica Mexicayotl* (Tezozomoc 1949: pars. 94–95), the Mexicas settled in territory belonging to the Tepanecs, the people of Azcapotzalco, and the Acolhuas, and they say, "Let us go to Tepanoayan and Azcapotzalco to beg . . . we will anger the people of Tepanoayan and the Azcapotzalcas."

74. RG 6:30–31, 58; 7:194, 200, 207; 8:127, 133, 138, 141, 147, 149.

75. "Ynauhteuc Tzompanco Citlaltepec, Huehuetocan, Otlazpan = ytlahuillanalpan, Toltitlan, Tepexic, Tepotzotlan = yhueytlal ytlahuillanal ytlatoc. Apazco 20 altepetlquiyacana. Tollan 20 altepetl quiyacana," (AC, 64). *Yhueytlal* may mean literally its "great land", in Molina (1970: s.v.) "Campo o tierra llana. teotlalli, vei tlalli, yxtlauatl"; "Llanura de campo. yxtlauatl, vey tlalli." For the translation of *itlahuilanal* and *ytlatoc*, see Zimmermann 1960:28, 29, 72, and Bierhorst 1992a: 130.

76. LT, 41, 535.

77. AGI, Mexico 112, ramo 3, no. 57. On the extent of the Teotlalpan, see also Cook 1949 and Vollmer 1972.

78. Zimmermann 1970:5. See the full discussion of section 4 of this memorial on p. 185.

79. Van Zantwijk 1969.

80. Zimmermann 1970:5. The text is somewhat corrupt, but the general meaning is clear. Zimmermann suggests several corrections following the corresponding text of Motolinía's "Memorial tetzcocano." See also Carrasco 1996:294.

81. Trautmann (1968:72–73) and Pérez Rocha (1982:16–18) have located some of them. Hodge (1996:35–36 n. 5), without naming or locating them, says they were towns that supported the palace of Tlacopan. She considers the provinces of the Codex Mendoza in this area as tributary provinces of the Empire.

82. AGN, Tierras 13, exp. 4, 320r.

83. This was done in 5 Acatl 1572 (AC, 55).

84. In the *Matrícula de Huexotzinco* the tortoise (*ayotl*) represents the personal name Yaotl (Prem 1974: fols. 483 and 713 and passim).

85. AGI, Indiferente 1529, facsimile in Brinckmann 1969, facing page 30.

86. AC, 60–61. Velázquez translates this toponym as the descriptive phrase "at the dam near the wooden canal." Cf. Lehmann 1938:287; Bierhorst 1992a: 123.

87. Pérez Rocha 1982:69.

88. SV, sec. 799.

89. Colín 1967: sec. 493.

90. AGI, Justicia 146; AGN-HJ 387, exp. 8.

91. AGN-HJ 290:1707v.

92. Ixtlilxochitl 2:107. See p. 128–32 on the Tenochca holdings in Tlalhuic.

93. AC, 49; Colín 1967: secs. 2615, 2616; documents from AGN, Tierras, cited in Strauss 1974: 87–88.

94. Trautmann (1968:74) identifies it as San Esteban Ahuazhuatepec in Tenango, according to the relación geográfica of Taxco (Tlachco), and he identifies this Tenango with present-day Tenango de Arista (or del Valle), but it is really another Tenango only one league distant from Tlachco (RG 7:118).

95. Zimmermann 1970:1.

96. Colín 1967: sec. 2449.

97. Ibid., secs. 706, 749.

98. Ixtlilxochitl 1975–77, 1:293–94, 300–301.

99. Ibid., 1:543; 2:84.

100. See below on Tecalco.

101. See below on Quauhtlaapan.

102. Hernández 1952:80, 91–92.

103. SV, sec. 296.

104. Ixtlilxochitl 1975–77, 2:145.

105. AGN, Tierras 2719, exp. 6; parish records of Cuauhtitlan.

106. AGN, Tierras 13, exp. 4, 320r.

107. Vetancurt 1961, 3:190; Pérez Rocha 1982:33.
108. RG 9:217.
109. Vetancurt 1961, 3:58–59; DA, 56–59.
110. AC, 54.
111. See discussion of Tizayocan and Tecalco in p. 119.

CHAPTER 8

1. Zorita 1941:91–92. See below, p. 211, on the concept of *señor natural*.
2. Baudot 1977:452–61. Cf. Hicks 1986:47; Carrasco 1994:73–79.
3. Ramírez de Fuenleal in CDI 13:253.
4. Ibid., 236.
5. Motolinía 1971:346. Cf. Zorita 1941:107–108.
6. Tapia 1858:561, 592. See below (n.25) on the meaning of *parias*. According to Tapia, the conquered people "were called *tequitin tlacotle,* which means they pay tribute like slaves." Molina translates *tlacoti* (s.v.) as "to work as a slave," but Olmos (1972:222) gives *nitequiti nitlacoti* as one of the many forms meaning "to serve as a servant or farmer" (servir de moço, de labrador). This expression is used in the *Crónica mexicayotl* (Tezozomoc 1949: sec. 118) to describe the condition of the Mexicas when they submitted to Azcapotzalco. Sahagún (1969a: 38, 185 [book 6, chaps. 8 and 34]) also uses it in a religious context meaning "to work or serve." The account of Tapia is probably related to Oviedo's (1851–55, 3:535–37) description of the tribute system.
7. Ixtlilxochitl 1975–77, 2:103–104.
8. Chamberlain 1939:130–137. I summarize the definition in Maravall 1964:71. From now on I will use "natural lord" to translate *señor natural*. See examples on p. 214 on Atlitlalacyan and pp. 302–10 on several towns of Oaxaca.
9. AC, 63–64.
10. RG 6:62–63. Atlitlalacyan was in the kingdom of Tollan within Tlacopan's domain, but it is not listed in any of the Codex Mendoza's provinces. See Table 7-2.
11. The kings of Tlachquiauhco, Zozollan, and Coaixtlahuacan were sacrificed during the reign of Moteuczoma Xocoyotzin (Torquemada 1975–83, 1:286–87, 295).
12. RG 7:126–27. Cf. p. 269.
13. RG 5:295; Tezozomoc 1975:348; Durán 1967, 2:202. See p. 355.
14. RG 2:102. See the quotation on p. 341.
15. Ibid., 300, 302, 306–308. See p. 280–83 on the province of Yohualtepec.
16. Ibid., 5:161–62, 407. See p. 362–63.
17. This is the case in Acatlan, Chillan, and Petlatzinco (ibid., 31–61). See p. 320.
18. Ibid., 36. See p. 320 on Acatlan.
19. Ibid., 35–36. See p. 320. This tradition recalls the myth in Motolinía (1971:10) on the nations that descended from the sons of Iztac Mixcoatl; Mixtecatl was one of them.
20. See p. 305 on the province of Coyolapan and p. 393–94 on the governors of the garrisons.
21. Durán 1967, 2:421–22.
22. Tezozomoc 1949: sec. 268; AGI, Justicia 1013, no. 1.
23. Tezozomoc 1949: sec. 200; AGI, Patronato 245, ramo 10.
24. Torquemada 1975–83, 4:334–35. In a similar statement López de Gómara (1988:111) does not use the word *parias*.
25. The word *parias* used in medieval Spain usually meant a yearly tribute paid to a Christian king by other kings, especially those of the Muslim petty kingdoms, as acknowledgement of his supremacy (Valdeavellano 1968:275, 410, 609–10). Some relaciones geográficas also use the word; see chapter 10, passim.
26. Ramírez de Fuenleal, in García Icazbalceta 1858, 2:179.
27. Ibid., 183.

28. AGN-HJ 284:2204–14.

29. HT-Ch, sec. 380.

30. Durán 1967, 2:202; Tezozomoc 1975:348–49.

31. Chimalpahin 1889:180.

32. Tezozomoc 1975:545; Chimalpahin 1987:118, 120.

33. AGN, Tierras 33, exp. 7; Tierras 18, 1st part, exp. 3. See p. 269.

34. AGI, Justicia 165, no. 1. See p. 262.

35. AGI, Justicia 179. There is little information on the situation of these towns under the Empire. Chillan is described in the SV (sec. 136); it paid tribute to Mexico (RG 5:169–73). About 1600 it was congregated with Xopala (Gerhard 1986:402); the latter town is present-day Jopala, Puebla. There is still a town called Chila in the map of the State of Puebla of the Comisión Geográfica Exploradora of 1908. Gerhard suggests that Xopala and Chila were Chapolicxitlan, conquered by Moteuczoma Ilhuicamina (Codex Mendoza, 8r). Mecatlan together with Chachalintla, Chumatlan, and Coahuitlan formed what García Martínez (1987:75 and map 2) calls a composite altepetl. Of these, Achachalintlan is recorded as a tributary of the Empire in the "Memorial de Tlacopan" (7.1-43). Today Mecatlán, Coahuitlán, and Chumatlán are municipios of Veracruz; there is a Chichilintla in Coyutla, Veracruz. See p. 384.

36. In Berdan et al. 1996 two categories of provinces are proposed, central (in the core area) and outer. The outer provinces are either tributary or strategic. The tributary provinces are those depicted in the Codex Mendoza, the strategic are regional groups of political entities subject in some way to the Empire but not recorded in the Codex Mendoza, and the polities not listed in the Codex Mendoza are called client states (Smith 1966:137). As I see it there were within the Empire different kinds of subordinate states. The core area included the dependent kingdoms of each of the three imperial capitals. In the outer areas there were political entities under a system of indirect rule with varying degrees of subordination; some of these are included both in the Codex Mendoza and in the "Memorial de Tlacopan," others are only in one of these documents, and still others are in neither one and are known only from other sources such as the *Relaciones geográficas*. The tributary provinces of the Codex Mendoza are the administrative units set up for the collection of tribute; some paid only to Tenochtitlan and others to all three capitals. There was not a uniform political administration in all the provinces.

The entities—not listed in the Codex Mendoza—that Berdan and Smith categorize as strategic provinces are units of very different kinds. For example, Cuauhchinanco and Xicotepec were kingdoms of the Acolhua group under Tetzcoco. The strategic province of Chiappan includes Apazco and Tollan, which were Tepanec kingdoms under Tlacopan; several of their sujetos are actually listed in the Codex Mendoza. Another strategic province, Ixtlahuacan, was a tributary dependency of Tlacopan. Tzompanco, although not listed in the Codex Mendoza, was part of the tributary province of Tepecuacuilco. Further discussion of their strategic provinces is not necessary here, but it should also be emphasized that the Codex Mendoza depicts separately two different kinds of units—the towns paying tribute in kind and the towns that constituted the military organization. Furthermore, a satisfactory account of the areas subject to the Empire but not listed in the Codex Mendoza should make use of the sources from the other two imperial capitals, in particular the "Memorial de los pueblos de Tlacopan"; the areas on the eastern borderlands, especially Tecuantepec, should also be taken into account.

37. Recent works include Berdan 1992, Kobayashi 1993, Mohar 1987 and 1990, Sepúlveda 1991, and Berdan et al. 1996.

38. A major emphasis has been placed on the process of expansion and its chronology. See Orozco y Berra 1960, Aragón 1931, Kelly and Palerm 1952, Barlow 1990, Tschohl 1964, Davies 1980, and Lameiras 1985. Hassig's book on war (1988) analyzes the campaigns of all the Tenocha kings from the military point of view with its logistical implications.

39. See the commentary of Kelly and Palerm (1952:265) and the section on sources in chapter 1 of this book.

40. Codex Mendoza, 3v, 5v–6r.

41. Ixtlilxochitl 1975–77, 2:108. The phrase "in the way described above" alludes to what he had

said earlier (ibid., 104) on the proportions in dividing the tribute among the three capitals. This subject is treated below.

42. Ibid., 150–51.

43. Ibid., 106–108.

44. Undoubtedly Hualtepec is badly written. Ixtlilxochitl (1975–77) repeats basically the same series of names in the other versions of his work. In the parallel text of the "Compendio histórico" (ibid., 1:446) he writes Yohualtepec, but he does not include it in the "Sumaria relación" (ibid., 1:544). In another list of conquests in the "Historia chichimeca" (ibid., 2:155), Hualtepec appears between Coyolapan and Tlappan. The key text for correcting the writing and identifying the towns is in the "Pintura de México" (ibid., 1:383), in which no. 31—between Cuetlaxtla and Cuauhtoxco—is Yehualtepec and no. 73—between Capolapan (*sic pro* Coyolapan) and Tlappan—is Yohualtepec. Evidently it is a case of two different towns: one is Yehualtepec (perhaps Yahualtepec), present-day Yehualtepec, Puebla, which would have been conquered in the Tepeyacac campaign; the other is Yohualtepec, present-day San Juan Igualtepec, Oaxaca, in the Mixteca Baja, which is the cabecera of a province in the Codex Mendoza and is also found among the conquests of Moteuczoma Ilhuicamina (Codex Mendoza, 8r, 40r).

45. Ixtlilxochitl 1975–77, 2:96, 124–27.

46. Ibid., 145. According to the Tenochca sources the conquests of Tepeyacac, Cuetlaxtlan, and Coaixtlahuacan took place during the reign of Moteuczoma Ilhuicamina.

47. Torquemada (1975–83, 4:331–35 [book 14, chaps. 6, 7, and 8]) specifies only Tetzcoca sources, but he generalizes on the three kingdoms of the Empire. In his chapter 6, about the officials at the court, he refers to an account book of Don Antonio Pimentel of Tetzcoco. His chapter 7, on land tenure, has data similar to Ixtlilxochitl's, and he also refers to his own chapter on King Techotlalatzin of Tetzcoco. His chapter 8 deals with royal revenue; he does not give his sources, but it is the same material known from López de Gómara (1988:110–11), Cervantes de Salazar (1971, 1:323–24), and others that refers primarily to Tenochtitlan.

48. Sahagún 1954:44–45, 58 (book 8, chaps. 14 and 17).

49. Codex Mendoza, 19v (see quotation on p. 75), 70r. Texancalli probably derives from the words for stone (*tetl*) and adobe (*xamitl*). The Codex Mendoza depicts two workers, one with a spade and the other with a basket and tumpline, implying that they were engaged in construction work. Siméon (1988: s.v.) derives texancalco from *texamatl* (literally "meal paper," interpreted as sheets of paper glued together). If this were so it should be *texamacalco*.

50. Durán 1967, 2:307.

51. In Nahuatl, hueycalpixqui is also the name of the steward in the head town of a tributary province, while calpixque (in plural) are the stewards of the subordinate towns, as is the case in Cuetlaxtlan, described below.

52. Torquemada 1975–83, 4:331.

53. Ibid., 332. See p. 18–19 for the meanings of the term *teuctli*. Judges (*teuctlatoque*) are sometimes described with this title, and in pictures its glyph is a headband (Sahagún 1954:56–58 and illustrations 83, 84, and 85 [book 8, chap. 17]). A local teuctli also participated in the collection and transfer of tribute. Cf. Zorita 1941:151, cited below, and examples in Carrasco 1976.

54. Torquemada (1975–83, 4:332) compares these officials with those of Spanish local government; he says the teteuctin were like *regidores* (councilmen), and the two leading ones like alcaldes (judges).

55. Torquemada (ibid.) compares the tequitlatoque and tlayacanque with the *merinos*, a term that was used in colonial New Spain for such officials. The officials called merinos in Spain were usually of higher rank (Valdeavellano 1968:510, 567).

56. Durán 1967, 1:116, 185.

57. Codex Mendoza, 66r. Torquemada's description recalls the envoys of Moteuczoma whom the Spanish encountered in Cempohuallan (Díaz del Castillo 1964:73).

58. Torquemada (1975–83, 4:334) compares this local teuctli with a regidor; López de Gómara (1988:110) calls him a *cogedor* (collector) and compares him with the Spanish *alguaciles* (constables).

59. Sahagún 1975:5 (book 12, chap. 2). The two tlayacanque were Cuitlalpitoc and Tentlil, mentioned in the chronicles of the conquest. Cf. Díaz del Castillo 1964:58 ff.

60. See pp. 367 and 373 on Tochpan and Tziuhcoac. Cf. the data on the various calpixques in the province of Tepecuacuilco, on p. 273.

61. Tezozomoc 1975:309, 338. See Ramirez de Fuenleal, cited above in p. 208, 217.

62. Ixtlilxochitl 1975–77, 2:104. See the beginning of this chapter.

63. RG 2:229.

64. Several reports not specific about the area described seem to stem from a common source; they are found in Oviedo 1851–55, 3:535–36; López de Gómara 1988:110; Cervantes de Salazar 1971, 1:322; and Torquemada 1975–83, 1:319. The data of Zorita (1941:142ff.) apply probably to the tramontane area that included both independent polities and the tributary province of Tepeyacac.

65. Torquemada 1975–83, 4:335.

66. This is said in the memorials of Tetzcoco and Tlacopan, and the descriptions of public works in Durán and Tezozomoc confirm it. See p. 407–409.

67. Tezozomoc 1975:666–67, 669. The text does not make clear whose camellones they were.

68. Ibid., 678; cf. Durán 1967, 2:467. See Sahagún 1952:6–9 (book 2, chap. 1) about the men fasting for Huitzilopochtli.

69. Codex Mendoza, 18v–19r.

70. Torquemada 1975–83, 1:239. Huexotzinco is also reported here as defeated by Axayacatl.

71. Durán 1967, 2:276–77.

72. Tezozomoc 1975:477.

73. See p. 354. This is a late source; it might be a tale based on the meaning of the town, since Cuezcomatepec means "Bin Hill."

74. Zorita 1941:91–92. See the full quotation in p. 207–208.

75. Ixtlilxochitl 1975–77, 2:108.

76. Motolinía 1971:395.

77. Sahagún 1969b, 2:317 (book 8, chap. 17). The Nahuatl text states that the king gave stewardships (calpixcantli) to the princes (tlazopipiltin) victorious in war (Sahagún 1954:53–54).

78. Zorita 1941:145, 151. The reference to lower lords is to those below the supreme lords or tlatoque; they must be either his second kind of lords (teuctli) or the third (calpoleque).

79. Moteuczoma Ilhuicamina advised his many sons who would not succeed him to take up warfare or crafts or painting and writing (tlacuilocayotl); this last term probably applies to the scribes or record keepers in the storehouses (Tezozomoc 1949: sec. 201). The Codex Mendoza also says that the calpixques were Mexicas. See the quotations in p. 75. On the calpixques of the core area, see Hicks 1978.

80. AC, 51. Compare the story about palace women stealing the tribute from Coaixtlahuacan in Chimalpahin 1987:136.

81. Ixtlilxochitl (1977, 1:393) notes that the calpixques in the tributary towns of the Tetzcoca kings were commoners.

82. Zorita 1941:74, 91–92, cited above in p. 207–208.

83. Torquemada 1975–83, 1:203.

84. Ibid., 242. See the full quotation on p. 233.

85. Motolinía does not transcribe the tribute that was depicted in the document he describes, but the corresponding text in the AC does. It would be necessary to make a detailed comparison of the data on kinds and quantities of tribute that are specified for the provinces that paid tribute to Tetzcoco, in Ixtlilxochitl (1977, 2:106–18, 145), in the Anales de Cuauhtitlan, and in the Tenochca sources. See Nielsen 1966.

86. Motolinía 1971:395.

87. AC, 64: "yn nohuian altepetl ytlacalaquil excan xellihuia Mexico Tetzcoco Tlacopan."

88. Molina (1970: s.v.) also translates excan as "en tres maneras" (in three manners). Cf. "nauhcan, en quatro partes, o lugares" (in four parts or places).

89. Motolinía 1971:395–96.

90. AC, 65.

91. Motolinía 1971:396. The document says "the same as is said above in the third house [casa] of those numerous towns." The word *casa* has not been used previously in the document; it must refer to each of the groups of towns: the first, the cities with kings; the second, the towns of tenant farmers; and the third, the province of Tochpan.

92. Ixtlilxochitl 1975–77, 1:444; 2:104, 106–108. See pp. 128–32, 172–75 and 201.

93. AGI, Justicia 1029, no. 10, fol. 10v.

94. This problem is discussed above in p. 36–38 on the kingdoms of the nuclear zone from whence comes the best information.

95. Zavala 1938:70. See the complete quotation in p. 68.

96. According to a petition by his son to the Crown (AGI, Mexico 95, ramo 1, no. 22).

97. Cf. Ixtlilxochitl 1975–77, 2:150–51, quoted above. See p. 220.

98. As one example, Tziuhcoac gave as tribute birds, rabbits, and deer (AC, 65).

99. For example, Durán 1967, 2:158–59, 180–81, 188.

100. Zorita 1941:91–92. See the complete quotation on p. 307–308.

101. No source says that the kings of these towns were among the direct dependents of Tenochtitlan or Tlacopan, nor are they included in the lists of the memorials of Tetzcoco and Tlacopan, which name the cities that paid tribute to the three capitals. See p. 253–61.

102. Pomar 1986:53.

103. RG 7:126.

104. Ibid., 3:143. See the quotation in p. 301.

105. Ibid., 271–72. See p. 342.

106. Ixtlilxochitl (1975–77, 2:107) writes Teochtepec, but the context and the comparison with Motolinía's "Memorial tetzcocano" leave no doubt that Tochtepec is meant.

107. Ibid., 103–104. See p. 210.

108. RG 2:229.

109. Zorita 1941:146–47.

110. Mohar 1987:305–20.

111. This contrast between Tziuhcoac and Tochpan does not appear in the data of the AC (pp. 64–65) or of Ixtlilxochitl (1977, 2:107).

112. RG 8:53.

113. Ibid., 3:36.

114. Ibid., 2:49.

115. Ibid., 3:90. The acquisition of goods for tribute by exchanging small cloaks is described in the same words in the relación of Atlatlauhcan. The authors of these two relaciones, of Atlatlauhca and Tecuicuilco, coincide literally on several points; they must have cooperated. See the commentary of Acuña (Ibid., 85–86). On these towns see the provinces of Coaixtlahuacan (Atlatlauhcan and Quiotepec) and Coyolapan (Tecuicuilco) on p. 297–310.

116. Ibid., 2:236.

117. Molina 1970: s.v.; Motolinía 1971:374.

118. Ixtlilxochitl 1975–77, 2:107.

119. Zorita 1941:142, 147, 150, 152; Sahagún 1959:17 (book 9, chap. 4). See p. 409–10 about the towns from which merchants went to the isthmus. Outside the control of the Triple Alliance, the people of Tonamecan gave to Tototepec tribute of cochineal that they went to the mountains to buy (RG 2:198).

120. Durán 1967, 2:162.

121. RG 2:255.

122. Ibid., 214.

123. Ibid., 255.

124. Torquemada 1975–83, 1:242.

125. Both writers are quoted on p. 137–38.

126. Pomar 1986:47. The Acolhuan expansion to the Pacific coast is not confirmed in other sources, but see p. 276 on the role of Tetzcoco in the conquest of Zacatollan.

127. Ixtlilxochitl 1975–77, 1:461.

128. Ibid., 484. The spelling of several toponyms has been corrected. In this context Tenayocan would not make sense because it did not pertain to the Acolhua kingdom.

129. AGI, Justicia 1029, no. 10, fol. 6r. See the discussion on Tecuantepec in p. 348–49.

130. Tenochtitlan remitted certain lawsuits to Tetzcoco (Motolinía 1971:334, 353). See p. 408 on Nezahualcoyotl as a builder.

131. López Austin (1985:278–80) relates each capital to a level of the universe: Tenochtitlan with the level of the sun and military affairs, Tetzcoco with the higher level of the creator gods and justice, Tlacopan with the lower world and cultivation. Thus, Tlacopan would have some special function connected with earthly activities, such as agriculture and commerce. Torquemada (1975–83, 1:127) describes the specialization of ethnic groups in different branches of the political organization in the kingdom of Techotlalatzin of Tetzcoco in the fifteenth century, before the Triple Alliance. The Tepanecs were the companions (*acompañados*) of the treasurer of Techotlalatzin. As to the functions of that treasurer, he says only that "he had charge of everything inside the palace." Elsewhere (4:331) Torquemada states that in the Empire of the Triple Alliance there were chamberlains and chief waiters (camareros y maestresalas) with names fitting the duties they performed, and they were "lords and the highest of the realm"; he refers to his chapter on Tetzcoco under Techotlalatzin. It is possible that in the Triple Alliance the Tepanecs held the same position as under Techotlalatzin of Tetzcoco, but one must take into account the possible confusion between Tepaneca (people of the lava field) and Tecpaneca (people of the palace). For the meaning of camarero in Spain, see p. 456n.49. On the participation of the Tlacopanec kingdoms in commerce, see p. 409.

132. As pointed out before, Zorita also says that each of the kings of the three capitals had his own provinces.

133. Ixtlilxochitl 1975–77, 2:145, 148–50; Durán 1967, 2:419.

134. Durán 1967, 2:328. Cuauhchinanco sent one of the officials—together with others from the three capitals—charged with settling a dispute over land between Mecatlan and Chillan. See p. 218.

135. RG 2:214, 217.

136. See p. 19–20 on the use of the word *provincia* in the sources.

137. For example, Barlow 1949b, Mohar 1987 and 1990, and Berdan 1980 and 1992.

138. Chapter 3 summarizes the most important conquests. The principal studies on this theme are Barlow 1990, Kelly and Palerm 1952, and Hassig 1988.

139. Gibson (1971, map 2) indicates the towns registered in the Codex Mendoza and those that paid tribute to the three capitals, undoubtedly according to the data of the "Memorial de Tlacopan," but he does not take into account the organization in different provinces or paragraphs that these sources give.

140. See the examples of Petlacalco (p. 111), Acolman (p. 117), Cuauhtitlan (p. 124), and Tlalhuic (p. 130), although they are all in the core area.

141. See p. 373–77 on Tziuhcoac, p. 273 on Tepecuacuilco, and p. 309 on Coyolapan.

142. The principal general studies are those of Barlow 1949b; Gibson 1956, 1964b, and 1971; Trautmann 1968; Vollmer 1972; Gerhard 1986; Davies 1987; and Berdan et al. 1996.

143. The "Memorial de Tlacopan" has been little used for the areas subject to the alliance. Gibson (1971, map 2) used it for one of his maps. Davies (1968) used it in his studies of independent areas. Berdan et al. (1996) practically ignore this important source. Many towns in the "Memorial de Tlacopan" appear also in the Codex Mendoza. In this book I give the complete identification in the lists that present the data of this codex; in the tables on the "Memorial de Tlacopan" they are identified only briefly; fuller information is given on the towns present only in this source.

CHAPTER 9

1. In the *Información de 1554* (Scholes and Adams 1957:44, 76) Malinalco and Xocotitlan are missing, but in their place there is a province called Apan. See below on Xocotitlan.

2. With the exception of Tonatiuhco, which is also in the Codex Mendoza province of Ocuillan, and some neighboring towns not in the Codex Mendoza that are in paragraph 7.3 of the "Memorial de Tlacopan."

3. Torquemada 1975–83, 1:201.

4. Cuahuacan, Cuauhtitlan, Tollan, Huitzitzilapan, and Tecpan (Kelly and Palerm 1952:287–90). According to Ixtlilxochitl (1977, 2:108), the conquest of Mazahuacan took place during the reigns of Nezahualcoyotl and Itzcoatl.

5. Codex Mendoza, 7v, 8r.

6. During the time of Quinatzin (grandfather of Nezahualcoyotl) the Tetzcocas fought against Chichimec and Metzca groups, driving them as far away as Metztitlan. At this same time the Mexicas recently installed in Tenochtitlan fought together with Azcapotzalco against Chichimec groups, and they expanded as far as the province of Atotonilco (Ixtlilxochitl 1975–77, 1:317–18, 429–30; 2:29). Atotonilco el Grande bordered upon Metztitlan (SV, sec. 354).

7. Durán 2:303; Tezozomoc 1975:441.

8. RG 8:128, 138–39. See p. 192–93.

9. Durán 1967, 2:231.

10. Tezozomoc 1975:364.

11. Durán 1967, 2:237.

12. Ibid., 285; Tezozomoc 1975:424.

13. AC, 55.

14. Codex Mendoza, 10r–v. According to Chimalpahin (1987:138), in 5 Acatl 1471, Axayacatl conquered Tepeticpac, Tonalli ymoquetzayan, Mazahuacan, and Xiquipilco. Of these places, Tepeticpac was a barrio of Xiquipilco (SV, sec. 801) and a name used also for Chiappan (see note 33 below). Barlow (1948:187–88) identifies Tonalli ymoquetzayan with Tonaliquizaya, a ranchería of Tetela del Río, Guerrero (Hendrichs 1945:214). However, the context favors placing it in Matlatzinco. Chimalpahin (1987:139) puts the conquest of Chiappan and Tlatelolco in 7 Calli 1473.

15. HMP, 231.

16. Chimalpahin 1889:148.

17. Durán 1967, 2:293.

18. The "Anales de Tula" (Barlow 1949a: 8) seems to agree with Durán, stating that in 1476 "here conquered Ocuillan; they destroyed the people of Cuauhnahuac"(nican tepeuh Ocuillan, oquimpopolo cuauhnavactlacah). But the AC (p. 57) on the same year is ambiguous: "Ocuillan was conquered; they destroyed the people of Cuauhnahuac" (nican tepehualloc Ocuillan quimpolloque quauhnahuaca). It is not clear whether, as Durán says, this was a struggle between those two cities or both were conquests of the Mexicas. Chimalpahin (1889:135; 1987:141) puts in that same year the Mexica conquest of Ocuillan, Cuauhnahuac, Tenantzinco, and Chontalcoatlan. The Codex Telleriano-Remensis (37r) depicts the defeat of Ocuillan by Tenochtitlan in 1476.

19. Ixtlilxochitl 1975–77, 2:144. Malacatepec (present-day Villa Allende, Mexico), Amatepec, and Cimatepec (which was an estancia of Oztoman [SV, sec. 167]) were on the frontier with Michoacan.

20. Tezozomoc 1975:442. For the Otomis of the Cuauhtlalpan and of the Metlatzinca (sic), see Durán 1967, 2:303.

21. Durán 1967, 2:306, 307; Tezozomoc 1975:446.

22. Kelly and Palerm 1952:274, 301–303. Toxico (present-day San Lorenzo Toxico in Ixtlahuaca, Mexico) is said to be one of the towns of tenant farmers of Tlacopan ("Memorial de los pueblos de Tlacopan," 5.2-8). The location of Cillan is given below.

23. Durán 1967, 2:319. There is an account of this war in Durán (319–20) and Tezozomoc (1975: 461–63, 467–69). No other source gives such a full description of this campaign. Torquemada (1975–83, 1:257) states only that the first thing Ahuitzotl did was to finish the temple his predecessor had started; he then went on to fight and defeat the Mazahuas, who had rebelled.

24. Durán 1967, 2:319. In Tezozomoc (1975–83, 1:461, 463) the rebels are the same, except in one passage he says Otomis instead of Cillan.

25. Among the tenant settlements of Tlacopan were Ahuazhuatepec, the name of the cabecera of

Xiquipilco; Ixtlahuacan, with its neighbors Toxinco and Tochcalco; and Zacapechco, a subject of Chiappan. See p. 202-203.

26. Durán 1967, 2:319.

27. RG 9:235.

28. SV, sec. 110.

29. RG 9:61.

30. Ibid., 235.

31. Ibid., 6:101-102. This is the same king of Xilotepec named in AC, 64.

32. SV, sec. 801. It is also found in colonial documentation (Sila or Cila) as the name of a hacienda, a mountain, and a tributary of the Lerma River in the area of Ixtlahuaca and Xiquipilco (Colín 1966: secs. 891, 914, 946, 978; 1967b: 783, 787, 788, 1063, 1075). The map of the Secretaría de Agricultura shows a Sila between Jiquipilco and Ixtlahuaca.

33. Codex Telleriano-Remensis, 39v. The toponym Chiappan or Chiauhpan (present-day Chapa de Mota, Mexico) means "spot of water" (*mancha de agua*) according to a relación geográfica of the region (RG 8:133, 142). Other places with a name also derived from *chiahuitl* or *chiauhtli* confirm this etymology. The glyph of Chiappan in the Codex Telleriano-Remensis (39v) is a puddle or spot of water with a banner in the center (Carrasco 1996:363-64, n. 52). This glyph could be read as Apan (water with banner), and this may explain the use of the name Apan in the *Información de 1554*. See p. 260-61 on Apan and the province of Xocotitlan. The full Nahuatl name of Chiappan was Chiappan (wet land) Tepeticpac (mountaintop) (DA, 139). In Otomi the equivalent of Tepeticpac is Anyãttoehoe (Urbano 1990:6; Uribe 1954-55:209; Andrews 1954-55:163), which is the modern name. The Otomi equivalent of Chiappan is Matzittzi, since Hueichiappan (Great Chiappan) is Antamatzittzi (Caso 1967:216) and Chiappantonco (Little Chiappan) is Marzitzi (Uribe 1954-55:209). Urbano (1990: s.v. *regadura*) gives *natzhittzi* as one of the words that translates *regadura* (irrigation).

34. A sujeto of Texopilco (RG 7:143; present-day Tejupilco, Mexico). Kelly and Palerm (1952: 305) identify Cozcacuauhtenanco with the present-day Cuautenango, Mexico, but there is no basis for this except the similarity of the names.

35. Sahagún 1954:2 (book 8, chap. 1); Chimalpahin 1889:136.

36. Torquemada 1975-83, 1:258. Cf. Chimalpahin 1987:158-59.

37. Sahagún 1969:206 (book 10, chap. 29).

38. Ixtlilxochitl 1975-77, 2:155.

39. Barlow 1990:84; Codex Mendoza, 13r. AC (pp. 57-58) records the conquest of Chiappan in 1484 and in 1488, and ATl (sec. 280) in 1490, but in contrast with the Codex Telleriano-Remensis they do not specify which they refer to. About that time conquests are also recorded in the isthmus region.

40. For the dedication of the temple under Ahuitzotl, the following attended: Coatlapan (*sic pro* Cuauhtlalpan), Xocotitlan, Mazahuacan, Xiquipilco, Cuauhuacan, Chiapan, and Xilotepec (Tezozomoc 1975:486). To settle in the region of Oztoman and Alahuiztlan after Ahuitzotl's victory, people went from, among other places, Cuauhtlapa (*sic*), land of the Otomi, Xilotepec, Chiappan, Mazahuacan, Xocotitlan, Xiquipilco, Cuauhuacan, Cillan, and Ocuillan (Durán 1967, 2:352-53; Tezozomoc 1975:534). Ahuitzotl's funeral rites were attended by "all the people of Cuauhtlalpan and Mazahuacan and all the Otomi nation of Xocotitlan, Chiapanecas, Xiquipilcas, and Xilotepecas" (Durán 1967, 2:393).

41. AC, 64. On the rulers of Tolocan, see below, p. 258.

42. In the lists of conquests by Moteuczoma Xocoyotzin there are two towns that could belong in this region, Tecozauhtlan and Teochiapan (Codex Mendoza, 16r), if we interpret the latter as Hueychiapan (present-day Huichapan, Hidalgo). They were towns in the kingdom of Xilotepec and garrisons against the Chichimecs (RG 9:217). Tecozauhtla was one of the sujetos of Xilotepec listed in the "Memorial de Tlacopan" (4.5-3) and was also in the province of Xilotepec in the Codex Mendoza (31r). In that case these conquests of Moteuczoma Xocoyotzin can be seen as battles against the neighboring Chichimecs. However, in place of Tecozauhtlan the AC (p. 69) give Tlalcozauhtitlan, a well-known town in Guerrero. Perhaps it is a matter of different readings of the same glyph. Another doubtful case

is found in the Codex Vaticano-Ríos (85v); in the year 9 Calli 1501—a year before his enthronement—there is a picture of Moteuczoma, dressed as Xipe, beside the glyph for Tolocan. Krickeberg (1952:256) interprets this as the conquest of this city. Facing it is the glyph for Xaltepec with a warrior attired for the sacrifice. It is not clear whether this event is connected with the preceding one.

43. The best discussion available is that of Menegus 1991: chap. 1, which presents material from AGI that I was not able to use here.

44. AC, 63–64.

45. Zorita 1941:74, 198.

46. Durán 1967, 2:267; Tezozomoc 1975:398–406, 420; Torquemada 1975–83, 1:250–51; Zorita 1941:198–201; Chimalpahin 1889:150.

47. In later times Tzinacantepec is said to be land of Axayacatl (Hernández 1952:82 and map of AGN-HJ, 277:67, which has a legend saying "Tzinacantepec ytlalpan ypilcha Axayacatzin").

48. Zorita 1941:200; RG 9:186; SV, sec. 365; RO, 42.

49. RG 6:48. Presumably this Axayacatzin was the future king Axayacatl, at that time tlacatecatl under Moteuczoma Ilhuicamina.

50. Sahagún 1961:181–83 (book 10, chap. 29).

51. Codex Mendoza, 10v.

52. Codex Telleriano-Remensis, 37v (1478). The glyph is just a net (*matlatl*) without the lower part of the body that denotes -*tzinco*, but in the preceding page (36r) there is a legend (without a glyph) saying that in 1472 the Mexicas started to wage war in the Valley of Matlatzinco, and the first incursion was at Tolocan. The same net is in 36v (without a legend) beside the glyph for war (1474).

53. RG 7:277, 280 (Teotenanco); SV, secs. 799 (Xocotitlan), 296 (Ixtlahuacan), 12 (Atlacomulco), 562 (Tlalchichilpa and Malacatepec).

54. RG 7:140.

55. See below, on Zoquitzinco in the province of Tolocan.

56. Chimalpahin 1958:3–5; HMP, 235.

57. Durán 1967, 2:307; Tezozomoc 1975:446.

58. Durán 1967, 2:319; Tezozomoc 1975:462.

59. Durán 1967, 2:334; Tezozomoc 1975:486.

60. Durán 1967, 2:353; Tezozomoc 1975:534.

61. Hernández 1952:79–99, and map from AGN-HJ, 277.

62. Ixtlilxochitl 1975–77, 2:144–45.

63. AGI, Patronato 245, ramo 1. In this document it is spelled Soquilcingo.

64. Hernández Rodríguez 1988:110. The same documents (104–108, 110, 115–120) give details about the lands of Ahuitzotl and the colonial names of the different towns that were distributed. See also Menegus 1991:61–72.

65. Hernández Rodríguez 1952:95–99; 1988:91–94 (the Nahuatl text is incomplete in the 1988 edition). See above on a possible conquest by Moteuczoma Xocoyotzin in Tolocan.

66. AGN, Tierras 13, exp. 4, fol. 320r.

67. AC, 55; Lehmann 1938: sec. 1131, p. 264.

68. Kelly and Palerm 1952:297–99; Codex Mendoza, 10v.

69. Durán 1967, 2:267.

70. Chimalpahin 1889:148.

71. HMP, 231.

72. ATI, sec. 106.

73. García Granados 1952–53, 1:130.

74. Serna 1892:287–88.

75. There is a Tzumpahuacan conquered by Moteuczoma Ilhuicamina (Ixtlilxochitl 1975–77, 2:109; Torquemada 1975–83, 1:128), but the context suggests the region of the Balsas; it could be Tzompahuacan in Chietla, Puebla, or Zumpango, Guerrero.

76. See Nicholson 1972:149 and Berdan 1996:115. Yet Gerhard (1986:53) and Hodge (1996:25, 33, 39, and 229, Appendix I) identify the Apan of the *Información de 1554* with modern Apan, Hidalgo.

If this were so, one would have to accept the idea that the paintings described by the witnesses in the *Información de 1554* did not contain a page depicting Malinalco and Xocotitlan and that Apan was another, completely different province that is lacking in the Codex Mendoza and the *Matrícula*. This presumed page would have been misplaced among other pages in the codex presented to the witnesses, since a plate on this Apan, in the domain of Tetzcoco, should have been next to other provinces in that region, such as Acolman and Atotonilco el Grande. See p. 152 about the status of Apan, Hidalgo, in the old Acolhua kingdom. Vollmer (1972:62, 73–74) proposes that the Apan in the *Información de 1554* was Oapan (Ohuapan), a town in the province of Tepecuacuilco. However, this source counts within Tepecuacuilco the cabecera with thirteen other towns, the same number of towns as in the Codex Mendoza.

77. The commentary cited above is written in handwriting of the eighteenth century; the reproduction of this plate in the book of Lorenzana (1770) demonstrates that the contents at that time were already the same as they are today. It is not certain that the *Matrícula* is exactly the same document shown to the witnesses, but the legend proves that the *Matrícula* must have had the additional glyphs.

78. As has already been said, the *Información de 1554* is based on the explanations of several witnesses of a pictorial that must have been very similar to the *Matrícula de Tributos*. In the *Matrícula* the cabecera of a province is usually in the lower left-hand corner of the page. The witnesses of the *Información de 1554* coincide in this manner of reading the document except when they describe the towns depicted in plate 20 of the *Matrícula*, which is, like plate 15, divided into sections (Tlalcozauhtitlan, Quiauhteopan, and Yohualtepec) delineated by vertical lines. Here they read as cabeceras the towns in the top parts of each section. If the plate they interpreted as Apan had the glyphs on the border higher than the rest, they could have taken one of them as the cabecera.

79. Scholes and Adams 1957:44, 76, 180.

80. These codices depict granaries made of planks that in the Codex Mendoza are called *trojes* and in the *Matrícula*, *cuezcomatl* in Nahuatl (plate 11, of Xilotepec) and *arcas, medidas*, or *escriños* in Spanish (not *escaños* as modern editions have transcribed it). Above each one the seed or grain contained in it is depicted, and usually each kind has a separate granary. The number of grains depicted over each granary varies; it is not clear what this might mean. In any case, for provinces such as Tolocan and Chalco the quantities are very large, showing a variation among the provinces greater than what is registered in the *Información de 1554*.

81. The name and the glyph for Chiappan have been discussed before in connection with Ahuitzotl's conquest. If Apan is equivalent to Chiappan, the Apan to which a son of Itzcoatl went to rule could refer to that Otomi town.

82. AC, 64.

83. SV, secs. 12, 296. See p. 202–203 on Ixtlahuacan.

84. Ixtlilxochitl 1975–77, 2:144.

85. RG 7:140.

86. Ibid., 140, 144–45. One of the sujetos of Temazcaltepec was Pipioltepec (143), which could have been the town of this name conquered by Moteuczoma Xocoyotzin (Codex Mendoza, 16r; Chimalpahin 1889:176). However other sources, such as the AC, give instead the name Xicotepec; this is a matter of two possible readings of the same glyph, making identification difficult (Barlow 1990:101, 122).

87. Chimalpahin 1987:158–59. Its location is given in RG 7:143.

88. RG 8:185.

89. Both are in AC, 67–68. The other lists give Çulan (Zollan) in place of the first, and instead of Tlatlayan give three names: Tlachinolticpan (Codex Mendoza, 15v), Tlachinollan (ATl, sec. 67), or Tlatlatepec (*Leyenda de los Soles*, in Tschohl 1989:252).

90. Ixtlilxochitl 1975–77, 2:144.

91. SV, sec. 38; RG 9:35–36. Cozamallan is the present-day Cutzamala de Pinzón, Guerrero.

92. AGI, Justicia 165, no. 1.

93. Codex Mendoza, 34r. Barlow (1949b: 25) adds Zoltepec and Temazcaltepec to the tributary province of Ocuillan.

CHAPTER 10

1. The Memorial of Don Hernando Pimentel includes some regions of the southern sector but does not give a complete picture; they could be understood as possessions of Tetzcoco in that sector, the same as Tlalcozauhtitlan according to Ixtlilxochitl.

2. Kelly and Palerm 1952:291–95. Barlow 1948 studies the history of the Mexica conquest of Guerrero. See also Litvak 1971a.

3. RG 7:117–25. Present-day locations are Atzala and San Francisco Acuitlapa in Taxco de Alarcón, Guerrero, and Pilcaya, Guerrero.

4. Ibid., 126–27

5. Torquemada 1975–83, 1:255. The name Maxtlaton is related to the tradition that Maxtlaton, the last Tepanec king of Azcapotzalco, fled to Tlachco when he was defeated by the Mexicas.

6. AGN, Tierras 33, exp. 7, 1572.

7. Kelly and Palerm 1952:287–90. Itzcoatl conquered Cuezallan, Yohuallan, and Tepecuacuilco and two other towns in the region that are not included in this tributary province: Zacualpan (Zacualpan, Mexico) and Iztepec (Ixtepec de San Simón in Arcelia, Guerrero). Barlow (1948) deals with the conquests of the Mexica kings in Guerrero.

8. Kelly and Palerm 1952:291–95.

9. Axayacatl conquered Oztoman and Poctepec, which Ilhuicamina had already taken (Codex Mendoza, 10v; AC, 57).

10. Durán 1967, 2:351–55. The towns from which the new inhabitants had come to settle these three towns are listed below, on p. 392. See p. 395–96 on Oztoman as a military colony.

11. Tezozomoc 1975:534. See p. 104–108 on Citlaltepec.

12. Most of the information on towns of this region that are cited in the following paragraphs are in the relación of Ichcateopan. Three other relaciones—of Chilapan, Tixtla, and Tzompanco—were prepared by a single author. This explains the similarities in the data from the different towns and makes more reliable the notable differences that are recorded.

13. RG 6:348. Cohuixco was a Nahuatl-speaking region whose boundaries cannot be precisely defined. See below.

14. Ibid., 285–91. Acapetlahuaya is today a town in the municipio General Canuto A. Neri, Guerrero.

15. Ibid., 293.

16. Ibid., 283.

17. Ibid., 328. Totoltepec is now a town in Teloloapan, Guerrero.

18. Ibid., 276–80. Tzicapotzalco is today Ixcapuzalco in Pedro Ascencio Alquisiras, Guerrero; the other town is Tlatlayan, Mexico.

19. Ibid., 324–25.

20. Ibid., 315–17. Coatepec is now Coatepec de los Costales in Teloloapan, Guerrero.

21. Ibid., 345.

22. Ibid., 349, 350. Mayanalan is today a town of Tepecoacuilco, Guerrero.

23. Ibid., 340, 342.

24. Ibid., 353.

25. Ibid., 264–65.

26. Ibid., 269, 271.

27. Ibid., 294–95.

28. Ibid., 5:112, 114 (Chilapan), 270–71 (Tixtla); 8:197–98 (Tzompanco). The towns named are present-day Tixtla, Mochitlán, and Zumpango, all in Guerrero.

29. The present-day town is Quechultenango, Guerrero. See p. 390 about the garrison.

30. AGI, Justicia 127, no. 1, questions 6 and 7 in the statement of Don Diego, cacique of Tzompanco, in the suit with Martín Dircio and Don Martín, cacique of Tixtla.

31. According to question 15 of the statement of Don Diego (ibid.), Oapan comprised "four cabeceras in one kingdom"; Ozomatlan, Tetelcingo, Tecociapa, and Apango are mentioned.

32. Ibid., question 3, witness 5, in the evidence of Don Martín.

33. Ibid., 195v, 207r.

34. Harvey 1971.

35. According to Sahagún (1981:187 [book 10, chap. 29]), the Cohuixcas spoke Nahuatl; they were also called Tlappanecs and were from Tepecuacuilco, Tlachmalacac, and Chilapan. However, the name Tlappanec was also given to the Yopitzincas or Yopimes, who spoke a different language. In a list of the "provinces" of the archbishopric of Mexico in 1571 (AGI, Mexico 112) "the province of la Coyxca" comprised the districts of Tzacualpa, Nochtepec, Tlachco, Huitzoco, Tlachmalacac, Tepecuacuilco, Yohuallan, Teloloapan, Cuezallan, Tetellan, and Tzompanco. In the north this province adjoined the province of Tlalhuic, in the west, Zoltepec, and in the south, Acapolco. Towards the east it was contiguous with the bishopric of Tlaxcallan, where there also were Cohuixca towns. The frontier between Cohuixcas and Coatlalpanecas is not well defined; see the section on Tepeyacac on p. 289. Neighboring on the Mixteca there was also the Nahuatl-speaking province of the Totoltecs, whose boundaries are not known; see p. 295 on Piaztlan. There are references to the province of Cohuixco and the Cohuixcas in RG 6:340, 348–49, 350, 352; DA, 170, 192; PNE 5:249; AGI, Justicia 127, no. 1 (evidence of Don Diego, cacique of Tzompanco, 5th question); and Dehouve 1990:54.

36. Four towns listed in SV could possibly be the cabecera of this province: Çigua (sec. 864), Çiguatlan, under the Crown (sec. 883), Çiguatanejo (sec. 894), and Ciguatlan, encomienda of Francisco Salcedo (sec. 901). For the various problems of locating the towns of this province, see Barlow 1949b: 8–12 and Acuña's introduction to RG 9 (439–62).

37. RG 9:453–56. Cayaco was on a plain one league from the sea and forty-seven leagues from Zacatula. It is more precisely located in SV, secs. 906, 907.

38. Torquemada 1975–83, 1:394. In colonial times the small population remaining in Mexcaltepec was settled in Atoyac (Gerhard 1986:405); modern maps still show Mexcaltepec to the north of Atoyac. Cuitlatec was spoken in the Balsas Basin area and the mountains to the south, as well as in some coastal towns, but no other source reports the existence of a large Cuitlatec kingdom. Torquemada uses the term *province* in the same chapter when referring to Pánuco (or Huaxteca) and to the "province or kingdom" of the Otomis. The Cuitlatec-speaking towns along the Balsas River and in the mountains to the south are discussed on p. 323.

39. Kelly and Palerm 1952:304–309.

40. Ixtlilxochitl 1975–77, 2:161–62.

41. Vega (1991) outlines the history of this region in her study of the Codex de Azoyú.

42. RO, 99, 100, 103, 105.

43. Dehouve 1990:61 and map 11.

44. Sahagún 1961:187 (book 10, chap. 29). For Cohuixco, see n.35 above.

45. Galarza 1972:24; Dehouve 1976:138, 146, 152.

46. Codex Mendoza, 13r. It is Acatl iyacac in AC (p. 67). There is another Acatepec in the "Memorial de Tlacopan" (7.2-15).

47. ATl, sec. 67. The Codex Mendoza (15v) gives Tlachinolticpac, which would be better identified with Tlanchinol, Hidalgo, near Metztitlan; it is named in SV, secs. 516 (as Tlachinolticpac) and 267 (as Tanchinoltiquipaque). Cf. Gerhard 1986:189–92. The AC (p. 68) give in its place Tlatlayan. All three names could be alternate readings of the same glyph. Barlow (1990:122) identifies Tlatlayan with Tlatlayapan to the south of Yancuitlan. Of the conquests of Moteuczoma Xocoyotzin, some writers have located Malinaltepec and Citlaltepec in Guerrero (Kelly and Palerm 1952:311, 313; Harvey 1971:612, fig. 8). I prefer to identify Malinaltepec with Yucuañe, near Tlachquiauhco (see p. 311). Citlaltepec is mentioned in the ATl (sec. 67), not agreeing with the other lists, which give Zacatepec, and it is difficult to identify. The interpretation of Kelly and Palerm of the Citlaltepec in the Codex Mendoza is not relevant here, since it is based on the page (17v) that depicts not Moteuczoma's conquests but the military district of the Basin. It is possible that there were more conquests in this region, since there had been an expansion to the Costa Chica, described below on p. 327–29.

48. SV, sec. 28; RG 3:284, 288, 289.

49. For the connection between Atzoyoc and Tlappan, see RO, 105; Toscano 1943; and Vega 1991.

50. Codex Mendoza, 8r; AC, 67.

51. Ixtlilxochitl 1975–77, 1:446; 2:108. That author's spelling is not consistent; he writes Tlauh-cocauhtitlan (1:108), Tlalcotzauhtitlan (1:383), and Tlalcozuauhtitlan (1:446).

52. Durán 1967, 2:307. Later it is mentioned as a conquest of Moteuczoma Xocoyotzin (AC, 68), but the Codex Mendoza (16r) gives in its place Tecozauhtla, which could be located in the area of Xilotepec. If it concerns this town of the Balsas, it is possible that Moteuczoma then assumed all rights to this tributary province in the same way that he took for himself the tribute from the Chinampan that previously had gone to Tetzcoco. See p. 172.

53. Barlow 1949b: 84.

54. AC, 67; Codex Mendoza, 8r. In Torquemada (1975–83, 1:218–19) it is spelled Cuauhteopan.

55. Durán 1967, 2:307.

56. Codex Mendoza, 8r; AC, 67; Ixtlilxochitl 1975–77, 1:446.

57. RG 2:129, 135. This information comes from the relación of Cuahuitlan, which treats primarily towns on the coast. Icpatepec is in the lists of conquests of Moteuczoma; its glyph in the Codex Mendoza (15v) is a ball of yarn or a warping frame. Durán (1967, 2:407) and Tezozomoc (1975:581) record the conquest of Icpatepec and Nopallan. See also Torquemada 1975–83, 1:293; Chimalpahin 1889:183 (with Tlachquiaiuhco and Nopallan); AC, 61; ATl, sec. 285. According to the Codex Telleriano-Remensis (42v), the Mexicas conquered Icpaltepec (*sic*). However, the glyph is a skein of thread, as in the glyph of Cuatzontepec. See p. 310 on the province of Coyolapan.

58. A. de los Reyes (1976:89) writes: "Tuctla, Yucuyaa, ñuuhuiya." Tuctla, Tutla, and Teutla can easily be understood as variant spellings for Teuctlan. Cf. Gerhard 1986:135.

59. In the lists of conquests of Moteuczoma Xocoyotzin, Teuctepec appears with Achiotla, Ço-çollan and Nochiztlan, which agrees with the identification suggested here. Cf. Torquemada 1975–83, 1:289; Chimalpahin 1889:176–77; Codex Telleriano-Remensis, 42r; AC, 60. Tezozomoc spells this toponym Tuctepec, but he also refers to its people as "Teuctepecas" (1975:625, 627). The Codex Mendoza (15v) records its conquest; in Nazareo's list it is written Teotepec (Zimmermann 1970:26). It has also been identified with a town near Coatlan, south of the valleys of Oaxaca; see below the discussion on paragraph 7.4 of the "Memorial de Tlacopan."

60. Durán 1967, 2:407; Tezozomoc 1975:581; Chimalpahin 1889:183, with Icpatepec and Tlach-quiauhco. There are towns named Nopallan in Tamazolapan and in Ixcatlan (Gerhard 1986:297, 317). The legend in the Codex Mendoza gives Xoconochco, which must be a divergent reading of the glyph that also signifies Nopallan. There is another Nopallan in the coastal area of Oaxaca. The possible conquest of this town is discussed on p. 331.

61. RG 2:279–324. The data in Herrera (1947, 9:198) on these towns undoubtedly comes from this relación.

62. RG 2:284, 287.

63. Ibid., 293, 295.

64. Ibid., 306–08.

65. Reyes 1976:91; notes by Acuña in RG 2:306n. 38; 3:282n. 1.

66. Codex Mendoza, 13v; AC, 67; ATl, sec. 64.

67. Codex Mendoza, 15v; Tlalotepec in ATl, sec. 67; Quiauhtepec in AC, 67. Sahagún (1954:3 [book 8, chap. 1]) and the Codex Telleriano-Remensis (43r) also give Iztactlalocan. Barlow (1990:119) identifies this Quiauhtepec with Quiotepec, in the Cuicatec region, but this is not possible. Quiotepec is not a corruption of Quiauhtepec but is derived from *quiyotl* (stalk), as explained in the relación of Quiotepec (RG 2:235).

68. RG 2:300, 302. Note that the author of the relación gives the same information on this town and on Xicayan almost word for word.

69. Torquemada 1975–83, 1:296.

70. RG 2:313, 314.

71. Durán 1967, 2:205. See p. 337 on Tochtepec. Barlow (1990:115, 137, and map following 134) identifies Poctlan with Teopochtla, conquered by Ahuitzotl according to the list in AC, 67; however, he also suggests locating Teopochtla in Santa María Teopoxco, near Teotitlan del Camino (1990:

87–88). Xiuhteczacatlan corresponds to Teopochtla in the Codex Mendoza (13r) and Zozollan in ATl (sec. 64). Herrera (1947, 9:198), in his description of the Mixteca, writes of "Patonala [*sic*] . . . and Tecomastla and Puctla, in the bishopric of Guaxaca [*sic*] where Montezuma had a garrison." The garrison must be that of Huaxyacac, but one could interpret this text to mean it was in Poctlan.

72. RG 2:319, 320.

73. Codex Mendoza, 6r; Ixtlilxochitl 1975–77, 2:107.

74. The war began in 6 Tochtli 1445 when Ilhuicamina requested the Chalcas to provide stone for the construction of the temple of Huitzilopochtli; it ended in 12 Calli 1465 (Chimalpahin 1889:113, 126–27).

75. Torquemada 1975–83, 1:227.

76. Tezozomoc 1975:305.

77. Codex Mendoza, 7v. Cf. Torquemada 1975–83, 1:227. Mount Chiconquiauhtepetl is mentioned in Chimalpahin 1889:83 (Nahuatl text) and 1987:85. The hacienda (or ranch) of San José Chiconquiahua or Chiconquiahuit is found in the municipio of Tlalmanalco (Colín 1966: secs. 427 and 484 and p. 420). For the hacienda and the mountain, see the map in García Mora 1981: fig. 1. Mamalhuaztepec is spelled Mamalhuazyocan in AC, 66; Mamalhuazocan in Torquemada 1975–83, 1:227; and Mamalihuazco in Ixtlilxochitl 1975–77, 1:299. It is the present-day Santiago Mamalhuazuca in Ozumba, Mexico. The Codex Mendoza also includes among the conquests of Ilhuicamina Teteuhtepec, which—given its place in the list—was probably in Chalco, as well as Totolapan and Atlatlauhcan in the Xochimilca region called Cuauhtenco.

78. Chimalpahin 1889:124–25. Siméon translates that they were torn to pieces, but actually they fled because they had condemned to this fate several Chalca lords who had dealt with the Mexicas. Cf. Chimalpahin 1987:132–35.

79. Durán 1967, 2:150; Tezozomoc 1975:304–305.

80. In Amaquemecan three princes kept the town (yeintin tlaçopipiltin yn quipieya altepetl; Chimalpahin 1987:134). In Axayacatl's time "The Chalca noblemen kept the four parts of Chalco . . . ; they were like kings in Amaquemecan" (yn chalca pipiltin yn izquican nauhcan Chalco tlapiayaca . . . ; ca yuhquin tlahtocapouhticatca Amaquemecan); two princes kept (tlapiaya omentin yn tlaçopipiltin) Tzacualtitlan Tenanco. In Tlamanalco four Chalca lords governed as nobles (*pillahtoque*) who received their orders from Axayacatl (Chimalpahin 1889:130, 132).

81. For example, in Chimalpahin 1889:149; 1987:120–21, 124–25; and many other cases in Durán 1967, 2:156ff.

82. Chimalpahin 1889:144–46; see also Chimalpahin 1987:143.

83. Chimalpahin 1889:178. Siméon translates this as "cultivated" instead of "set up boundaries."

84. See the discussion about Cuauhquechollan in the next section, on Tepeyacac, and p. 152 on the Tetzcoca calpixcazgo of Tetitlan. Perhaps Tlacopan also received tribute from Caltecoyan (cf. Table 7-1).

85. Parsons et al. 1982:362–63.

86. Chimalpahin 1889:154, 157, 159–63; 1987:110, 111.

87. "Ynin Chalco tlahtoque oc nahuililhuitique yn Mexico yn moteuhcçauhque" (Chimalpahin 1889:155–56, and another example on 160). Siméon's translation is incorrect; see Chimalpahin 1987:156.

88. Tezozomoc 1949: secs. 272, 273, 300–301; Chimalpahin 1889:212–13.

89. Tezozomoc 1949: sec. 315; Chimalpahin 1889:181.

90. ENE 7:260–61. One must keep in mind that this was written in Chimalhuacan and that the informants were from that town and from Tenanco.

91. On the Chalco region see Ruhnau 1988 and Schroeder 1991.

92. The glyph in the Codex Mendoza and the *Matrícula de tributos* is a head with the top painted red. This agrees with the name Cuatlatlauhcan, but the *Relaciones geográficas* says the name means red eagle, which would be Cuauhtlatlauhcan. This is the way the HTCh (sec. 403) writes the name in a report cited below.

93. The *Suma de visitas* identifies as Coatlalpaneca towns Epatlan (sec. 248), Itzocan (sec. 292), Te-

pexoxoma (sec. 540), Tlatequetlan (sec. 213), Tlilapan (sec. 542), and Teopantlan (sec. 559). Tezozomoc (1975:609) tells us that when Moteuczoma Xocoyotziun returned from the conquest of Tototepec, he was welcomed in Itzocan by the "Huehuetecas mexicanos settled there, and Tepapateca, Tlatlapanalan, Chietlan named coatlalpanecas." This "province" of Coatlalpan coincides with the region settled by the Nonocalcas, according to the HTCh (Kirchhoff 1940).

94. Durán 1967, 2:161–62; Tezozomoc 1975:309.

95. Torquemada 1975–83, 1:228.

96. In the "Historia chichimeca," Ixtlilxochitl (1977, 2:107, 109) attributes the conquest of Tepeyacac and other towns to Nezahualcoyotl before relating the death of Itzcoatl and the succession of Moteuczoma in an incomplete passage. Later, he mentions again the conquest of several of those towns, but without naming Tepeyacac. Nor does he cite Tepeyacac among the conquests made together with Ilhuicamina in the "Sumaria relación de la historia" (1:544).

97. HTCh, sec. 355; Carrasco 1948b.

98. Kelly and Palerm 1952:291–95.

99. AC, 53, 67; HTCh, secs. 369–87.

100. Scholes and Adams 1957:50, 83.

101. Durán 1967, 2:334; see table 13-2. For the location of Acapetlahuacan, see Motolinía 1971: 269 and RG 5:209. The present-day names of the other towns are: Atzitzihuacan, Puebla, and Hueyapan and Tlamimilulpan in Tetela del Volcán, Morelos. Yaotehuacan has not been identified.

102. RG 7:267.

103. Durán 1967, 2:444.

104. RG 7:85.

105. Ibid., 5:226.

106. Tezozomoc 1949: sec. 268; AC, 63.

107. For the various regions in this province, see Martínez 1964 on Tepeyacac, Paredes 1991 on the Coatlapanec region of Itzocan, Reyes García 1977 on Cuauhtinchan, Olivera 1978 on Tecalli, and Jäcklein 1978 on Tepexic.

108. RG 5:69, 73, 77, 83; SV, secs. 120, 521.

109. SV, sec. 248.

110. Tezozomoc 1949: sec. 200. In this source the name is Tepexic Mixtlan. The marriage is also described in a document concerning Don Gonzalo Montezuma Mazatzin, the king who helped the Spanish, prepared by his grandson Don Joaquín de San Francisco Montezuma (AGI, Patronato 245, ramo 10).

111. HTCh, sec. 403.

112. AGN, Tierras 2697, exp. 58, book 2, fol. 2r. There are some suspicious points in this documentation, which is a copy made in 1788.

113. AC, 52.

114. Codex Mendoza, 12r.

115. AGN, Tierras 2697, exp. 58, book 2, fol. 6r. It was an estancia of Don Gonzalo Mazatzin of Tepexic in 1533. In the eighteenth century it was San Martín Atezca in the district (partido) of Tepeji de la Seda.

116. These towns are discussed below in connection with secs. 7.2 and 7.3 in the "Memorial de Tlacopan."

117. RG 5:233–34.

118. Tepexic ("Memorial de Tlacopan," 7.2-13) could be an exception, but given the context of that list it must be Tepejillo in the Mixteca and not the Tepexic in the province of Tepeyacac.

119. See below, p. 322, on paragraph 7.4 of the "Memorial de Tlacopan."

120. Their patron god was Ometochtli, and therefore the pulque god Totoltecatl must have been the patron of Piaztlan and of this "province" (RG 5:32, 34, 57, 58). The god Totoltecatl is mentioned in Sahagún (1958:106–107, 142–43). Totollan as a specific town has not been identified, but the name occurs in other documents from this region. Tetellan and Hueyapan, south of Popocatepetl, obtained salt from Piaztlan, Chiauhtlan, Chilapan, and Totollan (RG 7:270), and farther west, Tetellan (Tetela del

Río, Guerrero) waged war with Totollan, "which is towards Zumpango" (RG 6:311). Among Ahuitzotl's conquests there is a town called Totollan in the AC (p. 67) and Huexolotlan in other lists (Codex Mendoza, 13r). Huexolotlan was also a conquest of the second Moteuczoma (Codex Mendoza, 16r). In the modern toponymy there is a hamlet called Cuapexco y Totola in the municipio of Atlixtac, Guerrero.

121. Torquemada (1975–83, 1:228) and Ixtlilxochitl (1977, 2:110) put the conquest of Piaztlan and Acatlan together with that of other towns difficult to identify. There is also a Piaztlan conquered by Moteuczoma Xocoyotzin (Codex Mendoza, 15v; AC, 67), but it could be the one in Pánuco (SV, sec. 452; Gerhard 1986:219, 222).

122. RG 5:57.

123. Tezozomoc 1975:477.

124. Durán 1967, 2:185–86, 195.

125. Tezozomoc 1975:338. He says the same about Cuetlaxtlan and gives it as a general practice (333).

126. Torquemada 1975–83, 1:222–23. Torquemada writes Tepzol, Tzapotla (as two words). Teuhçoltzapotla was in the province of Cuauhtochco (Codex Mendoza, 48r).

127. Codex Mendoza, 7v. The death of Cuauhtlatoa of Tlatelolco (6r) is another example.

128. AC, 51.

129. Seler 1902–23, 2:52; Jiménez Moreno 1940:9.

130. RG 2:49.

131. AGI, Escribanía de cámara, 162A. See below on Tecomatlan.

132. Durán 1967, 2:341.

133. There is not enough space here to cite all the conquests. Many towns are difficult to locate, and there is no documentation on the conditions of their subjection to the Empire. See the data compiled in Kelly and Palerm 1952:301–317; Barlow 1990: chaps. 13 to 15; and especially Tschohl 1964.

134. RG 3:220–21.

135. Ibid., 245.

136. Herrera 6:326.

137. Codex Mendoza, 12r.

138. RG 2:367. Nocheztlan was conquered by Moteuczoma Xocoyotzin (Codex Mendoza, 15v).

139. RG 3:232–33.

140. Ibid., 239.

141. Ibid., 143.

142. Ibid., 148.

143. AGI, Escribanía de cámara, 162A: 531v, 532r. For the relation between Yanhuitlan and Tecomatlan, see Spores 1967:94, 140, 168.

144. RG 2:167–68. The Quiotepec referred to was probably Santiago Quiotepec in the municipio of San Juan Bautista Cuicatlán, Oaxaca, but the present-day San Juan Quiotepec, Oaxaca, in the district of Ixtlán, is not far away.

145. Ibid., 142–44. Cuauhtla is the present-day San Miguel Huautla, Oaxaca.

146. Ibid., 147.

147. Ibid., 150.

148. Ibid., 153.

149. Ibid., 157.

150. Ibid., 48–51. The purchase of tribute in exchange for small blankets is described in the same words as in the relación of Tecuicuilco (see below on p. 309). For tribute acquired through commerce, see also p. 231–32.

151. Ibid., 229, 233.

152. The relación calls this language Quiotla or Quioteca, similar to Mixtec (ibid., 235, 236).

153. Ibid., 236–37. The small blankets, called "tapatíos" in the relación, were the kind used as money.

154. Ibid., 239–40.

155. Ibid., 3:29–30.

156. Ibid., 3:36–37. Tepehuitzillan is also listed in the "Memorial de Tlacopan" (7.2-59) as a tributary of the Empire.

157. Cuauhxilotitlan is also listed in the "Memorial de Tlacopan" (7.2-46).

158. RG 3:46–48.

159. Barlow 1949b: 120.

160. Codex Mendoza, 16r. According to the relación, Eztitlan (present-day Estetla) is derived from *eztli*, "blood." If it were interpreted as Iztetlan, "place of a claw or fingernail," it could be the town of that name conquered by the same Moteuczoma; in the Codex Mendoza (16v) it is written as Iztitlan, and the glyph is a claw.

161. Durán 1967, 2:436–37; Tezozomoc 1975:614–15, 619–20.

162. By Ahuitzotl according to the ATl, sec. 64, but usually Zozollan is given as a conquest of Moteuczoma Xocoyotzin (Ixtlilxochitl 2:179; Codex Mendoza, 15v).

163. Torquemada 1975–83, 1:285–87; cf. Ixtlilxochitl 1975–77, 2:183.

164. Cortés 1973:56, 94.

165. Suárez de Peralta 1990:111. That writer was familiar with the Mixteca area; his brother was the encomendero of Tamazolapan (145).

166. For the political geography and history of the Mixteca, see Dahlgren 1954 and Spores 1967 and 1984.

167. Durán 1967, 2:225–31; Tezozomoc 1975:354–61. The first royal envoys sent to Coatzacualco were four principales accompanied by twenty-eight merchants, according to Tezozomoc. According to Durán, they were messengers who served as couriers and ambassadors. Later, merchants passing through this area discovered the corpses of the envoys and went to Tenochtitlan to report it. Both Durán and Tezozomoc relate this episode. Durán (1967, 2:225) puts the massacre on the way out from Mictlan near Huaxyacac; Tezozomoc (1975:355), in Mictlancuauhtla. Mictlan, in the Valley of Oaxaca, has been confused with Mictlancuauhtla on the coast in the tributary province of Tochtepec. It should be noted that Tezozomoc mentions Otlatlan among those defeated in this war, which could be present-day Otlatitlan, Veracruz, also in the province of Tochtepec.

168. Sahagún 1959:17–19 (book 9, chap. 4).

169. Durán 1967, 2:238. Cf. Tezozomoc 1975:363–64.

170. Durán 1967, 2:231.

171. Tezozomoc 1975:360.

172. Otlatitlan, Veracruz, in the Tochtepec region, is too far away, but—as has been seen—Tezozomoc also puts the death of the Mexican ambassadors in Mictlancuauhtla. The Miahuatecs could perhaps be the people of that name in the isthmus.

173. RGL, 253; see also OM, 273.

174. Kelly and Palerm 1952:276, 278, 305–309, 311–17. On Cuatzontlan, see below on p. 310; for the location of Huilotepec, see p. 343, 348. Tschohl (1964:68–87) discusses the conquests of Ahuitzotl in the Valley of Oaxaca.

175. RG 2:178, 181.

176. Ibid., 214–16. In the "Memorial de Tlacopan," Cuauhxilotitlan is in paragraph 7.2, which includes the towns of the Mixteca, and not in 7.4, which comprises the central valleys.

177. Compare this with the glyphs in the Codex Mendoza for Tlapacoyan (50r) and gold (57r, 70r). Teocuitlatla also occurs on 13v among the conquests of Ahuitzotl, but the glyph represents only gold.

178. In RG 2:269 it is Santa Ana Tacolabacoya. For the various names of this town, see García Martínez (1969:52n. 98, and 137n. 320; Gerhard 1986:90, 92). Forms such as Tacalapacoya, Texquilabacoya, and Teuquilapacoya are corruptions of Teocuitlapacoyan; Tlapacoyan is a simplified form.

179. In the "Memorial de Tlacopan" (7.4-5) it is also written as Octlan. The modern name of Ocotlan in Tzapotec is Lachi tzu; *lachi* means "plain" (Zúñiga 1986:135), *tzu* probably corresponds to the ancient form *nizòo*, which Córdoba (s.v.) gives for wine. The Mixtec name is Ñundedzi, "place of pulque" (Reyes 1976:91). An unidentified Macuiloctlan was conquered by Moteuczoma Xocoyotzin in 1515 (AC, 61), and a barrio of Coaixtlahuacan was also named Octlan (Spores y Saldaña 1975: secs. 149, 154, 156).

180. RG 3:170–72.

181. Ibid., 2:330.

182. Ibid., 3:162. For the Tzapotec state organization, see Whitecotton 1977:127–32.

183. RG 3:79.

184. Ibid., 2:269–71. Iztepec is the present-day Santa Cruz Mixtepec, Oaxaca (296n. 1).

185. Ibid., 335. The modern name is Teotitlan del Valle, Oaxaca.

186. Ibid., 3:256–57. The towns cited are the present-day Tlacolula de Matamoros, Oaxaca, and San Pablo Villa de Mitla, Oaxaca.

187. Ibid., 260.

188. Ibid., 2:252, 255, 256. Itztepexic is the present-day Santa Catarina Ixtepeji, Oaxaca.

189. Ibid., 3:90, 95. These towns are the present-day Teococuilco de Marcos Pérez, San Juan Atepec, Santiago Zoquiapan, and Santa María Jaltianguis (all in Oaxaca). As for the small cloaks, see p. 231 on the tribute goods acquired through commerce.

190. Codex Mendoza, 16v. The "Memorial de Tlacopan" lists in paragraph 7.4 another Xaltianquizco, which can be located near Acapulco, Guerrero.

191. See the map in RG 3:127 and Gerhard 1986:275. Today there is a Huazantlán del Río Cerro del Marqués in San Mateo del Mar, Oaxaca. Guazonteca was the name of the Huave language (RG 3:110). There was another Cuatzontlan in Coatzacualco (RG 2:119). This could be one of the towns that encircled the Mexica merchants in Cuauhtenanco during the reign of Ahuitzotl (Sahagún 1959:3 [book 9, chap. 2]).

192. Durán (1967, 2:417), in the heading of his chapter 55, says it deals with the conquest of Cuatzontlan and Xaltepec, but the text is about Icpatepec and Xaltepec. Tezozomoc (1975:597–99) writes only of Cuatzontlan and does not mention Icpatepec. One might think that it is about Icpatepec and Xaltepec in the Mixteca, but the description of the war, both in Durán (1967, 2:421) and Tezozomoc (1975:599) alludes to the residents of Tecuantepec and other towns in the isthmus. The confusion between Cuatzontla and Icpatepec must have originated in the reading of the glyphs for *icpatl* (thread) and *cuatzomitl* (skein or leashes, "los lisos de la tela" in Molina), although they are quite different in the Codex Mendoza; compare Cuatzontepec in the province of Coyolapan (44r) and Icpatepec, conquest of Moteuczoma Xocoyotzin (15v). The Codex Telleriano-Remensis (42v) records the conquest of Icpaltepec (*sic*) in 1512, but the glyph is a skein, as in Cuatzontepec. The illustration in Durán (1967, 2: plate 40) depicts the war with only one town, whose glyph is hair (*cuatzontli*) above a mountain, that is, Cuatzontepec. For Xaltepec, see p. 346.

193. The "Memorial de Tlacopan" includes in paragraph 7.4 Teotitlan (7.4-3), Tlaliztacan (7.4-7), Coatlan (7.4-9), Cimatlan (7.4-11), and Miahuatlan (7.4-15). See Table 10-3. In paragraph 7.2 are listed Tecuicuilco (7.2-61), in the Sierra Juárez, as well as Coyolapan (7.2-70), Etlan (7.2-69), and Cuauhxilotitlan (7.2-46) of this province in the Codex Mendoza. See Table 10-2.

194. See below the discussion of paragraph 7.4 of the "Memorial de Tlacopan."

195. Torquemada 1975–83, 1:222; Jiménez Moreno 1940:9. See the previous section on Coaixtlahuacan.

196. See the compilation of sources in Kelly and Palerm (1952:311–17). The toponym Malinaltepec is found in various regions. Today this town is known by its Mixtec name, which has led several authors to identify this conquest of Moteuczoma with other towns, especially Malinaltepec, Guerrero.

197. Durán 1967, 2:479–82; Tezozomoc 1975:660–61.

198. Torquemada 1975–83, 1:270–71.

199. Tezozomoc 1975:660; Torquemada 1975–83, 1:271.

200. It could be San Agustín Tlacotepec, east of Tlaxiaco, or perhaps the Acatepec in the municipio de Caltepec, Puebla, which is listed in the "Memorial de Tlacopan" (7.2-15).

201. For the ethnic composition of this region, see Kirchhoff 1940.

202. Muñoz Camargo 1984:176–77. This statement is not trustworthy. These names are part of a list of conquests attributed to Axayacatl, as Ahuitzotl's successor, which includes Huexotzinco and Cholollan.

203. Ixtlilxochitl 2:107. It is a list that also includes Tepeyacac and Coaixtlahuacan.

204. Tezozomoc 1975:532. The relación of Cozcatlan says nothing about subjection to the Empire, but it does not answer questions 14 and 15 on government (RG 5:93–105).

205. RG 3:198.

206. The relación of Acatlan (ibid., 5:31–61) includes descriptions of this town and of Chillan, Petlatzinco, Icxitlan, and Piaztlan. It is obvious that the reports express the same point of view, but they are not copies of each other; there are sufficient differences to make clear that each report really refers to its own town. Piaztlan is discussed in connection with paragraph 7.3 of the "Memorial de Tlacopan," because Durán and Tezozomoc, in their lists of towns that came to Tenochtitlan for Tizoc's inauguration, associate it with Chiauhtlan and the Cohuixca region. Barlow (1990:102, 114) adds Acatlan and Piaztlan to the province of Yohualtepec; Petlatzinco, Chillan, and Icxitlan, to the province of Coaixtlahuacan.

207. RG 5:43.

208. Ibid., 48.

209. Torquemada 1975–83, 1:228; Ixtlilxochitl 1975–77, 2:110.

210. RG 5:35, 36.

211. Ibid., 53. Today it is San Miguel Ixitlán, Puebla.

212. Ibid., 37, 44, 49, 58.

213. Ibid., 3:90, 95.

214. See p. 392 on the imperial garrison near the Coatzacualco frontier.

215. Çomatlan could be Ozomatlan, which was the name of a sujeto of Ohuapan (RG 6:351), but Ohuapan is listed in the "Memorial de Tlacopan" (7.3-12) and was part of the province of Tepecuacuilco. Another possibility is Camotlan, a frequent toponym and a town in the province of Coyolapan in the Codex Mendoza.

216. Sahagún 1954:3 (book 8, chap. 1). However, the Spanish text spells it as Tlaopan (Sahagún 1969b, 2:285).

217. Codex Mendoza, 13r. Cf. p. 357, 384.

218. In Chollollan, Oztoman was a barrio in the cabecera of Tecpan (SV, sec. 114), and the gentile name Oztomeca is used for the merchants who traveled to distant lands.

219. Coçollan (sic) appears four times in the "Memorial de Tlacopan." Two other examples (7.2-35, 7.2-43) have been identified in Table 10-2. There is also Cuecallan (7.3-11), interpreted as Cueçallan.

220. RG 6:109–22; it is also written as Citlaltomahua. For its location, see Gerhard 1986:41.

221. There are other cases of towns with two names, one of which is an abbreviation of the other. Cf. Chontalcoatlan/Coatlan (in Tlachco), Teocuitlapacoyan/Tlapacoyan (in Coyolapan), Tlaltizapan/Tizapan (in Tochpan), and Ayoxochiquillatzallan/Xochiquillatzallan (RG 2:299–305).

222. Xaltianquizco is also the name of a Tzapotec mountain town conquered by Moteuczoma Xocoyotzin. It is mentioned above in the province of Coyolapan.

223. RG 6:309–11. This Totollan is of doubtful identification. See p. 295 on Piaztlan and the "province" of the Totoltecs.

224. Ibid., 9:35, 36. The Suma de visitas also gives the Tarascan name for Capollalcololco, which is Xanineo (place of corn), and confirms that it bordered on Axochitlan. In the eighteenth century it was called Tehuehuetla (Solano 1988, 2:407), and it is now San Juan Tehuehuetla in the municipio of San Miguel Totolapan.

225. RG 6:300–301. Tlacotepec is today in the municipio of General Heliodoro Castillo, Guerrero.

226. Torquemada 1975–83, 1:295.

227. Codex Mendoza, 13v. The Tlacotepec in the Mixteca and the one on the isthmus are also in regions conquered by Ahuitzotl.

228. RG 6:305–306. See Gerhard 1986:301–302 on Otlatlan.

229. Codex Mendoza, 13r.

230. The SV (sec. 95) gives Opilcingo as one of the towns adjacent to Cacahuatepec.

231. For the extent of the independent Yopis, see Ortega (1940) and Davies (1968:157–73). Barlow (1949b: 20n. 69) refers to Ortega, but in his map Yopitzinco is of greater extent. As Ortega indicates (1940:51–52) the estancias of Chilapan reached as far as Chacalinitla (today a congregación of

Ayutla de los Libres, Guerrero) beside the Omitlan River. Farther west the area not subject to the Empire could have extended towards the north. Tixtla and Mochitlan were founded by a cacique, sent by Moteuczoma, called Tzapoteuctli (RG 5:270), but the people of Tixtla rebelled and fled to the coast (AGI, Justicia 127, no. 1, fols. 195v, 199r, 209v–210r). This suggests that the area not subject to the Empire was more extensive in this direction. Perhaps Cuezalcuitlapillan, which the Mexica did not succeed in subjugating, was in Yopitzinco or its vicinity (Torquemada 1975–83, 1:258).

232. This is what Davies (1968:162) suggests.

233. Motolinía 1971:468. See also Zorita 1941:92.

234. Codex Mendoza, 13r. It is Acatl iyacac in AC (p. 67) and Acatlicpac in Nazareo (Zimmermann 1970:26). There was also an Acatepec near Tototepec, the Mixtec kingdom on the coast (Davies 1968:185). Other possible identifications are Acatepec (in paragraph 7.2-15 in the "Memorial de Tlacopan") and the hill called Acatepec where the Mexica garrison of Huaxyacac was located (RG 3:162).

235. Ayotlan is a very frequent toponym, however. Another Ayotlan on the bank of the Balsas River near Zacatollan (SV, sec. 855) could represent the province of Cihuatlan; it was in the mountains four leagues from La Villa (RG 9:454–55). Another Ayotlan was contiguous with Xamiltepec and Pinotecpan; probably it was part of the Mixtec kingdom of Tototepec (SV, sec. 32). Closer to the Valley of Oaxaca is the Mixe town of San Pablo Ayutla, Oaxaca. Given the scarcity of information, any one of these could be the town named in this paragraph.

236. SV, sec. 28. According to this article (from visita no. 50), Ayotlan had two estancias, Tututepeque and Suchitonala, that paid tribute separately. Visita no. 84 registers again the three towns in different articles: Ayutla (sec. 93), Tututepec (sec. 775), and Suchitonala (sec. 499). The relación of Xalapan (RG 3:284–88) and the RO (pp. 27–28) also describe the three towns as cabeceras.

237. RG 3:285–88. The maritime towns subject to Ayotlan were Cuahuitlan, Cuauhtzapotlan, Cintla, Tepetlapan, Copalitech, Xalapan, and Nexpan. Some of these will be mentioned below as conquests of the Empire.

238. Torquemada 1975–83, 1:296.

239. In the Codex Mendoza (16r) Quetzaltepec and Cuezcomaixtlahuacan are the conquests numbered 34 and 35; Iztactlalocan is number 9 (15v). Sahagún's list (1954:3 [book 8, chap. 1]) includes Iztactlalocan, Quetzaltepec, and Cuezcomaixtlahuacan. Cihuapohualoyan is not in any list of conquered towns.

240. Barlow (1990:125, 126) cites the Itinerario de Apan, Mexican manuscript no. 272 in the Bibliothèque Nacional, Paris. Gerhard (1986:108) identifies Cuezcomaixtlahuacan with Tecomaixtlahuacan, a town north of the present-day Juxtlahuaca, but Sahagún (1954:3 [book 8, chap. 1]) records the two as different conquests. Kelly and Palerm 1952 (316n. 43) put Cihuapohualoyan in the Mazatec region, following map 57 of the Colección Orozco y Berra, but according to H. Cline (1959:634) this map is a copy of the map by Patiño, from the relación geográfica of Veracruz (also published in RG 5:333–36), that does not include such a town.

241. Durán 1967, 2:425–31; Tezozomoc 1975:602–10. The illustration in Durán (1967, 2: plate 41) shows only Quetzaltepec.

242. Davies 1968:198–202; Barlow 1990:107, 117; Hassig 1988:227, 229–30.

243. Codex Telleriano-Remensis, 43r.

244. Codex Mendoza, 13r; AC, 67. ATl (sec. 64) gives Pantlanala. Barlow (1990:83) suggests locating it in Totolapilla, on the Tecuantepec River.

245. Durán 1967, 2:428; Tezozomoc 1975:605.

246. Durán 1967, 2:428. In Tezozomoc (1975:603, 605–606) the place where these towns guarded the road against the Mexicas is Quetzatlypan (Quetzalatl ipan); Quetzalotlytempan (Quetzalatl itempan) is the river.

247. Torquemada 1975–83, 1:296. Tezozomoc (1975:607) alludes to the "neighboring huaxtecs" during the attack on Quetzaltepec, although he says later that the army returned to Tenochtitlan by way of Itzocan. Cf. Sahagún 1954:3 (book 8, chap. 1), who names Cuextlan in his list of Ahuitzotl's conquests between Iztactlalocan and Quetzaltepec. Perhaps there was some confusion with the 1513 war against the Huaxteca, when Quatzalapan (*sic*) was conquered (Torquemada 1975–83, 1:296). This campaign is discussed on p. 378 in regard to Oxitipan.

248. Vega 1991:85–86 and fol. 30.

249. SV, sec. 651.

250. See the topographic map 1:1,000,000 of the Secretaría de Programación y Presupuesto, leaf Ciudad de México.

251. Gerhard 1986:155.

252. The chronicles state that the two towns were east of the Quetzalatl River. According to the proposed location, Tototepec was in the basin of the Nexpan River; more to the east one has to cross two rivers, the Copala and the Marquelia, before reaching the Quetzalatl.

253. Tototepec is found in the Codex Telleriano-Remensis, cited above, and the list of conquests of Moteuczoma in the AC (p. 67) in a position that corresponds to the Huilotepec in the Codex Mendoza (15v). Vega (1991:22 and fol. 12) interprets as Huilotepec the glyph of a town conquered in 1412–18 and identifies it with the Huilotepec conquered by Moteuczoma according to the Codex Mendoza. Quetzaltepec is found in all the lists of conquests and in Sahagún 1954:3 (book 8, chap. 1). In Torquemada it is associated with Cihuapohualoyan in the campaigns of 1514–16. It does not appear in the Codex Telleriano-Remensis, and it is notable that while this codex paints the conquest of Tototepec in 1513 and that of Iztactlalocan in 1515, Chimalpahin (1889:184) registers that of Alotepec in 1513 and in 1514 that of Quetzaltepec and Iztactlalocan. Alotepec seems to be the same, then, as Tototepec. It is possible that *alo* (large parrot) was read instead of *tototl* (bird). In any case, Alotepec is a known toponym; a Mixe town, Santa María Alotepec, curiously very near San Miguel Quetzaltepec, has the same name today. There was also another Alotepec, subject of Guamelula (Gerhard 1986:128–29), described in 1593 as a sujeto of Tututepec, probably the Mixtec kingdom on the coast (Spores and Saldaña 1973: secs. 28, 29, 30). Given the scarcity of data, mistakes in the interpretations of the toponyms, and the existence of several towns with the same name, it is practically impossible to prove or reject any hypothesis that attempts to solve these problems.

254. Codex Mendoza (13r) gives Tepechiapan. AC (p. 67) and ATl (sec. 64) both list Nexpan. The *Leyenda de los Soles* has Xalapan (Tschohl 1989:251). These three names are probably alternative readings of a glyph in which little dots have been read as either chía seeds, lime (*nextli*), or sand (*xalli*). Tepechiapan has not been identified. For the old location of Nexpan and Xalapan, see the relaciones of Xalapa, Cintla, and Acatlan in RG 3:281–94. Modern toponymy offers Jalapa in Cuauhtepec, Guerrero, and Nexpa in Florencio Villareal, Guerrero. The Nexpa River is the principal one in this region. There is also a Nexpan on the Costa Grande fifteen leagues from Zacatollan (SV, sec. 875).

255. Codex Mendoza, 13v; AC, 67. Several toponyms in the lists of conquests have been located by some writers in Guerrero. However, these toponyms are also found in other regions, and it is more likely that the conquered towns listed were not in Guerrero. Thus, Nantzintlan, Huehuetlan, and Mazatlan, conquered by Ahuitzotl, were probably in Xoconochco (Tschohl 1964:177–78), although Kelly and Palerm (1952:306) and Harvey (1971:611, fig. 7) place them in Guerrero. See also note 47 above on the province of Tlappan as regards Malinaltepec and Citlaltepec.

256. RG 2:61–93. Chichicapan is the present-day San Baltasar Chichicapan, in the district of Ocotlán; the other toponyms are found in the district of Miahuatlán, each one in several towns with different appellations and in different municipios. Modern spelling of these names is Amatlán, Miahuatlán, Coatlán, and Ozolotepec.

257. Ibid., 79.

258. Ibid., 83–84.

259. Tezozomoc 1975:625. Barlow (1990:105–106, 117) considered the location of Teuctepec uncertain. Hassig (1988:222–23) puts it in the Chatino region; apparently he identifies it with Santa Lucía Teotepec, Oaxaca. I think Teuctepec can be identified with modern Santa María Tutla in the Mixteca. See above the section on the tributary province of Yohualtepec. The reference to a river and to the sea (Durán 1967, 2:439–40) might be a misunderstanding of the picture of a flood caused by a river named Tozac recorded in Codex Telleriano-Remensis (42r) in the same year as the conquest of Teuctepec.

260. For the inauguration of the Coatlan temple, see p. 410–11.

261. RG 2:88–90.

262. Ibid., 66–67.

263. Ibid., 70.

264. For the Peñoles, see p. 303. Kelly and Palerm (1952) suggest other locations of the conquests of Moteuczoma Xocoyotzin that are not at all certain. See also Barlow 1990 and Hassig 1988. The best discussion of the problems in identifying these conquests is that of Tschohl (1964:124–58).

265. For the Tototepec kingdom, see Davies 1968 and Spores 1993.

266. RG 2:131, 132. These towns are described in the *Suma de visitas:* Cuahuitlan (sec. 480) and Potutla (sec. 455) disappeared in the eighteenth century (Gerhard 1986:391), but there is still today a ranch called Cahuitán in Santiago Tapextla, Oaxaca. Pinoteca (sec. 454) is today Santiago Pinotepa Nacional, Oaxaca, and Pinoteca la Chica (sec. 456) is Pinotepa de Don Luis, Oaxaca. Icpatepec, a town in the Mixteca Baja, is discussed on p. 281 with the tributary province of Yohualtepec.

267. RG 2:189, 203.

268. Codex Ramírez 1975:68. Tschohl (1964:20–29) analyzes in detail the history of this report, which originated in the Codex Cozcatzin.

269. The Nopallan in the Mixteca has been discussed above in connection with the tributary province of Yohualtepec. The Codex Telleriano-Remensis (42v) registers its conquest, together with that of Quimichtepec, in 7 Tecpatl 1512, and the legend states "that they are towards the province of Tototepec." Torquemada (1975–83, 1:295) notes the war against Nopallan in the eleventh year of Moteuczoma Xocoyotzin but does not say where it was; this might refer to the same town as that in the Codex Telleriano-Remensis. Quimichtepec is found in the lists of conquests (Codex Mendoza, 16r), but its location is uncertain.

270. AC, 65. The text is not complete; it ends with a series of glyphs that are not explained. See Bierhorst 1992:134.

271. Something similar occurs with the provinces of Tziuhcoac and Tochpan in the Codex Mendoza. In the Tetzcoca sources and the "Memorial de Tlacopan" each of the towns in these two provinces heads a list of towns.

272. In the discussion that follows, the number in parentheses after a toponym indicates its position in the list of the Codex Mendoza.

273. The town now called Mixistlan is spelled Mixitlan in the sources (RO, 67, 73).

274. RG 2:101–102. See the citation below.

275. Barlow 1949b: 93–94.

276. SV, sec. 281. According to the RO (pp. 65–67, 82), the other "nations" of Villa Alta were the Caxones, the Benecichas, the Bixanas—three Tzapotec groups—and the Mixes. The identity of the Guatinicamames (or Guatinicamanes) and the Chinantecs of Villa Alta is obvious, because the list of the two groups of towns is given and they are practically the same. The Chinantec towns in Villa Alta were Lachixila, Lobani, Petlapa, Tuavela, Yaci, Teutalcingo, Lacoba, and Lalana. The Guatinicamames were Ycisi [*sic*], Coban, Lalana, half of Teutalcingo, Toabela, Tlapa [*sic pro* Petlapa], and Lachixila which is an encomienda. Teotalcingo still exists in the municipio of Santiago Choapan. San Juan Lalana is another municipio that also includes Asunción Lacova. San Juan Petlapa is the cabecera of the municipio that also includes San Juan Tovela and Santa María Lovani. Asunción Lachixila is in the municipio of Santiago Camotlan. Yaci (Ycisi is probably a mistaken reading of Yasi) is the present-day Santiago Jocotepec (Chance 1989:14).

277. Cortés 1973:56, 128–29. See also Díaz del Castillo 1964:186, 210, 305. López de Gómara (1988:128) gives a similar report but mistakenly writes Tututepec for Tochtepec.

278. See Weitlaner 1961 and Barlow 1990:179–80 on Coatlicamac and the Guatinicamames.

279. SV, sec. 392; RO, 66, 73; Cortés 1973:56–57. The lists of conquests of Moteuczoma Xocoyotzin include a Malinaltepec (Codex Mendoza, 16r), but it must be the one near Tlachquiauhco, present-day Yucuañe.

280. Sahagún 1954:51 (book 8, chap. 17); 1975:58 (book 12, chap. 21).

281. RO, 67, 81.

282. Díaz del Castillo (1964:361–63, 424) does not locate it precisely; he says that he arrived at Guazpaltepec, during a trip from Ahuilizapan to Coatzacualco, before crossing a wide river, after which he went to Uluta (in Coatzacualco [RG 2:119], present-day Oluta, Veracruz). Motolinía also gives an approximate location of this "province"; he describes the rivers that flow into the Papaloapan

and gives the name Cuauhlcuezpaltepec (*sic*) to a river between the Chinantlan and Tuxtlan rivers; it must therefore be the Tesechoacán River. He also says that the so-called Estero de Dios in the Papaloapan River was the boundary between Otlatitlan and Cuauhcuetzpaltepec (Motolinía 1971:229, 230). See Gerhard (1986:88–89, 377–80) on the vicissitudes of Guazpaltepec during the colonial period.

283. Díaz del Castillo 1964:59.

284. Cortés 1973:57–58.

285. Ixtlilxochitl 1975–77, 2:107, 109. It has been noted above on p. 479n.96, in connection with Tepeyacac, that the conquests Ixtlilxochitl attributes to Nezahualcoyotl and Itzcoatl are assigned by other sources to Ilhuicamina.

286. Torquemada 1975–83, 1:223.

287. Ibid., 258.

288. Codex Mendoza, 16v; Sahagún 1954:3 (book 8, chap. 1).

289. RG 2:101–102.

290. Ibid., 3:271–72.

291. Ibid., 5:284.

292. Ibid., 291.

293. Sahagún 1959:17, 22, 48–49, 51 (book 9, chaps. 4, 5, 10, 11).

294. Ixtlilxochitl, 1977 1:498. Sahagún apparently excludes the Tetzcoca merchants from the expeditions to the coast.

295. Ixtlilxochitl (1977, 2:107–108) also gives a list of tribute goods similar to those in the Codex Mendoza, but he also includes labor for cultivating a cacao plantation (in addition to cacao beans as tribute) and the provision of nursemaids and servant women for the palace.

296. Tschohl (1964:88–123) has treated in detail the conquest and extent of Xoconochco. See Gerhard (1979) for the identification of the towns. More recent studies are those of Rojas (1989) and Voorhies (1989). Gasco and Voorhies (1989:80) enumerate the documents of several archives that mention the towns of Xoconochco province as listed in the Codex Mendoza, but they do not take into account the other towns in the "Memorial de Tlacopan" and the lists of conquests.

297. Barlow 1949b: 94; 1990:83 and maps, pp. 125, 134.

298. Codex Mendoza, 15v; AC, 67. Cf. Barlow 1990:107. See p. 327–29 on the Tototepec conquered by Moteuczoma Xocoyotzin.

299. SV, sec. 832 (Xaltepeque), sec. 392 (Malinaltepeque).

300. RG 2: map following p. 126. This would place Xaltepec in the area of present-day Jesús Carranza, Veracruz. Two towns in this area (Coapiloloyan in Hidalgotitlan, Veracruz, and Coapiloloyita in Jesús Carranza, Veracruz), might be the Cuappilollan conquered by Ahuitzotl (AC, 67; Codex Mendoza, 13v), as suggested by Kelly and Palerm (1952:304–307). However, Torquemada (1975–83, 1:258) reports this conquest in an account that starts with the conquest of Cozcacuauhtenanco (in Matlatzinco; see p. 253, 262), although it is not clear in his text whether he is still talking about the same area. In Codex Mendoza, Cuappilollan is depicted next to towns in the isthmus.

301. AGI, Contaduría 972A.

302. SV, sec. 396.

303. Durán 1967:357; Tezozomoc 1975:537, 599. There was a Miaguatlan in the mountain Tzapotec area, in the partido of Taua, that is, the present-day San Juan Tabaa, Oaxaca, in the district of Villa Alta (SV, sec. 396), and a Miautlan (*sic*) in Coatzacualco (RG 2:119).

304. In the "Memorial de Tlacopan" it is written Mapachtepec Atlan Omitlan, without commas to separate the names, although this manuscript usually separates all toponyms with commas. The Florentine Codex, in a series of gentile names given below, writes Atlan Omitlantlaca.

305. SV, sec. 501.

306. RG 1:178–79.

307. Pineda in ibid., 264. For the distribution of the languages, see Voorhies 1989:8–11.

308. Codex Ramírez:68; Torquemada 1975–83, 1:239. Coatolco (Guatulco) and its surrounding area were part of the Mixtec kingdom of Tototepec.

309. Tezozomoc 1975:354–61.

310. Sahagún 1959:3 (book 9, chap. 2). The gentile names have been changed to place-names with the spelling favored in this book.

311. Another Cuatzontlan in Coatzacualco (RG 2:119) was not part of Anahuac Ayotlan.

312. RGL, 253; OM, 272.

313. Durán 1967, 2:357–61; Tezozomoc 1975:537–44.

314. Durán 1967, 2:383–89; Tezozomoc 1975:550–58. The lists of conquests include more towns, some of doubtful location (Codex Mendoza, 13v; AC, 67). See also Barlow 1990:81–84.

315. Codex Mendoza, 13v. This could be a first attack on the Tototepec on the Costa Chica, conquered later by Moteuczoma. ATl (sec. 64) gives Pantlanala in its place; it is probably Patlanallan (Place of Wings) in the province of Yohualtepec. Its glyph is a bird with its wings spread; it may have been confused with that of Tototepec.

316. Durán 1967, 2:417–22; Tezozomoc 1975:597–600. For Cuatzontlan in the province of Coyolapan, see p. 310.

317. AC, 68; Codex Mendoza, 14r.

318. Barlow 1990:107.

319. Tribute from Tecuantepec passed through Tlachquiauhco en route to Tenochtitlan (Tezozomoc 1975:661). See the quotation in the section on Tlachquiauhco on p. 310–11.

320. RG 3:114–15.

321. Durán 1967, 2:421–22.

322. AGI, Justicia 1029, no. 10, fol. 6r.

323. Durán 1967, 2:419. This king of Tlacopan was Tlaltecotzin, according to Tezozomoc (1975: 597–98), which must be another name for the second Totoquihuatzin.

324. See chapter 12 about the Cuatzacualco frontier.

325. Chiappan, a conquest of Ahuitzotl, is the present-day Chiapa de Corzo, Chiapas, according to Barlow (1990:80, 90, 92, 130, 137). The war may have been carried that far, but what the chronicles describe is a campaign against the Otomis of Chiappan and Xilotepec.

326. Díaz del Castillo 1964:167. See the quotation on p. 393.

327. Díaz del Castillo 1964:387–88; Herrera 1947, 9:315–16; Remesal 1964:376. Tschohl (1964: 181–90) treats this subject in more detail and cites later sources that demonstrate the independence of Chiappan.

328. In the Codex Mendoza the glyph for Huitztlan is the same on the page depicting Xoconochco (47r) and among the conquests of Moteuczoma (15v). Xoconochco is also on this page of Moteuczoma's conquests, but the other versions of the lists of conquests give Nopallan in its place.

329. Their present-day names are Huixtla, in Soconusco, and Huistán, in Los Altos.

330. Köhler 1978:69.

331. Pantepec is listed in the "Memorial de los pueblos de Tlacopan" (7.1-27), and Tecpatlan was near Xoxopanco (RG 5:166).

332. Codex Mendoza, 13v.

333. Sahagún 1959:18 (book 9, chap. 4).

334. Note, for example, some that are cited in other parts of this study: Ixhuatlan, Quetzaltepec, Mixtlan, Chinameca (cf. Chinantlan), Miautlan (cf. Miahuatlan), Mazatlan, Soconusco, Michoacan, and Cuazontla (RG 2:118–19). At times it is impossible to decide to which town a document refers.

335. Cortés (1973:57–58) writes "Mazamalco o Cuacalcalco"; cf. Díaz del Castillo 1964:185–86.

336. Münch 1983:24–25.

337. Kelly and Palerm (1952:308) include Coatzacualco among the conquests of Ahuitzotl. But this town cannot be considered as conquered; Tezozomoc (1975:538) says that Coatzacualco was one of the towns (such as Xoconochco, Chinantlan, and Ayotlan) that prepared for war at the same time as Xochtlan, Amaxtlan, Izhuatlan, and Xolotlan, but he gives as conquered only the towns on the Pacific coast (Tezozomoc 1975:383–89). Durán (1967, 2:383–89) never mentions Coatzacualco in this war.

338. Durán 1967, 2:389.

339. Crónica de Itzcuin-Nehaib, in Recinos 1957:79; Título de Totonicapan 1983:200 and 264n. 359.

340. Memorial de Sololá 1950:117. Cf. Crónica de Itzcuin-Nehaib in Recinos 1957:84.

341. Muñoz Camargo 1984:184; Torquemada 1975–83, 1:299–300.

342. Gerhard 1986:86.

343. Santiago Huatusco was still a town and municipio in 1921. H. Cline (1961:646) identifies it with the town called Tucho in the map of the relación geográfica of Veracruz (cf. RG 5:335 and map). The town written Guatusco in this map is obviously San Antonio (RG 5:334). On the other hand, the Guatusco mentioned as located four leagues from Cuetlaxtlan in the relación of this town was obviously Santiago (RG 5:295).

344. Medellín Zenil 1952.

345. Codex Mendoza, 17v; LT, 124, 424–28. H. Cline (1961:648 and 674n. 62) identifies the Guacultenango in the map of the relación of Veracruz with Xaltenango in the municipio of Coscomatepec, Veracruz, and with Cachul Tenango (*sic*) in the LT. Cf. Quacultenango in RG 5:334 and map.

346. LT, 586. Torquemada (1975–83, 1:223) writes it in two words, Tepzol Tzapotlan. The *Matrícula de tributos* has only the glyph without a legend.

347. Relación sacada 1940:206, no. 64.

348. This Isteyuca, the Itzteyocan in the Codex Mendoza, should not be confused with the Istayuca that in the same LT (p. 586) is "Ystaiuca, also known as Pucta, in Veracruz, at Río de Alvarado." See p. 337.

349. Gerhard 1986:86.

350. Aguilar 1938:97. Cortés (1973:199) writes that he moved Medellín to a new site twenty leagues inland "in the province of Tatactetelco." The city of Medellín asked for the town spelled Tatatelco in 1525 (ENE 1:84). In colonial tribute documents Tatatetelco is located in the area of the Alvarado River (ENE 9:37). Zonguiluca (Tzoncoliuhcan) bordered on Tlatlatelco (SV, sec. 843). Torquemada (1975–83, 1:223) spells it Tlatlactetelco. In the modern toponymy Tlaltetela is a town in the municipio of Axocuapan, Veracruz.

351. RG 5:335n. 45 and map.

352. Mota y Escobar 1939–40:207.

353. Durán 1967, 2:182–83; Tezozomoc 1975:333.

354. Durán 1967, 2:197–99. More importance is given to the intervention of Tlaxcallan and the other tramontane kingdoms in Tezozomoc (1975:343ff.), ATl (secs. 269–72), and Torquemada (1975–83, 1:224). According to the last, the towns of Cuetlaxtlan had been founded by Tlaxcaltecs.

355. Tezozomoc 1975:348–49.

356. Durán 1967, 2:202–203.

357. Torquemada 1975–83, 1:225.

358. RG 5:295.

359. Durán 1967, 2:247; Tezozomoc 1975:370–72. The relación of Huaxtepec states that Moteuczoma Ilhuicamina ordered plants to be brought when they set out to conquer towns in the direction of Chiappan and Veracruz (RG 6:201).

360. Sahagún 1975:5 (book 12, chap. 2). Tezozomoc (1975:684) also calls Pinotl the calpixque who welcomed the Spanish.

361. In Molina (1970: s.v.): "Pinotlatoa. ni. hablar en lengua estraña" (to speak a foreign tongue); "Tenitl, hombre de otra nación y boçal" (man of another nation, rude). Sahagún 1961:187 (book 10, chap. 29) applies these names to the Popolocas (included in the same paragraph with the Yopis, perhaps by mistake) and the name Pinotl to the Olmecas, Vixtotins, and eastern Mixtecas, probably those of the Cuetlaxtlan region.

362. Durán 1967, 2:181, 200; Tezozomoc 1975:331, 346.

363. Teoixhuacan is today Ixhuacan de los Reyes, Veracruz (cf. RG 5:334, 369). The other towns are the present-day Chichiquila, Quimixtlán, and Zautla, all in Puebla.

364. LT, 276–77; Gerhard 1986:375.

365. Kelly and Palerm (1952:295n. 30a) cite García Payón (p. 303).

366. Kelly and Palerm (1952:295n. 30) cite Barlow (1947:270n. 40) to locate it west of Huatusco.

367. Durán 1967, 2:276; Tezozomoc 1975:325.

368. See the discussion in Kelly and Palerm 1952:269n. 37.

369. Torquemada 1975–83, 1:223.

370. Ixtlilxochitl 1975–77, 2:107. In the Memorial of Don Hernando Pimentel the towns that paid tribute to the three kingdoms of the alliance were Cuetlaxtlan, Cuauhtochco, and Ahuilizapan, together with Coaixtlahuacan and Tepeyacac.

371. Torquemada 1975–83, 1:228; Ixtlilxochitl 1975–77, 1:383, 446; 2:109–10.

372. Codex Mendoza, 10v.

373. Ixtlilxochitl 1975–77, 2:149, 150.

374. Ibid., 155.

375. Codex Telleriano-Remensis (40r) depicts only the glyph of Xicochimalco. The legend also reports the conquest of Aoliçapan (that is, Ahuilizapan), which editors of this codex have misread as Atlicapa or Atizapan. Xicochimalco is a conquest of Ahuitzotl in the Codex Mendoza (13r), but this might refer to another town of the same name in southern Guerrero (see p. 322).

376. According to the Codex Mendoza (48r, 49r); the tribute goods are different in AC (pp. 64, 65).

377. RG 5:315. Xamloluco is obviously Xalcomolco (367, today Jalcomulco, Veracruz); Cotaxtla is Cuetlaxtlan. Espiche, also written as Hospichan (289, 334) is probably the Oxichan in the list of tributary towns in the province of Cuetlaxtlan.

378. Herrera 1947, 9:211–12. Herrera used the *Relaciones geográficas*, but his report differs from the information in RG 5:315.

CHAPTER 11

1. Pomar 1986:47.

2. Ixtlilxochitl 1975–77, 2:107–108. Elsewhere (1:446) he names all these towns but does not distinguish between those conquered by Nezahualcoyotl alone and those conquered by all three kings. Ixtlilxochitl's accounts of the early conquests and the establishment of tributary provinces are discussed in chapter 8.

3. Although these provinces were conquered by Nezahualcoyotl according to Ixtlilxochitl, later they paid tribute to the three capitals. The AC (p. 65), in enumerating the tribute from these provinces, names specifically Nezahualpilli of Tetzcoco, Moteuczoma of Tenochtitlan, and Totoquihuatzin of Tlacopan. Motolinía (1971:395–96) identifies only Nezahualcoyotl.

4. Tetzcoco's share in Tolocan and Mazahuacan has been discussed in chap. 9, and the province of Tlalcozauhtitlan in chap. 10.

5. García Martínez (1987:365–66 and nn. 2, 6) reports that the Tlapacoyan in Puebla was a late colonial settlement of people from Chillan or Chicontlan and suggests that the Tlapacoyan that was the cabecera of this province can be related in some way to Mexicaltzinco. This is another name for Mexcaltzinco, which is in the "Memorial de Tlacopan" (7.1-39). There is another Tlapacoyan in Veracruz that originally was a sujeto of Xalatzinco (PNE 5:248). It is too far from the other towns in this province.

6. In the census it is written Acatzacata and is a barrio of Zautla, Puebla. The 1960 map of the Secretaría de la Defensa Nacional, Hoja Teziutlan, writes Acazacata and places it about five kilometers north of Zautla. In Carrasco 1996:500–501, I reluctantly reported the identification with Zacatlan.

7. Quimichtlan had an extensive territory, because it bordered on Xalapan in the north and on Tepeyacac in the south. It was the original point of a migration that ca. 1380 settled in Xalapan (RG 5:234, 345).

8. Cortés (1973:35) writes Caltanmi for the town I interpret as Tzauctlan (Zautla, Puebla); in a later passage (105) he refers to the towns of Cecatami and Xalatzingo. López de Gómara (1988:167) says that the town was called Zaclotan and the valley, Zacatami; later, he writes Zacatami and Xalacingo for the two towns named by Cortés. Díaz del Castillo (1964:96) calls it Zocotlan. Caltanmi, Cecatami (Zacatami), and Zaclotan (Zocotlan) must all be corrupt forms of Tzauctlan. Xalatzinco was farther to the northeast, but its territory bordered on Tzauctlan; when the Spaniards left Tzauctlan

and Iztaquimaxtitlan for Tlaxcallan, they went through settlements belonging to Xalatzinco (Díaz del Castillo 1964:97, 98). On Xicochimalco (Xico, Veracruz) and Teoixhuacan (Ixhuacán de los Reyes, Veracruz), see p. 384

9. Cortés 1973:36; López de Gómara 1988:69 (postas de hombres en parada hasta México).

10. Muñoz Camargo 1984:104, 152–53, 176. Torquemada (1975–83, 1:381–85) reports the traditional history of the migration of the Totonac and the ruling dynasty of Zacatlan.

11. Durán 1967, 2:265, 337, 339–40, 345.

12. Torquemada 1975–83, 1:384.

13. Tezozomoc 1975:441.

14. RG 5:161–62.

15. Ibid., 407.

16. Muñoz Camargo 1984:183. Tozapan, farther north, is in paragraph 7.1 of the "Memorial de Tlacopan." Torquemada (1975–83, 1:278) in a similar context mentions only Tetellan and Iztaquimaxtitlan.

17. Ixtlilxochitl 1975–77, 1:446, 484; Durán 1967, 2:248. Tlatlauhquitepec is also listed among the conquests of Moteuczoma Ilhuicamina in the Codex Mendoza (8r), AC (p. 67), and Chimalpahin (1987:135). It appears again as a conquest of Moteuczoma Xocoyotzin in Chimalpahin 1889:184.

18. RG 5:385.

19. Ibid., 155.

20. Library of Congress, Kraus Collection, MS 140, fol. 432v.

21. In the AC (pp. 64, 65) and Ixtlilxochitl (1977, 2:107) which describe the tribute from these two provinces, there is no such contrast.

22. See the relación of Fr. Nicolás de Sancto Paulo (ENE 16:56–62).

23. The conquests of these regions are the principal topic of Kelly and Palerm 1952. See also Davies 1968 and Melgarejo 1970.

24. Ixtlilxochitl 1975–77, 2:107. Later, Nezahualcoyotl, together with Ilhuicamina, undertook another war in the Cuexteca area, which was part of his patrimony, but the conquered towns that he enumerates are in other regions (109).

25. Tezozomoc 1975:310, 311; Durán 1967, 2:327. Tamapachco, or Tamachpa as Tezozomoc spells it, is probably the present-day Temapache, Veracruz.

26. See Kelly and Palerm 1952:296–317. Here I name only the towns that are most important and that best illustrate the constant repetition of the same conquests.

27. Codex Mendoza, 12r. Cf. Durán 1967, 2:303–304; Tezozomoc 1975:440–44.

28. Durán 1967, 2:327–28; Tezozomoc 1975:479.

29. Ixtlilxochitl 1975–77, 2:155.

30. Torquemada 1975–83, 1:258.

31. In Molina's dictionary, *muerto* is *micqui* or *micquetl;* the bean (*etl*) in the glyph points to the second form. The pictures of conquests in the Codex Mendoza (10v, 12r) register Miquiyetlan of Axayacatl and Miquetlan of Tizoc; the glyph in both cases is a naked corpse, whose pierced nose indentifies it as either a Totonac or a Huaxtec.

32. Melgarejo (1970:17 and table following 109) identifies Tlaltizapan with Tierra Blanca and Ocelotepec with Zanja del Tigre, hamlets in Tuxpan, Veracruz. Kelly and Palerm (1952:298 and 300n. 21) suggest identifying Ocelotepec with Occentepetl, which is in the lists of conquests in the ATl (secs. 61 and 62). But, *occentepetl* is not a toponym, it means "one other town"; probably it was a text or glyph the writer did not know how to read.

33. Ixtlilxochitl 1975–77, 2:107.

34. Motolinia 1971:395.

35. AC, 65.

36 In his forthcoming edition of the *Matrícula*, Luis Reyes García (n.d.) points out that Motolinía explains that the kings of the three capitals were shown on the top of the document and the tribute depicted in the center. He suggests that the lists of towns could have been depicted on the two sides. Following this idea I suggest that the first part of the list was painted on one side of the painting from top

to bottom and the second part on the other side from bottom to top, so that at the bottom of the document the beginning of Tochpan was next to the end of Micquetlan. It is possible that the scribe of the "Memorial de Tlacopan" read the toponyms along horizontal instead of vertical lines.

37. SV, secs. 449 (Papantlan) and 525 (Tochpan). I keep the spelling of the document.

38. In the map of the Secretaría de Agricultura y Fomento 1930: III-d.

39. RG 5:176–77.

40. LT, 229. The present-day name of this town is Metlaltoyuca, in the municipio of Francisco Z. Mena, Puebla.

41. In the "Memorial de Tlacopan" they are 7.1-25 and 7.1-27. See Table 11-5. In the map of Puebla made by the Comisión Geográfica Exploradora in 1908, and the map of the Secretaría de Agricultura in 1930, leaf "Pachuca," both Atlan and Pantepec are shown in the extreme north of the state. The map drawn by the Departamento Cartográfico Militar for the Comisión Intersecretarial Coordinadora del Levantamiento de la Carta Geográfica de la República, leaf "Pachuca" (1957), puts Pantepec where previous maps put Atlan, and the latter is not in the map. Pantepec is the cabecera of the municipio of the same name. Atlan is not found in the 1980 census of Puebla.

42. SV, sec. 135.

43. See Gerhard (1986:119–24) on the colonial towns and villages of this region. Melgarejo (1970:98) locates Tetzapotitlan in Zapotitlan, formerly a hamlet in Castillo de Teayo.

44. Codex Mendoza, 10v.

45. Chimalpahin 1889:157; 1987:159.

46. Codex Mendoza, 16r.

47. Davies 1968:34. It is spelled Chicoaque in the Codex Telleriano-Remensis (33r). Tezozomoc, in referring to the steward of this province, writes in one case *xiuhcoacatl* but in another *tziuhcoacatl* (Tezozomoc 1975:668, 494). The serpent that is the glyph of Tziuhcoac in the Codex Mendoza (54r) is very different from the *xiuhcoatl* in other codices (Seler 1902–23, 1:841).

48. AC, 64. Macuextlan looks like a good toponym, but it is not documented in other sources. It could be Macuxtepetla, a hamlet in Huejutla, Hidalgo. See also Macustepetla or Macuextepetlapa in Gerhard 1986:149. Given its place in the list and its absence in the other sources, one can think that it was outside Tziuhcoac, the same as Tlapacoyan. It is also possible that the amanuensis of the *Anales de Cuauhtitlan* had copied Tziuhcohuac Macuextlan instead of Tziuhcohuac iuan Cuextlan, that is, Tziuhcoac and Cuextlan; the association of Cuextlan with toponyms of this region occurs in other cases; for examples see Durán 1967, 2:205 and Tezozomoc 1975:318, 325.

49. The analysis of these lists is similar to that of Davies (1968:64), although it differs on several points.

50. SV, secs. 135 (Cicoaque) and 525 (Tuspa).

51. Barlow 1949b: 55; Kelly and Palerm 1952:267n. 32; Davies 1968:34-35; Ekholm 1953:413, 418; Meade 1962, 1:100 cited in Stresser-Péan 1995:103. The pre-Spanish cabecera of Tziuhcoac was moved to Chicontepec at an early date (Gerhard 1986:137).

52. Cf. Davies 1968:33.

53. SV, sec. 135.

54. Melgarejo 1970:66.

55. RG 7:58.

56. SV, sec. 135; Davies 1968:65.

57. RG 7:60. For Metztitlan, see Davies 1968:29-65 and Lameiras 1969.

58. Information on Hueyacocotla and Tototepec is very deficient. They are not mentioned as conquered or as tributaries of the Empire. Hueyacocotla carried on wars with Metztitlan (RG 7:67). See also Davies 1968:56-65.

59. See paragraph 7.1 of the "Memorial de Tlacopan" and Map 11-3. Farther inland, the identification of the Cozcatecutlan in the Codex Mendoza with Coxcatlan, near Tancahuitz in San Luis Potosí, which Barlow proposed, complies with the search for the communication route to the province of Oxitipan in the north, which is discussed below.

60. Ixtlilxochitl 1975–77, 2:107. There seems to have been a copying error in the text that com-

bined the name of the province with that of the steward. In all probability "Tizcohuacalaotl" should be read as "Tziuhcoac a Yaotl."

61. Barlow 1949b: 52. Oxitipan, eight leagues from Valles, bordered on Tanxocon and Tambolon (SV, sec. 424). Davies (1968:65) notes that Tambolon is a ranch in the municipio of Ciudad Valles. Tancanhuitz is the present-day Pedro Antonio Santos.

62. Nazareo in ENE 10:126.

63. Torquemada 1975–83, 1:296.

64. Ibid., 312. On the division between Cacama and Ixtlilxochitl, see Ixtlilxochitl 1975–77, 2:190–92 and Torquemada 1975–83, 1:303–11.

65. Durán 1967, 2:304.

66. Mazacintla was a ranch of Jalpan, Querétaro, in the 1921 census. It is southeast of Jalpan and near the Moctezuma River in the map of the Secretaría de Agricultura y Fomento.

67. Muñoz Camargo 1984:177.

68. Durán 1967, 2:275–76.

69. Cortés 1973:32. Cf. López de Gómara 1988:68.

70. Díaz del Castillo 1964:73, 75. Cf. Torquemada 1975–83, 2:86.

71. AC, 63.

72. Ixtlilxochitl 1975–77, 2:218.

73. García Granados (1952–53: sec. 755) compiles the different sources on this event.

74. Tezozomoc 1975:325.

75. Díaz del Castillo 1964:62–75; López de Gómara 1988:54; Ixtlilxochitl 1975–77, 2:203–204.

76. Díaz del Castillo 1964:77–79; López de Gómara 1988:59. Díaz writes Cingapacinga and López de Gómara, Tizapancinca.

77. RG 5:346, 360.

78. Ibid., 349–70. These towns are Xilotepec, Cuacuauhtzintlan, Chapultepec, Naolinco, Acatlan, Chiconquiyauhco, Colipa, Cihuacoatlan, Tepetlan, Almoloncan, Maxtlatlan, Chiltoyac, Atezcac, Xalcomolco, Coatepec, Xicochimalco, and Ixhuacan.

79. Ibid., 358.

80. Cortés 1973:34; Díaz del Castillo 1964:95.

81. There is another Xicochimalco in paragraph 7.4 of the "Memorial de Tlacopan" which treats of the Valley of Oaxaca and the Pacific coast. The report of Codex Telleriano-Remesis (40r) in 1493 deals probably with the Veracruz town, since it mentions in the same year the conquest of Ahuilizapan. Ixtlilxochitl (1977, 2:148–49) reports the conquest of Ahuilizapan and other towns in the same area by Nezahualpilli, but places the event in 1481. On the other hand the Codex Mendoza (13r) and other lists of conquests might refer to the town named in the "Memorial de Tlacopan" because it is listed with towns in the Pacific coastal area.

82. Cortés 1973:35; Díaz del Castillo 1964:95. The name of this town is written differently in the various sources. Cortes writes Ceyxnacan; Díaz del Castillo, Tejutla; and López de Gómara (1988:68), Theuhixiuacan.

83. RG 5:155, 167. These towns are described separately, but the answer to the question on their government is literally the same. The relación of Hueytlalpan also includes a description of Zacatlan, a town discussed above in the section on Tlapacoyan. Hueytlalpan itself is the same as Teotlalpan in the province of Tlatlauhquitepec in the Codex Mendoza (see Table 11-2).

84. RG 5:171. The two towns are described together.

85. Ibid., 190.

86. Motolinía 1971:206, 322. See the quotation in p. 137.

87. SV, secs. 134, 135, 526. San Diego Tuzapan is north of the San Marcos River near Chicualoque Pass in the Mapa del Estado de Puebla de la Comisión Geográfica Exploradora (1908) and in the 1958 map of the Secretaría de la Defensa Nacional, Hoja Coatzintla.

88. Durán 1967, 2:327–28; Tezozomoc 1975:440–44. Muñoz Camargo (1984:149, 163) and Torquemada (1975–83, 1:360, 370) mention Tozapan as one of the towns settled by the Teochichimecs who came after the Chichimecs of Xolotl and also settled in Tlaxcallan.

89. Torquemada 1975–83, 1:267. Kelly and Palerm (1952:311, 313) report it as conquered by Moteuczoma Xocoyotzin. What they interpret as Huejutla, Hidalgo, is the Huexolotlan of the Codex Mendoza and the AC, but the glyph in Codex Mendoza is a turkey (*huexolotl*) not a willow (*huexotl*), as it would be if the town were Huexotla.

CHAPTER 12

1. See p. 118–19, especially in regard to the data in AC, 53–54.

2. See Table 13-2 and the following commentary on Cuauhquechollan and its subjects.

3. RG 9:217–18.

4. For example, Ixtlilxochitl 1975–77, 2:104, 108, 110, 145, 149, 155, 162, 181, 183.

5. López de Gómara 1988:111. Cf. Torquemada 1975–83, 4:335.

6. Pomar 1986:93.

7. Muñoz Camargo 1984:76–77.

8. Covarrubias [1610]: s.v. *guarnecer*. The definitions of the *Oxford English Dictionary* are worth noting: "garnison: 3. A body of men stationed in a fortress or other place for purposes of defence," and "garrison: 4b. A body of soldiers stationed in a fortress or other place for purposes of defence, etc." The definitions are identical with that of Covarrubias.

9. Gorenstein (1966) and Davies (1987:173–76). Hassig (1984:15–16, 19–20) has refuted the arguments of Gorenstein and Davies.

10. Covarrubias [1610]: s.v. *presidio*. See also Ixtlilxochitl 1975–77, 2:108; Torquemada 1975–83, 1:222, 225, 279, 307, 312. On the relación of Tepecuacuilco, see the quotation given below from RG 6:348.

11. "Parecer de la Orden de San Agustín," in Carrasco 1968:121.

12. Oviedo 1851–55, 3:537.

13. There is a passage in ATI (secs. 13, 14) on Axayacatl's war against Moquihuix of Tlatelolco in which *motetlaquehui* has been translated as "enlist mercenary soldiers" (alistar soldados mercenarios). This is based on the meaning that Molina gives: "tlaqueuia. ninote, alquilar obreros,"(to hire workers); tlaqueualli. alquilado o mercenario" (hired one, mercenary). But he also gives "tlaqueuia. nite. buscar, o alquilar a alguno para que haga mal a otro" (to look for or hire someone to harm someone else) and "tetlaqueualiztica. alquilando, o con traición" (hiring, or by treachery). The context suggests that the enlisted or sought-for persons were those who betrayed the Tlatelolcas, as related in the preceding paragraphs (secs. 10–12). The HMP (p. 237), in a brief description of this war, explains that Moquihuix, according to the wife, said that "he prevailed over the people of Cuetlaxtlan and of Mexico and to do that he hired the neighboring people" (ganó a los de Cotasta y a los de México, y para ello alquilaron los comarcanos). In the *Leyenda de los Soles* there is another text that uses *tlaquehuia* and is difficult to interpret; it is not even clear that it refers to soldiers (*Leyenda de los Soles*, p. 83 in the MS; Velázquez 1945:127; Lehmann 1938:384; Bierhorst 1992a: 159). At other times and in other regions some polities established on their frontiers new settlements with military responsabilities, such as the colonies of Otomis in Tlaxcallan and the Matlatzincas in Michoacan. In Cholollan the Toltec-Chichimecs, after defeating the Olmecs with the help of Chichimecs they had brought in, settled them in towns surrounding Cholollan. The land given to the Chichimecs is described as their *ypatiuh* (payment), which Molina (1970: s.v. *patiuhtli*) translates as "paga, precio de lo que se vende, o soldada" (payment, price of what is sold or salary, soldiers' pay). But the full account of this event shows that it is used in the broad sense of reward, not a soldiers' pay (HTCh, secs. 267–310; cf. Reyes García 1977:24).

14. Weber (1978, 2:1015–20) gives a brief typology of the armies in patrimonial societies. In the classical world, colonists with military obligations (*klerouchoi*) were especially important in the Hellenic period (Tarn 1964:62, 146, 188).

15. Ixtlilxochitl 1975–77, 2:171.

16. These pages are those depicting Citlaltepec with neighboring towns and the garrisons in conquered regions; see the comparison of these documents in chapter 4 and the discussion of Citlaltepec in chapter 5. Berdan at al. (1966) do not consider fols. 17v–18r of Codex Mendoza as a depiction of

military units separate from the tributary provinces. They subsume the towns in these pages in either their tributary or their "strategic" provinces.

17. The place-name glyphs in the Codex Mendoza begin in the upper left-hand corner and are read from top to bottom. If more space is needed, they continue along the lower border towards the right and from there along the right-hand border from bottom to top. In the *Matrícula de tributos* they begin in the lower left-hand corner and continue to the right and then along the right-hand margin from bottom to top. In some cases they continue to the left along the top or form another line, above the first, that is read from right to left; in one case (plate 20) the glyphs of each of the three provinces represented are in vertical lines above the painting of the tribute and are read from botton to top.

18. Folios 21v–22r on Acolhuacan and 24v–25r on Huaxtepec also have to be seen as a unit in the open codex. In 17v and 18r the garrisons are not, strictly speaking, in rows; they occupy the space where in other pages the tribute is depicted. But there is no systematic correspondence between the two codices in regard to the order in which tribute goods are painted, although in general the Codex Mendoza depicts from top to bottom what the *Matrícula* puts from bottom to top.

19. According to some reports, every conquered town received a garrison. The map includes only towns with important fortifications or sizable garrisons of warriors.

20. The glyph for Quecholtetenanco has no legend. It consists of a base of stones (tetl) with a wall (*tenamitl*) on top of it, and above this a quechol (flamingo) feather (*quecholli*) with a red appendage (*tlahuitl*). Barlow (1949b: 128) read this as Quecholtenanco; it should be Quecholtetenanco (or Tlauhquecholtetenanco). In other glyphs of the Codex Mendoza that depict a wall over stones, the legend says Tetenanco (in Tlachco province [36r] and Tepeyacac province [42r]); however, in other sources these towns are usually called simply Tenanco. In this case, Quecholtenanco, as will be seen below, is the form that is found in written documents.

21. See p. 353 on the two settlements called Huatusco.

22. Barlow 1949b: 90.

23. Ibid., 128; PNE 5:277. There was another Quecholtenango north of Itzmiquilpan, probably the same as the Tenanco subject of Metztitlan (SV, secs. 293, 517). It would also be a good place to have a frontier fort.

24. Another entry names Cachultenango together with Tequila and Chichiquila, and places them "en el río de Alvarado" (LT, 424–28).

25. Gerhard 1986:213. But Quecholtenanco is also found in a list of towns that in 1599 had to provide workers for the sugar mill in Orizaba; they are towns located between Quimixtlan and Zongolica (Zavala 1987, 3:263).

26. Tezozomoc 1975:532. It is also possible to see in these settlers of Yancuitlan an antecedent for the garrison of Zozollan.

27. H. Cline 1961:648.

28. Medellín 1952:18 and map on p. 20.

29. Clavijero 1982:228.

30. Durán 1967, 2:177–83, 197–203; Tezozomoc 1975:325–33, 343–49; Codex Mendoza, 8r.

31. RG 5:315.

32. Codex Mendoza, 37r. There is a relación geográfica for Oztoman (RG 6:281–91). See p. 322 on its position in the "Memorial de Tlacopan."

33. There was a Poctepec (RG 6:314) subject to Cuetzallan, a town in the province of Tepecuacuilco; another Poctepec was a sujeto of Tetela in the same region (309).

34. Torquemada 1975–83, 1:218; Ixtlilxochitl 1975–77, 1:383; 2:109.

35. AC, 67; Codex Mendoza, 10v.

36. Tezozomoc 1975:521–36; Durán 1967, 2:347–55. See p. 270 on the conquest of Oztoman.

37. Durán 1967, 2:238–39; Tezozomoc 1949: sec. 202; 1975:363–64. See p. 305–307 on the conquest of Huaxyacac.

38. Codex Mendoza, 15v; Durán 1967, 2:436–37.

39. Codex Mendoza, 10v (Axayacatl); Chimalpahin 1987:159 (Ahuitzotl).

40. López de Gómara (1988:91, 94) tells of thirty thousand men, in Moteuczoma's garrisons two

leagues from Cholollan, who came from Acacingo and Azacan. This Azacan must be a copying error; Cortés (1973:46) says Acacingo and Yzcucan (*sic pro* Itzocan).

41. Sahagún 1963:4 (book 11, chap. 1); 1969b, 3:223. Tschohl (1964:164, 184) has noted this location of Atzaccan.

42. LT, 346.

43. RG 2:118, 121.

44. Díaz del Castillo 1964:185.

45. Codex Ramírez 1975:131.

46. Sahagún 1959:18 (book 9, chap. 4).

47. Tezozomoc 1975:538.

48. *Relaciones . . . de Yucatán* 1983, 2:420.

49. Ixtlilxochitl 1975–77, 1:498.

50. Díaz del Castillo 1964:167.

51. The data in the Codex Mendoza indicate that Atlan was the most important military center on the Pánuco frontier. Díaz del Castillo, however, gives the above list of garrisons in regard to the struggle of the Mexicas against Juan de Escalante, who had stayed in Veracruz when Cortés went to Mexico, and in several passages he refers to the Mexica garrison in the region of Tozapan. He identifies it as "that garrison that Moteuczoma had near Tozapan" (1964:167) and "on the coast near Tozapan" (169); or "Almeria, which are towns between Tozapan and Cempohuallan" (519). On another occasion he describes the arrival in Mexico of messengers from towns of the north coast who came to surrender peacefully. They were from "Tuzapan, Mascalzingo [Mexcaltzinco], and Nautlan" and affirmed that they had assisted the Spanish during the battle against Escalante (279). Cortés (1973:122) writes "Tazapan and Mascalcingo and Nautan"; López de Gómara (1988:180), "Accapan, Mixcalcingo, Nautlan"; and Torquemada (1975–83, 2:263), "Tuzapan, Maxcaltzinco and Huauhtla." All this suggests that the Mexica garrison between Tozapan and Nauhtlan had been Mexcaltzinco. This town is 7.1-39 in the "Memorial de Tlacopan"; see p. 381 on its location. Cf. Gerhard 1986:383, 386, and García Martínez 1987: map 2 and p. 157n. 2 on Mexicaltzingo. The archaeological site of Vega de la Peña near Tlapacoyan, Veracruz, could have been this garrison or another in the same zone. The expression "la raya de Pánuco" (border of Pánuco) that Díaz el Castillo uses in reference to a place between Tozapan and Nauhtlan was applied to a very large area. In the SV it is applied to Tamiahua (sec. 530) and to Xochicuauhtla (Suchicuautla, sec. 488), more to the north of the place described by Bernal, but also to Tonatiuhco (Tonatico, sec. 529), situated south of Tozapan; therefore, it could be used as much for Mexcaltzinco as for Atlan.

52. The titles registered in these pages of the Codex Mendoza are found in various other towns and at different levels of the governmental hierarchy. It is not possible to compile in this study all the material available on these titles.

53. Piho 1972a.

54. The spelling would be *teuctli* in the system followed in this book.

55. Sahagún (1952:57–58 [book 3, Appendix, chap. 6]) states that the young men of the telpochcalli could rise to be tlacatecca and tlacochcalca but not tlacateuctli and tlacochteuctli. However, the situation is more complicated; there were also the titles of tlacateccatl teuctli and tlacochcalcatl teuctli. See Piho 1972b.

56. Codex Mendoza, 65r. The *tequihua* (officer) also wear the temillotl; following them on the same page are four brave warriors with pikes and emblems with the titles of tlacatecatl, tlacochcalcatl, *huiznahuatl*, and *ticocyahuacatl*; the last two wear the temillotl, but since the emblem covers the head, one cannot see whether the first two also have this headdress (67r).

57. Tezozomoc 1975:530; Sahagún 1981:106 (book 2, chap. 27). Cf. Piho 1972a.

58. These are the *quauhnochtli*, the *tlillancalqui*, the *atenpanecatl*, and the *ezguaguacatl*, depicted in fol. 65r; the huiznahuatl is on 66r. In other scenes, several of these officials are depicted carrying out their different activities.

59. Tezozomoc 1975:534–35.

60. Durán 1967, 2:50, 56, 218; Tezozomoc 1949: secs. 97, 111, 202.

61. RG 6:348. See p. 74 on the Codex Mendoza.

62. Sahagún 1959:2 (book 9, chap. 1).

63. See p. 104–108 on Citlaltepec, and p. 118 on Tizayocan.

64. Codex Mendoza, 37r, 44r, 47r, 48r, 53r.

65. Tezozomoc 1975:363–64, 533–36. Cf. Durán 1967, 2:238–39, 351–55.

66. Tezozomoc 1975:531–36; Durán 1967, 2:352–53. See p. 271 on the province of Tepecuacuilco and p. 406 on the settlers of the military colonies.

67. RG 6:290. For all the towns in the Oztoman region, see p. 271–72.

68. Ibid., 293.

69. Ibid., 324, 325.

70. Ibid., 277.

71. Ibid., 328.

72. Torquemada 1975–83, 1:286.

73. Durán 1967, 2:412.

74. Ibid., 112, 334; RG 7:85, 267. For Cuauhquechollan, see p. 291.

75. RG 5:73.

76. Muñoz Camargo (1984:183) lists Zacatlan, Tozapan, Tetellan, Iztaquimixtitlan, and Tzauctlan as participants in the war of Moteuczoma Xocoyotzin against Tlaxcallan. For all these towns, see p. 363, 384.

77. This is the Cingapacinga of Díaz del Castillo (1964:77–79); López de Gómara (1988:59); and Ixtlilxochitl (1977, 2:205). Cf. Gerhard 1986:386. The present-day towns are Xico, Veracruz, and Ixhuacán de los Reyes, Veracruz.

78. Cortés 1973:35 (Sienchimalen [the first and last *en* are misreadings of *cu*] and Ceyxnacan); López de Gómara 1988:68 (Sicuchimatl and Theuhixuacan). Both these towns are described in the relación of Xalapa (RG 5:369). According to Díaz del Castillo (1964:95), the people of Xicochimalco (Socochima) were friends of Cempohuallan and did not pay tribute to Moteuczoma.

79. RG 5:358. Acatlan is present-day Acatlán, Veracruz, north of Jalapa.

80. Ibid., 3:198. See p. 320.

81. Ibid., 5:35–36, 48, 57. See p. 320.

82. Ibid., 2:49.

83. Ibid., 167.

84. Ibid., 3:30.

85. Ibid., 6:310.

86. Ibid., 300.

87. Torquemada 1975–83, 1:295.

88. RG 5:271.

89. SV, sec. 28.

90. As has been said, Barlow identifies the Quecholtenango of the Codex Mendoza with another town of the same name south of Chilapan, but its association with Cuauhtochco shows that it is better to identify it with the one in the Teohuacan region.

91. RG 3:143.

92. Ibid., 2:102.

93. Durán 1967, 2:383–85; Tezozomoc 1975:559ff.

CHAPTER 13

1. Durán 1967, 2:156; Tezozomoc 1975:307.

2. Durán 1967, 2:164. Tezozomoc 1975:314–15.

3. Durán 1967, 2:186.

4. Tezozomoc 1975:335.

5. Durán 1967, 2:237.

6. Ibid., 281. Tezozomoc (1975:419) gives a similar account.

7. Durán 1967, 2:284–85. Cf. Tezozomoc 1975:424.

8. Durán 1967, 2:303.

9. Tezozomoc 1975:441. There is no explanation of what Huaxyacac is doing there; Colima might be the unidentified town in the province of Cihuatlan.

10. Durán 1967, 2:327–29; Tezozomoc 1975:479–81.

11. Tezozomoc 1975:522. The reference to Coaixtlahuacan is a mistake that Tezozomoc repeats in other passages of his chronicle. There is another example where the confusion is evident; see below in Table 13-1 the towns that came to the installation of Tizoc. In another passage he writes, "all the people of the lands of Coayxtlahuacan and the mountain people of Tolocan" (524); probably he means Ixtlahuacan, not Coaixtlahuacan. Another passage is harder to interpret: "the towns of Tierra Caliente, Coayxtlahuacan, Toluca and many other towns" (535).

12. Durán 1967, 2:384–86. Cf. Tezozomoc 1975:551–53.

13. Durán 1967, 2:238.

14. Tezozomoc 1975:364.

15. Ibid., 531–32.

16. Ibid., 531–36. The list of settlers is on pp. 533–34; on p. 535 the new settlers are enumerated again. This list is almost the same as the previous one and finishes with Coaixtlahuacan, Tolocan, "and many other towns." In comparison with the previous list, Tolocan is in place of Matlatzinco, and Coaixtlahuacan must be in error for Ixtlahuacan. The same error occurs on p. 462 (cf. Durán 1967, 2:319). Durán's list of settlers is almost exactly the same as that of Tezozomoc; the comparison shows that the Coatlapan of Tezozomoc should be Cuauhtlalpan, not Coatlalpan (the same error occurs in Tezozomoc [1975:486]), but the two regions are mentioned together at the installation of Tizoc (Durán 1967, 2:306). The numbers of settlers are somewhat different in the two sources.

17. Durán 1967, 2:133–35; Tezozomoc 1975:287–89. Torquemada (1975–83, 1:210) says that Il-huicamina asked Tetzcoco and Tlacopan for help in constructing the temple of Huitznahuac.

18. Durán 1967, 2:226–27. Cuacuatlaca corresponds to Quaquata, another name for the Matl-atzincas (Sahagún 1961:181–82 [book 10, chap. 29]). Tezozomoc (1975:354–57) does not explain which tasks were performed by the people of each town.

19. See below for the lists of the rulers convoked for the inauguration of the temple and of those who attended the funeral ceremonies for Ahuitzotl. For Ahuitzotl's conquests in this region, see p. 251.

20. Palerm (1973) compiles all the information on this topic.

21. Torquemada 1975–83, 1:219.

22. Ixtlilxochitl 1975–77, 1:444, 445.

23. Durán 1967, 2:373. Cf. Tezozomoc 1975:560.

24. Durán 1967, 2:485–89; Tezozomoc 1975:662–66.

25. *Huicalli* is a participle derived from the verb *huica*, which Molina (1970: s.v. *uica*) translates as "yr con otros, o yr acompañando, o en compañia de otros" (to go with others or in the company of others); *inuicalhuan* means "their companions." *Huica* also means to lead or rule; cf. Molina 1970: "teuica temama. el que gouierna, o rije a otros" (he who governs or rules others), and the passive form "vicaloni. súbdito" (subject). Torquemada (1975–83, 1:127) calls "acompañados" (companions) the peoples that Techotlalatzin of Tetzcoco assigned to each of the four high officials of his kingdom (see p. 470n.25).

26. Sahagún 1959:17, 24, 45 (book 9, chaps. 4, 5, and 10). The list in Sahagún's chapter 5 does not include Tlatelolco or Xochimilco.

27. Tezozomoc 1975:306. Durán (1967, 2:155–56) says only that the people of Tepeyacac had killed all the Mexica, Tetzcoca, and Tepanec merchants.

28. Tezozomoc 1975:334–35; Durán 1967, 2:185–86.

29. Tezozomoc 1975:537. Durán (1967, 2:357) in addition to giving the provenance of the imperial merchants, also refers to the tramontane peoples; he names Mexicas, Tetzcocas, Tepanecs, Xochimilcas, Chalcas, and Tlahuicas as well as Chololtecs and Tlaxcaltecs, who were not part of the Empire.

30. Durán 1967, 2:172.

31. Tezozomoc (1975:625) states that Teuctepec was confederated with Coatlan. But he might have confused the name of the temple at whose inauguration the captives were sacrificed, or that there may be a connection between the temple and the city of the same name in Oaxaca. See p. 281, 330.

32. Durán (1967, 2:439) identifies this temple as the coateocalli, "house of different gods," located in the temple of Huitzilopochtli. Tezozomoc (1975:625) calls the temple Coatepetl and Coatzocalli (*sic pro* Coateocalli), which suggests the temple of Huitzilopochtli. Coatlan was the temple of Huitzilopochtli's mother, where the *xochimanque* (flower craftsmen) celebrated their festival in the month Tozoztontli and where they made sacrifices to the *centzonhuitznahua* as the month Quecholli came to an end (Sahagún 1981:57, 191 [book 2, chap. 22, and appendix 2]).

33. Durán 1967, 2:442–43; Tezozomoc 1975:626–30. Tezozomoc (p. 626) counts the prisoners captured in Teuctepec by the soldiers of Acolhuacan, the Tepanec towns, Chalco, Tierra Caliente, the Chanampan towns, the mountain people of Cuauhtlalpan, the towns of the Four Lords, Matlatzinco and Mexico, Nauhtecs, Matlatzinco, and Mexicas.

34. Durán 1967, 2:295–97. Tezozomoc (1975:431–32) gives a similar report.

35. Tezozomoc 1975:454–55. In his enumeration of towns he states after Cohuixco that it is what they now call Tierra Caliente, bordering on the Marquesado. The expression "Tierra Caliente" in other passages of Durán and Tezozomoc seems to be synonymous with Tlalhuic or the Marquesado (for example, in Durán 1967, 2:392–93; cf. below, Table 13-4), but it is possible that in some cases it also included Cohuixco. Durán does not list the towns represented at Tizoc's funeral.

36. Durán 1967, 2:306.

37. Tezozomoc 1975:446.

38. Durán 1967, 2:307; Tezozomoc 1975:446. Each column gives the town in standardized spelling. The text usually refers to the rulers and stewards of a town or of its people with a gentile name.

39. Tezozomoc makes the same mistake in other places. See in p. 405 the list of participants in the Oztoman war.

40. RG 6:345.

41. Ibid., 5:57. See p. 295.

42. PNE 5:266–69.

43. Ibid., 202; Gerhard 1986:320. Cuitlatenanco is also cited as a tributary of Tenochtitlan (AGN, Tierras, vol. 34, exp. 4).

44. Guamuchtitlan (PNE 5:209).

45. See Table 7-2.

46. Durán 1967, 2:319. See p. 251.

47. Ibid., 334–35; Tezozomoc 1975:486–87. The toponyms have been extracted in the order in which they are presented, and the spelling has been standardized. In Tezozomoc the names in sections 2, 3, and 4 are given in an unbroken list. In Durán the names of the corresponding sections are in different paragraphs, each of which names the towns convoked by a group of ambassadors. Tezozomoc is placed in the first column because he follows the hierarchical order of the Empire.

48. Written Suchiaca in RG 6:41–51; Suchiacan in DA, 163. It should not be confused with Xochiyocan in the "Memorial de Tlacopan" (5.2-4), which is probably Santa Ana Xochuca in Ixtapan de la Sal, Mexico.

49. It is an estancia of Tepeyacac in SV, sec. 532. Now it is Oxtotipan in Tepeaca, Puebla.

50. Durán 1967, 2:335.

51. The spelling of place names have been standardized. This digression and the lists of towns are completely lacking in Tezozomoc; probably it was not part of the original chronicle that was the source used by both authors. See p. 114–20 on the tributaries of Tenochtitlan in Acolman, and p. 146–53 on the tributaries of Tetzcoco.

52. Tezozomoc 1975:500, 514–15. It is not said where the captives brought by the people of Tolocan were put. Chimalpahin (1889:158) gives the four groups that had captives for the sacrifice in a somewhat different way: he lists Tlalhuactlipan (instead of Tlacopan), Chinampan, Acolhuacan, and Matlatzinco (instead of Cuauhtlalpan). For the location of the barrios of Tenochtitlan, see Caso 1956.

53. Tezozomoc 1975:494; Durán 1967, 2:340.

54. Durán 1967, 2:341; Tezozomoc 1975:494.

55. Durán 1967, 2:392, 393; Tezozomoc 1975:568–70.

Glossary

altepetl.   City or town.

amate.   Bark cloth.

barrio.   Ward or subdivision of a town or city.

cabecera.   Capital or head town.

cacique.   Chief or local ruler.

calpixcayotl.   The office of a calpixque.

calpixcazgo.   Tributary province or district.

calpixque.   Steward or tribute collector (in Nahuatl "calpixqui" is the singular form and "calpixque" the plural).

calpolli (calpulli).   Social subdivision; ward; barrio.

chalchihuite.   Green stone; jade.

chinampa.   Garden on land reclaimed from wetlands.

Chinampan.   Area of the southern Basin of Mexico where chinampa gardening predominated.

cihuacoatl.   In Tenochtitlan, the title of the highest official, next to the king.

cuauhtlalpan.   "Forest land," a mountainous area west of the Basin of Mexico; or "eagle land," (war land) a battlefield; or a type of military land tenure.

cuauhtlalpanecs.   Mountain people (Spanish "serranos"); people from Cuauhtlalpan.

estancia.   Rural outlying settlement, usually subordinate to another place.

municipio.   In Mexico, local administrative units within each state.

nauhteuctin.   The Four Lords, the rulers of Colhuacan, Itztapalapan, Mexicatzinco, and Huitzilopochco.

parcialidad.   Major subdivision of a city or kingdom.

parias.   Tribute in goods of high value given by one ruler to another.

petlacalcatl.   The governor or chief steward in charge of a storehouse.

petlacalco.   Storehouse.

pilli (pl. pipiltin).   Noble.

pinolli.   Ground parched maize.

presidio.   Fortress garrisoned by soldiers.

principals.   Notables or officials.

real cédula.   Royal decree.

relación.   Report.

renteros.   Tenant farmers.

sujeto.   A town subordinate to another, or a rural dependency of a town or city.

teccalli.   Noble house.

telpochcalli.   Youths' house.

tequitlato (pl. tequitlatoque).   Lesser official; foreman of drafted laborers.

teuctli (pl. teteuctin).   Lord (Spanish "señor"); person of high status; person of authority at various social and political levels.

tlacatecatl.   A military title.

tlacochcalcatl.   A military title.

tlatepotzca.   Tramontane.

tlatoani (pl. tlatoque).   King.

tlatocaaltepetl.   Governing city; capital.

tlatocayotl.   Kingdom, Kingship.

visita.   Tour of inspection; a settlement ministered to by nonresidential clergy.

xochiyaoyotl.   "Flower war"; ceremonial battle.

Bibliography

ARCHIVES AND MANUSCRIPT COLLECTIONS

Archivo General de Indias, Seville
Archivo General de la Nación, México City
Archivo Histórico, Instituto Nacional de Antropología e Historia, Mexico City
Bibliothèque Nationale, Fonds Mexicain, Paris
Library of Congress, Kraus Collection, Washington
Newberry Library, Ayer Collection, Chicago

PUBLICATIONS

Acuña, René, ed.
    1982–88   *Relaciones geográficas del siglo XVI.* 10 vols. Mexico City: Universidad Nacional Autónoma de México.

Aguilar, Francisco de
    1938   *Historia de la Nueva España.* Ed. Alfonso Teja Zabre. Mexico City.

Anales de Cuauhtitlan
    1938   [Untitled] In Lehmann 1938, Part 1.
    1945   "Anales de Cuauhtitlan." In Velázquez 1945.
    1992   "Annals of Cuauhtitlan." In Bierhorst 1992a and 1992b.

Anales de Tlatelolco
    1939   "Unos Annales Históricos. . . ." In Mengin 1939.
    1948   *Anales de Tlatelolco: Unos annales históricos de la nación mexicana y Códice de Tlatelolco.* Ed. and trans. Heinrich Berlin, with an analytical summary by R. H. Barlow. Mexico City: Antigua Librería Robredo.

Andrews, Henrietta
    1954–55   "Otomi Place-names in the State of Mexico." *Revista Mexicana de Estudios Antropológicos* 14:161–64.

Anunciación, Fray Domingo de la
    1939–42   "Parecer de fray Domingo de la Anunciación, sobre el modo que tenían de tributar los indios en tiempo de la gentilidad." In *Epistolario de Nueva España, 1505–1818,* 7:259–66.

Aragón, Javier O.
    1931   "Expansión territorial del imperio mexicano." *Anales del Museo Nacional de Arqueología, Historia y Etnografía,* 4th series, 7:5–64.

Arenas, Pedro de
    1982   *Vocabulario manual de las lenguas castellana y mexicana.* 1611. Reprint, Mexico City: Universidad Nacional Autónoma de México.

Aubin, J. M. A.
    1885   *Mémoires sur la peinture didactique et l'écriture figurative des anciens Mexicains.* Paris.

Barlow, Robert H.
    1947   *The Codex of Tonayan.* Carnegie Institution of Washington Notes on Middle American Archaeology and Ethnology, no. 84. Washington, D.C.
    1948   "Apuntes para la historia antigua de Guerrero." In *El occidente de México: Cuarta reunión de mesa redonda sobre problemas antropológicos de México y Centro América,* Section 3: 181–190. Mexico City: Sociedad Mexicana de Antropología.

1949a   "Anales de Tula, Hidalgo." *Tlalocan* 3, no. 1: 2–13.
1949b   *The Extent of the Empire of the Culhua-Mexica.* Ibero-Americana 28. Berkeley and Los Angeles: University of California Press.
1987–94 *Obras de Robert H. Barlow.* 5 vols. Ed. Jesús Monjarás-Ruiz, Elena Limón, and María de la Cruz Paillés H. Mexico City: Instituto Nacional de Antropología e Historia/ Universidad de Las Américas.
1987   *Tlatelolco: Rival de Tenochtitlan.* Vol. 1 of *Obras de Robert H. Barlow.* Ed. Jesús Monjarás-Ruiz, Elena Limón, and María de la Cruz Paillés H. Mexico City: Instituto Nacional de Antropología e Historia/Universidad de Las Américas.
1989   *Tlatelolco: Fuentes e historia.* Vol. 2 of *Obras de Robert H. Barlow.* Ed. Jesús Monjarás-Ruiz, Elena Limón, and María de la Cruz Paillés H. Mexico City: Instituto Nacional de Antropología e Historia/Universidad de Las Américas.
1990   *Los mexicas y la Triple Alianza.* Vol. 3 of *Obras de Robert H. Barlow.* Ed. Jesús Monjarás-Ruiz, Elena Limón, and María de la Cruz Paillés H. Mexico City: Instituto Nacional de Antropología e Historia/Universidad de Las Américas.

Baudot, Georges
1977   *Utopie et histoire au Mexique: Les premiers chroniqueurs de la civilisation mexicaine (1520–1569).* Toulouse: privately published.

Berdan, Frances F.
1980a   "The Matrícula de Tributos—Introduction." In *Matrícula de tributos* 1980: 9–11.
1980b   "The Matrícula de Tributos—Provincial Tribute." In *Matrícula de tributos* 1980: 27–43.
1992   "The Imperial Tribute Roll of the Codex Mendoza." In Codex Mendoza 1992, 1:55–67.
1996   "The Tributary Provinces." In Berdan et al. 1996: 115–35.
———, et al.
1996   *Aztec Imperial Strategies.* Washington, D.C.: Dumbarton Oaks Research Library and Collection.

Bierhorst, John, ed.
1992a   *History and Mythology of the Aztecs: The Codex Chimalpopoca.* Tucson: University of Arizona Press.
1992b   *Codex Chimalpopoca: The Text in Nahuatl with a Glossary and Grammatical Notes.* Tucson: University of Arizona Press.

Boehm de Lameiras, Brigitte
1986   *Formación del estado en el México prehispánico.* Zamora: El Colegio de Michoacán.

Boturini Benaduci, Lorenzo
1974   *Idea de una nueva historia general de la América septentrional.* Mexico City: Porrúa.

Brinckmann, Lutz
1969   *Die Augustinerrelationen Nueva España, 1571–73: Analyse eines Zensusmanuskripts des 16. Jahrhunderts.* Beiträge zur mittelamerikanischen Völkerkunde, no. 8. Hamburg: Museum für Völkerkunde und Vorgeschichte.

Broda, Johanna
1978   "El tributo en trajes guerreros y la estructura del sistema tributario mexica." In Carrasco and Broda 1978: 113–74.

Brumfield, Elizabeth M., and John W. Fox, eds.
1994   *Factional Competition and Political Development in the New World.* Cambridge: Cambridge University Press.

Calnek, Edward E.
1974   "Conjunto urbano y modelo residencial en Tenochtitlan." In *Ensayos sobre el desarrollo urbano de México,* 11–65. Comp. Alejandra Moreno Toscano. SEP-Setentas 143. Mexico City: Secretaría de Educación Pública.
1976   "The Internal Structure of Tenochtitlan." In *The Valley of Mexico: Studies in Pre-*

Hispanic Ecology and Society, 287–302. Ed. Eric R. Wolf. Albuquerque: University of New Mexico Press.

Carochi, Horacio
1983   *Arte de la lengua mexicana*. 1645. Reprint, Mexico City: Universidad Nacional Autónoma de México.

Carrasco, Pedro
1950   *Los otomíes: Cultura e historia prehispánicas de los pueblos mesoamericanos de habla otomiana.* Mexico City: Universidad Nacional Autónoma de México.

1966   "Documentos sobre el rango de tecuhtli entre los nahuas tramontanos." *Tlalocan* 5:133–60.

1968   "Relaciones sobre la organización social indígena en el siglo XVI." *Estudios de Cultura Náhuatl* 7 (1967): 119–154.

1971*a*   "Social Organization of Ancient Mexico." In *Handbook of Middle American Indians.* Vol. 10. Austin: University of Texas Press.

1971*b*   "Los barrios antiguos de Cholula." In *Estudios y documentos de la región de Puebla-Tlaxcala,* 3:9–88. Puebla, Mexico: Instituto Poblano de Antropología e Historia.

1974   "Sucesión y alianzas matrimoniales en la dinastía teotihuacana." *Estudios de Cultura Náhuatl* 11:235–41.

1976   "Estratificación social indígena en Morelos durante el siglo XVI." In Carrasco et al. 1976: 102–17.

1977   "La sociedad mexicana antes de la Conquista." In García Martínez et al. 1977, 1:165–288. Mexico City: El Colegio de México.

1979   "La aplicabilidad a Mesoamérica del modelo andino de verticalidad." *Economía y sociedad en los Andes y Mesoamérica. Revista de la Universidad Complutense* 28, no. 117: 237–43.

1984*a*   "Royal Marriages in Ancient Mexico." In Harvey and Prem 1983: 41–81.

1984*b*   "The Extent of the Tepanec Empire." In *The Native Sources and the History of the Valley of Mexico*, 73–92. Ed. J. de Durand-Forest. BAR International Series 204. Proceedings of the 44th International Congress of Americanists, Oxford, England.

1988   "La organización social de los nahuas en la época prehispánica." In *La antropología en México: Panorama histórico*, 3:465–531. Ed. Carlos García Mora. Mexico City: Instituto Nacional de Antropolgía e Historia.

1989   "Los mayeques." *Historia Mexicana* 39:123–66.

1991   "The territorial structure of the Aztec empire." In *Land and Politics in the Valley of Mexico*, 93–112. Ed. H. R. Harvey. Albuquerque; University of New Mexico Press.

1994   "The Provenience of Zorita's Data on the Social Organization of Ancient Mexico." In *Chipping Away on Earth: Studies in Prehispanic and Colonial Mexico in Honor of Arthur J. O. Anderson and Charles E. Dibble*, 73–79. Ed. Eloise Quiñones Keber. Lancaster, Calif.: Labyrinthos.

1996   *Estructura político-territorial del imperio tenochca: La triple alianza de Tenochtitlan, Tetzcoco y Tlacopan.* Mexico City: El Colegio de México/Fondo de Cultura Económica.

n.d.   "La historia tepaneca." In *Historia del Estado de México.* Zinacantepec, Mexico: El Colegio Mexiquense, forthcoming.

———, et al.
1976   *Estratificación social en la Mesoamerica prehispánica.* Mexico City: Secretaría de Educación Pública/Instituto Nacional de Antropología e Historia.

Carrasco, Pedro, and J. Broda
1978   *Economía política e ideología en el México prehispánico.* Mexico City: Nueva Imagen.

Carrasco, Pedro, and Jesús Monjarás-Ruiz, eds.
1976   *Colección de documentos sobre Coyoacán.* Vol. 1. Colección Científica 39. Mexico City: Instituto Nacional de Antropología e Historia.

1978   *Colección de documentos sobre Coyoacán.* Vol. 2. Colección Científica 65. Mexico City: Instituto Nacional de Antropolgía e Historia.

Caso, Alfonso
    1956   "Los barrios antiguos de Tenochtitlan y Tlatelolco." In *Memorias de la Academia Mexicana de la Historia*, 15:7–62. Mexico City.
    1967   *Los calendarios prehispánicos*. Mexico City: Universidad Nacional Autónoma de México.
Castillo Farreras, Victor M.
    1974   "Matrícula de tributos: Comentarios, paleografía y versión." In *Historia de México*, 2:231–96. Barcelona and Mexico City: Salvat.
    1991   "La Matrícula de tributos." In *Matrícula de tributos: Nuevos estudios* 1991, 19–35.
Cedulario Cortesiano
    1949   *Cedulario Cortesiano*. Comp. Beatriz Arteaga Garza and Guadalupe Pérez San Vicente. Mexico City: Editorial Jus.
Cervantes de Salazar, Francisco
    1971   *Crónica de la Nueva España*. Ed. Manuel Magallón. 2 vols. Biblioteca de Autores Españoles 244, 245. Madrid: Atlas.
Chamberlain, Robert S.
    1939   "The Concept of Señor Natural as Revealed in Castilian Law and Administrative Documents." *Hispanic American Historical Review* 9:130–37.
Chance, John K.
    1989   *Conquest of the Sierra: Spaniards and Indians in Colonial Oaxaca*. Norman: University of Oklahoma Press.
Chavero, Alfredo
    1901   *Pinturas jeroglíficas de la Colección Chavero*. 2 vols. Mexico City: Juan E. Barbero.
Chimalpahin Quauhtlehuanitzin, Domingo de San Antón Muñón
    1889   *Annales*. Trans. Rémi Siméon. Paris: Maisonneuve et Ch. Leclerc.
    1950   *Diferentes historias originales de los reynos de Culhuacan, y México, y de otras provincias. El autor de ellas dicho don Domingo Chimalpain. 5. relación*. Mitteilungen aus dem Museum für Völkerkunde 22. Trans. and ed. Ernst Mengin. Hamburg: De Gruyter.
    1958   *Das Memorial Breve acerca de la fundación de la ciudad de Culhuacán*. Trans. and ed. Walter Lehman and Gerdt Kutscher. Stuttgart: Kohlhammer.
    1963   *Die Relationen Chimalpahin's zur Geschichte México's*. Vol. 1 of *Die Zeit bis zur Conquista 1521*. Ed. Günter Zimmermann. Hamburg: Gram, De Gruyter.
    1987   *Troisième relation et autres documents originaux de Chimalpahin Quauhtlehuanitzin*. Trans. Jacqueline de Durand-Forest. Paris: L'Harmattan.
Ciudad Real, Antonio de
    1976   *Tratado curioso y docto de las grandezas de la Nueva España: Relación breve y verdadera de algunas cosas de las muchas que sucedieron al padre fray Alonso Ponce en las provincias de la Nueva España siendo comisario general de aquellas partes*. Ed. Josefina García Quintana and Víctor M. Castillo Farreras. 2 vols. Mexico City: Universidad Nacional Autónoma de México.
Clark, James Cooper, ed.
    1938   *Codex Mendoza: The Mexican Manuscript Known as the Collection of Mendoza and Preserved in the Bodleian Library, Oxford*. 3 vols. London: Waterlow and Sons.
Clavigero, Francisco Javier
    1982   *Historia antigua de México*. Sepan cuantos 29. Mexico City: Porrúa.
Cline, Howard F.
    1959   "The Patiño Maps of 1580 and Related Documents: Analysis of 16th Century Cartographic Sources for the Gulf Coast of Mexico." *El México Antiguo* 9:633–92.
Cline, Susan L.
    1986   *Colonial Culhuacan, 1580–1600*. Albuquerque: University of New Mexico Press.
Codex Aubin
    1981   *Geschichte der Azteken: Codex Aubin und verwandte Dokumente*. Quellenwerke zur alten

Geschichte Amerikas 13. Trans. and ed. Walter Lehmann und Gerdt Kutscher. Berlin: Ibero-Amerikanischen Institut.

Codex Chimalpopoca
  1938   *Die Geschichte der Königreiche von Culhuacan und Mexico.* Ed. Walter Lehmann. Stuttgart and Berlin: Kohlhammer.
  1945   *Códice Chimalpopoca: Anales de Cuauhtitlan y leyenda de los Soles.* Trans. Primo Feliciano Velázquez. Mexico: Universidad Nacional Autónoma de México.
  1992a *History and Mythology of the Aztecs: The Codex Chimalpopoca.* Trans. John Bierhorst. Tucson and London: University of Arizona Press.
  1992b *Codex Chimalpopoca: The Text in Nahuatl with a Glossary and Grammatical Notes.* Ed. John Bierhorst. Tucson and London: University of Arizona Press.

Codex Cozcatzin
  1994   *Códice Cozcatzin.* Ed. Ana Rita Valero de García Lascuráin. Trans. Rafael Tena. Mexico City: Instituto Nacional de Antropología e Historia/Universidad Autónoma de Puebla.

Codex Mariano Jiménez
  1967   *Nómina de tributos de los pueblos Otlazpan y Tepexic. Códice Mariano Jiménez.* Mexico City: Instituto Nacional de Antropología e Historia.

Codex Mendoza
  1925   *Colección de Mendoza o Códice Mendocino, documento mexicano del siglo XVI que se conserva en la Biblioteca Bodleiana de Oxford, Inglaterra.* Ed. Jesús Galindo y Villa. Reprint, Mexico City: Cosmos, 1979.
  1938   *Codex Mendoza: The Mexican Manuscript Known as the Collection of Mendoza and Preserved in the Bodleian Library, Oxford.* Ed. James Cooper Clark. 3 vols. London: Waterlow and Sons.
  1992   *The Codex Mendoza.* Ed. Frances F. Berdan and Patricia Rieff Anawalt. 4 vols. Berkeley: University of California Press.

Codex Osuna
  1947   *Códice Osuna.* Ed. Luis Chávez Orozco. Mexico City: Instituto Indigenista Interamericano.

Codex Ramírez
  1975   *Códice Ramírez, manuscrito del siglo XVI intitulado: Relación del origen de los indios que habitan esta Nueva España según sus historias.* In Tezozomoc 1975: 17–149.

Codex Telleriano-Remensis
  1899   *Codex Telleriano-Remensis: Ms. Mexicain no. 385.* Bibliothèque Nationale. Facsimile edition. Introduction by E.-T. Hamy. Paris.

Codex Vaticano-Ríos
  1900   *Il manoscritto messicano Vaticano 3738, detto il codice Ríos.* Facsimile edition. Rome: Danesi.

Codex de Xicotepec
  1995   *Códice de Xicotepec.* Ed. Guy Stresser-Péan. Mexico City: Gobierno del Estado de Puebla.

Codex Xolotl
  1951   *Códice Xolotl.* Ed. Charles E. Dibble. Mexico City: Universidad Nacional Autónoma de México.

Codex de Yanhuitlan
  1940   *Códice de Yanhuitlan.* Facsimile edition. Ed. Wigberto Jiménez Moreno and Salvador Mateos Higuera. Mexico City: Museo Nacional.

Colección de documentos inéditos . . . de Indias
  1864–84 *Colección de documentos inéditos relativos al descubrimiento, conquista y organización de las antiguas posesiones españolas de America y Oceanía, sacados de los archivos del reino y muy especialmente del de Indias.* Madrid: Frías.

Colín, Mario
   1966   *Indice de documentos relativos a los pueblos del estado de México: Ramo de Tierras del Archivo General de la Nación.* Mexico City: Biblioteca Enciclopédica del Estado de México.
   1967   "Indice de documentos relativos a los pueblos del estado de México: Ramo de Mercedes del Archivo General de la Nación." *Boletín de la Sociedad Mexicana de Geografía y Estadística,* 105. Mexico City.
   1968   "Indice de documentos relativos a los pueblos del estado de México: Ramo de Indios del Archivo General de la Nación." *Boletín de la Sociedad Mexicana de Geografía y Estadística,* 107. Mexico City.
Cook, Sherburne F.
   1949   *The Historical Demography and Ecology of the Teotlalpan.* Ibero-Americana 33. Berkeley: University of California Press.
Córdoba, Fray Juan de
   1942   *Vocabulario castellano-zapoteco.* Facsimile edition. Ed. Wigberto Jiménez Moreno. Mexico City: Instituto Nacional de Antropología e Historia.
Corona Sanchez, Eduardo
   1973   "Desarrollo de un señorío en el Acolhuacan prehispánico." Master's thesis, Escuela Nacional de Antropología e Historia, Mexico City.
Cortés, Hernán
   [1538] "Carta al Consejo de Indias." In *Colección de documentos inéditos de . . . Indias* 3:535–45.
   1973   *Cartas de Relación.* Sepan Cuantos 7. Mexico City: Porrúa.
Covarrubias, Sebastián de
   [1610] *Tesoro de la lengua castellana o española.* Facsimile edition. Madrid: Ediciones Turner, n.d.
Dahlgren, Barbro
   1954   *La Mixteca: Su cultura e historia prehispánicas.* Mexico City: Universidad Nacional Autónoma de México.
———, ed.
   1979   *Mesoamérica: Homenaje al doctor Paul Kirchhoff.* Mexico City: Secretaría de Educación Pública/Insituto Nacional de Antropología e Historia.
Davies, Claude Nigel Byam
   1968   *Los señoríos independientes del Imperio Azteca.* Mexico City: Instituto Nacional de Antropología e Historia.
   1980a   *The Toltec Heritage: From the Fall of Tula to the Rise of Tenochtitlán.* Norman: University of Oklahoma Press.
   1980b   *The Aztecs: A History.* Norman: University of Oklahoma Press.
   1987   *The Aztec Empire: The Toltec Resurgence.* Norman: University of Oklahoma Press.
Dehouve, Danièle
   1976   "Dos relatos sobre migraciones nahuas en el estado de Guerrero." *Estudios de Cultura Náhuatl* 12:137–54.
   1990   *Quand les banquiers étaient des saints: 450 ans de l'histoire économique et sociale d'une province du Mexique.* Paris: Editions du Centre National de la Recherche Scientifique.
Descripción del arzobispado
   1897   *Descripción del arzobispado de México hecha en 1570 y otros documentos.* Ed. Luis García Pimentel. Mexico City: Terrazas e Hijos.
Díaz del Castillo, Bernal
   1964   *Historia verdadera de la conquista de la Nueva España.* Ed. Joaquín Ramírez Cabañas. Mexico City: Porrúa.
Dibble, Charles E.
   1995   Preface to Stresser-Péan 1996: 7–8.
———, ed.
   1951   *Códice Xolotl.* Mexico City: Universidad Nacional Autónoma de México.

Diccionario de autoridades
  1963   *Diccionario de autoridades*. Facsimile edition of *Diccionario de la lengua castellana*. Real Academia Española, 1726. 3 vols. Madrid: Gredos.

Diccionario de historia de España
  1952   *Diccionario de historia de España*. 2 vols. Madrid: Revista de Occidente.

"Documentos de Texcoco"
  1903   "Documentos de Texcoco." In *Colección de documentos para la historia mexicana*, Part 6. Ed. Antonio Peñafiel. Mexico City: Secretaría de Fomento.

Durán, Fray Diego
  1967   *Historia de las Indias de Nueva España e Islas de la Tierra Firme*. Ed. A. M. Garibay K. Mexico City: Porrúa.

Durand-Forest, Jacqueline de, trans. and ed.
  1987   *Troisième relation de Chimalpahin Quauhtlehuanitzin*. Vol. 2 of *L'Histoire de la vallée de Mexico selon Chimalpahin Quauhtlehuanitzin (du XIe au XVIe siècle)*. Paris: L'Harmattan.

Dyckerhoff, Ursula
  1970   "Die 'Crónica Mexicana' des Hernando Alvarado Tezozomoc: Quellenkritische Untersuchungen." Ph.D. diss., Hamburg University.

————, and Hanns J. Prem
  1978   "Der vorspanische Landbesitz in Zentralmexiko." *Zeitschrift für Ethnologie* 103: 186–238.

Ekholm, Gordon F.
  1953   "Notas arqueológicas sobre el valle de Tuxpan y áreas circumvecinas." In *Huastecos, totonacos y sus vecinos: Revista Mexicana de Estudios Antropológicos* 13, nos. 2–3:413–21. Mexico City.

Epistolario de Nueva España
  1939–42 *Epistolario de Nueva España, 1505–1818*. 16 vols. Ed. Francisco del Paso y Troncoso. Mexico City: Porrúa.

Estas son las Leyes
  1941   "Estas son las leyes." In *Relaciones de Texcoco y de la Nueva España*, 280–86.

Galarza, Joaquín
  1972   *Lienzos de Chiepetlan*. Mexico City: Mission archéologique et ethnologique française au Mexique.

García Granados, Rafael
  1952–53 *Diccionario biográfico de historia antigua de Méjico*. 3 vols. Mexico City: Universidad Nacional Autónoma de México.

García Icazbalceta, Joaquín, ed.
  1858   *Colección de Documentos para la Historia de México*. 2 vols. Mexico City.
  1941   *Nueva colección de documentos para la historia de México*. 5 vols. Reprint of the 1886–92 edition. Mexico City: Chávez Hayhoe.

García Martínez, Bernardo
  1969   *El Marquesado del Valle*. Mexico City: El Colegio de México.
  1987   *Los pueblos de la Sierra: El poder y el espacio entre los indios del norte de Puebla hasta 1700*. Mexico City: El Colegio de México.

————, José Luis Lorenzo, Ignacio Bernal, and Pedro Carrasco
  1977   *Historia General de México*. 2d ed. Vol. 1. Mexico City: El Colegio de México.

García Mora, Carlos
  1981   *Naturaleza y sociedad en Chalco-Amecameca*. Mexico City: Biblioteca Antropológica del Estado de México.

García Payón, José
  1947   "Sinopsis de algunos problemas arqueológicos del Totonacapan." *El México Antiguo* 6:301–32.

Gasco, Janine, and Barbara Voorhies
　1989　"The Ultimate Tribute: The Role of the Soconusco as an Aztec Tributary." In Voorhies 1989: 48–94.

Gemelli Careri, Giovanni Francesco
　1983　*Viaje a la Nueva España.* Trans. and ed. Francisca Perujo. Mexico City: Universidad Nacional Autónoma de México.

Gerhard, Peter
　1970a　"A Method of Reconstructing Pre-Columbian Political Boundaries in Central Mexico." *Journal de la Société des Américanistes* 59:27–41.
　1970b　"El señorío de Ocuituco." *Tlalocan* 6:97–114.
　1979　*The Southeast Frontier of New Spain.* Princeton, N.J.: Princeton University Press.
　1986　*Geografía histórica de la Nueva España, 1519–1821.* Mexico City: Universidad Nacional Autónoma de México.

Gibson, Charles
　1956　"Llamamiento general, repartimiento, and the empire of Acolhuacan." *Hispanic American Historical Review* 36:1–27.
　1964a　*The Aztecs under Spanish Rule: A History of the Indians of the Valley of Mexico.* Stanford, Calif.: Stanford University Press.
　1964b　"The Pre-conquest Tepanec Zone and the Labor Drafts of the Sixteenth Century." *Revista de Historia de América* 57–58:136–45.
　1971　"Structure of the Aztec Empire." In *Handbook of Middle American Indians*, 10:376–94. Austin: University of Texas Press.

Glass, John B.
　1964　*Catálogo de la Colección de Códices.* Mexico City: Instituto Nacional de Antropología e Historia.

González Aparicio, Luis
　1973　*Plano reconstructivo de la región de Tenochtitlan.* Mexico City: Instituto Nacional de Antropología e Historia.

González Sánchez, Isabel
　1969　*Haciendas y ranchos de Tlaxcala en 1712.* Mexico City: Instituto Nacional de Antropología e Historia.

Gorenstein, Shirley
　1966　"The Differential Development of New World Empires." *Revista Mexicana de Estudios Antropológicos* 20:41–67.

Guzmán, Eulalia
　1938　"Un manuscrito de la colección Boturini que trata de los antiguos señores de Teotihuacan." *Ethnos* (Stockholm) 3:89–103.

Harvey, Herbert R.
　1971　"Ethnohistory of Guerrero." In *Handbook of Middle American Indians*, 11:603–18. Austin: University of Texas Press.
──────, ed.
　1991　*Land and Politics in the Valley of Mexico.* Albuquerque: University of New Mexico Press.
──────, and Hanns Prem, eds.
　1984　*Explorations in Ethnohistory: Indians of Central Mexico in the Sixteenth Century.* Albuquerque: University of New Mexico Press.

Hassig, Ross
　1984　"The Aztec Empire: A Reappraisal." In Spores and Hassig 1984: 15–24.
　1988　*Aztec Warfare: Imperial Expansion and Political Control.* Norman: University of Oklahoma Press.

Hendrichs Pérez, Pedro R.
　1945　*Por tierras ignotas: Viajes y observaciones en la región del Río de las Balsas.* Mexico City: Editorial Cultura.

Hernández Rodríguez, Rosaura
  1952   "El Valle de Toluca: Su historia, época prehispánica y siglo XVI." *Boletín de la Sociedad Mexicana de Geografía y Estadística* 74, nos. 1–3: 7–124.
  1988   *El Valle de Toluca: Epoca prehispánica y siglo XVI.* Toluca: El Colegio Mexiquense.

Herrera y Tordesillas, Antonio
  1947   *Historia general de los hechos de los castellanos en las islas y tierra firme del mar océano.* 15 vols. Madrid.

Hicks, Frederic
  1978   "Los calpixque de Nezahualcoyotl." *Estudios de Cultura Náhuatl* 13:129–52.
  1982   "Tetzcoco in the Early Sixteenth Century: The State, the City and the Calpolli." *American Ethnologist* 9:230–49.
  1984   "La posición de Temascalapan en la triple alianza." *Estudios de Cultura Náhuatl* 17:235–60.
  1986   "Prehistoric Background of Colonial Political and Economic Organization in Central México." In *Supplement to the Handbook of Middle American Indians.* Vol. 4, *Ethnohistory*, 35–54. Austin: University of Texas Press.
  1992   "Subject States and Tribute Provinces: The Aztec Empire in the Northern Valley of Mexico." *Ancient Mesoamerica* 3:1–10.
  1994   "Alliance and Intervention in Aztec Imperial Expansion." In Brumfiel and Fox 1994: 111–16.

Hinz, Eike; Claudine Hartau; and Marie-Luise Heimann-Koenen
  1983   *Aztekischer Zensus: Zur indianischen Wirtschaft und Gesellschaft im Marquesado um 1540.* 2 vols. Hannover: Verlag für Ethnologie.

Historia de los mexicanos por sus pinturas
  1941   "Historia de los mexicanos por sus pinturas." In *Relaciones de Texcoco y de la Nueva España*, 209–40.

Historia tolteca-chichimeca
  1976   *Historia tolteca-chichimeca.* Trans. and ed. Paul Kirchhoff, Lina Odena Güemes, and Luis Reyes García. Mexico City: Centro de Investigaciones Superiores en Antropología Social del Instituto Nacional de Antropología e Historia/Secretaría de Educación Pública.

Hodge, Mary G.
  1984   *Aztec City-States.* Studies in Latin American Ethnohistory and Archaeology No. 3. Memoirs of the Museum of Anthropology, University of Michigan, 18. Ann Arbor.
  1996   "Political Organization of the Central Provinces." In Berdan et al. 1996: 17–45.

Horcasitas, Fernando
  1978   "Los descendientes de Nezahualpilli: Documentos del cacicazgo de Tetzcoco (1545–1855)." *Historia Novohispana* 6:145–85.

Hunt, Eva
  1972   "Irrigation and the Socio-Political Organization of Cuicatec Cacicazgos." In *The Prehistory of the Tehuacan Valley.* Vol. 4, *Chronology and Irrigation*, 162–260. Ed. Frederick Johnson. Austin: University of Texas Press.

Información de 1554
  1957   In Scholes and Adams 1957.

Ixtlilxochitl, Fernando de Alva
  1975–77   *Obras históricas.* 2 vols. Ed. Edmundo O'Gorman. Mexico City: Universidad Nacional Autónoma de México.

Jäcklein, Klaus
  1978   *Los popoloca de Tepexi (Puebla): Un estudio etnohistórico.* El Proyecto México de la Fundación Alemana para la Investigación Científica 15. Wiesbaden: Franz Steiner Verlag.

Jimenez Moreno, Wigberto
  1940   "Ambiente Histórico del Códice." In *Códice de Yanhuitlan* 1940, Part 1.

Kelly, Isabel, and Angel Palerm
1952 *The Tajin Totonac:* Part 1, *History, Subsistence, Shelter and Technology.* Institute of Social Anthropology Publication no. 13. Washington, D.C.: Smithsonian Institution.

Kirchhoff, Paul
1940 "Los pueblos de la Historia Tolteca-Chichimeca; Sus migraciones y parentesco." *Revista Mexicana de Estudios Antropológicos* 4:77–104.
1963 "Dos tipos de relaciones entre pueblos en el México antiguo." In *A Pedro Bosch-Gimpera en el septuagésimo aniversario de su nacimiento,* 255–59. Mexico City: Instituto Nacional de Antropología e Historia.

Kobayashi, Munehiro
1993 *Tres estudios sobre el sistema tributario de los mexicas.* Mexico: Centro de Investigaciones y Estudios Superiores en Antropología Social/Kobe City University of Foreign Studies (Japan).

Köhler, Ulrich
1978 "Reflections on Zinacantan's Role in Aztec Trade with Soconusco." In *Mesoamerican Communication Routes and Cultural Contacts,* 67–73. Ed. Thomas A. Lee, Jr., and Carlos Navarrete. Papers of the New World Archaeological Foundation, no. 40. Provo, Utah: Brigham Young University.

Krickeberg, Walter
1952 "Moctezuma II." *Saeculum* 3:255–76.
1961 *Las antiguas culturas mexicanas.* Mexico City: Fondo de Cultura Económica.

Lameiras, José
1969 "Metztitlán: Notas para su etnohistoria." Master's thesis, Escuela Nacional de Antropología e Historia, Mexico City.
1985 *Los déspotas armados: Un espectro de la guerra prehispánica.* Zamora: El Colegio de Michoacán.

Lehmann, Walter, trans. and ed.
1938 *Die Geschichte der Königreiche von Colhuacan und Mexico.* Stuttgart and Berlin: W. Kohlhammer.

León-Portilla, Miguel, and Carmen Aguilera
1986 *Mapa de México Tenochtitlan y sus contornos hacia 1550.* Mexico City: Celanese Mexicana.

Leyenda de los Soles
1938 Untitled.In Lehmann 1938, Part 2.
1945 "Leyenda de los Soles." In Velázquez 1945.
1992 "Legend of the Suns." In Bierhorst 1992a.

Libro de las tasaciones
1952 *El libro de las tasaciones de pueblos de la Nueva España.* Ed. Francisco González de Cosío. Mexico City: Archivo General de la Nación.

Licate, Jack A.
1980 "The Forms of Aztec Territorial Organization." *Geoscience and Man* 21:27–45.

Los Lienzos de Tuxpan
1970 *Los Lienzos de Tuxpan: Códices de Tierras.* Ed. José Luis Melgarejo Vivanco, photog. Manuel Alvarez Bravo. Mexico City: La Estampa Mexicana.

Litvak King, Jaime
1971a *Cihuatlan y Tepecoacuilco, provincias tributarias de México en el siglo XVI.* Mexico City: Universidad Nacional Autónoma de México.
1971b "Las relaciones entre México y Tlatelolco antes de la conquista de Axayacatl: Problemática de la expansión mexica." *Estudios de Cultura Náhuatl* 9:17–20.

Lockhart, James
1992 *The Nahuas after the Conquest.* Stanford, Calif.: Stanford University Press.

López Austin, Alfredo
1985 "El dios enmascarado del fuego." *Anales de Antropología* 22:251–85.

BIBLIOGRAPHY

López de Gómara, Francisco
  1988   *Historia de la conquista de México*. Ed. Juan Miralles Ostos. Sepan Cuantos 566. Mexico City: Porrúa.

Lorenzana, Francisco Antonio
  1770   *Historia de Nueva España escrita por su esclarecido conquistador Hernán Cortés, aumentada con otros documentos y notas*. Mexico City: Imprenta del Superior Gobierno.

Maldonado Jiménez, Druzo
  1990   *Cuauhnáhuac y Huaxtepec (tlalhuicas y xochimilcas en el Morelos prehispánico)*. Cuernavaca: Universidad Nacional Autónoma de México, Centro Regional de Investigaciones Multidisciplinarias, Cuernavaca.

Mapa Quinatzin
  1885   "Mappe Quinatzin." In Aubin 1885: 74–106.

Martin, Cheryl E.
  1985   *Rural Society in Colonial Morelos*. Albuquerque: University of New Mexico Press.

Martínez, Hildeberto
  1984a   *Tepeaca en el siglo XVI: Tenencia de la tierra y organización de un señorío*. Mexico City: La Casa Chata.

———, ed.
  1984b   *Colección de documentos coloniales de Tepeaca*. Colección Científica 134. Mexico City: Instituto Nacional de Antropología e Historia.

Matrícula de Huexotzinco
  1974   *Matrícula de Huexotzinco (Ms. mex. 387 der Bibliothèque Nationale Paris)*. Ed. Hanns J. Prem. Graz, Austria: Akademische Druck- und Verlagsanstalt.

Matrícula de tributos
  1974   "Matrícula de tributos: Comentarios, paleografía y versión." In *Historia de México* 2:231–96. Ed. Victor M. Castillo Farreras. Barcelona and Mexico City: Salvat.
  1980   *Matrícula de tributos (Códice de Moctezuma)*. Ed. Frances F. Berdan and Jacqueline de Durand-Forest. Graz, Austria: Akademische Druck- und Verlagsanstalt.
  1991   *Matrícula de tributos: Nuevos estudios*. Mexico City: Secretaría de Hacienda y Crédito Público.

Meade, Joaquín
  1962   *La Huasteca veracruzana*. 2 vols. Mexico City: Citlaltépetl.

Medellín Zenil, A.
  1952   *Exploraciones en Quauhtochco*. Jalapa: Gobierno del Estado de Veracruz, Departamento de Antropología.

Melgarejo Vivanco, José Luis, ed.
  1970   *Los Lienzos de Tuxpan: Códices de Tierras*. Ed. José Luis Melgarejo Vivanco, photog. Manuel Alvarez Bravo. Mexico City: La Estampa Mexicana.

"Memorial breve"
  1958   "Memorial breve acerca de la fundación de la ciudad de Culhuacan." In Chimalpahin Quauhtlehuanitzin 1958: 3–128.

Memorial de Sololá
  1950   *Memorial de Sololá: Anales de los cakchiqueles; Título de los señores de Totonicapán*. Ed. Adrián Recinos. Mexico City: Fondo de Cultura Económica.

"Memorial de Tlacopan"
  1939–42   "Memorial de los pueblos sujetos al señorío de Tlacupan, y de los que tributaban a Mexico, Tezcuco y Tlacupan." In *Epistolario de Nueva España*, 14:118–22.
  1970   "Memorial de los pueblos." In Zimmermann 1970: 5–8; plates 6–8, facsimiles.

Méndez Martínez, Enrique
  1979   *Índice de documentos relativos a los pueblos del Estado de Puebla: Ramo Tierras del Archivo General de la Nación*. Colección Científica. Mexico City: Instituto Nacional de Antropología e Historia.

Menegus Bornemann, Margarita

1991   *Del señorío a la república de indios: El caso de Toluca, 1500–1600.* Madrid: Ministerio de Agricultura, Pesca y Alimentación.

Mengin, Ernst, trans. and ed.

1939   "Unos Annales Históricos de la Nación Mexicana: Die manuscrits mexicains nr. 22 und 22 bis der Bibliothèque Nationale de Paris," Part I, "Die Handschrift nebst Übersetzung"; Part II, "Der Kommentar." *Baessler-Archiv* 22, nos. 2–3:60–168; no. 4:115–39.

Mohar Betancourt, Luz María

1987   *El tributo mexica en el siglo XVI: análisis de dos fuentes pictográficas.* Mexico City: Centro de Investigaciones y Estudios Superiores en Antropología Social.

1991   *La escritura en el México Antiguo.* 2 vols. Mexico City: Plaza y Valdés.

Molina, Alonso de

1970   *Vocabulario en lengua castellana y mexicana y mexicana y castellana.* Mexico City: Porrúa.

Molins Fábrega, Narciso

1956   *El Códice Mendocino y la economía de Tenochtitlan.* Mexico City: Libro-Mex.

Monjarás-Ruiz, Jesús

1980   *La nobleza mexica.* Mexico City: Edicol.

1991   "Tlatelolco, la otra cara de los mexicas." In *Homenaje a Julio César Olivé Negrete,* 417–30. Mexico City: Universidad Nacional Autónoma de México.

Montoto de Sedas, ed.

1927–32   *Colección de documentos inéditos para la historia de Ibero-América.* 14 vols. Madrid: Compañía Ibero-Americana de Publicaciones.

Mota y Escobar, Alonso de la

1939–40   "Memoriales del obispo de Tlaxcala fray Alonso de la Mota y Escobar." *Anales del Instituto Nacional de Antropología e Historia* 1:191–306.

Motolinía, Toribio de Benavente

1971   *Memoriales o Libro de las cosas de la Nueva España y de los naturales de ella.* Ed. Edmundo O'Gorman. Mexico City: Universidad Nacional Autónoma de México.

Münch, Guido

1976   *El cacicazgo de San Juan Teotihuacan durante la Colonia, 1521–1821.* Colección Científica 32. Mexico City: Instituto Nacional de Antropología e Historia.

1983   *Etnología del Istmo veracruzano.* Mexico City: Universidad Nacional Autónoma de México.

Muñoz Camargo, Diego

1984   "Descripción de la ciudad y provincia de Tlaxcala." *Relaciones geográficas del siglo XVI.* Vol. 4.

Muriá, José María

1973   *Sociedad prehispánica y pensamiento europeo.* SEP-Setentas 76. Mexico City: Secretaría de Educación Pública.

Muriel, Josefina

1948   "Reflexiones sobre Hernán Cortés." *Revista de Indias* 9:229–45.

Navarro de Vargas, Joseph

1909   "Padrón del pueblo de San Mateo Huitzilopochco, inventario de su iglesia y directorio de sus obvenciones parroquiales." *Anales del Museo Nacional de Arqueología, Historia y Etnología,* 3d series, 1:555–99.

Nazareo, Pablo

1939–42   "Carta al rey don Felipe II . . . México 17 de marzo 1566." In *Epistolario de Nueva España,* 10:89–129.

Nebrija, Antonio de

1973   *Vocabulario de romance en latín. Transcripción crítica de la edición revisada por el autor (Sevilla, 1516).* Ed. Gerald J. MacDonald. Philadelphia: Temple University Press.

Nicholson, H. B.
     1972   "Tepepolco, the locale of the first stage of Fr. Bernardino de Sahagún's great ethno-
              graphic project: Historical and cultural notes." In *Mesoamerican Archaeology: New
              Approaches*, 145–54. Ed. Norman Hamond. Austin: University of Texas Press.

Nielsen, Hjørdis
     1966   "The 2:2:1 Tribute Distribution in the Triple Alliance: Analyzing the Tetzcocan
              Manuscripts." *Ancient Mesoamerica 7*, no. 2 (Fall 1996): 207–14.

Noguez, Xavier
     1978   *Tira de Tepechpan: Códice colonial procedente del Valle de México*. 2 vols. Mexico City: Bib-
              lioteca Enciclopédica del Estado de México.

Nueva colección de documentos para la historia de México
     1886–92   *Nueva colección de documentos para la historia de México*. Ed. Joaquín García Icazbalceta.
              5 vols. Mexico. There is a 2d edition of vols. 1–3, Mexico: Salvador Chávez Hay-
              hoe, 1941.

Nuevos documentos
     1946   *Nuevos documentos relativos a los bienes de Hernán Cortés, 1547–1947*. Mexico City:
              Archivo General de la Nación/Universidad Nacional Autónoma de México.

Offner, Jerome A.
     1983   *Law and Politics in Aztec Texcoco*. Cambridge: Cambridge University Press.

Olivera, Mercedes
     1978   *Pillis y macehuales: Las formaciones sociales y los modos de producción de Tecali del siglo XII al
              XVI*. Mexico City: La Casa Chata.

Olmos, Andrés de
     1972   *Arte para aprender la lengua mexicana*. Ed. Rémi Siméon. Facsimile of 1875 Paris edi-
              tion. Guadalajara: Edmundo Aviña Levy.

Origen de los mexicanos
     1941   "Origen de los mexicanos." In *Relaciones de Texcoco y de la Nueva España*, 256–80.

Orozco y Berra, Manuel
     1960   *Historia antigua y de la conquista de México*. 4 vols. Mexico City: Porrúa.

Ortega, Miguel F.
     1940–41   "Extensión y límites de la provincia de los yopes a mediados del siglo XVI." *El Mex-
              ico Antiguo 5*:48–52.

Oviedo y Valdés, Gonzalo Fernández de
     1851–55   *Historia general y natural de las Indias, islas y tierra firme del mar océano*. 4 vols. Madrid:
              Real Academia de la Historia.

Palerm, Angel
     1973   *Obras hidráulicas prehispánicas en el sistema lacustre del Valle de México*. Mexico City: Sec-
              retaría de Educación Pública/Instituto Nacional de Antropología e Historia.

Papeles de Nueva España
     1905–1906   *Papeles de Nueva España*. 2d series, *Geografía y Estadística*. 6 vols. Ed. Francisco del Paso
              y Troncoso. Madrid: Sucesores de Rivadeneyra.

Paredes Martínez, Carlos
     1991   *El impacto de la conquista y colonización española en la antigua Coatlalpan (Izúcar, Puebla) en
              el primer siglo colonial*. Cuadernos de la Casa Chata. Mexico City: Centro de Investi-
              gaciones y Estudios Superiores en Antropología Social.

Parsons, Jeffrey R., et al.
     1982   *Prehispanic Settlement Patterns in the Southern Valley of Mexico: The Chalco-Xochimilco Region*.
              Memoirs of the Museum of Anthropology, University of Michigan, no. 14. Ann
              Arbor: University of Michigan.

Paso y Troncoso, Francisco del, ed.
     1905–1906   *Papeles de Nueva España*. 2d series, *Geografía y Estadística*. 6 vols. Madrid: Sucesores de
              Rivadeneyra.

1939–42   *Epistolario de Nueva España, 1505-1818.* 16 vols. Mexico City.
Paso y Troncoso, Francisco del, and Faustino Chimalpopoca Galicia, eds.
1897   "Lista de los pueblos principales que pertenecían antiguamente a Tetzcoco." *Anales del Museo Nacional de México,* 1st series, 4:48–56.
Peñafiel, Antonio, ed.
1897   "Manuscrito americano número 4 de la Biblioteca Real de Berlín. Título de tierras del pueblo de Santa Isabel Tola." *Colección de documentos para la historia mexicana,* part 1. Mexico City: Secretaría de Fomento.
Pérez Rocha, Emma
1982   *La tierra y el hombre en la villa de Tacuba durante la época colonial.* Colección Científica 115. Mexico City: Instituto Nacional de Antropología e Historia.
n.d.   "Privilegios en lucha: La información de doña Isabel Moctezuma." Mexico City: Instituto Nacional de Antropología e Historia, forthcoming.
Pérez-Zevallos, Juan Manuel
1981   "Organización del señorío xochimilca." In Ramos et al. 1981.
Piho, Virve
1972a   "La jerarquía militar azteca." *Atti del XL Congresso Internazionale degli Americanisti* 2:273–88. Rome.
1972b   "Tlacatecutli, tlacochtecutli, tlacateccatl y tlacochcalcatl." *Estudios de Cultura Náhuatl* 10:315–28.
1974   "Esquema provisional de la organización militar mexica." *Actas del XLI Congreso Internacional de Americanistas* 2:169–78. Mexico City.
Pomar, Juan Bautista de
1986   "Relación de la ciudad y provincia de Tezcoco." In *Relaciones geográficas del Siglo XVI,* 8:21–113.
Prem, Hanns J.
1989   *Geschichte Altamerikas.* Munich: R. Oldenbourg.
——, ed.
1974   *Matrícula de Huexotzinco.* Graz: Akademische Druck- und Verlagsanstalt.
Proceso inquisitorial
1910   *Proceso inquisitorial del cacique de Tetzcoco.* Mexico City: Publicaciones del Archivo General de la Nación.
Quiñones Keber, Eloise, ed.
1944   *Chipping Away on Earth: Studies in Prehispanic and Colonial Mexico in Honor of Arthur J. O. Anderson and Charles E. Dibble.* Lancaster, Calif.: Labyrinthos.
Ramos, Rebeca; Ludka de Gortari Krauss; and Manuel Pérez-Zevallos
1981   *Xochimilco en el siglo XVI.* Cuadernos de la Casa Chata 40:105–81. Mexico: Centro de Investigaciones Superiores en Antropología Social.
Recinos, Adrián, trans. and ed.
1950   *Memorial de Sololá: Anales de los Cakchiqueles.* Mexico City: Fondo de Cultura Económica.
1957   *Crónicas indígenas de Guatemala.* Guatemala: Imprenta Universitaria.
Relación de la genealogía y linaje
1941   "Relación de la genealogía y linaje de los Señores que han señoreado esta tierra de la Nueva España. . . ." In *Relaciones de Texcoco y de la Nueva España,* 240–56.
Relación de los obispados
1904   *Relación de los obispados de Tlaxcala, Michoacán, Oaxaca y otros lugares en el siglo XVI.* Ed. Luis García Pimentel. Mexico City, Paris, and Madrid.
Relación sacada
1940   "Relación sacada de los libros de S.M. en enero de 1560 del valor de lo que producen los pueblos de yndios de N. España pertenecientes a la corona real descontado el diezmo de las cosas que se paga." *Boletín del Archivo General de la Nación* 11:201–21.

Relaciones geográficas del siglo XVI
 1982–88   *Relaciones geográficas del siglo XVI.* 10 vols. Ed. René Acuña. Mexico City: Universidad Nacional Autónoma de México.

Relaciones de Texcoco y de la Nueva España
 1941   *Relaciones de Texcoco y de la Nueva España: Pomar- Zurita.* Mexico City: Chavez Hayhoe. [Reprint of vol. 3 of *Nueva colección de documentos para la historia de México.* Edited by Joaquín García Icazbalceta. México City: 1891.]

Relaciones . . . de Yucatán
 1983   *Relaciones histórico-geográficas de la gobernación de Yucatán.* 2 vols. Ed. M. de la Garza et al. Mexico City: Universidad Nacional Autónoma de México.

Remesal, Fray Antonio de
 1964   *Historia general de las Indias Occidentales y particular de la gobernación de Chiapa y Guatemala.* Biblioteca de autores españoles 175. Madrid: Atlas.

Reyes, Antonio de los
 1976   *Arte en lengua mixteca* [1593]. Reprint of the edition by H. de Charency, Paris, 1890. Vanderbilt University Publications in Anthropology No. 14. Nashville, Tenn.

Reyes García, Luis
 1977   *Cuauhtinchan del siglo XII al XVI: Formación y desarrollo histórico de un señorío prehispánico.* Wiesbaden: Franz Steiner Verlag.
 1979   "La visión cosmológica y la organización del imperio mexica." In Dahlgren 1979.
 n.d.   "*Matrícula de tributos: Códice de Moctezuma. Introducción y comentarios.* Mexico City: Fondo de Cultura Económica, forthcoming.

Reyes García, Luis, Eustaquio Celestino Solís, Armando Valencia Ríos, Constantino Medina Lima, and Gregorio Guerrero Díaz
 1996   *Documentos nauas de la Ciudad de México del siglo XVI.* Mexico City: CIESAS/Archivo General de la Nación.

Robertson, Donald
 1959   *Mexican Manuscript Painting of the Early Colonial Period: The Metropolitan Schools.* New Haven: Yale University Press.

Rodríguez Shadow, María
 1990   *El estado azteca.* Toluca: Universidad Autónoma del Estado de México.

Rojas, José Luis de
 1986   *México Tenochtitlan: Economía y sociedad en el siglo XVI.* Mexico City: El Colegio de Michoacán/Fondo de Cultura Económica.
 1987   "El control del granero del imperio y la consolidación del estado mexica." In *Almacenamiento de productos agropecuarios en México*, 29–38. Ed. Gail Mummert. Zamora: El Colegio de Michoacán.
 1989   "El Xoconochco: ¿una provincia aislada del imperio?" *Revista Española de Antropología Americana* 19:91–107.
 1991   "La organización del imperio mexica." *Revista Española de Antropología Americana* 21:145–69.

Rosas Herrera, Gregorio, trans.
 1946   "Verba sociorum Domini Petri Tlacahuepantzi." *Tlalocan* 2: 150–69.

Ruhnau, Elke
 1988   *Die politische Organisation im vorspanischen Chalco.* Beiträge zur mittelamerikanischen Völkerkunde, 18. Hamburg: Museum für Völkerkunde und Vorgeschichte.

Ruiz Medrano, Ethelia
 1991   *Gobierno y Sociedad en Nueva España: Segunda Audiencia y Antonio de Mendoza.* Zamora: Gobierno del Estado de Michoacán/El Colegio de Michoacán.

Sahagún, Bernardino de
 1950–82   *Florentine Codex: General History of the Things of New Spain.* Trans. and ed. Arthur J. O. Anderson and Charles E. Dibble. Santa Fe, N.M.: School of American Research and the University of Utah.

(Sahagún, Bernardino de) continued

  1952 Book 3. *The Origin of the Gods.*
  1953 Book 7. *The Sun, Moon, and Stars, and the Binding of the Years.*
  1954 Book 8. *Kings and Lords.*
  1959 Book 9. *The Merchants.*
  1961 Book 10. *The People.*
  1963 Book 11. *Earthly Things.*
  1969a Book 6. *Rhetoric and Moral Philosophy.*
  1975 Book 12. *The Conquest of Mexico.*
  1981 Book 2. *The Ceremonies.*

 1958 *Ritos, sacerdotes y atavíos de los dioses.* Trans. and ed. Miguel León-Portilla. Fuentes Indígenas de la Cultura Náhuatl. Textos de los informantes de Sahagún, 1. Mexico City: Universidad Nacional Autónoma de México.

 1969b *Historia general de las cosas de Nueva España.* 4 vols. Ed. A. M. Garibay K. Mexico City: Porrúa.

Scholes, France V., and Eleanor B. Adams, eds.

 1957 *Información sobre los tributos que los indios pagaban a Moctezuma: Año de 1554.* Documentos para la historia del México colonial, vol. 4. Mexico: Porrúa.

Scholes, France V., and Ralph L. Roys

 1948 *The Maya Chontal Indians of Acalan-Tixchel: A Contribution to the History and Ethnography of the Yucatan Peninsula.* Carnegie Institution of Washington Publication 560. Washington, D.C.

Schroeder, Susan

 1991 *Chimalpahin and the Kingdoms of Chalco.* Tucson: University of Arizona Press.

Seler, Eduard

 1902–23 *Gesammelte Abhandlungen zur Amerikanischen Sprach- und Alterthumskunde.* 5 vols. Berlin.

Sepúlveda, María Teresa

 1991 "El tributo real en la Matrícula de tributos." In *Matrícula de tributos: Nuevos estudios 1991*, 103–52.

Serna, Jacinto de la

 1892 "Manual de ministros de indios para el conocimiento de sus idolatrías y extirpación de ellas." *Anales del Museo Nacional de México* 6:261–480.

Siméon, Rémi

 1988 *Diccionario de la lengua náhuatl o mexicana.* Trans. Josefina Oliva de Coll. Mexico City: Siglo XXI.

Simpson, Leslie Byrd

 1934 *Studies in the Administration of the Indians in New Spain.* Ibero-Americana 7. Berkeley: University of California Press.

Smith, Michael E.

 1986 "The Role of Social Stratification in the Aztec Empire: A View from the Provinces." *American Anthropologist* 88:70–91.

 1987 "The Expansion of the Aztec Empire: A Case Study in the Correlation of Diachronic Archaeological and Ethnohistorical Data." *American Antiquity* 52:37–54.

 1996 "The Strategic Provinces." In Berdan et al. 1996: 137–50.

Solano, Francisco de, ed.

 1988 *Relaciones geográficas del arzobispado de México: 1743.* 2 vols. Madrid: Consejo Superior de Investigaciones Científicas.

Southall, Aidan W.

 1956 *Alur Society: A Study in Processes and Types of Domination.* Cambridge, England: Heffer.

 1988 "The Segmentary State in Africa and Asia." *Comparative Studies in Society and History* 30:52–82.

Spores, Ronald

 1967 *The Mixtec Kings and Their People.* Norman: University of Oklahoma Press.

1984   *The Mixtecs in Ancient and Colonial Times.* Norman: University of Oklahoma Press.
1993   "Tututepec: A Post-Classic Period Mixtec Conquest State." *Ancient Mesoamerica*
        4:167–74.
———, and Ross Hassig, eds.
1984   *Five Centuries of Law and Politics in Central Mexico.* Vanderbilt University Publications
        in Anthropology, no. 30. Nashville, Tenn.
Spores, Ronald, and Miguel Saldaña, eds.
1973   *Documentos para la Etnohistoria del Estado de Oaxaca: Indice del Ramo de Mercedes del Archivo
        General de la Nación, México.* Vanderbilt University Publications in Anthropology,
        no. 5. Nashville, Tenn.
1976   *Documentos para la Etnohistoria del Estado de Oaxaca: Indice del Ramo de Indios del Archivo
        General de la Nación, México.* Vanderbilt University Publications in Anthropology,
        no. 13. Nashville, Tenn.
Strauss, Rafael
1974   "El área septentrional del Valle de México: Panorama agrohidráulico prehispánico."
        Master's thesis, Escuela Nacional de Antropología e Historia, Mexico City.
Stresser-Péan, Guy, ed.
1995   *El Códice de Xicotepec: Estudio e interpretación.* Mexico City: Fondo de Cultura Eco-
        nómica.
Suárez de Peralta, Juan
1990   *Tratado del descubrimiento de las Indias.* Mexico City: Consejo Nacional para la Cultura
        y las Artes.
Suma de visitas
1905   *Suma de visitas de pueblos por orden alfabético.* Vol. 1 of *Papeles de Nueva España.* 2d series,
        Geografía y Estadística. Ed. Francisco del Paso y Troncoso. Madrid: Sucesores de Ri-
        vadeneyra.
Tapia, Andrés de
1858   *Relación hecha por el señor Andrés de Tapia sobre la conquista de México.* In García Icazbal-
        ceta 1858, 2:554–94.
Tarn, William W.
1964   *Hellenistic Civilisation.* 3d ed. Rev. by the author and G. T. Griffith. Cleveland and
        New York: World Publishing Company, Meridian Books.
Tezozomoc, Fernando Alvarado
1949   *Crónica mexicayotl.* Trans. Adrián León. Instituto de Investigaciones Históricas, 1st
        series, Prehispánica 3. Mexico City: Universidad Nacional Autónoma de México.
1975   *Crónica Mexicana.* Ed. Manuel Orozco y Berra. Reprint of 1878 edition. Mexico
        City: Porrúa.
Título de Totonicapán
1983   *El Título de Totonicapán.* Trans. Robert M. Carmack and James L. Mondloch. Mex-
        ico City: Universidad Nacional Autónoma de México.
Torquemada, Juan de
1975–83 *Monarquía Indiana.* 7 vols. Ed. Miguel León-Portilla. Mexico City: Universidad Na-
        cional Autónoma de México.
Toscano, Salvador
1943   "Los códices tlapanecas de Azoyú." *Cuadernos Americanos* 10, no.4: 127–36.
Tovar, Juan de
1972   "Relación del origen de los Yndios que havitan en esta Nueva España según sus his-
        torias." In *Manuscrit Tovar: Origines et croyances des indiens du Mexique*, 9–113. Ed.
        Jacques La Faye. Graz: Akademische Druck- und Verlagsanstalt.
Tratado de Teotihuacan
MS[1621] *Tratado del principado y nobleza del pueblo de San Juan Teotihuacan.* MS. mexi-
        cain 243. BNP. Fotocopias de Troncoso, legajo 51. Archivo Histórico del Instituto
        Nacional de Antropología e Historia, Museo de Antropología. Mexico City.

Trautmann, Wolfgang

1968   *Untersuchungen zur indianischen Siedlungs—und Territorialgeschichte im Becken von Mexiko bis zur frühen Kolonialzeit.* Beiträge zur mittelamerikanischen Völkerkunde 7. Hamburg: Museum für Völkerkunde und Vorgeschichte.

1981   *Las transformaciones en el paisaje cultural de Tlaxcala durante la época colonial.* El proyecto México de la Fundación Alemana para la Investigación Científica, 17. Wiesbaden: Franz Steiner Verlag.

Tschohl, Peter

1964   "Kritische Untersuchungen zur spätindianischen Geschichte Südost-Mexikos: Teil I, Die aztekische Ausdehnung nach den aztekischen Quellen und die Probleme ihrer Bearbeitung." Ph.D. diss., Universität Hamburg.

1989   "Das Ende der Leyenda de los Soles und die Übermittlungsprobleme des Códice Chimalpopoca." *Baessler-Archiv,* n.s., 37:201–79.

Urbano, Alonso

1990   *Arte breve de la lengua otomí y vocabulario trilingüe español-náhuatl-otomí.* Ed. René Acuña. Mexico City: Universidad Nacional Autónoma de México.

Uribe, Oscar

1954–55   "Toponímicos otomíes." *Revista Mexicana de Estudios Antropológicos* 14:207–12.

Valdeavellano. Luis G. de

1968   *Curso de Historia de las instituciones españolas: De los orígenes al final de la Edad Media.* Madrid: Revista de Occidente.

Valle P., Perla, ed.

1993   *Memorial de los indios de Tepetlaoztoc o Códice Kingsborough.* Colección Científica 263. Mexico City: Instituto Nacional de Antropología e Historia.

Vega Sosa, Constanza, ed.

1991   *Códice Azoyú: El reino de Tlachinollan.* Mexico City: Fondo de Cultura Económica.

Velázquez, Primo Feliciano, trans. and ed.

1945   *Códice Chimalpopoca: Anales de Cuauhtitlan y leyenda de los Soles.* Mexico City: Universidad Nacional Autónoma de México.

Vetancurt, Fray Agustín de

1961   *Teatro Mexicano.* 4 vols. Madrid: Porrúa Turanzas.

Veytia, Mariano Fernández de Echeverría y

1944   *Historia antigua de México.* 2 vols. Mexico City: Editorial Leyenda.

Vollmer, Günter

1972   "Mexikanische Regionalbezeichnungen im 16. Jahrhundert." *Jahrbuch für Geschichte von Staat, Wirtschaft und Gesellschaft Lateinamerikas,* 9:40–101.

Voorhies, Barbara, ed.

1989   *Ancient Trade and Tribute: Economies of the Soconusco Region of Mesoamerica.* Salt Lake City: University of Utah Press.

Weber, Max

1978   *Economy and Society.* Ed. Guenther Roth and Claus Wittich. Berkeley: University of California Press.

Weitlaner, Roberto J.

1961   "The Guatinicamame." In *A William Cameron Townsend en el vigésimoquinto aniversario del Instituto Lingüístico de Verano,* 199–205. Mexico City.

————, and Carlo Antonio Castro G.

1954   *Papeles de la Chinantla.* Vol. 1, *Mayultianguiz y Tlacoatzintepec.* Serie Científica 3. Mexico City: Instituto Nacional de Antropología e Historia.

Whitecotton, Joseph W.

1977   *The Zapotecs: Princes, Priests and Peasants.* Norman: University of Oklahoma Press.

Zamora Acosta, Elías

1979   "El control vertical de diferentes pisos ecológicos: Aplicación del modelo al Occidente de Guatemala." *Economía y sociedad en los Andes y Mesoamérica: Revista de la Universidad Complutense* 28 (117):245–72.

Zantwijk, Rudolf van
  1967   "La organización de once guarniciones aztecas: Una nueva interpretación de los folios 17v y 18r del Códice Mendocino." *Journal de la Société des Américanistes de Paris* 56:149–60.
  1969   "La estructura gubernamental del Estado de Tlacupan (1430–1520)." *Estudios de Cultura Náhuatl* 8:123–55.
  1985   *The Aztec Arrangement: The Social History of Pre-Spanish Mexico.* Norman: University of Oklahoma Press.
  1994   "Factional Divisions within the Aztec (Colhua) Royal Family." In Brumfiel and Fox 1994: 103–10.

Zavala, Silvio
  1938   "Las encomiendas de Nueva España y el Gobierno de don Antonio de Mendoza." *Revista de Historia de América* 1 (2):59–75.
  1982   *Asientos de la gobernación de la Nueva España.* Mexico City: Archivo General de la Nación.
  1984   *El servicio personal de los indios en la Nueva España.* Vol. 1, *1521–1550.* Mexico City: El Colegio de México/El Colegio Nacional.
  1987   *El servicio personal de los indios en la Nueva España.* Vol. 3, *1576–1599.* Mexico City: El Colegio de México/El Colegio Nacional.
  1989   *El servicio personal de los indios en la Nueva España.* Vol. 4, *Suplemento a los tres tomos relativos al siglo XVI.* Mexico City: El Colegio de México/El Colegio Nacional.

———, and María Castelo
  1939–46 *Fuentes para la historia del trabajo en Nueva España.* 8 vols. Mexico City: Fondo de Cultura Económica.

Zimmermann, Günter
  1960   *Das Geschichtswerk des Domingo de Muñon Chimalpahin Quauhtlehuanitzin.* Beiträge zur mittelamerikanischen Völkerkunde, 5. Hamburg: Museum für Völkerkunde und Vorgeschichte.

———, ed.
  1970   *Briefe der indianischen Nobilität aus Neuspanien an Karl V und Philipp II um die Mitte des 16. Jahrhunderts.* Beiträge zur mittelamerikanischen Völkerkunde, 10. Hamburg: Museum für Völkerkunde und Vorgeschichte.

Zorita, Alonso de
  1909   *Historia de la Nueva España.* Book 1, Vol. 9, *Colección de libros y documentos referentes a la historia de América.* Madrid: Victoriano Suárez.
  1941   "Breve y sumaria relación de los señores y maneras y diferencia que había de ellos en la Nueva España. . . ." In *Relaciones de Texcoco y de la Nueva España,* 65–205.

Zúñiga, Rosa María
  1985   *Toponimias zapotecas: Desarrollo de una metodología.* Colección Científica 117. Mexico City: Instituto Nacional de Antropología e Historia.

Index

This index is in two parts; the second part contains only toponyms, primarily native place-names, most of them Nahua. Spanish colonial or present-day names are given only when necessary for identifying indigenous settlements. The names of saints are included when they are part of a modern toponym and also to distinguish homonyms. When the same toponym is used for different places, there is a separate entry for each one, indicating its location. Most entries are written with the standardized Nahuatl orthography; alternate spellings and plural forms are given in parentheses. Present-day names that begin with *J* or *S* come from Nahuatl forms that begin with *X*, *C*, or *Z̨*.

TOPONYMS

541